PENGUIN BOOKS

CLOSED CHAMBERS

Edward Lazarus served as a law clerk to Supreme Court Justice Harry A. Blackmun from 1988 to 1989. He is also the author of *Black Hills/White Justice*, which the *Harvard Law Review* praised as "meticulously researched and eloquently written." Lazarus has contributed to such publications as *The New York Times*, *The Washington Post*, *The Atlantic*, and the *Los Angeles Times*. He also appears as a commentator on CNN and MSNBC. Lazarus is a graduate of Yale College and Yale Law School, and is currently in private practice.

CLOSED CHAMBERS

The Rise, Fall, and Future
of the Modern Supreme Court

EDWARD LAZARUS

PENGUIN BOOKS

For Amanda

PENGUIN BOOKS
Published by the Penguin Group
Penguin Group (USA) Inc., 375 Hudson Street, New York, New York 10014, U.S.A.
Penguin Group (Canada), 10 Alcorn Avenue, Toronto, Ontario, Canada M4V 3B2
   (a division of Pearson Penguin Canada Inc.)
Penguin Books Ltd, 80 Strand, London WC2R 0RL, England
Penguin Ireland, 25 St Stephen's Green, Dublin 2, Ireland (a division of Penguin Books Ltd)
Penguin Group (Australia), 250 Camberwell Road, Camberwell, Victoria 3124, Australia
   (a division of Pearson Australia Group Pty Ltd)
Penguin Books India Pvt Ltd, 11 Community Centre, Panchsheel Park,
   New Delhi – 110 017, India
Penguin Group (NZ), cnr Airborne and Rosedale Roads, Albany, Auckland 1310, New Zealand
   (a division of Pearson New Zealand Ltd)
Penguin Books (South Africa) (Pty) Ltd, 24 Sturdee Avenue, Rosebank,
   Johannesburg 2196, South Africa

Penguin Books Ltd, Registered Offices:
80 Strand, London WC2R 0RL, England

First published in the United States of America by Times Books,
a division of Random House, Inc. 1998
Published with a new afterword by Penguin Books 1999
This edition published in Penguin Books 2005

10 9 8 7 6 5 4 3 2 1

Copyright © Edward Lazarus, 1998, 1999
All rights reserved

Please direct all reprint and other rights requests concerning the Afterword, and all inquiries
about nonprint rights in Closed Chambers to: Writers Representatives LLC, 116 W. 14th Street,
New York, NY 10011. Please direct all inquiries about print rights to Random House Inc.,
1749 Broadway, 18th Floor, New York, NY 10019.

THE LIBRARY OF CONGRESS HAS CATALOGED THE HARDCOVER EDITION AS FOLLOWS:
Lazarus, Edward P.
Closed Chambers: the first eyewitness account of the epic struggles
inside the Supreme Court / Edward Lazarus.–1st ed.
p.   cm.
Includes bibliographical references and index.
ISBN 0-8129-2402-9 (hc.)
ISBN 0 14 30.3527 4 (pbk.)
1. United States. Supreme Court—History.   2. Clerks of court—United States—History.
3. Judicial process—United States—History.   4. Political questions and judicial power—
United States—History.   I. Title.
KF8742.L39   1998
347.73'16—dc21   97-35708

Printed in the United States of America
Set in Goudy
Designed by Robert C. Olsson

AUTHOR'S NOTE

Although part of this book is written as a memoir, it is mainly a work of research and reportage. Naturally, my experience as a law clerk for Justice Harry A. Blackmun was indispensable to that process. The clerkship gave me unusual access to sources knowledgeable about the Court and armed me with questions others might not think to ask. It also gave me a significant advantage in evaluating and interpreting publicly available primary source material about the Court, in particular the unpublished draft opinions and memoranda contained in the papers of various former Justices.* Finally, the clerkship left me with specific memories and a general view of life at the Court against which to evaluate the information I subsequently gathered.

At the same time, in describing the private decision-making of the Justices, I have been careful to avoid disclosing information I am privy to solely because I was privileged to work for Justice Blackmun. In other words, I have reconstructed what I knew and supplemented that knowledge through primary sources (either publicly available or provided by others) and dozens of interviews conducted since 1992. Indeed, some of the more controversial revelations in the book, including events that occurred during my clerkship year, are things of which I was unaware—or dimly aware—at the time.

For expanding my knowledge of Court history and its inner workings, I am greatly indebted to the many people who spoke to me on the condition that I would not reveal their names. (To avert speculation, I

---

*Especially important for my research were the papers of Thurgood Marshall, publicly available at the Library of Congress. Unless otherwise noted, these were the source for the many internal Court documents, including the drafts and memos of other Justices, that I quote or refer to in the book.

should make clear that Justice Blackmun was not among them.) With some regret, I have chosen not to identify through footnotes the material gleaned from these confidential interviews. I recognize that this approach makes it more difficult for the reader to evaluate some of my assertions, but I have made this sacrifice in order to further shield the identity of those who helped me. I can add only that, in deciding what confidential source material to use, I have done my best to sift out information that was not independently corroborated or inherently credible in light of my own experience.

When *Closed Chambers* was first published, some among the Court's self-designated protectors accused me of violating the Court's confidentiality rules and of breaking faith with the institution. These charges were wrong on many levels. In addition to misstating the Court's rules and mischaracterizing my conduct, they relied on a skewed concept of loyalty. It does no service either to the Court over the long term or to our democracy to yield unquestioningly and forever to the Justices' considerable efforts to limit public scrutiny of their decision making or, as is commonplace, to mythologize that decision making. Worse still, the Justices have expanded their own demand for secrecy.

In response to the publication of my critical assessment of the Court's decision making, and in light of my status as a former law clerk and my use of other former clerks as sources for my book, the Court reportedly has changed the confidentiality rules governing law clerks. The Justices now demand absolute secrecy about the Court's work not only during a clerk's one-year tenure, but for eternity. This new omerta is regrettable.

I undertook *Closed Chambers* with two basic premises in mind: first, as discussed above, that we allow nine unelected, life-tenured judges the power to decide many of our most important legal social questions because we believe that they engage in a reasoned and deliberative process of decision making that differs substantially from the trade-offs of everyday politics in the other branches of government; and second, that it is, therefore, impossible to assess the legitimacy and quality of the Court's functioning without discussing critically both the Court's internal decision making and the opinions that the Justices produce.

Inside the Court, it is certainly important that Justices engage in freewheeling discussions with each other and with their law clerks. Protecting the open nature of these discussions by discouraging premature or irresponsible disclosure is, naturally, a significant concern. But the Court is not unique in this respect. The same need for confidentiality applies to discussions taking place in the other branches of government, yet we recognize that this concern must be balanced against the need for evaluation and public accountability. Accordingly, with the exception of agencies associated directly with national security, the government does not demand, nor should we permit, long-term gag orders on its employees. On the contrary, outside of the judiciary, we welcome critical assessments by former members of the other branches of government—and consider them essential to understanding and advancing our democracy. I wrote *Closed Chambers* with these examples in mind.

This is not to say that individuals who once held positions of confidence in government should consider themselves free, willy-nilly, to break those confidences as soon as they depart from their jobs. Of course, they should not. A duty of circumspection remains—even as it must be recognized (as it always has been) that the bonds of secrecy diminish over time and must be balanced against the public interest and the call of history. In adopting its new gag rule, the Court ignores this balance and establishes for itself a rule of secrecy surpassed only by the CIA.

Despite its reaction, the Court has little to fear. If experience is any guide, former law clerks have a fine record for discretion in discussing the Court's work, though some disclosures are made. *Closed Chambers*—a book based mainly on the public record, but which also contains some revelations of nonpublic material obtained through standard journalistic means—does nothing to change that.

At the same time, it is not trivial that the Court, a public institution, seems bent on insulating its internal processes from scrutiny. The Justices are the most important legal officers not only in this country, but in the world. Assessing the quality of their work is in our immediate best interest and in the long-term best interest of the institution. That the current Justices apparently feel otherwise reflects an unhealthy and undemocratic defensiveness. As in the other branches of government, the best defense against the criticism of former employees is not to impose unrealistic and unjustified secrecy rules. It is simply for the Justices to do their jobs conscientiously and well.

ACKNOWLEDGMENTS

During the research and writing of this book I incurred many debts of gratitude. This project would have foundered long ago but for the help of dozens of former clerks who agreed to speak with me candidly about life inside the Court. I also received crucial assistance from the staff of the Library of Congress (home to the papers of Justices Harry A. Blackmun, Thurgood Marshall, William J. Brennan, William O. Douglas, and Robert H. Jackson) and from George Kendall of the NAACP Legal Defense Fund (who allowed me significant access to the case files of Warren McCleskey).

My agents, Glen Hartley and Lynn Chu, once again did a magnificent job taking care of the business side of my writing life. I am also indebted to Joni Evans and Susan Kamil for signing up this book and to Steve Wasserman, my first editor, for his wise counsel and patience. Geoff Shandler, who inherited the project from Steve, took on the book as if it had been his own and did a superb job guiding me through the sometimes tricky shoals of publishing.

Many people commented on portions of the manuscript or otherwise helped shape my ideas. In particular, Vik Amar, Ian Ayres, Evan Caminker, Erwin Chemerinsky, Gia Cincone, Cynthia Gorney, Michael Small, Joe Onek, Jeff Powell, Roger Teich, and Clyde Spellenger let me borrow their extraordinary expertise and saved me from errors great and small. Jonathan Feldman, Bob Kagan, and Anthony Weller, unsurpassable friends, pored over my chapters, sometimes more than once, and dispensed sanity-saving advice, encouragement, and support. So did my father, Arthur Lazarus, Jr., in yet another gift of familial love.

I would never have undertaken this book were it not for the two judges who honored me with clerkships in their chambers: Judge William A. Norris and Justice Harry A. Blackmun. They gave me the privilege of seeing the world of law from their side of the bench. They taught me about the integrity and passion that go into the craft of judging. And, most treasured of all, they embraced me as part of their extended families. I know Justice Blackmun would not have agreed with some of the views I have expressed here. But I trust that he would have valued the independent judgment I have exercised—an independence that he, by shining example, helped instill.

Last, I thank my wife and soul mate, Amanda, the enduring beauty who walked by my side through the five years of this enterprise. She kept me whole.

Los Angeles
April 2005

CONTENTS

CLOSED CHAMBERS

There can be but few men in the society who will have sufficient skill in the laws to qualify them for the stations of judges. And making the proper deductions for the ordinary depravity of human nature, the number must be still smaller who unite the requisite integrity with the requisite knowledge.

—Alexander Hamilton (Federalist No. 78)

The Highest Court in the Land

They looked like rock 'n' roll fans camped out for the night in front of a box office. Huddled under ponchos, sheets of plastic, or converted trash bags, several dozen people formed a ragged line on the sidewalk and talked quietly as a steady late-night rain soaked their makeshift waterproofing. Up front, two policemen kept sullen watch over the still-growing crowd.

But the location was not a box office, and the event was not a rock concert. It was the Supreme Court of the United States, and the occasion was the deciding of *Planned Parenthood of Southeastern Pennsylvania v. Casey,* the abortion test case of 1992 that many expected would mark the death of *Roe v. Wade* and a woman's constitutional right to obtain an abortion.

Some who stood vigil were partisans, lawyers for various legal and political organizations. Others were soldiers from the protracted street war over abortion rights. One woman, in her fifties, had worked on the underground abortion network in the pre-*Roe* days when California girls were hustled across the border to Tijuana for quick operations. The man next to her, a midwesterner, was part of Operation Rescue's army of anti-abortion crusaders. He had been a "baby doe," a volunteer on the abortion clinic barricades, provoking arrest in the name of the unborn.

Carol Urich, first in line, forty-eight and wheelchair bound, had never been to the Court before. Still, *Roe v. Wade* had defined her political identity and she wanted to bear witness at the making of its history. Her mother had suffered through an illegal abortion in 1933, and Carol, pro-choice in memoria, was still haunted by the fear and pain of that story. So she and dozens of others with memories and convictions no less searing braved the rain and the long night just to sit silently in the Court's majestic chamber as the Justices, the nine high priests of American law, announced *Roe*'s fate.

The Court itself, a Greek-style temple commanding the crest of Capitol Hill, loomed above them in the dim light of the storm. Set atop a broad marble plaza and thirty-six steps, the Court stands in a splendid isolation appropriate to its place at the pinnacle of the national judiciary, one of the three independent and "coequal" branches of American government. Once dubbed the Ivory Tower by architecture critics, the Court has a Corinthian colonnade and massive twenty-foot-high bronze doors that guard the single most powerful judicial institution in the Western world.

Lights still shone in several offices to the right of the Court's entrance, and an occasional silhouette passed across the windows. A few in the crowd outside speculated whether the figure was a janitor, a law clerk, or perhaps even one of the Justices. Others wondered aloud about why Court business might still be going on so late at night.

As I watched them, I thought back to a similar scene three years earlier: July 2, 1989, the eve of the Court's decision in another landmark abortion case, *Webster* v. *Reproductive Health Services*. Then, too, I had been present as a small cross section of America lined up for seats at the next morning's session. On that night, though, my view had been from inside the Court, my shadow observed by the murmuring crowd below.

From July 1988 through July 1989 — in Court parlance October Term 1988 — I served as one of four law clerks to Justice Harry A. Blackmun, the author of *Roe*. This book is an outgrowth of that incomparable experience, meant to capture the judgments and feelings I formed while working for him and to examine how they have changed over what is now more than eight years of reflection.

At the outset, I confess that during my year of total immersion in the world of the Court—often ninety hours a week inside the building itself—I found myself almost inadvertently following Pericles' advice to the citizens of ancient Athens: to look upon their home and fall in love with her.[1] From the solemnity of the velvet-draped courtroom to the ornate brilliance of the gold leaf on the library ceiling, from the cloistered silence of the private corridors to the chatter of tourists admiring the Great Hall, the Court radiates a sense of tradition and higher purpose that even in a cynical age inspires belief in the sanctity of law and the possibility of justice. To contribute even in a fleeting way to the history of this place is an honor deeply felt by every one of its employees and creates a powerful loyalty to the institution. Over the course of my year there, I certainly came to share this devotion.

At the same time, what I saw inside the Court—how it worked or failed to work, the strengths and weaknesses of the Justices who presided while I was there, the role of clerks like me—all this left me with an irrepressible sense of disquiet. Part of this book is an attempt to explain and analyze that disquiet. All of this book is an attempt to give both lawyers and the lay public a better understanding of a particularly significant and tumultuous period in the Court's history.

It is at most a small exaggeration to say that legal rules and litigation have become Americans' civil religion and that if we share one sacred text, it is our Constitution. Whether the issue is abortion, race discrimination, sexual harassment, the environment, criminal justice, religious liberty, freedom of speech, or almost any other aspect of how we live and even how we die, Americans have come almost routinely to expect the courts, especially the Supreme Court, to take sides on every issue of national urgency and help resolve our most vexing social problems.

As a result, pilgrims like those who braved the rain to witness the Court's decision in *Casey* have become commonplace. So have political marches on the Court and demonstrations on its steps. And the confirmation hearings for prospective Justices, from the repudiation of Robert Bork to the inquisitions of Clarence Thomas and Anita Hill, have been transformed into political theater of the highest consequence. All this, it seems, marks a national recognition of how important control of the Court has become to shaping the contours of our government and the spirit of our society.

But for all the attention we now pay to it, the Court remains shrouded in confusion and misunderstanding. Indeed, amid the hedging and dodging of the confirmation hearings, the frequent headlines about legal precedents saved or overturned, the charges and countercharges of "politicizing" the judiciary, and much misleading talk about judicial "activism," "strict construction," and "original intent," I fear that we now feel more but think less about the essential questions of how the Court reaches its decisions, why its integrity and vitality matter so much, and what role it should play in our democracy.

No single volume can address these issues comprehensively. But I hope that what follows will add some measure of light and clarity to what, regrettably, has been a rapidly gathering dusk.

I came of age with an essentially idealized image of the Supreme Court, an image defined by the events of July 24, 1974. On that day, the Court ordered President Richard Nixon to turn over to the Watergate special prosecutor, Leon Jaworski, a series of highly incriminating tape recordings that the president previously had withheld on the ground of "executive privilege." Although three of the participating Justices had been appointed by Nixon, the Court's judgment against the president was unanimous.* And although releasing the tapes would brand him both a liar and a probable felon, Nixon respected the authority of the Court and complied with its ruling. Seventeen days later, he resigned.

Today I carry with me a very different image of the Court. It is of an institution broken into unyielding factions that have largely given up on a meaningful exchange of their respective views or, for that matter, a meaningful explication or defense of their own views. It is of Justices who in many important cases resort to transparently deceitful and hypocritical arguments and factual distortions as they discard judicial philosophy and consistent interpretation in favor of bottom-line results. This is a Court so badly splintered, yet so intent on lawmaking, that shifting 5–4 majorities, or even mere pluralities, rewrite whole swaths of constitutional law on the authority of a single, often idiosyncratic vote. It is also a Court where Justices yield great and excessive power to immature, ideologically driven clerks, who in turn use that power to manipulate their bosses and the institution they ostensibly serve.

In my mind, these two images of the Court—an idealized past and the more recent nightmare—are powerfully linked. The year 1974 is a fair marker for the birth of our current political age. With Nixon's resignation and the winding down of the Vietnam War, the tumultuous sixties drew to a close and bequeathed to us the deep divisions that make up our "culture war." Watergate itself provided a further legacy, leaving us heirs to an unraveling of character in our public life.

---

*A fourth Nixon appointee, then Associate Justice William Rehnquist, recused himself from the case.

Such is government today. Along a broad front, we relive the hatreds of the sixties in shattering struggles over abortion, gay rights, affirmative action, religious expression, the death penalty, and the role of the federal government. These struggles, moreover, now play out in a post-Watergate world in which the public has grown cynical about its institutions even as the members of those institutions appear to have grown cynical about themselves and their mission.

Others have written about the epidemic of partisanship and lack of character in our government's elected branches and the cycle of recrimination and disaffection it has created.[2] This book is about the creeping of that toxic combination into the delicate ecosystem of the Supreme Court. It is about how, through the steady stream of litigation and through the process of nomination and confirmation, the Court has absorbed the same rancor that now swamps the rest of government. It is about how the severity of these divisions has corroded the Court's institutional culture and driven the Justices to disregard the principles of decision making—deliberation, integrity of argument, self-restraint—that separate the judicial function from the exercise of purely political power. It is about a Court whose inner workings are dangerously at odds with the source of its authority within our constitutional scheme.

The fault line at the Court, as in the elected branches, traces the rages of the sixties. In constitutional terms, this was the era of the "Rights Revolution," when the Justices, under the guiding hand of Chief Justice Earl Warren, significantly changed the meaning and scope of the nation's foundational law. Starting with *Brown* v. *Board of Education*, the Court moved dramatically to end race discrimination in America, to establish a right of sexual privacy, and to expand the rights of the poor, of criminal defendants, and of religious minorities. Along the way, the Court substantially enhanced its role in the nation's political life as well as the role of the federal government (sometimes at the expense of the states) in protecting the Constitution's newly established safeguards.

From the perspective of the more liberal Justices and their supporters, today's Supreme Court—the Rehnquist Court—has been engaged in a sustained and evil counterrevolution, undermining or destroying the civil rights and civil liberties that the Warren Court properly championed. In curtailing affirmative action and civil rights enforcement, in limiting the right to abortion and enhancing the power of police and prosecutors, in rushing executions and curbing the power of the federal government, including the judiciary, the Rehnquist Court, it is said, has been turning back the clock on social progress and retreating from the institution's own duty to enforce the constitutional promises of liberty and equality.

Conservatives, both within and without the Court, approach the innovations of the Warren era from the opposite corner. In their view, the Warren Court's exaltation of egalitarianism, criminals' rights, and sexual freedom was a prime factor in creating the legal and moral decay of the current age. And, to them, most if not all of the Rights Revolution was illegitimate from the outset, a judicial coup d'état that established the Court as a "superlegislature," overturning with no constitutional authority the judgments of elected representatives. According to conservatives, the Rehnquist Court's retrenchments, while certainly welcome, remain significantly incomplete. To them, in several vital areas, and especially in those decisions reaffirming *Roe* and expanding the rights of women and gays, the relatively liberal and moderate Justices have succeeded in compounding the cardinal sins of Chief Justice Warren's day.

In light of such pervasive and continuing internal division, the question for the Court, as for the rest of government, has been whether the institution's own integrity can withstand the corrupting force of bitter disagreement. And the answer, thus far, is dismal.

Under the pressure of the conservative, anti-Warren counter-revolution, the Justices on the Rehnquist Court have broken into self-contained ideological factions who exchange, almost routinely, increasingly harsh accusations of hypocrisy and illegitimacy. On both sides, these charges have often been deserved.

In crucial cases, narrow Court majorities transformed constitutional law on the basis of opinions the Justices knew to be wholly inadequate and unconvincing. Individual Justices sought to advance their political agendas by employing legal arguments in which they themselves did not believe or methods of interpretation they had uniformly rejected in the past. Neither side respected precedent, except when convenient; both sides tried to twist the Court's internal rules to attain narrow advantage. In short, from William Brennan to Antonin Scalia, the Justices abandoned the power of persuasion for the power of declaring partisan victory by sweeping the chess pieces from the board.

This sort of decision making is more than unseemly or unfortunate. It is antithetical to the Court's role in our system of government. We have vested in the Court broad authority to interpret the Constitution in the belief that unelected and therefore independent judges can wield powers of reasoning, imagination, and wisdom that will raise their decisions above the trade-offs of everyday politics and the naked act of voting.[3] The *method* of their decision making is the irreplaceable source of the Justices' legitimacy. Thus, when they disregard the traditions of law, invoke intellectually dishonest arguments, engage in glaring inconsistencies, and reduce their deliberations to the shallow calculus of five votes beats four, they call their own reason for being into question.

The enterprise of the Court, the process of constitutionalism, depends on the Justices' ability to persuade us (and one another) that their choices among competing arguments, however imperfect, represent reasoned, dispassionate, honest attempts to decide cases in a principled way. We accept the imperfection—the certainty that judges will sometimes err or overstep their bounds—because we maintain a faith that, in the run of things, better arguments will triumph over lesser ones. And we depend on the judges themselves to undertake the process with a sense of self-doubt and humility that leaves open the constant possibility of reassessment and change.

To fulfill this mission, a body of nine independent, opinionated judges whose views in hard cases often prove irreconcilable must above all preserve a decency of process. For the system to work, for Justices in disagreement to achieve an exchange of ideas, undertake a search for common ground, or even reach an agreement respectfully to disagree, there must first be trust and belief in mutual good faith. There must be a sense that reasons matter more than specific outcomes. There must be a sense that both sides are advancing legal arguments because they believe in them.

This is not simply a matter of finding the "vital center," so much in vogue in today's political rhetoric. It is a matter of finding ways to acknowledge and accommodate even our most passionate differences, the ones where no common ground exists. For the Justices, this process demands a strong measure of empathy for opposing points of view and an emphasis on their common commitment to the enterprise of the Court itself. It means understanding when to stand on principle, when to put a matter off, and when simply to yield. It means submerging one's ideology and self-expression beneath the Court's larger duty to maintain clarity, coherence, and continuity in the law.[4]

Despite the weaknesses of human nature and the presence of other dark periods in the Court's own history, this is not an idle hope. Early in the nineteenth century, at the outset of the republic, Chief Justice John Marshall presided over a Court remarkable for its cohesion despite the prevailing atmosphere of crisis and recrimination between Federalist and Republican partisans. Through Marshall's own instinct for building consensus and, most important, through the power of collegial discussion, the Justices of that era overcame sharp divisions and succeeded in separating the interests of the Court and of the Constitution from politics.[5]

Earl Warren, too, even as he pursued a far-reaching agenda, was usually vigilant in nurturing the Court's institutional integrity. As a general matter, he understood that the greatest exercises of the Court's authority called for the widest possible agreement within the Court itself. In that vein, he worked diligently to achieve unanimity, not only in the first landmark of *Brown* v. *Board of Education* but whenever the Court addressed the issues of race, which so divided the nation. He forged broad alliances in other areas as well and, perhaps most important, exerted his considerable force of personality to ensure that those serious disagreements that did occur took place mainly within the framework of principled debate, not partisan maneuvering.[6]

The cost to the country of the Court's current deficiencies is potentially enormous. As our leaders across the spectrum of government abandon ethical and institutional constraints in pursuing their clashing agendas, we have begun to lose our belief in one of the nation's founding principles, that of representative democracy—the idea that those we trust with high office will distill and transcend public opinion to fashion wise policy.

In electoral politics, our current fancy for term limits, for "outsider" candidacies like that of Ross Perot, and for resolving complex issues through ballot initiatives are just a few expressions of the frustration-born populist impulse abroad in the land. And our elected representatives, for their part, seem to have lost either the faith or the courage to act in that capacity. Daily, they respond to what the public thinks at each polling-spun moment, creating a kind of fickle government by referendum. At the same time, through gimmickry such as blue-ribbon commissions and narrow-gauged constitutional amendments, they seek to remove from themselves the power to make the hard, politically inconvenient decisions that the nation's problems require.

This populist trend is now pressing hard against the Court's front door. Vocal critics, doubting the very idea of judicial review, are now aiming at the judiciary the same antirepresentative assault already launched against the rest of government. Robert Bork, the leading conservative spokesman on issues of law, has called for a constitutional amendment that would make "any federal or state court decision subject to being overruled by a majority vote of each House of Congress."[7] Only with this basic rewriting of our original national charter, Bork concludes, can the "Supreme Court . . . be brought back to constitutional legitimacy."*

From every quarter, proposals for new constitutional amendments— to balance the budget, protect the flag, fix term limits, limit campaign spending, reinstate school prayer, or guarantee crime victims' rights— have sprouted like weeds. Whatever their individual purposes, collectively they represent an implicit judgment that the Court's own interpretive methods have become corrupted, and that its common law processes for keeping faith with the Constitution should be replaced by a system of constitutional plebiscites.

This hyperdemocratization of the Constitution is dangerous on at least two levels. First, the more constitutional law is left to majority vote, the less secure become the interests of those dissenting citizens whom the Bill of Rights was meant to protect. Second, and more generally, a populist attack on the Court would turn the Constitution's nature on its head. For the Constitution is a "republican" document, one committed to the idea of democracy as crucially tempered through reflection and deliberation. The Constitution's Framers designed the Court to be a center for such thinking, a safe harbor for our most enduring basic values. If we abandon that idea, or if we allow the Justices to abandon it for us, we forsake the genius of our national design.

The Court is both a microcosm and a model for the nation as a whole. The ruptures in its culture are ones we share and partially impose. And, by the same measure, the Court's mending could be an inspiration for our own.

In the short run, the cure for what ails the Court lies solely with the Justices. It is their duty, under the shield of life tenure, to recognize the

---

*In a similar vein, some conservatives are now calling for a much more active use of the impeachment process to remove judges whose decisions they dislike.

pathologies affecting their work and to restore the vitality of American constitutionalism. Ultimately, though, the long-term health of the Court depends on our own resolve—on whom, through our elected and accountable representatives, we select to join that institution. Our divisions will be with us always, and they force us to a choice: will our Justices have the wisdom and character to nurture what Abraham Lincoln in his first inaugural address called "the bonds of affection [that] passion may have strained"? Or will they simply be a mirror in which we view our most divided selves at work?

Most books about the Supreme Court deal broadly and, by necessity, somewhat superficially with virtually the full range of important legal issues that come before the Court. This book takes a different approach. It is limited almost exclusively to a few issues, chosen to be illustrative of the whole: the death penalty, race discrimination, and abortion. This is not because I believe other issues—such as free speech, religion, or the separation of powers—to be less important. Rather, I believe that dealing comprehensively with the Court's varied caseload renders impossible a complete understanding and critique of how the Court really does its work.

My intent has been to use a relatively sharp lens to look deeply into the Rehnquist Court—to explore in detail the substance and history of the disputes that so intensely divide the Justices, to explain how those disputes tear at the fabric of the Court's internal culture, to provide a clear window into the unsettling interactions of Justices and law clerks as they write the law of the land, and, ultimately, to evaluate the arguments and strategies of the various factions at the Court.

Some parts of this book are written as a pure history of the Court and of constitutional law. Other parts are explicitly judgmental and embody my current assessment of the Court's actions past and present. Still other parts consist of a memoir written by someone who participated in the trench warfare that has consumed the Court in recent years.

I chose this approach—juxtaposing history, memoir, and analysis—in order to combine rigorous evaluation with a vivid portrait of the extreme intellectual and emotional intensity that builds inside the Court's closed environment as it grapples with the most explosive legal issues of our day. I have also tried to use the contrast between what I felt then—as a clerk in the heat of battle—and what I think now as a way of diagnosing what has gone wrong at the Court.

After an introductory chapter, I focus at considerable length on the death penalty. In my experience, the cases involving capital punishment exerted an enormous influence, both ideological and emotional, on the Court's work. This influence, moreover, has gone almost wholly unnoticed and unappreciated by outsiders to the Court.

At the same time, the issue of the death penalty provides an especially revealing view into the Court's work as a whole. Death penalty cases, both now and in the past, cut to the root of the Court's ideological divisions. In the terrible context of a choice between life and death, these cases raise many of the issues that have divided the legal world since the Civil War, including issues about the Court's own role and authority.

For these reasons, I use the death penalty (with an emphasis on the role of race in its imposition) to explain the essentials of Chief Justice Warren's Rights Revolution—to trace its origins and intent, to sketch out its opposition, and to describe its gradual eclipse. I also use the Court's capital cases to explain when and how both the liberal and the conservative factions at the Court came to abandon the Court's own deliberative processes and disregard basic tenets of the rule of law.

Chronologically, my discussion of the death penalty cases carries the narrative of judicial revolution and counterrevolution up to the full-scale bloodletting that commenced with President Ronald Reagan's nomination of Robert Bork to succeed Justice Lewis Powell. In my view, that nomination fight—full of deceptions on both sides—unleashed yet a new level of rancor and self-destructiveness in the nation's legal culture generally and at the Court in particular.

The story of the Court in the late 1980s and early '90s is of this spirit of faction and recrimination. And to tell this story—which makes up the heart of the book—I shift focus from the death penalty to the issues of race and abortion, which, more than any others, have defined the modern Court. There, I explain exactly how the warping factors of polarization and a failure of integrity profoundly affected the Court's decisions as the Justices and their clerks savaged one another over the most divisive matters in American life and what hand the Court should have in them. On questions calling for the most careful judicial response, the Justices again and again provided only the most political.

The Court today has found some measure of peace on the issue of abortion. And the holdovers from the era of Warren and Nixon are gone. But the battles at the Court, as in the country, continue with great force, especially over the issues of race and states' rights—the twin shadows of the Civil War that haunt us still. The current Court remains a place shattered, one lacking not only a center but a leader and shared sense of purpose.

So this book is meant as both an indictment—a revelation of how a Court can come to lose its essential character—and a hopeful plea that, as a new generation at the Court searches for its balance, such character may be restored.

THE MARBLE PALACE

A Clerk's Eye View

Every great institution has a culture all its own, an ethos, a way of doing things that shapes its work. The Supreme Court is no exception. To begin to fathom the Court requires at the outset an introduction to the environment inside the building and, particularly, in the offices and corridors behind guarded latticework gates where the law of the land is defined.

Growing up in Washington, D.C., the son of an attorney, I visited the Supreme Court on school field trips and heard many stories about it, but certainly never imagined working there. My father had argued cases at the Court, and I dreamed of doing so myself one day. But to me, as I imagined to most, the place remained unreal, a movie set complete with Greek temple–like building and nine black-robed protagonists. The Court spoke to me (to the extent that it did), as it spoke to the world, exclusively through the cold type of its opinions and the news reports that summarized them.

At Yale Law School, my friends and I read hundreds of Court opinions as we sharpened our skill in the high art of debunking their logic and consistency. For many of us, Court watching became a natural avocation, a kind of domestic Kremlinology, in which written pronouncements and thirdhand gossip were combined to support weighty prognostications. The nine actors on the stage—an ensemble cast from Chief Justice John Marshall's Court to William Rehnquist's—took on names, faces, personalities, and legal philosophies, ranging from the invidious to the heroic.

It was shortly after my arrival at law school that I first really learned about clerking—the highly prized opportunity to serve as assistant to a judge, usually for one year after graduation. Clerking held the immediate attraction of providing a once-in-a-lifetime opportunity to observe the judicial system from the judge's side of the bench and to participate in the heady process of deciding real cases, in which palpable, sometimes enormous, human interests were at stake. More crassly, clerkships also serve as door openers, jobs of sufficient prestige to launch promising careers and especially significant first steps for those inclined toward legal academia.

That said, clerkships vary widely in their nature and quality. Applying within the federal court system alone, a law student must choose between district court judges (who preside over trials) and circuit court judges (who hear appeals on the issues raised at trials), geographic regions of the country, old judges and young ones, prestigious and not so prestigious, liberal and conservative, smart and pedestrian. A good clerkship—full of intellectual exchange and shared respect—can be both a joy and a remarkable education. A bad clerkship, rancorous and distrustful, amounts to a year's sentence in an especially cloistered ring of hell.

On the one hand, clerks for Judge "Crazy Eddie" Weinfeld (now deceased) of the Southern District of New York knew they had to be in the office at 7:00 A.M. to cut the judge's morning grapefruit. On the other hand, they would learn a lifetime's worth of civil procedure and good lawyering during the ninety hours a week spent laboring for this incredibly wise man. By contrast, a stint with Judge Frank Easterbrook on the Seventh Circuit Court of Appeals was known (when I was applying) as the Maytag clerkship. Easterbrook—a former law professor and trailblazer in the field of "law and economics"—is so self-sufficient he reputedly hardly ever asks his clerks to do any interesting work.

In the best of circumstances, as one prominent federal judge put it, "by accepting a judge's clerkship offer a young lawyer becomes a part of the judge's extended family, a disciple, an ally, quite possibly a friend."[1] In any event, a clerk is forever marked by the judge for whom he or she worked, bonded to that judge's reputation and inevitably dependent on that judge for many years of professional and personal references.

At the undisputed top of the clerkship pyramid is the Supreme Court, where clerks have been serving since 1882, when Justice Horace Gray (at his own expense) hired a recent Harvard Law School graduate. Not until 1922 did Congress appropriate money for the Justices to hire one clerk each at a salary of $3,600 per year—about a tenth of what they are currently paid. Then, as now, Justices relied on friends in the legal academy or elsewhere to suggest candidates. As a Harvard law professor, for example, Felix Frankfurter sent Justice Oliver Wendell Holmes Harvard's best graduates. Over time, as the Court's caseload increased, so did the number of clerks. Currently, every Justice is entitled to four clerks, though Chief Justice Rehnquist and Justice John Paul Stevens employ only three.*

Landing one of the better clerkships (on any court) depends on that time-worn combination of merit, who you know, and blind luck. Judges look for superior grades and, usually, membership on a law review. No less important is a letter of recommendation from at least one professor (usually a former clerk) who is "plugged in" to the clerkship network— who either knows a number of judges personally or has developed a reputation for writing trustworthy evaluations. With some judges, liberal and conservative, political compatibility plays a role. And, of course, having a friend in the chambers of a judge to whom you are applying never hurts.

Generally speaking, the most sought-after clerkships are those with "feeder" judges, an elite group of about twenty mostly appellate judges with track records of having their clerks land subsequent clerkships at the Supreme Court. (As a general rule, Supreme Court Justices require a year of experience clerking on a lower court.) Most feeders are just excellent judges who hire top law graduates every year and train them well. But even with first-rate judges, politics and personal relationships play a part.

Judge Alex Kozinski, for example, is uniformly recognized as one of the smartest members of the federal bench, an outspoken conservative with a razor-sharp wit. He is also a former clerk to both the late Chief Justice Warren Burger and Justice Anthony Kennedy—who was still on the Ninth Circuit when Kozinski worked for him. As part of his own hiring process, Kozinski is famous for organizing poker games at elite law schools to which he invites leading clerkship contenders. More to the point, he not only is friendly with several conservative Supreme Court Justices but actually conducts screening interviews of applicants under serious consideration by Justice Kennedy. It is hardly surprising, then, that Kozinski clerks often continue on to the Supreme Court and that

---

*Each retired Justice is also entitled to one clerk. These clerks frequently moonlight as fifth clerks for active Justices.

Justice Kennedy's picks often mirror Kozinski's seeming preference for men as well as for members of the Federalist Society, a nationwide association of conservative law students and graduates.*

From the perspective of a law student, a Supreme Court clerkship is as much an honor as it is an actual job, a title, like Rhodes Scholar, that distinguishes you for life. One cannot plan for this position; the odds are too long. But one can yearn to join this Round Table of the law, and many law students do. For every office to which you might aspire, from the partners' offices at the best firms to the faculty offices at the best schools and the most powerful offices in government—from the office of Harvard Professor Laurence Tribe to that of Chief Justice Rehnquist and former Secretary of State Warren Christopher—former Supreme Court clerks abound. (They are easily identified. Somewhere in their offices, usually prominently placed, they almost always display an autographed portrait, framed in basic black, from the Justice for whom they clerked.)

Each Justice has his or her own predispositions and system for hiring clerks. All else being equal, Chief Justice Rehnquist is said to prefer tennis players. Justice John Paul Stevens, who practiced law and first sat on the bench in Chicago, hires many of his clerks from the better midwestern law schools. Justice Hugo Black always used to hire one southerner. Former clerks to Justice Byron White say that you knew your interview was going well if he took you on a tour of the courtroom. For many years, Justice Thurgood Marshall delegated the entire selection process to a committee of trusted ex-clerks. One hears other stories, ranging from silly—did Justice White, yelling, "Think fast," really throw a basketball at an applicant who claimed athletic prowess?—to the disturbing—Justice Brennan, despite his civil libertarian credentials, once reneged on a clerkship offer after the FBI approached him with concerns about the prospective clerk's left-wing allegiances.†

Not surprisingly, when Justice Blackmun granted me an interview, I went to some lengths to find out his modus operandi. The several former Blackmun clerks I checked with painted a remarkably consistent pic-

---

*Conservative judges have no monopoly on such arrangements. Hardly a year went by, for example, that Judge Skelly Wright, a prominent liberal on the Court of Appeals for the District of Columbia Circuit, did not place at least one of his almost uniformly liberal clerks with Justice Brennan. With the exception of Blackmun, the liberal Justices have also shared the conservatives' propensity for hiring male clerks.

†The almost-clerk was Michael Tigar, the noted attorney and law professor who recently served as defense counsel to Terry Nichols in the Oklahoma City bombing trial.

ture. After arriving at the Court, I would be escorted at 11:00 A.M. sharp to the Chambers, where I would spend twelve minutes ostensibly waiting for the Justice but actually being interviewed by the Justice's two secretaries, Wanda Martinson and Wannett Smith. If the "2 W's" didn't take to me, the ex-clerks agreed, the interview with the Justice would be irrelevant.

At 11:12, give or take fifteen seconds, Justice Blackmun would descend from the Justices' Library on the second floor, enter the Chambers—almost certainly clad in an old cardigan—and introduce himself. (Ex-clerks' warning: Don't imitate the unfortunate applicant who jumped to his feet and stepped straight into a trash can.) The Justice would then lead me into his office, where for forty-five minutes or so he would pepper me with scripted, basically routine questions about my family and background. (Ex-clerks' warning: Call him "Mr. Justice.") In addition, he would make at least five remarks disparaging himself and the value of a clerkship in his Chambers. (Ex-clerks' warning: Be prepared for him to caution you that he was very old and might die during your clerkship.)

In general, so the conventional wisdom held, the interview would provide no opportunity for me to distinguish myself, and I would leave the room wholly unenlightened about whether I had won the job. Don't worry, the ex-clerks said. Everybody feels this way.

All of the above was, in fact, very good advice, and I have given it myself to Blackmun clerkship applicants who have asked. Like much good advice, though, it was really all wrong.

It is true that Justice Blackmun did appear at 11:12 A.M. (on February 12, 1988, in my case), after allowing me about ten minutes' banter with Wanda and Wannett. And, as promised, the Justice was wearing a cardigan. Walking through the door to my right, he extended a hand. "Hello," he said in a deep and slightly graveled voice, "I'm Harry Blackmun"—to which, of course, I felt like responding, "No kidding."

The Justice ushered me inside his office, and I had a moment to scan the room. In an instant, I knew this experience would be anything but perfunctory and that before it was over he would have something of the measure of me, and I of him.

As soon as I walked in, somewhat desperate for topics of conversation, I noticed hanging on the far wall, amid a sea of memorabilia, a full-sized Louisville Slugger baseball bat mounted on a wooden slab. It was a Mel Ott model, the Justice said, styled for the New York Giants right fielder whose distinctive hitting technique and 511 career home runs made him one of the game's immortals. The bat was a gift, Justice Blackmun explained, from his clerks for October Term 1974. That term, the Justice continued, he'd written an opinion in a baseball case, *Flood* v. *Kuhn*. . . .

Like most law students, I knew this. Blackmun's opinion in *Flood* (upholding baseball's "reserve clause" against an antitrust challenge brought by the St. Louis Cardinals outfielder Curt Flood) was Court legend. Its entire first section has nothing to do with law. Instead, as a sort of preamble, Blackmun had penned a tribute to the game, complete with a list of more than seventy players whom he had selected as his favorites. Justice White was so put off by this extrajudicial show of sentimentality he refused to join that section of the opinion.

What I hadn't known, but the Justice now told me, was that through inadvertence the opinion's list of all-stars failed to include the redoubtable Mel Ott. And with that admission, Justice Blackmun walked over to a bookcase (on one shelf of which sat a Wheaties cereal box commemorating a Minnesota Twins World Series victory), and pulled out volume 407 of his personal copy of *U.S. Reports*—the thick volumes where Court opinions are published. Blackmun opened to the *Flood* opinion and showed me where in an infinitesimal script that I would come to know all too well he had written "Mel Ott?" in the margin next to where the Hall of Famer's name should have appeared in the opinion. With a rueful grin, the Justice also showed me the engraved plaque beneath the bat. "I shall never forgive myself," it read—his reaction on being informed of Ott's omission.

Justice Blackmun's office overflows with similar adornments. Each comes with a story and reveals part of the man. We touched upon a few more that morning: a magnificent stand-up desk that had belonged to Judge John Sanborn of the Eighth Circuit Court of Appeals, for whom the Justice had clerked more than fifty years before; a careworn pocket copy of the U.S. Constitution (always at hand), a gift from Justice Hugo Black; the sword of a grandfather who had fought for the Union in the Civil War. Some we did not discuss—photographs of friends and colleagues, or a swatch of torn fabric in a block of clear plastic, a memento from when a bullet had crashed through the Justice's apartment window and torn into an empty chair. Along one wall stood a small shrine to Abraham Lincoln: framed quotations, a silhouette, and documents bearing the signature of the president who had ended slavery and preserved the nation.

From across a broad, nearly bare desk, the Justice began his questioning, the talk of family and upbringing and general interests of which I had been warned. The purpose by now was clear. Rather than a grilling, he wanted simply to see how we'd get along for forty-five minutes or so—and how, together with three other clerks, two secretaries, and a messenger, we might get along for what, if he hired me, promised to be the most arduous year of my life.

Much of the time it sounded as if he was trying to talk me out of the job. More than once he alluded to the hard work and long hours. And with a self-deprecation hard to imagine (or believe) in a Supreme Court Justice, he insisted that his was the least desirable clerkship at the Court, in part because his colleagues were more intelligent and better teachers than he.

As with everyone who interviews with Justice Blackmun, the conversation eventually turned to *Roe*. Standing before a window, the weak February light catching a certain weariness in his deeply etched face, the Justice asked whether I would mind working for a man who had excited such fury. You could see that he lived with the heavy mantle of that case every day of his life, and he wanted me to recognize that for a year and maybe longer, in some small way, that weight might rest on me too.

In what seemed little more than an instant, the interview was over. He was thanking me for coming. I was looking swiftly about the room on the likely chance I would never see it again. Thinking back, I realize how much of Justice Blackmun's character I brushed against that morning: his overwhelming sense of duty, often agonized and joyless, to the Court and to the country; his nearly obsessive concern for detail; his appreciation of the impact of his work on others' lives; and, most of all, his deep, almost romantic, belief in the idea of the United States as a nation committed to broad principles of moral governance. This was a man who had kissed the cheek of a man—his grandfather—who had risked his life in the war that freed the slaves and enshrined in our Constitution the words "equal protection of the laws." The spirit of that struggle, the sense of its incompletion, fairly radiated from the man.

I'm sure most clerks for most justices have such stories, different in feeling or tone perhaps but amounting to the same thing—the first casting of the nearly familial bond between judge and clerk. Now I can say that I have kissed the cheek that kissed the cheek . . . and in all the times I sat in that office and looked at his grandfather's sword, it never failed to remind me, as it must remind the Justice still, why we were there.

* * *

The sidewalks and the subway cars of the nation's capital fairly teem with executive or legislative branch employees, their plastic photo-identification cards dangling from neck chains discreetly (but never too discreetly) tucked away in breast pockets. This faintly obnoxious status symbol lets its bearer pass through the tight security at federal office buildings.

Security is no less vigilant at the Supreme Court, but its employees never flash ID cards at the entrance. I remember reporting to work on my first day at the Court, walking through the front entrance, and being waved through the metal detector by the police officer at the door. Every officer on the Court's force had memorized pictures of the thirty-six incoming clerks before we arrived. It was like belonging to a secret club whose members knew one another before ever exchanging names.

Only later did I come to appreciate the full meaning of this ritual of recognition. It was but the first of a thousand manifestations of an essential truth about the Court that finds little place in the mountainous literature describing and analyzing it: the Court is far more than just an office building where nine Justices and their staffs conduct the nation's most important legal business. The Court consists of a minisociety unto itself, not unlike a small town—insular, intensely private, and deeply settled into a pattern of rituals, routines, and idiosyncrasies in almost every facet of its functioning.

To take a mundane example: Among the most important types of communication that circulate regularly among the Justices is the "join memo," a written commitment by one Justice to join the proposed opinion of another. Say Chief Justice Rehnquist sends around a draft of a proposed majority opinion in a given case. In order for that draft opinion to become the "Opinion of the Court" (and, thereby, the law of the land), four other Justices—totaling a majority—must join it.[2]

Join memos come in several varieties. Least welcome, for the author of the proposed opinion, is the blackmail type—really not a join memo at all—in which a Justice writes that he or she would gladly join *if only* the author would change X, Y, and Z. Such extortionist demands often arrived gloved in flattery, as in one Justice William Douglas wrote to Justice Stanley Reed: "I like your opinion in No. 18 very much. You have done an excellent job in a difficult field. And I want to join you in it. *But—*"[3] Sometimes an opinion author will find a colleague's suggestion meritorious. But often whether the author adopts the proposed change depends mainly on how close a case it is, in other words, how badly the author needs the other Justice to join in order to obtain or preserve a majority.

More welcome by far is the unconditional join memo accompanied by suggestions that the original author may take or leave at his or her discretion. The suggestions may be good ones, and, regardless, the author Justice can tally another join.

Most welcome of all, though, is the unconditional, no suggestions, nothing-but-a-join memo that simply communicates to the opinion author in a single sentence, "I'm with you." Yet even these one-line notes can become the subjects of considerable comment in the introverted, self-reflective world of the Court.

The issue is one of style. Most Justices, as far back as the sixties at least, circulated join memos using the polite phrasing "Please join me" (under a caption identifying the case in question) to indicate their agreement to sign on to a draft of an opinion. Deviation from the norm opened a Justice to uncharitable comment. Former Chief Justice Warren E. Burger's imperious "I join" was said to reflect his legendarily self-centered personality.

But "Please join me" is a formulation containing obvious ambiguities. By its terms alone, the phrasing does not make clear who is joining whom in what. To understand the meaning of "Please join me," one had to refer to past custom and usage—a fact that, in a completely silly and inconsequential way, reflected one of the most substantial jurisprudential debates at the Court.

Ever since his 1986 appointment, Justice Antonin Scalia has waged a full-scale campaign against methods of statutory interpretation that depend on assembling historical evidence and in favor of textual exegesis—that is, affixing meaning by looking solely at the words of a law itself. "Please join me" lacks the linguistic clarity to which Justice Scalia is partial and, accordingly, he adopted his own join memo formulation: "I would be pleased to join." (Others at the Court were quick to toss back their own niggle, of course, that this conditional phrasing begged the question If what?)

And, as if Scalia's deviation weren't tradition shattering enough, Justice Anthony Kennedy (early in 1988, his first full term as a Justice) followed Scalia's lead. Among tea leaf readers and prognosticators inside the Court, this was seen as proof positive that Justice Kennedy already had fallen under the intellectual sway of the Court's most dynamic conservative.[4]

Such byplay, the Court's version of gossiping over the back fence, arises inevitably from its size and self-sufficiency. The Court is a remarkably small place considering its profoundly important function, employing fewer than 300 persons, most of whom stay for many, many years. Moreover, the Court building, though by no means posh except for the public rooms, houses a cafeteria, snack bar, gymnasium, wood shop, police force, custodial staff, barbershop, seamstress, print shop, library, nurse, in-house law office, gift shop, and curator. As a consequence, from the beginning of the workday until its end—whether that day be a marshal's assistant's standard shift or a law clerk's fourteen-hour grind—the Court's employees virtually never venture outside its walls.

All of which is simply to say that, from the elevator operators (nearly all black women, who remind one that Washington is basically a southern town only a few decades removed from Jim Crow) to the Justices themselves, everyone at the Court operates in the intensely pressured environment within a hermetically sealed system. Justice Holmes once described himself and his brethren as nine scorpions trapped in a bottle. I think of the Justices more like nine princes—actually seven princes and two princesses—sharing a single castle, with much of the color, ceremony, and scheming (especially among the courtiers) such an arrangement would entail.

No doubt most of the petty wrangling, gossiping, favor trading, friendships, romances, prides, and prejudices of the castle's functionaries are of no real significance to the Justices' work. Did it really matter that Justice Thurgood Marshall's clerks inevitably entered into guerrilla warfare with the Justice's martinet of a secretary—a kind of revolving Hatfields and McCoys dating back to when the secretary padlocked the office refrigerator so the clerks could not use it? Well, no.

However, feuds, friendships, and feelings within the tiny community that is our Supreme Court inevitably creep into the quality and content of its work. Did it matter that after Justice William Brennan retired in June 1990, Chief Justice Rehnquist moved him into a small, inhospitable second-floor office and, despite Brennan's physical incapacity, took away his Court car and driver? I think it did. It was hurtful, not just to Brennan but to his friends in the building, to other Justices who could perhaps imagine caning their way down a remote hallway, and more generally to the mood inside the Court. As in any small community, slights (and favors, too) are mulled, magnified, remembered. A stone is dropped in the pool; the ripples reach every shore.

Life at the Court has a distinct rhythm, each term resembling a baseball season. The summer, from the end of June until roughly Labor Day, is the off-season. The Court stands in recess, rendering no decisions except for the rare emergency motion. Most of the Justices leave town for much of this period to rejuvenate and relax.

For the clerks, this is the time for an orientation—to the extent there is one. Immediately upon arriving in July, you begin to get a feel for your co-clerks, the Justice's messenger, and the vitally important secretaries. This group, together with the Justice, constitutes a "Chambers," the Court equivalent of a nuclear family, with all the risk of dysfunction that entails. At best, these are the people you will come to rely on, trust, and even love as you help and support one another through a long year at close quarters. At worst, some become slackers, or rivals, or even enemies to be overcome as you try to do your own work as well as you can. Most Chambers, like most families, find some middle ground.

In the Blackmun Chambers, each outgoing clerk designated two days to train his or her successor. I remember that time as a giant blur, a jumble of shorthand explanations of procedures I couldn't quite grasp, mixed in with a number of "don't worry, you'll figure it out as you go alongs." In quick order, we were trained in the Court's computer system, introduced to its librarians (who double as research assistants), and given a building tour—all of which meant that, after a week, we were on our own yet knew basically nothing except perhaps where to find the two magnificent freestanding spiral marble staircases.

The saving grace for every new clerk was a book called *Supreme Court Practice* (by Robert Stern, Eugene Gressman, and Stephen Shapiro, all former clerks) that each of us kept no more than an arm's length from our desks.[5] *Stern & Gressman*, as it was known, contained just about everything there was to know about the Court's procedures. It explained the basics, such as the fact that the Court hears appeals coming from both state supreme courts and federal courts of appeals (known as circuit courts, which, for their part, review the decisions of federal district courts). It reminded us that the Supreme Court reviews only issues of *federal* law, that the Court agrees to decide only a small fraction of the cases where the parties request review, and that the Court selects which

cases to decide primarily to resolve important issues of law and *not* to
correct case-specific errors in a lower court's rulings. Mostly, though,
Stern & Gressman was filled with technical knowledge that only a
Supreme Court clerk or practitioner could possibly want to know. In
other words, it was our Bible.

In the Blackmun Chambers, we also received a forty-page memorandum, "Helpful Hints for Blackmun Clerks," that explained in detail
what our Justice expected of us as incoming cases made their way
through the Court's cycle of business. That cycle is triggered when the
losing party to a lawsuit files a petition for certiorari (cert.), a formal request that the Court hear the case. If at least four Justices (not even a
majority) want to grant the petition, the Court schedules the case for argument.* The parties file written briefs; the Justices hear oral argument;
then they meet in conference and take a tentative vote. Afterward,
opinions are drafted and circulated; revisions are made. Then, finally,
the Court announces its decision. At every stage, with the exception of
the Justices' private conference, the clerks had some role to play—reading, assessing, commenting, advising—and (in our case) communicating
with Blackmun through the impersonal medium of typed "Mr. Justice
notes" placed on the top of a file cabinet at the entrance to his inner
sanctum.

Nor did all our tasks relate to cert. petitions and argued cases. The
Court also handled a steady stream of emergency applications, usually
requests for a stay to keep a lower court decision from taking effect. Each
Justice was responsible for supervising one or more of the thirteen federal
appellate (circuit) courts. Generally, a party seeking a stay would apply
first to the appropriate supervising Justice, who then would either handle the application individually, or, much more often, refer it to the entire Court for consideration. Justice Blackmun oversaw the Eighth
Circuit (including Minnesota, Missouri, and Arkansas), which meant
that many of the stay applications to our Chambers came from death row
inmates in Missouri or Arkansas seeking to avert impending executions.
Of all the instructions we received in "Helpful Hints," the most detailed
and forcefully phrased told us how to process and assist the Justice with
these.

---

*As with every rule, there are exceptions. On rare occasions, the Court will grant a petition and
decide a case summarily (without argument), but this practice is strongly disfavored by some Justices
and rarely used. Also, more frequently, the Court will grant a cert. petition, vacate the ruling of the
lower court, and return the case to that court for reconsideration in light of a new Supreme Court
decision that has been handed down since the time of the lower court's ruling.

By September, we had mastered the basics of our guidebooks, and, after Labor Day, the preseason began. The Justices returned to look over their new clerks. Then they attacked the backlog that had accumulated over the summer: more than 1,000 petitions for cert., whose fate the Justices determine in a single marathon session at the end of September. They also started preparing in earnest for the cases already granted review the previous spring and scheduled to be heard in October.

Opening day is the first Monday in October. At precisely 10:00 A.M., the marshal of the Court solemnly intones the medieval French words "Oyez, oyez, oyez," handed down for over 1,000 years from Norman days through the English common law. And then: "All persons having business before the Honorable the Supreme Court of the United States are admonished to draw near and give their attention for the Court is now sitting. God save the United States and this Honorable Court!" With that, the Justices (always in three groups of three) emerge from behind velvet drapes and take their seats.

The term builds steadily in workload, tension, and fatigue. Opinion assignments pile up in each Chambers as the Court hears and decides cases faster than the written opinions can be crafted. In December, January, and February, the Court hands down its judgments in some relatively straightforward and easily resolved cases. But the big cases, and the close ones, the ones where several Justices forcefully dissent, or where swing Justices straddle the fence and consider writing something of their own, these linger and grow in number, month after month, exerting a viselike grip on all other work that has to be done.

To give some idea of what goes on during the dog days of the term—March and early April—what follows is a list of the functions a law clerk typically performs during this period: drafting majority opinions, drafting dissents, drafting concurrences (opinions that agree with the result reached by the majority opinion but for somewhat different reasons), writing "bench memos" (which help a Justice prepare for a case the Court is about to hear), writing post–oral argument memos (which amend views set forth in bench memos), commenting on draft opinions, dissents, and concurrences circulated by other Chambers, recommending which new petitions for certiorari the Court should grant, and advising on emergency applications, often including last-minute requests for stays of execution.

Juggling these daunting assignments seven days a week for weeks on end produces a mind-numbing exhaustion and also exacts a physical toll. Longtime staffers around the building would joke about the "Blackmun diet," the workaholic's method for shedding pounds. Clerks invented remarkable routines for keeping themselves sharp; one, late at night during the winter months, propped open the security gates on the Court's main floor so that he could run circuits around the building.

As April progresses, some tasks fall away as the Court hears its last set of cases for the term and issues some of the major opinions from cases argued in the fall. The pace of work, however, only quickens. With the exception of a case or two for which reargument might be ordered for the following fall, before recessing for the summer the Court issues opinions in every one of the cases it has heard each term.* Most of these opinions, in a weekly cavalcade of major rulings, are handed down in the last two months of the term, with one or two monumental decisions always lingering until the very last day. This rush to the finish generates all the exhilaration of a great pennant race. Then the cycle starts over again.

Within this structure for the term, each week also follows a pattern. I learned to consider Wednesday the first day of the week. Sometime in the middle of the afternoon, without fail, an employee from the Court clerk's office would walk into each Chambers and, with a hair-raising *thwunk,* slam down a large stack of cert. petitions, then give a mildly apologetic shrug and walk back out the door.

These were the so-called paid petitions for certiorari, ones from litigants who could afford their own counsel, court costs, and printing. They came in at the rate of roughly forty per week, neatly bound and color coded (white for the petition itself, red for the response, yellow for the petitioner's reply, and gray if from the United States, regardless of its status as a party).

On Thursdays, another even larger stack would be delivered—the IFP's (*in forma pauperis*), petitions from indigent parties, often prisoners, representing themselves. These petitions were sometimes handwritten, occasionally illegible, and often inscrutable. But from Thursday's pile a number of the Court's landmark cases have emerged, such as *Gideon* v.

---

*In the mid-1980s the Court was hearing an average of roughly 150 cases each term, but the number has been significantly smaller in recent terms. The Court issued only 87 opinions during October Term 1993 and 84, 75, and 80 opinions in each of the subsequent terms. The reason for this dramatic drop in numbers is the source of much speculation. Justice Souter has suggested, rightly I believe, that the decrease has been caused, at least partially, by a "diminishing supply" of federal statutes to fuel pathbreaking litigation and by a "relative homogeneity" of views in the lower federal courts, resulting from twelve years of Reagan-Bush judicial appointments. With conservative judges dominating virtually all the appellate courts, many fewer conflicts arise for the Supreme Court to resolve. See David J. Garrow, "The Rehnquist Reins," *New York Times*, October 6, 1996, sec. 6, p. 65.

Wainwright from 1963 (establishing a constitutional right to counsel in state criminal cases), which began as a petition, carefully printed in pencil, from Clarence Earl Gideon, Prisoner No. 003826, serving a five-year sentence in a Florida jail for breaking and entering.[6]

These Wednesday and Thursday deliveries shaped the week because they determined which and how many petitions would be assigned to each clerk. Given the enormous task of selecting anywhere from 80 to 150 cases for full consideration, from what has grown to be more than 6,000 petitions received each year, most of the Justices pool their resources to expedite the evaluating process.[7] Rather than each Justice considering every case independently, a clerk for one Justice in the "cert. pool" circulates an advisory memo to all the Justices in the pool. This "pool memo" summarizes a case and assesses whether it is "certworthy"—that is, whether it raises a sufficiently important and controversial issue to merit the Supreme Court's attention. Although the Justices do not follow the pool memo recommendations slavishly, in practice they carry great weight.

When I clerked, six Justices (Rehnquist, White, Blackmun, O'Connor, Scalia, and Kennedy) participated in the cert. pool. Justices Marshall and Stevens worked with their own clerks to determine independently which cert. petitions merited a grant. Remarkably, Justice Brennan did all his cert. work on his own, with little assistance even from his clerks.

Currently, every Justice except Stevens participates in the cert. pool, and the disappearance of Justices outside the pool has, quite rightly I think, generated concern both inside and outside the Court. As a member of the pool, I well recall how helpful it was to be able to check my judgments in close cases with clerks in the Stevens and Marshall Chambers. And I wonder whether Justice Stevens and his clerks alone can effectively perform this checking function.[8] Others also have questioned whether the Justices have excessively delegated their cert. decisions to whichever clerk writes the pool memo in a given case.[9] In recent terms, Justices Kennedy and Scalia have both proposed reforms adding additional checks to the cert. pool system, but the Court has yet to adopt any major changes.

For a clerk in the pool, which petitions (averaging four per week) you catch in the rotation determines the nature of your week. Some, indeed most, petitions clearly do not raise issues appropriate to Court review, and the pool memo can be finished in a few hours or less. These cases end up on the "dead list," a voluminous roster of cases the Justices won't even bother to discuss at conference. By contrast, writing the pool memo for a petition involving capital punishment (these are specially marked for attention), or for a complex civil case, or for almost any case in which the decision whether to recommend a grant is close, can take a day or even two of nonstop research, writing, and thinking. With bad luck, cert. work might devour most of a week, pushing off the usually more interesting and rewarding work of assisting your Justice with cases the Court is actually deciding.

Cert. work, moreover, cannot be put off for more than a few days because more petitions arrive every week and the pool memos must be finished by 10:00 A.M. of the Wednesday before each of the Justices' biweekly Friday conferences. If your memos are not handed in to the Chief Justice's Chambers by the deadline, your name goes on the "late list," an ignominy calculated to earn the wrath of your Justice not only for your being late but also for the inconsideration you have thus shown (on his or her behalf) to the other members of the Court.

Fridays, at least the Fridays when the Justices met in Conference, were the most suspenseful and momentous days at the Court. At a few minutes to ten, the Justices would begin their perambulations through the plush red-carpeted halls toward the Conference Room located in the Chief Justice's suite directly behind the courtroom. Justice Kennedy, tall and on the lanky side, would fairly bound down the hall, arms swinging. Justice Marshall, old and mountainous, would lumber, wheezing slightly with each labored breath. By 10:00 sharp, they would all have assembled in the wood-paneled sanctum sanctorum for the ritual handshake commencing the Conference. Under the presiding portrait of Chief Justice John Marshall, the Justices would take their assigned seats at the long mahogany table, sharp pencils and yellow pads neatly arrayed at each place; then the junior Justice would shut the door against the outside world.

A few hours later the Justices would emerge, often individually, sometimes in groups of two or three, exchanging a few last words. As they retreated down the red carpet, their gaits would mirror their moods after a morning's decision making. Clerks would gather in doorways to gauge their bosses' success and speculate about which cert. petitions the Justices had granted and how the big cases had come out.

Weekends were quiet around the Court—no tourists or journalists, few secretaries. They were times when you could wander unimpeded through the portrait gallery of former Justices, trading stares with Holmes, Brandeis, Taney, Vinson—the great and not so great of bygone eras—or sit alone in the majestic courtroom, imagining trenchant arguments past and future.

Those oral arguments take place on Mondays, Tuesdays, and Wednesdays for two consecutive weeks each month. Except for a few mornings devoted to handing down decisions late in the term, these argument days, at most forty a term, constitute the sole personal interaction between the Court and the public, including the legal community. As a consequence, they are accompanied by a heightened level of commotion and excitement.

I loved walking from my office into the Great Hall to watch the preargument processional. Kept company by the marble busts of former Chief Justices, lawyers in dark pinstripes and tourists in lesser fashions would line up to pass through metal detectors manned by Court police officers immaculate in their dress blues. Advocates from the Solicitor General's Office (which represents the United States before the Court), some resplendent in morning coats and all solemn in demeanor, would strut past, chests puffed out, in a beeline for the courtroom.

There is something exquisite about the room's proportions, intimate but not cramped, magisterial but not overwhelming. From the pews of the courtroom, the panorama of lush marble, rich drapery, and gleaming appointments inspires an awe heightened by the dignity and ceremony of the proceedings themselves.

The Justices preside from a raised dais behind an imposing, dark mahogany bench. At their feet rest green-and-white china spittoons, relics now used as trash cans. Each Justice has his or her own black leather chair, formerly of varying styles according to a Justice's taste, but now almost uniform, with unnaturally straight, high backs. Rocking and swiveling as is their wont, the Justices look out on law clerks and invited guests to their left, journalists to the right, and counsel for the parties arrayed straight before them at long tables flanking a small lectern. Behind the lawyers sit members of the Supreme Court bar, then the public in pews toward the back. High above the Justices' heads, directly in view, a large frieze depicts a mythological battle between the Manichaean forces of Good and Evil.

The arguments themselves often fail to live up to the atmosphere. Most cases the Court hears involve dry stuff even for lawyers and raise issues that do not lend themselves to exploration in one hour of oral argument. As counsel drones on about some complex statutory scheme better described in previously submitted written briefs, the Justices do not always feign interest. They trade quips and trivia questions with their neighbors or ask desultory questions mainly to stay awake.

But many arguments do stir the blood. For the legally inclined, few sights are more riveting than an immensely skilled, exquisitely prepared advocate threading his or her way through the shark-infested waters of a hard case—parrying questions at every turn, conceding points where possible, standing ground where necessary. While the Court today may not hear arguments like Daniel Webster's in the *Dartmouth College* case of 1819, which, at least according to lore, moved the audience to tears ("It is a small college . . . yet there are those who love it"), the best attorneys can still capture a swing vote in a close case and carry the day. Or they can simply amaze with the agility of their minds.

On the other hand, much of the advocacy before the Court is mediocre, some downright contemptible. I remember one death penalty case where the Court was very closely divided, the outcome clearly in doubt, with the lives of dozens of condemned prisoners hanging in the balance. The lawyer for the defendant simply did not understand that the Court does not respond to pleas for mercy or other emotional arguments that might move a lay jury. It responds to arguments about the meaning of the law—in this case the Constitution—and she gave none.

These are the moments, as a clerk, when you want to jump up, rush to the podium, knock the incompetent lawyer out of the way, and carry on yourself. But you cannot. So you watch helplessly as an attorney, ignorant of potentially winning arguments, faces stony contempt, annoyance, sometimes even ridicule, from the bench. The client, rarely present, pays the price.

On some argument days, most often Mondays, the Court also hands down decisions. Once upon a time, according to a practice long ago abandoned as impractical, the Justices read their entire opinions from the bench. Today, the authoring Justice gives a brief explanation of the ruling. For Justice White, this meant clearing his throat and uttering one unintelligible sentence. Most Justices—especially those with a flair for the dramatic, such as Scalia and Kennedy—seem to revel in the moment and go to some length to make the cases accessible to the lay audience in the courtroom.

I always thought this appropriate. The Justices may discharge in their written opinions what Justice Robert Jackson called their obligation "to do our utmost to make clear and understandable the reasons for deciding cases as we do."[10] Nonetheless, I was struck repeatedly by the symbolic importance of having the Justices meet face to face with even a token representation of "We the People,"[11] whose laws and Constitution their opinions define. The Court's decisions, after all, are exercises of enormous coercive power that reorder many, even millions, of individual lives, indeed society itself. The subjects of that authority are entitled, I think, to see the faces behind the printed words.

On rare occasions, public announcement of a decision is accompanied by an expression of extreme disagreement by a Justice in dissent. A few times each term, a Justice will care so deeply about a case and feel so strongly that the Court has reached the wrong result that he or she will follow the announcement of the majority opinion by reading portions of his or her dissent.

Justice Stevens, an extraordinarily courteous man, is among those least inclined publicly to excoriate his colleagues from the bench. Still, he did it severely the term I clerked, when *Texas* v. *Johnson* (the first flag-burning case) was handed down.[12] I doubt anyone who was there has forgotten the moment.

In *Texas* v. *Johnson*, the Court ruled that the First Amendment's guarantee of free speech prohibited the state of Texas from prosecuting Gregory Lee Johnson for "flag desecration" after he burned an American flag as part of a political protest at the 1984 Republican National Convention. At oral argument it had been evident that Johnson's treatment of the flag infuriated Stevens, a World War II navy veteran. He became uncharacteristically testy with William Kunstler, Johnson's flamboyant attorney, who, for his part, was provocatively gleeful about his client's insulting conduct.

At the time, I wondered whether somewhere deep down Justice Stevens accepted the majority's view (axiomatic to almost all the clerks) that, purely as an intellectual matter, Johnson's burning of the flag was a constitutionally protected political statement. But no person, even a supremely rational one such as Justice Stevens, reaches every decision solely by the cold light of reason.* And he did not seem to have in this

---

*In this respect, Stevens's response resembled that of Chief Justice Earl Warren when facing a similar case during the Vietnam War. Explaining why he thought flag burning could be criminalized, Warren candidly told his clerks: "Boys, it's the flag. I'm just not going to vote in favor of burning the American flag." Ed Cray, *Chief Justice: A Biography of Earl Warren* (New York: Simon & Schuster, 1997), p. 452.

case. As he read his dissent from the bench, Stevens's voice was raw emotion. As he reached the peroration, his face was flush, his eyes just shy of tears.

"The ideas of liberty and equality have been an irresistible force in motivating leaders like Patrick Henry, Susan B. Anthony, and Abraham Lincoln, schoolteachers like Nathan Hale and Booker T. Washington, the Philippine Scouts who fought at Bataan, and the soldiers who scaled the bluff at Omaha Beach," Stevens closed. "If those ideas are worth fighting for—and our history demonstrates that they are—it cannot be true that the flag that uniquely symbolizes their power is not itself worthy of protection from unnecessary desecration. I respectfully dissent."

I still feel strongly that the Court majority was right and Stevens wrong in *Texas v. Johnson*. But tears do not often well on the high bench, and the purity of Stevens's conviction made an indelible impression. Every night, on the rooftops of the stately federal buildings that line Pennsylvania Avenue, a host of flags are spotlit against the dark sky. When I see those flags now, I'm always carried back to Stevens's speech in the courtroom. I don't look at them quite the same way as before.

Aside from chance encounters, clerks did not meet Justices other than their own until a welcoming cocktail party near the end of the summer recess. I remember a dazzling but awkward event, thirty-six clerks mingling (sort of) with most of the Justices and much of the upper echelon Court staff. For a while, the clerks from each Chambers tended to congregate among themselves, diplomats from nine separate nation-states, wine cups in hand, appraising their counterparts around the chandeliered room.

One of my best friends from law school was clerking for Justice White, and he took the bold step of introducing me to his boss. Even at seventy, White maintained the strong-shouldered physique and erect bearing of the world-class athlete he'd been in his youth. All-American halfback at the University of Colorado, Rhodes Scholar, NFL rookie of the year in 1938, top of his Yale Law School class, clerk to Chief Justice Fred Vinson, friend and adviser to Jack Kennedy, White was (as one admirer put it) both Clark Kent and Superman.

Wordlessly, we shook hands, his intense blue eyes bearing down on me. I felt his hand squeezing mine, harder, then harder still, like kids do in sixth grade. Instinctively, in bewilderment or self-defense, I started squeezing back, and we stood there for a moment, forearms bulging, looking at each other. Eventually, he grunted, approvingly I think, cuffed me on the arm, and moved away into the crowd.

I had heard about White's notorious physicality. Former clerks loved to talk about his aggressive play in the thrice weekly staff basketball game. By the time I arrived, a bad back had forced White to the sidelines, but on the fourth floor, immediately outside the "highest court in the land" where we played, a battered old locker still bore his name scrawled on a yellowed strip of athletic tape. Some said White didn't confine taking out his aggressions to sports. The story was he'd once pinioned another Justice's clerk against a wall for drafting a particularly biting dissent from one of White's opinions.

Although I dismissed this tale as the Court's version of an urban legend, nothing that happened during the term changed the impression left by my initial encounter with an oddly competitive, gruff, even ornery man. White openly prided himself on circulating his opinions with unrivaled speed and, partly as a consequence, on authoring more majorities than anyone else. Often the swing vote in close cases, he seemed to revel in being unpredictable and almost invariably disappointed whichever Chambers tried most obsequiously to lobby for his vote. Evidently, he didn't want you to kowtow; he wanted you to squeeze back.

For many clerks, the pace of work and the compartmentalized structure of the Court provided little opportunity to become friendly with the Justices outside their own Chambers.* By the same token, getting to know your own Justice—not only his (or her) jurisprudence, but his work habits, predispositions, and peeves—was of paramount importance to any clerk seeking to be effective, in both carrying out instructions and offering advice.

Becoming acquainted happened naturally, of course, with the passing of time, but the process was also abetted in most Chambers by various time-honored practices. Around 9:30 on weekday mornings, Justice Brennan and his clerks would have coffee in the Chambers and chat about Court business or whatever came to mind. Justice Kennedy often

---

*In 1973, Justice Rehnquist, new to the Court, suggested setting up a "coffee hour" for clerks and Justices on oral argument days, but Chief Justice Burger shot down the idea and it has never been revived.

lunched with his clerks during the relative leisure of Saturdays at the Court. Ever the raconteur, Justice Marshall would assemble the knuckle-heads (as he liked to call his clerks) and amuse or astonish them with tales of triumph and sorrow from his civil rights days. The Rehnquists had their tennis games; and the Whites played golf for money on a putting course they set up in their offices.

With Justice Blackmun, breakfast was the ritual through which the nearly familial bond between judge and clerk, elder and neophyte, was formed. Every weekday from September to July, at approximately 8:10, Blackmun, flanked by my co-clerks and me, would walk past the enor-mous bronze statue of Chief Justice John Marshall on the Court's ground floor and head into the public cafeteria for the first meal of the day. By this time the Justice would have been at work for the better part of an hour. We would still be rubbing sleep from our eyes.

Despite occasional mornings of excruciating silence, these breakfasts were one of the great rewards of a Blackmun clerkship. Breakfast was personal time, largely unencumbered by Court business, the time when we learned that the Justice had worked on a dude ranch to help put him-self through Harvard College, that he loved junk mysteries, that he could sing the fight song of rival Dartmouth—perfectly on pitch. From the frequency with which he picked at his food or ate almost nothing we could see how often he was disregarding Justice Black's first words of ad-vice to him: "Never agonize!" More than once we witnessed Blackmun's unspoken pain at having to vote to put another man to death.

There is a cynical saying attributed to the "legal realist" school of thought that the outcomes of cases are determined as much as anything by "what the judge ate for breakfast." If so, Blackmun was the only Jus-tice to reach his decisions in public. More seriously, I would say that much of the essence of Justice Blackmun's jurisprudence would have been evident to anyone who watched our breakfasts closely, though in an entirely different sense from that imagined by the realists.

Our first breakfast together, only our second meeting, was on a Mon-day. One of the Court's police officers came over to welcome the Justice back from the summer recess. I remember that Blackmun asked the offi-cer about his wife and children, whom he knew by name.

As we went through the line, I ordered pancakes. Shyly, but with a certain insistence, the Justice warned me off. "The pancakes aren't so good on Mondays," Blackmun advised in tones too low for the cook to hear. "The griddle goes stale over the weekend."

Justice Blackmun looked after my welfare many times during our breakfasts together, prodding me to eat when I lost weight, urging me to get more rest when I was dragging. And I saw him ask after dozens of spouses and children, never showily or politically, just from interest and concern. It is simply his way, and when you read his opinions you can sense it.

I have no doubt that Harry Blackmun has been the most empathetic Justice in recent times, and very likely in the history of the Court. He has been the Justice most concerned with the human drama behind the briefs and memoranda that flood his desk, the Justice most appreciative that legal cases arise from the unseen anguish of real people, which the law can either soothe or inflame, the Justice most likely to weave silken threads of sympathy across the gap between what is law and what is just. Scholars will long debate the merits of Blackmun's compassionate jurisprudence. Whatever their judgment, those of us who worked for him will remember breakfast as the place where we learned how to align our thinking with his.

I recall vividly the first time Justice Blackmun asked for my recommendation on a matter pending before the Court. It was around 9:30 in the evening. I was at my desk, hemmed in by a small mountain range of legal papers, staring out the window of my shared second-floor office at one of the Court's lovely flagstone courtyards. The phone rang, two short tones indicating a caller from outside the building—in this case, from Minnesota, where the Justice was preparing to return to Washington, shortly after Labor Day, for the start of the term.

I had spent the better part of the day preparing for, anticipating, and rehearsing for his call—none of which lessened my anxiety. I was twenty-eight years old. The sum total of my legal experience amounted to a one-year clerkship with Judge William A. Norris on the Ninth Circuit Court of Appeals in Los Angeles, seven weeks as a summer associate with a small Washington, D.C., litigation firm, and a semester advising federal prison inmates in Danbury, Connecticut, as part of the Yale Law School clinical program.

I had met Justice Blackmun once—in my interview; I had spoken to him twice more, first when he had asked me if I would serve as his clerk, and, second, when he'd telephoned to welcome me to his Chambers upon my arrival in early July. I suspect that most relatively ambitious law students occasionally dream of having a Justice of the Supreme Court ask for their recommendation on a legal issue whose resolution will grace the front page of the next day's *New York Times*. I certainly had. Yet as I reached to pick up the phone, my mind was fixed on something else, that old gypsy curse: may all your dreams come true.

The case that prompted the Justice's call was historic, groundbreaking, intricate—and controversial. In 1980, the U.S. Department of Justice (joined by the NAACP) had filed suit against the city of Yonkers, New York, claiming that its officials had violated both the Constitution and the 1968 Fair Housing Act by deliberately manipulating the location of public housing in order to perpetuate residential segregation. In 1985, after a fourteen-month trial, a highly respected federal district court judge, Leonard Sand, agreed. Yonkers officials, Sand found, had committed a vast array of "consistent and extreme" unconstitutional and illegal acts in an effort to keep minority residents out of predominantly white neighborhoods.[13]

But Judge Sand's determination that Yonkers had broken the law by no means ended the case. As often happens when a community has committed broad-based acts of discrimination—as in school segregation cases, for example—once liability is established, the question becomes one of remedy. How do you rework community structures built on a bedrock of decades of discrimination, and, in turn, what do you do if the community resists that reworking?[14]

In this case, Judge Sand ordered the city to adopt a fair housing policy, to build 200 public housing units on sites dispersed throughout Yonkers, and to make plans for many additional units of subsidized housing in previously segregated neighborhoods. At first the city categorically refused, but, after over a year of negotiation between Judge Sand and the parties, the city formally agreed—by signing a consent decree—to a timetable for implementing the judge's remedial order.

Not two months later, however, the city balked again. Four members of the seven-member city council, recognizing the political benefits of resisting desegregation in racially divided Yonkers, decided to flout the law. In a series of votes in June and July of 1988, the council adamantly refused to undertake the housing obligations agreed to in the consent decree.

Judge Sand first cajoled, then demanded, and finally threatened the city and its recalcitrant officials with contempt of court. As a last resort, Sand ruled that if the council did not adopt the necessary legislation by

August 1, he would fine the city $100 a day, doubling every day until the legislation passed ($1 million by Day 14 and $200 million by Day 21). In addition, he would fine each council member voting against the legislation $500 a day, with the possibility of incarceration after Day 10. In Judge Sand's view, Yonkers's noncompliance with a legitimate court order threatened "the very foundation of the system of constitutional government," and he simply wasn't going to put up with it any longer.

Despite this threat, four city council members—Henry Spallone, Nicholas Longo, Edward Fagan, and Peter Chema—continued to block any effort to comply with the consent decree. And when, as threatened, Judge Sand held the city and the four naysayers in contempt, they appealed. The Court of Appeals for the Second Circuit unanimously upheld Sand's contempt citation, which left the city and the council members in a precarious spot.[15] They could appeal again to the only court still open to them, the Supreme Court, but in the interim (while they prepared and the Court considered their cert. petitions), the fines would accrue to disastrous proportions. They needed the Court to take the unusual step of issuing an immediate stay—preserving the status quo—while the appeals process inched forward.

Emergency stay petitions come to the Court in a blizzard of paper, especially when multiple parties are involved. All of the council members plus the city filed their own memoranda (complete with lengthy appendices and portions of the record below). In opposition, the government and the NAACP responded separately.

From the clerk's office at the Court, nine copies of all the filings are loaded onto a gurney and wheeled around to the Justices' Chambers. In the Blackmun Chambers, the Justice's messenger—a recent college graduate who serves a variety of administrative purposes—would deliver these papers to whichever of the four law clerks whose turn it was. We kept to a strictly maintained rotation posted on the back of an office door. When the Yonkers petitions came in, my name was up.

As soon as I looked at the papers, I knew this case would be contentious. Yonkers and the council members originally had applied for a stay of their fines to Justice Marshall, in his capacity as supervising "Circuit Justice" for the Second Circuit Court of Appeals. The application must have brought forth vivid memories and an ironic smile. In September 1958, as lead counsel for the NAACP, Thurgood Marshall had argued and won Cooper v. Aaron, the seminal case involving resistance to court-ordered desegregation.[16] Faced with a virtual insurrection by

Arkansas officials opposed to desegregating Little Rock's schools, the Supreme Court, unanimously and in the strongest possible terms, had reaffirmed its power and intention to implement *Brown* v. *Board of Education*[17] and force the immediate enrollment of black children in the local high school.

Indeed, Marshall had spent much of his life as the nation's premier attorney attacking precisely the kind of discrimination and obstructionism for which the Yonkers defendants were being sanctioned, and he had little patience with their arguments. Although Marshall referred the Yonkers stay applications to the Conference (meaning he submitted them for consideration by all nine Justices), his accompanying memo indicated that he would deny the stays and made clear what he perceived to be the negligible basis, legal and moral, for their request.

Judge Sand's contempt order, however, met with a very different reception in another corner of the Court. Like many of the conservative judges whom President Ronald Reagan had appointed to the federal bench, Justice Scalia objected to using judicial power to remedy broad-based societal injustices. And he was particularly skeptical of intrusive remedies, such as Judge Sand had ordered in the Yonkers case. In Scalia's view, federal judges had little business (as had become increasingly common in the wake of Warren Court decisions expanding constitutional rights) appointing themselves de facto overseers of school districts, prison systems, highway projects, and the like, in the name of remedying past wrongs. To Scalia, Judge Sand was already suspect in his capacity as ongoing supervisor of Yonkers's public housing. That Sand had actually ordered individual city council members, on pain of fines or even prison, to vote for legislation implementing a particular court-ordered housing plan, to Scalia smacked of judicial tyranny.

So the battle of memos was joined. Justice Scalia fired off what several other Justices (some fondly and others not) referred to as a Ninogram— generally a one- or two-page, single-spaced, and always colorful legal polemic on a pending case. Hand-delivered, usually without warning, in innocuous manila envelopes, these diatribes would provoke consternation and anger from Scalia's adversaries, amusement and appreciation from his allies.

The Yonkers Ninogram, crafted in characteristically tangy rhetoric, took up two of the council members' arguments.* First, Scalia argued

---

*Justice Scalia did not challenge Judge Sand's sanctions against the city, only those against the individual officeholders.

that Judge Sand's contempt citation impinged on the council members' "legislative immunity"—their right to perform their function as duly elected legislators free from coercive legal sanctions. "It seems to me," Scalia wrote, "that some degree of immunity for legislative acts must inhere in the doctrine of separation of powers and that that doctrine must have some application in the federal-state context."

Second, Scalia argued that a court order forcing each legislator to vote yes on the Yonkers housing plan, contrary to their own convictions, had "a certain gulag quality to it, reminiscent of the confessions of error exacted in the Stalinist trials of the 1950's." Scalia indicated that he was "strongly in favor" of granting cert. in the case and staying the council members' portion of Sand's "deeply disturbing" order.

Marshall received Scalia's memo with contempt. In his unmistakable loopy, grease pencil scrawl, he disparaged in the margin: "Might have been helpful if he had cited one case or other authority."

The Ninogram sent an electric charge through the rest of the Court. Although the council members were asking only that their fines be stayed until the Court decided whether to review their claims,* latent in their request were fundamental and fiercely contested questions about the mission of the Court generally and, more specifically, about the leading role it had played since 1954 in combating race discrimination.

In *Cooper* v. *Aaron*, the Justices had shown a single-minded determination to squelch defiance of judicial desegregation orders. In a display of unity and conviction unprecedented in Court history, all nine Justices individually signed the Court's opinion excoriating Arkansas officials for their defiance. And in the thirty years since *Cooper*, although the Justices had split over remedial issues such as the constitutional limits on affirmative action and school busing, the Court had never once countenanced deliberate disobedience of court-ordered desegregation.†

But with the advent of three Reagan appointees, and the appointment of Chief Justice Rehnquist, who (as an Associate Justice) had voted to overturn a slew of the Warren Court precedents, such traditions were no longer sacrosanct. These justices belonged to schools of thought

---

*In other words, the granting of a stay did not mean that the Court necessarily would review the merits of the council members' claims, only that it would suspend the accrual of their fines pending the filing and, in turn, the disposition of the council members' petitions for certiorari.

†Notably, in the Yonkers case, the council members did not challenge the legitimacy of the underlying consent decree ordering the city to remedy its segregated housing system. They challenged only Judge Sand's method of forcing their compliance with the decree.

uneasy with *Brown* itself and downright hostile to the "Rights Revolution" of the Warren Court, which *Brown* had ushered in. Judicial actions that might strike a Brennan or a Marshall as the height of judicial statesmanship smacked of judicial tyranny to a Rehnquist or a Scalia. Once Justice Scalia distributed his memo identifying the Yonkers case as potentially useful for reshaping the prevailing legal landscape, the vote on the stay applications inevitably developed into a kind of quickie litmus test for a Justice's allegiance in the escalating civil war over the Court's purpose and identity.

I remember placing Scalia's and Marshall's memos side by side on my desk, staring from one to the other. As a technical matter, the legal standard for deciding whether to grant the council members a stay was not whether they had a winning argument but whether they raised the sorts of issues on which the Court was likely to grant review, whether they had a reasonable probability of prevailing on the merits, and whether they would suffer serious hardship if no stay were granted.

Based on these criteria, the council members' stay applications had much to commend them. The issue of how much freedom from outside coercion legislators have when performing their elected duties was a substantial one and very topical at the time. While the Yonkers stay applications were pending, a fairly similar case was brewing right across the street from the Court in the Capitol, where Congress had passed a resolution cutting off funds to the District of Columbia unless its city council members voted to rescind a local gay rights ordinance. Moreover, the council members' legislative immunity argument had at least some grounding in past Court decisions, including several written (ironically) by Justice Brennan. As for the question of hardship to the council members if stays were not granted, that pretty much answered itself.

Justice Marshall's memo, on the other side, mounted a strong defense of Judge Sand's system of fines and pointed out several significant anomalies in the Yonkers case that might make it a poor vehicle for the Court to use even if a majority wanted to address the legislative immunity question. But underlying Marshall's writing as much as the legal argument was an implicit expression of outrage at the prospect of granting even temporary relief to elected officials who had used their offices to perpetuate racial segregation and thumb their noses at Sand's orders. If the Court wanted to consider the scope of legislative immunity, it could wait for a case where the legislators did not have such dirty hands and where no message would be sent giving aid and comfort to racial obstructionists.

By the time I spoke to Justice Blackmun at 9:30, the skirmish was all but over. Galvanized by Scalia's memo, in short order the more conservative Justices—Rehnquist, O'Connor, and the newly appointed Kennedy—joined him in voting to grant the council members' stay applications and indicating that they intended to vote to grant cert. once the members filed petitions with the Court. These four votes were sufficient to ensure that the Court eventually would hear the council members' claims, and, in order to preserve the status quo until the case actually came before the Court, Justice Stevens agreed to provide the necessary fifth vote for a stay.

As the requisite five-vote majority fell into line, Justice Marshall, as much resigned as angry, instructed his clerks to transform their internal defense of Judge Sand into a dissent to be published the following morning, when the Court officially issued the stays. With the Justice's gruff instructions ("Print it!") ringing in their ears, two of Marshall's clerks worked frantically to get the dissent into shape in the few hours they had. Their writing focused on exactly what had found no place in Scalia's memo about judicial overreaching and the council members' prerogatives: the Yonkers council members' belligerent refusal to abide by a legitimate judicial order vindicating the rights of the city's minority citizens.

That Marshall decided to publish a dissent was a powerful statement in itself. Dissents from Court decisions granting preliminary stays are almost unheard of—precisely because they are so preliminary. When granting such a stay (usually on the basis of hurried consideration of hastily prepared arguments), the Court has not yet even decided whether to review the case, much less how the underlying legal issues should be resolved. Apparently Justice Marshall had no desire to wait and see whether the majority made more substantial and galling decisions down the road.

Picking up the phone to talk to Justice Blackmun, I already knew that he opposed granting the stays—which was no surprise given his consistently liberal record in race discrimination cases. Still, I had to advise the Justice about whether he should go on the public record joining Marshall's published dissent as Justice Brennan, Marshall's closest ally on the Court, had done soon after it circulated.

I told Blackmun that I thought Marshall's dissent, though fairly convincing, felt premature to me and also prejudged some legal issues that seemed too tricky to decide without fuller briefing and consideration. I don't know how much sense I made. We talked for a while, back and forth, question and answer, as I thought how glad I was that this was his decision, not mine. In the end, the Justice chose not to join Marshall's dissent.

Down the hall, the Marshall Chambers were rueing the loss. Like a good general rallying dispirited troops, Justice Brennan walked down the hall from his Chambers to the office of the two Marshall clerks who had worked on the case. Hero to a generation of liberal law students, the mastermind behind many of the Warren Court's most celebrated achievements, Brennan congratulated Marshall's clerks on the job they had done with the dissent. One of the clerks was celebrating her birthday. Thinking back, she still remembers Brennan's words, precious and unexpected, as the finest gift she could have received.

Later that term, the Justices voted to hear the council members' case and, sixteen months later, on January 10, 1990, the Court ruled 5–4 that Judge Sand's contempt order had been an "abuse of judicial discretion."[18] Chief Justice Rehnquist's opinion dodged the legislative immunity issue, which had so troubled Scalia, as well as every other issue of potential import and interest beyond the specifics of the Yonkers case itself. The Court merely held that Judge Sand "should have proceeded with such contempt sanctions first against the city alone in order to secure compliance with the remedial orders. Only if that approach failed . . . should the question of imposing contempt sanctions against [the council members] even have been considered."

Justice Brennan wrote a dissent joined by Justices Marshall, Blackmun, and Stevens. "The Court's decision today," Brennan observed derisively, "creates no new principle of law; indeed, it invokes no principle of any sort." Throughout his opinion, Brennan pointedly quoted from Marshall's landmark victory in *Cooper* v. *Aaron,* an opinion—a promise of commitment—that Brennan himself had drafted in what seemed like another age. Instead of closing with the customary "I respectfully dissent," Brennan pointedly omitted the "respectfully." It no longer fit his feelings. It no longer fit the Court.

The Grand Canyon

Inside the Court, constitutional law cases, especially cases involving deeply felt and closely contested issues—such as freedom of speech or of religion, the right to privacy or to equal protection of the laws—make everyone's blood run faster. With few exceptions, these are the cases where the stakes seem highest, the allegiances strongest, and the consequences most enduring, as the Court discharges its most far-reaching duty as self-described "supreme" arbiter of the nation's highest law.

Even among the most important and controversial cases, there is a hierarchy of tension, excitement, and foreboding. Naturally, the abortion cases—each another pitched battle in what has become a social, political, and legal civil war—exact a large emotional toll on virtually everyone in the building. But day in and day out, the cases that most influence the psyche of the Court, the cases that seem to follow one after another in a never-ending cavalcade, and that every week demand another forced march over the same bloody legal ground, the ones that chronically anger and fray nerves, are the capital cases, where the penalty is death.

Not a week goes by when the unpaid cert. petitions don't include several from indigent prisoners on death row. They are unmistakable, red-flagged ("CAPITAL CASE") for special consideration. Each of these demands close attention, in part because a person's life is at stake but also because the Court's death penalty jurisprudence is enormously complicated, technical, and to some observers inherently self-contradictory. Capital case petitions often raise a multitude of claims, ranging from newly discovered evidence to challenges to police, prosecutorial, or judicial misconduct, as well as alleged flaws in the state death penalty statute under which the defendant was originally sentenced.

To assess whether any of these claims is important or novel enough, in a legal sense, to warrant review by the Court requires a clerk to master dozens of prior decisions and many varying state death penalty regimes. Much also depends on a dizzying array of procedural rules separating live claims from those which, through neglect, delay, or some other circumstance, are now barred from the Court's consideration.

The technical difficulty of deciding whether to grant review in a capital case is compounded by the consequences that follow from the decision. Most immediately, of course, the individual petitioner's life is at stake and may be spared if the Court decides to hear his claims. More broadly, every grant of cert. in a capital case sets off a chain reaction. Like an accident in a tunnel, each grant of cert. causes enormous backups in the system.

Suppose, for example, the Court grants review to determine if an aspect of the California death penalty statute is unconstitutionally vague. As a practical matter, every California execution will then be stayed until the Court decides the issue—a delay of as much as a year—as will every execution in any other state that has a provision similar to the one challenged in California. Or suppose the Court grants cert. to decide whether the Constitution bars prosecutors seeking the death penalty from introducing evidence showing the crime's impact on the victim's family. Immediately, every death penalty defense attorney in the country would start ransacking his client's case to see if a claim of this sort could be asserted plausibly. If so, that death row defendant's march toward execution almost certainly would be halted until the Court rendered its decision.

Find a stalled car and line up behind it: this is standard operating procedure for zealous death penalty defense lawyers, for whom success is often measured by delay. But at a Court badly split over the constitutional limits on the death penalty, their strategy means that, in capital cases, the normally uncontentious process of deciding which cases to hear is constantly freighted with an enormous consequence—creating another traffic jam—and thus is transformed into a source of chronic strife between the sides of the death penalty debate.

Still more unsettling are the emergency stay applications that punctuate the steady drumbeat of death penalty cert. petitions. These always eleventh-hour and usually last-ditch efforts to stop a scheduled execution—or, conversely, last-minute efforts by states to overturn lower court orders halting scheduled executions—descend on the Court sometimes as often as once a week. And each one triggers a tense ritual (to be described in detail later on) of rushed appraisals, late-night phone conferences, and the tallying of life against death.

Even the most frivolous stay application from the most despicable murderer forces on every person working the case a kind of involuntary moral accounting, a taking of sides. The closer cases, the ones where the defendant might actually be innocent or where he presents a fairly strong constitutional claim, can leave a stench of ill will that lingers long after the condemned man has been either executed or spared.

All of which is simply to say that through the cert. process, the emergency stays, and the inordinate number of capital cases that it chooses to review and decide, death pervades the Supreme Court every day and at times dominates it.

During October Term 1988, the Court decided several major death penalty cases. In *Stanford* v. *Kentucky*, the Court ruled 5–4 that the Eighth Amendment's ban on "cruel and unusual punishments" did not prohibit the execution of sixteen- and seventeen-year-olds.[1] The same day, the Court handed down *Penry* v. *Lynaugh*, where by the same 5–4 vote it held that states, in this case Texas, were not barred from executing mentally retarded persons. At the same time, a different coalition of five Justices required Texas to allow jurors at least to consider evidence of mental retardation as a "mitigating factor" when deciding whether to sentence a particular individual to death.*

In another case, *South Carolina* v. *Gathers*, the Reagan administration had requested that the Court overrule *Booth* v. *Maryland*, a controversial 1987 decision that had barred prosecutors from presenting "victim impact" evidence (evidence of how the victim's death affected his family and community) to jurors weighing a death sentence. In a decision even more acrimonious than *Booth* itself, a bare majority in *Gathers* reaffirmed *Booth*'s prohibition.[2]

---

*The two holdings in *Penry* were supported by different majorities, with only Justice O'Connor, the opinion's author, a member of both. The Chief Justice and Justices White, O'Connor, Scalia, and Kennedy voted to permit the execution of mentally retarded persons. Justices Brennan, Marshall, Blackmun, Stevens, and O'Connor voted to require Texas to permit the introduction of retardation as mitigating evidence at sentencing. 492 U.S. 302 (1989).

In my view, however, the most telling death penalty case of the 1988 Term was one in which the Court never published an opinion. It disposed of the case, *Tompkins* v. *Texas*, with an opaque two-sentence statement: "The judgment below is affirmed by an equally divided Court. JUSTICE O'CONNOR took no part in the consideration or decision of this case." This is how the Court announces its version of a tie, by which the ruling being appealed is automatically upheld. In keeping with the Court's unbroken rule, the announcement made no mention of how the Justices had arrived at their deadlock or what they thought about the competing arguments in the case. *Tompkins* v. *Texas* slid quickly into obscurity, almost as though the case had never happened.

Yet it had. The Justices had granted cert., read the briefs, heard oral argument, voted, and reached a tentative judgment that in all likelihood would have spared a man's life—only to not so decide. The process by which the Justices reached this result says as much about the Court's handling of these vexing cases as its brief public statement said little.

The facts of *Tompkins* were classic for a death case: appalling and depressing. Sometime shortly before midnight on January 25, 1981, Phillip Tompkins, a person of extremely limited mental capacity (an IQ of roughly 70), was driving around Houston smoking dope when he rear-ended a car driven by Mary Diana Berry, a twenty-four-year-old hospital pharmacist. When Berry stopped to survey the damage to her car, Tompkins abducted her to a remote area near Houston's Astrodome, bound her to a tree, and gagged her with a large wad of bedsheeting. Tompkins then took Berry's automatic teller card, went to her bank, and withdrew $1,000 from her account.

In the meantime, Berry died, slowly and excruciatingly, as she suffocated on the oversized gag Tompkins had stuffed into her throat. When her body was discovered two days later, it was evident from the scratches and bruises that she had struggled ferociously to free herself.

The next day, the police arrested Tompkins and he confessed to the crime. In rambling, dull-witted, and agonizing detail, Tompkins recounted how he had abducted Berry to get money to take his girlfriend (Pizza) to Austin. While they were driving around, Berry had carefully explained to Tompkins how to use her bank card. According to Tompkins, he then tied and gagged her so that she couldn't call the police while he made the trip to her bank. When Tompkins returned, Berry wasn't moving. He felt for her pulse but couldn't find one. Tompkins said he then drove to a phone and dialed the police, only to hang up when they answered. Next, he went to a friend's house and played cards.

Tompkins, a black man accused of killing a white woman, went on trial for his life before an all-white jury. When jury selection began, the jury venire (the pool of prospective jurors) included thirteen blacks, but during voir dire (juror examination) the prosecutor had eight of them struck "for cause." The prosecutor then eliminated the remaining five using peremptory challenges (by which each side may disqualify a certain number of prospective jurors without giving any reason).

Once the jury was impaneled, the defense succeeded in having Tompkins's confession suppressed. It had been obtained in violation of his right to counsel. Nonetheless, the prosecution produced ample evidence that Tompkins was responsible for Berry's death. A night janitor at the bank saw Tompkins use the automatic teller machine at roughly 2:30 A.M. on the night of Berry's disappearance. One of the bank's automatic cameras captured the moment on film. Upon Tompkins's arrest, police found Berry's bank card as well as others of her belongings in his possession. Police also discovered in the trunk of Tompkins's car severed electrical cord that matched the cord used to bind Berry's ankles.

Under Texas law, to find Tompkins guilty of "capital" murder, the jury had to conclude beyond a reasonable doubt first, that he killed Berry *intentionally* and, second, that he did so while either robbing or kidnapping her. Tompkins's lawyers introduced no evidence on either of these points; in fact, they put on no defense at all. Rather, they simply argued, in their closing remarks, that Berry's binding and gagging indicated Tompkins did not intend to kill her. Absent such intention, he was not guilty of capital murder.

Proceeding on this theory, Tompkins's lawyers asked the judge to instruct the jury that it could find him guilty of any of three lesser offenses: noncapital intentional murder (intentional murder but not committed during a robbery or kidnapping); involuntary manslaughter; or negligent homicide. The judge agreed to instruct the jurors as to noncapital intentional murder but refused to give them the option of finding Tompkins guilty of either involuntary manslaughter or negligent homicide. So instructed, the jury found Tompkins guilty of capital murder and, on June 15, 1981, sentenced him to death.

Tompkins (through his counsel) appealed his conviction on many grounds, but by the time the case reached the Supreme Court, only two claims survived.[3] First, Tompkins alleged that the prosecutor's use of peremptory challenges to excuse all the eligible blacks from his jury violated *Batson* v. *Kentucky*,[4] a 1986 ruling forbidding prosecutors from using their peremptories to exclude jurors on the basis of race. This *Batson* claim (as I shall call it) raised one of the most frequent and troubling issues in the death penalty debate—the degree to which capital punishment, mainly a punishment of the South, is often if not inevitably tainted by racism.

Second, Tompkins argued that under another Supreme Court precedent, the 1980 case *Beck* v. *Alabama*,[5] the trial judge had been constitutionally required to give the jury the option of convicting him of involuntary manslaughter or negligent homicide. This *Beck* claim touched a different but no less critical theme in the Court's death penalty jurisprudence: that jury deliberations must be structured so that jurors do not impose death sentences "arbitrarily"—that is, without careful and rational thought about the background of the individual defendant and the circumstances of the crime involved.

When you are a clerk, each case comes to you neatly packaged, a stack of color-coded pamphlets held together by a rubber band. The essential history of the case is there: an "Excerpt of Record," containing the lower court opinions and other relevant items from previous proceedings, the cert. petition and the other side's response, the competing briefs of the parties, and, in many cases, briefs from amicus curiae (friends of the court), who offer gratuitous (and sometimes excellent) advice on cases related to their fields of special interest.

For every capital case, inside this pristine stack of papers lies chaos, a terrible story of human tragedy and legal bedlam. When you open up the state-side briefs, you can be certain that you will be confronted with a gruesome account of the taking of human life, gory details stretched out over the maximum number of pages and bled deliberately (and irrelevantly) into the legal arguments. The defendant's brief, by contrast, deliberately glides over the suffering and depravity into the legal issues, as though the only human values at stake are the defendant's life and the integrity of a legal system in which due process is alleged to be skirted or ignored.

Tompkins was no exception. The state's brief hammered home the pain of Mary Diana Berry's last minutes; and to some effect, especially among some of the women clerks, for whom the image of Berry—alone, at night, chosen entirely at random, dying torturously—touched a common chord of fear. Then Tompkins's lawyers, bolstered by amicus briefs from the ACLU and the NAACP Legal Defense Fund, conjured up a nightmare vision of a soon to be irreversible and wholly undeserved conviction and sentence, the product of racism and caprice.

Every clerk and judge has his or her own method for digging into a case. Mine, especially in capital cases, was to set aside the briefs of the parties and first read the opinions of the lower court judges. These tend to frame the legal issues in a less partisan manner than the briefs. More important to me, the quality and tone of the opinions below often gave me a sense of how conscientiously the lower courts had handled the case and a gut feeling about whether something might be amiss.

During the 1988 Term, I must have read more than 1,000 lower court opinions. Roughly speaking, they fell into two categories. The good ones, even the ones with which I ultimately disagreed, always made a serious attempt to convince the reader that they were right. Logic and precedent (or history, where appropriate) melded with the relevant facts of the case to draw me along as if to an inescapable conclusion. Bad opinions announced themselves, sometimes blatantly, as shams. They did not reason; they concluded. Flimsy rationales were substituted where logic belonged. Precedents were not applied or accounted for; they were willfully misread or shunted aside with the back of a judicial hand.

I cannot remember a set of lower court opinions more distressing (and less judicial) than those of the Texas courts in *Tompkins*. Why this is so requires some explanation. Let's start with Tompkins's jury instruction, or *Beck*, claim.

In a group of landmark 1976 capital cases (known collectively as *Gregg v. Georgia*),[6] the Supreme Court permitted the reinstitution of the death penalty after a four-year ban. Striking down some newly drafted state death penalty statutes while upholding several others, the three centrist Justices who controlled the Court (Stewart, Powell, and Stevens), insisted that death is a qualitatively different punishment from any other and that, accordingly, the Constitution requires states to observe special procedural safeguards in its use. Under *Gregg*, "any decision to impose the death sentence [must] be, and appear to be, based on reason rather than caprice or emotion."[7] And, to that purpose, juries in capital cases must be "carefully and adequately guided in their deliberations,"[8] so as to avoid "arbitrary" sentences of death.

The Court's decision in *Beck* v. *Alabama* (written by Justice Stevens) was one of many rulings aimed at fulfilling *Gregg's* promise to bring rationality to the capital sentencing process. The defendant in *Beck* (like Tompkins) had been accused of the capital crime of intentional killing in the course of a robbery. The evidence left no doubt that Beck had participated in the robbery that led to the victim's death, but some question did exist whether he had intended the killing—which he said occurred when his accomplice unexpectedly hit the victim.

If the jury believed Beck's story, he was guilty of *noncapital* felony murder, not the capital crime with which he was charged. Alabama, however, unique among the states, did not permit its judges in capital cases to give juries the option of convicting on such a "lesser included offense." This meant that the Beck jury faced the uncompromising choice of convicting Beck of capital murder or acquitting him altogether.

The Supreme Court found that this thumbs up–thumbs down approach injected an unconstitutional degree of arbitrariness into the jury's deliberations. The problem was this: in cases such as *Beck*, jurors may be convinced that the defendant is guilty of a serious violent felony in which an innocent life has been taken; at the same time, they may have some doubt about whether the defendant is guilty of capital murder. But if the only choice is to convict on capital murder or to acquit altogether and let a violent felon go free, what juror would not be sorely tempted to resolve his doubts in favor of conviction on the capital offense? As the Court observed, "The failure to give the jury the 'third option' of convicting on a lesser included offense would seem inevitably to enhance the risk of an unwarranted conviction. Such a risk cannot be tolerated in a case in which the defendant's life is at stake."[9]

Under the Constitution, the Texas Court of Criminal Appeals (the state's highest court for criminal cases) was required to follow the rule of *Beck* or explain why it did not apply. The court did so by concluding that *Tompkins* was "factually distinguishable" from *Beck*. "In *Beck*," the Texas court asserted, "the defendant testified at trial and denied that he killed his victim or intended his victim's death, whereas [Tompkins] did not testify or present any evidence from any source that he possessed only the intent to rob or kidnap Berry."

Of course all cases are "factually distinguishable" from one another; each involves a different set of facts. The question for a conscientious judge—one who distills the essential principles underlying prior cases and assesses their application to new circumstances—is whether the distinguishing facts make a difference as to what legal rule should apply.[10]

The Texas court did not bother to explain why Beck's failure to testify or put on a defense should void his constitutional right to proper jury instructions. Nor could it. Regardless of whether Tompkins put on a defense, the prosecution was constitutionally required to prove every element of capital murder beyond a reasonable doubt; and the defense, even without putting on an affirmative case, was entitled to argue to the jury that the prosecution had failed to carry that burden. The Court's concern in *Beck* was to ensure that jurors had an alternative to acquittal when the evidence of capital murder was doubtful. That concern did not vary with the style of defense the accused chose to employ.

In law school, one of the bits of jargon that a student inevitably picks up is that when the facts of a new case raise the same issue in the same way as an already decided case, the new case is "on all fours" with the decided case, and its rule should govern. *Tompkins* was not quite on all fours with *Beck*, but I judged it a solid three. In both cases, the defense had tried to raise a reasonable doubt as to whether the defendant had intended to kill his victim—a necessary element of capital murder. And in both cases the jury was denied the option of convicting on a nonintentional lesser included offense.

The distinction between the two cases was that in *Beck* the jury could choose between only capital murder and acquittal, whereas the *Tompkins* jury did have a third option. It could have found Tompkins guilty of noncapital intentional murder—that is, intentional murder but one not committed during the course of a robbery or kidnapping. The appropriate question for the Texas court to have asked was whether this third option, even though it did not match up with Tompkins's claimed lack of intent, was sufficient to satisfy the constitutional concerns behind *Beck*. Yet on this point the Texas court wrote nary a word.*

---

*In addition to ignoring *Beck*, the Texas appellate court concocted the following rationale for why Tompkins was not eligible for a jury instruction on either involuntary manslaughter or negligent homicide.

Under Texas law, a person commits negligent homicide when he is *unaware, but ought to be aware*, of a substantial and unjustifiable risk that death will result from his actions. According to the Texas Court of Criminal Appeals, Tompkins could not have been found guilty of negligent homicide because his elaborate method of trussing Berry to the tree "very tight" indicated that he must have been aware of the risk he created to her life.

Under Texas law, a person commits involuntary manslaughter when his "reckless" conduct results in a killing. Recklessness, in turn, is defined as being *aware of and consciously disregarding* a substantial

The Texas court's rejection of Tompkins's *Batson* claim was even more troubling. Decided in 1986, *Batson* was the most recent ruling in the Court's century-old effort to weed out racial bias from criminal trials. This line of cases started after the post–Civil War enactment of the Fourteenth Amendment, which required states to provide blacks as well as whites with "equal protection of the laws." In an 1880 case, *Strauder* v. *West Virginia*,[11] the Court had struck down Jim Crow laws overtly excluding blacks from jury rolls. When states replaced these laws with ones that were unbiased on the surface but allowed jury commissioners discretion to disqualify blacks—who miraculously never seemed to have the right qualifications—the Court banned these practices too.[12]

Yet while the Court guarded against racist conduct that kept minorities out of grand juries and off jury rolls, it was much less rigorous in policing the winnowing process by which lawyers approved prospective jurors to sit on actual cases. In 1965, the Court ruled in *Swain* v. *Alabama*[13] that a prosecutor could legitimately take race into account when using peremptory challenges to eliminate potential jurors so long as he did so for reasons "related to the case he is trying."

Under *Swain*, a prosecutor violated the equal protection clause only if he eliminated minority jurors "in case after case, whatever the circumstances"—that is, not as a trial tactic but as a way of excluding minorities solely because of their race. Thus, a defendant could not win merely by showing discrimination in his own case, even if the prosecutor struck every black from the jury. The Court demanded evidence that the prosecutor in question had an established pattern of race-based challenges inexplicable as trial strategy. (Moreover, trial stategy included such race-tainted thinking as a prosecutor's generalized view that blacks are prone to vote to acquit other blacks.)

---

and unjustifiable risk. According to the Texas court, Tompkins could not have been found guilty of involuntary (reckless) manslaughter because he trussed Berry in such a way as to allow "some movement of [her] knees and shoulders" and thus did not "consciously disregard" the risk to her.

Here the Texas court constructed a classic catch-22. Tompkins cannot have been simultaneously *too aware* of the risk to Berry for a charge of negligent homicide and *not aware enough* of the risk for a charge of involuntary manslaughter. In other words, he couldn't possibly have been too reckless to be negligent yet too negligent to be reckless. Legally (as well as metaphysically), no middle ground exists between the two potential charges. Tompkins was either aware of the risk or not aware, and if the evidence was sufficiently ambiguous to make unclear which it was, then the jury should have been allowed to decide between the two. Indeed, even if Tompkins's conduct fell into some heretofore unknown middle category between negligence and recklessness, it would have made no sense to follow the Texas court's path and allow the jury to decide only on the much more serious charge of intentional murder. Yet this is where matters stood.

The practical effect of *Swain*'s acceptance of trial-related, race-based peremptories and its heavy burden of proof for systemic discrimination was virtually to immunize prosecutors from constitutional scrutiny and to perpetuate the widespread occurrence of all-white juries. Often indigent, few black defendants possessed the resources to investigate, over a number of cases, the race of persons tried in particular jurisdictions, the composition of the jury venires and petit juries, and the manner in which prosecutors exercised peremptory challenges. In many places, no such records existed and proof was simply impossible.

In *Batson*, after more than twenty years' experience and an avalanche of scholarly criticism, the Court acknowledged that *Swain* had invited prosecutorial abuse and race-tainted trials.[14] In those few cases in which black defendants had been able to compile statistics, the results painted a graphic picture of racially tainted prosecutions. Routinely, it seemed, southern prosecutors used 80 percent or more of their peremptories to strike black jurors from cases involving black defendants. In Dallas, Texas, the instructional manual in the prosecutor's office advised its lawyers to conduct jury selection to eliminate "any member of a minority group." Prosecutors struck nine of every ten eligible black jurors compared with one of every two whites.

As a remedy, *Batson* revoked *Swain*'s permission to use race-based peremptories (even as trial strategy) and significantly eased *Swain*'s burden of proof. Rather than having to show a pattern of discrimination in case after case, minority defendants could now rely solely on evidence from their own trials to prove discrimination. Initially, a minority defendant would have to show only that the prosecutor used peremptory challenges to strike members of the defendant's race and that these strikes, together with "any other relevant circumstances," raised an "inference" that the prosecutor's jury selection was racially motivated. (This first step is known as a prima facie case, a set of facts that, if left unrebutted, gives rise to an inference that the allegation at issue is true.)

If a minority defendant succeeded with this showing, the burden would shift to the prosecutor to rebut the inference of discrimination. Specifically, the prosecutor would have to come forward with a "neutral explanation" for each strike that was "related to the particular case." Then, in the final step, the trial judge was supposed to assess whether the prosecutor's explanations were credible (or instead pretextual) and, thus, determine whether the defendant had proven racial bias. The *Batson* Court clearly hoped that this new order of proof would succeed where *Swain* had failed and finally vindicate both the right of minority defendants to impartially chosen juries and the right of minority citizens to serve on those juries without race-based interference from the state.

Although Phillip Tompkins went on trial for his life in 1981, when the Court handed down *Batson* five years later, his appeal was still pending in the Texas courts. As a result, Tompkins received retroactively the benefit of *Batson*'s new rule, and his case was sent back to the trial court for a hearing into the constitutionality of the prosecutor's peremptory jury strikes.

Tompkins had little trouble carrying his initial burden (making his prima facie case) of raising an inference of discrimination. The raw facts of the case were sufficient. Tompkins was black, and the prosecution had used peremptories against all five eligible black jurors. And the hearing brought out much more. Testimony showed that Tompkins's prosecutors, like others in the Harris County D.A.'s Office, were particularly wary of selecting blacks as jurors because in their view many blacks "have preconceived notions about law enforcement and government" and blacks as a group are inclined to be sympathetic toward black defendants. As the principal prosecutor in Tompkins's case admitted, race is "something you have to look at" during jury selection.

With the prima facie case established, the burden shifted to the prosecution to rebut the inference by giving neutral explanations for its five peremptory strikes. *Batson* itself, moreover, specifically deemed not neutral the sort of "intuitive judgment"—to which Tompkins's prosecutors admitted—that black jurors "would be partial to the defendant because of their shared race."

Tompkins's prosecutor did offer neutral justifications for each of the five peremptories. She justified two strikes on the ground that the would-be jurors had expressed reservations about the death penalty. The prosecutor next testified that she'd struck a third juror, Isabella Thomas, because her "whole case" depended on circumstantial evidence and she was skeptical of her ability to follow circumstantial evidence law.* And Frank Samuel was allegedly challenged because the prosecutor thought he might be illiterate. The only specific "reason" the state advanced for challenging the fifth black juror, Leroy Green, was his employment by the U.S. Postal Service.

---

*In fact, at the time of jury selection the prosecution's case consisted mainly of *direct* and not circumstantial evidence: to wit, Tompkins's confession, which was not excluded from evidence until later in the proceedings.

Under *Batson*, it was now the trial judge's job to assess, given all the facts and circumstances, whether these explanations were genuine or a cover-up for racial bias. The Texas trial judge, however, made no such evaluation. Instead, the judge either rubber-stamped the prosecution's explanations or, where these appeared obviously inadequate, provided embellished explanations on the prosecution's behalf.

When Tompkins appealed, the Texas Court of Criminal Appeals recognized the total inadequacy of the trial judge's inquiry and even the plain error of some of the judge's findings. But rather than reverse the ruling and award Tompkins a new trial, the appeals court conducted its own inquiry and either excused the trial judge's errors or made up its own explanations for the prosecutor's strikes—and found *them* to be race neutral.

The Texas courts' treatment of the challenge to Leroy Green was representative. Evidently the trial judge felt uncomfortable accepting Green's post office employment as a legitimate reason for striking him. After all, although on direct examination the prosecutor had said that she "had not had very good luck with postal employees," on cross-examination she admitted to actually having enjoyed good luck with postal worker jurors in past cases. Faced with this, the trial judge substituted his own neutral justification in place of the prosecutor's. He concluded that the prosecutor's challenge of Green must have stemmed from Green's somewhat uncommunicative demeanor and "vacillation" regarding his ability to apply certain legal principles.

The state court of appeals could not accept this approach. After all, *Batson* demanded that the prosecutor produce genuine neutral explanations, not have the trial judge do it for her. And the appellate court realized that "the sole reason given" for striking Green was his job at the post office. But rather than reverse the trial judge's clearly erroneous finding, the appeals court decided to evaluate the postal worker justification for itself.

In so doing, the appeals court seemed to appreciate that *Batson* required that the prosecution's explanation not only be neutral and genuine but also be *related to the case on trial*. The court expressed "some difficulty understanding the relevancy" of Green's job to his standing as a juror and complained that the prosecutor had not "undertaken to enlighten us further on the subject." Nonetheless, the court accepted the prosecutor's explanation as "racially neutral," on the falsely modest ground that "it is not the office of this Court to judge her credibility."

This disclaimer concluded the Texas courts' *Batson* shell game (which they also employed in reviewing the peremptory strike against the "illiterate" Frank Samuel, despite Samuel's reading and comprehension of complicated legal materials during voir dire). The trial judge, who was supposed to evaluate the credibility of the prosecutor's justification, instead made up a justification of his own. Next, the appellate court scorned the trial court's justification and resurrected the one actually given by the prosecutor. Then the appellate court endorsed the prosecutor's justification, despite obvious credibility problems, on the ground that the trial court—and not it—had responsibility for evaluating the prosecutor's veracity. Voilà. Tompkins loses.

The state court opinions in *Tompkins* reminded me of a handful of cases I had worked on while clerking for Judge Norris on the Ninth Circuit. The judge would call me into his office after reading a particularly outrageous lower court ruling, toss the offending text onto his desk, and practically shout: "This just can't be the law." As decided by the Texas courts, *Tompkins* just couldn't be the law.

At the Supreme Court, the Justices heard a relatively straightforward oral argument in *Tompkins* on Tuesday, December 6, then discussed the case at their next Friday Conference. Finding out who voted which way and why at these closed-door meetings was the most memorable regular occurrence of a Blackmun clerkship. The buzzer signaling the end of Conference would sound, and the Justices' haphazard recessional would begin. Most times during the 1988 Term, Justice Blackmun and Justice Brennan would walk slowly together down the long red carpet of the south corridor as Brennan, who was ill, steadied himself on Blackmun's arm. They would pause before the door to Brennan's Chambers, framed against the light filtering in from the courtyard. Their heads, inclined slightly, would almost touch as they exchanged a few last words. After a moment, the brotherhood would part, and Justice Blackmun, lost in thought, would complete his return journey, gliding wordlessly into his office, gently shutting the door.

Soon thereafter Justice Blackmun would call his clerks in to report on Conference. For the argued cases (as opposed to the cert. dispositions), he would summarize the remarks of each of the Justices, in order of seniority. It was mesmerizing: Blackmun's thespian voice rumbling through the comments of his colleagues, punctuated occasionally by a sentence or two of brilliant imitation that never failed to astonish and amuse.

Only eight Justices participated in the *Tompkins* discussion. Justice O'Connor recused herself apparently because her husband, until recently, had been a partner at the D.C. law firm (Miller & Chevalier) that was representing Tompkins, pro bono. Her absence almost certainly favored Tompkins. As a general rule, O'Connor rarely sided with capital defendants, especially in cases such as this one, which called for second-guessing the judgments of a state court.

Even with this advantage, Tompkins achieved mixed results. On the *Beck* issue, Chief Justice Rehnquist and Justices White, Stevens, Scalia, and Kennedy sided with Texas. They read *Beck* as requiring no more than that a jury in a capital case be given *some* "third option" between conviction on capital murder and acquittal. Tompkins's jury had received exactly this.

Justices Brennan, Marshall, and Blackmun disagreed. In their view, the third option called for in *Beck* had to conform to the particular element of capital murder that was in doubt. In Tompkins's case, that element was his intent to kill—not (as the jury instructions suggested) whether Berry's death took place during a robbery or kidnapping.

Tompkins prevailed, however, on his *Batson* claim. Only the Chief Justice and Justice White thought the prosecutor's justifications sufficient. Justices Brennan, Marshall, Blackmun, Stevens, and Kennedy agreed that the prosecutor had violated *Batson* and that the judgment of the Texas courts had to be reversed. On this issue, Justice Scalia was still on the fence.

As the senior Justice in the majority on both the *Beck* and *Batson* issues, Justice Stevens enjoyed the right to assign who would write the Court's opinion. (Justice Kennedy was the only other Justice in the majority on both issues.) Stevens elected to keep the case for himself.

In 1946, having graduated first in his class from Northwestern Law School, Stevens had clerked for Justice Wiley Rutledge, whose trademark was the devoted parsing of the facts of criminal cases in search of a just result. As a court of appeals judge in Chicago, Stevens had developed much the same practice he had admired in his former boss. And this trait was greatly in evidence when he circulated his *Tompkins* draft opinion at the beginning of March.

Its reasoning hewed closely to the majority's views at Conference. With respect to Tompkins's *Beck* claim, Stevens distinguished *Beck* on the ground that the jurors in *Tompkins* were given a third option between acquittal and convicting on capital murder. If "they found that [Tompkins] had committed a serious, violent crime but did not believe he deserved to be executed for his act—they could have convicted him of noncapital [intentional] murder."

The bulk of the twenty-eight-page draft, however, was devoted to the *Batson* issue and to admonishing state courts to start taking seriously their responsibility to curb race-based peremptories. Together with one of his clerks, Justice Stevens exerted considerable energy and care tracing the Texas courts' treatment of the peremptory challenges against the prospective jurors Thomas, Samuel, and Green. In each case, Stevens faulted both the district and appellate courts for frustrating *Batson's* command to root out the race-based exclusion of blacks from juries and giving rubber-stamp approval to the prosecutor's actions. Accordingly, he proposed sending the case back to the Texas courts to do their job again, properly.

For Tompkins himself, the bottom line of Stevens's draft was a substantial victory. The Court's *Batson* ruling would mean a new trial and reprieve from death row. Even though Tompkins had not convinced the Justices that the Constitution entitled him to additional lesser included offense instructions, the judge at a new trial could still choose to instruct the jury on involuntary manslaughter and negligent homicide—and a fair-minded judge probably would, even when not constitutionally compelled. On balance, that seemed a pretty fair result, in terms of both developing constitutional law and meting out justice to Phillip Tompkins.

For Justice Stevens, the wait for responses now began. When a Justice circulates a draft opinion, he or she is hoping, especially in a close case, for a couple of quick joins. Having a few other Justices sign on to your draft right away creates a sense of momentum toward "getting a Court"—securing the crucial four other votes necessary to guarantee a majority. The response a circulating Justice emphatically does not want is dead silence or, even worse, questions and criticism from one of the Justices who had cast a friendly vote at Conference. In *Tompkins,* with the Court split 5–3 on *Beck* and 5–2–1 on *Batson,* Stevens could ill afford any defections.

Justice Scalia responded first to Stevens's circulation, on March 5, and his message was unsettling. As expected, Scalia readily joined the *Beck* section. But whereas at Conference he had been uncertain about

Tompkins's *Batson* claim, now Scalia was skeptical. Specifically, he expressed deep reservations not only about Stevens's application of *Batson* to Tompkins's case but more fundamentally about the wisdom of *Batson's* entire formula for proving discrimination.

Batson had borrowed its three-step burden of proof scheme—(1) establishment of prima facie case; (2) rebuttal by neutral justification; and (3) evaluation of that justification's credibility—from cases involving Title VII, the civil rights law that bars race and gender discrimination in employment. Title VII law, however, was a bête noire for many conservative jurists, including Justice Scalia, who thought it encouraged frivolous lawsuits.

In particular, they considered Title VII's initial prima facie case requirement too easy to satisfy. As Scalia explained, it shifted the burden of proof to employers "even when there was no *real* prima facie case, in the ordinary sense—that is, no showing that would be strong enough, if entirely unrebutted, to support a verdict."* *Batson's* decision to incorporate Title VII's plaintiff-friendly regime into the jury selection context, Scalia continued, was "a bad idea and should be abandoned as soon as possible." Scalia expected that his disagreement with Stevens's draft was "too fundamental to be accommodated." He said he would "await Byron's dissent"—a common Court euphemism for "I foresee joining the dissent."

Scalia's memo immediately rendered Stevens's position precarious, at least with respect to his discussion of Tompkins's *Batson* claim. True, Stevens didn't need Scalia's vote; he had four others. But he did need Justice Kennedy, who in his first full term on the Court so regularly consulted Scalia and so often followed his lead that clerks joked about how thin the carpet had worn between their Chambers.

Three days later the other shoe dropped. Kennedy sent Stevens a terse note. "I share some of Nino's concerns." Then followed the ominous "I will await further writing."

With Kennedy waffling, Stevens had to do something or face the likely prospect that the Court would deadlock 4–4 on Tompkins's *Batson*

---

*Scalia's memo in *Tompkins* marked the beginning of his ultimately successful campaign to change the burden of proof regime in Title VII cases. In *St. Mary's Honor Center v. Hicks*, 509 U.S. 502 (1993), over Justice Souter's strong dissent, a bare majority led by Justice Scalia revised Title VII's proof scheme and made it more difficult for employment discrimination plaintiffs to prevail in their suits.

claim. If that happened, the *Batson* issue would drop out of the case and the Court would issue opinions only regarding Tompkins's *Beck* challenge.

For Tompkins, this would mean a complete reversal of fortune: instead of overturning the Texas courts and voiding his conviction and sentence, the Court would affirm the Texas courts and leave him on death row. And Stevens had to act quickly. Justice White, the Court's fastest opinion writer, was drafting a dissent from Stevens's handling of the *Batson* claim. If White's dissent circulated, Scalia and Kennedy might join it before Stevens could tender some compromise to entice them back into his fold.

On March 13, Stevens responded, painstakingly, to Scalia. Addressing his attack on the Title VII and *Batson* burden of proof regime, Stevens assured Scalia that he understood and agreed that the initial prima facie case requirement for *Batson* claims should be different from and tougher than that used in Title VII. A defendant seeking to prove discrimination in the use of peremptories (in contrast to a plaintiff in an employment discrimination case) should have to raise a *genuine* inference that such discrimination had actually occurred before a prosecutor would be forced to explain any strikes. To demonstrate his earnestness, Stevens volunteered to remove from the opinion all references to Title VII cases.

Having conceded this much, however, Stevens tried to persuade Scalia that his desire for a rigorous prima facie case requirement had no bearing on how *Tompkins* should be decided. Stevens pointed out that Tompkins unquestionably had established a prima facie case, even under the kind of rigorous standard Scalia was advocating. "I wonder, therefore," Stevens summed up, "if another case might provide a better vehicle for detailed consideration of the elements of the prima facie case."

A week went by, then two, with no response from either Scalia or Kennedy to Stevens's offer to meet them much more than halfway. On March 28, Justice White, who had written the majority opinion in *Swain*, which *Batson* had revamped, circulated a dissent on Tompkins's *Batson* claim. In six characteristically terse pages, he accused Stevens of unduly interfering with state criminal processes. "The majority apparently believes," White wrote, "that state trial courts will not follow *Batson* and cannot be trusted fairly to pass upon the credibility of the prosecutor and the reasons he offers for the use of peremptories, a view that I do not share." White argued that the states should be left to their own devices for implementing *Batson*. He made no attempt to make sense of the Texas courts' mutually inconsistent treatment of the strikes against the jurors Thomas, Samuel, and Green and even had no problem accepting the prosecutor's postal worker rationale. "Judgments like this," he concluded, "are what peremptories are all about."

Two days later, Justice Stevens received a thanks-but-no-thanks letter from Scalia. He had decided to join White's dissent. The Chief did the same, leaving the fate of Stevens's *Batson* discussion in the hands of Justice Kennedy's Chambers—from which only silence emanated.

In the meantime, the liberal Justices had started writing draft opinions of their own. As senior Justice among the three dissenters on the *Beck* issue, Justice Brennan had asked Justice Blackmun to take the assignment. On May 3, Blackmun distributed a draft attacking Stevens's view on the *Beck* issue. In Blackmun's view, *Beck* required not just any third option, but a *plausible* third option given the facts of the case. And the third option in Tompkins—noncapital intentional murder, in other words, intentional murder *not* committed in the course of a robbery or kidnapping—was simply not plausible.

The evidence that Mary Diana Berry had died during a robbery or kidnapping was overwhelming. No reasonable juror could have concluded otherwise. Indeed, the jurors could not have convicted Tompkins of noncapital intentional murder unless they deliberately disregarded their obligation to apply the facts to the law as instructed by the trial judge.

The express purpose of *Beck*, as well as many cases before and after, was to reduce the potential for arbitrariness in capital sentencing.[15] It made no sense, Blackmun therefore argued, to interpret *Beck* as being satisfied by a third-option instruction that would actually make the process less rational by inviting juries to disregard their oaths and return compromise verdicts at odds with the evidence.

Blackmun closed with reference to the "particularly bitter irony" of Tompkins's suppressed confession. As even the Texas court of appeals had admitted, the outcome of Tompkins's case would surely have been different if the jury had heard his admission to killing Berry unintentionally. The Justices could right that wrong, Blackmun admonished, merely by giving *Beck* the meaning it deserved.

The Marshall Chambers was also preparing a writing, a concurrence in Stevens's imperiled *Batson* draft. At age eighty, Justice Marshall very much disliked writing separate concurrences; he preferred to let the

Opinion of the Court speak for him. But discrimination in jury selection had been a special concern of his for fifty years, and it was one of the few areas where he, as a Justice, had staked out his own ground and played a decisive role in reforming the law.[16]

Marshall had been fighting discrimination in jury selection practically since the first day he took over as the NAACP's lead lawyer in 1938. That year a sixty-five-year-old black president of a junior college refused to take the strong hint of Dallas, Texas, court officials and excuse himself from jury service. Two white men dragged the man out of the courthouse and threw him down the front steps, but he picked himself up and marched through an angry crowd back into the jury room. Marshall journeyed from New York to investigate and, remarkably, convinced the governor to order out the Texas Rangers to ensure no further unlawfulness at the Dallas courthouse.[17]

Over the next two decades, one of Marshall's priorities at the NAACP was to orchestrate a campaign of lawsuits to enforce flagrantly violated federal laws and Supreme Court decisions outlawing all-white juries. As a Justice, Marshall wrote the Court's opinion in *Peters* v. *Kiff*,[18] extending to white defendants the right not to have blacks struck from their juries. Marshall also mounted a sustained campaign against race-based peremptories and pushed strongly for the Court to abandon its weak-willed ruling in *Swain*. When the Court was considering *Batson*, Marshall took the extraordinary step of circulating to his colleagues a series of studies documenting racial bias in the use of peremptories. He bolstered these with anecdotes about his own in-the-trenches encounters with race-tainted jury selection. And Justice Powell's majority opinion in *Batson* reflected Marshall's influence.

But Marshall himself was still not satisfied. A lifetime of experience had led him to an overwhelming skepticism, a sense that even *Batson*'s easing of the burden of proof for showing racial bias could never curb the practice of race-based peremptories. Neutral explanations for such strikes, Marshall felt, would be too easily manufactured and not easily enough exposed. Concurring in the judgment of the *Batson* Court, he wrote separately to insist that the goal of race-neutral jury selection "can be accomplished only by eliminating peremptory challenges entirely."

What Marshall explicitly recognized (and *Batson* papered over) was that serious judicial inquiry into the motives behind peremptories was fundamentally at odds with their concept. The whole point of peremptory challenges is to permit each side to excuse a prospective juror for a funny look or having green eyes—for no reason at all, based on gross generalizations and stereotypes, or on nothing more than a whim. To later require a prosecutor to give specific, race-neutral, and case-related reasons for using a peremptory is both too easy and too hard. Too easy because such reasons are readily concocted; too hard because an honest, nonracially motivated prosecutor may well not have had a specific, case-related reason for each peremptory strike.

Justice White resolved this tension by basically abandoning any serious effort to look behind whatever neutral justifications a prosecutor might put forward. He recognized that, in the face of a probing inquiry into prosecutorial justifications, peremptories would cease to be peremptories.

And that was precisely what Justice Marshall thought *should* happen. If the Constitution prohibits prosecutors from excluding jurors on the basis of racial stereotypes, then the Court should do away with the institution that provides for the use of stereotypes. For Marshall, peremptory challenges might have had a lineage stretching deep into the history of the English common law, but they had no grounding in the Constitution. By contrast, the principle of selecting jurors without resort to race rested solidly on the Fourteenth Amendment. If the two were at odds, as Marshall was certain they were, the nonconstitutional practice of peremptories had to yield.

Marshall obviously thought these views were borne out by Texas's efforts to explain the peremptories in *Tompkins*. Indeed, he was so upset by the case that it provoked one of his rare forays into oral argument, where his questions—often flippant or badgering—seemed more expressions of disgust with a lawyer's argument than requests for response. "What's wrong with a postal worker?" he had barked harshly at Texas Assistant Attorney General Charles Palmer. Marshall's *Tompkins* draft was certain to be flavored with the same derision.

That dissent, however, never saw the light of day. On May 16, more than six months after *Tompkins* was argued, Justice Kennedy formally switched his vote on the *Batson* issue. He no longer echoed Scalia's concerns about *Batson*'s burden of proof. He had developed a whole new line of reasoning. Although Kennedy still found the Texas court of appeals's *Batson* discussion "difficult to accept," he had done his own review of the *Batson* hearing and had concluded that the Texas district court had it right all along.

In the early days of the case, Kennedy had visited Marshall in his

Chambers, evidently in the hope of developing a relationship with his sometimes prickly colleague. Trying to build bridges, surrounded by Marshall's collection of Kenyan tribal crafts, Kennedy had joked about the absurdity of the prosecutor's stated rationales in *Tompkins*, in particular the postal worker excuse.*

Now all that talk was forgotten. Writing to the Conference, Kennedy did not explain why it was satisfactory for the trial court to justify the prosecutor's challenges on grounds different from those offered by the prosecutor (as with Juror Green). Nor did he evaluate the discrepancies in the prosecutor's testimony (as with Jurors Samuel and Thomas), or defend the postal worker justification, or discuss how the Texas appellate court could have been so wrong in disparaging the district court's work. Nonetheless, Kennedy claimed to have found reasons in the record for why a prosecutor might want Thomas, Samuel, and Green off the jury. In short, where once Kennedy and Marshall had both seen the miasma of southern racism, now Kennedy had come to see just ordinary lawyering; he voted on both the *Beck* and *Batson* issues to affirm Tompkins's conviction.

Kennedy's change of heart, even if not entirely unexpected, was a bombshell. Justices do not often switch votes after Conference, and they do so very rarely (not more than a few times a term, collectively) when the switch radically changes the outcome of a case. Kennedy already had submarined a tentative 5–4 liberal victory by switching positions in a major civil rights case, *Patterson* v. *McLean Credit Union*.[19] Apparently uncomfortable providing the swing vote against his natural allies on the Court, he had now changed sides again. His revised vote guaranteed that the Court would split 4–4 on the *Batson* issue, strictly along political lines: Rehnquist, White, Scalia, and Kennedy on one side; Brennan, Marshall, Blackmun, and Stevens on the other. It also meant that the Court's opinion would speak only to Tompkins's *Beck* claim, rejecting it 5–3.

Although he had written the opinion, Justice Stevens was heartsick at this result. Fair trial procedures were a particular concern of Stevens, and he had invested himself deeply in the prospect of using *Tompkins's*

---

*Ironically, Kennedy himself revealed this conversation (without naming the case) in a glowing tribute he wrote about Marshall after his retirement. In his tribute, though, Kennedy recalls only his bonding with Marshall, conveniently neglecting that he changed his view in *Tompkins* and brought the Court to a result Marshall abhorred. Of course, because the record in *Tompkins* is buried in Marshall's papers, Kennedy's selective memory has never been noted. See Kennedy, "The Voice of Thurgood Marshall," 44 *Stanford Law Rev.* 1221 (1992).

claim to refine and strengthen *Batson*. From the first day, he had worked hard to keep Scalia's and Kennedy's votes. And for naught. Most important, the bottom line of Stevens's opinion would now read as an affirmance of Phillip Tompkins's conviction and sentence, rather than as a reversal (and likely retrial) on *Batson* grounds.

It was more than Stevens, never comfortable in death cases, could stomach. Very much a lawyer's lawyer, the Justice next to Marshall with the most actual litigation experience, he had a long-standing practice of never voting to affirm a death sentence in a case where he thought serious trial error had occurred and a proper objection been raised. *Tompkins* was such a case.

On May 19, three days after Kennedy's switch, Stevens wrote the Chief. "After further reflection, I have decided to change my vote on the *Beck* issue in this case. I remain convinced that the opinion states the correct rule, but, as Harry has demonstrated [in his dissent], there is a real risk that its application in this case distorted the jury's deliberations. . . . In all events, I am now persuaded that the best disposition of the entire case . . . is a simple affirmance by an equally divided Court."

In the 200-year history of the Court, I very much doubt that the author of an opinion has changed his vote even a handful of times to assure that the Court does not issue his own opinion. I question whether it had ever happened before. Too much effort has been expended, too much ego engaged. Yet Stevens scuttled his opinion, even while agreeing with the legal principle it expounded, rather than put his imprimatur (as well as the Court's) on Tompkins's sentence of death.

Stevens's vote change may have cleared his conscience, but it provided cold consolation to Tompkins, who was once again under imminent threat of execution. From his perspective, an affirmance was an affirmance. Regardless of whether the Court issued an opinion, Tompkins was back on death row, waiting for Texas to set another execution date and for his lawyers to dredge up other claims that might win him a reprieve.

As a clerk, you inevitably lose track of what happens to capital case defendants, except perhaps for those who are executed during your term at the Court. The others, even those whose appeals, cert. petitions, or stay applications you have worked on, disappear into the dark well of state and federal habeas proceedings, which can stretch on for years. At most, a few of the more notorious names pop up on the inside pages of a newspaper.

I daresay much the same is true for the Justices, even though, over time, the cases of most death row inmates cycle through the Court repeatedly, as they seek relief from their sentences one way or another. But there are too many people awaiting execution, too many cert. petitions and stay requests, even too many executions, to keep track of every one.

I worked many hours on Phillip Tompkins's case, but I never knew what happened to him until I called his lawyer in connection with this book. I doubt that any of the Justices yet know. In the end, although the Justices had no way of anticipating it, Tompkins was not executed. As his volunteer lawyers at Miller & Chevalier prepared to file a state habeas corpus petition (the next step in the death penalty defense process), a young associate attended a death penalty defense conference sponsored by the NAACP Legal Defense Fund, which spearheads the national legal campaign against capital punishment. Among the mountain of advice the LDF experts dispensed was the suggestion that defense lawyers double-check the credentials of expert witnesses who testified at trial.

In Texas, one of the critical questions jurors must answer in deciding whether to sentence someone to death is whether the defendant poses a risk of "future dangerousness" to society. At the penalty phase of Tompkins's trial, the state had put on the stand an expert named Jean Matthews, who claimed a master's degree in psychology from Florida State University and work toward a psychology doctorate at MIT and Harvard. Matthews testified that she had treated Tompkins while he was jailed in Virginia on a burglary charge, and, on that experience, she concluded that he would pose a serious risk of future dangerousness.

Jean Matthews did receive a master's degree from FSU. The degree was in music; her specialty was trombone. She never attended Harvard or MIT. Her only training in psychology was a college introductory course taken as a freshman. Police officials in Virginia remembered her—as a quack. Because Tompkins had the resources of a major D.C. law firm behind him, and thanks to what the lead attorney, Emmett Lewis, called "99 percent luck," an associate named Mary Lou Soller contacted FSU, sensed something fishy, and uncovered Matthews's deception.

Based on Matthews's fraudulent testimony, Tompkins's attorneys filed a clemency petition (joined by an embarrassed Texas Attorney General's Office) with Gov. Bill Clements. The governor commuted Tompkins's sentence to a life term, and he is eligible for parole in the year 2002. The state also indicted Matthews for perjury.

Today, looking back, I remain stunned by the Court's handling of *Tompkins*, and not only by the wild finish. Now, as then, I believe *Tompkins* was a relatively easy case. After I had studied *Beck* and *Batson*, then read the record, it seemed clear to me that these cases virtually compelled the Court to rule for Tompkins on both his claims.

Tompkins's *Batson* claim had presented the Justices with evidence of serious corruption in the administration of the criminal law. Here was a case where, in all likelihood, the prosecutor had not only committed race discrimination in seeking a lily-white jury but skirted the truth in explaining her challenges in court. Here was a case where two Texas courts had turned a blind eye to the discrimination and the deception, even though both courts essentially admitted to finding the prosecutor's explanations incredible.

As the Justices knew, there were dozens, even hundreds of cases like Tompkins's, in which prosecutors, state courts, or both abused or avoided *Batson*'s command. Yet three other Justices, in a capital case with seemingly egregious facts, joined a White dissent that expressed complete confidence in the ability and willingness of state courts to observe and protect federal constitutional rights.

The corrosiveness of this fact extends far beyond Phillip Tompkins's case. The Supreme Court had made a crucial promise in *Batson*, the promise of juries free from race-biased selection. In refusing to enforce that promise, in countenancing deception by prosecutors, and in allowing state courts to render *Batson* meaningless, the Justices were fostering precisely the kind of legitimate mistrust of the judicial system that pervades the black community and destroys the possibility of a shared vision of justice. This was a terrible failure in an area of the Court's highest responsibility.*

On a smaller scale, the resolution of Tompkins's *Beck* claim was also discouraging. I was as satisfied as one can be from the removed perspec-

---

*The Court decided many more *Batson* cases after its nondecision in *Tompkins*, each time extending its scope. In the last few years, the Court has extended the ban on race-based challenges to civil cases (as well as criminal) to defense attorneys (as well as prosecutors), to cases involving white defendants (as well as minorities), and to challenges based on gender (as well as race). But while the Court can congratulate itself on superficially expanding its fight against discrimination in jury selection, it has yet to hand down a single opinion (like Justice Stevens's *Tompkins* draft) admonishing state courts to apply *Batson* rigorously and instructing them how to do so. In the absence of such exhortation, *Batson*'s ever broader rule is honored mainly in the breach. Across the South, practitioners will tell you that *Batson*, as applied, is simply a trap for lawyers so incompetent that they can't manufacture plausible cover-ups for racially motivated strikes. As of 1991, for example, the state courts of North Carolina had upheld not a single *Batson* challenge. Paul H. Schwartz, "Equal Protection in Jury Selection? Implementation of *Batson v. Kentucky* in North Carolina," 69 *North Carolina Law Rev.* 1533 (1991).

tive of the Court that Tompkins was not guilty of intentional murder. Stuffing a gag in a woman's mouth while leaving her nose uncovered and otherwise unharmed is a peculiar method for accomplishing a deliberate killing, especially for someone who carried a knife. In the written confession the jury never saw, Tompkins explained to the police in excruciating detail exactly matching the physical evidence how he had tied Berry up, even leaving her some slack, to prevent her from getting help while he used her bank card. When he returned to untie her, she was dead. Some confessions, even self-serving ones, ring true. Tompkins's did.

Even if Tompkins's jury had never observed his confession, all of us at the Court had. We knew that the failure of the trial judge to give the jury the *meaningful* choice of convicting him of involuntary manslaughter or negligent homicide almost certainly had resulted in precisely the miscarriage of justice against which *Beck* was intended to guard: a man guilty of a terrible but not capital offense was sentenced to death because the jury had no other reasonable choice except acquittal.

How could it be that the Court refused to correct this evident injustice not only in the particulars of Tompkins's case but in the plain flouting of federal constitutional law by the courts of Texas? In *Beck,* a majority of the Court worried that even well-meaning jurors faced with the possibility that a heinous felon would go free would disregard their legal oaths and convict someone for a capital crime he did not commit. Did not the Justices do precisely this in Tompkins's case? They were willing to let him die, wrongly, unconstitutionally one would have thought, rather than risk letting him go free.

At the end, the Justices lined up exactly as one might have predicted before the case was briefed or argued—liberals on one side, conservatives on the other, a gorge between them and no bridge across even in an easy case. The conservatives were wrong in their view of the law, but the more important point of *Tompkins,* the reason it still strikes me as a case of such compelling symbolism, has little to do with which side was at fault in this instance.

Tompkins, at its essence, is about the grand canyon dividing the Justices—deepening and widening for more than a legal generation. The soil of shared experience and principles, of compromise and understanding, had washed away. Across a seemingly unbridgeable gap, the Justices yelled back and forth about a number of the most crucial issues affecting our legal culture: race, state court justice, the death penalty, and the extent and use of their own power to do right. Their voices fell short of the distance. And a dim-witted man named Phillip Tompkins and the rule of law were left to free-fall.

How this could happen is the central problem of the modern Court, and to begin to understand it one must start far in the past.

THE PENALTY OF DEATH

The Spirit of Scottsboro

Legal doctrines are shaped like family trees. Each generation of decisions is derived from ones that came before as, over time, each branch of the law grows and spreads or, occasionally, withers and dies away. The most recent decisions almost always draw their strength by tracing back through an ancestral line, choosing among parents, uncles, and cousins according to the aptness of their bloodlines. Rarely, a branch of doctrine is disowned, repudiated, and left vestigial until perhaps revived in another legal era.

As a consequence, Justices tend to think about cases vertically as opposed to horizontally—that is, they think about previous cases in the same line of doctrine much more than they think about other cases in different areas of law that the Court might be hearing at the same time. This is the essence of precedent and also the importance of context and history to contemporary legal argument. The Court is forever looking backward, and, for that reason, today's debates are unintelligible without an understanding, with respect to each legal issue, of how the Court got to where it is and of where the past might drive it next.

On March 25, 1931, a fight broke out between a group of white youths and a group of black youths on a freight train traveling through rural Alabama from Huntsville to Chattanooga, Tennessee. Both sides were riding the rails illegally, moving north in search of relief from a depression world of breadlines and unemployment. The blacks got the better of the sparring and pushed the whites off the train. The losers then complained to a local stationmaster, who notified railroad agents ahead.

Forty miles up the track, a posse stopped the train. Nine black teenagers and two young white women, Victoria Price and Ruby Bates, were taken off. Someone, no one knows exactly who, said something about rape, and, in an instant, the nine blacks found themselves hauled off to the nearest jail (in a small town named Scottsboro), charged with the most infamous crime known to the South.

Six days later, with a retinue of National Guardsmen protecting them against a lynch mob, the black defendants—confused, illiterate, ignorant of the law, and far from home—were arraigned on the charge of gang-raping the two white girls from the train. By this time, the entire region was aflame with stories of the alleged "heinous and unspeakable crime," which the local press agreed "savored of the jungle, the way back dark ages of meanest African corruption."[1]

Apparently to avoid making any particular lawyer culpable for defending the indefensible, the trial judge appointed "all the members of the [local] bar" to represent "the boys" (as they were constantly referred to) for the limited purpose of their arraignment. All nine entered pleas of not guilty, despite the fact that no one stepped forward to take responsibility for the defense and one leading member of the local bar even joined up on the prosecution's side.

On April 6, only twelve days after the incident on the train, the young blacks went on trial for their lives. They still did not have a lawyer, although a friend of some of their parents, an attorney from Tennessee named Stephen Roddy, came forward to help informally with the defense. Intimidated from the start, Roddy refused a formal appointment as counsel; he excused himself on the grounds that he'd had no time to prepare and was unfamiliar with Alabama's rules of procedure. After much back-and-forth with the judge, a Mr. Milo Moody, "an ancient Scottsboro lawyer of low type and rare practice," agreed to give the defense a whirl.[2]

The Scottsboro boys were tried in four groups over four days in a town that had taken on the appearance of an armed camp. The proceedings took place before a standing room only crowd, from which women and minors were excluded on account of the subject matter. For three days in a row, Price and Bates (prostitutes, as it turned out, who were held up as the flower of southern womanhood) told four separate all-white juries their increasingly lurid tale of how all nine of the defendants held knives at their throats, pinned down their legs, tore off their clothes, and raped them over and over again. Despite a host of obvious discrepancies in the girls' story (which Bates later recanted), the absence of physical injury, the fact that one of the boys was virtually blind and another incapacitated by venereal disease, the defense put on essentially no case.

On the fourth day, the juries sentenced eight of the nine defendants to death. The ninth case, that involving thirteen-year-old Roy Wright, ended in a mistrial when eleven jurors held out for the death penalty, even though the state had asked only for life imprisonment because of the defendant's age.

The International Labor Defense (the legal arm of the Communist Party of the United States), which had taken an interest in the Scottsboro case from its inception, immediately denounced the verdicts as a legal lynching. The ILD volunteered to defend the boys in their appeals, fought off the NAACP's efforts to take over the defense, then lost no time running with a case tailor-made for their radical politics. Separate from the Communists, a tidal wave of mainly northern protest— telegrams, letters, and petitions from hundreds of ordinary folk as well as the likes of Albert Einstein, Fiorello La Guardia, and H. G. Wells—descended on Alabama officials. This outrage was matched by an equally vociferous defense of the verdicts from southern politicians and editorialists.

Within weeks, the Scottsboro case (like the Sacco-Vanzetti case a decade earlier) became a national cause célèbre. On one side, Communists, emerging black civil rights groups, and some white liberals took aim at the racial caste system of the South. On the other, southerners (even some who thought the Scottsboro verdict suspect) defended the death sentences as if they believed their entire way of life would somehow "fall like a house of cards if *any* black accused of assaulting *any* white (and especially a white woman) escaped extreme punishment."[3]

After the highest court in Alabama upheld the defendants' convictions on appeal, the Scottsboro case moved inexorably to the U.S. Supreme Court.[4] There, daily, the Justices confronted organized demonstrations demanding freedom for the black youths and, according to Justice Harlan Fiske Stone, even rushed their deliberations to put an end to the picketing.[5] Then, on November 7, 1932, as the nation voted in a New Deal for America, the Justices overturned the Scottsboro convictions by a 7–2 vote. Reading his majority opinion from the bench, Justice George Sutherland held that Alabama had denied the Scottsboro boys effective assistance of counsel and thereby deprived them of due process of law as mandated by the Fourteenth Amendment.[6]

Sutherland summarized the defendants' predicament: "Young, igno-rant, illiterate, surrounded by hostile sentiment, hauled back and forth under guard of soldiers, charged with an atrocious crime, regarded with especial horror in the community where they were to be tried, [the de-fendants] were thus put in peril of their lives within a few moments after counsel for the first time charged with any degree of responsibility began to represent them." According to Sutherland, "The failure of the trial court to give the defendants reasonable time and opportunity to secure counsel" was "a clear denial of due process."

So too was the trial judge's failure to appoint "effective" counsel once the defendants were unable to secure lawyers on their own. In a capital case, the Justices ruled, "it is the duty of the court, whether requested or not, to assign counsel for [the defendant] as a necessary requisite of due process of law." In Scottsboro, this duty had been grossly slighted, and, as a consequence, the Court ordered the defendants' convictions reversed.

The Court's ruling, however, did not end the case. Alabama persisted in retrying most of the defendants. Those retried were convicted again, and two, Haywood Patterson and Clarence Norris, were resentenced to death. Again they appealed, this time claiming that Alabama had de-nied them their Fourteenth Amendment right to equal protection of the laws by conducting the trial before a jury from which all blacks had been systematically excluded.

Remarkably, the Supreme Court agreed to hear Norris and Patterson's appeal, making the Scottsboro case one among a handful ever to be re-viewed twice by the Court. And, once more, the Court reversed the con-victions.[7]

A half century earlier, the Court had ruled that laws explicitly ex-cluding blacks from jury service violated the equal protection clause of the Fourteenth Amendment.[8] The wrinkle in the Norris and Patterson situation was that Alabama law did not explicitly exclude blacks. In-stead, such exclusion was a matter of unbroken practice. As one jury commissioner testified, not a single Negro in his county ever had been judged competent to serve.

Writing for the Court, Chief Justice Charles Evans Hughes found this presumption of race-based incompetence "so sweeping and so contrary to the evidence" that it could not stand. "For this long-continued, un-varying and wholesale exclusion of Negroes from jury service," Hughes wrote, "we find no justification consistent with the constitutional man-date."

Yet even this second victory at the Supreme Court did not end the Scottsboro boys' legal travail. Alabama convened a new grand jury (including one black man), which returned yet another two-count indictment for rape against both Norris and Patterson. Both were convicted yet another time, by yet another all-white jury, and Norris again received a sentence of death. More appeals and requests for clemency, ultimately successful, followed. Eventually, all the Scottsboro boys went free, but not until they had served, in aggregate, more than 100 years in jail for a crime they almost surely did not commit.

The Supreme Court's decisions in these cases deeply affected the lives and spirit of black Americans, especially those in the South, whose experience with the criminal justice system consisted mainly of fear, too often realized, of a one-way ride to the chain gang or the hangman through a gauntlet of beatings, sham trials, and the baying of a mob. Now, when life was at stake, they would for the first time be guaranteed lawyers and at least the possibility of a black face (and voice) in the jury room.

More generally, the Scottsboro rulings marked a significant advance for a Supreme Court that, in the decades since the Civil War, had sanctioned and legitimized segregation in public schools and public transportation, prohibitions on intermarriage, and several methods of disenfranchisement (such as literacy tests, poll taxes, and the grandfather clause). As then Harvard Professor (and later Justice) Felix Frankfurter noted at the time, in the Scottsboro cases, a Supreme Court noted for using the Fourteenth Amendment to ward off regulation of business had finally turned the same words to their "more immediate purpose of protecting black men from oppressive and unequal treatment by whites."[9] Very tangibly, Scottsboro helped spur the growth of a dynamic and powerful civil rights movement and was one of the first stops on the long road toward *Brown* v. *Board of Education*, the demise of Jim Crow, and formal black equality before the law.

The import of the Scottsboro cases, however, was not limited to the issue of race. These decisions were at the leading edge of the defining legal development of the twentieth century: the so-called due process revolution, in which the Court, over the following decades, held state governments accountable to almost all the protections of individual liberty recognized in the Constitution's Bill of Rights.

While this may sound like a matter of mere legal technicality, it is anything but. Today we take for granted that the guarantees of personal liberty contained in the Bill of Rights—such as the Sixth Amendment right to counsel at issue in the first Scottsboro case—apply to the federal government and state governments alike. For most of this country's history, however, quite the opposite was true, and even now it is not strictly so.

Before the adoption of the Fourteenth Amendment in 1868, the Bill of Rights applied *only* to actions of the federal government.* In other words, to the extent that state governments recognized such fundamental rights as freedom of speech and religion, protection against unreasonable searches and seizures, or the right to jury trial, it was by dint of their own laws or state constitutions, not because the Bill of Rights required it.

This legal regime did not change until after the Civil War. In constitutional terms, the Union victory ushered in two profound and related changes: it ended slavery, and it marked the ascendancy of national power over the concept of "states' rights," which had provided much of the legal underpinning for southern secession.

Following the Confederate defeat, in the era known as Reconstruction, the Republicans dominant in Congress moved quickly to extend basic liberties, including citizenship, to the freed slaves. At the same time, they moved to compel individual states to obey many of the constitutional limitations previously imposed on the federal government and to establish the federal government in place of the states as the main protector of citizens' rights.[10] To these ends, Congress initiated a constitutional revolution. It adopted three new amendments, starting with the Thirteenth (in 1865), which outlawed slavery in every state, and culminating with the Fifteenth (in 1869), which guaranteed blacks and former slaves the right to vote in state and federal elections.

In the center stood the Fourteenth Amendment, ratified in 1868, whose capacious clauses opened the door to an entirely new system of federal constitutional regulation of state law and law enforcement. "No State," it declared, "shall make or enforce any law which shall abridge the privileges or immunities of citizens of the United States; nor shall any State deprive any person of life, liberty, or property, without due

---

*As Chief Justice John Marshall explained in an 1833 case, *Barron v. Mayor of Baltimore*, "The Constitution was ordained and established by the people of the United States for themselves, for their own [federal] government, and not for the government of the individual states." 32 U.S. (7 Pet.) 243 (1833).

process of law; nor deny to any person within its jurisdiction the equal protection of the laws." Anticipating resistance to these provisions, especially in the South, the amendment also authorized Congress to intervene in local and state affairs to enforce these new guarantees.

The question remained—and still remains—how broad a definition the Court would give to the new constitutional provisions, especially the Fourteenth Amendment. While this amendment required states to respect "privileges and immunities" and afford "due process" and "equal protection," it was by no means self-evident what these terms meant. For example, did the privileges or immunities or due process clauses impose all the restrictions of the Bill of Rights on the states? If not, which restrictions were not included and why? Seen differently, might the concepts of "privileges or immunities" and "due process" safeguard any rights not specifically mentioned in the Bill of Rights, such as, for example, a right to privacy or to freedom of contract? Reaching answers to these and similar questions has been the central enterprise of the last one hundred years of constitutional law and has generated almost every controversial decision of our time—from capital cases to *Miranda* and *Roe v. Wade*.

As a matter of history, until the turn of the twentieth century, the Court gave an extremely narrow construction to the Fourteenth Amendment. In a series of cases, it refused to invoke the amendment either to much protect black citizens or to apply any of the specific limits of the Bill of Rights to the states. In the *Slaughterhouse Cases* of 1873, for example, a closely divided Court ruled that the privileges and immunities clause required no more than that states observe a narrow group of rights—such as the right to travel to and from the nation's capital—either guaranteed elsewhere in the Constitution or implicit in a citizen's relationship to the federal government.*

At a Court mirroring the nation's rapid retreat from the ideals of Reconstruction, the clauses requiring states to observe due process and provide equal protection of the laws received equally cramped interpretations.† And the practical result was to leave states to their own devices

---

*Despite much scholarly criticism, the Court has never revisited its emasculation of the privileges and immunities clause. Instead, the Court has infused the due process clause with much of the meaning that might better be borne by its now vestigial cousin. See, e.g., Akhil Amar, "The Bill of Rights and the Fourteenth Amendment," 101 *Yale Law Journal* 1193 (1992).

†In the *Civil Rights Cases*, for example, the Court reached the by no means obvious conclusion that the Fourteenth Amendment's ban on race discrimination applied only to official state action and not to the actions of private individuals. This doctrine, too, remains accepted law. Other Court rulings, such as the endorsement of separate facilities for whites and blacks, have proven less enduring. See *Plessy v. Ferguson*, 163 U.S. 537 (1896).

and permit the apartheid of Jim Crow to become the southern rule of law.

Gradually, starting near the turn of the century, the Court did begin to find some specific guarantees of the Bill of Rights included in the concept of due process protected by the Fourteenth Amendment.* More specifically, it absorbed or "incorporated" into the Fourteenth Amendment those aspects of the Bill of Rights that (as Justice Benjamin Cardozo described them in an oft-quoted phrase) were "so rooted in the traditions and conscience of our people as to be ranked as fundamental."[11] So, in 1925, sixty-seven years after the ratification of the Fourteenth Amendment, the Court first applied to the states the First Amendment's "fundamental" guarantee of freedom of speech.[12]

In the area of criminal procedure, the perennial question for the Court became which of the Bill of Rights's many rules for assuring fair trials and shielding defendants from coercive state power should similarly be deemed sufficiently "fundamental" to be incorporated into "due process" guaranteed by the Fourteenth Amendment. Here the Court's first Scottsboro decision—applying the Sixth Amendment's right to counsel to defendants in state capital cases—broke significant new ground. It was the first major decision imposing one of the Constitution's criminal procedures on the states. And, more than that, Scottsboro was the harbinger of a major shift in legal culture, by which, over time and especially under Chief Justice Earl Warren, the Court resurrected the promise of the Fourteenth Amendment and applied to the states nearly every one of the procedural protections of the Bill of Rights.†

Today we take for granted that states may not use in court evidence obtained in violation of Fourth Amendment limits on searches and seizures (*Mapp v. Ohio*)[13] or the Fifth Amendment's right against self-incrimination (*Miranda v. Arizona*).[14] We know intuitively that states must observe the Sixth Amendment requirement of trial by a jury of one's peers (*Duncan v. Louisiana*)[15] and the Eighth Amendment's prohibition on "cruel and unusual punishments" (*Robinson v. California*).[16]

---

*The Court at this time, notorious for its concern with protecting business interests, started the process of incorporation by requiring that states obey the Fifth Amendment's prohibition against taking private property without payment of just compensation. *Chicago, Burlington, and Quincy Railroad Co. v. Chicago*, 166 U.S. 226 (1897).

†The Supreme Court has yet to incorporate (and thereby apply to the states) the Second and Third Amendments, the Fifth Amendment's guarantee of indictment by grand jury, and the Seventh Amendment's guarantee of a jury for civil trials.

The blood of the Scottsboro cases courses through all these decisions as well as other Warren Court landmarks, which forced state law enforcement officials to observe federal constitutional standards for the protection of individual rights. At their core, the Scottsboro cases were about the abuse of state authority and, specifically, the infusion of race hatred into the law and the possibility that a southern court, after essentially a sham trial, might commit what the Supreme Court in 1932 itself labeled "judicial murder." Scottsboro was a potent symbol of what could go wrong locally in the American judicial system and a spur to both those who would expunge bigotry from the system and those seeking to enforce national standards of justice upon the states.[17]

The criminal law rulings of the Warren Court, in some cases reversing long-standing precedent, reflected a firm conviction that the sins of Scottsboro lay deeply ingrained in the fabric of state criminal law processes, and had to be expunged. Swept up in the optimistic ferment of the 1960s and emboldened by the world-altering achievement of *Brown* v. *Board of Education*, the Warren Court resolved to make criminal justice in America more evenhanded, decent, and humane. Fashioning what became known as the Rights Revolution, that Court enshrined in constitutional law a deep skepticism about the willingness of state officials, left to their own devices, to conduct "fair" investigations and trials. And the Justices opened wide the federal courts to ensure state compliance with these new constitutional commands.

Many of the most divisive battles at today's Supreme Court are in essence referenda on this legacy of Scottsboro—on the idea that racism is endemic; that state judicial systems, especially in the South, cannot be trusted; and that the federal courts and, ultimately, the Supreme Court must serve as the guarantors of social justice. Nowhere in the law has this legacy had a deeper effect than in the area of capital punishment. For the advocates, scholars, and judges seeking to root out racism and forge a stronger bond between morality and law, the death penalty—the ultimate and irreversible potential abuse of state power—made a natural target. And the Warren Court's expanded definition of "due process" provided a host of new legal tools with which to mount an assault.

As late as 1962, no Justice ever had suggested that the death penalty might be categorically unconstitutional. But in retrospect, from the moment of Scottsboro, it seems almost inevitable that, someday, someone would. What happened with that suggestion, and to the principles supporting it, is in large part the story of the modern Court.

Sand in the Machine

The first shot in the war over the constitutionality of the death penalty was fired from the Chambers of Justice Arthur Goldberg, a deeply religious man and consistently liberal jurist who considered the death penalty morally offensive. In the summer of 1963, Goldberg faced six pending cert. petitions in capital cases, each raising disturbing questions about race bias in sentencing, the adequacy of defense counsel at trial, or the appropriateness of executing the mentally impaired. None of the six claimants raised the issue whether the death penalty per se might violate the Eighth Amendment's cruel and unusual punishments clause. Still, Goldberg wanted to push his colleagues on this issue, as did his young, anti–death penalty clerk Alan Dershowitz.

Through August, Goldberg and Dershowitz labored over a lengthy memorandum laying out the legal case for why the Court should declare capital punishment unconstitutional. They didn't have much to work with. Two turn-of-the-century federal death penalty cases had raised the question whether execution by either firing squad or electrocution violated the Eighth Amendment's ban on cruel and unusual punishments. Both times, the Court had answered no. Also, in a 1947 case, the Justices had ruled that it was not cruel and unusual punishment for Louisiana to send a man back to the electric chair after its accidentally botched first attempt at electrocution ended in scarring and torture but not death.[1]

The Court had reversed a significant number of death sentences in the 1940s and '50s, and also several times chosen a capital case as the vehicle for incorporating another constitutional protection into the due process clause.[2] But the Justices always had managed to strike down questionable death sentences on relatively narrow grounds (as in the Scottsboro cases) and never suggested that the penalty itself might pose constitutional problems.

This history, though, did not faze Goldberg. In a memorandum to the Conference, he rested his case on two precedents.[3] The first was a 1910 case, *Weems* v. *United States*,[4] in which a man convicted of falsifying a public document was sentenced to fifteen years of *cadena temporal*— "hard and painful labor," to be carried out while hamstrung with chains. Striking down this punishment, the Court reasoned that the Eighth Amendment's prohibition on cruel and unusual punishments not only must include those punishments that were considered barbaric or excessive at the time of the Founding Fathers but also "may acquire meaning as public opinion becomes enlightened by humane justice." The *cadena temporal*, the Court concluded, was excessive by 1910 standards of decency and, accordingly, violated the Eighth Amendment.

Because before 1960 the Court applied the cruel and unusual punishments clause only to punishments meted out by federal courts, it had few occasions to reconsider *Weems's* formula for determining an Eighth Amendment violation. Indeed, the Court did not decide another Eighth Amendment case until 1958, when, in *Trop* v. *Dulles*, it reviewed whether the federal government could punish an army deserter by stripping him of his citizenship. A fractured Court concluded that "denationalization" was cruel and unusual. And more to the point, Chief Justice Warren, writing for a plurality of four Justices, reaffirmed the central tenet of *Weems* that the Eighth Amendment "must draw its meaning from the evolving standards of decency that mark the progress of a maturing society."[5]

Writing five years later, Goldberg believed that precisely such "evolving standards of decency" condemned the death penalty as unconstitutionally "barbaric and inhuman." The vast majority of "civilized nations," he observed, "had abolished capital punishment," and the worldwide trend was "unmistakenly in the direction of abolition." At home, nine states plus Puerto Rico and the Virgin Islands had done away with the death penalty, and recent polls indicated that 50 percent of Americans opposed its retention.

To the obvious rejoinder that a punishment about which opinion is fairly divided cannot be said to violate contemporary standards of decency, Goldberg countered with his vision of the Court as a moral beacon for society. In "certain matters," he admonished his colleagues, "this

Court has traditionally guided rather than followed public opinion in the process of articulating and establishing progressively civilized standards of decency."

Goldberg's suggested abolition of the death penalty—an idea that neither the Court nor the rest of the legal community had much studied—stunned his colleagues.[6] Ever the politician, Chief Justice Warren (already on record rejecting Goldberg's basic argument)[7] expressed serious concern that the Court had spread its political capital too thin to invest itself in yet another big controversy. In light of the Supreme Court's ongoing fight with southern states over the implementation of *Brown*, attacks on the Court over its recent barring of school prayer, and the highly controversial decision of the previous term requiring widespread redistricting according to a one-person, one-vote principle of apportionment, Justice Douglas summed up the Chief's view as "It would be best to let the matter sleep for a while."[8]

Other Justices spurned Goldberg's thesis purely on its merits. Justice Hugo Black, for example, flat out rejected the idea that "evolving standards of decency" could render cruel and unusual a punishment routinely imposed in the age of the Founding Fathers. Often literal in his interpretation of the Constitution's language, Black observed that several provisions—such as the Fifth Amendment's declaration that no person "shall be subject for the same offence to be twice put in jeopardy of *life* or limb"—implicitly endorsed the death penalty.[9]

Such criticisms prevented Goldberg from getting the four votes needed to grant cert. in any of the pending capital cases. This failure, however, which the Justice seems to have anticipated, did not stop him from expressing publicly his desire to see the Court look at the death penalty more closely. When the Court denied cert. in the six pending capital cases, Goldberg published a "dissent from denial" in one (*Rudolph* v. *Alabama*), a case like Scottsboro involving a black man sentenced to death for raping a white woman. Although Goldberg did not air his internal memo's attack on the death penalty per se, his dissent urged the Court to address whether capital punishment specifically for rape unconstitutionally violated "evolving standards of decency," or was unconstitutionally excessive for a crime that did not take human life, or (as a third option) was "unnecessarily cruel" in achieving the permissible aims of punishment. Significantly, Goldberg carried two other Justices with him. Brennan and Douglas both signed on to his dissenting statement.

Dissents from denials of cert. send a signal to the legal community.

They declare that an issue has caught the attention of at least one Justice, who feels strongly enough about the matter to issue a rare public comment effectively inviting other litigants to raise it again. For three Justices—one short of the number capable of forcing the whole Court to hear an issue—to join in a dissent from denial was tantamount to taking out a classified ad seeking new cases.

Coming at the dawn of the era of "public interest" law, Goldberg's *Rudolph* dissent found an avid readership among the burgeoning ranks of young, ambitious, liberal-minded lawyers seeking to deploy their skills in the cause of social justice. At a time when recourse to elected legislatures seemed doomed to filibuster or failure, the federal courts of the Warren era provided a wide-open alternative for seeking dramatic reforms.

Brown, of course, was the model. This singular victory had been the culmination of a twenty-five-year campaign against the constitutional doctrine of "separate but equal" meticulously orchestrated by the talented attorneys of the NAACP's Legal Defense Fund. For a generation, Thurgood Marshall's cadre of LDF lawyers—representing everyone from the most anonymous black at a lunch counter sit-in to Martin Luther King—had challenged state-sponsored bigotry in a thousand courtrooms across the South. Along the way, they had beaten down a host of entrenched racist practices, from restrictive covenants for residential housing to all-white primaries and juries. Astonishingly successful, the *Brown* campaign became the blueprint for further efforts at social reform, copied by (among others) advocates for the nascent feminist movement and those who sought greater legal rights for the poor.

At the Legal Defense Fund itself, Goldberg's published dissent catalyzed a long-standing concern about race bias in capital punishment into an entire new *Brown*-style litigation campaign. These civil rights lawyers were inspired by cases such as that of Charles Hamilton, a black man sentenced to death in the late 1950s not for actually raping a white woman but merely for breaking into her home "with intent to ravish." That Hamilton's death sentence (eventually overturned by the Supreme Court because the state had denied him a lawyer at his arraignment), seemed so disproportionate to the crime and inconceivable for a white man simply reinforced the raw numbers, which revealed that of the roughly 450 Americans executed for rape between 1930 and 1960 almost 90 percent were black. (Blacks made up roughly 12 percent of the national population.) Indeed, more than half of the 3,800 Americans executed for any crime during that period were black, and this percent-

age did not factor in the dozens of other blacks who would have been officially executed but for the efficiency of southern lynch mobs.

Goldberg's invitation to bring death penalty test cases to the Court
was precisely the encouragement needed to spur the LDF into committing several staff lawyers to a campaign toward abolition. They also hired
an outside lawyer to act as commanding general, the role Thurgood Marshall had served in the march toward *Brown*.

The LDF's choice was a young law professor from the University of
Pennsylvania, Anthony Amsterdam, a former federal prosecutor, law
clerk to Justice Felix Frankfurter, and by common account the finest
lawyer of his generation.[10] Tall, athletic, coffee guzzling, cigar smoking,
and surpassingly brilliant, Amsterdam became the subject of a nearly
endless supply of what sound like legal fish stories—he dictated a brief
from memory at four in the morning from a roadside pay phone a hundred miles from the nearest law library—except that in his case many of
the tales are demonstrably true.[11]

Working at a frenzied pace and with an almost religious zeal, Amsterdam and his colleagues set out to prove that death penalty sentencing violated the Fourteenth Amendment's equal protection clause, which, as
one of the amendment's leading sponsors had stated, "prohibits the
hanging of a black man for a crime for which the white man is not to be
hanged."[12] As a starting point, the LDF lawyers focused on cases in
which black men had received the death penalty for raping white
women—the crime for which evidence of racial bias in sentencing
seemed most graphic.[13] And to lay the groundwork for a legal claim, they
hired a respected criminologist, the University of Pennsylvania sociolo-
gist Marvin Wolfgang, to conduct a statistical analysis of racial patterns
in death sentences for rape.

While Professor Wolfgang accumulated the necessary data, LDF
lawyers sought with considerable success to postpone all pending rape
trials as well as any executions based on rape convictions. At the same
time, the LDF started cloning the litigation strategy of *Brown*—which
meant trying to chip away at the legal underpinnings of the death
penalty one side issue at a time until the institution practically fell of its
own weight. To this end, Amsterdam and his cohorts developed three
"procedural" challenges to the death penalty, that is, challenges to the
way the capital punishment was meted out rather than to the validity of
the penalty itself.

First, they attacked the usual practice of the judge excusing potential jurors who expressed reservations about the death penalty. States authorized this culling of "scrupled" jurors on the supposition that such jurors would be partial to the defense. The LDF hoped to turn this logic on its head. The Constitution guaranteed every criminal defendant a jury composed of a "cross section" of the community. Excusing scrupled jurors eliminated a segment of the cross section and, arguably, skewed the jury toward that part of the community more inclined both to convict and to impose a death sentence.

Second, the LDF challenged what was known as the single verdict procedure, used in most death penalty jurisdictions. Under this system, the same jury that determined whether a capital defendant was guilty or innocent *simultaneously* decided whether the defendant found guilty should receive the death penalty. By forcing a defendant to introduce whatever evidence he wanted the jury to consider during sentencing even before the jury had rendered a verdict, the single verdict system put the defendant to several potentially excruciating (and the LDF believed unconstitutional) choices at trial.

Without tracing all the tactical permutations of the single verdict, suffice it to say that in 1959 the American Law Institute, a highly respected organization of legal scholars and practitioners, had recommended doing away with the system. In its place, the ALI recommended that capital trials be "bifurcated" into separate phases for the determination of guilt and, where necessary, the determination of appropriate sentence. The LDF planned to argue that the ALI's proposed bifurcation was not only a good idea but constitutionally mandated as a necessary element of due process of law.

Third, the LDF prepared an attack on the way juries in most states decided whether to impose a death sentence. When jurors deliberate over the question of guilt or innocence—in any kind of case, civil or criminal—they do so only after receiving extensive instructions from the presiding judge about the legal rules that should frame their verdict: for example, what are the elements of the crime with which the defendant is charged? What standard of proof should be applied, what lesser included offenses considered?

Most capital juries, though, in their separate role as sentencers, received absolutely no legal guidance about how to separate those convicted felons who deserved to die from those who did not. Jurors reached this decision on whatever basis they individually chose, rational or capricious, fair or biased. Such unconstrained discretion originally had been intended to allow juries to show occasional mercy. Recent practice, though, followed a very different pattern. In a nation where thousands of capital crimes were committed each year, only about one hundred criminals annually received the death penalty. The overwhelming majority of these were black, poor, or so physically repulsive as to seem outside the bounds of human sympathy. And this skewing became the basis of an LDF due process–based claim that unconstrained jury discretion simply gave free rein to arbitrariness, irrationality, and racial bias in the jury box.

The moving force behind the LDF lawyers' multiprong strategy was as much expediency as a deep belief in the procedural reforms they sought. If the LDF could convince courts to adopt their proposed reforms, hundreds of death row inmates would have their sentences overturned. In the meantime, the procedural challenges provided effective means for stopping executions across the country, as Amsterdam's team pleaded with judges to halt the killing until the exact requirements of due process could be sorted out. Working at a furious pace, they intervened in every case—from the trial level to last-minute stay applications—in which a black man might be executed for raping a white woman. As one LDF attorney, Michael Meltsner, recalled, they wanted to keep their clients alive "by raising every legal argument available, whether in the long run the new procedures improved the quality of criminal justice or worked like sand poured in a machine."[14]

Many judges, especially in the federal courts, cooperated. For any judge the least bit reluctant to send someone to the chair or the gas or the gallows, the LDF strategy offered solid legal grounds for putting off the decision, perhaps indefinitely, pending final resolution of the procedural challenges by the Supreme Court. While the lower courts waited for the cases to percolate up through the system, the stays of execution came rolling in.

In April 1966, Professor Wolfgang finished his rape sentencing study, and his results were precisely what the LDF had hoped for and expected. Of 119 convicted rapists executed in twelve southern states between 1945 and 1965, Wolfgang found that 110 were black. And after attempting to control for other factors that might account for this apparent gross disproportion, Wolfgang concluded that "in less than one time in a thousand could these [racial] associations have occurred by the operation of chance."[15]

The LDF put forward Wolfgang's finished study in a test case involving William Maxwell, a young black man convicted and sentenced to death in Garland County, Arkansas, for raping a thirty-five-year-old white woman after breaking into her home. By the time the LDF introduced the Wolfgang study into Maxwell's case, his conviction and sentence were already four years old, and it is worth pausing to examine Maxwell's odyssey through the Arkansas and federal court systems to see exactly how the LDF exploited legal procedures to stymie state efforts to carry out executions.

After his 1962 conviction and sentence, Maxwell was entitled as a matter of law to appeal to the Arkansas Supreme Court. He did so, arguing in part that death penalty sentencing for rape in Arkansas was racially biased. Maxwell's appeal, though, came two years before Wolfgang even started his statistical study. His lawyers were armed with no hard evidence at all, and the Arkansas Supreme Court rejected the appeal.

After this defeat, Maxwell had the right to file a petition for certiorari in the U.S. Supreme Court. Although the Court has the power to consider any issue of *federal* law raised in a state criminal case, it reviews only a tiny fraction of those that come before it—ten or twenty of several thousand each year. The Justices do not announce the basis for their selections, but they look for cases that raise broadly significant unresolved questions or ones containing issues over which the lower courts have divided. Maxwell's unsupported claim of racism stood no chance of sparking interest at the Court; indeed, his attorney opted not even to file a petition.

Instead, Maxwell and his lawyer explored an entirely separate avenue of potential relief. They sought a writ of habeas corpus, by which, generally speaking, a judge may free any detained person if that detention is shown to be unlawful. As Justice Brennan, the writ's leading champion, wrote: "Its root principle is that in a civilized society, government must always be accountable to the judiciary for a man's imprisonment: if the imprisonment cannot be shown to conform with the fundamental requirements of law, the individual is entitled to his immediate release."[16]

The "Great Writ," as habeas corpus is known, has roots deep in the English common law, tracing its lineage back as far as Magna Carta and the earliest stirrings against monarchical power. In this country, the Framers deemed the writ so important that they specifically prohibited its suspension in the Constitution.[17] The power of issuing the writ, moreover, was one of the first prerogatives Congress gave to the federal courts.

Despite this pedigree, the scope of the writ was limited. Until the

Civil War, federal courts could grant habeas relief only to federal prisoners. That changed in 1867, when the post–Civil War Congress decided
to entrust federal judges with a spare key to southern jails. Concerned
that resentful southern officials would trump up charges against freed
blacks and northern sympathizers, Congress extended federal habeas jurisdiction to "any person," including state prisoners, "restrained or deprived of liberty in violation of any federal right."

The subsequent history of habeas corpus will be discussed later. Suffice it to say here that by the 1960s, as a practical matter, pursuing a writ
of habeas corpus gave prisoners a second (and sometimes third and
fourth) chance to argue in court that their convictions or sentences were
unlawful. Because many states offered their own forms of habeas corpus,
most criminal defendants could follow as many as three paths of judicial
review: direct appellate review of conviction, state habeas review, and
federal habeas review. On each go-round, moreover, the prisoner might
appeal all the way to the Supreme Court (as might the state if relief were
granted by a lower court).

Nor was a prisoner limited to one habeas petition. As long as he (or
she) did not deliberately withhold claims, a prisoner could file successive
habeas petitions raising new arguments or bringing forth new evidence.
On federal habeas, where there was the best chance of success in vindicating constitutional rights, a prisoner could usually proceed with claims
never raised or raised unsuccessfully in the state courts.[18] And while this
process was unfolding, a prisoner often (though not always) received the
retroactive benefit of changes in constitutional law—a fact of no small
import during the Warren era. Thus, a conviction, even if obtained in
accordance with the Constitution as defined at the time of trial, might
subsequently be deemed unlawful as the Court reformed the rules of the
game.

Proponents of this costly, complex, and time-consuming redundancy
argued that habeas corpus review, especially in federal court, was absolutely necessary to correct a system in which state courts consistently
slighted constitutional rights. The problem was as old as the republic
and recognized explicitly by Justice Joseph Story as early as 1816: "The
Constitution has presumed," he wrote, that "State attachments, State
prejudices, State jealousies, and State interests might sometimes obstruct . . . the regular administration of justice."[19]

Reflecting this sentiment, the Warren Court's liberal block, led by
Justice Brennan, read congressional grants of habeas power as broadly as

they could so as to keep open federal courts to the hundreds of prisoners who claimed (often justifiably) to have been the victims of police coercion and deceit, incompetent counsel, biased juries, or unscrupulous judges. With characteristic idealism, Brennan and his allies argued over strenuous dissents from more conservative justices (especially John Harlan) that the costs to the finality of state convictions and in the resources of federal courts were a small price to vindicate more fully the Constitution's promise of liberty. Congress evidently agreed. After reviewing the federal habeas rules in 1966, the legislature placed its imprimatur on virtually all the Court's liberalizing measures.

This expansive approach to habeas review greatly assisted abolitionist lawyers in their campaign to prevent the carrying out of any executions. The LDF and its affiliated attorneys could keep running their clients up and down the habeas ladder, reraising issues rejected by the state courts on direct appeal, unearthing new claims, and all the time watching for and trying to create new developments in the law, until (as frequently happened given the quality of much state court justice) they uncovered a constitutional violation warranting a grant of the writ or at least a claim worthy of a stay.

Willie Maxwell's case well illustrates the steps of the habeas waltz. After failing in his direct appeal, he filed for and was denied federal habeas relief in 1964. He appealed that denial and lost. He filed for a writ of certiorari, which the Court denied in 1965. Shortly thereafter, just as Professor Wolfgang was finishing his rape sentencing study, Arkansas set Maxwell's execution for September 1966. At this late stage, Amsterdam and the LDF stepped in.

As noted earlier, federal law at the time permitted the filing of successive habeas petitions presenting new evidence or new legal claims so long as the defendant had not deliberately withheld the new material in previous petitions. Accordingly, the LDF filed a second federal habeas petition for Maxwell and chose his case to bring forward Wolfgang's now completed study. With Maxwell's execution rapidly approaching, the lawyers also raised their challenges to the single verdict system, the removal of "scrupled" jurors, and the lack of guidance given capital juries. In other words, they threw in every decent argument they possessed—in the hope of piquing the interest of the federal district judge wielding the all-important power of the writ.

It didn't work. Judge J. Smith Henly rejected as insubstantial all Maxwell's claims, including the one based upon Wolfgang's statistics.

"Statistics are elusive things at best," Henly concluded skeptically, "and it is a truism that almost anything can be proved by them."[20]

After Judge Henly's ruling, Maxwell's case (slowed by a year of technical squabbling) moved to the Eighth Circuit Court of Appeals, but even before that the LDF's failure to impress a federal court with Wolfgang's documentation of racial bias spurred a fundamental change in legal strategy. Starting in 1967, the LDF decided to stop limiting its intervention to cases involving black defendants and, in particular, southern black rapists.

In the wake of their failed statistical argument, the LDF group concluded that they "could never win unless the fact that a high proportion of blacks were subject to execution emerged as but one distasteful aspect of a far greater evil."[21] In other words, they would have to challenge the death penalty not only for its racial biases but fully and completely (along the line Justice Goldberg had outlined) as morally bankrupt and wrong.

Ethical considerations also pushed the LDF lawyers to abandon their exclusively race-based approach. They now had developed a spectrum of procedural arguments against the death penalty—challenges to standardless sentencing, the single verdict, and jury selection—none of which was race based and each of which could be used in every capital case. Amsterdam and his cohorts were fielding calls from all over the country asking for help in capital cases. After the LDF lawyers realized their legal theories could, at a minimum, gain stays of execution in most pending cases, they felt a pressing moral obligation to expand their work.

The new strategy was straightforward.[22] The LDF (now often joined by the ACLU) would raise its entire range of capital punishment arguments in all cases where execution was imminent. They would defend whites as well as blacks, murderers as well as rapists, and do so in every one of the forty-two jurisdictions, north and south, that still maintained the death penalty. The idea was to create a de facto death penalty moratorium, to stop every execution both for its own sake and to build up a backlog of prisoners on death row. As Michael Meltsner explained, "The politics of abolition boiled down to this: for each year the United States went without executions, the more hollow would ring the claims that the American people could not do without them; the longer death-row inmates waited, the greater their numbers, the more difficult it would be for the courts to permit the first execution."[23]

This was psychological as well as legal warfare. In every capital case that eventually came before the Court, the LDF wanted the specter of a potential bloodbath—the sudden lifting of hundreds of stays of execution—to be firmly implanted in the Justices' minds. The group was betting that no judge and no court would choose to play God en masse.

Accordingly, LDF lawyers orchestrated a nationwide network of death penalty defenders. They developed a "Last Aid Kit"—a collection of draft briefs, motions, and habeas petitions that local counsel all across the country could use to apply for stays of execution. They organized friendly lawyers and scholars to help with the campaign and obtained a million-dollar Ford Foundation grant to fund their effort.

The campaign succeeded. Nineteen sixty-eight was one of the most violent years this country has known. Thousands of American soldiers and tens of thousands of Vietnamese died in an increasingly unpopular war. Student demonstrators torched draft cards and occupied college campuses. The Black Panthers and other radicals built bombs of their own. Richard Daley's police busted heads at the Democratic Convention in Chicago. Assassins killed Robert Kennedy and Martin Luther King. Then, the cities burned. Amid this tornado of wrath, for the first year in the country's history, not a single person was executed for a crime.

In June 1968, the Supreme Court handed down *Witherspoon v. Illinois,* its first decision tackling one of the LDF's three main procedural challenges to the death penalty.[24] Illinois, as did almost every capital punishment state, allowed the prosecution to exclude from capital case juries anyone with "conscientious scruples against capital punishment." During jury selection at Witherspoon's 1960 trial, the prosecution eliminated forty-seven such prospective jurors after the trial judge announced, "Let's get these conscientious objectors out of the way, without wasting any time on them."

Justice Potter Stewart's majority opinion struck down the prevailing standard for "scrupling" a capital jury on the ground that dismissing any juror opposed to the death penalty made the jury unconstitutionally prone to return a death sentence. The Court held that although the state might legitimately exclude jurors who would "automatically" or "invariably" vote against the death penalty, it could not exclude those who merely "voiced general objections to the death penalty or expressed conscientious or religious scruples against its infliction."

Underlying this ruling was a belief that a jury purged of death penalty opponents could not perform its essential function of expressing "the conscience of the community on the ultimate question of life and death." This was especially true, Stewart concluded, in a nation where the latest polls indicated fewer than half its citizens still believed in capital punishment.[25] "Culled of all who harbor doubts about the wisdom of capital punishment," Stewart wrote, ". . . such a jury can speak only for a distinct and dwindling minority."

A majority of the Justices, furthermore, seemed to express their own serious doubts about the penalty. In a footnote discussing the division of popular opinion on the subject, Stewart inserted a famous excerpt from Arthur Koestler's abolitionist novel, *Reflections on Hanging*: "The division is not between rich and poor, highbrow and lowbrow, Christians and atheists: it is between those who have charity and those who have not. . . . The test of one's humanity is whether one is able to accept this fact—not as lip service, but with the shuddering recognition of a kinship: here but for the grace of God, drop I." If, as seemed likely, a prospective Eighth Amendment challenge to the death penalty would turn on the Court's sense of society's "evolving standards of decency," Stewart seemed to be hinting strongly at the result such decency required.

But while that fight lay ahead, *Witherspoon* by its own terms handed the LDF an enormous victory. Because the Court's decision was to be applied retroactively, every prisoner on death row sentenced by a jury on which "scrupling" had taken place under pre-*Witherspoon* standards was now entitled to resentencing. Practically everyone on death row could present some sort of *Witherspoon* claim and with the LDF's help could tie up the execution process for years.

State officials recognized *Witherspoon*'s likely consequences. "I'm so mad, I'm speechless. We don't know what to do," one Texas D.A. told a reporter. Arthur Bolton, the attorney general of Georgia, thought the Court's decision would "definitely end capital punishment in Georgia."[26]

The lawyers at the LDF agreed. The moratorium was on in full force. Even if the effect of *Witherspoon* gradually played out, they had other procedural challenges working their way through the courts—more sand in the death penalty machine. As the Court was handing down *Witherspoon*, the attorney general of the United States, Ramsey Clark, taking an unprecedented position on behalf of a sitting president, asked Congress to abolish the federal death penalty. In a *New York Times* article at year's end, Jack Greenberg, Thurgood Marshall's successor as head of all LDF litigation, declared that the "national courtroom campaign" had achieved a "de facto national abolition of the death penalty."[27] The war seemed all but won.

The Strike of Lightning

In the fall of 1968, the Eighth Circuit (having sat on the case for almost a year) finally ruled on Willie Maxwell's second habeas petition. It dismissed all his claims, including the race discrimination argument based on Professor Wolfgang's study. About Wolfgang's work, then Judge Harry Blackmun (a mathematics major at Harvard) concluded that "whatever suspicion [Wolfgang's study] may arouse with respect to southern interracial rape trials as a group over a long period of time . . . we feel the statistical argument does nothing to destroy the integrity of Maxwell's trial."

The LDF lawyers filed a cert. petition with the Supreme Court, hoping the Justices would give more favorable consideration to their various arguments, especially the much labored over discrimination claim. For their part, the Justices were eager to come to grips with the many issues surrounding the death penalty—except, apparently, the issue of race discrimination. The Court granted cert. in Maxwell's case but limited review to his nonrace-based challenges to the single verdict system and to the unfettered discretion given capital juries in passing sentence.

Thus, ironically, although the challenge to racism that had fueled the abolitionist movement from the outset was now moribund, the LDF's procedural claims remained promising. Indeed, after oral argument on March 4, 1969, the Justices voted 8–1 to reverse Maxwell's death sentence. Three Justices—Warren, Brennan, and Douglas—wanted to strike down both the single verdict system and the practice of giving capital juries unfettered sentencing discretion. Justices Abe Fortas and Thurgood Marshall (making a majority) agreed on the single verdict issue but did not vote to limit jury discretion. Justice Harlan leaned toward this position as well, which meant as many as six votes to strike down the single verdict system and hand the LDF a victory even more useful and far reaching than *Witherspoon*. Justices White and Stewart, meanwhile, wanted to reverse Maxwell's death sentence but for the much narrower reason that jury selection in his case had violated the Court's *Witherspoon* decision of the previous year. Justice Black alone among the nine voted to affirm Maxwell's conviction and sentence.

Chief Justice Warren asked Douglas to take on the majority opinion. The choice proved a history-making mistake. Not content with striking a solid blow against the death penalty, Douglas went for a knockout punch. He circulated a draft majority opinion that declared unconstitutional *both* the single verdict system and unfettered discretion for capital juries—a view that had not commanded five votes at Conference. When Fortas and Marshall refused to go along, Douglas redrafted, dropping the discretion issue, and his revised opinion quickly garnered the necessary four joins. But now Justice Brennan insisted on writing separately to set forth the jury discretion arguments Douglas had omitted.

The delay proved disastrous. The Court was already operating in lame-duck fashion. The previous June, Chief Justice Warren had tendered his resignation to President Lyndon Johnson and was set to step down as soon as a successor was confirmed. Johnson nominated Justice Fortas to be the next Chief, but his confirmation stalled when conservative senators (furious over Fortas's record in criminal cases and buoyed by allegations of impropriety) launched a successful filibuster. In October 1968, with his nomination doomed, Fortas had Johnson withdraw his name. But with only a month before the Humphrey–Nixon presidential election, Johnson had no time to put forward a second choice, and after the election, the choice of Warren's replacement passed to Richard Nixon, whose "law and order" platform promised dramatic change at the Court.

As Nixon mulled over whom to nominate, scandal continued to dog Fortas. On May 5, 1969, while the Justices continued to fuss over *Maxwell*, an article in *Life* magazine revealed that Fortas had been engaged in a highly improper moneymaking scheme while on the bench. Nine days later, Fortas resigned in disgrace, leaving a second huge gap in the Court's once formidable liberal facade.

Fortas's departure wrecked the *Maxwell* coalition. It deprived Douglas of his certain majority for striking down the single verdict system and left Harlan holding the key fifth vote. Although Harlan initially had indicated agreement with Douglas, once his vote became pivotal, he demanded that the Court reargue *Maxwell* the following fall.

By the time of reargument, Warren Burger had replaced Earl Warren as Chief Justice and, after Nixon's failed nominations of Clement Haynesworth and Harold Carswell, Harry Blackmun had taken Fortas's seat (although as the author of the Eighth Circuit's *Maxwell* opinion he was recused from the case). With only eight Justices participating, the Court remained deadlocked on the LDF's challenge to the single verdict system. Harlan returned to his original view, stating in conference that he could not "imagine a more flagrant violation of due process."[1] But with Burger substituted for Warren, Douglas could still muster only four votes. In the end, eight years after a jury sentenced Maxwell to death, the Justices decided to duck the single verdict issue entirely and reverse Maxwell's death sentence (as Stewart and White had wanted all along) on the basis of *Witherspoon*.*

The Court could dispense with *Maxwell*, but it could not avoid the underlying issues. More than 500 prisoners were on death row waiting for resolution of the LDF's single verdict and jury discretion challenges, and the Justices took them up again the next term in *McGautha v. California*.[2]

In the interim, the balance of the Court had shifted significantly. This time, Blackmun as well as Burger would be eligible to hear the cases, which meant (entirely because of Abe Fortas's misconduct) that in the space of a year the abolitionists had seen two sure allies replaced by two new Justices, whom President Nixon had selected specifically to reflect a sizable national backlash against the "activist" decisions of the Warren era.

Republicans had been running against the Warren Court since 1964, when Barry Goldwater featured as a central part of his presidential campaign a jeremiad against its contribution to a "suicidal drift" away from constitutional government and moral order. Although Goldwater lost badly, his message still resonated in the hearts and minds of conservative journalists, a number of jurists, and a wide spectrum of middle America.

---

*On the same day the Court considered *Maxwell*, it heard argument in *Boykin v. Alabama*, 395 U.S. 238 (1969), which involved the rare instance of a death sentence imposed for robbery. In *Boykin*, for the first time, the LDF challenged the death penalty on Eighth Amendment grounds—arguing that it was disproportionate for robbery and, therefore, cruel and unusual punishment. At Conference, only three Justices (Warren, Brennan, and Douglas) concurred in this view. A majority of the Justices did agree, though, that Boykin's robbery conviction should be reversed because his confession introduced at trial was involuntary. This decision to reverse made superfluous any decision on the broader Eighth Amendment question, and the Justices let its resolution pass for another day.

Respected judges (such as the much revered Learned Hand) and a number of prominent theorists expressed deep concern that, in fashioning their Rights Revolution, the unelected, life-tenured Justices of the Warren Court had usurped the powers of the government's democratic branches and set themselves up as "Platonic guardians" of American society.[3] For these critics, the Justices' proper role was to discern not whether the actions of the democratic branches were "fair" or "right" or "compassionate" but whether they violated some specific prohibition of the constitutional text as informed by the historical intentions of those who drafted it.

Less theoretically, the Warren Court's ban on organized prayer in public school classrooms, its apparent "coddling" of criminals, and the continued forced integration of schools and society at large had sparked resentment among many laypeople who feared that judicial efforts to reweave the nation's social fabric had imperiled some of their most deeply held beliefs. In the temper of the times, crime and, specifically, the Warren Court's extension of defendants' rights to the states emerged as a successful campaign issue for conservative candidates. In 1966, Ronald Reagan in California and Claude Kirk in Florida captured governorships by promising to be tough on criminals and, in particular, to accelerate the execution process for prisoners on death row. Richard Nixon's law and order campaign rode the same public concerns into the White House.

In naming new Justices, Nixon clearly intended to redeem his campaign pledge to turn the Court around. He elevated Warren Burger from his seat on the D.C. Circuit Court of Appeals in large part because of Burger's outspoken opposition to judicial extensions of defendants' due process rights. Harry Blackmun (a fellow Minnesotan and boyhood friend of Burger), Nixon's third and finally successful choice to replace Fortas, was reputed to be a studious but unadventurous judge whom the administration could count on to follow Burger's lead in checking Warren Court excesses.

From the LDF's perspective, the appointments could hardly have been worse. As an appeals judge, Burger was on record rejecting the LDF's single verdict challenge. Even more damning, Blackmun had written the Eighth Circuit's repudiation of both the LDF's procedural claims. At his confirmation hearings, moreover, Blackmun had stated that, despite personal doubts about the death penalty, he considered its imposition largely "a matter for the legislature."

The mood of the country further dimmed the LDF's hopes. The spring of 1970 was filled with urban explosions. Three members of the Weathermen, an underground radical group, accidentally blew themselves up while building a bomb in a Greenwich Village apartment. Another person was killed in a similar incident on the Lower East Side. A pipe bomb tore apart a Manhattan nightclub, injuring seventeen. Just before the trial of black militant H. Rap Brown, someone blew up the courthouse. Several of Brown's followers died shortly thereafter when their car exploded. President Nixon responded to the bombings with legislation, quickly enacted, imposing the death penalty for interstate transportation of explosives when death resulted.

In the wake of the invasion of Cambodia, students took to the streets and National Guardsmen shot four dead at Kent State. State troopers killed two more and injured nine at Jackson State in Mississippi. Vice President Spiro Agnew denounced a "damn zoo" of "deserters, malcontents, radicals, incendiaries, [and] civil and uncivil disobedients." Images of urban riots, rampant crime, constant protest, and upheaval dominated the public consciousness.

On the narrow issue of the death penalty, public opinion turned around. As the Court took up *McGautha* in the fall of 1970, supporters of capital punishment, 42 percent of Americans in 1966—what in *Witherspoon* Justice Stewart called a "distinct and dwindling minority"—constituted 51 percent and climbing. At the Justice Department, where in 1967 Johnson's Attorney General Ramsey Clark had called for an end to the federal death penalty, the new solicitor general, Erwin Griswold, submitted a brief on behalf of the United States opposing the LDF.

The once fence-sitting Court now emphatically rejected both the LDF's single verdict and jury discretion arguments. Writing for a 6–3 majority (including both Nixon appointees), Justice Harlan had rethought his previously stated view that the single verdict system was a "flagrant" violation of due process. Now, while conceding that the coupling of trial and sentencing posed "cruel" dilemmas for a defendant, Harlan found such "nice calculations" about strategy an unavoidable and constitutionally unobjectionable part of the criminal process.[4]

On the issue of unfettered jury discretion, Harlan gave voice to a deep skepticism that society could ever separate effectively those crimes for which death should be imposed from those for which it should not. Such failed attempts stretched from as far back as the Book of Exodus to the modern law's ineffective struggle to define first-degree murder. In light of this uninspiring history, Harlan concluded that offering meaningful guidance to sentencing juries in capital cases was a task "beyond present human ability." And absent such ability, he continued, states were entitled to assume "that jurors confronted with the truly awesome responsibility of decreeing death for a fellow human will act with due regard for the consequences of their decision."

Justice Brennan replied with an especially scorching dissent. In his view, by refusing to require states even to attempt to devise sentencing standards, the Court had completely abdicated its responsibility to "bring the power of reason to bear on the considerations relevant to capital sentencing." Brennan expressed confidence that states could effectively channel jury discretion. But if, as Harlan contended, the human mind was incapable of creating a rational capital sentencing scheme, Brennan saw very differently the course the Court must take. "Even if I shared the Court's view that the rule of law and the power of the States to kill are in irreconcilable conflict," he wrote acidly, "I would have no hesitation in concluding that the rule of law must prevail."

Brennan's *McGautha* dissent, however, obscured his real views. Though he professed that states could bring their death penalty laws in line with due process, Brennan had already become convinced—to the point of almost religious conviction—that capital punishment was so totally degrading to human dignity that it violated the Eighth Amendment's prohibition on "cruel and unusual punishments" no matter the circumstances.

McGautha caused Brennan to lose hope that the Court would ever come around to his view,[5] and, fearing a further entrenchment of the death penalty, he tried to forestall the Court from granting cert. in any of the many pending cases that raised Eighth Amendment claims. His efforts ran aground. The LDF was pushing the issue hard as probably its last, best hope for abolition. Also, Justices Black and Stewart were pressing their colleagues to tackle the Eighth Amendment, which, after all, had shadowed the Court's death penalty debate since its inception. Accordingly, in June 1971, just before their summer recess, the Justices granted cert. in four cases that would become known collectively as *Furman* v. *Georgia*.[6]

Neither Black nor Harlan, *McGautha*'s author, would see the cases argued. Both resigned before the end of the summer and died before year's end. As their replacements, Nixon continued to nominate perceived strict constructionists, a term generally understood as referring to those who wanted to curb or even reverse the Warren Court's expansion of rights for accused criminals. Lewis Powell and William Rehnquist certainly fit this mold.

Powell was a Virginia patrician and past president of the American Bar Association who had overseen the reluctant desegregation of Richmond's schools. As the former chairman or president of the Richmond School Board, the State Board of Education, the Richmond Family Services Society, the Richmond Citizens Association, the State Library Board, and the Virginia Constitutional Revision Commission, he naturally resented the Warren Court's newfangled restrictions on local authority. This was especially true in criminal law. As one of the country's leading private practitioners, he had served on President Johnson's Crime Commission, where (in a minority report) he urged that the Warren Court had "swung the pendulum too far in affording rights which are abused and misused by criminals." So vehement was Powell's opposition to the Court's *Miranda* ruling, forcing police to read suspects their rights, he even proposed a constitutional amendment to overrule the decision.

Rehnquist was a product of Goldwater Republicanism and the Nixon Justice Department. After a clerkship with Justice Robert Jackson in 1952–53, Rehnquist had moved to Arizona, where, while building a successful law practice, he became active in Goldwater GOP politics and spearheaded a number of conservative political causes. At the time of his nomination, Rehnquist headed the Justice Department's Office of Legal Counsel, which made him, in essence, the chief legal adviser to Attorney General John Mitchell. In that role, Rehnquist had urged sharp cutbacks in federal habeas corpus, defended the legality of wiretapping, preventive detention, and "no-knock" searches, and urged strong countermeasures to even nonviolent civil disobedience by protesters he denounced as "the new barbarians." Rehnquist particularly infuriated the civil liberties establishment when he provided legal justification for the dragnet arrests of several thousand 1971 May Day antiwar protesters by Washington, D.C., police.*

The new appointments certainly did nothing to ease the LDF's daunting task of convincing the Court to accept its basic argument that the Eighth Amendment prohibited any punishment that, if evenly applied, would be unacceptable to contemporary standards of decency. But the

---

*These arrests were later declared illegal, and the government ended up paying a $3.3 million court judgment to the protesters.

LDF pushed forward. At oral argument in January 1972, Anthony Amsterdam insisted that the death penalty persisted in America solely because juries imposed it infrequently and against only the abject outcasts of society. "The short of the matter," he concluded, "is that when a penalty is so barbaric that it can gain public acceptance only by being rarely, arbitrarily and discriminatorily enforced, it plainly affronts the general standards of decency of the society."

These arguments were a classic appeal to Warren Court sensibilities, a test of whether the Court still saw itself as an institution principally charged with the righting of social wrongs while interpreting a Constitution filled with "majestic generalities" that gathered meaning over time.[7] When the *Furman* decision finally came down on June 28, the very last day of the term, it became clear that the Justices were no longer certain themselves.[8] By a surprising 5–4 vote, the Court struck down the death penalty in America, but each of the nine Justices wrote his own opinion, a splintering unprecedented in the 150 years since the Justices abandoned the practice of expressing their views seriatim.

As one scholar has aptly described the 50,000-word production (the longest collection of opinions ever), *Furman* was the Court's version of a "badly orchestrated opera, with nine characters taking turns to offer their own arias."[9] Not one of the five in the majority saw fit to join any of the others' opinions, and, consequently, each wrote only for himself. At least the four dissenters (the solid bloc of Nixon's appointees), though writing separately, acceded in each other's opinions.*

Only two of the Justices, Brennan and Marshall, embraced the crux of the LDF position. Brennan's lengthy opinion was built on essentially the same rickety scaffolding that had supported Justice Goldberg's internal memo of 1963. Capital punishment—inflicted in "arbitrary fashion," decisively "rejected throughout society," patently "unnecessary," and "uniquely degrading to human dignity"—could not be squared with what Brennan distilled to be the Eighth Amendment's central command that all punishments conform with "the evolving standards of decency which are the mark of a maturing society."

Justice Marshall liked to joke how his wife, Sissy, was nagging him to "string up" all the bad guys, but behind the gallows humor his opposition

---

*The exception here is Justice Blackmun's dissent, which is highly personal in tone and was not joined by the others.

to the death penalty had become so powerfully felt he prepared much of his *Furman* opinion during the summer before the Court heard argument. A lifetime of experience in southern courtrooms and a stint during the Korean War investigating the cases of black G.I.'s sentenced to death had schooled Marshall in the ugly realities of who was executed and why. Yet his opinion did not dwell overmuch on discrimination. Instead, Marshall argued that capital punishment could serve only two possible functions, retribution or deterrence. The Justice first rejected retribution as a legitimate aim of criminal sentencing, then dismissed the idea that the death penalty had served as a deterrent to crime. Because it served no legitimate purpose, capital punishment in Marshall's view was simply an excessive cruelty visited solely on the weakest members of society. Unwilling to believe that a compassionate people could accept such a system, Marshall concluded on their behalf that an enlightened citizenry would recoil at its handiwork. "Assuming knowledge of all the facts presently available regarding capital punishment," he wrote, "the average citizen would, in my opinion, find it shocking to his conscience and sense of justice. For this reason alone capital punishment cannot stand."

Justice Douglas refused to accept the "evolving standards of decency" standard for determining a cruel and unusual punishment. Rather his opinion focused mainly on the way American society has inflicted the death penalty on the disadvantaged. He thought the Court should have recognized this inevitable bias in *McGautha* and could now rectify that mistake.

The surprise votes in *Furman* came from Stewart and White, both of whom had joined Harlan's majority opinion in *McGautha*. Although Stewart was not swayed by Amsterdam's moral arguments, he had become a captive of the LDF's moratorium strategy. By his own account, Stewart spent long nights fretting about the now 600 men (their number growing) on death row whose lives hung on the thread of his vote, wondering why they had been sentenced to die when thousands of others guilty of similar or worse crimes had received only jail sentences.[10] For Stewart (as he had written in *Witherspoon*), capital punishment was a weak and fading institution that in all likelihood would disappear with a slight nudge from the Court. Rather than face the specter of a national bloodbath, he found constitutional error in capital punishment's infrequent and seemingly arbitrary imposition. The death penalty, Stewart wrote, was "cruel and unusual in the same way that being struck by light-ning is cruel and unusual." The Eighth Amendment did not permit it to be so "wantonly and freakishly imposed."

White's approach was more hardheaded. Assuming capital punish-ment served a legitimate function of the criminal law, specifically the de-terrence of future crimes, he found nothing repugnant about it. But White could not fathom how a punishment imposed "with great infre-quency even for the most atrocious crimes" could alter human behavior. If the nation was not tough-minded enough to use capital punishment as an instrument of social policy, continuing with the current smattering of executions resulted in nothing more than the pointless extinguishment of human life. Simply put, in White's view of the Eighth Amendment, states had to put to death either more people or none at all.

The four dissenting Justices sounded common themes, each accusing the majority of far overstepping the judicial role. The majority, they claimed, had abandoned the task of assessing whether challenged legis-lation violated a specific constitutional provision and had set themselves up instead (in Justice Rehnquist's words) as "a roving commission . . . to strike down laws that are based upon notions of policy or morality sud-denly found unacceptable by a majority of the court."

The dissenters were incredulous at how, only one year after *McGau-tha*, the Court could suddenly have discerned a contemporary moral re-pugnance to executions. This "precipitate" discovery and "instant evolution of the law" flew in the face of eighty years of unbroken case law directly or implicitly upholding the death penalty against Eighth Amendment challenge. Furthermore, it simply wished away a continued public commitment to the option of capital punishment. As for the ma-jority's more practical rejection of the deterrent value of occasional exe-cutions, the dissenters argued that such judgments about social utility were for legislators—not judges—to make.

In counterpoint to the majority's alleged elevation of personal pre-deliction over impartial judgment, Justice Blackmun's short personal statement sounded the deepest chords of judicial self-discipline and re-straint. "Cases such as these provide for me an excruciating agony of the spirit," he wrote. "I yield to no one in the depth of my distaste, antipa-thy, and, indeed, abhorrence, for the death penalty, with all its aspects of physical distress and fear and of moral judgement by finite minds." But Blackmun could find no warrant for these views in the Constitution, and thus, however reluctantly, he decried the majority's collective action as judicial expropriation "in the modern guise of the Eighth Amendment" of authority vested in the elected branches of government.[11]

One cannot read Justice Blackmun's dissent, openly acknowledging the "temptation" of his personal preferences, without recognizing how much he wanted to be persuaded to join the majority. Yet even for the sympathetic minded, *Furman* is a decision that utterly fails to persuade.

Partly that failure stems from the inherent difficulty in making the Goldberg-Brennan argument that a punishment clearly contemplated by the Framers and consistently practiced since that time had suddenly become cruel and unusual even though most of contemporary American society continued to support its use. Opponents of the Warren Court habitually criticized the liberal Justices for reading into the Constitution their contemporary notions of fairness, regardless of text or tradition. Whatever the merits of these charges generally, they struck home in *Furman*. In shifting the basis for their arguments from the Constitution's explicit ban on race discrimination to more amorphous claims of personal morality, the abolitionists had moved their cause from the strongest to the weakest sector of the Warren Court's enterprise—the place where the political views of the liberal Justices outstripped the logic of legitimate legal argument.

In the end, however, *Furman*'s failure was as much institutional as intellectual. For five Justices to issue one of the most far-reaching constitutional rulings in the Court's history without even agreeing among themselves on a legal rationale betrayed the very rule of law they claimed to be upholding. That rule depends on a shared language of principle, a common understanding of where the law has been, where the law should go, and how to travel the distance between. It depends on continuity, a sensible accounting of how long-standing ideals compel contemporary conclusions.

Furman contains none of this: no communal judgment, no explanation of how the decision reconciled the Court's meandering from *Witherspoon* to *Maxwell* to *McGautha*, no effort to take into account the profound changes in both public attitudes and the Court's own composition. Instead, five Justices abandoned the Court's institutional responsibility to justify and give coherence to a dramatic shift in the law.

Eighteen years before, when the Court had reversed itself in *Brown*, it did so in a self-conscious and much worked at unanimity that the Justices maintained throughout two decades of school desegregation cases. In this sense, *Furman* was *Brown's* antithesis. Gone was any effort toward accommodation or persuasion or the felt need to deliver an opinion as an institution with a past and a future, and not as individuals. Not one of the Justices in the majority thought to reconsider his vote rather than march forward in total disarray.

The LDF naturally celebrated *Furman's* triumph of result over reason. Amsterdam called the decision "the biggest step forward that criminal justice has taken in 1000 years." Jack Greenberg predicted that capital punishment would end permanently in the United States, and, privately, Chief Justice Burger agreed.[12]

But the splintered quality of the *Furman* majority cast serious doubt on these conclusions. Only two Justices, Brennan and Marshall, had found the death penalty unconstitutional in all circumstances. Douglas, White, and Stewart had stated only that capital punishment *as currently implemented* violated the Eighth Amendment. Nothing in their writings—especially White's and Stewart's complaints about the infrequency of imposition—prohibited states from designing new death penalty schemes to address their concerns.

Chief Justice Burger's dissent had specifically noted *Furman's* technically limited reach. The scope of ruling is determined by the narrowest view still necessary to command a majority of the Court—which meant *Furman* extended only as far as either Stewart's or White's opinion (depending on which was *more* limited). With that in mind, Burger invited states to enact new death penalty laws that, by providing specific standards for capital sentencing, might satisfy one or the other of them. Thus, for all the hurrahs among the abolitionists, it was by no means clear whether *Furman* would prove an irresistible flood tide sweeping away capital punishment forever or the high-water mark of the abolitionist wave broken and spent on the broad beach of the law.

Backlash

The response to *Furman* was overwhelming. Despite the infrequency with which juries imposed the death penalty, the general public rebelled at Court-imposed abolition. Polls that in March 1972 had registered 50 percent approval for capital punishment showed a sudden jump to 57 approval by November and moved steadily higher during 1973. President Nixon denounced the decision and vowed to restore the federal death penalty for certain extraordinary crimes, such as treason or hijacking. Voters in California endorsed a ballot initiative seeking restoration of that state's death penalty by a 2–1 margin. Within a year of *Furman*, nineteen state legislatures had passed new death penalty statutes. Sixteen more would shortly follow suit.

Although the new laws varied significantly, all were designed to meet Stewart's and White's objection in *Furman* that absolute jury discretion in capital sentencing produced arbitrary and freakish results. In response, roughly half of the states reinstituting the death penalty took the natural step of eliminating jury discretion altogether. They made the death penalty mandatory upon conviction for certain categories of crimes. Louisiana, for example, mandated capital punishment for defendants convicted of specified types of intentional homicide—such as when the defendant was guilty of a prior murder, killed in the course of committing another major felony, or killed a police officer. Even more draconian was North Carolina's new law. It required the death penalty for all "first degree" murders.*

---

*This definition raised the additional problem of identifying which murders should be classified as "first degree"—a question that had confounded the criminal law for generations.

A second group of states attempted a more nuanced answer to *Furman*. Rather than abolish jury discretion, these states adopted so-called "guided discretion" statutes, which sought to structure and control the way capital juries reached their sentencing decisions. The prototype for these laws was the Model Penal Code drafted by the judges, scholars, and practitioners of the American Law Institute. Their model law limited capital punishment to the crime of murder, replaced the single verdict system with one that separated the guilt and sentencing phases of a capital trial, and provided rigorous appellate review of all death sentences. Responding to *Furman*'s demand for greater "rationality" in the death penalty, the ALI proposal further provided that a capital jury could return a sentence of death only if it found the murder in question to have involved at least one designated "aggravating circumstance." These circumstances included factors such as a defendant's prior conviction for a violent crime, the committing of multiple murders, murder for monetary gain, murder during the course of a major felony such as rape, robbery, arson, burglary, or kidnapping, or murder that was "especially heinous, atrocious or cruel, manifesting exceptional depravity."

At the same time, the ALI model provided "mitigating circumstances" for the jurors to consider if they found at least one aggravating circumstance. Such mitigating factors included the defendant's lack of significant criminal history, the defendant's acting under duress or believing the actions justified under the circumstances, the defendant having killed when very young, or the defendant having committed the crime under severe emotional distress or other mental impairment short of insanity. The ALI model authorized a jury to return a death sentence only when it found one or more aggravating circumstances to exist and no mitigating circumstances "sufficiently substantial to call for leniency." There was no escaping broad judgment calls on matters such as whether a murder was especially heinous or cruel or whether the accumulated mitigating circumstances were sufficient to merit leniency. Still, in theory at least, the model statute would create a more rational process for separating those defendants who deserved the death penalty from those who did not.

The cycle of litigation started all over again, and the moratorium on executions continued as the LDF (now actively joined by other groups, such as the Southern Poverty Law Center) interceded in every capital case in the country. Led again by Anthony Amsterdam, abolitionist lawyers claimed that the guided discretion statutes were too vague and malleable to eliminate the arbitrariness of capital sentencing while the mandatory sentencing laws simply shifted the absolute discretion condemned in *Furman* from juries to the police and prosecutors, who decided whether to charge a defendant with a capital crime. And, of course, the abolitionists continued to press their central argument that capital punishment was so morally repugnant that it violated the Eighth Amendment.

By October 1974, as the number of inmates sentenced to death under the new laws surpassed 150, the Justices granted cert. in *Fowler v. North Carolina*, a challenge to that state's mandatory death penalty scheme, arguably the nation's harshest. Much as had happened in *Maxwell*, however, developments at the Court ran the case aground. On New Year's Eve, Justice Douglas suffered a severe stroke, which, despite the Justice's legendary physical stamina, left him partially paralyzed, unable to control his bodily functions, and teetering on the edge of mental incompetence. As spring approached, Douglas tried to resume his duties, but the doctor-defying effort was beyond him. In and out of the hospital, Douglas often fell asleep at oral argument or had to excuse himself from the chamber to recover from bouts of pain.

Desperate to participate in *Fowler*, Douglas had himself wheeled into the hushed courtroom as the April 21 oral argument commenced. When the case was taken up at the weekly Conference, though, he was already back in the hospital. In his absence, the remaining Justices deadlocked 4–4 and decided to have the case reargued the next term rather than wait on Douglas's vote.

After the summer break, with Douglas unimproved, the Conference concluded that his unstable mental condition called for a drastic curtailment of his authority. Secretly, the Justices decided to nullify Douglas's participation in pending cases by ordering reargument in every case where he held the deciding vote.* This arrangement left the new death penalty statutes in continued limbo, until finally, mercifully, on November 11, 1975, Douglas agreed to retire.

The Justices returned to the issue of the death penalty at a special Saturday conference in mid-January 1976. By this time, President Gerald Ford had filled Douglas's seat with John Paul Stevens, a judge from the Seventh Circuit Court of Appeals who enjoyed a reputation as a scrupu-

---

*Justice White alone objected to stripping Douglas of power. He argued that under the Constitution only Congress through impeachment could take away a Justice's authority. The others put their plan into effect nonetheless.

lous judicial craftsman, a lawyer's lawyer on the bench. Formerly a clerk
to Justice Wiley Rutledge and then an accomplished antitrust attorney,
Stevens had won unanimous confirmation from a Senate eager to embrace a keenly intelligent nominee with no obvious ideological ax to
grind.

At the death penalty conference, the reconstituted Court had sorted
through which of the many pending capital cases to review. More than
400 people now had been sentenced to death under a wide assortment of
post-*Furman* statutes, and the Justices had to decide which if any passed
muster under *Furman*—or whether they should revisit *Furman* itself. In
the end, the Court granted cert. in five death penalty cases, challenges
to the mandatory sentencing schemes of North Carolina and Louisiana
and the guided discretion statutes of Georgia, Florida, and Texas. (These
cases are generally referred to collectively by the name of the lead case,
Gregg v. Georgia.)

The Ford Justice Department immediately took sides. In support of
the state attorneys general defending the challenged statutes, Solicitor
General Robert Bork filed a seventy-six-page brief and appeared at the
March oral argument to assert, in essence, that the dissenters in *Furman*
had been right: the Constitution left the issue of capital punishment to
the people's elected representatives. In the four years since *Furman*,
those representatives had spoken resoundingly, and the Court should let
their will be done.

Anthony Amsterdam—so brilliant in *Furman* that even the grudging
Justice White said he'd never seen a better oral advocate—again spoke
for the abolitionists, but this time to very different effect. As the two
days of argument unfolded, there was no mistaking the costs of Amsterdam's long years of total immersion in the abolitionist cause. His intense
moral and emotional commitment had rendered him tone deaf to the
changing tune of the country and the Court. At one point Justice Powell asked whether Amsterdam could "conceive of any crime as to which
you would consider the death penalty an appropriate response." He
could not. Not for air piracy resulting in hundreds of deaths; not for the
commandant of Buchenwald. Powell kept up the hypotheticals. What
"if some fanatic set off a hydrogen bomb and destroyed New York City"?
Still no. The exchange persuaded Powell that Amsterdam was a "nut."
Worse still, Amsterdam's perceived fanaticism seemed touched by an
unappealing self-righteousness. After argument, one Justice was heard to
comment, "Now I know what it's like to hear Jesus Christ."[1]

At Conference on April 2, only Justices Brennan and Marshall endorsed the LDF's basic Eighth Amendment argument attacking the morality of the death penalty. Having been rebuffed by more than thirty state legislatures in their assessment of contemporary American morality, these two stalwarts still believed that, if only Americans "were better informed," they too would conclude that capital punishment was destructive of human dignity, "shocking, unjust, and unacceptable." In any event, Brennan and Marshall saw the Constitution and the Court as protecting Americans from their vengeful "baser selves." The Eighth Amendment, they maintained, prohibited the satisfaction of national "bloodlust" in a country already haunted by "too much crime, too much killing, [and] too much hatred."

All seven other Justices, including both Stewart and White from the *Furman* majority, voted to uphold at least some of the new death penalty regimes. Three—Burger, White, and Rehnquist—were definite about upholding all five. Blackmun and Powell leaned in this direction but were troubled by North Carolina's particularly rigid and harsh mandatory law, what Stevens called a "monster." Stevens and Stewart were for striking both mandatory sentencing statutes as needlessly bloodyminded responses to *Furman*, which obscured but did not cure the arbitrariness of capital sentencing.* Stevens and to a lesser degree Stewart also objected to Texas's law, the least finely tuned of the guided discretion statutes.†

The confused lineup presented Chief Justice Burger with one of those occasional instances where the power to assign the majority opinion held the prospect of affecting the outcome of the case. He could have adopted the strictly impartial route of assigning the case to one of the Justices taking the middle ground (say Justice Powell), to reflect what appeared to be an emerging majority to strike down at least the North Carolina law. But, in a move that typified Burger's unpopular tenure as

---

*Of course, mandatory laws were the perfect cure for Stewart's "struck by lightning" objection to the death penalty, but the Justice was uneasy with a remedy that meant both significantly more executions (i.e., blood on his hands) and a return to a system that most states had abandoned long before *Furman*.

†Although the Texas law provided a bifurcated trial, its channeling of jury discretion was limited to asking three questions: whether the defendant had "deliberately" caused death; "whether there is a probability that the defendant would commit criminal acts of violence that would constitute a continuing threat to society"; and whether, if the victim had provoked the defendant, the defendant's killing was nonetheless an "unreasonable" response. If the jury answered yes to these questions, a death sentence was imposed automatically.

Chief, he tried to exploit the lack of clarity at Conference to advance his own view of how the cases should be resolved. Burger assigned the opinions to the like-minded Byron White—whose qualms about an irresolute public undermining the purpose of executions disappeared entirely in the wake of the post-*Furman* clamoring for the death penalty.

It soon became clear, however, that White could not command a majority for upholding all five statutes. Although Blackmun was willing to go along, Powell was not. In *Furman*, he had argued passionately in dissent that capital punishment was solely the business of the states and their legislatures. But that was history. *Furman* was now on the books, and Powell took seriously the principle of stare decisis—that, generally, the Court should let past decisions stand even if wrongly decided. Rather than attempt to turn the clock back to pre-*Furman* days, Powell wrote in his Conference notes for *Gregg*, "I accept *Furman* as precedent." For Powell, this meant at a minimum that the Constitution imposed some restrictions on how the death penalty was implemented. And even the most limited constitutional restrictions would prohibit North Carolina's step backward to mandating death for all first-degree murderers.

Even before White circulated a draft opinion, Powell was exploring a common middle ground with Stewart, and together they took Stevens, the Court's newcomer, to lunch at the Monocle (a favorite Capitol Hill watering hole) to propose joining forces in a centrist "troika" on the capital cases. By the time dessert arrived, for all practical purposes the three had agreed to take the opinion of the Court away from White and forge an opinion of their own. Later they worked out a compromise on the specifics. Powell agreed to strike down both mandatory sentencing laws while Stewart and Stevens reluctantly swallowed Texas's bare-bones attempt to guide jury discretion. (With respect to both positions, the coalition was guaranteed majorities. Brennan and Marshall would concur in striking down the mandatory laws, while Burger, White, and Rehnquist would lend their votes to upholding the others.)

As a matter of form, Stewart, Powell, and Stevens decided to issue opinions covering all five capital cases as equal and indivisible coauthors rather than have one or another take the lead in any individual case. No plurality of Justices had ever written as an undifferentiated bloc, though the self-conscious solidarity of Stewart, Powell, and Stevens appeared to echo *Cooper v. Aaron*, where every Justice individually had signed the Court's unanimous opinion to emphasize their resolve to overcome southern resistance to *Brown*. In semi-imitation, Stewart, Powell, and

Stevens seemed to be sending a message that they meant to bring moderation, order, and consistency to the Court's pinball ride through the law of death.

Reading the five jointly rendered opinions, one cannot help but feel the authors' tense struggle to identify and protect the rule of law in the face of an issue that had riven both Court and country. All around them they saw the shadow of lawlessness. On one side, the unrelenting mandatory death statutes "plainly invite[d] . . . jurors to disregard their oaths" and ignore evidence of capital murder whenever they felt the death penalty inappropriate.[2] On the other side, the option of abolishing the death penalty invited vigilantism. "In part," the troika wrote, "capital punishment is an expression of society's moral outrage at particularly offensive conduct. This function may be unappealing to many, but it is essential in an ordered society that asks its citizens to rely on legal processes rather than self-help to vindicate their wrongs."[3]

Charting a middle course between these dangerous shoals, Stewart, Powell, and Stevens accepted one basic premise of the abolitionist crusade. They agreed at the outset that "death is different" from every other punishment—unique in its severity and irrevocability. Because of this qualitative difference, the troika concluded, "there is a corresponding difference in the need for reliability in the determination that death is the appropriate punishment in a specific case."[4] And because of that heightened need for reliability, they ruled that, although states could carry out capital punishment, they had to do so with care and caution—preferably with such safeguards as bifurcated capital trials, rigorous appellate review, and serious efforts to give juries guidance about what sorts of crimes merited the death penalty and what sorts of criminals deserved to die.

From diametrically opposing perspectives, the *Gregg* dissenters—from Brennan to Rehnquist—denied that the guided discretion statutes provided anything more than the illusion of regularity for a process that they considered intrinsically ungovernable.[5] But by overriding these skeptics, and by deeming capital sentencing standards not only possible but constitutionally necessary, Stewart, Powell, and Stevens set a new death penalty agenda for the Court. As the controlling plurality of a fractured Court, the centrists in effect had appointed themselves overseers of the newly approved yet highly regulated business of capital punishment. They had promised implicitly that the system could be made to work—indeed, that *they* would make it work—and with death rows in guided discretion states overflowing with more than 200 convicts, challenges to that extravagant promise would be upon them in almost an instant.

The burden of this position was deeply felt across the Court. When the Court handed down *Gregg* and its companion cases on the last day of the 1975 Term, Justice Stewart's voice cracked with emotion as he announced the joint opinions. That night, after delivering an anguished dissent to a somber courtroom, Justice Marshall suffered a mild heart attack.

For months, Justice Powell had been severely distressed over his personal responsibility for the prospect of renewed executions after an eight-year moratorium. Back in April, he had explored the possibility of upholding the Georgia, Florida, and Texas laws only for future cases while vacating the entire backlog of pending death sentences. He had abandoned the idea when no one could come up with a single authority for upholding a law as constitutional while allowing it to be applied only prospectively. As Powell's biographer aptly observed, "The strange suggestion [of prospective application] . . . was an attempt to distance himself from the consequences of his own acts."[6]

After the opinions came down, Powell was given another chance to forestall their effect. Amsterdam immediately filed for a rehearing before the Court, a request that is routinely made in many cases and just as routinely denied. Along with the rehearing petition, Amsterdam asked Justice Powell (as the Circuit Justice for the states involved) to stay all executions until the Court could consider his request. Enticed by the prospect of a three-month delay while the Court stood in summer recess, Powell decided tentatively to grant the stay.

When he heard what was in the offing, Chief Justice Burger went through the roof. He threatened to call a special one-day summer session of the Court to overturn the stay if Powell granted it—a stratagem that Chief Justice Vinson had used successfully in 1953, when Justice Douglas had granted a last-minute stay of execution to the convicted spies Ethel and Julius Rosenberg. After receiving reassurance from Justices Stewart and Stevens (and some goading to show a little backbone from Justice Brennan), Powell went ahead, and Burger's threat proved empty. But the summer did not last forever, and in the fall the whole Court denied Amsterdam's rehearing petition, lifting the stay. For every prisoner on death row—and for the Justices of the troika who now controlled their fate—the clock started ticking again.

The Death Watch

When I started clerking for Justice Blackmun in July 1988, ninety-four people had been executed in the twelve years since *Gregg*, almost exclusively in southern states, especially Texas and Florida. During the same period, death row populations in the thirty-five states that had reinstituted the death penalty after *Furman* spiraled steadily upward. Every year across the country roughly an additional 150 people received the death penalty. In 1988, those awaiting execution numbered more than 2,000.

At the Court, the advent of the next execution and the handicapping of who would be next to die were ever present. Each week, as regularly as clockwork, the Clerk's Office would distribute the death list—a simple photocopied sheet that listed every execution then scheduled in the United States. In the Blackmun Chambers, we divided the list into two categories, executions coming out of the Eighth Circuit (for which Justice Blackmun served as supervising Circuit Justice) and all the others. My co-clerks and I divided up both sets of cases according to a strict rotation, putting our initials next to the cases fate assigned to our responsibility.

Some of these cases would "go away." A state or lower federal court would issue a stay of execution while it conducted a hearing or held argument on one or more of the inmate's claims. In other cases, no such reprieve—either for the inmate or for the Court—was forthcoming. As time wound down, attorneys for the condemned would besiege the Justices with applications for a stay or petitions for cert. Whatever legal arguments these papers might include, they always alleged that a serious, indeed fatal, injustice was about to transpire. And these allegations invariably triggered a furious response from the attorney general of the state involved.

The Court tried to prepare as far in advance as possible for these execution-night ordeals. Each Chambers received copies of both sides' lower court filings as soon as they were made—often a day or two before the scheduled execution. This practice, born of necessity, permitted the Justices and their clerks to get a running start on the issues in the case. Next, the Circuit Justice for the state in question would circulate a memo summarizing the parties' claims and counterclaims as soon as they became reasonably certain, usually less than twenty-four hours in advance.

Sometimes the Circuit Justice's memo made clear on the basis of past experience whether the Court (or a lower court before it) would grant a stay. At the time, for example, an inmate whose conviction and death sentence were still under direct appellate review (as opposed to habeas consideration) was certain to receive a stay somewhere along the line. By contrast, an inmate on the second or third round of federal habeas who raised only fact-specific claims (such as that the evidence at his trial was constitutionally insufficient) was very likely to be executed on or near to schedule.

Quite a few cases, though, were not nearly so predictable. Many stay applications required fine judgments about what had happened in the case and what legal precedents suggested or required. A single vote among the Justices often made the difference between a stay and an execution. These occasions were spent in tense assessments and reassessments of an inmate's final claims, frantic arguments with clerks in other Chambers over the merits of the case, and rounds of reluctant and stilted phone calls to a Justice's home, often continuing past midnight, about where matters stood as the last grains of sand passed through someone's hourglass. Such evenings were sheer, bleary-eyed agony, no matter what the outcome.

For those of us on the death watch in any particular case, our most important resource was the deputy court clerk in charge of the capital cases, Chris Vasil, a lawyer from Cleveland who specialized in judicial administration. Then in his late thirties, shy and unassuming, Chris was the Court's liaison to the states' attorneys, defense lawyers, lower courts, and prison officials involved in each impending execution. For each case on the death list, he made sure that every Chambers received all the legal papers. As cases heated up, Chris often received advance warning about the likely course they would take: which claims the defense lawyers intended to bring; what the chances were that a lower court would issue a stay; and, if a lower court did grant a stay, whether the state attorney general would ask the Justices to overturn it. Many of the state attorneys and the lawyers from the death penalty defense bar—tooth and nail adversaries over and over again—distrusted and even despised each other. But they all trusted Chris and confided in him their strategies so that he could prepare the Court for what might be heading its way.

In the evenings before executions (which always seemed to be scheduled between midnight and dawn), Chris would walk the incoming papers around to every Chambers. He always knew where matters stood: Had the state courts acted? How far along was the federal habeas petition? On what grounds were the inmate's claims being denied? Did he think the case would make it to the Court and, if so, when? Chris gave his answers in a soft, sorrowful voice, almost a whisper, and he had a way of leaning his slight frame toward you when he spoke that seemed to recognize implicitly the gravity of what was taking place and how hard he thought your job was.

Once a last-minute stay application or cert. petition was filed, the clerks on the death watch would while away the time as the Court's verdict gradually took shape. I remember how the votes from other Chambers, sealed in plain manila, would come sliding under the door with a portentous whoosh. The Circuit Justice's Chambers kept the official tally and conveyed the results to Chris. If a majority favored granting a stay, he would call the state attorney general's office or the prison to halt the execution, sometimes only minutes away. A few states insisted that Chris preface his calls with secret code words (such as the prison superintendent's mother's maiden name), to guard against a yet to be attempted sabotage. In most of the death states, the responsible official knew Chris's voice, and that was enough.

Chris described his role as the "air traffic controller" of the death penalty. He was that and more. Chris served as the Court's institutional memory, witness to and participant in almost every capital stay since they became regular fixtures of Court life in 1982. He still remembers vividly his first night on the death watch, when a former cop turned murderer from Virginia, Frank Coppola, was scheduled to die. The Court had no fax machine back then, no instant way to receive last-minute applications. Just minutes before the midnight execution, Coppola's lawyer from the ACLU appeared at the Court's back door, stay papers in hand. Chris literally ran through the halls to pick them up. To Chris's relief, the Court granted a stay that night, although Coppola was put to death soon thereafter.

In those days, lower courts communicated their eleventh-hour decisions over the phone, dictating to Chris or his boss, who then transcribed the rulings for distribution to the Justices. Many of the Clerk's Office staff would wait to see what the Justices would do. Down the hall in the Public Relations Office, the Court press corps would be waiting too. Over the years, Chris watched the technology improve and helped design a streamlined system for handling stays at the Court. As scheduled executions became more routine, the extraneous staff and the journalists starting going home on time.

When Chris arrived at the Court, only four men had been executed in the six years after *Gregg*. Since then, he has watched the hostility grow between prosecutors and abolitionists, as both sides pushed the system to its limits. He has seen men saved from execution simply by the fortuity that the prison and the Court were located in different time zones. He has watched battles over stay applications rage until dawn. He has seen men killed who he thought might be innocent. Each time, he was the one who made the call, the one who had to report that the Court of last resort finally and for the last time had said no.

Those calls were plain hell. Chris hated the death penalty, thought it wrong in every case, and believed it only reduced the state to the level of the people it wanted to kill. The prosecuting attorneys kidded him about it. The abolitionists knew him too well to try to take advantage. I never talked to Chris directly about his views, and I don't know any clerks who did. It seemed potentially disrespectful. Chris's labored neutrality was a badge of his extraordinary professionalism. He never took sides, even if you had the sense he wanted to desperately.*

As clerks, we did not bear the burden or enjoy the comfort of this enforced professional neutrality. Certainly, the ultimate power to grant or deny a stay rested with the Justices. Still, when the final arguments reached the Court, the Justices were almost always long since home for

---

*Though still the Court's deputy clerk, Chris Vasil no longer handles the emergency stages. That thankless task is now done by Cynthia Rapp.

the night, isolated from the tall stacks of paper in which the crucial elements of the case lay buried. The Justices counted on their clerks to distill for them the essence of the case, the facts, the issues, and the precedents that should inform their vote. They relied on us for advice.

Our roles were circumscribed by which Justice we worked for. Justices Brennan's and Marshall's clerks knew in advance that their bosses would vote to grant every stay application and to vacate every death sentence. Clerks in the Rehnquist, Scalia, and White Chambers could be almost as certain of their Justices' contrary view. Even in these Chambers where the final vote was certain, clerks had to decide which cases were worth writing in, fighting about, and lobbying colleagues on—and which ones were foregone conclusions better left alone.

Those of us who worked for Justices Blackmun, Stevens, O'Connor, and Kennedy, despite the different inclinations of our bosses, shared a middle ground where, in many cases, no fixed rule or policy dictated our Justice's vote. Accordingly, our choices and judgments were even more complicated and consequential than our colleagues'. How we described a given case, which facts we put in and which we left out, how we characterized the competing arguments, and how insistently we put forward our own points of view—these things mattered deeply and, at least in a few instances, undeniably made the difference between life and death.

In narrow terms, death penalty stay applications and last-minute cert. petitions brought up purely legal questions: Did the applicant raise a sufficiently novel and important claim to warrant Court review? Did he raise a claim substantially similar to one the Court was already considering? If so, were the claims "procedurally barred" or otherwise defective as the basis for a stay or cert. grant? But these legal questions often had no clear answers, and the recommendations we as clerks advanced inescapably reflected a set of beliefs about capital punishment, about the morality of vengeance, about the integrity of the system by which guilt and punishment were assessed, and about the role of the Court in overseeing that system.

At the most abstract level, most of us, by the oppressive moonlight of an execution eve, mulled over the philosophical, ethical, and religious arguments for and against the death penalty. Both sides routinely trotted out conflicting biblical authority, from Exodus's "Thou shalt not kill" to the admonition in Leviticus that "he that kills any man shall surely be put to death." Few clerks during my term seemed moved by religious arguments; if they were, it was (on the abolitionist side) by a fairly general belief in the inherent sanctity of human life and the possibility of redemption and rehabilitation for even the most savage members of society.

More commonly voiced was the idea that society had no business "playing God," deciding who shall live and who shall die. This argument harkened back to the philosophical origin of the modern abolitionist movement and the Enlightenment legal reformer Cesare Beccaria's assertion that the social contract did not vest in government a legitimate power to kill members of the community. Beccaria also had opposed capital punishment as simply barbaric.[1] Some clerks certainly agreed and enjoyed pointing out the company of nations—North Korea, Iran, pre-Mandela South Africa—that shared with the United States the rare distinction of retaining the penalty.

Death penalty proponents (or those comfortable with capital punishment) at some level dismissed these considerations, as Immanuel Kant did, as essentially sentimental and misplaced.[2] Far from being immoral or disrespectful of the sanctity of life, the death penalty to them was a supremely moral statement, a confirmation of human dignity through the elimination of those—from Adolf Eichmann to Ted Bundy—who purposefully destroyed human life. Killing the perpetrators of terrible crimes was an appropriate expression of a community's anger, an affixing of responsibility for evildoing, and a passionate affirmation of a community's devotion to moral life.[3]

For the most part, however, clerks steeped in legal training thought not from philosophy to experience but rather the other way around. The universe of our beliefs was shaped foremost by the cases with which we came into contact week by week and, more specifically, through our observation (albeit at a distance), first, of the many stunningly vicious criminal acts people are capable of committing and, second, of the discouragingly inconsistent process by which guilt and punishment for those crimes is determined.

Even now, eight years after I left the Court, the images of murder and mayhem stick in my head almost as vividly as that year, when I often would wake up thinking about them. Many of the crimes shared a sick sexual aspect. On the pages that crossed my desk, a man sodomized a grandmother with an umbrella before killing her, small children were raped, then beaten to death. One stay vote, much contested because of the legal issues raised, involved a man convicted of the savage rape and murder of a young housewife. The assailant had sliced open the woman's stomach, and evidence suggested he had inserted his penis into the wound.

In another category are the seemingly random killings that terrorize by their very purposelessness, the ones committed for fun or for no reason at all, the kinds of crimes that make you think, This could happen to me. After robbing a cabdriver, two young Georgians stripped their victim at knifepoint and shoved him into the trunk of the car. They laughed as the driver begged for mercy, then took a joyride and sank the car, driver and all, in a pond.[4]

For someone like me, who had no religious scruples against the death penalty, the redundant examples of gratuitous torture and death overwhelmed categorical claims (such as Brennan's and Marshall's) against the death penalty. I didn't become convinced that any particular murderer "deserved" to die or even that the death penalty was a good idea. But I did lose the capacity to believe that the death penalty was evil per se, that because of some abstract ideal of human dignity, under no circumstances could the state extinguish a life. Some human conduct was that terrible. I saw it every week.

Yet finding justification for the death penalty did nothing to assuage my unease with its imposition. One of the natural results of a legal education is a heightened concern for "process," an attention (some might say bordering on obsession) to the reliability and fairness of the way the decisions are reached. This concern lay at the heart of *Gregg* and the Court's other death penalty rulings emphasizing the uniqueness of the death penalty and the need for especially careful regulation of capital sentencing. Although couched in terms of the Eighth Amendment, these decisions simply followed the rule of thumb judges routinely employed to assess how much process is "due" before a decision is made: the higher the stakes, the more exacting the process—and no stakes could be higher than death.

By that standard, the capital stay applications made a shocking impression. In general, capital cases seemed to magnify the human frailties of the system. Police and prosecutors, under pressure to solve a community's most gruesome and well-publicized crimes, strained too hard for arrests, convictions, and death sentences. Local trial judges, often elected and under special scrutiny, failed to enforce constitutional safeguards and sometimes created constitutional violations of their own.

Despite constitutional prohibitions, police coerced confessions, coached witnesses at lineups and in their testimony, and on occasion even perjured themselves on the stand. Prosecutors withheld potentially exculpatory evidence from defense attorneys and maneuvered to try black defendants before all-white juries. Judges improperly shifted burdens of proof from the prosecution to the defense and failed to remain impartial during trials. In an arena calling for the most solemn and rational of judgments, passion and prejudice reigned.

Although in the vast majority of cases that crossed my desk evidence of the defendant's guilt bordered on irrefutable, the frequency and willfulness of constitutional violations not only impeached the integrity of the system but made the prospect of mistake seem inevitable. And it was. In Texas, for example, prosecutors in a cop-killing case knowingly used perjured "eyewitness" testimony to obtain a guilty verdict and death sentence against Randall Dale Adams.[5] Moreover, the state's lawyers hid the perjury from the defense by illegally withholding the eyewitness's prior contradictory statements to the police. Despite this blatant misconduct, over the next twelve years, the Texas Attorney General's Office did everything possible to defend Adams's conviction and sentence. He won his freedom anyway. It turned out that another witness for the state—its star witness, who had cut a deal with prosecutors after being linked to the car and gun involved in the shooting—was the actual killer. By this time, he had killed again.

In a second Texas case, a sixteen-year-old white girl was raped and killed at a high school where she had gone to compete in a volleyball tournament. Suspicion immediately fell on the janitorial staff and especially Charles Brandley, a black man who supervised a staff of four whites. During a rushed investigation, the Texas authorities did everything possible to finger Brandley for the crime. They ignored every piece of evidence or lead that pointed in any other direction, "lost" potentially exonorating physical evidence taken from the girl's body, and were so suggestive with witnesses that they ended up creating false testimony. At Brandley's trial, the prosecution used its peremptory challenges to strike all the blacks from the jury, deepening the racist cast of a case in which one police officer had told Brandley that either he or a white man had committed the crime, and "since you're the nigger, you're elected." The all-white jury convicted Brandley and sentenced him to death.[6] Nine years later, after a court-ordered investigation conducted over the state's continued objection and resistance, it became obvious that two of the white janitors had committed the crime.[7]

Compounding such rare but horrifying cases were much more frequent problems in the system for deciding which defendants properly convicted of murder also deserved to die for their crimes. The capital stay applications were replete with instances of seemingly inappropriate and occasionally incomprehensible death sentences. Some of these cases stemmed from prosecutorial and judicial misconduct, usually a prosecutor's deceptive or overly inflammatory statements to a sentencing jury. By far the most serious problem in capital sentencing, however, was the chronic ineptitude of defense counsel.

It was no accident that the greatest common denominator among the inmates on death row was poverty. Clients of the world's great defense attorneys (and even the good ones) don't receive death sentences. Most of the time prosecutors don't even try for them. Almost without exception, a prerequisite for receiving a death sentence is the inability to hire a lawyer sufficiently talented or motivated to mount a credible defense either at trial or at the separate sentencing proceeding, which followed on conviction.

In many states, no standards governed appointed counsel in capital cases. And the lawyers who were appointed, whatever their qualifications, received minimal compensation. Louisiana provided a maximum of $1,000 for all pretrial preparations and trial work. Kentucky allowed $2,500, and other states did much the same. The result was any number of nightmare representations: lawyers who were drunk, lawyers who never bothered to read the pertinent death penalty statute, lawyers unable to cite a single twentieth-century criminal case except *Miranda,* lawyers who fell asleep or never showed up during trial, lawyers who failed to conduct investigations, lawyers who argued during the sentencing phase that the defendants deserved to die.[8]

Although these are some of the most outrageous examples, as a routine matter hopelessly unqualified and underpaid attorneys failed to prepare adequately for trial or to raise crucial objections and present a rigorous defense. Naturally, inept defense counsel increases the possibility of erroneous conviction. Less dramatically, by depriving the jury of the defendant's side of the case (such as justifications or lack of intent to kill), poor defense lawyers substantially increase the probability that a defendant will be convicted of capital murder as opposed to some more appropriate lesser offense.

Even more crucially, appointed counsel often failed to undertake the time-consuming task of assembling the "mitigating" evidence that, regardless of conviction, might save a defendant from receiving the death penalty during the sentencing process. The sentencing phase provided each defendant with an opportunity to present himself in sympathetic, human terms and call upon the jury's sense of mercy. Under law, a capital defendant was entitled to present witnesses (doctors, relatives, coworkers, or himself) and argue, on the basis of childhood abuse, diminished mental capacity, or any other mitigating circumstance, that his life should be spared. Although such appeals frequently proved successful when made, time and again lawyers neglected to assemble and submit this crucial evidence, even when readily available. Death row housed a host of wretched creatures—victims of severe retardation, child molestation, incest, or physical abuse. Many of these surely would not have been there but for the incompetence of their attorneys.

In sum, the death penalty stay applications infiltrated the Court's cloistered haven from two diametrically opposed directions. On one side, the applications, as did no other cases, forced the Justices to confront the ugly details of American society's dark violent streak, details that made comprehensible (and to some laudable) the popular choice to put some criminals to death. On the other side, the stay process provided the Court with an ongoing audit of how well the states complied with the nation's supreme law in imposing the death penalty—and the results were grim.

The stay process presented the Justices with a herculean challenge. They needed to compel, coerce, and convince state police, prosecutors, and judges to be more scrupulous in their observance of the Constitution. At the same time, the Justices could not so paralyze the system that, in effect, they deprived the states of their right under *Gregg* to carry out the death penalty. If they failed at the former, the Court would be in the position of acquiescing in and even putting its imprimatur on the taking of human life, however despicably lived, despite regular violations of our bedrock law. If they failed at the latter, they would be usurping the people's legitimate right to execute the worst transgressors of the social order.

Success, even an approximation of success, at such a thorny venture called for the Justices' constant engagement with each aspect of the system of capital punishment—the police, prosecutors, defense attorneys, and judges on every level. Success required accommodation within the Court to command obedience from the participants and understanding from the public. It required the sort of sustained judicial statesmanship that had marked the Court's imperfect but beneficent assault on segregation.

Under the circumstances, I would have thought that the death penalty stays would have spawned an almost constant discussion among the Justices about how best to supervise the machinery of death. But by the time I came to the Court, the Justices engaged in no death penalty debate, no exchange or modification of views. On the long nights when someone's life hung in the balance, or in the days that followed, the Justices essentially never conferred with one another. In five Chambers (those of Brennan, Marshall, White, Rehnquist, and Scalia), the votes were certain or all but certain regardless of the facts of the case at hand. The remaining four Justices made no attempt to join forces and steer the Court in concert. Everyone's views seemed to be frozen, locked in a position long since determined. The process of what Justice Felix Frankfurter had extolled as "reason called law" seemed especially absent exactly where it most belonged.[9] I wondered how and why that process had died.

The Lone Ranger

On January 17, 1977, Gary Gilmore, killed by a Utah firing squad, became the first person executed in the United States since the moratorium on the death penalty began in 1967. In some sense, though, Gilmore's execution didn't count. He was what came to be known as a volunteer. Gilmore wanted to be killed—he saw death as a matter of "blood atonement" for his sins—and he not only refused to challenge his death sentence but actively resisted attempts by the LDF, the ACLU, and even his mother to intervene on his behalf.[1]

No one was executed in 1978, only two persons in 1979, zero again in 1980, and one more in 1981. This negligible record reflected a return to much the same situation as held before *Furman*. Anthony Amsterdam and the death penalty abolitionists (whose ranks swelled after *Gregg*) started the litigation cycle all over again, armed with a host of new substantive and procedural challenges to capital punishment.

In the abolitionists' view, the Stewart, Powell, and Stevens plurality opinion in *Gregg,* promising rational and coherent sentencing, begged as many questions as it answered. For their part, the Justices seemed to agree that *Gregg* was only the starting point for identifying and refining a constitutional framework for imposing the death penalty. They decided fifteen major capital cases between 1976 and 1982. In all but one, the Court imposed new restrictions, reversing or vacating the death sentence under review.

The Court abolished capital punishment for rapists[2] and for participants in crimes that resulted in death who did not themselves commit murder or at least intend that the murder take place.[3] The Justices told states not to limit the kinds of mitigating evidence (such as evidence of mental impairment or an abusive childhood) that capital defendants could submit for consideration by the sentencer.[4] They also forced states to narrow or dispense with "vague" aggravating factors—such as that a murder was "outrageously or wantonly vile."[5] Such catchall categories were so intrinsically malleable and potentially all-inclusive that they undermined the overall purpose of identifying those especially contemptible murders for which capital punishment should be reserved.[6]

In all these cases, the Court was sharply divided, sometimes to the point, as in both *Furman* and *Gregg,* where no majority emerged for any single point of view. The *Gregg* troika, now often joined by Blackmun, tried to steer a middle course between Brennan's and Marshall's persistent abolitionism and Burger, White, and Rehnquist, who thought the Court had gone too far and urged the centrists to abandon their ill-conceived role as "fine tuned calibrator[s] of depravity."[7] The result was a stalemate as the Court struggled to put on line the death penalty prototypes it had okayed in *Gregg.* Every one of the Court's fifteen cert. grants put dozens of cases on hold. And every one of the fourteen decisions in which the capital defendant prevailed required a host of resentencings.

In the lower courts, moreover, the LDF, the ACLU, and local abolitionist groups were scouring the trial records of every capital case for evidence of reversible errors. Often, indeed usually, these efforts bore fruit. In addition to finding many violations of the Court's special rules for capital sentencing, zealous abolitionist lawyers uncovered literally hundreds of examples of police, prosecutorial, and judicial misconduct unrelated to the death penalty. Under the microscope of Anthony Amsterdam and his colleagues, improper jury instructions, coerced confessions, improper searches and seizures, and violations of the right to counsel jumped out of the transcripts of capital trials. Even in cases in which state officials dotted every constitutional *i*, defense counsel at trial was often so deficient as to deprive the capital defendant of the *competent* representation the Constitution requires. As a consequence, somewhere in the appellate process, whether on direct review or on habeas (especially federal habeas), an astonishing 65 percent or more of capital convictions or sentences were overturned.[8]

On the states' side, frustrations mounted. For six years, the state attorneys general's offices had been staring at the green light of *Gregg,* yet capital punishment existed in form only. As time passed, state prosecutors and politicians readily blamed the abolitionists for manipulating technicalities, concocting constitutional errors where none existed, and always dragging their feet through the redundancy of habeas review. As the Court added new death penalty regulations, the states started to blame the Justices as well.[9]

Within the Court, Justice Rehnquist was particularly critical of his colleagues for allowing abolitionists to block death sentences. The events preceding the Florida execution of John Spenkelink, the first person executed after *Gregg* to have opposed the carrying out of his sentence, typified what Rehnquist saw as the guerrilla litigation tactics of abolitionist lawyers and the timorous failure of federal judges, including the Justices, to ensure that the death penalty could be administered promptly.

In 1973, Spenkelink had been convicted of murdering a traveling companion in his sleep.[10] His conviction was affirmed on direct appeal in 1975. Then, in the course of the next four years, Spenkelink filed twice each for state and federal habeas relief—unsuccessfully every time. As his scheduled execution approached, abolitionist lawyers—distraught at the impending breach of their twelve-year moratorium on opposed executions—began a last-ditch round of appeals.

On May 22, three days before Spenkelink was slated for electrocution, former Attorney General (and abolitionist) Ramsey Clark went to Florida intending to "bear witness" in protest against the execution. Instead, a lawyer from the ACLU convinced Clark that previously unnoticed flaws in Spenkelink's trial showed that he'd been deprived of his constitutional right to effective assistance of counsel. The ACLU attorney then prevailed on Clark to intervene on Spenkelink's behalf.

By Clark's own account, Spenkelink's court-appointed trial lawyer had made any number of blunders in handling the case.[11] The "clincher" for Clark was his failure to bring to the attention of the sentencing jury the fact that when Spenkelink was eleven, he had discovered the body of his father, an unhappy World War II veteran, after he committed suicide by inhaling from the exhaust pipe of the family car. Prison psychologists had attributed much of his subsequent criminal history to this family trauma, and Clark was convinced that no jury would have returned a death sentence if they had known that Spenkelink was a "second generation casualty of World War II."

A natural course at this point would have been for Clark to file a "successive" habeas petition with a state or federal judge in Florida. But neither Clark nor the ACLU expected a Florida-based judge, so close to the circumstances of a highly political and emotionally charged case, to respond sympathetically to their claim. After all, they were arguing that after six years of intensive litigation it had just been discovered that not only Spenkelink's trial counsel but also the separate counsel who had handled his four previous applications for state and federal habeas relief were constitutionally deficient. Taking advantage of the very broad power of every federal judge to grant a stay, Clark went looking for one who might be more favorably inclined to halt an execution or, as he put it self-servingly, "a very courageous, very independent, open-minded and fair judge."

At 11:00 P.M. on the twenty-second, Clark rang the doorbell of Elbert Tuttle, a federal appeals court judge based in Georgia, highly esteemed for his tough stands against segregation in the 1950s and '60s but now long since semiretired. Tuttle did not disappoint. As a judge on "senior status," he didn't think he had the power to issue a writ of habeas corpus. Still, after hearing Clark's allegations, he did grant a stay of execution to permit an evidentiary hearing on their merits. The next morning, an apoplectic Florida attorney general flew to Washington to ask the Supreme Court to take the extraordinary step of vacating Tuttle's stay.[12]

When the Court refused the Florida attorney general's request, Justice Rehnquist decided to emphasize his disagreement by publishing a solo dissent.[13] He scolded Clark for blatantly "forum shopping" to find a sympathetic judge and ridiculed his expedient, ineffective assistance of counsel claim, which Rehnquist derided as simply "an insurance policy of sorts, to spring on the federal judge of his choice if all else fails." In Rehnquist's view, these practices amounted to typical abolitionist sandbagging, part and parcel of the strategy of reserving new claims for the last minute. If the lawyers waited long enough, conscientious judges, faced with potential complicity in taking a life, would grant stays for no other reason than that time was too short for them to grasp the contentions of the parties. This was a perfectly natural tendency, Rehnquist recognized, but one federal judges, armed with the extraordinary power to grant stays and writs, must resist.

As it turned out, Florida electrocuted Spenkelink a mere six weeks later (after the Fifth Circuit lifted Judge Tuttle's stay), but another two-year de facto moratorium followed. In April 1981, after not a single new execution, Justice Rehnquist's frustrations spilled over again.[14] On April 27, the Justices denied cert. in a relatively routine capital case, *Coleman v. Balkom.* The Court had previously denied cert. in Balkom's unsuccessful direct appeal, and this petition stemmed from his failed attempt at state habeas relief.

It was the kind of case in which, by his own admission, Rehnquist ordinarily "would have [had] no hesitation joining my colleagues in denying [cert.]" But in Rehnquist's view, times were no longer ordinary. The abolitionists, he wrote, were making a "mockery of our criminal justice system." And while the Justices themselves fiddled with the "arcane niceties" of its capital jurisprudence, they were "undermin[ing] the integrity of the entire criminal justice system" and abetting the creation of an approaching "state of savagery." A vicious child killer, Rehnquist observed, was loose in Atlanta, where vigilantes now roamed the streets. Closer to home, urban violence had claimed a member of the Court's own family and sent the institution into shock and mourning. Not four blocks from the Court building, a young assistant in the library, walking with his wife, had been shot to death during a robbery despite giving over his money.[15]

To restore respect for the rule of law and to vindicate the rights of states both to deter crime and to seek retribution, Rehnquist argued for a drastic change in the redundant, time-consuming cycle of death penalty review. In particular, he took aim at the federal habeas process, in which individual federal judges had the power to disregard state court rulings on federal law and to order a prisoner's release or resentencing. Up to now, the court had rarely granted review when capital cases came up on direct appeal from state courts. Instead, the Justices would deny cert. and let capital defendants file for habeas relief in the lower federal courts, which would then investigate and decide their claims. Only after this process was complete would the Justices seriously consider whether a capital case was sufficiently important to merit their attention. In *Balkom,* Rehnquist proposed that the Court do exactly the opposite: it should decide the merits of *every* capital case coming up from the state courts before the habeas process even started.

This was a Swiftian "modest proposal," which (as Justice Stevens pointed out) would reserve more than half the Court's calendar for capital cases. The result, though, if adopted, would have been for the Court to short-circuit the entire habeas process and dispose of every federal claim in every capital case after the first go-round of state appellate review. For, once the Supreme Court decides a case, its ruling is conclusive and bars the parties from raising their claims again. In the capital context, as Rehnquist hoped, this meant no federal habeas review and, thus, that death sentences "would presumably be carried out."

No one joined Rehnquist's dissents, but it's doubtful that he hoped or expected others would. These were the sorts of idiosyncratic writings that earned him the moniker the Lone Ranger for his often lonely and always vigilant patrol of the Court's right wing. As his *Spenkelink* and *Balkom* dissents indicate clearly, Rehnquist's judicial philosophy made few concessions to the Warren Court's reshaping of American law. In general, Rehnquist readily agrèed that his legal opinions hadn't "changed much" since his law school days.[16]

Certainly, his views on the death penalty and habeas corpus, specifically, were nearly identical to those he expressed as far back as his 1952–53 clerkship with Justice Robert Jackson, immediately before the dawn of the Warren era. During that year, Rehnquist had participated in two extremely important and controversial capital cases. Indeed, when writing in *Spenkelink* and *Balkom*, Rehnquist borrowed so heavily in language and outlook from his death penalty experiences with Jackson, one cannot escape the sense that, in taking on the death penalty defense bar and in seeking to cut short the appellate process, he was self-consciously reconvening the legal battles of his youth.

In March 1952, at the height of McCarthyism and the Korean War, Julius and Ethel Rosenberg were convicted of conspiracy to commit espionage as part of a Communist spy ring organized to funnel atomic secrets to the Soviet Union. At sentencing, the presiding federal district judge, Irving Kaufman, an outspoken anti-Communist who many thought had grossly favored the prosecution during trial, charged the Rosenbergs with a "diabolical conspiracy to destroy a god-fearing nation" and sentenced them to death. Theirs was the only capital sentence for espionage ever imposed on civilians in peacetime, and the trial, verdict, and sentence immediately became the subject of one of the century's most virulent national and international debates.

Inevitably, the Rosenberg case made its way to the Court. In fact, it plagued the Justices from October 1952, when it first came up on direct review, until the Rosenbergs' execution in July of the next year. In their first cert. petition, the Rosenbergs claimed that while they had been charged under the Espionage Act, the real charge against them was treason; therefore, their conviction was illegal because it was obtained without observing the Constitution's special requirements for a treason trial.[17] The petition was denied just barely, by a 6–3 vote, after an especially tense conference, with Justices Black and Frankfurter strongly in favor of review. (Justice Harold Burton was the third, less adamant vote.) Two weeks later, on a petition for rehearing, the Justices turned down the case by the same vote.

The case once more returned to the Court at the end of March 1953, after a divided court of appeals rejected the Rosenbergs' first habeas petition. This time the issue was whether the U.S. attorney prosecuting the case (the top Communist hunter Irving Saypol) had engaged in misconduct so serious as to deprive the defendants of a fair trial.[18] Justice Black was certain that the Rosenbergs' trial had been a travesty and that a new one was essential. Justice Frankfurter argued with equal vehemence that the Court had "a duty" to review the case either to affirm or to remove the taint of injustice that colored the proceedings. Despite Frankfurter's emotional appeal, the remaining Justices voted to deny.

For several weeks thereafter, the Court held off formally ruling on the cert. petition while Frankfurter agonized about making some accompanying public comment. Then, just as Frankfurter decided not to write, Justice Douglas abruptly reversed himself and announced his intention both to dissent from the denial of cert. and to condemn U.S. Attorney Saypol for conduct so "wholly reprehensible" that he had deprived the Rosenbergs of a fair trial.

Frankfurter immediately seized on Douglas's turnabout and moved to reopen the Conference's decision denying cert., a ploy that Rehnquist complained to Jackson "would be allowing one justice—WOD [Douglas]—to force the hand of the Court and get the result which he now so belatedly wants."[19] But Jackson, while sharing his clerk's anger, thought Douglas was bluffing. Dissenting from a denial of cert. gave Douglas a cost-free chance to blow his own sanctimonious horn while embarrassing the Court for seeming to turn a blind eye to allegedly serious prosecutorial misconduct. What if the Justices voted to grant cert? Was Douglas really so anxious to have the Court dragged into the Rosenberg mess? Jackson didn't think so. And he had no intention of letting Douglas get away (at the Court's expense) with an act of grandstanding that Jackson described to Frankfurter as "the dirtiest, most shameful, most cynical performance that I have ever heard in matters pertaining to law."[20]

As a way of forcing Douglas's hand, the next day at conference Jackson announced that he would now make a fourth (with Black, Frankfurter, and Douglas) to grant cert. rather than have the Court deny cert. with one Justice (Douglas) publicly casting doubt on the Rosenbergs' convictions. As the Justices then set about discussing how and when to hear the appeal, Douglas backed down. He announced that rather than hear the case, he would simply withdraw his proposed dissent from denial. Jubilant that "the SOB's [Douglas's] bluff was called," Jackson now switched back to a denial—which returned the Justices to exactly where they had been after the original Conference vote to reject the case.

On Saturday, June 13, five days before the Rosenbergs' scheduled execution and two days before the close of the Supreme Court term, the couple's legal team returned to the Court seeking a stay of execution or, alternatively, an oral argument on the issue of whether the Court should grant a stay. Accompanying their plea for a stay, the lawyers presented three new claims of trial error (each rejected as a basis for habeas relief by both Judge Kaufman and the Second Circuit) that they hoped the Court would eventually hear.

At conference that afternoon, the Justices voted 5–4 to deny the Rosenbergs' request to hold oral argument.* By the same tally, but with a different lineup, they also denied their request for a stay outright. In the process, Justice Douglas continued to infuriate his brethren with his erratic behavior.

Of the five Justices who voted to deny the Rosenbergs a stay, Burton was at least willing to hear oral argument on the issue. That should have made a majority for holding oral argument. But Douglas, despite having voted *for* granting the Rosenbergs a stay without bothering with oral argument, switched sides and provided the crucial fifth vote *against* their more modest request to argue orally for the very stay he was on record supporting.

In any event, on Monday morning, June 15, the emotionally exhausted Justices took the bench before a teeming courtroom and announced that they had denied the Rosenbergs relief. While the room

---

* In those days, the Court held conference on Saturday rather than Friday.

broke into pandemonium, the Justices adjourned for the summer, but as they retreated through the velvet drapes behind the bench, one of the Rosenbergs' lawyers, John Finerty, began bellowing that he was moving orally, then and there, for a writ of habeas corpus from the high court itself. A bewildered Chief Justice Vinson, though steadfastly opposed to any intervention on the Rosenbergs' behalf, told him to file papers with the clerk.

The Justices met again at two o'clock to discuss Finerty's habeas filing, which charged that Prosecutor Saypol had made knowing use of perjured testimony. With Communist-inspired Rosenberg riots breaking out in Paris and mobs threatening the U.S. embassy in London, the Justices voted 7–2, with Frankfurter and Black powerfully opposed, to deny Finerty's petition. More than that, the Justices agreed among themselves to cauterize this running sore of a case. As difficult as it might be, regardless of what issues might come up, they pledged that this would be their last decision respecting the Rosenbergs. No Justice would act on his own to reopen the matter, and the Rosenbergs' execution would go forward.

Even though the Court was in summer recess, the next day brought yet another startling and disturbing twist. Two new lawyers, Fyke Farmer and Daniel Marshall (who represented not the Rosenbergs but rather a West Coast radical named Irwin Edelman, seeking to intercede on the couple's behalf), came to the Court to present an entirely new legal challenge to the Rosenbergs' trial and death sentences. The gist of their novel argument, contained in a sixty-one-page habeas petition, was that the United States, in prosecuting the Rosenbergs under the Espionage Act of 1917, had proceeded under the wrong statute. Because the conspiracy charged in the Rosenbergs' indictment included conduct continuing until May 1948, they should have been charged under the Atomic Energy Act of 1946. And under the 1946 act, the Rosenbergs could not have been sentenced to death without the recommendation of a jury and without proof of a specific intent to injure the United States. Neither of these requirements had been met in the original trial, over which Judge Kaufman had presided.

Despite the Justices' cloture agreement of the previous Monday, Douglas agreed to meet with Farmer and Marshall (together with representatives of the Justice Department) at 11:30 A.M. on Tuesday. The Justice listened for two hours and was stunned by the apparent validity of the argument. During the afternoon, Douglas did his own research into which statute should have applied to the Rosenbergs' crimes, only to have reinforced his growing conviction that the prosecution had made a colossal, potentially fatal, error.

While Douglas deliberated amid increasing speculation, Chief Justice Vinson, at Justice Jackson's behest, met privately with Attorney General Herbert Brownell to draw up a contingency plan in case Douglas exercised his power to grant an in Chambers (one Justice) stay. That the Chief Justice should engage in a private discussion (much less a strategy session) with the chief counsel for one side of an imminently pending matter was highly irregular, improper, even bizarre, but it testified to the extreme anxiety and anger that Douglas's whole course of conduct had provoked.

That anger only intensified the next morning when, at 11:00, Douglas granted the Rosenbergs a stay pending a hearing on the applicability of the Atomic Energy Act of 1946. An hour later, while the Rosenbergs' support group celebrated and the rest of the nation tried to absorb this shocking move, Brownell filed his preplanned motion to reconvene the Court to overturn Douglas's stay. And Chief Justice Vinson (over Justice Black's objection) called the Court back into a virtually unprecedented special session the next morning.

Oral argument on Thursday, June 18, conducted by exhausted and ill-prepared attorneys, was hopelessly confused and essentially pointless. As Frankfurter was later to record, all the Justices' minds were made up before they took the bench and, although they met in Conference afterward, the principal concern of the majority was to delay the announcement of their decision until the next day in order to provide the illusion of real deliberation.[21] By a final 6–3 vote, with Black, Frankfurter, and Douglas in dissent, the Court vacated Douglas's stay. The Justices announced their decision at precisely noon on the nineteenth. In less than nine hours, Ethel and Julius Rosenberg were dead.

Both sides within the Court saw a terrible failure of the rule of law. An outraged Justice Black was convinced that the full Court lacked constitutional authority to void Douglas's stay and, worse still, had used its self-created power to send two people to their deaths under plainly illegal sentences. Justice Frankfurter, who harbored lasting doubts about the validity of the Rosenbergs' death sentences, considered the institutional failure to give meaningful consideration to the case "the most disturbing single experience" of his tenure on the Court. As a clerk and close friend of Frankfurter, Philip Elman, recalled, "We knew the Supreme Court was one institution that worked the way it was supposed to work, where people got a fair shake, where equal justice under law was more than a slogan. And here the whole thing was falling down and we were shattered."[22]

Members of the majority drew from the Rosenberg case a very different lesson. "To permit our judicial processes to be used to obstruct the course of justice destroys our freedom," Justice Tom Clark wrote for himself and his five colleagues. "Unlike other litigants [the Rosenbergs] have had the attention of this Court seven times; each time their pleas have been denied. Though the penalty is great and our responsibility heavy, our duty is clear." In his own separate opinion, Justice Jackson lambasted the last-minute tactics of Farmer and Marshall, whose intervention (though pointing up a serious potential flaw in the Rosenbergs' sentence) he saw as "a threat to orderly and responsible representation." Even before the last round of desperate motions, Justice Sherman Minton had coined a new phrase for criminals' seeking to avoid their just punishments; he dubbed it to "pull a Rosenberg."[23]

Rehnquist had even less sympathy than his boss for the Rosenbergs. They were "fitting candidates" for execution, he wrote Jackson. "It is too bad that drawing and quartering has been abolished." Rehnquist couldn't understand why the "highest court of the nation must behave like a bunch of old women" whenever it confronted a capital case.[24]

Now, as a Justice, Rehnquist was watching as death row inmates "pulled Rosenbergs" on a grand scale. Tellingly, he quoted from the majority opinions overturning the Douglas stay not once but twice in his *Spenkelink* dissent. In *Spenkelink*, as with the Rosenbergs twenty-six years before, he thought that the forces of abolition were demeaning the rule of law and that it was high time for the Court to usher other "fitting candidates" to their appointed fate.

If the Rosenberg case illuminated Rehnquist's long-held opinions about the death penalty and what he saw as last-minute legal obstructionism, another landmark case of the 1952 Term, *Brown* v. *Allen*, made clear his hostility to federal habeas corpus and, more generally, his extreme devotion to states' rights, the hallmark of his later jurisprudence.[25] The issues facing the Court in *Brown* arose from the redundant nature of federal habeas review. Before a state prisoner could file for federal habeas, his constitutional claims already would have been ruled on by state courts during direct appellate review. These challenges would also have been the subject of an unsuccessful cert. petition to the Supreme Court at the end of that state appeals process. In *Brown*, the Justices had to decide what weight or effect a *federal* judge reviewing a habeas petition should give both to prior *state* court rulings and to the Supreme Court's own subsequent denial of cert.

Though clouded by legal technicality, the stakes in *Brown* were enormous. For thirty years, inch by inch, the Court had been widening the door to federal habeas review, gradually asserting the federal judiciary's post–Civil War mandate to oversee the constitutional integrity of state criminal trials. That trend would be all but erased if the Court ordered federal habeas judges to defer to prior state court rulings on the very issues that they were called upon to decide. Much the same result would follow if habeas judges had to consider a denial of cert. by the Supreme Court as tantamount to an affirmance of prior state court rulings.

One might wonder why all this was so important. State judges, the same as federal judges, took an oath to uphold the Constitution and laws of the United States and were duty bound to resolve fairly claims based on their violation.[26] In passing the Habeas Corpus Act of 1867, however, Congress had concluded that the states that had seceded from the Union could not be trusted to respect the liberty and equality of *all* their citizens—in particular blacks and southern Unionists—and that federal courts had to be available to enforce constitutional commands.[27] The wisdom of that congressional skepticism was more than borne out, even if for half a century the Supreme Court and the country turned a blind eye to lynchings, Klan terror, and Jim Crow.

Eventually, though, the federal government, including its judiciary, slowly began to reassume the responsibilities it had fought for at Gettysburg and assumed after Appomattox. In 1919, a confrontation between black farmers (organizing against oppressive white landlords) and a local deputy sheriff in Arkansas turned into a shoot-out around a crowded black church that left the deputy dead and a companion wounded. The sheriff then rounded up 300 locals who avenged the killing in every corner of the county. For a week, they hunted down every black farmer who didn't manage to hide in the surrounding woods or swamps. In the end, as many as 200 blacks and 5 whites had died. A star chamber of white landlords put a dozen black ringleaders on trial for murder; armed mobs ensured the guilty verdicts and sentences of death.[28]

The black defendants complained that their trials had been shams, kangaroo courts conducted before all-white juries, with verdicts enforced by gun-toting thugs, based on confessions extracted from people who were beaten with chains. Despite reams of evidence, the state courts rejected their appeals. Then, on their filing for federal habeas, the federal district judge deferred to the state court rulings denying their claims.

When the case, *Moore v. Dempsey*,[29] reached the Supreme Court in 1923, Justice Oliver Wendell Holmes, writing for a majority of six, held that federal courts simply could not ignore allegations of such gross injustice. The defendants' charges of mob intimidation, if true, he declared, clearly stated a violation of their due process rights. A federal habeas court, he continued, was obligated to assess and to rule on these due process claims and could not, as had happened here and in the past, simply defer to state court rulings. Over a dissent written by the scarcely veiled racist Justice James McReynolds, Holmes ordered a federal district court to hold a full hearing on the matter. In the end, the twelve condemned men went free.*

Like the Scottsboro cases that came a decade later, *Moore* was an early spark in what would become the great prairie fire of the civil rights movement, which, in turn, rekindled the old debate between those who championed the federal government as the central instrument for securing the general welfare of the people and those who took up the old-time slaveholder rallying cry of "states' rights." At the Court, the defenders of states' rights, if not yet routed, were on the run. In the most famous footnote in Supreme Court history, Justice Harlan Fiske Stone, with a suspicious glance toward Jim Crow, suggested that the Court might subject to especially "searching judicial inquiry" state actions directed against "discrete and insular minorities."[30] And, in practice, by the end of the 1940s, the Justices had done away with restrictive racial covenants for real estate that perpetuated segregated neighborhoods, had started chiseling away at the doctrine of separate but equal, and had continued the incremental expansion of due process, increasing federal regulation of state court justice.

---

*Eight years before, the Court had refused to order a habeas hearing in a virtually identical case, *Frank v. Magnum*, 237 U.S. 309 (1915), in which a southern mob dominated the trial of a Jewish businessman, Leo Frank, accused of killing a thirteen-year-old girl. Frank was convicted of murder, sentenced to death, and ultimately lynched after the governor of Georgia commuted his sentence. Justice Holmes had dissented in the Frank case. As a general matter, before *Frank* and *Moore,* federal courts had limited their habeas inquiries to the issue of whether the challenged verdict had been rendered by a court of competent jurisdiction.

In the political arena, the same progressive movement, however glacial, was under way. President Harry Truman called on Congress to enact antilynching legislation, to outlaw the poll tax, to end segregation on interstate transportation, to enforce fair elections, and to create a permanent national civil rights commission. At the 1948 Democratic National Convention, Minneapolis Mayor Hubert Humphrey, in a defining moment for his political party as well as his own career, declared in support of Truman's civil rights agenda that the time had arrived "to get out of the shadow of states' rights and walk forthrightly into the bright sunshine of human rights."[31] Democrats from the old Confederacy objected so strongly that they broke off to form their own States' Rights (or Dixiecrat) Party and ran Strom Thurmond of South Carolina unsuccessfully for president.

The expansion of habeas corpus was but a small part of this slow nationalization of the law, but by Rehnquist's arrival at the Court in 1952, its impact was being strongly felt. Federal habeas petitions were multiplying and promised to expand exponentially if the Court (as it would) continued to broaden the definition of due process (which served as the legal basis for habeas claims). State judiciaries, particularly in the South, had begun to complain bitterly as individual federal judges increasingly subjected their work to the sharp and sometimes embarrassing scrutiny of federal habeas review.

The questions facing the Court in *Brown* v. *Allen* went to the nub of this mounting conflict, and, appropriately, the four defendants in the case were all black men sentenced to death in North Carolina for crimes against whites.* In that too familiar context, the Justices faced a stark choice between further entrenching federal supervision of state court justice or turning their backs on the legacy of *Moore* v. *Dempsey*.

The twenty-seven-year-old Rehnquist made no bones about where he stood. The future Chief Justice wrote his boss, Justice Jackson, three times during the opinion-drafting process, each time squarely supporting the narrowest view of federal habeas. In a memo playfully entitled "HABEAS CORPUS, THEN AND NOW, Or, 'If I Can Just Find the Right Judge, Over these Prison Walls I Shall Fly . . . ,' " Rehnquist advocated that prior state court rulings coupled with a denial of cert. by the Supreme Court "should be *res judicata* so far as any further federal intervention in the case is concerned." More simply put, he believed that state court

---

*Two of the defendants had been convicted of rape, the two others of murder.

judgments rejecting due process claims should be final and unreviewable in federal court except when the Supreme Court itself granted direct review.*

Rehnquist rejected outright the notion that state courts, particularly southern state courts, might too frequently neglect constitutional protections in their criminal trials. "We should trust the state cts to enforce [due process]," he insisted. "Why [state judges] are less well equipped to find facts than a federal district judge, I don't know. True, this ct has reversed many state convictions. . . . But in fact many of these were borderline cases . . . when this ct was bending over backwards to comfort the prisoners even where there was no showing of prejudice."[32]

Rehnquist candidly placed the habeas debate into the context of the deeper legal and political rift over states' rights generally. Liberals, he pointed out, had cried foul when in the late nineteenth and early twentieth centuries "this ct exrecised [sic] a strict supervision over state economic legislation, ratemaking, etc. . . . But they [sic] very factions which most loudly damned the old court for its position on property rights are the most vocal in urging that this ct and other federal cts strictly supervise the state cts on matters of 'civil liberties' and procedural due process." To Rehnquist this was sheer hypocrisy. "What these forces fail to recognize," he continued, "is that the vice of the old court was not that it imposed the wrong views on the states, but that it imposed any views at all. In the field of liberty as well as property the states must be left to work out their own destinies within broad limits."

Rehnquist's states' rights philosophy had implications far beyond habeas, of course. As it had been for more than one hundred years, states' rights was the intellectual armor of those sympathetic to or at least willing to accept the subordination of blacks in the South. And as evident from the advice Rehnquist gave Jackson in other notable cases, he shared none of the Justices' growing concern with race discrimination in the South and saw their emerging commitment to curb racist practices as an assault on inalienable state perogatives.

One such case was *Terry v. Adams*, a challenge to the exclusion of blacks from Texas elections. In a 1944 case (*Smith v. Allwright*)[33] that marked one of Thurgood Marshall's greatest victories as an advocate, the

---

*Federal habeas, Rehnquist wrote, should be limited to those highly exceptional cases that involved newly discovered evidence after the state proceedings ended or in which, because of the absence of counsel, an inmate did not have the chance to effectively litigate claims in state court.

NAACP had convinced the Justices to outlaw "white primaries" whereby southern political parties excluded black voters from participating in the selection of electoral candidates. Rather than comply with the spirit of the Court's ruling, many jurisdictions came up with ingenious methods for continuing to shut out the black electorate. During Rehnquist's clerkship eight years later, the NAACP returned to the Court to challenge one of these: the primary practice of the Jaybird Democratic Association of Fort Bend County, Texas.

The Jaybirds held a primary every year identical in all respects to the subsequent official Democratic Party primary except that the Jaybirds excluded blacks from their vote. Although the Jaybirds had no official tie to the Democratic Party, by remarkable coincidence, the winner of their "private" primary always won the regular state-sanctioned primary, which the Court had opened to black voters. In *Terry* v. *Adams*,[34] the Court had to decide whether the Jaybirds' shadow primary was a "state action" infringing blacks' Fifteenth Amendment right to vote.

Writing Jackson about *Terry*, Rehnquist allowed that he was having "a hard time being detached about this case" and complained caustically about liberal colleagues in the building whose attitude he summed up as " 'Now we can show those damn southerners,' etc." Rehnquist took "a dim view of [their] pathological search for discrimination." Or, as he warned in another memo, "It is about time the Court faced the fact that the white people on [*sic*] the South don't like the colored people."[35] In Rehnquist's view, the Court should stay out of local affairs and the business of social engineering.

Notably, when it came time for Rehnquist to counsel Jackson about what to do in *Brown* v. *Board of Education,* he based his emphatic conclusion that "*Plessy* v. *Ferguson* was right and should be re-affirmed" on much the same states' rights argument he had put forward against federal habeas. "If this Court," Rehnquist wrote, "because its members individually are 'liberal' and dislike segregation, now chooses to strike it down, it differs from the McReynolds court [striking down economic legislation] only in the kinds of litigants it favors and the kinds of special claims it protects."[36]

The Court rejected Rehnquist's suggested states' rights approach to segregation in *Brown* v. *Board of Education* and *Terry* v. *Allen*. And it rejected his approach to federal habeas in *Brown* v. *Allen*. With respect to habeas, the Court directed federal district judges to assess petitions from state prisoners independently from any prior state court judgments.[37] In addition, the Court told those judges to regard prior denials of cert. by the Supreme Court as stating absolutely no view on the merits of a petitioner's claims. The Justices could not possibly review every potentially meritorious habeas petition and, thus, cert. denials often reflected nothing more than the Court's crowded docket and its decision to review only cases presenting broadly significant legal issues. All told, *Brown* v. *Allen* was a sweeping victory for proponents of federal habeas, clearing the way for federal judges to independently review every constitutional claim arising from state criminal trials.

As a Justice, Rehnquist has never sought to revisit *Brown* v. *Board of Education*, and, during his confirmation hearings, he even sought to distance himself from his contemporaneous opposition to desegregation.* Nevertheless, he stuck close to his states' rights philosophy, one aspect of which continued to be his active opposition to federal habeas. Indeed, Rehnquist's 1981 dissent in *Coleman* v. *Balkom* was actually a renewal, twenty-eight years after the fact, of his quarrel with the Court's decision in *Brown* v. *Allen* allowing lower federal courts to second-guess state court legal judgments. In *Balkom*, as in *Brown* (but by a different method), Rehnquist sought to prevent inmates from reraising before federal judges the same claims that state courts already had rejected. The states, he wrote in *Balkom*, "are also entitled to due process of law"[38]— and as a Justice, precisely as he had as a clerk, Rehnquist intended to serve steadfastly as their champion.

---

*In December 1971, Rehnquist wrote the Senate Judiciary Committee that the "Random Thought on the Segregation Cases" memo "was prepared by me as a statement of Justice Jackson's tentative views" and was not "an accurate statement of my own views at the time." A study of Jackson's draft writings in *Brown* v. *Board of Education*, a comparison with Rehnquist's other memos to Jackson during his clerkship, and the recollections of Rehnquist's co-clerks all contradict this claim. See Bernard Schwartz, "Chief Justice Rehnquist, Justice Jackson, and the *Brown* Case," 1988 *Supreme Court Rev.*, p. 245.

Stay of Execution

Diametrically opposed to Rehnquist stood Justices Brennan and Marshall, the rear guard of the Warren Court. One of Brennan's greatest triumphs was his authorship, in 1963, of the Court's most expansive habeas decision, *Fay v. Noia*.[1] In *Fay*, Brennan not only embraced *Brown v. Allen*'s expansive definition of habeas but also gave state prisoners an almost unlimited right to have their claims heard in federal court even when they failed to comply with state procedural rules that would have barred their claims in the past. For both Brennan and Marshall, the touchstone for habeas was an almost heroic vision of federal judges as knights-errant righting constitutional wrongs wherever they could be found. And in their view, neither procedural technicalities nor Rehnquist's notion of respect for state courts should be allowed to impede that paramount mission.

From hard experience, Justice Marshall knew the system was rife with errors to correct. Although winning *Brown v. Board of Education* had made him famous, Marshall's messiahlike reputation in black communities across the South had first arisen from his years defending the accused in criminal cases. Alone among the Justices, he had wrestled hand-to-hand with the evil of state judicial systems warped by race hatred and fear. In rural Tennessee, Marshall himself had almost been lynched by local police while representing twenty-five blacks against charges of murder and assault. With characteristic dark humor, he enjoyed recalling these days; he always knew his client was innocent, he'd recount, when the jury returned a sentence of only life imprisonment.[2] Through Marshall's glasses, the opportunity for meaningful federal review of state criminal proceedings was no abstraction. It was the minimum justice required.

Quite apart from the issue of racism, Marshall and Brennan believed the idea of parity between state and federal judges to be a pernicious myth. As a general matter, state judges tended to be less intelligent, less competent, less well-trained, and less broadly experienced than federal judges, who usually were selected from the highest ranks of the legal profession. Equally important, in contrast to federal judges, who enjoyed the vital security of life tenure, most state judges had to stand periodically for election. This accountability to a local electorate inevitably made state judges more concerned with the personal and political consequences of their decisions, especially in highly emotional or controversial cases. All things considered, Brennan and Marshall thought federal judges much better suited to decide (as well as more receptive to) claims of constitutional right.[3]

Brennan's and Marshall's allegiance to federal habeas review was also closely connected to their unyielding opposition to the death penalty. In capital cases, federal review was vital in terms of both correcting injustices and slowing down the process. On habeas, the Fifth and Eleventh Circuits (which included most of the southern states) overturned capital convictions or death sentences in the vast majority of the cases they decided, even though state courts in the same cases previously had found no constitutional violations.[4] To Brennan and Marshall, those reversals were proof positive that, as long as the death penalty continued, federal oversight was an absolute necessity.

As for the death penalty itself, Brennan and Marshall moved in almost mirror image to Rehnquist. While Rehnquist sought a return to pre-Warren approaches to capital cases, Brennan and Marshall adamantly refused to accept or reconcile themselves to the Burger Court's reinstitution of capital punishment in *Gregg*. After 1976, no matter what the circumstances, Brennan and Marshall voted to reverse or vacate every death sentence that came before the Court, whether in the form of an argued case, a cert. petition, or an application for a stay. Often, Brennan's and Marshall's position amounted to nothing more than maintaining a continuous judicial vigil against the death penalty. For example, when the Court denied cert. in the many death penalty cases each term raising no substantial issue of federal law, Brennan and Marshall simply took turns issuing a single sentence of formulaic protest:

"Adhering to our views that the death penalty is in all circumstances cruel and unusual punishment prohibited by the Eighth and Fourteenth Amendments, we would grant certiorari and vacate the sentence of death." Clerks within the building joked, not facetiously, that the computers in the Brennan and Marshall Chambers were programmed to call up this symbolic dissent on the press of a single key.

In the argued cases and in the many cert. petitions and stay applications that raised more substantial issues, Brennan and Marshall supplemented their blanket objection to the death penalty with a detailed critique of whatever aspect of the capital process the defendant called into question. Collectively, these frequent opinions established a case-by-case record—a sort of running catalog—of what these committed enemies of the death penalty saw as the endemic breakdowns and iniquities of the system.[5]

Brennan and Marshall did not pretend that their abolitionist position could be squared with the Court's precedents. Instead, they self-righteously excused themselves from following stare decisis—the principle of acceding to past decisions, especially ones (as *Gregg* came to be) that the Court repeatedly reaffirmed. According to Brennan and Marshall, the Court was so fundamentally wrong in its interpretation of the Eighth Amendment that they were bound "by a larger constitutional duty . . . to expose the departure and point toward a different path."[6]

Whatever the duo's justification, their acid stream of abolitionist dissents ensured that the issue of capital punishment continually ate away at the connective tissue of the Court community. After *Gregg*, the Court handed down a number of decisions further restricting the death penalty. But every success for Brennan's and Marshall's short-term goal of stalling executions only made an eventual backlash more certain.

The conservatives started by trimming federal habeas. As early as 1976, they categorically barred state prisoners from relitigating on federal habeas alleged violations of their Fourth Amendment (search and seizure) rights.[7] They also partially overruled Brennan's habeas-friendly opinion in *Fay v. Noia* by sharply cutting back on the ability of inmates to raise on federal habeas constitutional complaints that they had failed to register at their original trials.[8]

The technical holdings in these cases were significant but not as important as the philosophical turn they signaled. Both rulings were based on precisely the parity of state and federal judges that the Warren Court had disparaged and gave much less weight to Brennan's and Marshall's concern with correcting constitutional violations than to Rehnquist's preoccupation with the costs that federal habeas imposed on state law enforcement.

The tide turned definitively in 1981, when the moderate Justice Stewart retired and President Reagan, fulfilling a campaign pledge to name a woman to the Court, nominated Sandra Day O'Connor to the vacant seat. Third in the same Stanford law school class from which her friend William Rehnquist graduated, O'Connor clearly fit the tough anti-Warren profile of a Reagan judicial appointee. A former prosecutor in the Arizona Attorney General's Office, majority leader of the state senate, and then a state judge who earned the nickname Iron Lady for both her demeanor and her rulings from the bench, O'Connor was about the last person who would encourage federal supervision of state affairs, especially the criminal law process. In fact, only one year before her nomination, while still an Arizona appellate judge, O'Connor had written a law review article echoing many of the concerns about federal habeas that Rehnquist had expressed. To her, such habeas review produced a "strange" and "imperfect" duplication of judicial effort ultimately demeaning to state courts.[9]

O'Connor's elevation to the Supreme Court did nothing to change this perspective. In her first term, she wrote an opinion reaffirming and expanding the Court's previous habeas cutbacks.[10] O'Connor also provided an important vote in a trilogy of highly technical death penalty cases that greatly expanded the definition of what legal errors in the capital sentencing process could be overlooked as "harmless." It was the first time since Gregg that the Court significantly "deregulated death."[11]

After only two executions the previous year, in 1983 the new majority took an even larger step. In Barefoot v. Estelle,[12] the Court ruled that federal appeals courts could treat death-sentenced habeas petitioners to a specially shortened version of the usual appellate process.

Texas already had set an execution date by the time Thomas Barefoot's petition reached the Fifth Circuit. Still, the appeals court had refused to stay his impending execution while it considered his case. Instead, with time running down, the circuit gave Barefoot's LDF lawyers two days in which to submit their briefs and prepare for oral argument—a process that would take weeks or even months ordinarily. (This, even though Barefoot presented a compelling legal claim challenging the testimony of state psychiatrists who declared him a 100 percent risk of "longterm future dangerousness" without ever examining him.)*

Barefoot's lawyers protested the Fifth Circuit's superfast-track treatment, but the Supreme Court's conservative majority upheld the circuit's actions. Courts of appeals, they ruled, need not assess the merits of a capital appeal according to their usual full briefing and argument schedules. Rather, circuit courts could decide death penalty appeals using special rapid-fire procedures as long as the defendants had an opportunity to present their claims and be heard—even if that opportunity consisted of only two days.

Indeed, the conservative Justices *encouraged* a variety of hurry-up tactics. Aside from speeding appeals, they lectured lower federal courts to counter all defense delaying tactics more aggressively. No stays should be granted in the absence of a "substantial showing" of a violation of federal law. Furthermore, the circuit courts should expedite all successive habeas petitions and also search these petitions for claims that should have been filed earlier. Such bypassed claims constituted "abuses of the writ" and should result in automatic denials of relief.

Although aimed at the lower courts, one major result of *Barefoot* was to further ensnare the Justices themselves in the ongoing war of attrition between state prosecutors and the death penalty defense bar. By encouraging expedited appellate review and discouraging the granting of lower court stays, *Barefoot* guaranteed that capital cases would reach the Court more rapidly and with executions already pending. In other words, the agony of last-minute, last-ditch appeals, thus far unusual at the Court, was about to become a terribly draining and divisive part of its routine.

Right from the beginning of the 1983 Term, the level of acrimony started to build. Several states, taking their cue from the Court's new get-tough attitude, starting scheduling executions immediately after a petitioner was denied habeas relief at the court of appeals level—even before the deadline for filing a cert. petition at the Court. The practical result of this scheduling was to cut short the Court's ordinary consideration of an inmate's cert. petition, and a number of Justices resented these attempts to rush the system, especially because a life was at stake.

---

*Future dangerousness was a major factor in the Texas scheme for determining when the death penalty was appropriate. In *Barefoot*, the state had used Dr. James Grigson on this point. Grigson was so notorious for testifying in favor of death and so successful in that testimony (defendants received death sentences in 115 of the 124 cases in which he was involved) that Grigson was commonly referred to simply as Dr. Death.

Despite such concerns, in three cases in rapid succession, the conservative majority refused to issue stays to allow for the filing of a cert. petition and for the Court's own deliberative process to run its usual course.[13] Implementing a new harder-nosed approach to emergency stays, the conservatives served notice that they would no longer force states to reschedule executions just so the Court could preserve the formality of denying a cert. petition that in their view would undoubtedly lack merit. Justices Brennan, Marshall, Stevens, and even Blackmun (in one case)[14] could complain all they wanted about a "rush to judgment" and "distort[ing] the deliberative process within the Court," but procedural niceties had become the handmaidens of abolition and the majority would abide them no longer.

These skirmishes, however, were mere prologue. In light of *Barefoot*, the attorneys general of several death penalty states started pressing the Court to overturn questionable lower court stays. Such requests (as in the Spenkelink case) always had failed in the past. It was standard practice for the Justices to defer to lower court judges, who were closer to the facts and nuances of particular cases. In January 1984, though, in *Woodard* v. *Hutchins*,[15] the majority decided to break what it now saw as a bad habit.

James Hutchins had been convicted of murdering three police officers and sentenced to death in 1979. He appealed unsuccessfully through the state system, then filed for federal habeas relief. The lower federal courts saw no merit in Hutchins's claims, and, in due course, the Court denied his cert. petition on January 11, 1984, two days before his scheduled execution. The following day, Hutchins filed a stay application and second federal habeas petition alleging three entirely new claims. The district judge assigned the case denied Hutchins's stay application but inexplicably failed to issue any ruling on the habeas petition.

With time running very short, Hutchins's lawyers asked Circuit Judge James Dickson Phillips to stay the execution on the ground that Hutchins was entitled to have his habeas petition acted on before being put to death. Phillips agreed and, at 12:05 A.M. on the thirteenth, issued a stay.

Phillips's intervention infuriated Justices Burger, Powell, Blackmun, Rehnquist, and O'Connor. Despite the Court's rule of vacating stays only in extraordinary circumstances, they vacated Judge Phillips's stay. In the majority's view, Hutchins should have raised his three new claims in his original habeas petition. By failing to do so, he had abused the writ and made himself ineligible for a stay, regardless of any irregularities in the handling of his petition. A few hours later, Hutchins was electrocuted without any court considering the merits of his second habeas petition.

Much the same set of events occurred twice more before the 1984 summer recess, each time provoking a more heated dissent. In *Hutchins*, Justices Brennan and Marshall had accused the Court of being "insensitive, if not ghoulish." By the third case they were accusing the conservatives of throwing caution "to the winds with an impetuousness and arrogance that is truly astonishing."[16] Such bitter accusations have appeared from time to time in Court opinions, but not often, and almost never in such close succession. The inflammatory rhetoric reflected hurt feeling, anger, and a certain amount of despair. These dissents were meant not to convince but to shame—even though the targets, equally indignant in their own right, were all but impervious to the charges.

October Term 1984 began where '83 left off. After several nasty battles at the end of the summer,[17] in November the acrimony of the stay war ratcheted up yet again. During the previous year, the conservatives had intentionally disregarded the Court's usual ways of doing business, but only in cases where the petitioner's claims seemed insubstantial. Now, as the Court took up the second habeas petition of Alpha Otis O'Daniel Stephens, an indigent black man sentenced to death for killing a white, the new majority seemed willing to foreclose even potentially meritorious constitutional claims in the name of streamlining the execution process.

The background to Stephens's case was the LDF's new campaign to attack the death penalty on racial grounds. Back in 1970, after their failure with Professor Wolfgang's statistical study alleging racism in capital sentencing for rape, the lawyers at the LDF had moved away from their original concern with race discrimination. Their resounding defeat in *Gregg*, however, had brought them back to the roots of their abolitionist campaign. Starting in 1978, the LDF had commissioned a series of state-of-the-art analyses to assess the role race played in several of the new capital sentencing schemes. The lead study—known as the Baldus study after its principal architect, David Baldus of the University of Iowa—examined more than 2,400 post-*Furman* homicides in Georgia and became the basis of a new claim that Georgia's post-*Gregg* system for imposing the death penalty was unconstitutionally biased against blacks.

By 1984, what had become the test case for the LDF's new discrimination claim, *McCleskey v. Kemp*,[18] had reached the Eleventh Circuit. Recognizing its importance, the appeals court arranged a special en banc (all judge) hearing. And while the parties to *McCleskey* prepared their arguments, the Eleventh Circuit started issuing stays in other Georgia death cases where race had surfaced as an issue. This practice preserved the basic legal principle that similar cases should be treated similarly and ensured that no inmate was executed only for it to be discovered, too late, that his conviction or sentence was constitutionally flawed.

The ensuing bottleneck, however, was also a main reason for the long delays in carrying out death sentences. Every time a circuit court decided to hear such a major challenge to the death penalty, abolitionist lawyers made sure that every capital defendant who could plausibly assert the same claim did so. Sometimes this was solely a tactic for seeking a stay; other times the abolitionists were conscientiously updating a petitioner's claims to reflect changes in a rapidly developing field of law. Often it was hard to tell one from the other.

In any case, the Eleventh Circuit, departing from its regular practice, rejected Alpha Stephens's attempt to claim racial bias and, thereby, scramble behind the temporary shield of *McCleskey*. By a 6–6 vote (ties going against the party seeking a stay), the judges of the appeals court rejected Stephens's habeas petition and denied him a stay. The Court ruled that Stephens, who was on second federal habeas, had failed to submit the evidence of Baldus's study at the proper time and, therefore, was barred under the abuse of the writ doctrine from bringing a *McCleskey*-style claim. Because Stephens had forfeited his race claim, no stay was appropriate.

Immediately after the Eleventh Circuit's ruling, with Georgia moving ahead with plans for his execution, Stephens applied to the Supreme Court for an emergency stay while he filed a cert. petition. On the vote of five Justices (Brennan, White, Marshall, Blackmun, and Stevens), the Court approved his stay request, halting his execution pending the outcome of *McCleskey*, "or until further order of this Court."[19]

In due course, Stephens filed his cert. petition—which challenged the Eleventh Circuit's use of the abuse of the writ doctrine to bar his claim. It came up for discussion at a Conference early in October, and the cert.-pool memo recommended a grant. At Conference, however, only three Justices voted to hear the case. White and Blackmun, despite having voted to grant a stay, now voted (without explanation) to deny review of Stephens's abuse of the writ claims.

Their votes were critical. Because this denial of Stephens's cert. petition would qualify as a further order, once the Court formally announced its decision, his stay would be dissolved. As a consequence, even though *McCleskey* was still pending in the Eleventh Circuit, and even though proceedings were suspended in all other cases involving *McCleskey*-type claims, Stephens would again find himself heading straight toward execution.

This turn of events devastated Justice Brennan, and he had the announcement of the Court's decision delayed while one of his clerks prepared a dissent. Brennan expected that an enlightened public would react in horror at the prospect of executing someone even as a pending case cast doubt on the constitutionality of his death sentence. And although Brennan recognized that openly impugning his colleagues might damage the Court's public standing, he'd reached the point where that was a price worth paying. On October 22, he circulated the statement of sheer outrage he intended to publish when the Court officially announced its denial of Stephens's petition. The Court's unexplained and inexplicable turnabout, Brennan concluded, "is at best an example of result-orientation carried to its most cynical extreme. At worst, it is outright lawlessness."

The proposed dissent caused a considerable reaction inside the Court but no reconsideration. An outraged Chief Justice Burger demanded that Brennan remove the sentence about "outright lawlessness" as a threat to the Court's esteem. In the only conversation about a death case he would have with Brennan all year, Burger threatened to respond with his own rejoinder if Brennan didn't comply. Brennan acquiesced and deleted the phrase, but the damage was done.[20] *The New York Times* ran an article accusing the Court of "a new, brazen insensitivity to the need for special care in death cases" and singling out Justices White and Blackmun for their unexplained, allegedly inconsistent votes. "Has the Court no dignity?" the piece queried at the end.[21]

The drubbing in the *Times* only aggravated the raw feelings in the building. Stephens, meanwhile, was pursuing a desperation third federal habeas challenging some of the jury instructions at his trial. Justice Stevens sent around a memo stating his lack of interest in the jury instruction issue but an intent to vote to grant Stephens another stay on the old ground of waiting for the Eleventh Circuit's race discrimination decision. Brennan and Marshall immediately jumped onboard. Then Blackmun, with the *Times* article on his desk, told his clerks that he had changed his mind and now agreed with Stevens. He also would vote to grant a stay.

Blackmun's about-face still left Stephens one vote shy of the five he needed. In an effort to prevent another defection, Burger circulated a Stephens "case history," relating the saga of his many appeals during the nine years since his original conviction. In this and other, similar memos, Burger's favorite tactic was to count up the number of judges who at some point had considered an inmate's claims. These tallies were wildly inflated (for example, Burger included dissenting judges who had voted to reverse convictions) and of dubious relevance, but the Chief held them out as proof of the scrupulousness of judicial review, no matter how undeserving its beneficiaries. Behind Brennan's and Marshall's backs, Burger also instructed the Court's Public Relations Office to release his histories to the press as a counter to the bad publicity generated by their dissents.

Amid these machinations, White stuck to his denial, and on December 11, the day of his scheduled execution, the Court refused Stephens any relief on his third habeas petition.[22] That night, his lawyers filed a last-ditch request for reconsideration, which generated another round of late-night phone calls between clerks and their Justices. Toward 11:00 P.M., the clerks began congregating in Chris Vasil's office to wait for any last-minute developments. Justice Brennan's Chambers was busy preparing another diatribe, while Justice Blackmun spoke with his clerks on an open phone line, double- and triple-checking his own separate dissent.

Around 11:30, with the Justices having denied Stephens's final appeal, the Court staff started shutting down the computers and the clerks headed home. About the same time, Georgia botched the first attempt to electrocute Stephens. He lingered for eight minutes, gasping for breath, before a second charge slowly killed him. For the dissenters, Stephens's agony only compounded an already severe injustice and deepened the wound the conservatives had inflicted on the Court itself.[23]

Two weeks later, after a barrage of negative publicity from Stephens's execution, the Court faced almost exactly the same situation. On December 10, the Justices had denied a cert. petition arising from the first federal habeas of the Georgia inmate Roosevelt Green, Jr., a black man convicted in the rape and murder of an eighteen-year-old white woman. Immediately before Christmas, Green returned to the Court with a petition for rehearing in which he raised a discrimination claim based on the

Baldus study and requested a stay. Although Green was still technically on first federal habeas (in contrast to Stephens's disfavored "successive" petition), again only Justices Brennan, Marshall, Stevens, and Blackmun wanted to postpone his execution until the court of appeals decided whether racism had corrupted his sentence.

In Green's case, though, Justice Powell was unavailable to provide a fifth vote either way. A few days before Green's rehearing petition came up, Powell had traveled to the Mayo Clinic in Minnesota for surgery to remove his recently diagnosed prostate cancer. Although a relatively routine procedure was forecast, during the operation Powell began hemorrhaging uncontrollably and almost died.[24]

From past experience, everyone knew that Powell was a possible—perhaps even a likely—vote to grant Green a stay. In deciding whether to grant emergency stays, he drew a sharp distinction between petitioners on first federal habeas (such as Green) and much disfavored repeat petitioners (such as Stephens). None of the conservatives, however, was willing to put the case over until his return; the Justices deadlocked 4–4 on Green's stay application in a situation where a tie meant death.

Justices Brennan, Marshall, Blackmun, and Stevens all went on the public record in dissent, but to no avail. Georgia electrocuted Green on January 9, 1985, prompting an incredulous *Times* editorial with the headline KILL HIM 4–4. The adverse reaction infuriated Burger, who some weeks later reluctantly decided to postpone any executions until Powell returned. Still, he and the other conservatives were achieving their goal. Green's was the twenty-second execution in the last twelve months, twice the number of the preceding eight years combined.

By 1985, the bruising arguments over the death penalty, beyond straining relations among the Justices, began to break down the internal rules that for decades had governed how the Court handled its docket. The crux of the problem was that while Burger, White, Powell, Rehnquist, and O'Connor (as in Stephens's and Green's cases) could prevent the Court from issuing stays of execution, they could not prevent the remaining minority from making two other kinds of decisions central to the consideration of capital cases.

First, under the Court's rules, a minority of four Justices was sufficient to grant cert. and force the entire Court to conduct full review of a case. Second, a mere three Justices could place a "hold" on any cert. petition that they considered related to a case already pending before the Court. The hold rule was meant to ensure that the parties to every case still in the judicial pipeline would receive the benefit of whatever changes in the law the Court might make in its upcoming decision.[25]

Given the Burger Court's close division between liberals and conservatives in the capital cases and the growing rancor on both sides, it was only a matter of time before the minority-based cert. and hold rules came into direct conflict with the majority rule governing stays. In capital cases, uniquely, a vote to grant cert. or to hold a case was not necessarily self-sufficient. When a capital defendant came to the Court with an execution date already set, a cert. grant or a hold vote wouldn't be effective unless the Court also issued the defendant a stay of execution. In the absence of a stay (requiring five votes), the defendant would be dead before the Court took final action on his case.

This asymmetry in procedures meant that in death cases in which an execution was set, the conservatives held an effective veto whenever the liberals voted to grant cert. or hold: they could simply refuse consent for a stay. It was thus only a matter of time before the question arose whether, in the recrimination-filled context of the capital stays, the conservatives would continue to honor the Court's nonmajoritarian traditions.

In short order, the conservative answer came back a resounding no. In February 1985, the Court considered the cert. petition of Morris Odell Mason, a schizophrenic, borderline mental retardate whose execution for the savage murder of an elderly woman was rapidly approaching.[26] At the time, the Justices were deciding another case, Ake v. Oklahoma,[27] which (once the opinions were completed) would recognize that the Constitution gives capital defendants a right to psychiatric assistance during their trials. In his cert. petition, Mason claimed he had received no such psychiatric assistance, and, accordingly, Justices Brennan, Marshall, Blackmun, and Stevens all deemed his case sufficiently related to Ake to warrant a hold. But, none of the other four Justices (Powell was still out after his surgery) would agree to lend the fifth vote necessary for a stay.* And so it stood, neither side blinking, time ticking away, Mason's life and the integrity of the Court's internal processes hanging in the balance, until the Fourth Circuit fortuitously granted Mason a stay of its own.

---

*The conservatives' obstinateness so infuriated Blackmun that he called Brennan to say he would vote to grant Mason's cert. petition outright if it would help prevent his execution.

The Court's minority-based rules were predicated on a level of trust and consideration among the Justices—the idea that, in certain matters, simply out of respect for one another's judgments, the entire Court would allow itself to be bound by a minority of its members. The capital cases, though, had destroyed that sense of community and mutual obligation.

Conservatives were fed up with Brennan and Marshall behaving like abolitionist agents in judicial garb. Their two automatic votes to grant or to stay or to vacate in every capital case mocked the Court's precedents and skewed the balance between its majority and nonmajority rules. From the conservative perspective, the liberals, including Blackmun and Stevens, were manipulating both the cert. rule and the hold rule, sometimes in combination, to delay legal executions. First, the liberals would grant cert. in what the conservatives saw as cases clearly unworthy of the Court's attention. These internal maneuvers worked hand in glove with abolitionists on the outside. Trying to take advantage of the three-vote hold rule was a favorite tactic of the death penalty defense bar. As soon as the Court granted cert. in a capital case, the LDF or some other group would be arguing in every cert. petition that their clients' cases were related and should be held until the Court issued its ruling—and, of course, that stays of execution should be meted out accordingly. In light of these tactics, the conservatives felt perfectly justified in exercising whatever power they could to keep executions on track.

From the liberals' perspective, the conservatives were now willing to subvert even the Court's own processes to keep the "Old Sparkys" of the South in business. For Justices uneasy about, if not unalterably opposed to state-sponsored killing, that was an insult touched with evil. The whole point of making the cert. and hold rules nonmajoritarian was to give a minority of Justices the power to prevent a majority from denying a cert. petition. Surely the majority should not be allowed to defeat those rules by withholding a stay and waiting for the petitioner's execution to moot his appeal.

What was really going on here, the more liberal Justices believed, was sheer hostility to capital defendants whatever the merits of their claims. Certainly Stevens and Blackmun considered themselves absolutely scrupulous in what cases they voted to stay and hold—conscientious in their effort to make the death penalty as fair and rational as possible. By contrast, no one could even remember the last time Burger or Rehnquist voted to stay or to hold a death case, no matter how appropriate. (Indeed, in his fourteen years on the Court, Rehnquist had pursued a kind of reverse abolitionism, only once voting to overturn a death sentence even on those occasions when his colleagues unanimously found that result to be compelled.) And the record of the other conservatives wasn't much better. The conservatives' new attitude was simply "Let's get it over with." That wasn't judicial; that wasn't even toughness; that just seemed mean and wrong.

After the near miss in Mason's case, Justice Powell returned to the bench, but the crisis only deepened. The conflict among the Court's rules came to a head on Labor Day weekend, a month before the start of the 1985 Term. The occasion was a stay application filed by Willie Jasper Darden, a black man who twelve years before had been convicted in a Florida court of killing a white man during a furniture store robbery, then making sexual advances on the victim's wife and wounding a neighbor who stumbled on the crime. After the Florida state courts affirmed Darden's conviction and sentence, his case moved to federal habeas. There, at one point, Darden almost won a new trial, but in the end, after a series of very close votes, the court of appeals denied him relief.

Florida set Darden's execution for September 4, 1985, substantially before his deadline for filing a cert. petition with the Court. Naturally, he applied for a stay to allow him to present his claims, and that application reached the Court on September 3.

Brennan and Marshall, of course, immediately voted to grant Darden a stay. And Blackmun and Stevens joined them. Both Blackmun and Stevens believed that every capital defendant deserved one complete round of federal habeas review, including the filing and disposition of a cert. petition at the Court. Notwithstanding the rhetoric of conservative Justices about the parity of state and federal judges, in practice the Court almost never granted cert. in capital cases coming up from the state courts. Rather, the Justices intentionally denied cert. and rolled the cases into federal habeas. They wanted more conscientious lower federal judges to assess a defendant's claims before deciding whether those claims were worthy of Supreme Court review.[28] In Darden's case, Florida was trying to cut that process short, and, on that score, Blackmun and Stevens voted for a stay.

By a few minutes after 6:00 P.M., all the votes were in, and Darden's stay application had failed by a now familiar 5–4. On hearing this news, with less than twelve hours before the execution, Darden's lawyers scrambled to think of some strategy to save their client. They knew that they had garnered four votes for a stay. They also knew that two years before, in another capital case where the Court had denied a stay 5–4, the conservative majority had promised that if only the applicant had "convinced four Members of the Court that certiorari would be granted . . . a stay would issue." In that case, *Autry* v. *Estelle*,[29] only two of the Justices voting to issue a stay (Brennan and Marshall) also would have voted to grant cert., so the conservatives were never put to the test.

Thinking back to *Autry*, Darden's lawyers decided to explore whether the four Justices who had voted unsuccessfully to grant their stay request were sufficiently interested in Darden's case also to vote to grant cert. If so, presumably the conservative majority would fulfill its promise from *Autry* and issue a stay. Accordingly, at 9:11 P.M. they faxed a letter to Chris Vasil addressed to Chief Justice Burger, asking for Darden's stay papers to be treated as a cert. petition and also renewing his request for a stay.[30]

Unbeknownst to Darden's lawyers, and as had never happened before, all four of the Justices who had voted to issue Darden a stay were also interested in granting cert. in his case. Brennan's and Marshall's votes were, of course, givens. Stevens was the next most likely vote. The key was Justice Blackmun.

Over time, Blackmun had shifted ground on the death penalty. Although he had once seen little role for the judiciary in regulating capital punishment, meticulous study of hundreds of cert. petitions and stay applications had begun to raise serious doubts in his mind about the fairness and reliability of state capital trials and sentencing procedures. Behind the closed door of his office or at home in the evening, Blackmun would pore over the capital cases, conjuring up the human faces behind each drama—the victim, the assailant, the witnesses and accomplices, and the families left grieving.[31] This personalizing approach caused more than one clerk to comment, only partially in jest, that if you wanted Blackmun's vote for a stay you had to keep him away from photographs of the deceased. But Blackmun's compulsive methodology also caused him to reflect almost daily on the awful responsibility of overseeing the taking of a life and made him increasingly concerned with the chronic irregularities he saw in the system.

In Darden's case, Blackmun thought he saw not only irregularity but the very real possibility of innocence. The most important of Darden's claims was that the prosecutor's closing argument in his case was so in-

flammatory it deprived him of a fair trial. Among other seeming impro-
prieties, the prosecutor had twice called Darden an "animal," suggested
that he belonged on a leash, and expressed the wish that he "could see
[Darden] sitting here with no face, blown away by a shotgun." In Blackmun's view, the physical evidence linking Darden to the crime was
equivocal; the case had boiled down to the word of two somewhat shaky
eyewitnesses against Darden's own proclamation of innocence. By assaulting Darden's humanity, Blackmun thought the prosecutor had impaired the jury's ability to compare the witnesses' credibility and decide
the case on the evidence rather than emotion.

Justice Stevens, always vigilant against flawed trials, had parsed the
case much the same way. Both he and Blackmun were firmly for granting
cert. and averting a potential tragedy.

As the requisite four votes to grant cert. rolled in, a game of judicial
chicken began. Despite their assurance two years previous about issuance of a stay to preserve a granted case for argument and decision, the
conservatives were balking. Burger was adamantly opposed to a stay.
From out of town, Rehnquist phoned in his vote to deny, as did White,
even though he had authored the *Autry* promise. O'Connor followed
suit.

As clerks scurried from one heated argument to another, Darden's fate
came to hinge on Justice Powell, who in capital cases, as in many other
areas of law, had emerged as the crucial swing vote. Despite his hostility
to federal habeas, and his abhorrence of abolitionist tactics, Powell was
not, as were Burger or Rehnquist (and increasingly White), totally immune to allegations of constitutional error. As Circuit Justice for Georgia and Florida, Powell served as the Court's point man on a
disproportionate number of capital cases, a chore that nourished his personal discomfort (evident in *Gregg*) with administering the death
penalty. On many late death watch nights, clerks remember seeing Powell's frail, almost ghostlike figure hovering around Chris Vasil's desk, supervising the final hushed communications between the Court and a
prison. Some clerks worried that the pressure of so often casting the crucial life-determining vote might ruin Powell's own fragile health.

The pressure was never greater than in Darden's case, but Powell, unlike Blackmun and Stevens, saw nothing in Darden's papers that called
his guilt into question or in any other way merited a cert. grant. He also
bristled at the anomaly of transforming Darden's stay application into a
cert. petition and then holding a vote without benefit of a formal con-

ference. He feared this last-minute switch might become another procedural loophole for the death penalty bar to exploit. Still, it was getting late; Darden's execution was scheduled for dawn; the Justices were scattered; and, as someone preternaturally concerned with decorum and tradition, Powell took the cert. grant "rule of four" very seriously. He drafted a statement emphasizing that he found "no merit whatever" in Darden's claims. Nonetheless, because of "the unusual situation," he would vote to grant a stay.[32] A minute before midnight, the order went out and Darden received a reprieve.

The next day, Powell circulated a rare angry memo. To him, Darden's twelve years of appeals, now extended by the Court's own acceptance of the case, symbolized everything that was wrong with the system. "I have no doubt as to the constitutionality of capital punishment," he wrote, but, because of the delays caused by federal habeas, "I have grave doubts as to whether it now serves the purposes of deterrence and retribution, the principal purposes we identified in *Gregg*."[33] Indeed, Powell was so upset he raised the possibility of dramatic reform: increase the number of Justices required for a cert. grant to five. That revision, of course, would eliminate the conflict between the current nonmajority cert. rule and the stay rule.

Several Justices replied to Powell's idea. Rehnquist was certainly amenable to making cert. grants in capital cases more difficult. Thirty years before, as a clerk, he had suggested requiring five votes to grant cert. for all cases coming up from the states. Rehnquist's desire had been to reduce Supreme Court supervision of state criminal trials. Powell's suggestion was just a capital case variation on the same theme.

Not surprisingly, Brennan countered from the opposite point of view. He considered it beyond argument that once four Justices voted to grant cert., the entire Court had to issue a stay. He agreed with Blackmun, who warned in a grave memo of his own that allowing a petitioner's execution after accepting his case for review would render the Court an "intellectually and morally bankrupt" institution. As a way of making certain that a stay issued automatically when four Justices voted to grant cert., Brennan proposed a special rule for death penalty cases (the mirror image of Powell's suggestion) reducing the number of votes required for a stay from five to four.[34] Rehnquist scoffed that this would allow a minority to "in effect control the operations of the Court, at least in the short run," although Brennan professed with childlike innocence to be interested only in the Court's smooth functioning.

In the end, the Court adopted neither Powell's nor Brennan's pro-posal. But what was most interesting and significant about both sugges-tions was that they shared a common premise. A main purpose of letting a minority of four Justices grant cert. was the idea that after briefing, ar-gument, discussion, and deliberation one or more Justices might change their preliminary view of a case; in the end, the original four granting cert. might command a majority for the final decision. In suggesting that five Justices be required for a cert. grant, Powell was in effect admitting that in the capital cases all the Justices' minds were made up in advance and that holding argument and discussing the cases in Conference had become an essentially hollow exercise. From the opposite perspective, Brennan agreed. He wanted a rule of four to issue stays because those were all the votes he could muster.

The remainder of the term gave ample support to Powell's and Bren-nan's underlying appraisal. At term's end, the Court rejected Willie Dar-den's claims by a predictable 5–4 vote. As if to reemphasize how reluctant his stay vote had been, Powell wrote the opinion.

In the aftermath of the Darden stay fight, Powell did decide as a mat-ter of policy that in all future cases he would vote to issue a stay when-ever four Justices voted to grant cert. He took a very different approach, however, to the nonmajority hold rule. In May 1986, while *Darden* was still pending, Brennan, Marshall, Blackmun, and Stevens voted to hold for *Darden* the cert. petition of Ronald Straight, who was also in need of an emergency stay. Again the liberals and conservatives stared each other down, but this time Powell refused to blink. He didn't think Straight's petition was sufficiently related to *Darden* to warrant a hold. Moreover, Straight was on second federal habeas, and Powell thought his new claims presented a clear instance of abolitionist "sandbagging." He felt the liberals were invoking the hold rule in bad faith, and he pre-ferred to see the sanctity of the rule broken rather than postpone an-other execution on mere pretense.

After another night of hair-tearing fury, Brennan fired off a pointed dissent, which Marshall and Blackmun joined.* Straining to find lan-guage sufficient to his outrage, Brennan wrote that by rejecting the hold rule the majority had rejected "those first principles of justice that ulti-mately define a system of law: the principles of uniform application of rules, of consistency, of evenhandedness, of fairness." He was certainly

---

*Justice Stevens, who had some reservations about the hold rule, did not.

right that if Straight had been anyone other than a capital defendant facing immediate execution, his case would have been held. But in the last few years, the conservatives had succeeded in turning the trope "death is different"—once the justification for especially exacting procedures—on its head.

During the 1986 summer recess, Blackmun reminisced on the past year in a speech at a gathering of judges from his prior court, the Eighth Circuit. This had been the hardest of his sixteen terms at the Court, he said, more difficult and more divisive. The "triggering mechanism" for the acrimony had been the *Darden* stay fight, which had deprived the Justices of their ordinarily convivial postsummer start. "If ever a man received an unfair trial, Willie Darden received an unfair trial," Blackmun rued. "This started it off," and now Darden was dead. The "brooding overtones" of the capital cases, he continued, bombarding the Court "one almost every other day," had clouded the whole year.[35]

Even as Blackmun spoke, he knew that yet darker storms were on the horizon. At the end of the term, the Court had granted cert. in *McCleskey* v. *Kemp*, the LDF's comprehensive claim that racism was inherent in the death penalty. In a sense, it was a claim as old as the Scottsboro decision. And like those landmark cases a half century before, *McCleskey* would force the Justices to confront the most deeply embedded problem of American society and consider the Court's role in its solution.

Of the 1985 Term, Blackmun had suggested that perhaps the Supreme Court's center had held, but "it had bled a lot." That loss of blood was not merely a matter of politics, liberal or conservative. The wound to the center was a wound to the most vital organ of the Court—to its ability to reach collective judgment, to deliberate on the nation's fundamental values and beliefs, and to translate those values and beliefs into a coherent rule of law. There are some disagreements so deep that the disputants share no moral ground and have no mutually recognized obligations to meet. Neither side can shake the other's convictions, and both are reduced to exchanging accusations of hypocrisy and bad faith.[36] The capital cases were driving the Court toward this polarized nightmare. And as the 1986 Term opened, the toughest challenges were yet to come.

A Cop Killer's Case

From the moment the Court reauthorized capital punishment in *Gregg* v. *Georgia*, it became all but inevitable that the NAACP's Legal Defense Fund and other abolitionists would construct a new test case challenging the death penalty on grounds of racial discrimination. Years earlier, in 1968, the Justices had sidestepped the race issue when they declined to review then Judge Blackmun's appellate decision in *Maxwell* v. *Bishop* rejecting the LDF's claim of racial bias in capital sentencing for rape. Soon thereafter, the abolitionist victory in *Furman* had made further litigation unnecessary. After the Court's turnabout in *Gregg*, however, the LDF urgently revived the race-based legal arguments that originally had inspired its anti–death penalty campaign.

Although *Gregg* marked a terrible setback for abolitionists, the Stewart-Powell-Stevens plurality opinion seemed to leave room for a renewed claim that racism and the death penalty were inextricably and unconstitutionally linked. From the abolitionists' perspective, the crucial aspect of the *Gregg* plurality was its repeated emphasis on the constitutional requirement that capital sentencing be "rational" and "reliable." Justices Stewart, Powell, and Stevens approved the guided discretion statutes at issue in *Gregg* because they assumed that the guidance provided by statutorily enumerated "aggravating" and "mitigating" circumstances would eliminate irrational and pernicious factors (including race) from capital sentencing. For the abolitionists, that theoretical assumption left wide open the possibility of showing the Court that, as the system really worked, the post-*Furman* death statutes, despite their new procedural safeguards, were as irrational and arbitrary (and racially skewed) as the statutes *Furman* had condemned.

To this end, the abolitionist godfather Anthony Amsterdam launched a new long-term LDF program to develop an all-encompassing race discrimination challenge based on increasingly sophisticated statistical studies of the post-*Furman* death statutes.[1] Obtaining generous foundation grants to underwrite the work of independent but liberal-minded legal academics, the LDF spawned a virtual cottage industry of race discrimination analyses. The touchstone for this effort was *Maxwell v. Bishop* itself, in which (on the court of appeals) Justice Blackmun had found the Wolfgang rape study "interesting and provocative" but insufficiently comprehensive to serve as adequate proof of racial discrimination. Amsterdam and the LDF were determined not to repeat that failure—which meant finding a jurisdiction with data complete enough to defy any claim of statistical insignificance, then subjecting those data to state-of-the-art mathematics.

What emerged as the lead study among the LDF projects focused on Georgia. There, Iowa Law School professor David Baldus oversaw the most exhaustive statistical analysis of the death penalty ever attempted, a study of more than 2,400 criminal homicide cases from 1973 to 1980.* Using questionnaires as long as 120 pages, Baldus's investigators pored through police reports, parole board records, and prison files, extracting and categorizing over 400 aspects of each case—from the exact nature of the crime to the strength of the evidence at trial and the background of the defendant. The idea was to take account of virtually every variable that might have influenced which homicide defendants ultimately received death sentences and, using rigorous mathematical analysis, to isolate exactly what role the illicit factor of race played in Georgia's capital decision-making process.[2]

Upon its completion in mid-1982, the Baldus study showed a dramatic disparity in the treatment of whites and blacks in Georgia's death penalty process but *not* the disparity one might have guessed. The analysis indicated (in contrast to the rape studies of the 1960s) that the post-*Furman* Georgia system generally did not result in a disproportionate

---

*Much of Baldus's work (undertaken with two colleagues, Charles Woodworth and Charles Pulaski) was funded by a grant from the Edna McConnell Clark Foundation. Although Baldus worked independently from the LDF, and enjoyed complete discretion to publish his results even if unfavorable to the LDF's interests, the LDF played a crucial role in obtaining and administering this grant money. Such a relationship does not impugn the integrity of Baldus's work, but it does indicate the degree to which his and most like studies were the work of academics with close ties to the abolitionist community and were undertaken, at least in part, with the abolitionist litigation campaign in mind.

number of black *defendants* receiving the death penalty. When adjusted for legitimate nonracial variables, the numbers showed essentially no link between the race of a homicide defendant and his chances for receiving a death sentence.

At the same time, the study did reveal a strong correlation between the race of the homicide *victim* and the prospect of a defendant being executed. Murderers—black or white—who killed whites were substantially more likely to receive the death penalty than those who killed blacks. In terms of raw numbers, killers of whites were eleven times more likely to receive death sentences than killers of blacks.[3] Baldus then adjusted these raw numbers to control for as many as 230 legitimate variables that might account for this discrepancy. Using what he considered his best statistical model, Baldus still found that killers of white people were 4.3 times more likely to receive the death penalty than killers of blacks.[4]

Looking at the numbers another way, Baldus found that, compared with other factors, the victim's race had a remarkably large influence on the final sentencing decision in homicide cases. Specifically, the fact that a murder victim was white had a greater influence on whether the defendant received a death sentence than did factors such as the defendant's prior history of committing violent crimes, the fact that the victim was a police officer, the fact that the victim pleaded for his life, or was handicapped, or that the killing took place during an armed robbery. Indeed, compared with thirty-nine factors deemed especially relevant to the capital sentencing process, race of the victim ranked twelfth in importance in determining whether a death sentence would result, surpassed only by such highly aggravating factors as the involvement of torture, rape, multiple murder, or the killing of a child.

The study further revealed that the victim's race played an especially powerful role in "mid-range" cases—those that fell between low-aggravation homicides (such as barroom brawls or quarrels between friends) and high-aggravation cases (such as multiple murders or murders involving rape or torture). In low-aggravation cases, virtually no defendants received the death penalty, regardless of the victim's race. High-aggravation cases presented the reverse picture. These cases were so heinous that the vast majority of defendants received death sentences no matter what the victim's race. In the intermediate cases, however—those where the death penalty was reasonably justifiable but not compelled—the race of the victim had a stunning impact on the ultimate sentence. For these cases, in which prosecutors and juries wielded the most discretion, a defendant who killed a white person faced odds of receiving the death penalty as much as 30 percent higher than if the victim were black.

The abolitionists had a straightforward historical explanation for why (according to Baldus's numbers) Georgia systematically placed a higher value on the lives of whites than on those of blacks. In their view, Baldus's numbers simply reflected the deeply ingrained double standard of southern life—that any black harming a white must pay an especially harsh penalty, whereas crimes against blacks warranted little concern.*

In the LDF's view, these social attitudes, several hundred years in observance, though less pronounced and no longer a part of the formal law code, still flourished in the choices made by southern prosecutors and juries at every stage of a potentially capital case. When blacks were killed, prosecutors too often declined to indict the perpetrator for murder, or accepted plea bargains, or decided not to seek the death penalty after trial and conviction. When prosecutors did follow through in black victim cases, capital juries more frequently failed to convict or shied away from ordering executions. At the end of the day, roughly 1 defendant in 100 received a death sentence when the victim was black. By contrast, 22 percent of black defendants in white victim homicides received the death penalty. In the South, in other words, capital punishment came with a "white victims only" sign.

The disparity between white victim and black victim cases was further exacerbated, LDF attorneys believed, by the influence of politics on prosecutorial decisions. As elected officials, often ambitious for higher office and possessing enormous discretion over the charging and sentencing process, local prosecutors pursued most vigorously the cases that their mainly white, middle-class constituents viewed as important. Capital cases were the headline grabbers, the ones in which an outraged public demanded results, the ones that could make or break careers. But across the South, the sad truth was—and Baldus's study only confirmed the daily experience of abolitionist lawyers—such political inspiration to seek and obtain a death sentence hardly ever arose unless the dead folks were white.

---

*This racial double standard appeared vividly in [Gunnar Myrdal's] pathbreaking study of black life in the South in which he found that any white could "strike or beat a Negro, steal or destroy his property, cheat him in a transaction and even take his life without much fear of legal reprisal." *An American Dilemma: The Negro Problem and American Democracy* (New York: Harper & Row, 1944), p. 65.

From the abolitionist perspective, the results of Baldus's study provided strong but by no means ideal evidence for challenging the death penalty. The numbers gave no support to what would have been the most straightforward case of race discrimination: that Georgia's prosecutors and juries were disproportionately singling out black *defendants* for the death penalty. As the LDF recognized, there was something awkward about arguing on behalf of convicted murderers (black or white) that their death sentences should be thrown out merely because of the coincidence that they had killed a white person instead of a black. Although the victim orientation of Baldus's findings did not diminish the role of racial bias in capital sentencing, it did mean that the LDF's clients, each one a convicted murderer, would be benefiting from a grievance that really belonged to the victim, or the victim's family, or the black community generally.[5]

Yet, awkward or not, the LDF was now in possession of the comprehensive study for which the whole abolitionist world had been waiting. Starting in mid-1982, LDF lawyers advanced discrimination claims and introduced the preliminary results of Baldus's study in as many Georgia cases as possible. They knew it was only a matter of time until a judge would decide to evaluate Baldus's work and return the explosive issue of race to center stage of the death penalty debate. On October 8, 1982, the inevitable process began. In the otherwise seemingly unremarkable case of Warren G. McCleskey, Federal District Judge Owen Forrester, a Reagan appointee and former drug enforcement prosecutor, ordered a full hearing on the LDF's Baldus-based discrimination claims, thereby anointing the last comprehensive challenge to the death penalty.

At approximately 2:15 P.M. on Saturday, May 13, 1978, four armed men, all black, robbed the Dixie Furniture Company, at 993 Marietta Street, N.W., in the midst of an unremarkable business district of Atlanta, Georgia. Having cased the store earlier in the day, three of the men— David Burney, Bernard Dupree, and Ben Wright, Jr.—lowered stocking masks over their faces, rounded up several store employees, and moved into Dixie's back offices in search of money.

The fourth man, Warren McCleskey, ran into the front of the store and disarmed Dixie's private security guard. McCleskey ordered the guard, his brother, and the two other Dixie employees who were present to lie on the floor, but not before one of them (Cassie Barnwell, a secretary and bookkeeper) managed to hit the store's silent alarm. Oblivious to the alarm, McCleskey continued to watch over the front while, in the rear, his cohorts forced the store manager to hand over an undetermined amount of cash (somewhere between $500 and $1,500).

At 2:20, Police Officer Frank R. Schlatt responded to the Dixie alarm. Officer Schlatt parked his squad car in front of the store and walked through the glass-paneled front door. Inside, a voice called out a warning—"The cops."[6] The next few moments passed in silence as Schlatt, gun drawn, walked roughly forty feet up the store's center aisle. Then, two shots. The first bullet entered Schlatt's right eye and lodged in his brain. The second shot hit his chest, deflecting off his cigarette lighter. Thirty years old, white, married with a child, Schlatt died almost instantly.

The four robbers fled as they had come, three out the back, McCleskey through the front. Speeding off in McCleskey's car, they faced two huge and unanticipated problems. One of them had shot a cop, maybe killed him. And in the ensuing panic, Ben Wright, the ringleader, had left his black jacket in the store.[7]

Not surprisingly, the black jacket proved the criminals' undoing. Within two weeks, the focus of the police investigation had fallen on what they described as Ben Wright's gang of "professional robbers"—all ex-cons, recently released, three of whom had served time together for armed robbery at the state's high-security Reidsville prison.

Several hours before dawn on May 30, fifteen police officers converged on the home of McCleskey's sister, routed McCleskey out of bed, and arrested him for robbing the Red Dot produce market, one of a series of robberies that police attributed to the same suspects as in the Dixie Furniture case. On being questioned about the Dixie case, McCleskey denied having anything to do with the robbery and shooting. He said he just knew what he'd read in the papers.

On the same day, the Atlanta police arrested David Burney. According to the police report, Burney initially denied any involvement in the Dixie robbery-murder but confessed after detectives promised that they would protect Burney and his family against what Burney feared would be reprisals by Ben Wright.

The next day Burney gave a formal written statement, revealing details of the Dixie holdup and naming his three accomplices. He also volunteered an answer to the all-important question of who had shot Officer Schlatt.

> Question: When the vehicle was driven away from the scene, was
> there any conversation about the shooting?
> Answer: Yes.
> Question: Can you tell us what was said and by whom?
> Answer: Warren [McCleskey] said that he had shot him [Schlatt]
> twice but did not know if he had killed him or not.

That same day, McCleskey decided to give the police a new statement. This time, he admitted being part of the Dixie Furniture robbery but denied shooting Schlatt. According to McCleskey, when Schlatt's police car pulled up to the store, he had hidden under a sofa ten feet from the front door. Schlatt had walked past him, only to be shot by someone farther up the store aisle. McCleskey claimed not to know who the triggerman was. During the getaway, no one had talked about it, he said.

The police apparently believed Burney's version of events and immediately issued statements to the press identifying McCleskey as Schlatt's killer. In the meantime, Bernard Dupree turned himself in, while Ben Wright—described by police as "mean and dangerous"—became the target of a nationwide FBI manhunt.

McCleskey's preliminary hearing (at which a judge evaluates whether the state has probable cause to indict the defendant for the crimes charged) was set for a week later, June 7. McCleskey was leery of the public defender's office, and his sister, Betty Myers, managed to retain a lawyer. For the set price of $2,500, Myers hired John Turner, a solo practitioner concentrating mainly on criminal matters who had several years' experience as a federal prosecutor in Atlanta. The fee was paltry for virtually any case, much less one involving a highly publicized cop killing and the possibility of a death sentence, but it was all Myers could afford.

At the preliminary hearing, it became apparent what a godsend Burney's and McCleskey's confessions were for the prosecutor. None of the Dixie store employees could positively identify McCleskey; indeed, some of their descriptions from the day of the robbery did not resemble him. Moreover, none of the employees had seen who shot Schlatt or even knew with any degree of certainty where in the store each of the robbers was at the time of the shooting. All the potential eyewitnesses had been facedown on the floor, with the ones at the back bound and blindfolded as well. The prosecution also had not recovered a murder weapon.

Still, the confessions were certainly sufficient to sustain robbery and murder charges against McCleskey and, accordingly, he was placed in the solitary confinement wing of the Atlanta jail to ponder whether he wanted to plead guilty or go to trial.* Bernard Dupree—who had turned himself in to the police but still denied any wrongdoing—occupied the cell directly above McCleskey's. They chatted through heating vents and connecting pipes.

The prosecutor, Russell Parker, an assistant district attorney with several years' experience, started putting together his theory of the case. He concluded on the basis of ballistic evidence that the murder weapon was a .38-caliber Rossi revolver, silver with ivory handles, that McCleskey and Wright had stolen in the Red Dot produce market robbery (for which McCleskey originally had been arrested).

Between Wright and McCleskey, McCleskey seemed the better candidate for the triggerman—and, hence, the death penalty. Burney's statement named McCleskey directly and also described McCleskey as carrying a silver revolver while Wright carried a shotgun. Cassie Barnwell claimed to have seen a silver gun in the hand of the robber at the front of the store—the role McCleskey played by his own admission. Being up front also put McCleskey in closest proximity to the shooting. On the other side, Wright's ex-con girlfriend, Mary Jenkins, told the police that Wright carried a silver .38 whereas McCleskey generally used a .45. Also, McCleskey said that he had used a black-handled .22 during the Dixie holdup.

At McCleskey's arraignment on July 20, the judge set trial for September 25. At this point, McCleskey's lawyer had yet to interview any potential witnesses. In Turner's view, the D.A. had "almost an air tight case."[8] Although he informed McCleskey that no eyewitnesses had yet identified him as one of the robbers, Turner consistently advised his client to plead guilty rather than risk the death penalty, which the D.A. intended to seek assuming the case went to trial.

Despite his confession, McCleskey wanted to risk a trial. He intended to put forward an alibi defense—that he had spent the afternoon of May 13 at his sister's house playing cards. McCleskey hoped to suppress or at least discredit his confession by claiming that the police had coerced

---

*Under what is known as the felony-murder rule, McCleskey could be tried for murder even if he did not personally shoot Officer Schlatt. In the eyes of the law, every coconspirator to a felony is criminally liable for a death that foreseeably results from the commission of that crime.

him into making up lies. And, thus, while Turner and Parker discussed the possibility of Parker accepting a guilty plea in exchange for a sentence of life imprisonment, no deal was ever offered and McCleskey refused even to consider the idea.

On September 6, less than three weeks before the scheduled trial, Turner got the defense rolling by filing a series of essentially boilerplate motions. He asked for copies of all statements McCleskey might have made in connection with the crime. Then, citing *Miranda* v. *Arizona* and *Escobedo* v. *Illinois*, he asked the court to "suppress any and all evidence obtained as a result of defendant's illegal interrogation and intimidation by police." Turner also sought on several grounds to preclude the prosecution from asking for the death penalty.

On September 20, Parker presented Turner with a list of an astonishing ninety-six potential witnesses for trial—including twenty-three investigating officers—a clear attempt to swamp the defense just before the trial (which was moved to October 8). Regardless, Turner was doing a fine job of self-sabotage. He still had not interviewed a single witness or hired an investigator to conduct interviews for him.[9] The sum and substance of Turner's defense efforts at this stage consisted of a few conversations with McCleskey and a few more with Parker to get a sense of the prosecution's case.

Turner finally looked at Parker's prosecution file—redacted police reports, witness statements, and the like—on October 5, the Friday before the Monday of trial. (By way of comparison, counsel for Burney and Dupree, whose trials were not scheduled for another month, had looked at the file weeks earlier.) Turner spent the better part of the day taking notes on the file, which Parker would not let him copy.

About midnight Turner went to the jail and asked McCleskey to think again about a guilty plea. McCleskey said that his mind was made up, but Turner asked him to mull it over until Sunday, when he would be back.

If Turner was counting on a last-minute change of heart, McCleskey disappointed him. As a result, Monday came and trial started and John Turner had exerted virtually no energy trying to develop testimony that might cast doubt on the prosecutor's case or make more difficult his burden of proving McCleskey guilty beyond a reasonable doubt: no competing ballistics expert, no effort to discredit the prosecution's theory about where McCleskey had obtained the missing gun, no attempt to determine from Dixie employees if one of the robbers at the back of the store might have walked up to the front, no guarding against surprise witnesses. Turner's attitude seemed to be, Why bother? After all, McCleskey's story was that he'd spent the afternoon at his sister's house and, later, playing cards. Anything having to do with the actual robbery-murder was, in his words, "peripheral to the main issue."[10]

Jury selection took up the better part of the first day. With Officer Schlatt's widow and a large contingent in attendance, Judge Sam Mackenzie presided as Parker "Witherspooned" the prospective jurors, a process by which the prosecution attempts to remove opponents of the death penalty from the jury panel. As discussed earlier, in the 1968 case *Witherspoon v. Illinois*, the Supreme Court had ruled that a defendant's Sixth Amendment right to an impartial jury precludes states from excluding persons with "conscientious scruples" against the death penalty. Prosecutors, however, were still allowed to disqualify jurors so adamantly opposed to capital punishment that they would be unable to perform their duty to apply the law to the facts of the case before them. Over Turner's objection, Parker succeeded in excusing several jurors in this fashion.

Both lawyers also excused jurors using their peremptory challenges. Of the forty-four prospective jurors considered for the McCleskey trial (excluding alternates), nine were black. Parker used nine peremptory challenges, seven to strike blacks from the panel. In the end, one black survived to join eleven whites on a jury of seven men and five women.

Putting on his case, Parker had a few surprises for Turner and McCleskey. Although at the preliminary hearing the D.A. had been unable to produce an eyewitness identifying McCleskey as one of the robbers, he now had two. At the time of the robbery, Cassie Barnwell, the secretary who had pulled the silent alarm, had been unable to give police even a description of the man who ran in the front of the store and held them at gunpoint. Later, she failed to pick McCleskey out of a police photo spread. The prosecution did not even bother to have Barnwell testify at McCleskey's preliminary hearing. Nonetheless, on the day of trial, Parker brought Barnwell to the courthouse. She walked into the courtroom just before the proceedings, observed three men sitting in the jury box flanked by two sheriff's deputies, and in a sudden epiphany realized she was "positive" one of them, Warren McCleskey, was the man from the Dixie robbery.

Mamie Thomas, Dixie's cashier, did an even more astonishing about-face. At the scene of the crime, she had told police that the robber at the front of the store had "bumps on his face" and a scar on the left side—a description ill fitting the smooth-skinned McCleskey. Like Barnwell, Thomas had failed to identify McCleskey from a photo spread. At the preliminary hearing, she had stood no more than five feet from McCleskey yet testified that she did not recognize anyone from the day of the robbery. Then at trial Thomas told the jury that she had lied at the preliminary hearing—that she was afraid to get involved—but she never forgot a face and was "one hundred percent sure" McCleskey had robbed her store.

Although Turner worked hard on cross-examination to discredit these witnesses, their words still corroborated the prosecution's most important evidence: McCleskey's now repudiated confession, which Parker went over in exquisite detail. No juror could have missed how closely it tracked the known facts about the crime.

The weaker part of Parker's case, by far, was his evidence that McCleskey was the triggerman. Mary Jenkins had changed her story and now testified that McCleskey had carried a silver .38 caliber revolver on the day of the robbery. But Turner countered pretty effectively, eliciting on cross-examination that Jenkins previously had told the police that Wright carried a .38 and McCleskey a .45.

The prosecution's star witness on the issue of who actually killed Schlatt was Ben Wright himself. It had taken the police most of the summer to catch up with Wright, who was finally apprehended in Arkansas in connection with yet another armed robbery. On the way back to Atlanta, Wright successfully negotiated a deal: He'd give up McCleskey in exchange for a twenty-year sentence on charges stemming from the Dixie robbery-murder.

On the stand, Wright was, if nothing else, unabashed. In a fairly standard tactic when dealing with the testimony of a witness with a criminal record, the prosecution started out by bringing to light Wright's prior criminal convictions (doing this to your own witness steals some of the other side's thunder). In Wright's case, these impeaching admissions filled three transcript pages and included jail sentences for robbery and theft offenses in 1957, 1960, 1963, 1966, and 1972, all the more remarkable given that Wright spent almost all the intervening periods in jail.

Still, Wright held up his end of the bargain. He walked through the planning and execution of the Dixie robbery. He explained how he and McCleskey had obtained the silver .38 caliber Rossi revolver in the holdup of the Red Dot produce market. He put that gun in McCleskey's hands on the day Schlatt was killed. And he described the conversation in the getaway car as the four accomplices contemplated a job gone awry:

> [McCleskey] said the police slipped up on him before he know it, said he slipped up on him, he didn't have no siren on . . . and he saw the police car pull up and said he went behind a sofa and crawled through to the front and when the police came in the door he had his gun out. I said, "You couldn't disarm the man or nothing like that?" He said "No." I said, "What did you do?" He said, "I told the man to freeze." I told him to freeze and the man turned around, and he said he shot him twice, and I don't know, I just—I punched him and grabbed him or something, you know, through an emotional thing and told him, said, "Man, you done fucked up, you done killed the police." He said, "Be cool, it's all right, ain't nobody going to say nothing about it."

It was certainly a credible account, but the witness became less so on cross-examination. Wright—the only other possible triggerman—admitted having a penchant for .38 caliber revolvers. More important, he displayed an attitude toward the truth that must have had Parker squirming.

Turner:	How many robberies have you committed that you haven't been charged with here in, say, Atlanta in the past year?
Wright:	I have committed two.
Parker:	Just two in the last year?
Wright:	I have committed the Red Dot and this place here.
Turner:	What about Tidwell's Furniture?
Wright:	Have I been identified in that?
Turner:	Did you rob it?
Wright:	Did anyone say I robbed it?
Turner:	I am asking you.
Wright:	No, sir, I didn't rob it. I am always innocent until proven guilty or being convicted of the crime.
Turner:	So until someone identifies you, you are innocent?
Wright:	That is the way the criminals operate.
Turner:	Are you a criminal?
Wright:	Yes sir.
	. . .

Turner: Let me ask you one last question. Would you lie to keep
            from getting convicted of murder in this case?
Wright: Every person will lie to keep from getting convicted.
Turner: Would you personally?
Wright: Me?
Turner: Yes, sir.
Wright: Yes, sir, I would.

Turner's defense consisted almost entirely of putting McCleskey on the stand to disavow his confession and put forward his alibi. Thirty years old, divorced, the father of a twelve-year-old daughter, McCleskey admitted to spending more than seven years—most of his adult life—in prison for a series of armed robberies committed in 1970.

Then he told the jury about how he and Ben Wright had met in Reidsville prison, becoming buddies after McCleskey's release. On the day in question, May 13, McCleskey claimed that he had lent Wright his car and that Wright had dropped him off at his sister's house. In the afternoon, he had borrowed his sister's car and gone to play cards, a betting game called skin. The first he heard about the Dixie robbery was when Wright returned his car, "about four o'clock or a little after."

McCleskey blamed his confession on police intimidation. The detectives had told him they had enough to "burn" him. Witnesses had seen his car at the scene and said they'd seen him there too. When McCleskey denied it, he said the police threatened to throw him out of a moving car—as a cop had done to a suspect in a highly publicized recent case. Later they had shown him Burney's confession.

After that, McCleskey decided he better cooperate. "I couldn't stand a chance of trying to fight it because, you know, I have been convicted once before for armed robbery . . . plus I knew I was on parole, and I didn't have a very good alibi." So he and the detectives "pitched in" and helped make the statement up; most of it, he insisted, was "false."

"Were you at the Dixie Furniture Store that day?" Turner asked.

"No," McCleskey insisted.

"Did you shoot anyone?"

"No, I didn't."

"Is everything you have said the truth?"

"Positive."

McCleskey's alibi was inherently suspect. If he was playing cards, why didn't he produce someone else from the game to corroborate his story?

On cross-examination, matters only got worse. Parker started asking McCleskey about conversations in jail where he allegedly admitted shooting Schlatt. Next, in an exchange that would later cause enormous controversy, Turner objected on the ground that Parker seemed to be referring to some kind of statement made by McCleskey and that all such statements should have been turned over to the defense. Responding, Judge Mackenzie said that Parker "has a statement that was furnished to the Court but it doesn't help your client" and that Turner was not entitled to it because it was not "exculpatory" (suggestive of innocence).*

When Turner continued to press his point, Judge Mackenzie told him that "this is not a statement of the defendant" and that "he [didn't] know that we are talking about any written statement." If Turner had a problem with the ruling, he could "use it in the appellate courts."

It quickly became apparent that Parker was setting McCleskey up for a knockout blow. He kept asking about jailhouse conversations: whether McCleskey had talked to Dupree or to the man in the adjoining cell about fabricating an alibi, about arranging to hurt Mary Jenkins so that she couldn't testify, and, most damning, about how he wouldn't have cared if a dozen cops had come through Dixie's front door, he would have shot his way out. McCleskey explained or denied it all, but it was obvious the prosecutor was holding some kind of trump card.

That trump card turned out to be a jailhouse informant, a lifelong burglar and forger named Offie Evans, whom McCleskey said he'd never heard of or talked to, but whom the prosecutor now called to the stand to wreak havoc with McCleskey's already meager defense. According to Evans, he had been placed in the cell next to McCleskey's after having been picked up for walking away from a halfway house. The two of them got to talking, Evans insinuating himself into McCleskey's confidence, telling McCleskey how "he knowed Ben [Wright] real good," until McCleskey started revealing details from the Dixie Furniture robbery.

Evans's testimony explained away the discrepancies in Mamie Thomas's eyewitness identification. By Evans's account, McCleskey had told him that Mary Jenkins (Wright's girlfriend) had made up his face to appear bumpy and scarred—exactly as Thomas had described it on the day of the robbery.

---

*Under the Supreme Court case *Brady* v. *Maryland*, 373 U.S. 83 (1963), the prosecution is constitutionally required to turn over exculpatory evidence to the defense.

Even more important, Evans corroborated Ben Wright's testimony that McCleskey was the one who shot Schlatt. And Evans gave the appearance of being a far more neutral witness. He said the prosecutor hadn't promised him anything for testifying. He was just telling it like it happened: McCleskey had told him that it was a choice between shooting the cop or getting caught. So McCleskey shot and said, "It would have been the same thing if it had been a dozen of them."

The jury took only two hours to return a guilty verdict.

The same jury then convened again to consider whether to sentence McCleskey to death. Under Georgia law (similar to that of a number of states), during this penalty phase the prosecutor must prove that the murder in question involved at least one of the statutorily enumerated aggravating circumstances distinguishing capital murder from ordinary murder. These circumstances included whether the murder involved torture, whether it was a murder for hire, or, as in McCleskey's case, whether the murder occurred during the course of another serious felony or the victim was a police officer.

At the same time, the law provided the defendant with the opportunity to present any mitigating evidence to suggest that the jury should not impose the death penalty. Such testimony often took the form of a personal statement by the defendant; favorable testimony about his character from family members, friends, or ministers; evidence that the defendant had been abused as a child, or was mentally or emotionally impaired. Assuming that the jury did find the presence of an aggravating circumstance qualifying the defendant for death, it still had absolute discretion to forgo that sentence if it so chose.

Parker argued passionately for the jurors to return a sentence of death. "Have you observed any repentance by Mr. McCleskey?" he asked them. "Has he exhibited to you any sorrow? . . . Have you seen any tears in his eyes for this act that he has done?"

Turner presented not an iota of the mitigating evidence that frequently proved decisive in averting a death sentence—nothing about McCleskey's illegitimate birth to skid row parents, his childhood spent selling bootleg liquor to patrons of neighborhood gambling houses to supplement the family income, or the many times he called the police to stop his stepfather from battering his mother. Turner later claimed he had asked McCleskey's sister about potential character witnesses; she denied he had done so. In any event, the jury went back to the jury room never having heard a word of testimony that McCleskey did not deserve death or for simple mercy, even from McCleskey himself.

Two hours later the jury sentenced Warren McCleskey to death, and Judge Mackenzie set an execution date a month hence, November 27, 1978.

John Turner looked at his client and asked whether he didn't wish now that he'd copped a plea.

Outside the courtroom, a tearful Mrs. Schlatt, surrounded by friends, told reporters that the death sentence "at least proved that the justice that [her husband] gave his life for really exists."

Equal Protection of the Laws

As Mrs. Schlatt appraised Warren McCleskey's sentence, no one could even have guessed that his case would generate two distinct landmark Supreme Court rulings, that the upholding of his death sentence would be compared with two of the most infamous decisions in American judicial history (*Dred Scott* and *Plessy* v. *Ferguson*), and that it would become for everyone with qualms about the death penalty a symbol not of justice but of its diametric opposite.

The case certainly started out as a fairly run-of-the-mill appeal, at least to the extent that the turmoil of capital litigation can ever be ordinary. John Turner stopped the execution clock by challenging his client's conviction on half a dozen grounds, all rejected by the Georgia Supreme Court in January 1980. McCleskey's case then moved to the U.S. Supreme Court, though without Turner, who (as is typical of the original defense counsel in capital cases) bowed out after the first round of appeal.

Instead, McCleskey's cert. petition was prepared by a volunteer named Robert Stroup, who decided to add a capital case to his normal practice of suing employers for age, sex, and race discrimination. It was common knowledge in Atlanta legal circles that death row inmates in Georgia often had difficulty finding competent counsel to handle their postconviction appeals, and the prospect of such work fit Stroup's conviction that lawyers had a duty to perform public service. Deciding that he should "put his money where his mouth was," Stroup called the Georgia Resource Center, the state's clearinghouse for death penalty legal defense, and the center suggested he take on McCleskey's case. Stroup agreed on the condition that someone from the LDF team in New York would act as a sounding board and double-check his legal work. Five years out of the University of Pennsylvania Law School, he was a novice at criminal law and knew better than to cut his teeth solo on a capital case.

The cert. petition Stroup prepared for McCleskey, filed in spring 1980, was essentially a formality. As noted earlier, neither capital defendants nor the Justices favored cert. grants on direct appellate review. Even in cases raising significant legal issues, the Justices almost always were inclined to deny cert. and push cases into habeas review, where a more complete factual and legal record could be developed before a federal district judge.

When, as expected, the Court denied cert. in McCleskey's direct appeal, Stroup moved the case to the next stop on the well-worn track of capital litigation: state habeas review. Although state judges generally granted habeas relief only in cases of irrefutable legal error (and sometimes not even then), the rules of federal habeas—in which a capital defendant stood a much greater chance of obtaining relief—required that a defendant first "exhaust" all his claims in state court. Accordingly, Stroup combed the record of McCleskey's trial for any ruling or occurrence that might reasonably form the basis of a legal challenge.

In all, Stroup alleged twenty-one grounds for vacating his client's conviction or sentence. Many of these were specific to McCleskey's trial—such as challenges to the highly suggestive pretrial jury box lineup, to the testimony of the jailhouse informant Offie Evans, to the prosecutor's closing argument, and to the competence of Turner's representation. Other claims put forth more broad-based legal theories, which the LDF was grooming for ultimate decision by the Supreme Court. These included generalized claims that Georgia's system of capital punishment was arbitrary and discriminatory as well as a comprehensive challenge to the way capital juries were chosen.

At a hearing before a state judge in January 1981, Stroup tried to develop what seemed to be his strongest claims. Grilling John Turner at length, Stroup effectively showed what a desultory job he'd done as defense counsel. He also got Evans to admit, after a lot of evasion, that in exchange for his testimony one of the detectives on the McCleskey case had "agreed to speak a word for me" with federal officials about a federal escape charge that had been hanging over his head at the time. (The charge was later dismissed.) This admission was potentially critical because the Supreme Court had ruled several times that due process required prosecutors to disclose any deals made with witnesses.

The state habeas judge, however, was unimpressed. He found Turner's representation adequate to meet the constitutional minimum and credited the prosecutor's categorical denial that he had struck a deal with Evans. With little comment, the judge denied these and McCleskey's nineteen other claims. After exhausting his state appeals, Stroup followed up with another essentially pro forma cert. petition to the Supreme Court (denied in due course), then sought habeas relief in federal district court.

Despite Stroup's strong belief that McCleskey's trial had been severely flawed, Federal Judge Owen Forrester didn't see anything in McCleskey's papers to warrant further investigation, much less the issuance of a habeas writ. On June 10, 1982, he issued an order denying McCleskey habeas relief without even holding a hearing.

Just at this moment, an accident of good timing intervened: the preliminary results of the Baldus study became available. For the LDF strategists in New York, this development raised the difficult question of whether their new trump card should be saved for a single carefully selected case (one with as favorable facts as a capital case could provide) or introduced in every case where a defendant's life might be saved. As in the past, the LDF decided to forgo orchestrating an especially favorable test case.

That decision was crucial for McCleskey, for it meant submitting the Baldus study in his case despite some obvious disadvantages. As a matter of pure numbers, McCleskey's case came out of Fulton County, an urban area where the statistics on discrimination were less strong than in Georgia's more rural counties. In addition, although cop killing technically ranked as a midrange crime (based on the number of death sentences that resulted from it), the allegedly cold-blooded ambush of Officer Schlatt (by a previously convicted armed robber no less) would undoubtedly taint McCleskey in the eyes of whatever judges presided over his case. Less significant but still relevant was the fact, unfortunate for a capital defendant claiming race discrimination, that the investigating detectives were black.

Still, the LDF pressed on. They filed a motion for reconsideration with Judge Forrester, including an affidavit describing the findings of Baldus's study. And Forrester—who'd been hearing about Baldus's research for some time—had his interest sufficiently piqued to grant Mc-Cleskey's motion and order a hearing the following summer.

To handle McCleskey's discrimination claims, the LDF dispatched Jack Boger, an Amsterdam protégé who oversaw all the Georgia capital cases. Boger was a southerner himself, born and educated in North Carolina, who had abandoned pursuit of a divinity degree to try his hand at the more worldly calling of public interest law. After law school at the University of North Carolina, he'd moved north to learn his trade at the liberal democratic New York firm Paul, Weiss, Rifkind, Wharton & Garrison. Fortuitously, Boger landed a choice pro bono assignment handling a Texas death case in the immediate aftermath of *Gregg*. The experience hardened his opposition to capital punishment, and when a position opened in the LDF's capital defense project in 1976, he jumped at the chance. Soft-spoken, serious, and intensely thoughtful, Boger became over the next six years one of the most respected and important architects of the national campaign for abolition.

Before Judge Forrester, Boger and Baldus adopted an unusual strategy. First, Boger had Baldus testify about how his study had been conducted and what conclusions it had reached. In addition, they invited both the Georgia Attorney General's Office and Judge Forrester to suggest their own sets of variables that might explain the apparent race-of-the-victim discrimination in the Georgia homicide cases. Baldus would then subject their proposals to whatever sort of statistical analysis they preferred.

The state declined the offer and chose instead to attack Baldus's data collection techniques. Forrester, though, was not so reticent. Drawing on his experience as a drug enforcement prosecutor, the judge identified several factors he thought accounted for the racial disparities. But when Baldus ran the numbers to adjust for the variables Forrester identified, the race of the victim effect actually came out *larger* than the 4.3 "death odds multiplier" Baldus's best model had produced.

Having failed to come up with his own explanation for the racial factor in Georgia's sentencing data, Forrester nonetheless decided that Baldus's work proved nothing. In an opinion that contained (as commentators later showed)[1] numerous mischaracterizations and outright mathematical errors, Forrester disparaged Baldus's database as flawed, his statistical procedures as invalid, and the results produced, even if credited, as insufficient to support a discrimination or arbitrariness claim against Georgia's death penalty system.[2]

Oddly enough, Forrester granted McCleskey's habeas petition anyway. After taking a closer look at the case, he zeroed in on the prosecution's relationship with its informant Offie Evans. To Forrester (the ex-prosecutor), Evans's acknowledgment that one of the detectives had offered to "speak a word" for him on his escape charge was exactly the sort of deal the Constitution (as defined in the case *Giglio* v. *United States*)[3] required prosecutors to disclose. Such a quid pro quo, of testimony in exchange for possibly reduced charges, certainly could induce a witness to lie and, in turn, might affect a jury's appraisal of a witness's credibility. Given the importance of Evans's testimony to the issue of whether McCleskey had acted with malice (making him subject to conviction for capital murder), Forrester concluded that Evans's credibility had been crucial to the success of the prosecution's case. In the judge's view, if the jury had known about Evans's deal, there was no telling how its deliberations might have turned out. Accordingly, he felt compelled to grant McCleskey's *Giglio* claim and order a new trial.

Despite the emergence of this side issue, on appeal by the state, the Eleventh Circuit Court of Appeals selected *McCleskey* as the case in which it would tackle the LDF's statistical challenge. Because it included all the most active death penalty states except Texas, the Eleventh Circuit had become something of a junior supreme court for capital cases, an initial proving ground for abolitionist arguments big and small.

To ease their asphyxiating docket, the circuit had adopted a number of capital case shortcuts. One was to identify test cases raising broadly relevant issues for immediate consideration by all the circuit's judges sitting en banc (rather than, as usual, by three-judge panels whose rulings might then be subject to en banc review). Then, the judges would hear the year's specially chosen en banc cases during a marathon session in June, the annual "death Super Bowl," as clerks referred to it.

With dozens of similar cases backing up behind it, *McCleskey* was the main event for Super Bowl 1984. The final tally was a very emotional 9–3 to reject the LDF's Baldus-based claims.[4] The court of appeals's decision differed from Judge Forrester's in one important respect. Whereas Forrester disputed almost every aspect of Baldus's work, the circuit court majority purported to "assume the validity" of Baldus's statistics. They just didn't agree that the study, even if accepted, proved anything of legal significance.

As an initial matter, the majority ruled that for McCleskey and the LDF to prevail, they had to prove that Georgia *intentionally* discriminated in *his* case. According to the majority, Baldus's numbers (indeed, any statistics standing alone) were insufficient to show such focused intent. In the first place, the court ruled that statistical analysis was "incapable of measuring" the virtually infinite number of qualitative differences between individual cases; and, second, to the extent that Baldus's study proved anything, it revealed "an essentially rational system" that did not "contain the level of disparity . . . so great as to lead inevitably to a conclusion that the disparity results from [discriminatory] intent or motivation."[5]

For Boger and the LDF, this defeat was disappointing but not devastating.* With respect to the race discrimination claims, they expected that whatever the Eleventh Circuit decided, its opinion would eventually prove no more than a dress rehearsal for the Supreme Court's ultimate resolution of the issue. Much more immediately disappointing was the Eleventh Circuit's decision, by an 8–4 vote, to reverse Forrester's judgment that the undisclosed deal with Offie Evans warranted a new trial for McCleskey. Courts of appeals rarely second-guess district court judges on such fact-specific rulings; it is, after all, the district judge who actually listens to the relevant witnesses testify and is in the best position to assess what really happened. But the Eleventh Circuit didn't think a detective's promise to "speak a word" for a witness was enough of an explicit "deal" to trigger a constitutional problem and also found that any potential prejudice to McCleskey was "harmless error"—the verdict in his case would have been the same regardless.

With McCleskey's life now in much more immediate jeopardy, the LDF moved forward. In the fall, Boger, Stroup, and Co. petitioned the Court to review their discrimination claims and, for good measure, the Eleventh Circuit's handling of the *Giglio* issue. Months passed with no word from the Justices, a sure signal that, just as many cases were lined up at the Eleventh Circuit waiting for final resolution of *McCleskey*, so *McCleskey* had become a "hold" for a case already pending at the Court.

In fact the Justices had held *McCleskey* for another of the LDF's death penalty challenges, *Lockhardt v. McCree*, a variation on the Court's 1968

---

*Although Boger thought the LDF stood some chance for success in the Eleventh Circuit (many of the judges were moderate Carter appointees), clerks at the court describe *McCleskey* as an all but foregone conclusion. As at the Supreme Court, over time the deluge of capital cases had sharply divided the Eleventh Circuit judges. Indeed, their attitudes toward capital punishment had become so rigid that in those cases heard by the circuit's ordinary three-judge panels, a death row inmate's prospects depended almost entirely on which three judges happened to be assigned to the case. When the circuit sat en banc, it often wasn't hard to count votes, even long before argument, and no one could foresee seven of the twelve judges accepting novel race-based claims that threatened to eliminate the death penalty altogether.

ruling in *Witherspoon* v. *Illinois* that disqualifying "scrupled" jurors produced juries unconstitutionally prone to return death sentences. The LDF was now back in *Lockhardt* arguing that eliminating scrupled jurors also produced juries unconstitutionally biased toward *convicting* defendants at the earlier guilt phase of their trials.[6]

McCleskey's cert. petition was held for *Lockhardt* because (as in many other cases) his LDF lawyers had long ago inserted this exact jury selection issue into his original habeas petition. The LDF's hope was to repeat their *Witherspoon* victory, by which dozens of death row defendants had received a second chance at sentencing—except this time the beneficiaries of a favorable ruling (presumably including McCleskey) would get entirely new trials.

The Court, however, soon dashed this abolitionist fantasy. With Justice Rehnquist writing, a majority held that, even if the death qualification process did tend to skew juries toward convictions at the guilt stage, that bias did not violate the defendant's constitutional right to an impartial jury.[7]

In addition to depriving McCleskey of a *Lockhardt*-based reprieve, Rehnquist's opinion foreshadowed real problems for McCleskey's race-based claims. The tone of Rehnquist's majority was openly disdainful of the LDF's "illogical and impractical" arguments as "a glib nonchalance," and displayed an undercurrent of annoyance with the very idea of opposing the death penalty. Whereas in *Witherspoon* Justice Stewart had spoken almost admiringly of scrupled jurors who shudderingly recognized their "kinship" with the condemned, Rehnquist in *Lockhardt* practically characterized such jurors as undeserving of citizenship.[8] At one time, Rehnquist's harsh tone had been his alone. Now it belonged to a majority of Justices. Weary with the death cases and resentful of abolitionist tactics, in *Lockhardt* they were visibly hardening against any new substantive challenge to the death penalty.

This development was especially dangerous for *McCleskey* because in several crucial respects the LDF's claims in *Lockhardt* and *McCleskey* were strikingly similar. In *Lockhardt*, much as in *McCleskey*, the case was made up primarily of statistical evidence (showing the "conviction proneness" of death-qualified juries) designed to confirm what judges steeped in capital cases already knew from experience and intuition. In both cases, an LDF victory would grind executions to a halt.

Behind the scenes, to an extent Boger and McCleskey's other lawyers could not have known, the Justices' deliberations revealed a deep impatience with precisely these types of claims. In the secret conference on *Lockhardt,* a number of Justices expressed outright contempt toward both the LDF's methods and goals. "Think of the consequences," Chief Justice Burger said as he opened the session. He, for one, was not going to be "bossed around" by social scientists. Justice Powell, the usual swing vote, seemed increasingly to resent the LDF's incessant efforts to subvert the Court's decision in *Gregg.* In his view, the constitutionality of the death penalty was "settled," and he would countenance no backdoor arguments that would effectively nullify that decision. Even Justice Blackmun was leery of the scope of the LDF's challenges. He saw *Lockhardt* as "typical Tony Amsterdam"—an all-or-nothing abolitionist approach.

The Justices do not announce the breakdown of their cert. votes, but if they had, the LDF would have seen how much trouble it was in for on *McCleskey.* When McCleskey's cert. petition finally came up for consideration at the end of May (after a second brief hold for a case involving a technicality of habeas), the Justices split straight down the fault line of their capital jurisprudence. Although *McCleskey* presented the most significant and well-developed challenge to the death penalty since *Gregg,* and although every death penalty state in the South was waiting for a resolution of the LDF's discrimination claims, not one of the five conservative Justices at the Court, not even Powell, voted to hear the case.

On the contrary, in a memo to the Conference, Powell strongly urged his colleagues to deny cert.[9] To Powell, the Baldus study actually confirmed his hopeful prognosis from *Gregg* that guided jury discretion would bring rationality to the capital sentencing process. After all, Powell noted, Baldus's own numbers showed that Georgia juries tended to return death sentences in highly aggravated cases while generally declining to do so in less aggravated ones. This pattern suggested that juries now engaged in "precisely the kind of careful balancing of individual factors that the Court required in *Gregg.*" Powell didn't find race-of-the-victim discrimination particularly troubling. If race discrimination was infecting the state's capital sentencing, he concluded, "one would expect . . . the Baldus study would show a bias based on the *defendant's* race." Yet, the "study suggests *no* such effect."[10]

For the conservative Justices, the most important consideration was their view that the Eleventh Circuit had reached the right result in rejecting the LDF's claims. They could see no possible advantage and some considerable disadvantages in granting cert., even if merely to ratify the Eleventh Circuit's judgment. The LDF's discrimination claims probed some of the Court's most tender spots. Not only did *McCleskey* call on the Justices to make a major pronouncement on the always emotionally charged issue of race, it required them to make that pronouncement according to their assessment of a complex statistical study whose intricacies, in truth, lay far outside their ken.

Judge Forrester had tackled the Baldus study head-on only to embarrass himself as an amateur statistician. The Eleventh Circuit judges, eyes glazing at concepts such as multicollinearity, had finessed any real evaluation of the study by "assuming" its validity. Then they had rendered the statistics pointless by setting the evidentiary standard for proving discrimination in the death penalty so high that no statistical undertaking could reach it.

The Justices were in no better position. Justice Powell frankly admitted that his "understanding of statistical analysis . . . range[d] from limited to zero." With the exception of Justice Blackmun, the other Justices were equally innumerate.

The Justices' general ignorance of social scientific methods, moreover, was reinforced by a sharp skepticism, especially among the conservatives. For forty years, conservative commentators had attacked *Brown* v. *Board of Education* for its reliance (in a footnote) on several primitive social scientific studies that sought to refute the idea of separate but equal by suggesting that segregation created feelings of personal inferiority in black children.[11] Over time, this specific criticism of *Brown*'s methodology blossomed into a more general suspicion that liberal lawyers and like-minded judges were using questionable soft science of hired-gun academics to advance their legal agenda.[12]

Although the Court had accepted social scientific evidence in proving certain kinds of claims (particularly those involving employment discrimination), this was an approval born of necessity, not knowledge or enthusiasm. Unsurprisingly, then, with an acceptable Eleventh Circuit decision in hand, the five conservatives wanted to leave the LDF's Baldus-based claims well enough alone.

Brennan, Marshall, Blackmun, and Stevens, however, forced *McCleskey* on the Court. Brennan's and Marshall's cert. grant votes were, of course, automatic. For Blackmun and Stevens, having watched for years as the LDF's race discrimination claims coalesced, the Court finally had no choice but to confront the relationship between race and death, whether the other Justices wanted to or not. Some issues are too important and too timely for the Court to duck. Their votes made the requisite four to grant cert. (though solely on the LDF's race-based claims, not the *Giglio* claim), and the Court set *McCleskey* for argument for the second week of October.

Two days after granting cert., in late May 1986, Chief Justice Burger privately informed the Reagan White House that he intended to resign at the end of the term and honor the president's request that he oversee the national celebration of the Constitution's bicentennial. Over the next three weeks, the administration quietly decided what to do about the vacancy. In a move that baseball fans would recognize as a double switch, the president's top advisers, most notably Attorney General Edwin Meese and Chief of Staff Donald Regan, recommended elevating Rehnquist to Chief Justice and filling Rehnquist's seat with Antonin Scalia, a judge on the D.C. Circuit Court of Appeals and bright star of the conservative movement.[13]

These recommendations, which Reagan adopted and announced publicly on June 17, clearly reflected the administration's determination to use its judicial appointment power to create a dramatically more conservative federal court system and, if possible, to undo what they considered the Warren Court's unwarranted expansion of civil rights and civil liberties. In fourteen years on the Court, Rehnquist had compiled an impeccable record on the issues that mattered most to the administration: he opposed a constitutional right to abortion, voted against busing and affirmative action, aggressively sought to constrict the rights of criminal defendants, frequently supported governmental limits on free speech, and interpreted the First Amendment as permitting prayer in public schools.

Burger had been conservative too (though not as consistently as Rehnquist), but he was an intellectual lightweight whose pomposity, pettiness, and outright dissembling had alienated his colleagues, even his natural allies. Rehnquist, by contrast, was brainy, a quick thinker with a straightforward, easygoing manner that smoothed his sometimes jagged-edged written opinions. Rehnquist's brand of conservatism already had considerably influenced the Court's criminal law and states' rights decisions. The administration hoped that, as Chief, he could succeed where Burger had failed at carrying forward a broad constitutional counterrevolution.

From Reagan's perspective, Scalia shared many of Rehnquist's ideological virtues. Conservative even in his youth, he exceeded Rehnquist in sheer intellect and dynamism. The only child of an Italian immigrant father who taught Romance languages at Brooklyn College, Scalia graduated as the valedictorian of both his Jesuit high school and his class at Georgetown University. At Harvard Law School he continued to excel, serving as an editor of the *Harvard Law Review* and finishing at the top of the class of 1960. As one former school friend recalled, "People just competed for second, he was so superior academically."[14]

Scalia started off in private practice at a first-rate firm, but his true bent was more scholarly, and in 1967 he joined the law faculty first at the University of Virginia and later the University of Chicago. From there he moved into government. In 1971 he became counsel to the Office of Telecommunications Policy in the Nixon administration and earned sufficient notice that Gerald Ford named him to head the Justice Department's Office of Legal Counsel, the closest thing the government has to a legal think tank. With Jimmy Carter's election in 1976, Scalia moved into political exile at the American Enterprise Institute, a brain trust where many of the nation's best conservative minds were hammering out the contours of what would become the Reagan Revolution. When the political tide turned again in 1980, Scalia was named by Reagan to the D.C. Circuit.

Scalia was brash, didactic, outspoken in his desire to reshape and limit the role of the federal courts, and he promised to bring to the Court more pure cerebral firepower than any Justice since Douglas had gone into decline. In many ways he resembled Robert Bork, his chief rival for the nomination. But Scalia was younger and thinner than Bork, didn't smoke, hadn't fired Archibald Cox in the famous Saturday Night Massacre of Watergate days, and would be the first Italian-American Justice. These factors made him easier to confirm and a better choice for the long run.

Once Reagan announced his pair of nominees, civil rights organizations, women's groups, and other liberal interests rapidly mobilized an opposition, concentrating their fire on the potentially more vulnerable Rehnquist. These groups quickly focused on Rehnquist's attitude toward societal discrimination. As the hearings opened, the LDF came forward with a detailed assessment of Rehnquist's voting record as an Associate Justice. In a section that garnered particular attention, the LDF had tallied eighty-three cases where the Court had been less than unanimous in deciding a civil rights issue involving racial minorities, women, or the elderly. By the LDF's count, in those cases, Rehnquist had voted against the civil rights plaintiff eighty-two times. In further support of their case that Rehnquist was an "extremist," Sen. Edward Kennedy and others noted that he had issued solo dissents in a record fifty-four cases and had been the lone voice advocating such reactionary (and impolitic) positions as giving tax breaks to segregated private schools and allowing states to force pregnant teachers to take unpaid leave five months before their due dates, regardless of their ability to continue working.

The testimony politically most damaging to Rehnquist suggested a pattern of support for and even participation in specific incidents of racial and religious discrimination. Exhibit A was Rehnquist's clerk memo to Justice Jackson advising him in *Brown* to reaffirm *Plessy* v. *Ferguson*'s doctrine of separate but equal. Next in the indictment was Rehnquist's aggressive opposition to desegregating Phoenix's public schools and accommodations, captured pithily in his own declaration at the time that "we are no more dedicated to an 'integrated' society than we are to a 'segregated' society."

More troubling still, a widely admired trial lawyer from San Francisco, James Brosnahan, testified that during elections in the early 1960s Rehnquist had gone to polling places to intimidate black voters by challenging their credentials—a practice, later outlawed, that was a hallmark of hostility toward blacks. And, finally, it was revealed that the deed to Rehnquist's Vermont summer home, purchased in 1974, contained a covenant prohibiting its sale or rental "to any member of the Hebrew race."

In response, Rehnquist (as he had during his 1971 confirmation hearings) attributed the thinking behind his incriminating *Brown* memo to Justice Jackson, denied ever "harassing" or challenging black voters, and professed ignorance of the bigoted restriction in his house deed. But in the eyes of his critics and even some fence-sitters, these responses compounded Rehnquist's sins by calling into question his veracity. As was evident to scholars familiar with Justice Jackson's papers, Rehnquist's explanation of his *Brown* memo bordered on the incredible.[15] Brosnahan's charges of voter intimidation were corroborated by several other apparently reputable witnesses. And it was hard to believe that a sophisticated lawyer like Rehnquist would make a major real estate purchase without examining the deed.

Had it not been for the presence of a rare Republican majority in the Senate, Rehnquist's nomination might have fallen into genuine difficulty. As it was, Judiciary Committee Chairman Strom Thurmond, the 1948 Dixiecrat candidate for president who certainly had shared Rehnquist's contemporaneous aversion to the expansion of civil rights, shepherded the nomination through his committee by a 13–5 vote. Rehnquist was then confirmed by the full Senate, 65 in favor, 33 opposed, the largest number of no votes ever lodged against a Chief Justice.

The Democrats had no energy left over for Scalia. With a ready wit, he charmed his way around those few tough questions about judicial philosophy Democratic senators threw his way. As one commentator remarked, Scalia gave his name and rank but withheld his serial number. On the day after the Senate voted on Rehnquist, Scalia won confirmation 99–0. Together, they took their oaths on September 16, three weeks before the opening of the term, a month before oral argument in *McCleskey*.

While the confirmation hearings wore on, the LDF prepared its brief in what had now become the first major test for the nascent Rehnquist Court. From the outset, the LDF had (as Baldus put it) "gone for broke" in *McCleskey*. In other words, Boger and his colleagues had advanced arguments so broad that the only practical remedy the Court could impose would be to suspend capital punishment in Georgia—and by extension in all the other southern states where similar discrimination was coming to light. That didn't change now.

From the moment his became the test case for the LDF's discrimination claims, McCleskey's lawyers faced a crucial choice. They could focus on his case: a midrange case in which the evidence of discrimination was strongest, a cop killing in a county where not one of sixteen other cop killers had received a death sentence. Such a strategy would have highlighted the sentencing disparities at his level of aggravation, the unbridled prosecutorial discretion in his case, and possible remedies short of shutting down Georgia's capital system.

But agenda-driven litigation inevitably brings competing obligations. A tension develops between achieving victory for the individual client and advancing the broader goals of the interest group molding a test case. Some of the most powerful arguments to get Warren McCleskey off death row would at best secure only a modest gain for the larger cause of abolition.* And with the once-in-a-generation opportunity provided by the Baldus study, the LDF strategists, while not ignoring arguments about McCleskey's particular case, pressed hard for a knockout blow.

The LDF advanced two separate legal theories for attacking the death penalty using Baldus's statistics. First, they argued that the race-of-the-victim disparities showed Georgia's death penalty system to be shot through with precisely the arbitrariness and capriciousness that the Court had suggested in both *Furman* and *Gregg* would violate the Eighth Amendment. Second, the LDF claimed that the Baldus study, coupled with evidence of historic discrimination in Georgia's system of criminal justice, proved that the state's capital sentencing system discriminated on the basis of race in violation of the Fourteenth Amendment's equal protection clause.

The LDF acknowledged that under Supreme Court precedent for proving violations of the equal protection clause, they had to show *intentional* discrimination by the state.[16] Still, they argued that Baldus's statistics and their other evidence was sufficient to raise an inference of intentional discrimination—both generally and in McCleskey's case. More particularly, according to the LDF, the court of appeals had failed to give them appropriate credit for showing that the race-of-the-victim disparities in the Georgia system were most likely caused by race discrimination and not some legitimate factor. Then the appellate court had failed to demand that Georgia give a neutral explanation for those disparities.

As the LDF pointed out, this order of proof—with the plaintiff first raising an inference of discrimination, which then shifts the burden to the defendant to advance a neutral explanation rebutting that inference—was the Court-ordained standard procedure in employment and jury discrimination cases. Under that procedure, McCleskey should have prevailed.

Both the LDF's Eighth Amendment and equal protection clause theories were, in essence, arguments that Georgia's experiment with guided discretion in capital sentencing had failed completely or very nearly so. If the LDF prevailed on its Eighth Amendment arbitrariness theory,

---

*The idea of centering the argument on the particulars of McCleskey's case was rendered considerably less attractive by the fact that McCleskey (who already had served time for armed robbery) stood convicted of a crime—killing a cop—that most judges would find unusually disturbing. Thus, the LDF's litigation strategy was strongly affected by its initial decision to introduce the Baldus study in every Georgia case, including McCleskey's, rather than to wait for an especially favorable test case.

every post-*Furman* death sentence in Georgia would have to be voided and the state's whole system revamped or scrapped. If the Court adopted the equal protection argument instead, presumably Georgia could save some death sentences by showing that defendants in highly aggravated cases would have been sentenced to die regardless of any racial bias involved. (Courts sometimes used this sort of harmless error analysis in employment discrimination cases.)[17] Still, Georgia executions would be brought to a standstill, and, if the state wanted to continue the death penalty, it would have to undertake another major statutory reform, further channeling the discretion of prosecutors and juries.

As wide-ranging as the LDF's claims were, Boger still felt guardedly optimistic about McCleskey's chances. The prospect of Scalia replacing Burger, one conservative for another, didn't seem as if it would make much difference to the close political balance of the Court. *McCleskey*, Boger judged, would be won or lost with the Justices at the Court's center, and he pitched his brief with an eye toward White and Powell.

In his 1976 concurring opinion in *Gregg*, Justice White had all but challenged the LDF to develop and present "facts" to the Court to disprove his assumption that Georgia's new guided discretion statute had solved the problem of arbitrariness in capital sentencing. Boger reminded White of that challenge now, arguing in essence that he was back with the evidence White had demanded.[18] (Boger had even used a statistical method—multiple regression analysis—that White had specifically sanctioned in a Title VII discrimination case the previous term.)[19]

As for Powell, he was the author of the crucial opinion from the previous year that established the framework for proving race-based jury discrimination claims on which the LDF was relying most heavily.[20] Indeed, the LDF had tailored its arguments precisely to fit Powell's methodology for proving race discrimination by prosecutors in jury selection. Powell had only needed to remain consistent to see merit in McCleskey's claims.

In Boger's mind, O'Connor and even Scalia were possible votes. But this was a hopelessly Pollyannaish view. Outside the Court, the cause of abolitionism was increasingly hard-pressed. The Reagan administration, as part of its ongoing campaign to discredit the activist legacy of the Warren era, had singled out judicial efforts to undermine the death penalty (Brennan's especially) as an egregious example of judicial overreaching. Conservatives were mounting a massive election drive to unseat the Chief Justice of the California Supreme Court, Rose Bird, on account of her court's always calculated and sometimes unprincipled obstruction of the state's highly popular death penalty. To date, Bird and her liberal allies on the Court had succeeded in preventing every single scheduled execution in the state, but nobody gave her a ghost's chance of winning reelection.*

On the opposite coast, the depth and power of this backlash were not lost on Gov. Bob Martinez, who was seeking another term in the Florida statehouse largely on the basis of his aggressive support for the death penalty. Clerks at the Court joked that they could anticipate which Florida counties would be scheduling executions by studying Martinez's speaking schedule.

All this formed the background against which *McCleskey* would be decided, which is to say that it was a highly inauspicious time for the LDF come forward with broad abolitionist arguments. Of course, Boger and his associates were not privy to the Court's unfavorable deliberations in *Lockhart* or to the fact that the conservatives, including Powell, had voted to deny cert. in *McCleskey*. More generally, they did not seem to realize how deeply the steady drumbeat of last-minute stay applications—culminating in still-echoing recriminations over Willie Darden and Ronald Straight—had deafened the Court's potential swing Justices to the merits of their legal claims. They must at least have realized that the tide of the country was running fast against them and that they were asking a no longer friendly Court to buck that tide.

Still, Boger was counting on the Justices to faithfully apply their precedents from other fields of law and do what no court had ever done: strike down a criminal sentence explicitly on the ground of race discrimination. He was driving a speeding car around a blind corner—straight into a brick wall.

As argument day for *McCleskey* approached, Eben Moglen, a new clerk for Justice Marshall, started work on his bench memo. The level of apprehension about the case was already extremely high. It was the biggest case of the October sitting, perhaps of the whole term, a case that had been simmering at the Court for a year, now moving toward boil. Although absolutely convinced of the merits of the LDF's arguments,

*In fact, the conservatives succeeded in unseating not only Bird but two other liberal Justices.

Moglen wasn't optimistic. "A loss is very likely indeed," he wrote Marshall, "but I think if we choose our ground right, we have some running room, and we should be able to make a real fight of it."

For Moglen, the right ground was undoubtedly that of race discrimination (as opposed to the Eighth Amendment). Under the Court's precedents, to prove a case of race discrimination (subject to rebuttal by the defendant), a plaintiff had to show: (1) disparate impact on a group entitled to special judicial protection (such as blacks or women); (2) the existence of sufficient discretion in the system to make discrimination against this class possible; and (3) a history of past discrimination.

The Baldus study fulfilled the first requirement. As for the second, the Georgia death penalty system was among the most discretionary. And no one could deny Georgia's history of maintaining a dual system of justice for blacks and whites. At a minimum, then, Moglen considered it irrefutable that the Justices should send McCleskey's case back to the lower courts to see if Georgia could come up with a plausible and legitimate explanation for Baldus's results. Fantasizing, Moglen couldn't resist predicting: "I think the state will necessarily fail and the party will start."

Separate from the technical merits of McCleskey's equal protection claim, Moglen advised Marshall to make a stand on the race issue rather than some Eighth Amendment argument because it was the alternative "which frees us most to talk about what's really going on here." In Moglen's view, *McCleskey* at its core was about the ancient southern rule governing what happened to any black so-and-so who dared kill a white. The Republican reformers who had framed the Fourteenth Amendment's equal protection clause had sought to blunt that rule. And, although the nation had left their work unfinished after Reconstruction, in the generation since *Brown,* the Court had revived their mission. In the last thirty years, the Justices had fought racism in schools, at lunch counters, in the workplace, and at the local pool. Would they now turn their backs on that quest for racial justice because the stakes were not swimming pools but a man's life?

What Moglen called "the immense rhetorical and substantive advantage" of focusing on race, however, was not so keenly felt in the Chambers of those Justices who might conceivably join Brennan, Marshall, Blackmun, and Stevens as a fifth vote to annul Georgia's death statute. In the center of the Court, the once powerful consensus to sweep away the vestiges of slavery and Jim Crow had shattered on the diamond-hard issues of remedy, specifically busing and affirmative action. In the face of public resistance and personal uncertainty, the Justices had come to disagree sharply over what role the judiciary could and should play in seeking to right historic wrongs and in pursuing the goal of equality under law. In seeking to build on achievements of the past, the civil rights community still won occasional victories at the Court (especially in gender discrimination cases), but they were hard fought and close, and each one seemed to dissipate what had once been a shared vision for reshaping the racial balance of society.

Nowhere was this shift on the issue of race more evident than in Justice White's Chambers. As President Kennedy's deputy attorney general, White had sent 600 federal marshals to Alabama to protect young "freedom riders" seeking to break the stranglehold of segregation on interstate bus travel. As a Justice, White had steadily supported judicial efforts to desegregate schools. But he was a critic of affirmative action and, during the 1980s, parted company with the liberal Justices in a series of cases involving racial quotas in employment. Most relevant to *McCleskey*, he was persistently skeptical of claimants seeking to prove discrimination by showing unequal racial outcomes as opposed to more direct proof of intentional discrimination.

A year before the Court granted cert. in *McCleskey*, when the preliminary results of Baldus's study were appearing in some of the LDF's emergency stay applications, White had put one of his clerks to work on a memo evaluating a prospective LDF equal protection challenge to the death penalty. The Baldus study, that clerk recalls, "cut no ice" with White. The racial disparities in the Georgia system just weren't stark enough to rule out every alternative except racial animus; they weren't *Yick Wo* numbers—referring to an 1886 case (*Yick Wo* v. *Hopkins*)[21] in which the Court had inferred intentional discrimination from a statistical disparity when the San Francisco Board of Supervisors granted a license to not one of 200 Chinese laundry owners while routinely granting licenses to non-Chinese. The state of Georgia already had advanced a legitimate neutral reason for every death sentence since *Furman*: the defendant had committed a murder involving at least one specially enumerated aggravating circumstance. White wasn't going to overturn that neutral justification for each death sentence without a "smoking gun"—and Baldus's 4.3 death odds multiplier simply didn't suffice.

Powell had reached a similar conclusion, though from another angle. As his authorized biographer put it, Justice Powell represented "the best of the old [southern] order," but it was still the old order and it had its history and limits on matters of race.[22] Powell had opposed *Brown* at the time it was decided, calling the ruling "wrongly decided" and declaring that he was "not in favor of, and will never favor compulsory integration."* In time, however, he came to embrace both *Brown* and the general idea of full equality for blacks. On race issues, as on so many others, Powell could be found at the center of the Burger Court. He accepted the principle of school desegregation but fought hard against busing. He accepted the principle of affirmative action but abhorred quotas. He appreciated the Supreme Court's role in undoing a legacy of racial oppression but resented the supervision of southern institutions by an armada of federal judges, which he likened to a second (and scarcely more tolerable) Reconstruction. In private, Powell admitted to an infusion of "Confederate emotion," a deep visceral consternation with hypocritical Northerners who distanced themselves from the national problem of racism by demonizing the South.

All in all, Powell was a man extraordinarily reluctant to level charges of racism. In 1986, he had dissented vehemently from a majority opinion that allowed defendants in capital cases arising from interracial crimes to question prospective jurors about possible racial bias. The ruling did no more than recognize that some jurors *might* harbor latent racist feelings, but the exceptionally sensitive Powell bristled at this "singularly unwise and unjustified presumption."[23] Powell had been stung by the racist label himself, and he would attach it to others on only the most damning evidence.

Even more broadly, the LDF's arguments in *McCleskey* struck at one of Powell's most deeply cherished beliefs about himself and the culture that had nurtured him. In Powell's eyes, the South had achieved a dramatic reformation on matters of race. His memory of the past, even of his own views, was far more benign than the historical record reflected; and in his eyes the binding up of racial scars was significantly more complete.[24]

The Baldus study was, in essence, a statistical debunking of Powell's myth of southern progress. It announced that, despite a host of behavior-

---

*Jeffries, *Justice Powell*, p. 140, quoting Powell's private correspondence. Ironically, these were precisely the views Rehnquist felt compelled to deny in order to win confirmation. They never posed a hindrance for Powell, perhaps because he eventually embraced *Brown* with an enthusiasm and sincerity Rehnquist never exhibited.

modifying rules and regulations adopted in the generation since *Brown*, a latent and perhaps ineradicable racism still pervaded the South, insinuating itself into the rule of law as surely as in the dreaded Black Codes of bygone days. In *McCleskey* specifically, the LDF was calling into question the very idea that rationality could replace caprice and prejudice in the death penalty and, for that matter, in all of southern criminal law. That question, in turn, begged others: Had the South really changed? Could it ever? The best of the old order surely had to answer these questions yes. And Powell did. Seizing on the fact that Baldus had found little race-of-the-*defendant* discrimination and some rationality in Georgia's capital sentencing, Powell took a glass three-quarters empty and declared it almost full.

Leslie Gielow, the clerk handling *McCleskey* for Justice Powell, recognized the handwriting on the wall. She was convinced that McCleskey and the LDF should prevail. She even approached the clerks in more liberal Chambers hoping to find arguments that might persuade her boss. It was true that the previous year Powell had written a strong equal protection opinion in *Batson* v. *Kentucky*, which lessened the evidentiary burden on a defendant trying to prove that a prosecutor had used peremptory challenges to exclude blacks from the jury. Powell in that case had adopted exactly the method of proof the LDF was suggesting in *McCleskey*: once the defendant demonstrated a racial pattern in a prosecutor's peremptory challenges, the burden shifted to the prosecutor to rebut this inference of discrimination with a legitimate and neutral justification for his strikes. Powell's *Batson* ruling governing a prosecutor's discretionary decisions during jury selection seemed perfectly suited for a case involving (in large part) a prosecutor's discretionary decisions leading up to a death sentence. And it was certainly a favorite clerk tactic to try to influence a Justice by hoisting him on the petard of his previous writings.

Gielow, though, despite considerable agonizing, never really pressed the case with Powell. She was new at her job and had the strong sense that her boss's mind was made up. It seemed to her that Powell had crossed the point of no return in *Gregg*, when he not only approved Georgia's capital punishment system but applauded it as among the nation's best. More liberal than the Justice she worked for, Gielow knew she'd have to pick her fights, and there was little point in wasting precious capital on a lost cause.

Clerks in other conservative Chambers shared her sense of helplessness. A number of them were impressed with the Baldus study and tried to get their bosses to give it careful attention. Several clerks, even one of Rehnquist's, suggested that the Court appoint a special master—an independent expert—to give the mathematically challenged Justices a neutral assessment of Baldus's methods and findings. The conservative Justices would have none of it, though.

The idea of appointing a special master presupposed that the conservative Justices were still open to convincing. But the evidence was increasingly to the contrary. Even before hearing oral argument, Justice White took the extremely unusual (and perhaps unprecedented) step of sending Justices Rehnquist, Powell, O'Connor, and Scalia a detailed memo—behind the liberals' backs—urging a unified vote to reject McCleskey's claims and laying out his *Yick Wo* analysis for dispensing with the Baldus study. In White's view, to accept the LDF's arguments in *McCleskey* would be to return the Court to the position it had taken in *Furman*, and he wanted to preempt any possibility of heading back down that road.

In this he succeeded. By the time Jack Boger stood before the bench at oral argument on October 15, for all practical purposes, the fix was already in, preset in White's memo and subsequent conservatives-only tête-à-têtes.

The conservatives made no secret of their hostility. Five minutes into Boger's presentation, Justice White hit him with a series of curt questions insinuating that the data collectors for Baldus's study had been insufficiently trained or incompetent. White always seemed to take great pleasure intimidating lawyers appearing before the Court, badgering them, often about small points, demanding a yes or no answer whenever his targets tried to offer a nuanced or qualified response. And he turned on Boger with enthusiasm.

"Who took the information from those [data] sources?" White demanded.

"They were taken under the direction of a coding supervisor—"

"I didn't ask you that. I asked you who did it."

White was apparently perturbed that the data collection and coding were done mainly by law students, as opposed to law graduates.

In the crowded gallery, David Baldus's heart sank. Boger was defending the integrity of the study well enough, but the look on White's face and the tone of his voice forecast disaster. White was leaning forward over the bench, his large, flushed face contorted into a nasty scowl; his every word dripped with contempt. Baldus couldn't understand how a careful and conscientious challenge to the death penalty, one that should have given pause even to those who would not ultimately accept it, could generate such complete disdain and hostility.

It was Justice O'Connor who bewildered Bob Stroup. Touching on one of the most difficult aspects of the case, she wanted to know what remedy Boger thought appropriate for race-of-the-victim discrimination. "Is it to execute more people?" O'Connor asked.

Stroup thought this totally inane. Obviously, that was the opposite of what he and Boger were advocating. But O'Connor's question was actually quite logical. If the problem in Georgia was undervaluing the lives of black victims, then why couldn't this problem be solved by reforming the system in a way that increased the number of death sentences for persons who killed blacks? The difficulty for Boger, which O'Connor's question exposed, was that his chief concern lay not with ensuring that black victims and white victims received equal justice but rather with abolishing the death penalty.

And that problem haunted the rest of Boger's argument. At the time of *Gregg*, the Court had struck down several mandatory death penalty statutes, holding that juries must be given some discretion about whether to impose the ultimate sentence. Now Boger was arguing that a discretionary system such as Georgia's resulted in racially biased sentencing.

"So this Court's cases that have, since *Furman*, opened up to allow more discretion, were wrongly decided, and we should move back toward less discretion?" O'Connor asked.

"Not necessarily," Boger responded. Yet, although he did his best to deny it, Boger was putting the Court between a rock and a hard place. Either the Justices could revive the idea of mandatory sentencing that they had buried only a decade before or they could do away with capital punishment altogether. In his final minutes, Boger tried to argue that Georgia's system was particularly "loose" and that there were "a number of solutions" to its problem of excess discretion short of a return to mandatory sentencing. But it was a vague answer out of the mouth of one of the nation's leading abolitionists, and it met a wall of skepticism.

Mary Beth Westmorland, an assistant attorney general of Georgia who had been handling the McCleskey case since early in the habeas process, argued for the state. She started, as the state advocates always did in death cases, with the terrible facts of McCleskey's offense—a cold-blooded cop killing. During Boger's argument, Powell had pressed this point; so had Scalia. Westmorland could sense from questions leveled at Boger that several Justices were surprised by the characterization of such a crime as "midrange" even though no other cop killers had received the death penalty in Fulton County. Westmorland scoffed at the midrange label and to great effect assured the Court that McCleskey was "a most aggravated case," wholly warranting a death sentence.

As for the racial disparities in the Baldus study, Westmorland suggested that the white victim cases were simply more aggravated than the black victim cases. Under questioning, she had to admit that the Baldus study was designed to control for precisely that qualitative difference. It was one reason why the 11.0:1 race-of-the-victim disparity in the raw numbers became a 4.3:1 death odds multiplier in the Baldus analysis. Once challenged, Westmorland retreated to a fallback the Eleventh Circuit had endorsed. "Each case is unique on its own individual facts," she declared. There was simply "no way" to take account of the virtually infinite variables that enter into a jury's decision to impose death. And in trying to quantify the unquantifiable, Baldus had not proved and could not prove racial discrimination.

The Justices took up McCleskey at their conference on Friday, October 17, but White did not wait even that long to resume his crusade. In a rare preconference memo (this one to all the Justices), he not only tried to undermine one of McCleskey's key claims but also called into question Boger's truthfulness. At oral argument, White had suggested that McCleskey was hard-pressed to argue that he was a victim of prosecutorial discrimination because, according to Judge Forrester, he "was offered a plea bargain and turned it down." Boger had responded that Forrester had gotten the facts wrong, that John Turner, McCleskey's original lawyer, had urged his client to plead guilty in exchange for a life sentence, but that the prosecutor had never offered a plea bargain, and McCleskey had decided against asking for one. Parker had confirmed this himself in a deposition before the state habeas court.

White, though, was not a Justice to take contradiction lightly. Immediately after argument, he ordered the entire habeas record sent overnight to the Court so that one of his clerks could evaluate what had happened. What White found, and reported in his memo, was that in his view Boger had deliberately misled the Court. White's proof was Turner's testimony at McCleskey's state habeas hearing that "the Prosecutor was indicating that we might be able to work out a life sentence if he were willing to enter a plea. But we never reached any concrete stage on that because Mr. McCleskey's attitude was that he didn't want to enter a plea."

White either didn't realize or ignored the fact that Turner gave this self-serving testimony in the context of trying to defend the competency of his representation of McCleskey, that the state had never claimed it offered McCleskey a plea bargain, that the prosecutor had specifically denied making such an offer, and that the issue of whether the prosecutor had offered a plea bargain had never been litigated. Instead, White was so suspicious of abolitionist lawyering that he was willing on flimsy evidence to implicitly accuse a leading lawyer at the nation's foremost civil rights organization of baldly lying to the Court.

Furthermore, on the same flimsy evidence, White was willing to torpedo the main part of McCleskey's equal protection argument. "It would be difficult to conclude," he confidently asserted to the Conference, "that McCleskey suffered racial discrimination at the plea-bargaining stage, and there is a reduced chance that racial considerations influenced the prosecutor to proceed to a sentencing hearing."

Whatever the effect of White's accusatory memo, his preargument campaign for a unified conservative front was fully realized. When the Justices discussed McCleskey the next day, they lined up precisely as they had at the cert. stage. Briefing and argument—which the conservatives had not wanted see in the first place—had changed nothing. Justices Rehnquist, White, Powell, and O'Connor voted to affirm the Eleventh Circuit; the newcomer, Justice Scalia, joined them; and Justices Brennan, Marshall, Blackmun, and Stevens voted to reverse.

Powell was eager to try his hand at the opinion, and, to White's disappointment (he wanted to write it), Rehnquist accommodated him. Gielow started working on a draft immediately, as Powell generally imposed on himself a one-month deadline for circulating draft majorities. Less than four weeks later, the work was done, and on November 13 Powell circulated his first draft.

Powell's basic opinion strategy was to avoid dealing with the substance of the Baldus study altogether.[25] In this regard, he closely tracked the reasoning of the Eleventh Circuit, first claiming to "assume the validity" of Baldus's study (though not without attacking it), then trying to show why the statistics were insufficient to support McCleskey's claims.

Powell tackled the LDF's equal protection argument first. Like the Eleventh Circuit, he began by stating that McCleskey could not prevail merely by showing the existence of generalized discrimination in the Georgia system. Rather, he had to prove "the existence of purposeful discrimination" and a "discriminatory effect on him" or, in other words, that "the decisionmakers in *his* case acted with discriminatory purpose."

Powell acknowledged that the Court had sometimes found statistical evidence (which by its very nature does not focus on individual cases) sufficient to raise an inference of such intentional discrimination against a specific individual. But he asserted that McCleskey could not follow that route here. Because McCleskey was challenging the sort of discretionary decision making "essential to the criminal justice process," the Court would demand he provide "exceptionally clear proof" of intentional discrimination. And, in Powell's view, no mere statistical study could meet that standard.

To Powell it was all but irrelevant that the Court had recently inferred intentional discrimination from statistical analysis in the context of jury selection and employment decisions. Capital sentencing was "fundamentally different." "Each jury is unique in its composition," Powell wrote, "and the Constitution requires that its decision rest on consideration of innumerable factors that vary according to the characteristics of the individual defendant and the facts of the particular capital offense." In other words, in Powell's view, a given jury's decision whether to impose a death sentence was an inscrutable process not susceptible to meaningful statistical analysis.[26]

As for the historical evidence of discrimination that the LDF had used to bolster Baldus's statistics, it was dismissed in a single footnote. According to Powell, although "the history of racial discrimination in this country is undeniable," McCleskey's historical evidence focused solely on "Georgia laws in force during and just after the Civil War." While he recognized the value of historical background as evidence, he declined to "accept official actions taken long ago as evidence of current [discriminatory] intent."

Powell was no more receptive to the LDF's Eighth Amendment theory that the influence of race rendered Georgia's capital punishment scheme arbitrary and capricious. The collective judgment of a capital jury was "often difficult to explain," he emphasized again, and the Baldus study did not do so. "The Baldus study can only demonstrate a *risk* that the factor of race entered into some capital sentencing decisions," Powell noted. "At most, the Baldus study indicates a discrepancy that appears to correlate with race."

Such an apparent correlation was not good enough. Some discrepancies were inevitable in a system that involved a degree of discretion—as capital sentencing necessarily did. But "where the discretion that is fundamental to our criminal process is involved," Powell continued, "we decline to assume that what is unexplained is invidious." Accordingly, he concluded that "the Baldus study does not demonstrate a constitutionally significant risk of racial bias affecting the Georgia capital sentencing process."

To rule otherwise, Powell warned in closing, would be to invite "similar claims as to other types of penalty" as well as other types of discrimination. Indeed, McCleskey's arguments knew no limit in a system that depended entirely on human choices, and, thus, ruling in his favor might well paralyze the entire criminal justice process.

To the skeptics around the Court—and they included most of the clerks—Powell's opinion was an obvious failure of logic and craft. Overall, his response to the LDF's statistical evidence seemed to be to have stuck his head in the sand. His suggestion that "at most the Baldus study indicates a discrepancy that appears to correlate with race" was (as one commentator noted), about as correct and vacuous as declaring that "at most studies on lung cancer indicate a discrepancy that appears to correlate with smoking."[27] Even more troubling was Powell's hear-no-evil, see-no-evil statement that the Court would "decline to assume that what is unexplained is invidious." The LDF asked for no such assumption. Rather, Boger had introduced the most comprehensive death penalty study ever undertaken precisely to show that no factor other than racial bias could plausibly explain the apparent disparities in Georgia's capital sentencing system. Justice Powell was the one guilty of making an unsupported assumption—namely that Georgia's race-of-the-victim disparities were "unexplained." Having apparently decided not to come to grips with this evidence, he opted instead to pretend it didn't exist.

Powell's avoidance of the hard issues was also specific. His treatment of the equal protection issue all but ignored the major thrust of the LDF's argument. Even if one accepted Powell's depiction of jury deliberations

as a virtually mystical group experience impervious to statistical analysis,* that did not address the LDF's principal charge that the race-of-the-
victim disparities in the Georgia system resulted from *prosecutorial*
misconduct—a subject on which statistics had several times been held
to be relevant and probative. Powell knew he was papering over this aspect of the case, but his potential rejoinders to the LDF's evidence of
racial bias were essentially foreclosed by prior opinions he had either
written or joined. So he deliberately ignored the LDF's most persuasive
arguments.

Powell's brush-off of the LDF's historical evidence was equally egregious. Far from relying solely on Georgia's practices before and just after
the Civil War (as Powell contended), the LDF was arguing that the
racist administration of Georgia's criminal laws had persisted through
the entire Jim Crow era and even after. Recognition of a dual system of
justice in Georgia and throughout the South had been a strong undercurrent in *Furman* (indeed, specifically noted by three Justices), had produced appalling statistics on capital punishment for interracial rape, and
had forced the Court itself to impose stronger and stronger checks on
blatant discrimination in jury selection and other aspects of the criminal
process. About all this Powell said nothing.

The deficiencies in Powell's opinion, however, had little effect at the
Court except to exacerbate the frustration, anger, and dismay in the liberal Chambers. On the day after Powell's draft circulated, O'Connor,
who had promised her clerks to give *McCleskey* the most careful consideration, signed on to the majority without a single qualification. Rehnquist and White followed suit in quick succession.

For the liberals, the quick joins were disappointing but no longer surprising. In November, while Powell's Chambers was drafting *McCleskey*,
they had received a full dose of the conservatives' thinking about the
death penalty in another capital case, *Tison* v. *Arizona*. *Tison* involved
two brothers sentenced to death for their part in a jailbreak. The Tison

---

*Why statistical analysis should not be effective for analyzing jury decisions in capital cases was
far from clear. In a unanimous decision from the previous term, the Court had endorsed the use of
Baldus-style multiple regression analysis in an employment discrimination case involving one hundred hiring agents and a number of hiring factors over the course of several years. See *Bazemore* v.
Friday, 378 U.S. 385 (1986). In that case, moreover, the Court had specifically stated that a statistical study need not take account of every conceivable variable to qualify as meaningful evidence of
discrimination. Powell never really explained why this case, also involving multiple decision mak-
ers and multiple variables, shouldn't govern the value of Baldus's study.

boys had smuggled guns into a prison to help their father and another man escape. During the getaway, their car broke down and the fleeing felons decided to flag a passing motorist and steal a replacement. When a car pulled over, they took the four occupants out into the Arizona desert, where the father, Gary Tison, shotgunned them to death. (Gary Tison later died of exposure after being stranded.)

The Tison brothers were convicted of murder (under the felony-murder rule), and, although the evidence showed that they had not intended the killings to occur, both received sentences of death. They appealed their sentences as violating the Supreme Court's ruling in *Enmund* v. *Florida*, a 1982 case that had imposed a "categorical rule: a person who has not in fact killed, attempted to kill, or intended that a killing take place or that lethal force be used may not be sentenced to death."[28] Under the close scrutiny of an outraged Arizona public, the Arizona Supreme Court squirreled around *Enmund* and affirmed the death sentences. The Justices then granted cert.

For the liberals, *Tison* should have been a sure winner. The Arizona Supreme Court had ignored *Enmund*'s "categorical rule"—which the Justices had reaffirmed just the year before—and *had* to be reversed. Nonetheless, at Conference, Rehnquist voted to affirm. So did White, even though he had written *Enmund* and offered no explanation of why its rule didn't control this case. Powell fell in line too, which meant (with Scalia a sure vote to affirm and the others solidly to reverse) that O'Connor held the crucial swing vote.

O'Connor had entered the room prepared to reverse because of *Enmund*. She admitted as much. But after seeing how White voted, she changed her mind. After all, White had written *Enmund*. If he thought it didn't prohibit sentencing the Tison brothers to death, that was good enough for her. O'Connor voted to affirm.

Shrewdly, Rehnquist assigned the majority opinion to O'Connor, knowing that giving her responsibility for writing would prevent O'Connor from changing her mind again. The problem, of course, was that she had no theory for how to get around *Enmund*—and White had offered none. She told her clerk to come up with something, and he did: allowing death sentences for persons guilty of felony murder who, while not intending to kill, nonetheless had shown a "reckless indifference" for human life.[29]

To the liberals, *Tison* represented an abomination of result-oriented judging, a senseless trampling of logic and precedent—and in pursuit of what? The taking of two lives. To the conservatives, *Tison*, like a number of other cases before it, didn't belong on the Court's docket in the first place and never would have been there but for the liberals' indefensible insistence on micromanaging (or subverting) capital punishment. Four innocent people had lost their lives because of the illegal and violent actions of the Tison brothers. They deserved the fate Arizona had assigned. The conservatives had no compunction about bending old law a bit to usher them on their way.

There was nothing to say between these two positions, no common vocabulary or assumptions, no purpose or subject for discussion. Majorities and dissents were written, votes cast, rulings handed down. So it was even in a case as fundamental and difficult as *McCleskey*. From start to finish, each side operated as if enclosed in its own cocoon. An "odd silence" descended over the case, one clerk recalls. It was the silence of mutual scorn.

Justice Brennan gave instructions to his clerk Mitt Regan about preparing a dissent in *McCleskey*. They agreed to write only on the Eighth Amendment issue—endorsing the LDF's claim that the infusion of racial bias had rendered Georgia's death penalty system unconstitutionally arbitrary and irrational. It was the issue Brennan had pioneered, the moral ground on which he wanted to make his stand. Besides, Blackmun had indicated a strong interest in writing on the equal protection issue, and Brennan was pleased to accommodate his ever more reliable ally. Brennan harbored no illusions that anything he might say would convince any of his opponents to change sides and deprive Powell of his majority. Brennan told Regan to take his time preparing a draft. They were writing "for the next generation," he said, not for colleagues on the Court, and they should do the best job they could.

While Regan toiled away, Justice Scalia, after sitting on Powell's draft for close to two months, offered his reaction. Despite Scalia's conservative credentials, the LDF had by no means given up on his vote beforehand. Certainly, Scalia was no friend to the LDF on race issues generally. As the child of modern-day Italian immigrants, he felt neither guilt nor responsibility for wrongs perpetrated against blacks long before his ancestors even dreamed of reaching America. Having excelled by the sheer force of his own brains and hard work, Scalia believed deeply in rewarding individual initiative and had little truck with the "group-think" that pervaded the claims of many traditional civil rights groups. Thus, he condemned affirmative action particularly "because it is based upon concepts of racial indebtedness and racial entitlement, rather than individual worth and individual need, and that is to say, because it is racist."[30]

Still, Scalia's hostility to restorative justice did not necessarily presage his views on a claim of present-day racial discrimination. Nor did he have an established record on the death penalty. As a judge on the D.C. Circuit, Scalia hadn't heard capital cases, and he had danced around those few death penalty questions posed during his confirmation hearings. Most important, perhaps, was the fact that Scalia was at heart an academic and, as such, more likely than most of his colleagues to recognize the rigor and power of Baldus's statistics.

Scalia's memo, dated January 6, proved the LDF half right. He did understand the power of Baldus's numbers, and he was obviously troubled by the statistical know-nothingness of Powell's opinion. But the bottom line for McCleskey was no different. In Scalia's view, Powell had pinned too much on wrongly alleged weaknesses in the Baldus study, as if a better statistical showing might have carried the day. "Since it is my view," he wrote, "that the unconscious operation of irrational sympathies and antipathies, including racial, upon jury decisions and (hence) prosecutorial decisions is real, acknowledged in the decisions of this court, and ineradicable, I cannot honestly say that all I need is more proof." In other words, Scalia basically agreed with the LDF that some racial bias in capital sentencing was inevitable. He was, however, willing to tolerate that bias and even thought that the other Justices, in candor, should admit they were too.

Scalia said that he intended to write a separate concurrence to record his point, but he never did. Most likely, he decided that Powell's opinion all but foreclosed another statistical challenge—and that was good enough.

As the month of January wore on with still no sign of Brennan's dissent, Chief Justice Rehnquist began to fume. Every week the Court delayed in handing down *McCleskey* was another week the LDF could use the case as the basis for getting holds and stays of executions in other cases. In the eight months since cert. had been granted, *McCleskey* had created a huge backlog of capital cases, and Rehnquist suspected that Brennan's tardiness was not the product of diligence but another of his abolitionist guerrilla tactics to clog up the system as much as possible while he still could. Indeed, Rehnquist became so angry that he threatened not to assign Brennan another majority opinion until he circulated a *McCleskey* dissent.

On January 30, Brennan finally distributed his rejoinder. At the outset, it traced the Court's commitment in past cases to free the death penalty from even the "*risk* that prejudice or other impermissible influences *might have infected* the sentencing decision." Then it made the case for why Baldus's statistics and the whole run of southern history compelled the "human moral judgement" that in Georgia the risk—indeed, the virtual certainty—of that infection was too great for any court to bear.

Brennan dismissed Powell's fear that crediting Baldus's statistics would lead to widespread challenges to numerous other aspects of criminal sentencing. "Such a statement seems to suggest a fear of too much justice," he replied. "The prospect that there may be more widespread abuse than McCleskey documents may be dismaying, but it does not justify complete abdication of our judicial role."

To Brennan, the nature of that judicial duty was evident from the Court's own history. By way of peroration, he pointedly called to mind the Court's sizable contribution to the history of American racism. It had been the Taney Court in *Dred Scott* that had ruled as a matter of constitutional law blacks possessed "no rights which the white man was bound to respect." So too, the Court had sanctioned segregation in *Plessy* v. *Ferguson*, stating that "if one race be inferior to the other socially, the Constitution of the United States cannot put them upon the same plane."

In recent times, Brennan continued, we have "sought to free ourselves from the burden of this history." But now, he lamented, the Court had left that work unfinished. The Court rejected McCleskey's claims "at our peril," Brennan closed, "for we remain imprisoned by the past so long as we deny its influence in the present."

Justices Marshall, Blackmun, and Stevens signed on to Brennan's opinion in short order. Justice Powell responded by tacking a scant two footnotes onto his opinion, a response that only demonstrated what small weight Brennan's uncompromising death penalty views carried with his opponents. Although Powell graciously described Brennan's dissent as "eloquent," he immediately emphasized that it must "of course" be read in light of his "often repeated opposition to the death sentence." As Powell observed with considerable justification, "The dissent's call for greater rationality [in capital cases] is no less than a claim that a capital punishment system cannot be administered in accord with the Constitution." In other words, Brennan's arguments based on precedent and history were just window dressing, an abolitionist gambit not to be fallen for.

While Brennan and Powell skirmished in their footnotes, Blackmun continued preparing his dissent based on the equal protection clause's promise of evenhanded justice. It finally circulated in early April. Mainly, Blackmun focused on exactly what Powell's jury-oriented analysis had ignored—the LDF's theory that the Baldus study revealed *prosecutorial* discretion run amok. Proof of race discrimination that the Court surely would have deemed sufficient in any context other than a capital case had been rendered deficient for no other reason than that a life was at stake. "The Court today seems to give a new meaning to our recognition that death is different," Blackmun observed. "Rather than requiring a 'correspondingly greater degree of scrutiny of the capital sentencing decision,' the Court relies on the very fact that this is a case involving capital punishment to apply a *lesser* standard of scrutiny under the Equal Protection Clause."

The greatest significance of Blackmun's dissent, however, lay not in its detailed parsing of why McCleskey should have prevailed under the Court's established equal protection precedents but in the simple fact that it was Blackmun who wrote it. This was the same man who, in *Maxwell* v. *Bishop*, had rejected the Wolfgang study of race discrimination in capital sentences for rape. This was the same man who had voted to uphold the death penalty in both *Furman* and *Gregg* because, despite "an excruciating agony of the spirit," he could see no constitutional grounds for prohibiting the punishment.[31]

It is certainly true that both the evidence and the law had changed in the two decades since *Maxwell*. Baldus's study, as a technical matter, was superior to Wolfgang's work. And the Court had developed a framework for proving discrimination claims that simply didn't exist when *Maxwell* was being decided. Blackmun had in fact written some of these opinions.[32] Even more important, perhaps, was the fact that Blackmun could build his ruling on the clear textual and historical mandate of the equal protection clause to eliminate racial disparities in the criminal law, rather than on the Court's erratic interpretation of the Eighth Amendment's more amorphous "cruel and unusual punishments" clause.

But Blackmun's conversion was above all testament to Oliver Wendell Holmes's famous adage that the "life of the law is not logic but experience." In sixteen years as a Justice, through thousands of cert. petitions, hundreds of death penalty stays, and as Circuit Justice overseeing the execution-eager Missouri Supreme Court, Blackmun had developed an intimate acquaintance with the viscera of the death penalty. With an unmatched meticulousness, he had read, analyzed, annotated, and absorbed tens of thousands of pages detailing the minute factual and legal details of capital cases across the country.[33] What moved Blackmun to speak out (indeed, almost shout) in *McCleskey* was not merely the thoroughness of the Baldus study or his decidedly Yankee view of southern history but his conviction born of experience that every day, in some courtroom across the South, race was playing a significant, pernicious, and unconstitutional role in the death penalty. The Baldus study did not prove this to him; it simply confirmed what Blackmun had come to know already.

Blackmun's dissent, quickly joined by the three other dissenters, elicited no response within the Court except the addition of another two footnotes to Powell's opinion. Before the ruling came down, Justice Stevens chimed in with a brief dissent of his own (joined by Blackmun). Stevens observed that "if society were indeed forced to choose between a racially discriminatory death penalty . . . and no death penalty at all, the choice mandated by the Constitution would be plain." But Stevens didn't see *McCleskey* as necessarily presenting this choice. The Baldus study suggested that the influence of race was negligible in "high aggravation" murders (as opposed to midrange cases). Logically, if Georgia were to narrow the category of death-eligible murders to the more aggravated group, its system might very well prove constitutional. Surely, Stevens argued, such a restructuring was "not too high a price to pay." He proposed sending the case back to the lower courts for further consideration of this middle-of-the-road approach.

Stevens's much-belated dissent, despite its commonsense appeal, made no impact either. Having secured the votes necessary for a majority months before, Powell dismissed this solution as "unconvincing."

Among the dissenters, only Marshall—the Court's first and sole black voice and the only Justice with any direct experience with criminal justice in the South—kept silent. Years later, upon his retirement, Justice O'Connor would recall a story that Marshall, the Court's most purposeful raconteur, had told at the *McCleskey* conference about his days defending blacks in the South:

I had an innocent man once. He was accused of raping a white woman. The government told me if he would plead guilty, he'd only get life. I said I couldn't make that decision; I'd have to ask my client. So I told him that if he pleaded guilty, he wouldn't get the death sentence.

He said, "Plead guilty to what?"

I said, "Plead guilty to rape."

He said, "Raping that woman? You gotta be kidding. I won't do it."

That's when I knew I had an innocent man.

When the judge sent the jurors out, he told them that they had three choices: Not guilty, guilty, or guilty with mercy. "You understand those are the three different possible choices," he instructed. But after the jury left, the judge told the people in the courtroom that they were not to move before the bailiff took the defendant away. I said, "What happened to 'not guilty'?" The judge looked at me, and said, "Are you kidding?" Just like that. And he was the "judge."

Leaning over the conference table, Marshall pointed his finger at no one in particular. "E-e-e-end of story," he announced. "The guy was found guilty and sentenced to death. But he never raped that woman." Marshall paused, flicking his hand, then added, "Oh well, he was just a Negro."[34]

O'Connor recalled how "particularly moved" she was by Marshall's cautionary tale—moved, but not convinced. The conservatives either did not believe in the continuing legacy of the world Marshall described or they blinded themselves to it. The Baldus study provided a unique window into the operation of Georgia's death penalty law, but while the LDF could press the Justices' faces against the glass, it could not make them see.

In *McCleskey*, the conservative Justices chose not to even look. Depending on the individual, that choice may have stemmed from a simple refusal to acknowledge the evidence, or a concern for the consequences of acknowledging the evidence, or an exasperation with the abolitionists who presented the evidence, or a conviction that a certain degree of racism, however regrettable, is an inevitable part of American society and law. Whatever the cause or combination of causes, this blinkering had been coming on for years as, in the face of seemingly endless litigation and abolitionist maneuvering, the conservative Justices increasingly closed themselves off from the persistent proof streaming into the

Court that the system of death penalty adjudication seethed with error and abuse.

The problem with this self-blinding was not that *McCleskey* was an easy case wrongly decided. The problem was it was a difficult case—full of hard choices about how to prove racism and what courts could do about it without tearing down the entire system of law. Yet *McCleskey* was decided as though it were easy. The *McCleskey* majority refused to engage seriously in two of the Court's most heralded undertakings: to bring reason to the death penalty and to root out racism from the criminal law. Instead, the conservatives withdrew the Court from these fields stealthily and with only cursory explanation.

This result was in a way the worst of all worlds. The Court did not advance boldly to eradicate race discrimination in capital sentencing, even at the risk of losing the death penalty itself. Nor, by contrast, did it retreat honestly and forthrightly (as Justice Harlan had done long ago in *McGautha*), conceding that the death penalty was permissibly imperfect and too intractable a puzzle for human wisdom to solve. Instead, the majority erected a facade of fairness and rationality, and pretended that the potential problems recognized in *Gregg* had been solved. And, in so doing, these Justices legitimized—for every participant in the death penalty system and for the public at large—a process that, at a minimum, they should have recognized as deeply flawed.[35]

The import of this development extended far beyond the issue of capital punishment. It culminated a sea change in how a majority of the Justices defined the Court's central mission and, in particular, its role in narrowing the gap between the nation's constitutional ideals and the truth of everyday experience. Fifty years before, in the Scottsboro cases, an idea had taken hold, a commitment by the Court that grew stronger every year, to breathe life into the moribund promises of the Fourteenth Amendment and to force state governments, especially in the South, to obey national standards for fairness and justice. In practice, this meant applying the Bill of Rights to the actions of every state government and, belatedly, extending the Constitution's protective umbrella to cover every citizen.

This spirit of Scottsboro inspired the great triumph of *Brown*. But its first home was in a host of criminal cases, mostly death cases, where the power of southern states unjustly threatened the lives and liberty of blacks. So it was, for example, in the 1940 case of *Chambers v. Florida*.[36] The day after an elderly white man was robbed and murdered near Fort

Lauderdale, the police (without a single warrant) arrested between twenty-five and forty black men and held them in complete isolation for six days while questioning, threatening, and abusing them. After six days the police released all but four "ignorant young colored tenant farmers," who, after another fifteen straight hours of interrogation, confessed to the crime. On that basis, they were convicted and sentenced to death.

Justice Hugo Black's majority opinion reversed the convictions and for the first time applied the Constitution's prohibition on coerced confessions to the states. It ended with a crescendo: "Under our constitutional system, courts stand against any winds that blow as havens of refuge for those who might otherwise suffer because they are helpless, weak, outnumbered, or because they are nonconforming victims of prejudice and public excitement. . . . No higher duty, no more solemn responsibility, rests upon this Court than that of translating into living law and maintaining this constitutional shield deliberately planned and inscribed for the benefit of every human being subject to our Constitution—of whatever race, creed or persuasion."

On April 22, 1987, Justice Powell announced the *McCleskey* decision from the bench. As of that moment, the duty Justice Black had invoked in *Chambers*, that driving imperative of suborning the authority of states to the call of equal justice—that spirit of Scottsboro—was dead. In part, the spirit was a victim of its own impressive achievements. The apartheid world of *Chambers*'s day was gone, its glaring inequities outlawed and its attitudes changed or driven underground.

But an autopsy would show also that, over time, this spirit of Scottsboro had been much abused and finally exhausted. Some Justices, such as Brennan and Marshall in their persistent abolitionism, had blatantly overextended it in the hope of writing their own sense of morality into law. Outsiders, such as the LDF, had sapped its energy through a crusader's overuse—reducing a noble sense of mission to a legal cliché. And finally, fatally, the spirit of Scottsboro simply fell prey to the unsympathetic, those who either had never welcomed its ambitions or thought its work was done, its day past.

The spirit of Scottsboro derived from an idealistic belief in the power of law to cure social ills and push all of us closer to realizing what Lincoln called the "better angels of our nature." The question for the Court as it prepared to recess for the summer of 1987 was what new animating spirit would take the place of the one that had passed.

THINGS FALL APART

Robert Bork and Civil War

O n June 26, 1987, two months after the Court's decision in
McCleskey, on the final day of the term, Justice Powell announced
his decision to retire. For the last decade, Powell had suffered several sur-
geries, the most debilitating the nearly fatal excision of a prostate cancer
in 1985. Three months shy of eighty, unable to keep weight on his ema-
ciated frame, and diagnosed by his internist at the Mayo Clinic as suffering from "chronic fatigue," Powell decided that he could no longer
sustain the physical effort necessary to meet his exacting standards for
serving as a Justice. Powell also wanted a Republican to name his successor and, with a presidential election coming in 1988, he chose not to
put that at risk by serving another term.*

Around the Court, Powell kept his decision secret. The Justice didn't
tell his own clerks until a day before the public announcement. The rest
of the Court found out only minutes beforehand. Powell's departure
would have been deeply felt under any circumstances. Coming at the
end of the term, with emotions ebbing at the completion of a long and
exhausting cycle, the effect was crushing.

Justice O'Connor wept upon hearing the news and, later in the day,
wrote Powell that she was "devastated." To the first female Justice, no
one could have been more courteous, helpful, or approachable than the
gentleman Virginian. Nor could anyone have shared more fully her high
sense of family orientation, civic mindedness, and cautious perfection-

---

*Powell could have served one more term and still resigned while Reagan was in office, but he
wanted to retire early enough so that the naming of his successor would not become an issue in the
election.

ism. "There is no one for whom I have greater respect and affection than you," O'Connor gushed uninhibitedly in a note. "In short, you are irreplaceable."

There were tears in Justice Blackmun's Chambers, too. And Justice Stevens became so choked up in the last conference with Powell that he could not speak. Perhaps the most telling sentiments came from Byron White, a man rarely known to praise and never to excess. "I have seen a good many Justices come and go," he wrote Powell, "but I'm quite sure that I shall miss you more than any of the others, and that is saying a good deal."[1]

In the lower echelons of the Court, the reaction was much the same. Grafton Gaines, Justice Marshall's elderly black messenger, a southerner with as different a background from Powell's as perhaps could be imagined, summed up the communal reaction. "Yes, it's a terrible day," he said in commiseration with Justice Brennan's secretary. "It's like a funeral around here."

This widespread and exceptionally deep sense of mourning reflected not only how much Powell was liked and admired but also the crucial role he played on a fiercely divided Court. Shortly before Powell's announcement, a leading civil liberties lawyer had called him "the most powerful man in America." And with good reason. By any number of statistical measures, Powell was the most important Justice on the Court. He was in the majority more often than any of his colleagues. Indeed, Powell's view of the law prevailed more than 90 percent of the time in fields as varied as abortion, affirmative action, environmental law, equal protection, federal crimes, federal jurisdiction, military law, obscenity, prisons, religion, search and seizure, securities law, and tax. Even more important, Powell was consistently the "swing" Justice on a Burger Court that divided 5–4 with unprecedented frequency. His vote provided a majority for one faction or another in close to 80 percent of the 5–4 cases, far more than any other Justice, and he almost always controlled the Court's decisions in the most contested areas of law, such as privacy, race, and the death penalty.[2]

Powell was forever carving out a middle ground. He had provided a solid fifth vote for reaffirming *Roe* v. *Wade* and a woman's privacy right to an abortion. At the same time, he had upheld numerous restrictions on free access to abortion and, in an especially controversial case, joined Burger, White, Rehnquist, and O'Connor in refusing to extend the same right of privacy to homosexuals engaged in consensual acts of sodomy within their homes.[3]

Powell split the difference on race cases as well. Although in the *Bakke* case he accepted the concept of racial preferences for college and graduate school admissions, Powell balked at the idea of fixed racial quotas. Similarly, in the context of employment, he sanctioned limited affirmative action, but only in the hiring of new workers, not to expose old ones to layoffs. (He thought the injury to a white worker who *lost* a job to affirmative action was significantly greater than the injury to a white job applicant who did not *obtain* employment in the first place.)[4]

In death penalty cases, even in the wake of *McCleskey*, Powell was still capable of joining the liberals on occasion. In *Booth v. Maryland*, he wrote a 5–4 majority (over furious dissents from both White and Scalia) striking down the use of "victim impact evidence" in capital sentencing. Before *Booth*, it was common practice in some states for prosecutors to bring in the victim's family members and have them describe their grief and sense of loss for the sentencing jury. Continuing his commitment to impose "rationality" on death sentencing, Powell found such emotional appeals "irrelevant to the decision whether a defendant . . . should live or die."[5]

In condemning the use of victim impact evidence, Powell was also troubled by its implicit suggestion "that defendants whose victims were assets to the community are more deserving of punishment than those whose victims are perceived to be less worthy." Considered this way, victim impact evidence raised a strikingly similar problem to the one Powell had glossed over in *McCleskey*—that the system was valuing some types of victims more than others. Some clerks even speculated that Powell's *Booth* opinion was something of a makeup for his authorship of *McCleskey*. Either way, *Booth* showed that Powell, unlike the four more conservative Justices, was still willing to reform the *procedures* of the death penalty, so long as those reforms did not restrict the availability of the penalty itself. In that sense, *Booth* was a typical Powellian compromise and a good example of how much he could disappoint the Justices to both sides of him on the political spectrum.

Powell's location at the political center of the Court was only one aspect of his significance. Justice Powell was also, in O'Connor's words, a "humanizing influence," an oasis of civility among increasingly fractious colleagues. On the Fourth Circuit, before which Powell had practiced, the judges would come down off the bench after oral argument to shake hands with the lawyers. Powell fairly radiated that old-fashioned gentility, and his gracious aura seemed to moderate the recriminations swirling around him. His very presence seemed to lower the volume of debate. It was, after all, hard to raise one's voice to the wraithlike, bespectacled Powell, and he never seemed to raise his.

Powell's colleagues understood the role he played and how dearly his civilizing presence would be missed. The previous term had provided them with a glimpse at their likely future as they watched Justice Scalia bring a new level of pugnaciousness to the Court. While at their best most of the Justices relied chiefly on experience or practical wisdom for their judgments, Scalia was a master of academic pyrotechnics who delighted in theory and spinning out new ideas, especially his own. At oral argument, Scalia could be so domineering (and at times rude) that Powell once wondered aloud, "Does he know we're all here?" At Conference, it was much the same; Scalia was didactic, even hectoring. And he showed no deference to his colleagues, all of whom save O'Connor were his elders by a generation. Even the venerated Powell could be the target of Scalia's scorn, as in *Booth* (the victim impact case), where Scalia "went ballistic" (as one clerk put it) and was heard disparaging Powell's intelligence around the building.

Announcing Powell's departure, Chief Justice Rehnquist knew he was "dropping a bombshell." Powell's retirement promised a major upheaval in the politics of the Court and threatened to shatter already fragile bonds of civility. There is a tradition at the Court that when a Justice retires, the other Justices purchase for him the chair he has used on the bench. The price is cheap, roughly five dollars per Justice, but in this case the act was especially dear. The loss of Powell inspired profound sadness and also, especially among the liberals, no small amount of dread.

The reaction at the White House, by contrast, was pure jubilation. From the outset of his presidency, Reagan had hoped for the chance to shift dramatically the balance of the Supreme Court. Already he could account for two of the Court's nine members. Yet his substitution of O'Connor and Scalia for Stewart and Burger, while shoring up the Court's conservative wing, had not materially affected the outcome of key cases. With Powell's departure, the prospect of a solid conservative majority was finally at hand.

So, too, was the ideal nominee: Judge Robert Bork, the sixty-year-old intellectual dean of the conservative legal world. In terms of experience and qualifications, a more perfect legal résumé would have been hard to imagine. Bork had been a tenured professor at Yale Law School, solicitor general of the United States (in the Nixon administration), a successful corporate lawyer, and, as of 1981, one of twelve judges on the D.C. Circuit (the nation's second most prestigious court).

Philosophically, Bork was perfectly in tune with the administration, in some ways even its bandleader. For more than thirty years, he had been in the forefront of conservative academics who savaged the post-*Brown* Court as an out of control "Imperial Judiciary" usurping authority from the democratically elected branches of government. More technically, Bork was the nation's premier advocate for interpreting the Constitution according to the "original intent" of the Framers, a controversial jurisprudence, which Attorney General Meese had adopted as the intellectual centerpiece of the administration's attack on liberal legal precedents.

In Bork's view, the most significant rulings of the Warren era (as well as like-minded ones of the Burger Court) were products not only of poor reasoning but of what he described as totally "indefensible" and "illegitimate" methods for interpreting the Constitution.[6] Among the opinions he considered utterly without constitutional foundation were the Court's reapportionment cases establishing the principle of "one-person, one-vote," cases striking down poll taxes and prohibiting the enforcement of racially restrictive real estate covenants, all decisions upholding affirmative action, or those based on a generalized "right to privacy," including *Roe* v. *Wade* and its precursor, *Griswold* v. *Connecticut*, establishing a right to use birth control.

Not surprisingly, the Democrats, who had regained control of the Senate in 1986, tried to head off Bork's selection. Senator Joseph Biden, the chairman of the Senate Judiciary Committee, warned the White House that choosing Bork, regardless of his credentials, would provoke an intense confirmation fight. When he was paid no heed, liberals on and off Capitol Hill starting girding for battle.

Within hours of Reagan's selection of Bork, Sen. Edward Kennedy, on behalf of the entire civil rights and civil liberties establishment, sounded the war cry. "Robert Bork's America," Kennedy warned with calculated hyperbole, "is a land in which women would be forced into back-alley abortions, blacks would sit at segregated lunch counters, rogue police could break down citizens' doors in midnight raids, school children could not be taught about evolution, writers and artists could be censored at the whim of government, and the doors of the Federal courts would be shut on the fingers of millions of citizens for whom the judiciary is—and is often the only—protector of the individual rights that are at the heart of our democracy."[7] So began a nomination battle of unprecedented rancor and ferocity, which ended when a man whom the Senate had approved unanimously to sit on the court of appeals was soundly rejected by the same body (58–42) for a seat on the Supreme Court.

I had just graduated from Yale Law School and was beginning a clerkship with Judge William Norris (a leading liberal on the Ninth Circuit) when Bork was chosen. To everyone I knew in the close-quartered world of legal academia, clerking, and judging, to everyone I knew with a serious interest or stake in legal policy, nothing was more important in that summer of 1987 than what happened in and around the Senate Caucus Room where the Bork hearings unfolded and Judge Bork himself jousted for more than thirty hours with Senator Biden's committee. I took sides; all of us took sides, passionately and irrevocably, as others before us had divided over the Rosenbergs' guilt or whether Nixon should be impeached.

The nomination, of course, was important on its own terms. Everyone understood that Bork's elevation to the Court would in all likelihood substantially alter the course of constitutional law. But the fears and allegiances that caused us so aggressively to choose up sides transcended even such considerable consequences. For liberals, the Bork hearings were more than a defense of hard-won victories regarding civil rights and civil liberties. They were a test of where the nation was headed, with one road leading toward a more just society and the other toward political recidivism and the moral straitjacket of the religious right.

For conservatives, the fight was no less fundamental. Bork's nomination was a chance to curb a rights-happy Court that had overstepped its authority and undermined the social order. More broadly, his nomination stood for a philosophical commitment to the value of limits, rules, and standards as opposed to the "anything goes" relativism that since the 1960s had come to prevail in everything from morality to legal interpretation. As *Time* magazine assessed the stakes, "All at once the political passions of three decades seemed to converge on a single empty chair."[8]

From the liberal perspective, the long fuse to the Bork hearings was lit the moment Ronald Reagan took office and began a concerted campaign to put his distinctive conservative stamp on both federal law and the entire federal judiciary. In that sense, the fury liberals unleashed on Bork was not personal to him but the culmination of more than six years of anger and frustration as they watched Reagan's revolutionaries swing wrecking balls at the edifice of legal rights they had been building for a generation.

The most obvious (but by no means the only) method for bringing the Reagan Revolution to the federal legal system was the judicial appointment process. Many presidents, Franklin Roosevelt quite effectively, have sought to appoint like-minded judges to the bench. Careful judicial selection is an obvious and natural way for any administration to perpetuate its political legacy through the long-term work of hand-picked, life-tenured judges. The Reagan administration, however, aiming in Ed Meese's words to "institutionalize the Reagan Revolution," raised this previously rather informal practice to something closer to a fine art.[9]

Under Attorney General William French Smith, the Justice Department had established an Office of Legal Policy to oversee a screening process that deliberately and substantially increased executive branch control over nominations. In a sharp break with tradition, the administration curtailed the role of senators in the choice of lower court appointees for their respective home states. (In the less partisan past, even senators of the opposing party had participated in the selection process.) Also, for the first time White House and Justice Department officials conducted detailed interviews with leading judicial candidates about their legal philosophies. Staffers at OLP minutely scrutinized candidates' written works for hints of political or legal apostasy. One leading contender for an opening on the D.C. Circuit was scrubbed because, despite superb credentials and an otherwise strong conservative background, he'd given small donations to a gun control group and to Planned Parenthood. Another candidate lost out because of ties to a legal aid society.

After winning reelection in 1984, President Reagan was on track to appoint more than half the federal judiciary before leaving office, and this fact loomed ominously over every group, legal and political, whose power derived from the rights explosion of the Warren era. Liberal interest groups geared up for a counteroffensive in the Senate, the body charged by the Constitution with advising in and consenting to the president's nominations. With Ted Kennedy as their champion, the civil rights and abortion rights communities—accusing Reagan of trying to "pack" the courts with right-wing extremists—worked furiously to head off the most reactionary judicial candidates and to torpedo those nominees who appeared most vulnerable.*

Starting in 1985, these efforts succeeded in a few highly publicized cases. Jefferson Sessions III became the first victim of confirmation scrutiny when the NAACP revealed his history of making oddball and offensive racist remarks.† A few other names were withdrawn before public hearings.

In general, though, despite a few close votes, Reagan succeeded in naming a cadre of unusually young, often enormously gifted ideologues to fill his large reservoir of judicial vacancies. Leading academics such as Richard Posner and Frank Easterbrook as well as rising conservative stars such as J. Harvie Wilkinson III and Alex Kozinski (both former Supreme Court clerks), invaded the courts of appeals with sparkling intelligence combined with a conscious desire to undo the liberal status quo. Other less sterling appointees understood well enough whom and how to follow. To liberals, the better appointees were evil geniuses, the lesser ones just evil.

By the time of Bork's nomination, a virtual civil war had broken out on several of the most prominent appellate courts, with Bork's own D.C. Circuit probably the most contentious. In 1987, of the twelve judges on the D.C. Circuit, Reagan had appointed seven—and all of these (including superstars such as Bork, Kenneth Starr, and Lawrence Silberman) were doctrinaire. Each of the five remaining judges were Carter

---

*Many liberals have harped on the Reagan administration's systematic effort to "pack" federal courts with like-minded judges. It is difficult to pinpoint a sound basis for objecting, however. Reagan was elected in part because of an expectation that he would use the presidency's appointment power to further his ideological agenda. That he did so, even with unprecedented zeal, was part of his mandate. By the same token, the Democrats who controlled the Senate had every right not to confirm his nominees because of their ideology or from a belief that ideologically motivated nominees (of whatever stripe) often make poor judges.

†Ironically, Sessions is now a U.S. senator from Alabama with a seat on the Judiciary Committee. In that position, he has played a significant role in holding up the confirmation of President Clinton's judicial nominees.

appointees, among them three of the nation's most prominent liberal jurists: Pat Wald, Abner Mikva, and Harry Edwards.*

Because of the way federal appellate courts work, the presence of even a one-vote Reagan majority allowed this solid bloc to control all the major cases coming before the circuit. Appellate judges hear and decide cases in randomly determined and frequently rotating panels of three. Under this system, depending on the luck of the draw, a controversial case might end up being heard by a panel consisting of two or even three liberal judges despite the preponderance of conservatives on the circuit. Although such a liberal panel might render a liberal decision, under the rules of the courts of appeals, that panel's ruling was not absolutely final.

By a simple majority vote of the circuit's judges, every panel opinion was subject to en banc review—a rehearing before all the judges on the circuit. In practice that meant, on the D.C. Circuit, that the seven Reagan appointees had sufficient votes both to reconsider and to reverse every three-judge panel decision they didn't like.

The liberal judges felt that the Reaganites were grossly abusing this power. According to the Federal Rules of Appellate Procedure, the en banc process is "not favored and ordinarily will not be ordered." In the past, when the liberals had dominated, the circuit judges had invoked the process mainly to resolve "intracircuit conflicts"—situations in which two separate three-judge panels had taken different views of the same legal issue. The Reagan conservatives, by contrast, were using the en banc process to revisit old circuit precedents they wanted to get rid of and to impose a conservative uniformity on important new cases. In the Reaganites' view, reconsideration en banc was appropriate for any decision they considered "clearly wrong" or "highly dubious," a description that they seemed to apply whenever a liberal panel decided a big case. To the liberals, the conservatives' stance was a naked power grab, and they publicly and loudly cried foul.[10]

The liberals registered other complaints as well. Although court of appeals judges are bound to follow rulings of the Supreme Court, the liberals thought the conservatives were ignoring rulings they didn't like on the flimsiest excuse. In the process, Judge Bork in particular, but others as well, exploited every opportunity to disparage liberal Supreme Court precedents or, as Judge Ruth Bader Ginsburg put it critically, "to conduct a general spring-cleaning of constitutional law."[11] The liberals also ac-

---

*Ruth Bader Ginsburg was also on the D.C. Circuit, but her views were less predictably liberal.

cused the conservatives of trampling the canon of judicial restraint, which held that, whenever possible, courts should avoid deciding constitutional questions (as opposed to statutory ones). The liberals felt the conservatives were reaching out to establish new constitutional law anytime they could—sometimes even deciding large questions that the litigants had studiously avoided raising.

Within the pressure cooker of the D.C. Circuit building (where all twelve judges had their chambers), the level of frustration and vitriol rose dramatically as the Reaganites blasted huge holes in the liberal status quo. In a total collapse of what one liberal judge called "the collegiality that is indispensable to judicial decisionmaking,"[12] several judges stopped speaking to each other. On the opposite extreme, one day in conference, Judge Mikva became so upset with Judge Silberman that he started wagging his finger in Silberman's face. Silberman shouted back something to the effect that if Mikva "weren't so old, I'd rip that finger off and shove it up your ass."

The circuit's written opinions took these screaming matches public, and, as in private, the conservatives swaggered while the liberals shook with an anger bordering on hysteria. And to one degree or another, this wrenching shift of power was taking place on all thirteen of the country's circuit courts.

The work of the new Reagan judges, moreover, was being fueled by the aggressive policies of the administration's Justice Department. Under Attorney General Edwin Meese and his coterie of committed deputies, the department reversed course on decades-old policy in fields ranging from school prayer to civil rights. To liberals this about-face was distressing on its own, but what felt even more sinister and dangerous were the methods Meese employed to force-feed the administration's views to the courts and to the country.

One lightning rod for liberal outrage was the office of the solicitor general, whose main task was to represent the executive branch of the United States in the Supreme Court.* The solicitor general is the only government official specifically charged by statute with being "learned in law," and the office, held by such legal giants as John W. Davis, Robert Jackson, Erwin Griswold, Archibald Cox, and Thurgood Marshall, enjoyed a lore-encrusted reputation for caring more about the long-term integrity of the law than about the short-term vagaries of politics.

---

*In full, the solicitor general is responsible for approving the government's position in every appellate court in the country.

In keeping with what Cox referred to as its "public trust," the Solicitor General's Office (an elite group of about twenty) prided itself on seeking not merely to win cases for its client, the United States, but to do justice. To that end, the solicitor general had a long-standing practice of "confessing error" in cases where a lower court ruled for the United States on the basis of a manifestly flawed legal theory. The solicitor general considered it his office's duty to advise the Supreme Court to overturn such erroneous decisions regardless of the short-term interest of the United States.[13]

Solicitors general enjoyed a reputation (sometimes exaggerated) for defending their office against undue influence by more partisan elements in presiding administrations. Despite considerable pressure from their own administrations, solicitors general were known to sidestep some disputes of great political import if the legal interest of the United States was unclear. (The solicitor general decided not to file a brief, for example, in *Roe* v. *Wade*.) On rarer occasions, when overruled by higher-ups in an administration and forced to take legal positions they found abhorrent, solicitors general have been known to issue silent yet public protests. (For example, in one particularly troubling McCarthy-era prosecution, the solicitor general refused to sign the government brief submitted to the Court.)

In part because of this record for candor and professionalism, the Solicitor General's Office enjoyed a uniquely cooperative relationship with the Supreme Court. When wading through cert. petitions, the Justices relied heavily on the solicitor general's filings to help them sort out which cases involving the United States deserved full Court review. In those cases chosen for argument, they counted on the office to submit briefs that were unusually scholarly, restrained, and, above all, scrupulously honest about the state of the law. Justice Powell once described the solicitor general as having a "dual responsibility," to the judicial branch as well as the executive. Around Washington, the solicitor general was even referred to as the Tenth Justice, in recognition that, although an advocate, he (there has yet to be a woman) was the Court's informal partner in the complex enterprise of shaping federal law.

The solicitor general's independence from politics, however, can easily be overstated. At bottom, the solicitor general is still a political appointee subject to the authority and direction of the president. While he certainly must strive to preserve his influence and integrity before the Court, his immediate responsibility is to shape and advocate the legal theories and philosophy of the administration he serves.[14] The Reagan administration's legal philosophy—one of the reasons it won election— was one of counterrevolution. And by reflecting that spirit, the Reagan Solicitor General's Office naturally became a leading target of liberal and moderate complaint.

To opponents of the Reagan Revolution, it was clear the administration was subverting what they declared to be the time-honored restraint and independence of the Solicitor General's Office, turning it instead into a shop of narrow partisans. Exhibit A was the administration's handling of the Bob Jones University case, which arose in Reagan's first year.[15] During the Carter administration, the IRS had denied tax-exempt status to Bob Jones, a Christian school that would accept black students only if they agreed not to date or marry outside their race. The university sued to restore its tax exemption, and the Reagan Justice Department, over the strenuous objection of Larry Wallace, the deputy solicitor general handling the case, insisted on urging the Court to overturn the ruling. (Reagan's solicitor general, Rex Lee, was recused from the case because of a conflict of interest.)

Outsiders saw the move as a crass bow to Reagan's supporters in the religious right. In subtle protest, Wallace, an apolitical career member of the office, notified the Court in a footnote that he did not "fully subscribe" to the position set forth in the government's brief. Nor did the Justices, who rejected the administration position 8–1, with Rehnquist the sole dissenter.

As Reagan's first term wore on and it appeared that Rex Lee might not be sufficiently zealous in his pursuit of the president's legal agenda, Brad Reynolds, the assistant attorney general for civil rights—a man described even by friends as "willful," "rigid," and "a bit of a bully"—began hounding Lee to insinuate himself into a greater number of controversial cases and to submit more confrontational briefs.[16] During his four-year tenure, Lee fought off the most revolutionary of the positions suggested by the conservative Young Turks in the department (he thought they would antagonize the Court). Lee's successor, Charles Fried, however, proved more amenable to the hard-liners.

Fried began his tenure (in *Thornburgh v. American College of Obstetricians and Gynecologists* and *Diamond v. Charles*) by becoming the first solicitor general to argue to the Court that it should completely overturn *Roe v. Wade*, a position Lee had hedged on in a similar case a mere three years earlier. According to Fried's take-no-prisoners brief, *Roe* was without "moorings in the text of our Constitution or in familiar constitutional doctrine" and "so far flawed" that the Court, despite several reaffirmations, should now abandon it. Similarly contentious filings in other hot-button cases, especially those involving affirmative action, prompted three former solicitors general (including the Nixon appointee Erwin Griswold) to criticize Fried publicly for "interven[ing] too often," being "too polemical," "weakening the rule of law," or, as one media report summarized, "turning [the] historic post into little more than a political mouthpiece for the President."[17]

As of Powell's resignation, the Court had rebuffed the administration's highest profile proposals for constitutional revision, most forcefully in opinions reaffirming the status quo on abortion, race, and religion. But Meese and his staff confounded liberals by seeking other avenues for imposing the administration's political will. They tried to change accepted notions of who made and defined the law.

In a series of speeches, Meese belittled the principle of judicial review and challenged the notion that the Supreme Court was the ultimate arbiter on questions of constitutional law. To the contrary, Meese asserted that each branch of government had an independent duty "to interpret the Constitution in the performance of its official functions."[18] He further alleged that the executive branch's view of the law (that is, the view he as attorney general put forward) was at least as authoritative as the views of either the Court or Congress. Meese accepted the binding effect of Supreme Court judgments *on the particular litigants of a given case* but not necessarily on others in similar situations. They should feel free to pursue their own views of the law.

In support of this flank attack on the Court, Meese invoked Abraham Lincoln's response to the infamous *Dred Scott* case, where the Court had struck down Congress's efforts to limit slavery in the territories and declared slaves to be property not persons. *Dred Scott* had been a dagger blow to moderates such as Lincoln, who hoped to end slavery through congressionally mandated attrition, and they sought ways to minimize the ruling without directly flouting the Court. Walking this tightrope, Lincoln accepted that he could not challenge *Dred Scott* as it applied to the parties in the case (meaning Scott and his putative masters), but he refused "to obey it as a political rule." Had he been in Congress, Lincoln continued, "and a vote should come up on a question whether slavery should be prohibited in a new territory, in spite of the Dred Scott decision, I would vote that it should." Generalizing from Lincoln's resistance to a ruling he considered suicidally wrong, Meese thought the Reagan administration should take the same attitude toward Court decisions it considered fundamentally flawed.[19]

To liberals, the proper analogy for Meese's attitude toward the Court was not Lincoln but the southern racists who, after *Brown*, resisted school desegregation by declaring the Court's ruling an exercise of "naked judicial power" that had "no legal basis."[20] In the liberal view, Meese and his fellow Reaganites, like the segregationists of the 1950s, were plundering the rule of law. The evidence loomed everywhere: from the flouting of Supreme Court authority to the subverting of the Solicitor General's Office, the "packing" of the federal courts, and the subterfuges of Iran-Contra. The administration, the liberals believed, had no notion of individual liberty, or legal limits, or restraint of any kind; it only knew power and how to tear down. For twenty-five years liberal lawyers, judges, and politicians had guarded the citadel of civil rights and civil liberties, trying to hold out against the steady siege of Republican presidents and the Burger Court. In recent years, the Reaganites had breached the outer walls, and, with Powell's resignation, they threatened to take the city. Scared and increasingly desperate, liberals saw Robert Bork as nothing less than a barbarian, who, devilish beard and all, was coming for the women and children.

Naturally, conservatives thought that the roles were reversed, that they were crusading to rebuild a world liberals and leftists had shattered and defiled in the 1960s. Almost everything the left cherished—from welfare entitlements to the sexual revolution—was born in the social, political, and legal upheaval of this decade. For Bork and his supporters, it had been a time of moral abdication, disorder, and decline.

From his base at Yale Law School, Bork had sallied occasionally into politics. He took to the pages of *The New Republic* to denounce the Civil Rights Bill of 1964 desegregating private hotels and restaurants as an unwarranted intrusion on the right of individuals to chose with whom to associate. He wrote position papers for Barry Goldwater in the 1964 presidential campaign and, four years later, organized academic support for Richard Nixon. When Congress challenged Nixon's legal authority to extend the Vietnam War to Cambodia, Bork provided a legal refutation. In the same vein, he offered theoretical grounding for prohibiting court-ordered busing.

The formative environment for Bork's views, however, was not the public arena of politics but the cloistered halls of academia, in particular Yale University and its preeminent law school. It is difficult to describe for anyone unfamiliar with this world the intensely personal nature of its philosophical disputes or the depth of the schisms that divided faculties and students in the late 1960s and the 1970s. Faculties broke apart, old friends stopped speaking, colleagues came to despise each other over the Vietnam War and how to deal with student sit-ins, strikes, and other acts of civil disobedience. One's stands on the war, on matters of race, and on student protest were tests of character as well as politics. Opponents were not merely wrong, they were evil or complicit in evil.

In Bork's own thinking, events at Yale in 1970 appear to have been decisive.[21] In April of that year, Yale was brought to a standstill when Black Panther Bobby Seale was charged with murder in a New Haven criminal court. Campus radicals whipped up frenzy and called for a student strike to publicize their claim that Seale could not get a fair trial in New Haven or anywhere else in America. Outside groups threatened "to bring Yale to its knees" through a campaign of on-campus violence. On April 23, at a feverish faculty meeting convened on a campus criss-crossed with roving bands of protesters, Yale President Kingman Brewster voiced sympathy with the students' appraisal of the American justice system and the professors voted en masse to countenance the unprecedented student strike. Despite this act of solidarity (or abject surrender, depending on one's perspective), four days later a suspicious fire struck the Yale Law Library, charring a wall of books. (A newspaper photo published the next day shows a stunned Bork observing the damage to his intellectual sanctuary. And, notably, Bork chose the memory of smoldering books as the starting point for his most recent attack on "modern liberalism.")[22]

To academics who spent their lives contemplating the meaning and consequences of freedom or its absence, who cherished the ideal of a university as a seat of learning and rational discourse, the disruption of domestic order and the complicity of some teachers and administrators in that attack were beyond forbearance. Bork's closest friend and mentor, the law professor Alexander Bickel, though opposed to the war, saw the campus and the country disintegrating into a "dictatorship of the self-righteous." The campus radicals, he declared, were engaging not in meaningful dissent but rather in intimidation, a kind of "vandalism . . . a series of curses which do not pretend any attempt at persuasion."[23]

That fall, having seen Bickel hung in effigy in the law school court-yard on alumni weekend, Bork started work on his first major article in constitutional law. It was a rumination on the First Amendment that, not coincidentally, placed especially radical forms of political dissent outside the realm of constitutional protection.[24]

When the Vietnam War ended and campus agitation subsided, the civil strife in academia did not. Whether the issue was affirmative action, multiculturalism, women's studies, or hate speech, the two sides perpetually replayed old themes and kept campus animosities fresh. What commentators now call the culture war was an everyday truth with an enormous power to divide and alienate.

Throughout his academic tenure, Bork remained deeply immersed in the debates over all these matters, and among professors at the top law schools he found himself in a distinct minority. (It is no surprise that after writing one book, in defense of his nomination, he has now written a second attacking liberal academia.) By law school standards, "right wing" has generally referred to traditional New Deal Democrats or libertarians (who were usually conservative on economic matters and agnostic or liberal on social issues). "Liberal" law professors were distinctly to the left in comparison to the country at large and included a healthy community of neo-Marxists. Cultural conservatives and Republicans such as Bork were uncommon, an endangered species at some schools. At the University of Chicago Law School, for example, often considered the nation's most conservative, the faculty comfortably favored Mondale over Reagan in the 1984 presidential election and, more remarkably, had narrowly preferred McGovern to Nixon in 1972.[25]

Intellectual trends in the law also left Bork relatively isolated. One of the most vibrant forces in legal academia was the Critical Legal Studies Movement (described by one of its leading members as a "political location for a group of people on the Left who share the project of supporting and extending the domain of the Left in the legal academy").[26] In terms of scholarship, this enterprise meant applying European literary criticism and neo-Marxist social thought to the study of legal doctrines. That, in turn, meant dismissing old notions of legal reasoning as historical artifact or the will of the dominant classes. For "the crits" (as they were known), law was a hegemonic struggle for power, and the vast body of judicial decisions reflected little more than a sinister desire to perpetuate the class, gender, or racial advantages of the lawmakers.

The crits deconstructed the law, exploding what they perceived as myths about the potential for objectivity or the value of tradition, history, and the common law. They deconstructed law schools, too. Duncan Kennedy, one of the movement's founders, went on tour as a CLS evangelist with such "modest proposals" as equalizing the pay of janitors and professors at Harvard (where he taught) and having them exchange jobs for a while. Heirs to a sixties radicalism, the charismatic leaders of CLS charmed students with their "context smashing" doctrines while a follow-up army of feminists, multiculturalists, critical race theorists, and champions of gay rights borrowed deeply from such attacks on the established order.

All this Bork detested with an undisguised vehemence, and the points of conflict were not only theoretical. In Bork's view (and by no means his alone), the ascendancy of liberals and leftists on law school faculties went hand in hand with a serious erosion in the standards of scholarship. Nowhere was this more true than in the hiring and tenure process, where the left (often with active support from students) championed diversity while the right defended their particular concept of excellence against the inroads of race and gender preferences.[27] In the spirit of the times, the ultimate symbol of meritocracy, *The Harvard Law Review*, added an affirmative action component to its grades- and writing-based selection process because the old system had produced a chronic numerical underrepresentation of minorities. To outraged conservatives like Bork, the student editors were simply parroting their teachers, who already had subordinated quality of published work to genetic makeup as the most important criterion for faculty eligibility.

Bork was in the forefront of such controversies. In speeches ever angrier and more ominous, he decried the spread of radical "egalitarianism" and "moral relativism," bemoaned the "decline of our institutions," and weighed in on the conservative side of various social issues. As a tenured professor, Bork could speak his mind freely. But he watched appalled as a young conservative political philosopher, Thomas Pangle, Yale's most popular undergraduate professor, lost a tenure fight that smacked of a political lynching. On a smaller scale, Bork saw intellectual intimidation among the students at the law school all the time.

To Bork, the Warren Court was guilty of sins analogous to those he observed among his colleagues. Just as leftist law professors wielded scholarship as a weapon to further their political aims, the liberal Justices of the Warren Court abandoned traditional legal reasoning in favor of a "results-first, premises to follow" approach. Rather than interpret the Constitution according to its original meaning and purposes, Justices Brennan, Douglas, Goldberg, Fortas, and some of their successors had updated the document to conform with their own fashionable ideas. Rather than carry out their limited mandate of enforcing the specific commands of the Constitution within the Court's sphere of special competence, these Justices had set themselves up as an all-powerful liberal elite imposing on the country their own notions of right and wrong, fair and unfair. What CLS preached in theory, liberal Justices had put into practice: for both, there were "no rules, only passions."[28]

Bork's own jurisprudence was a furious rejoinder to both his academic and his judicial foes.[29] He proposed a much more circumscribed judicial role. In a representative democracy, Bork asserted, political judgments are to be made by the democratic branches of government and may be overridden by the unelected judiciary only if in violation of some explicit constitutional command. The meaning of the Constitution, he argued, must be determined according to the intention of its "framers"—"those who drafted, proposed, and ratified its provisions and various amendments." All that counted, according to Bork, was "how the words used in the Constitution would have been understood at the time." And "the judge's responsibility is to discern how the framers' values, defined in the context of the world they knew, apply in the world we know." No "evolving standards of decency." No Arthurian Round Table imposing morality from above. Just law determined by a factual inquiry.

It was the judicial philosophy of a severe skeptic, someone who thoroughly distrusted the very idea that judges could reason from text, history, precedent, or social convention to achieve a legitimate modern meaning for the Constitution. The process of using such conventional legal tools had been so utterly betrayed, so obviously abandoned by both the Warren Court and the main community of legal scholars that Bork sought to place the Constitution's meaning beyond their reach—in the intentions of persons long dead. The alternative, he believed, was to leave the judiciary without real constraint and thereby surrender the meaning of the law to the personal prejudices of whatever Justices sat on the Court at a given time. While the crits might consider that inevitable, to Bork it was nothing less than a judicial coup d'état.[30]

From this perspective, President Reagan's pattern of judicial appointments, the aggressive positions taken by Reagan judges and Charles

Fried once in office, even Edwin Meese's attack on the scope of judicial authority were not only justified, they were imperative. For the liberals, history began in 1954 when the Court moved to the forefront of the struggle for black equality and civil rights. They equated the rule of law with the expansive precedents of the Warren Court. But for conservatives, that was exactly backwards.

Like abolitionists confronting *Dred Scott*, Bork and his followers thought the Court itself was behaving unconstitutionally.[31] In this sense, the legal aspects of the Reagan Revolution were really, in their eyes, a counterrevolution. It was the Warren Court that had thrown precedent, tradition, and legal reasoning to the winds. The Reaganites simply wanted to restore order from chaos and corral the judiciary within the bounds it formerly had observed.

Against this background, the Bork nomination proceeded on two levels. The first was that of an especially nasty political campaign. With uncharacteristic unity, liberal interest groups from organized labor to the National Organization for Women (mainly under the umbrella of the Leadership Conference on Civil Rights), mounted a highly effective grassroots and media campaign assailing the nominee. The basic tactic was to instill fear. Through millions of pieces of direct mail, full-page newspaper ads, and negative television spots featuring Gregory Peck's trust-inducing voice, Bork was made out to be something of a monster, a man who favored sterilizing women who worked in dangerous workplaces, supported poll taxes and literacy tests to keep blacks from voting, wanted to repeal basic civil rights laws, and invited government intrusion into every private act.

The bases for these charges were Bork's legal opinions and other published writings, but the liberals stripped his words and positions of all nuance and in some cases, twisted them beyond recognition. (Believing, as Bork does, for example, that—before the Twenty-fourth Amendment—the Constitution did not prohibit poll taxes is certainly debatable as a matter of law, but it is not the same as believing, as Bork does not, that poll taxes were a good thing.) As the best analysis of the nomination concluded, "What remained was neither lie nor truth. It was half-truth. Like the half-truths of the Reagan years, it played well."[32]

The White House strategy was scarcely more honest. Chief of Staff Howard Baker and other officials around the Oval Office tried mightily to cast Bork as a "moderate," a more academic facsimile of the departing Powell. But they were betrayed by both Bork's extensive published record and the hard-core conservatives in the Justice Department, who delighted that one of their own was poised to transform the Court. The most telling blow of the Bork campaign, however, was probably the one never delivered. During the late summer, when senators were most susceptible to persuasion, President Reagan went on an extensive vacation and did nothing to support his beleaguered nominee.

In the field of public relations, Bork was no help to himself. Hardly telegenic, he came off during the hearings as aloof even when lobbed softball questions by Senate supporters. His response to Sen. Alan Simpson's query about why he wanted to be a Justice of the Supreme Court captured everything about Bork's failure as a nominee-cum-candidate. Bork could muster no better than that it would be "an intellectual feast just to be there and to read the briefs and discuss things with counsel and discuss things with my colleagues."

The liberals' political campaign paid direct dividends. Once the nomination became a close fight, Bork's fate (in a Senate now controlled again by the Democrats) rested with the more conservative Southern Democrats, represented on the Judiciary Committee by Howell Heflin of Alabama. Thanks in large part to the Voting Rights Act and to several Supreme Court opinions that Bork had criticized, blacks had become a powerful constituency in the cotton belt. As Louisiana's Bennett Johnson said to a group of freshman senators from his region (most of whom owed their election to black support), "I know how you're going to vote, and you, and you, and you." He was right. Once he was tarred by his opponents as anti–civil rights, Bork's support in the South vanished. Of the twenty-two senators from the Old Confederacy, a paltry six voted to confirm him.

There was some justice to this lopsided result. Over time, Robert Bork might have moderated his views about civil rights. But for black Americans with a memory, he had been on the wrong side of all the major battles. When the Supreme Court handed down *Baker v. Carr*, requiring fair apportionment of state legislatures and opening the door to the election of blacks, Bork complained bitterly of judicial overreaching. When Congress ordered southern businesses to accept black patronage, he decried the "unsurpassed ugliness" of forcing shopkeepers to "serve persons with whom they do not wish to associate."[33] Even Bork's support for *Brown v. Board of Education* was hedged and full of criticism. In the sweep of his career, Bork had been a naysayer to the life-altering achievements of the civil rights era and had devalued the Constitution as a refuge for minorities.[34] He had stigmatized these achievements as illegitimate, impugned their integrity, and agreed to stand behind them more as a matter of courtesy than of principle.

It was this legacy that brought former Texas Representative Barbara Jordan, the first black to serve in Congress from the South since Reconstruction and a leading figure during Watergate, to testify against Bork. The "primary basis" for her opposition was simply the accumulated experience "of living fifty-one years as a black American born in the South and determined to be heard by the majority community."[35] In the final vote on Bork's nomination, she and other blacks made themselves heard, distinctly.

In addition to politics, the Bork nomination was about law. Apart from issues of race, it served as a national referendum of sorts on two issues: the attractiveness of Bork's jurisprudence of "original intent" and whether the Constitution includes a right to privacy protecting such things as the use of contraception and a woman's choice to obtain an abortion. The end result was first to discredit Bork (in the eyes of much of the lay public) as a constitutional thinker and, second, to establish a belief in the right to privacy as a prerequisite (at least in the short term) for anyone aspiring to be confirmed to the Court. While both these developments were victories for the liberals, they changed few minds among those who had opinions beforehand and only deepened resentment among conservatives, who in the future would use artifice as an additional method for securing judicial confirmations.

Liberals had been massing their attack on Bork's jurisprudence long before his nomination was even announced. In 1985, Attorney General Meese had made this interpretive method the fulcrum of his attack on the Court, especially its decisions protecting abortion rights and those enforcing a stricter separation of church and state than Meese thought justifiable.[36] In a rare public diatribe, Justice Brennan had responded that original intent jurisprudence was "little more than arrogance cloaked as humility"—a false pretense that the Framers' intent could be discovered and, more damningly, a political choice against claims of the minority versus the majority cloaked in the robes of neutral historicism.[37] Even the more moderate Justice Stevens felt compelled to upbraid the attorney general for neglecting those historical facts that did not jibe comfortably with his political preferences.[38]

During Bork's hearings, the case against original intent was made to the point of exhaustion by panels of mainly liberal legal scholars, who took turns at the long, baize-covered table from which witnesses testified. They pointed out, to start with, that it was far from obvious why the Constitution, replete with clauses of indefinite content, designed with the evident purpose of applying to unseen and unforeseeable changes in the structure of American society, should be interpreted exclusively by reference to the vision of persons dead for more than 200 years. At a minimum, Bork's choice of approach was itself based on a value judgment commanded by neither constitutional text nor history and repudiated by a long line of distinguished Justices dating back to John Marshall. Originalist arguments had been rattling around for a long time, as had critics, such as Justice Brandeis, who described the Constitution as "not a straight jacket" but "a living organism" and identified its "capacity of adaptation" as the cause of its endurance "as the fundamental law of an ever-developing people."[39]

Even Charles Fried (though Reagan's solicitor general and a Bork supporter) agreed that the practical and theoretical objections to originalist reasoning were "devastating."[40] Judges were by no means expert in the distinct discipline of history. On the contrary, many of their forays into historical analysis were embarrassingly amateurish.[41]

But even if judges doubled as historians, they would have no objective way to decide whose intent should count in interpreting the Constitution—that is, who should qualify as a "Framer." The drafters of the document? The people who ratified it in separate state conventions? And even if one could resolve that problem, how would a judge reconcile the sometimes conflicting views of leading figures in the founding generation? Furthermore, shouldn't it matter to an originalist that the Framers themselves—many of whom believed the lessons of experience to be more important than those of history*—apparently didn't think "origi-

---

*As Thomas Jefferson wrote James Madison at the end of his presidency: "Some men look at constitutions with sanctimonious reverence and deem them like the ark of the covenant, too sacred to be touched. They ascribe to the men of the preceding age a wisdom more than human and suppose what they did to be beyond amendment. I knew that age well; I belonged to it, and labored with it. It deserved well of its country. It was very like the present, but without the experience of the present; and forty years experience in government is worth a century of book-reading; and this they would say themselves, were they to rise from the dead." Quoted in Jack Rakove, *Original Meanings: Politics and Ideas in the Making of the Constitution* (New York: Knopf, 1996), p. 367.

nal intent" (as Bork would practice it) was the proper way to interpret the Constitution.[42]

The most powerful indictment of original intent jurisprudence, however, was simply that it could not deliver what Bork promised, namely a method for interpreting the Constitution that curbs judicial discretion and prevents unelected judges from seizing power from the people's representatives. As his own testimony revealed, the practice of originalism was full of exactly the kind of subjective, value-laden, inescapably political judgments that Bork claimed to abhor.

The false promise of originalism was revealed most clearly in Bork's defense of *Brown*, a decision so widely accepted as "right" that no nominee could realistically repudiate it. Before the Judiciary Committee, Bork embraced *Brown* as not only consistent with the Framers' original understanding of the Fourteenth Amendment's equal protection clause but even "compelled" by it.[43] This was an odd testimonial for an originalist to make, for the historical record is powerfully to the contrary. The debates surrounding the adoption of the Fourteenth Amendment provide ample evidence that some of its main sponsors thought about and specifically rejected the idea that "equal protection" prohibited segregated schools. Speaking directly to the issue, the amendment's floor manager assured the House of Representatives that "civil rights do not mean that all children shall attend the same school." And as if to drive home the point, the same Congress that crafted the equal protection clause continued segregation in the one school system it administered, that of the District of Columbia.[44]

Despite this evidence regarding original intent, with a Houdini-like deftness, Bork managed to escape the seemingly inescapable conclusion that *Brown* was wrongly decided. Instead, Bork argued that the Fourteenth Amendment, as originally understood, embodied a *general principle of racial equality* and that, by 1954, the time of *Brown*, "it had been apparent for some time that segregation rarely if ever produced equality."[45]

But this is only the most tepid and unscientific form of originalism and certainly not one consistent with Bork's insistence on interpreting the Constitution according to "how the words . . . would have been understood at the time." At the time of the Fourteenth Amendment's ratification, most people recognized a sharp distinction between "political equality" and "social equality." They didn't think social slights, such as separate trolley cars or even separate schools, deprived people of equal protection of the laws.

Far from adhering to his avowed methodology, Bork had distilled one plausible general principle—no racial discrimination—from the language of the equal protection clause and the context (emancipation) in which it was framed. This wasn't the only general principle Bork might have chosen. Using the same method, he might have settled on the broader principle that equal protection of the laws commands that the majority cannot discriminate against any minority when that discrimination reflects prejudice. Or he might have chosen the even farther-reaching principle that the amendment outlawed all forms of official prejudice, including, for example, prejudice against women.[46]

The point is not that Bork chose the wrong principle (though many would argue that he did). The point is that he made a choice—one based not on what the Fourteenth Amendment's Framers thought about a specific question but on his own judgment about which of a number of general principles best fit the amendment's protean words. Text, context, history, even moral philosophy all informed Bork's selection, as they would for any judge. Yet Bork persisted in denying the exercise of his own judgment and in denouncing others more candid than himself.

The Bork hearings demonstrated to the public what had long since been evident to students of Court history: that originalism is potentially every bit as malleable as other methods of interpretation. *Dred Scott,* for example, the pro-slavery decision Bork excoriated as the wellspring of judicial activism, is shot through with originalist rhetoric. Justice Hugo Black, no devotee of judicial restraint, defended many of his most activist opinions as reflecting not his own judgment but that of the founding generation. As Richard Posner, perhaps Reagan's finest judicial appointee, would later conclude in assessing Bork's views, "Originalism is not an analytic method; it is a rhetoric that can be used to support any result a judge wants to reach."[47]

That is certainly how liberals looked on it. They saw an astonishing congruence between the alleged command of history implicit in original intent jurisprudence and the reactionary agenda of Bork and his political patrons. It was history that permitted school prayer, history that condemned affirmative action, history that knew no right to privacy, history that exalted states' rights. To liberals, such conclusions were no more than the products of a closed mind and a carefully selective memory. Such a man, they thought, knew no integrity and had to be stopped.

* * *

Bork's opponents, however, conducted a jurisprudential charade of their own. One of the liberals' principal concerns was Bork's outspoken opposition to *Roe* v. *Wade* and the very strong possibility that his elevation to the Court would provide a fifth vote (together with those of Rehnquist, White, O'Connor, and Scalia) for overturning a woman's right to obtain an abortion. While polls conducted by the Democrats showed that they might not make much political headway attacking Bork as antiabortion, the public was very receptive to a similar but broader attack that Bork opposed the "right to privacy" on which *Roe* v. *Wade* was premised. Accordingly, with the strong backing of women's groups, Senator Biden and other liberals made Bork's antiprivacy views a central part of his inquisition.

Bork's objection to a constitutional right of privacy boiled down to a single question: given that the Constitution itself never mentions the word *privacy*, where does the right to privacy come from? In his view, the Court had never provided a satisfactory answer, and even a brief look at the relevant cases lends credence to his assessment.

The turning-point privacy case of the modern era, and the one most often debated at the hearings, was *Griswold* v. *Connecticut*,[48] in which the Justices, by a 7–2 vote, used privacy grounds to strike down a mostly dormant and completely antiquated Connecticut statute making it a crime to use birth control. Although strong in number, the Justices in the majority splintered badly over how to justify their decision.

Justice Douglas, in an opinion now often ridiculed, found constitutional "zones of privacy" in "penumbras, formed from emanations" of a smorgasbord of constitutional provisions, specifically the First, Third, Fourth, Fifth, and Ninth Amendments.

Justice Goldberg, joined by Chief Justice Warren and Justice Brennan, considered the Ninth Amendment the best mooring for a right to privacy. He wanted to tie the right to that amendment's enigmatic instruction that "the enumeration in the Constitution, of certain rights, shall not be construed to deny or disparage others retained by the people." Privacy, in Goldberg's view, was among those "other" rights the people retained.

Justices Harlan and White thought the right to privacy came from the Fourteenth Amendment's guarantee that no state shall "deprive any person of life, liberty, or property without due process of law." For Harlan, the due process clause protected basic values "implicit in the concept of ordered liberty," and "marital intimacy," including the right to use contraception, was among those values. To bring the full machinery of the criminal law to bear on such private conduct, a state would have to provide a justification far more compelling than the purely moral preference that supported Connecticut's birth control law.

Justices Black and Stewart, in dissent, subscribed essentially to Bork's view that the Constitution contains no freestanding right to privacy. While they derided the Connecticut birth control law as "uncommonly silly," Black and Stewart could find no constitutional provision prohibiting state legislatures from passing stupid laws. As Black put it, "I like my privacy as well as the next one, but I am nevertheless compelled to admit that government has a right to invade it unless prohibited by some specific constitutional provision." As one commentator remarked, expanding on Black's point, "Whenever you get such a potpourri of constitutional provisions as suggested . . . in *Griswold*, the feeling must grow that the answer was not found in the Constitution at all."[49]

By the time of *Roe*, the Justices in the majority (again, seven) had more or less agreed to locate the right to privacy in the Fourteenth Amendment's due process clause. But this was an approach beset with serious problems. By its very language, the due process clause does not place any substantive constraints on government. It cautions that no state could deprive a citizen of life, liberty, or property *without due process of law*. In other words, the clause's text seems focused on procedural regularity and, taken that way, a duly enacted statute (such as Connecticut's birth control law) surely passed its test.

It was undeniably true that the Court sometimes had given substantive content to the due process clause—that is, it had read the clause as imposing limits on the *content* of legislation rather than dealing solely with the *processes* by which laws were adopted and applied. Scholars had coined an oxymoron for this doctrine under which the Court singled out what it deemed to be particularly "fundamental" rights for special protection. They called it "substantive due process." But it was also true that this countertextual doctrine was the source of some of the Court's most reviled decisions, cases Chief Justice Hughes referred to as the Court's "self-inflicted wounds."

In *Dred Scott*, for example, Chief Justice Roger Taney had used substantive due process to insist that Congress could not deprive southerners of their slave "property" by outlawing slavery in the territories. Then, after the Civil War, a Court uncommonly committed to laissez-faire capitalism had found a substantive right to "freedom of contract" implicit in the due process clause—almost precisely as the modern Court had discovered a right to privacy. From the turn of the century until the mid-1930s, the Court used this reading of the due process clause to strike down regulations on business, including maximum hour, minimum wage, and other labor statutes as well as central provisions of Franklin Roosevelt's New Deal.

The debate over substantive due process and the right to privacy will be discussed at greater length in a subsequent chapter. Suffice it to say here that a large collection of constitutional scholars of every political stripe share Bork's antipathy for substantive due process. Of all the doctrines of constitutional law, it has been the basis for the Court's most extensive and least defensible forays into policy making, both liberal and conservative. Even many politically liberal scholars who defended the idea of a right to privacy in certain specific cases nonetheless admit that the Court stretched the concept beyond all logic in extending that right to cover obtaining an abortion. And, at a minimum, any fair-minded constitutionalist must at least concede that the Court's foray into the right to privacy lies at the furthest reach of its power, the place where constitutional law borders on constitutional invention.

Yet, with their poll numbers and their constituencies firmly in mind, the Senate Democrats not only embraced the right to privacy but enshrined it as a litmus test for confirmation to the Court. In so subordinating constitutional interpretation to the demands of a single suspect doctrine, they invited precisely the charge they leveled against Bork and his supporters: that they had no regard for the integrity of the law or of the Court but only wanted their political point of view to prevail. Reducing the hearings to a referendum on reproductive rights may have been good liberal strategy, but it pushed the Court even deeper into the quicksand of partisan politics.

Liberals rejoiced when the Senate rejected Robert Bork. I counted myself among them. During the hearings, my co-clerks and I had spent more than a few off-hours thinking up and funneling to friends on the Senate committee staff questions that would expose the weaknesses and contradictions in Bork's positions. Years later, I'm still glad Bork lost. His subsequent writings—including his recent proposal that Congress be given the power to override Supreme Court decisions—have only reinforced the conclusion that Bork would have been an intemperate and partisan Justice, arrogant about a judicial philosophy he only selectively practiced and could not effectively defend.

But, that said, I have come to appreciate, as I did not even consider at the time, the deep and lasting damage that the liberals' approach to the Bork hearings visited upon the Court. Skewering Bork on the issue of privacy ushered in the era of "stealth" nominees, during which a chief qualification for the Court became a lack of public comment coupled with a denial of private comment on *Roe v. Wade*, the most disputed case of the modern era. The Bork experience also established intense political campaigning and special interest lobbying as a fixed part of the nomination process. Such truth-twisting campaigning made a casualty of candor in the selection of life-tenured appointees to our highest court. The lobbying ate away the thin but crucial divide between law and politics—the public belief that the Supreme Court is not merely another political institution and that judges can and should stand above the expedient trade-offs of the day.[50]

But the problem that the Bork hearings created for the Court penetrated far deeper than the institution's image and was more serious and immediate than such an almost quaint concern with keeping law and politics separate. The development of law, especially constitutional law, involves a delicate alchemy. If history is any judge, there is no single "right" approach to interpreting the Constitution. Certainly, neither the Justices nor the academics who dissect their work have ever agreed on one. Just as Bork's jurisprudence of original intent suffered from the inherent weakness of too closely linking the law to an unknowable past, other modes of interpretation potentially cast the law adrift without reference to the text, history, and structure of the document that is the charter of both our government and our liberties.

The most we can expect and what we must demand from the Court as it expounds the law is an integrity born of consistency and sincerity. Legitimate constitutional arguments are not limitless; they may take several forms familiar to law. They may be based on history, on precedent, on the text, on inferences from the way our government is structured, on appeals to ethics, or on prudential considerations about the consequences of a decision. Often, these modes of argument are used in combination, melded into a convincing whole. And none is perfect for every circumstance. Deciding which modes of argument best suit the facts and circumstances of a given case is both an inevitable moral choice and the essence of judging.

To undertake this process as a body of nine independent, opinionated judges, whose views in hard cases often prove irreconcilable, depends on a decency of process. For the system to work, for Justices in disagreement to achieve an exchange of ideas, undertake a search for common ground, or even reach an agreement respectfully to disagree, there must first be trust and belief in mutual good faith. There must be a sense that both sides are advancing legal arguments because they believe in them deeply and not as a stratagem for imposing their will on the law. There must be a sense that reasons matter more than results. The power to interpret carries the responsibility of good faith and self-denial. When these are destroyed, nothing remains but counting votes and the exercise of raw power.

Bork's mentor, Alex Bickel, had written shortly before his death in 1975 that our system "cannot survive a politics of moral attack."[51] Whether or not that is true as a general matter, the delicate process of collective judicial decision breaks under the weight of unrelenting ideology and the arrogance of certainty. That was the highest cost of the Bork nomination. Before the hearings ended, the possibility of trust, good faith, and self-doubt had been vanquished. Each side was convinced of its own virtue while, at the same time, believing that no tactic, no hypocrisy, no lie was too low or base or simply wrong for the other side to forgo. Both sides concluded that the best recourse in the future would be to fight fire with fire.

The final vote on Robert Bork's nomination (he refused to withdraw even when defeat was inevitable) was a beginning, not an end. Conservative political commentators, blaming liberal "dirty tricks" for their setback, exhorted followers to carry on Bork's war against the imperial liberal judiciary.[52] Meanwhile, Reagan's attorney general urged top Justice Department officials to avoid seeking consensus and to "polarize the debate" on prominent legal issues.[53] Liberals deluded themselves into thinking that, a bit of mendacity aside, they had found a true mission in upholding "the rule of law" against the forces of darkness.

The Justices, split 4–4 and waiting, had their own allegiances, of course, as well as friends and protégés in the thick of the fight. Watching the hearings from their respective Chambers, they were one step removed from the full emotional force of the conflagration. But that was inescapably a short-term isolation.

By the time of Bork's nomination, the ligatures of trust within the Court were already strained to the breaking point. Weekly confrontations over the death penalty and sharp divisions over race, abortion, and religion had seen to that. By the end of the hearings, the storm of civil war was hard against the Court's front door. Every month, the backlog of controversial cases grew as the Justices anxiously delayed decisions until joined by a tiebreaking ninth.

Regardless of Bork's defeat, it was only a matter of time until Reagan succeeded in putting a new conservative on the Court. And when he did, the battle would shift with all its ferocity from the Senate Caucus Room to the Court's inner chamber—and some of us, still tracking blood, spoiling for the next round, would shift with it.

The Cabal Against the Libs

After Robert Bork's defeat, the moderate and conservative factions within the Reagan administration split over whom next to put forward for the Court. Howard Baker, Reagan's middle-of-the-road chief of staff (who had warned against nominating an ideologue such as Bork to begin with), favored Anthony M. Kennedy, a judge on the Ninth Circuit Court of Appeals with a consistent if fairly bland conservative record. Kennedy's qualifications were best summed up as "confirmable," which was exactly what Baker was looking for after the Bork debacle.

Although Kennedy could hardly match Bork's academic and professional record, he was an impressive achiever. The son of a prominent Republican lobbyist in Sacramento, California, he was valedictorian of his high school class, earned election to Phi Beta Kappa at Stanford, and graduated near the top of his class at Harvard Law School. After law school, Kennedy returned to Sacramento, where he eventually took over his father's lawyer-lobbying business. Between rounds at the state capitol, he demonstrated a continued interest in the more academic side of law by teaching a course on the Constitution at a local law school, McGeorge.

In his private life, the lanky, baby-faced Kennedy was a modern George Washington, a nose-to-the-grindstone straight arrow, viceless to the point of being a bit of a "priss" in the eyes of some colleagues, so old-fashioned in his sensibilities that he moved his family into his parents' home after their deaths. An observant Catholic and former altar boy, happily married and a father of three, Kennedy managed to keep an unblemished reputation despite a dozen years working for the liquor industry in the back-scratching and sometimes palm-greasing world of the California legislature.

In politics, Kennedy, like a number of young California conservatives, had latched on to Ronald Reagan's 1966 gubernatorial campaign, which featured the same tough-on-crime, cut taxes, and reduce spending platform that would eventually carry him to the White House. Through financial contributions to the Reagan campaign and ties to Edwin Meese (Reagan's closest adviser), Kennedy landed the choice assignment of drafting a proposed spending cap amendment to the state constitution. Although the amendment failed at the ballot box, in 1975 Reagan repaid Kennedy for his loyal service by recommending him to President Ford for an open slot on the federal Court of Appeals for the Ninth Circuit. At age thirty-nine, Kennedy became the youngest federal appellate judge in the country.

In twelve years on the bench, Kennedy attracted a stellar cast of conservative clerks (who would later prove instrumental in the campaign for his Supreme Court nomination) but wrote relatively few memorable opinions. As a rule, he spurned liberal or innovative legal claims. He upheld death sentences when more progressive judges might have struck them down.[1] He crafted the country's first appellate opinion rejecting the controversial "comparable worth" standard for equalizing pay between men and women.[2]

Kennedy also threw out a novel lawsuit brought by one hundred black and white families who alleged that a group of real estate brokers were violating federal housing laws by "steering" black families away from predominantly white neighborhoods. The hundred families had established the basis for their civil rights claim by posing as prospective home buyers to test whether the brokers treated the blacks differently from the whites. The results of the experiment showed a distinct pattern of bias; still Kennedy ruled that the "tester" families had no right to sue. In his rather narrow view (which the Supreme Court would later unanimously reject),[3] because the testers were only posing as buyers and had no real intent to purchase homes, they had not suffered the "legal injury" necessary to sustain a lawsuit.[4]

Kennedy did pioneer one significant judicial retrenchment: he carved out a new "good faith" exception to the "exclusionary rule," which forbids prosecutors from using evidence obtained in violation of the Fourth, Fifth, or Sixth Amendments. In a leading opinion, subsequently endorsed by the Supreme Court,[5] Kennedy authorized trial courts to accept evidence seized by police officers who acted in good faith reliance on a search warrant even when that warrant later turned out to be defective.

Despite this solid conservative pedigree, Kennedy did not rate especially well with the Reaganites in Washington. Most of his work was cautious. Unlike Bork or Scalia, Kennedy almost never used his judicial office as a bully pulpit from which to assail the liberal excesses of the Supreme Court or other judges. In the blunt assessment of Brad Reynolds, Meese's influential deputy, this predisposition to write opinions "within the four corners of the case" rendered Kennedy "mechanically competent, but not much else."[6]

Kennedy's liberal colleagues on the Ninth Circuit agreed with Reynolds's judgment and, specifically for that reason, they tried through various back channels to promote his nomination.* In the liberals' calculus, Kennedy was the best they could hope for from the Reagan White House: someone not especially ideological, a person who thought of himself and wanted others to think of him as "lawyerly" and "reasonable." In their experience, Kennedy could be talked to, perhaps occasionally even convinced, or at least lured into compromise. He was the sort of judge who might "grow" (i.e., move left) once on the Court. Or so the liberals convinced themselves.

In Washington, hard-liners such as Reynolds and Meese feared exactly this potential flexibility: the risk that Reagan's final choice for the Court would turn out to be a Powell clone—a middle man and balancer—robbing conservatives of a clear-cut Court majority. Or worse yet, that he'd be another Harry Blackmun, a generally conservative appellate judge who turned steadily more liberal after Nixon put him on the Court. A specific source of concern was Kennedy's opinion in a 1980 case in which members of the U.S. Navy had challenged Pentagon regulations banning homosexuals from the service. Kennedy had upheld the military's policy, but characteristically his opinion was narrowly drawn and, to the dismay of conservatives, almost solicitous of gay rights. Although Kennedy ultimately deferred to the military's judgment about personnel, he intimated that, in nonmilitary contexts, the constitutional right to privacy might well protect homosexuals engaged in "consensual homosexual behavior."[7]

This kind of thinking was inexcusable in the eyes of many Reaganites.

---

*Several Ninth Circuit judges also feared that the administration would select another of their colleagues, Clifford Wallace, whom they saw as much more rigid and ideological than Kennedy.

Kennedy not only seemed to subscribe to the dubious doctrine that the Constitution contained a right to privacy but apparently even contemplated that this right might be broad enough to cover homosexual conduct. (By comparison, when faced with a similar case, Robert Bork had scoffed at the notion of any such privacy right for gays.)[8]

More disturbing still, if Kennedy were so accepting of a right to privacy, could he be trusted to vote to overturn *Roe*? High-placed former Kennedy clerks—Judge Alex Kozinski, Richard Willard (chief of the Justice Department's Civil Division), and Carolyn Kuhl (a deputy solicitor general)—could swear up and down on the basis of their private conversations that Kennedy could be trusted on the matter. But such assurances couldn't vanquish all doubts or, for that matter, placate anti–gay rights Republicans such as Sen. Jesse Helms, whose reaction upon hearing about Kennedy's gay rights opinion was a definitive "No way, José."[9]

At the White House, Reagan's legal advisers winnowed the field of potential nominees down to Kennedy and Douglas Ginsburg, a forty-one-year-old former antitrust scholar and D.C. circuit judge whom Meese and company sized up as a clone of Bork without his crippling paper trail. In the final deliberations, Kennedy faded as his fellow Californians Meese and William French Smith (Reagan's first attorney general) both weighed in for Ginsburg. In addition to harboring doubts about Kennedy's ideological purity, his old associates from Sacramento "seemed to think of him as a nice guy who didn't quite measure up."[10]

Reagan announced his selection of Ginsburg on October 28, and within hours the nomination started sinking. Journalists revealed that during the 1970s, while a professor at Harvard, Ginsburg had occasionally smoked marijuana with friends and around students. Reporters also discovered that his wife, a physician, had performed abortions. As conservatives in Congress went ballistic over these moral failings, another report charged Ginsburg with a potentially significant conflict of interest. It seemed that during his time at the Justice Department, Ginsburg had argued positions favoring the cable industry while failing to disclose his own $140,000 investment in a cable company.

In little more than a week, Ginsburg's nomination imploded, and the White House, for their third choice, immediately resurrected Mr. Confirmable. Kennedy did not disappoint. Despite the earnest efforts of the Washington press corps, no skeletons emerged from his closet during his hearings. On substantive matters, Kennedy tiptoed masterfully through the potential minefield of Senate questions. Where Bork had spoken confrontationally about a Constitution of fixed and determined meaning, Kennedy floated puffballs about a Constitution that "provides a dynamic mechanism for creative achievement in a framework that preserves our values."

On the all-important issue of privacy, Kennedy followed a script that would become standard for future nominees: he endorsed the *idea* that the Constitution included some sort of right to privacy but retreated to meaningless platitudes when pressed to define how extensive that right might be. As he suggested in one exquisitely circular response, "The concept of liberty in the due process clause is . . . quite sufficient to protect the values of privacy that Americans legitimately think are part of their constitutional heritage."[11] This definition effectively begged the question of which "values of privacy" should be deemed "legitimately" part of our constitutional heritage (is abortion?); and crucially Kennedy never offered his view. Still, such nonanswers effectively finessed the privacy issue. Liberals, too exhausted by the Bork fight to offer significant resistance, could claim that he passed their right-to-privacy litmus test. Conservatives, meanwhile, could comfort themselves with the vacuousness of Kennedy's testimony and the many private winks and nods they had received that, on abortion and other key topics, Kennedy was their man down the line. In the end, both sides held their breath while voting overwhelmingly to confirm.

Kennedy wasn't installed at the Court until mid-February 1988, too late to hear many cases for that term. One case he did arrive in time for was *Patterson v. McLean Credit Union*. The result of Kennedy's participation was enough to give liberals ample cause to wonder whether their much-cherished victory over Bork would turn out to be pyrrhic.

When McLean Credit Union of Winston-Salem, North Carolina, hired Brenda Patterson as an accounting clerk in 1972, she was the first and only black at the company. Although securing the clerk's position was a "dream come true" for Patterson, according to her legal complaint, once she started work, her supervisors regularly harassed and demeaned her. Among other alleged offenses, they singled out Patterson for humiliating work assignments (such as sweeping the office), which were never given to white clerks, and responded to her complaints about overwork by reminding her that "blacks are known to work slower than whites by nature." After being laid off without warning in 1982, Patterson sued her former employer for money damages, claiming that McLean Credit had violated her contract rights as guaranteed by a civil rights law known as Section 1981.

This civil rights provision had a complicated judicial history. Its parent statute, the 1866 Civil Rights Act, represented Congress's first attempt to capture the achievements of the Civil War and give legal content to the new promise of freedom that the Thirteenth Amendment granted black Americans. Prior to the Act's passage, in the first year after the Confederate defeat, the ideal of true emancipation had proven largely illusory for many blacks in the South. Routinely, whites refused to sell blacks property or employ them for a fair wage. Instead, former masters sought to replace emancipated slaves with black laborers held in check through a system of rigged personal service contracts that essentially amounted to debt peonage. Vigilante groups used violence and intimidation to restore something close to the old order, rounding up freedmen to work for their former masters, torturing those who refused.

To remedy these oppressive conditions, Congress (over President Andrew Johnson's veto) passed the Civil Rights Act, which spelled out the rights and responsibilities of citizenship that blacks were now supposed to enjoy. "Citizens, of every race and color, without regard to any previous condition of slavery or involuntary servitude, . . . shall have the same right . . . to make and enforce contracts, to sue, be parties, give evidence, to inherit, purchase, lease, sell, hold and convey real and personal property, and to full and equal benefit of all laws . . . as is enjoyed by white citizens, and shall be subject to like punishment, pains, and penalities, and to none other." The act further provided criminal sanctions for its violation and allowed aggrieved parties to file civil suits for damages in federal court.

As with many of the potentially far-reaching enactments of the Reconstruction period, the 1866 Civil Rights Act lay dormant for the better part of a century. To the extent that the statute outlawed official governmental discrimination, it was in practical terms superseded in 1868 by the Fourteenth Amendment's equal protection clause, which gave constitutional status to the principle of equal treatment for blacks under law. Both the Fourteenth Amendment and the 1866 act might also have been read to prohibit a broad range of discriminatory practices by private persons and institutions. The judiciary, though, explicitly limited the Fourteenth Amendment to governmental discrimination and implied that the same limit applied to the 1866 act. As a result, the 1866 act became largely vestigial.

In 1968, however, the Warren Court, as part of its larger enterprise of desegregating American society, gave the 102-year-old law new life. That year, in *Jones v. Alfred Mayer Co.*, the Court ruled 7–2 that Congress did intend the 1866 act (in contrast to the Fourteenth Amendment) to reach private discrimination. Specifically, the majority ruled that a black man could use that part of the act dealing with property rights (known today as Section 1982) to sue private white homeowners who refused to sell him real estate in their segregated neighborhood. If the act were read otherwise, Justice Stewart concluded for the majority, "Negro citizens . . . would be left with a mere paper guarantee . . . that a dollar in the hands of a Negro will purchase the same thing as in the hands of a white man."[12]

Building on this ruling, in a 1976 case (*Runyon v. McCrary*), the Court applied the same analysis to Section 1981, the 1866 act's ban on discrimination in the "making" and "enforcement" of contracts. In *Runyon*, a black woman named Sandra McCrary sued Richard Runyon for refusing to enroll her child in his lily-white child-care center. The Court (again over dissent) ruled that this private act of racism violated Section 1981.[13]

Brenda Patterson's claim against McLean Credit raised a second-generation definitional question about the breadth of the statute. Patterson alleged discrimination *during the course of her employment*. McLean Credit countered that such on-the-job discrimination did not fall within Section 1981's ban on discrimination in the "making" and "enforcement" of contracts. The lower courts had sided with McLean Credit, and the Supreme Court had agreed to resolve the issue.

On its face, *Patterson* did not seem a likely candidate to become a watershed case. The direction of the Court's decision was, naturally, a matter of enormous import to Brenda Patterson, but it was of only middling significance in the broader context of civil rights.[14] More recent civil rights laws, specifically Title VII of the Civil Rights Act of 1964, clearly outlawed the sort of on-the-job discrimination of which Patterson complained; she undoubtedly could have brought suit under that statute. She had chosen the alternate route because (in contrast to Title VII) the older Section 1981 allowed juries to award punitive (as well as compensatory) damages against an offending employer. Section 1981 also did not contain Title VII's two-year limit on the award of back pay. A Court ruling that Section 1981 did not cover Patterson's complaint would reduce the scope of remedies available for on-the-job discrimination. But, in general terms, it wouldn't leave a large hole in the overall umbrella of civil rights law.

Chief Justice Rehnquist, however, saw *Patterson* as a potential vehicle for advancing a much broader agenda. Although the parties had litigated the case on the assumption that the Court's 1976 *Runyon* decision (extending Section 1981 to private parties) was settled law, Rehnquist thought otherwise. He had dissented in *Runyon* and (as did some commentators) still held firmly to the view that neither Section 1981 nor any other part of the 1866 Civil Rights Act could properly be read as outlawing race discrimination by private parties.

The previous year, Rehnquist had reraised his objections to *Runyon* in a Section 1981 case in which the Court was considering whether discrimination against Arabs and Jews qualified as "race" discrimination prohibited by a statute originally designed for the benefit of blacks. This case, too, had involved private discrimination, and Rehnquist thought it better decided not by defining "race" for the purposes of the statute but rather by overruling *Runyon* and making Section 1981 inapplicable altogether. At the time, Justices White (who also had dissented in *Runyon*) and Scalia had echoed Rehnquist's view. Justice O'Connor had expressed some reservations about *Runyon* as well, but, lacking a majority, Rehnquist had dropped the issue and the Court had ruled unanimously that discrimination against Arabs and Jews was race discrimination prohibited by the act.

Now, with Kennedy having replaced Powell (who had been in the *Runyon* majority), Rehnquist recognized that he might have the votes to prevail. So as he opened the Justices' conference on *Patterson*, the Chief transformed the case into a potential blockbuster by putting into play the entire notion—central to the post-Warren conception of civil rights—that the 1866 Civil Rights Act outlawed private acts of race discrimination. Even though McLean Credit hadn't asked the Court to reconsider *Runyon*, Rehnquist suggested that the Court hold *Patterson* over until the next term and order the parties to brief and argue the fundamental underlying question of whether *Runyon* should be overruled.

Faced with the Chief's proposal, the Justices split exactly as might have been expected. White gladly seconded the suggestion. O'Connor and Scalia reiterated their serious doubts about whether both *Runyon* and also *Jones* had been correctly decided. They, too, supported reargument.

Justices Brennan, Marshall, Blackmun, and Stevens lined up on the other side. Brennan and Marshall thought *Runyon* correctly decided, period. Blackmun and Stevens had been less certain that *Runyon* was right at the time it was decided.[15] Nonetheless, they felt strongly that it was settled law and that the conservatives had advanced no good reason for calling it into question. All agreed, moreover, that Rehnquist's gambit was especially inappropriate in a case where the parties—who ordinarily frame the issues to be decided—had not asked the Court to reconsider its prior ruling.

In the liberals' view, the conservatives' proposal was reckless. As Stevens stressed, the force of the Court's past precedents should be especially strong in cases of statutory (as opposed to constitutional) interpretation. Whereas Congress is often powerless to affect Court rulings that interpret the Constitution, when Congress believes the Court has misinterpreted a statute, it can negate the purported mistake simply by amending the law. Yet in the case of *Runyon*'s interpretation of Section 1981, Congress had done no such thing. On the contrary, it had accepted the Court's ruling without a murmur (despite its close attention to civil rights enforcement), in a sense ratifying *Runyon* with silence. If Congress had no complaint with *Runyon*'s assessment of *congressional* intent, the liberals insisted, the Court had no business setting aside stare decisis and second-guessing itself.

As junior Justice, Kennedy was last to speak at conference and the deciding vote. He cast his lot with the Chief and made a fifth to reconsider *Runyon*.

For the liberals, Kennedy's decision was devastating, a declaration seemingly calculated to announce that he was no Powell (who had been in the *Runyon* majority) or timid either. And when Rehnquist sent around a draft opinion ordering the parties in *Patterson* to brief and argue the merits of *Runyon*, the liberals screamed their protest. In a dissent joined by Brennan and Marshall, Blackmun angrily accused the majority of seeking to unravel the entire fabric of judicial protection for minorities that the modern Court had woven around the Civil Rights Act. "I am at a loss," he wrote, "to understand the motivation of five Members of this Court to reconsider an interpretation of a civil rights statute that so clearly reflects our society's earnest commitment to ending racial discrimination, and in which Congress has evidently acquiesced."[16]

Even the usually unflappable Stevens was moved to anger. "If the Court decides to cast itself adrift from the constraints imposed by the adversary process and to fashion its own agenda, the consequences for the Nation—and for the future of this Court as an institution—will be even more serious than any temporary encouragement of previously rejected forms of racial discrimination," he lamented in a separate dissent (also joined by the others). "The Court has inflicted a serious—and unwise— wound upon itself today."

The conservatives took umbrage at these accusations, especially Kennedy, who wrote Rehnquist privately that he found the dissents "most disappointing." Nor did Rehnquist let them pass unchallenged. "One might think from the dissents of our colleagues that our decision . . . is a 'first' in the history of the Court," the Chief responded sarcastically. And "one would also think from the language of the dissents that we had decided to overrule *Runyon* v. *McCrary*." That was nonsense, Rehnquist assured. In revisiting a controversial precedent, the Court was merely doing what it regularly had done from time to time. If anyone was acting improperly, it was the liberals—by trying to exempt from ordinary reconsideration every decision that favored civil rights plaintiffs.

From a purely technical standpoint, the liberals' reaction to the reargument order in *Patterson* was disproportionate. Rehnquist was surely correct that the Court occasionally rethought precedents involving statutory interpretation (particularly ones, such as *Runyon*, that had met with some scholarly criticism). In fact, just five weeks before their conference in *Patterson*, the Justices had voted unanimously to overturn a statutory precedent in a much less controversial field of law.[17] Furthermore, the Court's decision to reconsider *Runyon* did not necessarily prefigure a decision to overrule it.

But the liberals were not responding on the level of legal technicality. To them, the majority's insistence on reaching out beyond the confines of the issues originally argued in *Patterson* marked a sharp turn in the road. Having listened to their conservative colleagues in conference, the liberals had concluded that, public pronouncements notwithstanding, for Rehnquist and his allies, the order to reconsider *Runyon* was simply the necessary first step before overruling it. More broadly, they saw *Patterson* as only the beginning of an extended post-Powellian nightmare, in which a narrow conservative majority, with little regard for precedent, tradition, or other notions of judicial restraint, took an ax to the great liberal oaks that had taken root under Chief Justice Warren and even Burger.

Particularly galling was the fact that the new conservative majority, as though flaunting its power, was announcing its anything but conservative approach in the area of civil rights, hallowed ground, where even the Burger Court had stepped softly around the landmarks of the Warren era. As everyone at the Court keenly appreciated, the docket for the next term was already brimming with potentially momentous cases where, depending on Kennedy, whole fields of law could be rewritten. And judging by Kennedy's strong allegiance to Rehnquist in *Patterson*, for the liberals a full-scale disaster loomed. The shrillness of their *Patterson* dissents reflected that apprehension, the cold fear that both their power and the principles they held dear were teetering at a cliff's edge in the face of a gale-force wind.

When I arrived to clerk at the Court in July 1988, there was no mistaking the high anxiety suffusing the liberal Chambers. The outgoing clerks indoctrinated the incoming group with cautionary tales from the year before, such as the case of Willie Watson, who (in a replay of the Roosevelt Green case from 1985) was executed after the Court, with Powell in retirement, split 4–4 over his stay application.[18] They briefed us about the major cases already on the docket for our term, such as the second round of *Patterson* and closely watched appeals involving sex discrimination, affirmative action, and capital punishment for minors. They warned us not to trust the work coming from the Solicitor General's Office: both because it aggressively pushed the Reagan legal agenda and, perhaps more important, because it sometimes played fast and loose with the interpretation of past cases. The outgoing clerks also gave us a sketchy sense of the politics of the Court, of what kinds of arguments in what kinds of cases had carried weight with O'Connor, White, or Kennedy—one of whom would have to be won over for the liberal wing to prevail in any given case.

But nothing in this crash course and nothing in law school and nothing in my imagination prepared us for the tidal wave of politically charged cases that term, or for the depth of the moral, philosophical, and personal schisms that divided the Justices, or for the guerrilla war that liberal and conservative clerks conducted, largely out of sight of those Justices, to control the course of constitutional law. It is fair to say, I believe, that during October Term 1988 the Court handed down more landmark decisions in more fields of law than in any other year in its history and that the term nearly ranks with the New Deal watershed of 1937 and the year of *Brown*, 1954, as among the most decisive in this century. Regarding civil rights, privacy, the death penalty, freedom of speech, separation of powers, the right to counsel, religious freedom, and states' rights, the Justices made important new law and set the Court on a course dramatically less sympathetic to the claims of minorities, criminal defendants, prisoners, death row inmates, and women seeking abortions.

The legacy of that term is very much with us today. The current Court, though it includes only five Justices from the Court of 1988–89, owes much of its character to events set in motion that year. It is not merely that the Court continues to erode or reverse outright liberal Warren and Burger Court precedents (though this is true). The more fundamental similarities are internal: the virtual disappearance of a meaningful center in favor of two sharply divided wings, the emergence of either Kennedy or O'Connor (depending on the area of law) as the controlling vote in almost every politically charged case, and the perpetuation of a Court culture that suffers from the same accusatory and uncompromising spirit of faction that now poisons American political society at large. These lamentable developments are in significant part a legacy of my term and what we, Justices and clerks together, wrought.

In December 1957, three years into the Court's post-*Brown* era, the young William Rehnquist, then a practitioner in Phoenix, published a much-discussed article complaining that the Justices' law clerks were disproportionately liberal in their politics and that they were "slanting" the work of the Court. In particular, Rehnquist charged that the majority of clerks showed "extreme solicitude for claims of Communists and other criminal defendants, expansion of federal power at the expense of State power, [and] great sympathy toward any government regulation of business." In Rehnquist's view, clerks were unconsciously allowing these decidedly liberal biases to affect their advice about which cases the Court should accept for review.[19]

A few months later, Yale Law Professor Alexander Bickel, a recent former clerk to Felix Frankfurter and already a force in constitutional scholarship, wrote an indignant rejoinder. Law clerks' "political views and emotional preferences," Bickel insisted, "while they enliven the lunch hour, make no discernible difference to anything in their work; and . . . as a group the law clerks will no more fit any single political label than will any other eighteen young Americans who are not picked on a political basis." In Bickel's view, clerks served the salutary and apolitical function of cross-fertilizing the Justices' deliberations with some of the creative ferment taking place in legal academia. "Only those who cannot conceive of intellectual disinterestedness," Bickel concluded, "those who, having despaired of our system of higher education, having totally despaired also of the nation's future—only those have cause to be uneasy that there are clerks at the Court."[20]

I cannot judge the nature and extent of clerk influence at the Court in the 1950s or whether that influence had a liberal political slant. Bickel's denial smacks of excessive protest and may also reflect that he had clerked for Justice Frankfurter, who, as much as any judge ever, knew his own mind. I can say with certainty that Rehnquist's mild suggestion of unconscious liberal bias in the cert. process does not even begin to capture either the very significant power that clerks wielded at the Court during my time (and in the several years subsequent) or the very conscious and abusive manner in which clerks wielded that power for partisan ends.

Every year the behind-the-scenes commencement of the new fall term is a cocktail party for Justices, clerks, and senior Court staff held roughly two weeks before the first oral argument in October. As clerks, we had already been at work for two months when Chief Justice Rehnquist, partway through the evening, gave us an official welcome and admonished us about our clerkly duties. The law clerk's actions, he reminded us, "reflect on the Justice, on the Court, and ultimately on the judiciary as a whole. . . . The law clerk holds a position of public trust and must comply with the demanding standards of that position."[21]

I remember looking around the room and thinking how quaint such lofty abstractions sounded. By the time Rehnquist spoke to us, the clerks of October Term '88 already were divided between two well-entrenched and hostile camps. Across the room we glared at each other, eyes hooded with distrust or outright contempt. We were already veterans of the nasty fight over the stay of fines in the Yonkers desegregation case. We had been through one execution and nearly come to blows over others narrowly averted. Preparation for the first set of argued cases was far enough along for us to know each other's politics and how cleverly we could pursue our respective views. Our thoughts were not of the "public trust" but of private strategies for the coming battle over the future of the Court.

Our contingent was unique in one vital respect. We were the first group of clerks, thirty-six in all, to include a critical mass of ideological conservatives. Four of our number had previously clerked for Robert Bork. One of these, Peter Keisler (a Kennedy clerk), had served on the White House team that advised and assisted Bork during his confirmation ordeal. Another, Andrew McBride (who worked for Justice O'Connor), had researched and critiqued *The Tempting of America*, Bork's best-selling, score-settling diatribe against his political and jurisprudential opponents. Several other clerks were protégés of leading Reagan judges, such as J. Harvie Wilkinson and Ralph Winter.

In all, ten clerks were active members of the Federalist Society, an organization founded in 1982 by law students, professors, and judges to serve (according to its brochure) as "a conservative intellectual network that extends to all levels of the legal community." In practice, Federalist Society membership was an identifying mark for Young Turks committed to a Reaganite judicial revolution or, as they put it, to challenging "the orthodox liberal ideology which advocates a centralized and uniform society." The Federalist Society was enormously effective. At its many sponsored events, the movers and shakers met the up-and-comers of the conservative legal and political world. Membership quickly became a prerequisite for law students seeking clerkships with many Reagan judicial appointees as well as for employment in the upper ranks of the Justice Department and White House.

These Federalist Society clerks shared a history. As graduates of predominantly liberal law schools, they were accustomed to being politically outnumbered, to having their views censured by both fellow students and professors, to being ostracized socially. According to one story, while at Stanford Law, Andrew McBride (a white male) attended a student meeting held to discuss the then controversial issue of whether the traditional Socratic method for teaching law had a tendency to "silence" women students. A scornful McBride interjected that the group suffering the worst silencing at Stanford wasn't women but the group to which he belonged: conservatives.

He had a point. Elite law schools were filled with organizations for black students, Latino students, Asian and Native American students, gay and lesbian students, women students. Conservatives were surrounded by faculty-student clinics pressing a liberal legal agenda on behalf of convicted criminals, the homeless, battered women, and the poor. The schools sponsored any number of leftist publications: journals of law and liberation, law and feminism, law and lots of things the conservatives staunchly opposed. Academic trends and hiring practices exalted feminism, egalitarianism, affirmative action and, at some schools, fostered a sneering bias against law and economics and corporate practice. In class and in the hallways, legal doctrines to which conservatives adhered were derided as insensitive and immoral. Their judicial heroes—Scalia, Bork, Rehnquist—were denounced not simply as wrongheaded but as bigots and fascists.

The conservative clerks at the Court shouldered heavy chips of resentment, airs of victimhood justified by numerous perceived wrongs, most notably the tarring of Robert Bork. At the same time, they were brash, snide, dismissive, and very much feeling their oats knowing that at the Court (unlike in law school), although outnumbered, they were ascendant—likely to have enough votes among the Justices to "win" most of the time. Put another way, the conservatives came to the Court with a desire for revenge, and they found a ready environment to pursue that goal. As McBride E-mailed his fellow conservatives in mid-September, "Everytime I draw blood I'll think of what they did to Robert H. Bork."

By Labor Day, the conservatives had partially separated themselves from the remainder of the clerks into what they self-consciously styled the Cabal. In part it was a social institution, a closing of ranks familiar to conservatives from law school. Once a week, without fail, the full cabal bonded over dinner at a Capitol Hill Chinese restaurant, Yang Chow. They also created their own separate E-mail network within the Court computer system that connected all the clerks. The conservatives sent one another a steady stream of messages trading information on cases and politically incorrect witticisms or ridiculing liberal clerks and Justices in the putdown brand of humor at which they excelled. Cabal members mocked the liberals as crusading cartoon characters (such as Batman), compared Justice Brennan to the money changers Jesus banished from the temple, and joked of Justice Blackmun leaving the Court in disgrace to earn a living as a psychic predicting future rulings for *The Star*.*

*A barbed sense of humor and a taste for pranksterism were common in Federalist Society ranks, and the fun was not always harmless. At Harvard, in 1992, in the annual parody put out by editors of the *Harvard Law Review* (the *Harvard Law Revue*), a group of conservative editors (including one slated to clerk for Scalia) spoofed the work of Mary Joe Frug, a feminist scholar at the New England School of Law who had been brutally stabbed to death on a Cambridge street in an unsolved 1991 murder. The specific target of the spoof was Frug's article "A Postmodern Feminist Manifesto" which, after much heated argument about the merit of its scholarship, the *Harvard Law Review* had

Much of this was harmless if juvenile, though it certainly escalated tensions with the liberal clerks, who resented being constant targets of ridicule. But the cabal was much more than a social club. It was a mechanism for imposing through peer pressure a strict ideological purity among the conservative clerks in different Chambers and of coordinating positions and strategy on death penalty stays, cert. petitions, and argued cases. Imposing social costs on individuals who considered deviating from a preestablished "party line" was a familiar tactic of the political left that the political right now freely borrowed.

The cabal was also the medium by which the smartest and most aggressive cabalists—McBride, John Manning, and Paul Cappuccio (a Scalia clerk from the term before who arranged to clerk six months for Kennedy)—shored up the work of weaker members in other Chambers. It further served as an idea factory for ways of drawing O'Connor and Kennedy closer to the orbit of their chief mentor at the Court, Justice Scalia. In short, the cabal was a structure stretching across all the conservative Chambers, dedicated to advancing an uncompromising Reaganite agenda at the Court. And it worked well.

The cabal imagined itself to be fighting a comparable group, which they generally referred to as the "dreaded Libs." Undoubtedly, many of us who worked for Brennan, Blackmun, Marshall, and Stevens, like members of the cabal, were possessed of an attitude. In our case, it was an overbearing self-righteousness. But the "libs" were not nearly so self-consciously coordinated as the conservatives. We employed no group-think to determine and advance a defined agenda. There was no need. Our mission was clear enough: to save as much of the liberal status quo as could be managed. Ours was strictly a rearguard action and, typically, whatever joint planning we managed—and we attempted some—was largely ad hoc and haphazard.

Those few attributes that the cabal and the libs had in common only exacerbated the division between them. Almost to a person, we were in our late twenties, driven by ambition, insecurity, or both; combative, unfamiliar with failure, and obsessively committed to the importance of our

---

printed posthumously (and still in draft form) to honor the law community's lost colleague. Her husband, Gerald Frug, was also a member of the Harvard faculty. Characteristic of the conservatives' takeoff was its title, the "He-Manifesto of Post-Mortem Legal Feminism." The parodists identified the author, supposedly speaking from the grave, as "Mary Doe," the "Rigor-Mortis Professor of Law, New England School of Law, 1981–91." The tenor of the article itself ran downhill from there, infuriating the many students and faculty members (including Gerald Frug) who were still in mourning.

"principles." For most, our postgraduate life experience consisted of one year followed by another of higher education punctuated by a narrow range of summer jobs and perhaps a year or two "off" somewhere along the way. We sought standing and power in the legal world, had attained it, and (many felt) deservedly so. All in all, these were not qualities that made for reflection, doubt, or self-restraint in carrying out our extraordinary tasks. They were qualities that made for trouble.

The opportunities for exercising the black arts of political or strategic clerking were myriad on both sides, though they differed from Chambers to Chambers depending on the work habits of each Justice. The cert. process was the focal point of frequent skirmishing as conservatives and liberals vied to control the Court's agenda.[22] There were those in the liberal camp who not infrequently would try to downplay in their cert. memos the certworthiness of certain kinds of cases (such as those involving the exclusionary rule) in which the result of full Court review would almost certainly be a significant liberal defeat. We called this tactic for trying to bury potentially dangerous cases the "defensive denial."[23]

At the same time, liberal clerks tended to scour death penalty cert. petitions for any issue even remotely worthy of the Court's attention and recommended cert. grants wherever defensible. The goal was to convince Blackmun and Stevens to join Brennan and Marshall in voting to grant, which they frequently would, even on relatively small questions, in their persistent quest to make individual state death penalty regimes more rational. The push for death penalty cert. grants was, of course, tied to the enterprise of stopping executions. Inevitably, abolitionist lawyers fashioned new cert. grants into legal justifications for new claims, holds, and stays. In this damming of the system, with different degrees of premeditation, we clerks played our beaverish part.

The cabal worked as a mirror image. The conservatives trivialized capital cert. petitions or buried open questions that at least the four liberal Justices might have liked to answer. At the same time, they pushed cases where they thought they had the votes to advance the Reagan Revolution in law.

What effect our cert. process machinations really had is difficult to gauge. In the first place, each side checked the other's work and, where necessary, called slanted or inaccurate cert. pool memos to the attention of their respective Justices. More important, each of the Justices usually had a good idea of what issues in what kinds of cases they wanted the Court to hear, especially in contentious areas of law. With the possible exception of one or two on each side, I doubt the Court granted any cert. petitions because of something clerks did and, if some clerks did manage to bury a few cases along the way, the same issues, assuming they were worth the Court's time, were sure to resurface.

This ineffectiveness did not, however, make our machinations inconsequential. The insidious seeking of advantage in the cert. work was a source of continual and escalating mutual recriminations. Dirty tricks breed hatred and distrust even when they don't work.

The danger of clerk bias and the potential for real mischief was much more intense and dramatic in the emergency death penalty stays. The arithmetic of the Justices was constant: no death row petitioner seeking a stay stood any chance of success unless he could capture both Blackmun's and Stevens's votes. These Justices shared a general approach to emergency stays, and their clerks often collaborated in handling them. As a rule, Blackmun and Stevens voted to grant stays to permit petitioners to complete one full round of federal habeas review. They would also reject applications filed by states to vacate stays previously issued by lower courts.

The sticky cases involved stay applications arising from successive habeas petitions, especially ones that lower courts had rejected because they believed the petitioner was either abusing the writ (raising claims that should have been raised in previous petitions) or raising claims that had been for some reason procedurally defaulted (forfeited) in earlier proceedings. In the most common scenario, a petitioner would raise a claim similar to one on which the Court already had granted cert. in another case. The lower courts would have rejected this claim on its merits, as an abuse of the writ, because of procedural default, or for some combination of all these grounds.

The job for clerks to Blackmun and Stevens was to evaluate these lower court decisions meticulously. As a matter of law, for example, the Supreme Court has no authority to consider claims that a state court *properly* has deemed defaulted under state procedural rules.* But determining whether a procedural default ruling was proper often called for fine judgments. A procedural default could be overlooked if the state courts did not apply the procedural rule in question consistently. Or the

---

*In lawyers' parlance, such a decision rested on an "adequate and independent state ground" and thus did not present a federal question subject to review by the Supreme Court.

default could be overlooked if the state court did not rely on its procedural default ruling and instead went on to evaluate the merits of a petitioner's claim. Lower court rulings, hurriedly written and cursory in every respect, often shed little light on these tricky yet decisive points.

In any event, as Blackmun or Stevens clerks, we were charged with the task of giving thorough and honest evaluations: did the petitioner present a good claim on the merits for a hold and stay? And, if so, was that claim nonetheless procedurally barred? Blackmun and Stevens considered both these matters very seriously, personally evaluating every case on its own merits. And they took no pleasure but some pride in rejecting abolitionism and permitting executions to go forward even while pursuing scrupulous treatment for claims in capital cases.

As their clerks, we received exacting instructions about how to handle the emergency death cases, including explicit warnings not to be overly influenced by abolitionists from the Brennan and Marshall Chambers. Thus, while we might search aggressively in each case for legitimate arguments in favor of a stay, as far as I know, none of us shaved the truth in presenting a petitioner's claims. In the end our bosses regularly voted to deny stays when circumstances required.

Quite a different attitude pervaded the cabal. Its members considered expediting executions a central part of their collective mission, and they pursued that goal passionately in both the argued cases and the emergency stay process. Their resolve reflected a powerful philosophical commitment to the right of states to execute vicious murderers, but it manifested itself in an amazing bloodthirst, a revelry in execution reminiscent of the celebratory crowds that years ago thronged to public hangings. When Missouri executed George "Tiny" Mercer on January 6, 1989, Robert Giuffra, a cabalist in the Chief's Chambers, exhorted the others: "In case anyone hadn't noticed, we had a successful execution last night. We need to get our numbers up after only 11 in 1988, and 5 since July 1988." Two weeks later, after Florida electrocuted the mass murderer Ted Bundy, the cabal celebrated.

The issue was not just good taste. It was, on some occasions, literally the difference between life and death. In most cases where Blackmun and Stevens joined Brennan and Marshall in favor of granting a stay of execution, Justice Kennedy held the deciding fifth vote. For Kennedy, the determinative issue was often whether the petitioner had abused the writ or forfeited his claims under state law. In contrast to Blackmun and

Stevens, Kennedy was predisposed to accept or be convinced of such procedural grounds for rejecting stay applications. And the cabal exploited this predisposition.

Several cabal members clerked for Justice Kennedy, and, with active encouragement (or sometimes direct pressure) from their conservative cohorts, they lobbied him to find abuse of the writ or procedural default wherever possible. Counterarguments, whether raised by defense counsel or by other clerks, were dismissed out of hand. This unyielding stance became important in the closest cases, the ones inevitably resolved long after the Justice himself had gone home. On these nights, the outcome depended in very large part on how a clerk characterized a petitioner's claim and the lower court rulings, what the clerk recommended and how strongly, even whether a clerk would place another late-night call to the Justice's home to apprise him of a new fact or argument.*

Ingeniously, one Kennedy clerk figured out that his boss was much more likely to grant stays of execution when the other Justices already were split 4–4—that is, when Kennedy's vote clearly would be the difference between a stay and death. To combat this tendency, this clerk made it a practice to get his boss to vote early on the emergency stays— before the real pressure mounted—knowing that a Kennedy vote to deny would be more easily obtained with other Justices' votes still outstanding.

All the cabalists moved lockstep in their hostility toward petitioners' claims, tilted the scales toward death whenever possible, and played to Kennedy's ingrained conservatism. And it is no exaggeration to say that for the inmate facing imminent execution who (as periodically happened) presented a strong but not overwhelming argument for a stay, one significant factor in the final vote was the pure fortuity of whether one of the cabal members in the Kennedy Chambers drew his case.

The polarizing effect of these dynamics cannot be overstated. For those of us who were abolitionist by conviction or near abolitionist from a distrust of a system that seemed rife with illegality, caprice, and uncertainty, watching our peers eagerly, almost laughingly, grease the tracks toward death was a chilling, nauseating experience. I still remember midnight screaming matches in the red-carpeted no-man's-land between the Blackmun and Kennedy Chambers as conservative clerks declared

---

*This issue of clerk judgments and characterizations also arose in the Chambers of Justice O'Connor, the next most likely fifth vote for a stay.

triumphantly that, yet again, they had found some technical reason—a lawyer's error, a quirk of timing—for denying a stay of execution without even considering the merits of the petitioner's claims. I still remember leaving the Court in the hours before dawn with the certain knowledge that before I returned for breakfast a man who I believed surely *by law* did not deserve to die would be dead. And I still remember the head-banging frustration that no argument I had mustered, no product of my intelligence, had made the least difference because the person I needed to convince thought me soft or stupid or both for not taking satisfaction in the too-long-delayed death of a convicted killer. The truth was that the cabalists took some pleasure in watching us libs "scream bloody murder" (as one joked)—and we provided this amusement routinely.

As extreme as this might seem, the broadest exercise of what has become known politely as clerk influence occurs not on the death watch but in the Court's written rulings. For while it is, of course, true that only the Justices cast votes at the Court and that no Justice would ever circulate or publish an opinion that he or she has not approved, during October Term '88 the vast majority of opinions the Court issued were drafted exclusively by clerks. Indeed, only Justices Stevens and Scalia made it a regular practice to participate in first drafts. The other Justices consigned themselves to a more or less demanding editor's role.

Chief Justice Rehnquist has written that having clerks draft opinions is "entirely proper" and that clerks are engaged in a "highly structured task," largely foreordained by the Court's conference discussion and specific instructions from a Justice.[24] Despite such reassurance, a number of scholars have started to complain about the baleful effects of clerk drafting.[25] Many have blamed the growth of the clerk bureaucracy for the increased splintering in the Court's rulings, the expression of three, four, or even more points of view, which, in many important cases, renders the Court's decisions confusing if not unintelligible to the lawyers and judges who are supposed to observe and apply them.[26] As these critics note, the fact that each Justice now runs a separate law firm with four eager associates has made it much easier for each Justice to give in to ego and put out separate concurring or dissenting opinions in a multitude of cases. Some clerks certainly encourage these independent writings. After all, every opinion represents another opportunity for a clerk (through his or her Justice) to make an impression on the law and to achieve a sliver of immortality as the ghostwriter for portions of the *U.S. Reports*.

In assessing these overabundant writings, some Court watchers have further lamented that the contemporary editor-Justices lack the distinctive voice of some great stylists of the past—Holmes, Brandeis, Cardozo, or Jackson—whose published opinions each bore the unique stamp of their exemplary minds. Other critics have remarked on the proliferation of excessively comprehensive, prolix opinions (which they attribute to clerks' inability to exercise the practiced judgment necessary to select among available arguments). These opinions often are also littered with legal jargon and further leadened by excessive and arcane footnotes—hallmarks of the youthful drafter's ill-wed combination of "hubris and self doubt."[27]

Still others have suggested that clerks are responsible for the rise of legal doctrines that depend on complicated multiprong tests as well as the Court's overfondness for the rhetoric of "balancing" as a description of its deliberative process in deciding particular cases. Such mechanistic forms of analysis—what one astute critic has called "strategies of insecurity"[28]—tend to hide rather than explain the Court's true basis for decision. No one really knows what it means to "balance legal interests," but these methodologies are handy tools for clerks struggling in the green glow of their computers to fashion drafts that sound reasonable and "legal."

This panoply of criticism is well taken but incomplete. Clerk drafting of opinions leads to at least two other less obtrusive yet substantial problems. First, there is a world of difference between writing and editing. The process of writing imposes an irreplaceable discipline on the process of reaching a fully considered decision. Finding the specific words to defend a tentative legal conclusion forces the author into a constant reexamination and reevaluation of previous beliefs. It exposes unforeseen strengths and weaknesses in an argument. It is an act of creation and imagination that strengthens and conditions the muscles of judgment.

Editing the draft of a clerk—especially in the generally hands-off, work-within-the-margins way that it was practiced by several Justices—is an act of relative disengagement that naturally tends toward excessive deference to the original author. This is bad in and of itself. It makes the process of opinion writing little more than a shortcut to reaffirming a Justice's original (but necessarily incomplete) view of a case rather than an extended opportunity to appreciate and come to terms with a case's hidden complexities. Simply put, seeing whether an argument "will write" just isn't the same as seeing whether an argument "will read."

More than that, the prevalence of editorial Justices means that most of the text of most Court opinions—the key words and phrases that make up the crux of a ruling—has been chosen and crafted by clerks. In the endlessly ongoing interpretation of Supreme Court opinions, the devil is in these details. How the facts of a case are characterized, how the Court's standard of review is phrased, which precedents and principles are marshaled to support the ruling, how other precedents and principles are distinguished, what if any exceptions to the scope of the Court's ruling are recognized, these are the matters that the entire legal community will fixate on and argue about as they interpret the Court's opinions year after year. And it is here, in wielding the enormous power of the first draft and, specifically, in the selection of words, structure, and materials, that clerks may exercise their greatest influence. For while everything they write passes through the filter of their Justices' scrutiny, this scrutiny is directed at an essentially complete product and often amounts to little more than a surface polish. Rarely do the Justices disassemble the drafts they've been given to examine the crucial choices that went into their design.

I do not mean to suggest that every clerk or even many clerks set out like Rasputins to write opinions by their own lights instead of their Justices'. Some clerks express genuine surprise and concern about the breadth of their power to shape the law of the land. But even well-meaning clerks—by dint of youth, narrow experience, ambition, and the very nature of the job—may become wayward influences on their Justices and on the Court. The vast majority of clerks serve a single Justice for a single year. They have almost no knowledge of what has happened at the Court in the past or deep sense of responsibility for what might happen in the future. They are in a rush to make an impression, to have their say, to be well regarded by their bosses, and to have themselves and their Justices prevail in the immediate contests in which they are involved. These goals, often pursued at the brink of exhaustion, do not make for clear thinking about distinguishing between a loyalty to one's own views as opposed to the views of one's Justice, and they take no account of the interests of the institution of which one is an integral but transient part.

More important, some clerks are not well meaning. Given the deep schism at the Court, the ideological fervor on both sides, the atmosphere of mutual resentment and distrust, and the docket of polarizing cases, those so inclined readily have found (and continue to find) a compelling motive to greatly overstep the appropriate role of a clerk. The line of propriety may not always be obvious, but many infractions have been egregious. Clerks have miscited or mischaracterized cases when giving advice. Clerks have stirred up bad feeling and sought to influence votes by telling their bosses exaggerated stories about how other Justices demeaned them behind their backs. Clerks have laced their opinion drafts with extreme theories in the hope that some would survive the editing process.

The clerk rumor mill buzzed (and buzzes still) with even darker, though unconfirmed, manipulations—of collusion between clerks and like-minded counterparts in the Justice Department, of a clerk invading the computers of his colleagues and altering opinion drafts, of a clerk exploring the possibility of running for public office while still at the Court. Some tales are given greater credibility than others, but all reflect and reinforce the intensely polarized environment inside the Court.

In too many Chambers, the opportunity for abuse has been abundant. The temptation was (and remains) especially great at the political center of the Court, in the Chambers of Justices O'Connor and Kennedy, both of whom are susceptible to clerks' arguments and delegate to them almost all the opinion drafting and doctrine crunching. These Justices have the power in their votes and in their writings to determine whether and how far the Court will tilt to the right. This centrality, naturally, makes them targets of every form of clerk machination and means that their politically divided clerks—both more liberal and more conservative than their bosses—fight incessantly and (in some cases) deviously to put O'Connor and Kennedy "on record" espousing views of the law as close to their own as possible. (Getting a Justice to endorse a particular position in writing inevitably has a long-term effect, as Justices are loathe to backtrack from their previously published views.)

During October Term '88, the hostility among the clerks or, more accurately, the open warfare of the cabal against the libs, was reflected in almost every aspect of Court life. We started the term arguing about everything and ended it in a silence punctuated occasionally by gloating or insults. In the clerks' lunchroom, we dispersed into a petulant cliquishness that we perpetuated at dinner, when small groups gathered to order in pizza or Chinese. On a physical level, we traded punishing fouls during our thrice weekly intramural basketball games.

From a liberal point of view, we were watching a bonfire consume our most deeply valued professional ideals, the very reason many of us had pointed ourselves toward law, and the cabal was having a time of it rubbing our noses in the ash. From their point of view, both personally and ideologically, we richly deserved our fate.

As a consequence of this unalloyed dislike, the "clerk network," the back channel by which, in the past, Justices had sought to reach common ground, became instead a font for endless sniping and antagonism. In too many of the Court's Chambers, clerks did not so much inform or counsel their Justices as devise clever prescriptions for avoiding compromise, seeking advantage, and sticking it to the opposition whenever possible. In short, for a significant number of clerks, the naked Machiavellianism of the Bork fight was not an end but a beginning and a lesson learned.

Of course, if the Justices themselves had not been susceptible and, in some cases, even eager for the polarizing advice of their clerks, none of this would have mattered. But from the outset of the 1988 Term, the widespread differences between the liberal and conservative Justices, barely held in check during Powell's tenure, assumed a new depth and intensity. With Kennedy's arrival, the possibility of a radical reorienting of constitutional law hung in the air like an electric charge, pulsing energy into the conservatives and sending the liberals into a kind of convulsive shock.

The power of youth, energy, and innovative thinking radiated from the conservative side. Though not a young man, Rehnquist seemed rejuvenated since his elevation to Chief Justice after a period of relative disengagement and a variety of troubles (including a dependence on painkillers) associated with a very bad back. Justice Kennedy was full of a novice's vitality. On long legs, he fairly bounded down the Court's wide hallways, addressing almost everyone he encountered in a tone of earnest enthusiasm. His every action seemed to advertise both an absolute delight with his position and an already formed resolve to place his mark on the law.

It was Justice Scalia, though, who came close to dominating the Court through his overwhelming intellect and imposing personality. To a degree greater than any of his colleagues, Scalia could lay claim to following a clear-cut and comprehensive jurisprudence. When interpreting a statute, he was a "textualist": he looked to the "plain meaning" of the statute's words and vigorously opposed attempts to divine legislative intent from extrinsic evidence, such as congressional committee reports and floor debates. (Scalia considered such evidence unreliable.) By contrast, when interpreting the Constitution, Scalia was a self-described "fainthearted originalist," who (like Bork) sought to define each provision according to the Framers' original understanding.*

Although Scalia sometimes deviated from these stated principles, generally speaking they lent his opinions an unusual power and rigor, which he amplified (and made intimidating) through the cleverest and most pungent prose style on the Court. On every important case, even ones on which he ended up in the minority, the gravitational pull of Scalia's ideas was strongly felt, particularly by Justice Kennedy, who, as a newcomer, was naturally drawn into the orbit of the Court's strongest sun.

On the other side, the must of age and old ideas prevailed. Justice Brennan, who started the term at age eighty-two, fell ill with an infected gallbladder in November, never recovered his strength, and even lost his voice for long stretches in the spring. In thirty years as a Justice, the jaunty Irishman from New Jersey had earned a glorious reputation as the Court's greatest diplomat. First as Earl Warren's trusted confidant and later as the acknowledged leader of the Court's liberals, Brennan with his charm, persuasiveness, and knack for compromise had built and sustained a sometimes fragile coalition that, remarkably, continued to prosper well into the Burger years. His triumphs were legion: forcing legislative reapportionment in *Reynolds* v. *Sims*,[29] protecting the rights of a free press in *New York Times* v. *Sullivan*,[30] forging a unanimous Court for ordering President Nixon to turn over his famed incriminating tapes.[31] Even his ideological enemies agreed that Brennan, "the playmaker" as he was sometimes called, had strategized and persuaded his way to being the most influential Justice of the modern era.

---

*By "fainthearted," Scalia meant that he couldn't promise that in an extreme instance he might not condemn a practice (such as ear clipping) that the Framers had condoned. Antonin Scalia, "Originalism: The Lesser Evil," 57 *Univ. of Cincinnati Law Rev.* 849 (1989). Scalia's approach to originalism, moreover, was subtly but importantly different from that of some other alleged practitioners, such as Bork. In Scalia's view, judges should interpret the words of the Constitution according to their publicly understood "original *meaning*" (as divined mainly from contemporary practices). Bork, by contrast, thought the Constitution's meaning should be determined by reference to the private *intent* of the original authors. See Antonin Scalia, *A Matter of Interpretation: Federal Courts and the Law* (Princeton: Princeton Univ. Press, 1997).

Yet by the fall of 1988, the legendary velvet touch had gone brittle. Where once Warren had lauded Brennan as "a unifying influence on the bench and in the Conference room,"[32] he had become an often bitter and unyielding partisan. Brennan was famous for holding up one of his hands, wiggling his fingers, and reminding colleagues of the all-important rule of five: that it always takes five votes, a majority, to make law at the Court. In former days, Brennan was notorious for walking the hall and buttonholing Justices to secure that fifth vote. Now, his flagrant abolitionism and increasingly shrill dissents in other areas of law estranged him from those Justices who might fill out the last finger of his hand. Brennan hardly ever spoke to the conservatives outside of conference, and had he bothered they would have been disinclined to listen.

Even crackerjack statesmen need an audience susceptible to being wooed. When Brennan had orchestrated his most brilliant coups, he was surrounded by a majority of colleagues who, despite specific differences of opinion, shared a general vision for the Court and of the law. They inhabited a common terrain, where negotiation was always possible; arguments over approach or detail could be worked out, circumvented, or transcended. But too many of those colleagues were now dead, and with their passing, the realm of the possible—the place where Brennan could work his political magic—all but disappeared. The balance of the Court had slipped away and left Brennan, in his old age, increasingly isolated and frustrated.

Worse yet, the triumphs of former days returned to haunt him. For crucial members of the Court, they made him an object of not just philosophical estrangement but active distrust. It was received wisdom among clerks, for example, that Justice O'Connor so distrusted Brennan—for having hoodwinked her in some unnamed past case—that she refused when her vote mattered to join his majority opinions for the Court.

Even in cases involving women's rights, where O'Connor was a likely ally, Brennan achieved only alienation. In 1987, when he wrote the Court's landmark opinion upholding affirmative action for women, O'Connor joined his draft, then a month later, in a pointed tit for tat, revoked her joinder when Brennan brushed off some concerns she'd expressed about his opinion.[33]

O'Connor's hard feelings were still evident in October Term '88, when the Court decided a major sex discrimination case, *Price Waterhouse* v. *Hopkins*,[34] involving a female accountant denied partnership amid comments about her unfeminine appearance and manner. Brennan left conference with five votes, including O'Connor's, for a fairly liberal interpretation of Title VII.

Rather than lock in O'Connor's vote by assigning her the majority opinion (a favorite Warren tactic), Brennan (who had a reputation for hogging the good cases) kept it for himself. Despite his courting of O'Connor with half a dozen drafts aimed at garnering her final endorsement of this standard, O'Connor (encouraged by her cabalist clerk) retreated two steps for every one Brennan took forward. She ended up writing her own, modestly different opinion, and Brennan had to settle for the distant second best of a plurality. It was a sign of the times. Even liberal victories were small and felt hollow.

Among the other liberals, Marshall—Brennan's closest ally and only a year his junior—was frequently disengaged. In midterm, the *National Review* published a nasty piece suggesting, among other jibes at the Court's left wing, that Marshall spent more time watching afternoon soaps in his office than working on cases.[35] His clerks could fume and accuse the cabal of talking to journalists out of school, but they could not deny.

Marshall remained a hero to tens of millions of people and was arguably the twentieth century's greatest symbol for American social and legal progress. On a personal level, he still served as a reservoir of gruff wit and pointed war stories.* With respect to the Court's docket of cases, though, he cast his vote and that was about all. With a minimum of guidance, his clerks did the work, and, in his own way, Marshall acknowledged as much. With characteristic gallows humor, he issued standing instructions in case he dropped dead at his desk. Rather than give a Republican president another appointment, he instructed his clerks to "prop me up and keep on voting."

Justice Blackmun, the third of the Court's octogenarians, was just hitting his stride as a full-fledged member of the Court's liberal wing, but he was too much a loner and too far under the shadow of *Roe* to command the attention of any more conservative Justices. Blackmun spent his days in a self-imposed exile in the spare and otherwise unused second-floor

---

*There were those who had begun to suggest that Marshall was growing senile, but I saw no evidence of it. On the contrary, at the once-a-term lunchtime audience he granted the clerks from other Chambers, he regularly bested his youthful interlocutors. Most memorable was his response to a particularly silly question asking what he would do, if all powerful, to solve the problem of racism in America. After a perfect pause and in perfect deadpan, he gave his response: "Kill all the white people."

Justices' Library. There, amid small mountains of books, he agonized over the social consequences of the Court's decisions and, with an unrivaled attention to detail, immersed himself ever more deeply in the compassionate jurisprudence that was increasingly becoming his trademark.

Alone among the liberals, Justice Stevens possessed the pure brains and quickness of mind to counter Scalia. Stevens's own views, however, were highly idiosyncratic, and he showed little inclination to construct a consensus around them. On the contrary, he seemed to revel in his solitary concurrences and dissents, which, in unequaled quantity, set forth an always intelligent but often quirky view of the law. As the weather grew colder, moreover, Stevens became increasingly an absentee—piloting himself and his wife to a condo in Florida for weeks at a time. For most of the winter, Stevens became the FedEx Justice, sometimes even telephoning his votes in to the Justices' weekly conference. That arrangement annoyed several Justices and, more important, deprived the Court of the one liberal whose overtures the other side might have respected.

The glaring contrast between the liberal and conservative Justices was reflected in almost every aspect of Court life and was on public display during every oral argument. I came to dread these sessions, where, from the cheap seats at the side of the courtroom, the liberal clerks would watch demoralized as the conservatives thoroughly dominated the proceedings. There was Scalia, ever witty, brilliant, and self-satisfied, leaning forward into his microphone to make mincemeat of those advocates with whom he disagreed or coming to the rescue of friendly counsel. The Chief, O'Connor, and Kennedy usually contributed sharp questions as well, a soprano and two tenors to complement Scalia's booming bass. In counterpoint, only the unfailingly polite Stevens interjected an occasional thought, while Brennan, Marshall, and Blackmun sat sphinxlike, seemingly depleted, as the legal principles they had championed and we now defended took a relentless beating.

One could not observe these proceedings without realizing how profoundly the Court was changing and how much more change was inevitable. In November, only a month after the start of the term, George Bush defeated Michael Dukakis for the presidency. With Bush's victory, all the liberals' Pollyannaish scenarios for holding the line at the Court vanished like so many rainbows at sundown. You could read in every one of our faces the same grim calculation: could Brennan, Marshall, and

Blackmun—each over eighty and all ill in their own ways—possibly hold on for another four years? Not a soul among us thought they could, which meant that the steady pace of our defeats would soon become a wholesale rout. In our corners of the building, every day felt like Dunkirk was that much closer and our job was simply to salvage for some distant future those scattered parts of the liberal legacy resilient enough to endure.

The conservatives, for their part, recognized the strength of their position and pressed the advantage aggressively along a broad front. Behind the scenes, small disputes having nothing to do with the many controversial argued cases took on enormous symbolic importance for both the way they were handled and their ultimate resolution. Typical was the perennial debate over how the Court should handle crank litigants who abused its appeals process. Year in and year out, the Court was plagued by a dozen or so seemingly unhinged souls who filed one frivolous application after another for some type of special writ or for certiorari in one of the convoluted lawsuits they had going. On every occasion, these people (nicknamed frequent filers) would take advantage of the Court's open-door policy, which provided a waiver of filing fees and printing costs for anyone who signed an affidavit claiming indigence. Their handiwork wasn't hard to spot; still, denying their repetitive and usually incomprehensible requests was an annoying, if small, waste of time.

The conservatives wanted to end the Court's indulgence of these barnacles on the system. Pursuing what they perceived as "the interests of justice," they proposed a limit on the number of unsuccessful applications a single litigant could file at the Court before forfeiting eligibility for treatment as an indigent. After that, if a frequent filer wanted to persist in trying the Court's patience, he would have to pay for the privilege.

The four liberals objected strongly. As a practical matter, they thought the administrative costs of keeping track of who was filing frivolous petitions and how often would take more staff effort than the current system. However, more was at stake than this question of efficiency. The Court's infinite indulgence of even the most persistent nuisance was the small cost of upholding a large principle: "equal access to the Court for both the rich and the poor,"[36] no matter how pathetic, or even demented. In that sense, justice in America was truly democratic. Everyone could receive the Court's attention, however perfunctory. They simply had to ask. It was a romantic notion, the stuff of sixth-grade civics classes. But it was deeply felt, and the liberals published emotional protests (and fumed privately) as the conservative majority, in a series of 5–4 votes, started turning away the worst of the Court's nuisances.*

The frequent filer rule was a small matter, but it marked the divide between the Court's factions. From the conservative perspective, there was nothing noble about encouraging nuisance litigation or in the ideal of a largehearted judiciary. Federal courts, including the Supreme Court, were institutions of limited scope and purpose, regrettably prone to self-aggrandizement and a misplaced vanity. Tolerating abusive litigants simply encouraged the dangerous idea that the judiciary should be the forum to which society brought its every problem and, in turn, fostered the seductive and wrongheaded notion among judges that they possessed the mandate to take every problem on.

The liberals, for their part, believed in exactly what the conservatives would deny—that the judicial system had an expansive role to play in solving the dilemmas of American society and protecting its less fortunate members—whether minorities, criminals, or women unwantedly pregnant. For all this, the frequent filers were a metaphor, a harkening to the Clarence Earl Gideons of the world—one of whose handwritten, unlettered cert. petitions might become the next landmark case. The conflict was of philosophies tragically opposed.

The Court, of course, had long been a home to ideological differences. Under Chief Justices Melville Fuller and William Howard Taft, Oliver Wendell Holmes was so eloquent in his departures from the majority that he earned the appellation the Great Dissenter. In the Warren era, first Felix Frankfurter and later John Harlan led several Justices in adamant dissents from many of the Court's myriad innovations. And the antagonism between Justices Black and Jackson is legendary.

It does not minimize these historic discords to recognize that the conflicts at the Court in October Term '88 and after possessed an altogether different depth and character. While Holmes became justly famous for his dissents in the areas of free speech and substantive due process, he also wrote more majority opinions than any Justice in the history of the Court, and, in several important respects, shared the political and social

---

*One indigent turned away in October Term '88, Jessie McDonald, had filed seventy-three motions at the Court in the previous eighteen years. See *In re McDonald*, 489 U.S. 180 (1989). At the persistent urging of Chief Justice Rehnquist and Justice Scalia, the Court (again over liberal protests) codified the conservative position by changing Rule 39, which governs in forma pauperis petitions, to provide for the exclusion of litigants judged to be abusive. 500 U.S. 13 (1991).

views of the very colleagues he sparred with on matters of law. Similarly, although Harlan objected vigorously to many Warren Court innovations in criminal procedure (such as *Miranda*), or to the Court's adoption of the one-person, one-vote standard for state apportionments, he also subscribed to a number of its leading liberal decisions. (For example, he championed both the right to free association and the right to privacy.) As a true conservative, moreover, Harlan had an unusually high regard for precedent and, therefore, scrupulously honored even those decisions from which he originally had dissented most strenuously.

The Rehnquist Court, in contrast, was distinguished by insurmountable ideological differences, both personal and jurisprudential, between two unvarying factions combined with a revolutionary spirit that threatened to liberate the Court from the traditions and precedents that ordinarily regulated the evolution of its doctrines. Although the Court was narrowly divided, and despite the liberals' hope of an occasional defection from White, O'Connor, or Kennedy (depending on the issue), there was an overwhelming sense that from *Roe* to *Miranda* to affirmative action, the death penalty, free speech, separation of church and state, federal-state relations, separation of powers, and the "takings" clause, no doctrine, no matter how well entrenched, was beyond repeal. Radical change seemed no more than one case—one cert. grant—away.

This combustible alignment had occurred before, albeit with the politics somewhat scrambled. In the mid-1930s, the Court was split into camps separated by diametrically opposing views of constitutionalism and law.[37] On one side massed the Four Horsemen, the octogenarian Justices Pierce Butler, James McReynolds, George Sutherland, and Willis Van Devanter, who together with William H. Taft and others deceased had held sway at the Court for a generation. Usually hostile to claims of civil rights or civil liberties, this old order had as its true hallmark a limitless devotion to the right of free contract and the protection of private property from government.

For the Four Horsemen, the principles of laissez-faire economics were not merely preferred but part of the natural order "beyond the right of official control." Although they swore allegiance to a brand of constitutional fundamentalism that required judges to "declare the law as written," with no textual mandate whatsoever, they freely read into the Constitution their own Darwinist notions of social policy. Using the protean doctrine of substantive due process as their sword, they ventured forth to defend the country against all manner of social and economic legislation—minimum wage laws, maximum hours laws, price controls, regulations of interstate commerce—and, thus, set themselves four-square against Roosevelt's New Deal efforts to lift the nation from depression.

Opposite the Four Horsemen stood the Three Musketeers, Justices Louis Brandeis, Harlan Fiske Stone, and Benjamin Cardozo. These "liberals" found no particular economic philosophy enshrined in the Constitution (certainly not "Mr. Herbert Spencer's *Social Statics*," as Holmes had put it in the most famous expression of their jurisprudence).[38] Though not all enamored of Roosevelt—Stone was close to Calvin Coolidge, who had appointed him—they were political progressives and legal pragmatists who looked out on a nation in crisis and recognized that its basic charter must be deemed flexible enough to meet "the social and economic needs of the time." To the Musketeers, the Justices had no right (as the conservatives had been doing for twenty years) to hold 120 million citizens hostage to their "own personal predilections" regarding economic policy. The Court's proper concern was solely with Congress's authority to enact a particular statute, not with its wisdom.

Between these two wings, Chief Justice Charles Evans Hughes and Justice Owen Roberts held the balance of power. And although Hughes (more inclined toward the liberals than Roberts) tried to steer a middle course and to avoid excessive confrontation with Roosevelt and the New Deal Congress, the Four Horsemen (whenever joined by Roberts) defied him. In a series of politically explosive, sweeping decisions, during the 1935 Term the Court ran a scythe through Roosevelt's legislative program, striking down the National Industrial Recovery Act (the centerpiece of the early New Deal) as well as measures designed to revive the nation's agriculture, coal industry, and wage scale.[39]

Inside the Court, all was turmoil. Every day of argument or conference, the Four Horsemen would ride to and from the Court together for the purpose of coordinating their positions. To counter these caucuses, the liberals started convening at Brandeis's apartment on Friday afternoons. Observing the certitude of his colleagues, Cardozo recognized that the schism in the Court was unbridgeable by reason. "I don't worry any more about whether I can influence the vote of the other Justices," he once remarked. "I'm satisfied now if I can get myself to vote right."[40] Cardozo's disillusionment with what he called a "cruel" time was echoed by his allies. Brandeis had some time ago given up on the conservatives. "When I first came to this Court," he wrote a friend, "I thought I would be associated with men who really cared whether they were right or wrong. But sometimes, Sonny, it just ain't so."[41]

The view from the other side was, if anything, even more dismissive. McReynolds, the surliest of the old guard, was a thoroughgoing anti-Semite and for all practical purposes refused to speak to either Brandeis or Cardozo. In the main, the Four Horsemen shared the view of their former leader, Chief Justice Taft, who, shortly before his death, derided the liberals as "hopeless" and vowed to stay on the Court as long as possible "to prevent the Bolsheviki from getting control."[42]

The result of these dynamics was a steady drift into the Court's most serious crisis since *Dred Scott*. As the Justices finished up the 1935 Term—deemed by Stone "one of the most disastrous in its history"—popular and political outcry against what New Dealers of every stripe viewed as the Court's "economic dictatorship" moved toward crescendo. Some communities responded to the Court's paralyzing jurisprudence by hanging the Justices in effigy. Even sober academics concluded that the Court's aversion to regulated capitalism confronted the country with "the question not how governmental functions shall be shared, but whether in substance we shall govern at all."[43]

As is familiar history to students of the Court, Roosevelt responded to its gutting of his legislative program with an unprecedented plan to change the course of constitutional law by expanding the Court's membership. The Court-packing scheme was overwhelmingly rejected as a dangerous and expedient meddling with the judiciary's constitutionally guaranteed independence. Still, Roosevelt prevailed. In 1937, Justice Roberts broke the impasse between Court and country when, in a new series of regulatory cases, he shifted to the liberal side in the so-called "switch in time that saved the nine."[44] Within a year, Van Devanter and Sutherland retired and Roosevelt replaced them with the staunch New Dealers Hugo Black and Stanley Reed. Then, in short order, Brandeis, Cardozo, Butler, McReynolds, and Hughes were gone as well—succeeded by the likes of Frankfurter, Douglas, and Jackson—and thus the Court was remade.

Any number of aspects of the Hughes Court of 1934, '35, and '36 reappeared in the Rehnquist Court of 1988 and '89. At both times, the Court stood at the storm center of the nation's political debate, even if the paramount issues had changed. At both times, the Court was divided into rival blocks composed of an old guard seeking desperately to preserve the status quo and a more youthful insurgency, supported by the sitting president, equally determined to rework the law. At both times, the course of the Court's decisions was determined by a Justice or two who stood at what passed for the center but who provided little ballast against a current of extremism.

Overall, the 1930s Court and the Rehnquist Court shared an over-abundance of dogma, which left little room for reason and even less for persuasion. Justice Stone was several times known to complain that cases were decided "without discussion and with no analysis" and opinions prepared in debilitating "great haste." Assessing the Justices' collective work as of 1936, he remarked that there had never been "a time in the history of the Court when there has been so little intelligent, recognizable pattern in its judicial performance as in the last few years."[45] As one observer suggested, the Court's groundbreaking pronouncements were based not on a set of carefully discerned constitutional principles but on the simple mathematical fact that "five is a larger number than four"—that is, they were based on pure power.[46]

The Rehnquist Court operated in like fashion. The Chief Justice actively discouraged discussion or debate at conference, even cutting off Justices who offered comments out of turn. In his assessment, the Justices' views were determined beforehand, and a lot of talk wasn't going to change anyone's mind.[47] As Scalia admitted with a note of disapproval, "To call our discussion of a case a conference is really something of a misnomer. It's much more a statement of the views of each of the nine Justices."[48] Even this description was a bit generous. Several of the Justices rarely elaborated on their theories of decision; Justice White frequently simply endorsed Rehnquist's views, and Justice Marshall's unadorned "I'm with Billy Brennan" became a virtual mantra.

As noted earlier, Rehnquist was fond of saying that, once the Justices voted, the details of any particular ruling would "come out in the writing." But at this stage, as well, the Chief put a premium on efficiency. He expected his clerks to produce opinion drafts a mere ten days after assignment. White imposed a similar rule on his clerks. Taking longer, even with the most complex or difficult case, triggered substantial consequences. Rehnquist doled out new opinion assignments according to which Justices had the fewest opinions outstanding. White, the all-world athlete, took this as a challenge and routinely beat the others in his self-created race to see who could author the most majorities each term. Other Justices bristled under the system, and Stevens finally complained to the Chief that his assembly-line approach was having an "adverse effect on quality."

Taken as a whole, the Justices' process of decision was desolate, unenriched by argument, doubt, or reconsideration. The senior Justice in the majority would assign the opinion for the Court. In fairly rapid order, the opinion would circulate, and then, usually within a day or two, the other members of the majority would give their endorsement. Weeks (or perhaps months) later, a dissent would appear, sometimes telling, often biting, and almost always irrelevant; the other side had long since moved on. Instead of some reevaluation or shoring up or (God forbid) an acknowledgment of worthy points made by the other side, the author of the majority, almost without exception, would respond to the dissent with a series of barbed footnotes. Indeed, in most cases, communication between the Court's factions consisted solely of accusations of bad faith, stupidity, or worse.

From start to finish, the process was an abdication of the Justices' paramount responsibility. Deep cynics in legal academia make fun of the idea that there is more to lawmaking and judging than the exercise of power. Journalists, in describing the Court's rulings largely in terms of their political consequences, perpetuate much the same view. It is a duty of the Justices to defy such thinking. Judging is an exercise of personal and institutional character. It is a delicate mixture of logic tempered by wisdom, reflection, imagination, and as much detachment as a trained mind can achieve. When exercised by a court of nine, judging requires a tense engagement between the competing arguments in a case—an honest statement of the most powerful theories underlying each side's view. The Court's role as interpreter of our most basic law demands no less.

Yet the Court during my clerkship delivered virtually none of this. Much as had happened during the political melee of the Bork hearings, each side at the Court resorted to whatever arguments lay closest at hand, regardless of their long-term integrity. In pursuit of their legal counterrevolution, the conservatives seemed to care little or nothing about consistency and continuity in their use of legal doctrine or whether their arguments held up under scrutiny. The liberals, for their part, reached predictable results through complacent means, resting on old law even when its foundations had been exposed as shaky or when it seemed ill-suited to the case at hand.

The casualty in this triumph of ends over means was, of course, the Court itself, which, unique among our institutions of government, must rely on its reputation (and not on a police force, an army, or the power of the purse) for its authority. It was as if the Justices on both sides were hell-bent on confirming the most destructive view of their own enterprise—that legal interpretation is driven by personality and politics rather than considered judgment. It was a charge, once almost unheard of from the Justices themselves, that each side now leveled at the other almost as a matter of routine.

Emperors are not supposed to accuse themselves of wearing no clothes. Over time, in the case of a court, such accusations inevitably raise an issue potentially devastating to a society based on the rule of law: if law is no more than power, no more than five votes supported by doctrines of convenience, why should we obey?

The Test of Sincerity

For law students, lawyers, judges, legal academics, and other persons especially concerned with constitutional or public law, two issues, centered on two cases, have dominated argument for the past forty years. First was the issue of race and *Brown* v. *Board of Education*, in which the Court belatedly redeemed the broken promise of constitutional equality and irrevocably altered the ground rules of American life. The second was the right to privacy and *Roe* v. *Wade*, the high-water mark of the modern Court's expansion of individual rights.

These issues also dominated October Term 1988. In cases whose names register mainly with lawyers—*Patterson* v. *McLean Credit*, *Wards Cove Packing Co.* v. *Antonio*, *Richmond* v. *Croson*, and *Martin* v. *Wilks*—the Court dramatically changed its approach to almost every significant aspect of civil rights law. On abortion, in *Webster* v. *Reproductive Health Services*, the Court approved an unprecedented set of state restrictions on a woman's right to obtain an abortion and reconsidered but ultimately did not overrule *Roe* v. *Wade*.

At the time, the rulings in these cases (and others as well) caused me great sorrow, anger, and frustration. The decisions seemed terribly flawed products of insensitivity and faulty reasoning. Looking back, I still harbor some of these feelings about some of the cases. My overwhelming reaction now, however, is quite different. I see many of the Justices' opinions, on both sides, not as just logically wrong and morally inadequate but as fundamentally dishonest, either by design or through gross negligence.

The Supreme Court, naturally, has an obligation to try to reach the "right" result in every case. No less important, though, is an obligation, rarely to be overridden, of sincerity. With respect to race and abortion, the Court was dealing with the most intractable social and political problem in America's history and with the most polarizing issue of the day. About such matters, Justices charged with deliberating and expounding on the nation's defining principles should not resort to blatant intellectual dishonesty. Yet they did, with great consequences for their own Court and to the country.

In *Brown*, in 1954, the Supreme Court committed itself and the nation to the idea, denied for centuries, of black equality. There were those who quibbled with the Court's authority to make that commitment[1] and those who actively and sometimes ingeniously sought to frustrate it. Still, the Court held its ground, and much of the country rallied to it. Despite police dogs, fire hoses, and even murder, Freedom Riders blazed trails of liberation across the South. Martin Luther King preached his dream of integration in the shadow of Abraham Lincoln on the Washington Mall. Congress restored to blacks their voting rights and outlawed Jim Crow, prohibiting the humiliating separation of blacks in many private walks of life—hotels, restaurants, every business over which the federal government could exercise control. Colored Only signs faded under the southern sun.

Yet the legacy of *Brown* has been marked by conflict and disappointment as well as progress. In the first fifteen years after the decision, there was painfully little mixing of races at most southern schools as local officials engaged in a campaign of "massive resistance." In Arkansas and Alabama, governors blockaded schoolhouse doors. Elsewhere, school boards closed down whole systems rather than integrate, or employed subtler tactics, such as adopting "freedom of choice" plans that perpetuated the old pattern of scholastic segregation.

The glacial pace of southern compliance led eventually to forced busing, North and South. After 1968, when an increasingly impatient Supreme Court ordered desegregation "*now*,"[2] federal district judges overseeing many school districts resorted to ever more elaborate transportation schemes to maintain a semblance of racial balance in their systems. White families responded with near riots in the streets and then a panicky exodus to the suburbs or to private schools.[3] The result has been to leave many urban school systems effectively resegregated and the noble promise of *Brown* largely unfulfilled.[4]

Outside the realm of public schooling, over forty years after *Brown*, the law and the nation as a whole still search for an adequate and shared definition of equality. The complete prohibition of official discrimination against blacks—a fact not fully decreed in law until the late 1960s*—inevitably raised the question of how members of a race hundreds of years in subjugation could be made full and equal citizens. Even as the country struggled to make good on its promise of equal rights, many came to believe that for blacks to achieve true equality, they would need, at least for some time, not neutral treatment but a helping hand. The "footrace" metaphor made famous by President Lyndon Johnson captured this view. "You do not take a person," he observed, "who, for years, has been hobbled by chains and liberate him, bring him up to the starting line of a race and then say, 'you are free to compete with all the others' and still believe that you have been completely fair."[5] In that spirit, affirmative action and the controversy surrounding it were born.

Even some opponents of affirmative action conceded that it had made America a "better country," helping to build a black middle class and bringing minorities, sometimes in significant numbers, into jobs and institutions they never had entered before.[6] At the same time, racial preferences caused resentment, injury, and backlash.[7] Affirmative action placed burdens on whites who never had discriminated against anyone and who felt, often with reason, that they were being leapfrogged by minorities less senior or less qualified than themselves. Some members of the minority community also complained that the existence of racial preferences diminished or cast doubt on their very real achievements.[8] And, more generally, the entire notion of affirmative action seemed to give leaden feet to Dr. King's soaring aspiration that every individual be judged not "by the color of their skin but by the content of their character."[9]

Briefly put, although *Brown* was a magnificent achievement in law, it was in many ways simply a beginning, a first step in a venture at which no society in human history ever has succeeded—the assimilation as equals of a racially distinct former slave caste. In the apt phrase of one scholar, the post-*Brown* era has been a seesaw of "remedies and resistance," an experiment in reworking the social order against the force of history, of prejudice, and, ultimately, of opposing claims to justice.[10]

---

*Not until the Court's 1967 decision striking down Virginia's prohibition on interracial marriage could one say with certainty that the Constitution definitively prohibited every law "designed to maintain White Supremacy." See *Loving v. Virginia*, 388 U.S. 1 (1967).

For more than forty years, the Court has played a leading role in shaping this endeavor. From the abolition of Jim Crow to the institution of busing and the occasional approval of affirmative action programs in academia and the workplace, the Court's task has been not to decide what is wise but to decide what is constitutional—what "equal protection of the laws" allows and requires. In a country that declared at its birth that "all men are created equal" and fought a terrible civil war to include among such "men" a race of emancipated slaves, no question could have been more important.

It was the first question of our term.

On October 5, 1988, the Court heard argument in *Richmond v. Croson*, a challenge to the constitutionality of what are known as minority business set-asides. The Richmond, Virginia, ordinance at issue had been enacted to address apparent discrimination in the city's construction industry. Although Richmond's general population was one-half black, in the five years before the set-aside's adoption in 1983, minority-owned prime contractors had received less than one percent of the $24.6 million the city dispensed for construction contracts. In addition, the major local construction trade associations included virtually no minority members. Having long endured the indignities of its Jim Crow ways, the city's elected black officials attributed these disparities to a history of racial discrimination and exclusion from the industry.

The Richmond set-aside was the product of a dramatic shift in the city's power structure. In 1982, as a consequence of legal victories equalizing voting rights, blacks had gained a five-member majority on the nine-member Richmond city council. Within a year, the council had passed the construction industry set-aside bill. This Minority Business Utilization Plan, as it was styled, required prime contractors awarded city construction contracts to subcontract at least 30 percent of each contract to one or more Minority Business Enterprises. The plan defined MBEs as businesses from anywhere in the country that were at least 51 percent owned and controlled by black, Spanish-speaking, Oriental, Indian, Eskimo, or Aleut citizens.

The litigation in *Croson* erupted over a contract to install stainless steel toilets at the city jail. Richmond had put the contract out to bid in September 1983, and the J. A. Croson Company had submitted what turned out to be the only timely proposal. Throughout the bidding process, and after it ended up as the sole bidder, Croson made some effort (how diligent was a matter of dispute) to arrange for an MBE subcontractor to supply the fixtures and, thereby, comply with Richmond's set-aside law. Croson, however, was unable to reach a satisfactory agreement with the one MBE that expressed interest (the MBE's price quote allegedly was too high), and the city was unwilling to grant Croson a waiver of the MBE requirement. In the end, Richmond decided to rebid the project, and Croson responded with a lawsuit.

Croson raised questions that the Justices had been struggling with for a decade. Did the equal protection clause prohibit affirmative action entirely? If not, what reasons or purposes were legally sufficient for adopting an affirmative action plan? More specifically, could affirmative action be used only as a remedy to address the effects of past discrimination or could it also be employed in a more forward-looking fashion, to increase "diversity" within social institutions?[11] Could affirmative action plans include quotas or only less definite preferences? And to what extent did an affirmative action plan have to take account of the rights of "innocent" persons, who had not themselves committed any discriminatory acts but who (because they were white or male) might be injured by the plan?

Ten years earlier, when the Court first considered the constitutionality of affirmative action in Regents of University of California v. Bakke[12] (involving a quota for minority applicants at the University of California at Davis medical school), no majority of five had emerged for any shared view. The most that could be gleaned from the Justices' differing opinions was that a bare majority of Justices believed that the equal protection clause permitted some degree of affirmative action. Justice Powell, who as usual held the swing vote, issued an especially qualified endorsement. He disapproved of systems involving rigid "quotas" while welcoming what he considered less definitive preferences.

In the intervening decade, little had changed. Four Justices of the 1988 Court (Rehnquist, White, O'Connor, and Scalia) either were on record opposing all affirmative action or had voted consistently to strike down those affirmative action programs that had come up for review.[13] Three Justices (Brennan, Marshall, and Blackmun) had yet to find an affirmative action program that they wouldn't approve. And Stevens harbored serious reservations about voluntary affirmative action plans intended solely to remedy past discrimination yet was much more amenable to forward-looking programs aimed at increasing racial diversity.

Amid this fragmentation, Powell had been the only Justice in the majority of every single affirmative action case, usually writing separately to split hairs over which affirmative action plans seemed too quotalike or imposed excessive burdens on innocent third parties.[14] With four Justices almost uniformly against affirmative action, the $64,000 question in *Croson* was whether Kennedy—Powell's replacement—would make a majority for a substantial shift to the right from Powell's case-by-case moderation and, if so, how far the Court would go.

The central legal issue facing the Justices in *Croson*—the one that prompted competing amicus briefs from the Reagan Justice Department and every major civil rights group—was what standard of review the Court should use to assess constitutional challenges to affirmative action. In evaluating the constitutionality of statutes, the Court does not look at every kind of law in the same light. Rather, some kinds of laws must be supported by a greater level of justification—a more important governmental purpose—than others. The level of justification the Court requires in a given case is its "standard of review," and, in practice, the Court's choice of standard often preordains the outcome of a case.

In equal protection law, the Court's selection of a standard of review operates roughly like a three-way light. Under the lowest standard of review, "rational relations" review—which it applies to run-of-the-mill legislation, such as tax rates or speed limits—the Court turns the light to its lowest setting—a dim twenty-five watts. In this semidarkness, almost all the potential flaws in a statute remain hidden. In technical terms, all the Court is asking itself is whether the challenged statute is "rationally" related to some conceivable "legitimate" purpose (any one will do). One critic described the Court's function in these circumstances as serving as a "lunacy commission," and the Justices almost never strike down legislation as "irrational."[15]

In some circumstances, the Court will turn up the light to its second setting, say seventy-five watts. For example, when a statute distinguishes on the basis of gender (such as a law that permits boys to drive at age sixteen while delaying girls until eighteen), the Court will look at the law under the stronger light—what is called "intermediate scrutiny." Specifically, the Court will ask itself whether the proposed rule is "substantially related to an important governmental purpose." Here, the state's legislative purpose must be "important" (not merely "legitimate"). In addition, the rule in question must "fit" its purpose, that is, it must be closely "tailored" (substantially related) to actually serve the legislature's stated objective and not miss the mark by much. Simply put, the Court takes a much more skeptical view of such laws because, given their subject matter, there is a heightened risk that the legislature has acted invidiously. Many laws, though not all, do not survive such review.

Finally, in some cases, the Court will turn the light on full power, under which every flaw in a challenged practice is starkly revealed. When legislation touches on a fundamental constitutional right, the classic example being discrimination against racial minorities, the Court subjects it to "strict scrutiny." Under this standard, the statute must be "necessary" to achieve a "compelling" state interest—and these are rare. Strict scrutiny is commonly thought of as the Court's doctrinal shorthand for saying "absolutely not," and scholars and lawyers refer to the standard as "strict in theory but fatal in fact."[16] Only a single challenged practice ever has survived strict scrutiny, and that was the infamous case of the Japanese internment during World War II. In a 1944 decision now much criticized and even reviled, the Court found that the wartime relocation and detention of Japanese citizens was necessary in light of the allegedly compelling military emergency of the time.[17]

Before *Croson*, no majority of the Justices ever had agreed on where affirmative action fit in this scheme. At one extreme, Justice Scalia believed that all racial classifications of whatever purpose not only merited strict scrutiny but were always invalid. Justice Powell, by contrast, also felt that the Court should subject all racial classifications to strict scrutiny, at least in name, but he implicitly watered down this "fatal in fact" test when assessing affirmative action programs. Justices Brennan, Marshall, and Blackmun agreed that affirmative action called for some level of heightened scrutiny, but they settled on intermediate scrutiny (75 watts) and, significantly, had never voted to strike down an affirmative action plan on that basis. Justice Stevens disdained the three-tier framework altogether ("there is only one equal protection clause," he was fond of writing)[18] and applied his own somewhat amorphous standard.

This disarray largely reflected the Justices' opposing views on the core meaning of the Fourteenth Amendment's command that no state shall "deny to any person within its jurisdiction the equal protection of the laws." To Justice Scalia, this requirement meant strict neutrality, "color blindness," without reference to or exception for the effects of historic discrimination. For the son of immigrant parents who came to America long after slavery ended and no doubt endured slights based on their own Italian heritage, there was no way to settle up for America's racist past—whether to blacks or to the Irish or to Jews. The best one could do, and what the Fourteenth Amendment required, was henceforth to treat every person individually, without reference to his or her race, religion, or gender.

Justices Brennan, Marshall, and Blackmun followed the opposite approach. For them, the equal protection clause took its meaning from precisely the history of slavery, of Jim Crow, and of the subordination of women and other minorities that Scalia would move beyond. In their appraisal, the central purpose of the equal protection clause was not so much to prohibit all racial distinctions but to serve as a shield against official prejudice and the subjugation or stigmatization of disadvantaged groups. However much we might want society and its laws to treat people solely as individuals, the harms of historic racism and sexism had been visited upon individuals because of their membership in distinct groups. For the present, therefore, color blindness could be no more than a shared goal, and affirmative action, the rebalancing of society's scales, a color- (or gender-) conscious tool for achieving it. As Blackmun summed up their philosophy in an oft-quoted statement, "To get beyond racism, we must first take account of race. . . . And in order to treat some persons equally, we must treat them differently."[19]

In choosing between these positions, or in finding some middle ground, the Justices in *Croson* were not writing on a clean slate. Especially relevant was the 1980 decision in *Fullilove* v. *Klutznick*, in which the Court upheld a 10 percent set-aside for "Negroes, Spanish-speaking, Orientals, Indians, Eskimos, and Aleuts" built into a $4 billion federal public works bill. This federal set-aside had been a rush job, tacked on to an emergency economic pump-priming measure, to make sure minority contractors, subject to considerable discrimination nationwide, received a piece of the action. Remarkably, Congress enacted the set-aside provision without hearings or committee reports and over only token opposition.[20]

Six Justices, split among three opinions, found Congress's action constitutional. After conducting what he termed a "most searching examination," Chief Justice Burger (writing also for White and Powell), concluded without announcing a specific standard of review that Congress's past experience with the problem of discrimination in contracting gave it an "abundant historical basis" for establishing a 10 percent set-aside. Powell wrote separately to reach the same conclusion under his weak strain of strict scrutiny. And the trio of Brennan, Marshall, and Blackmun applied intermediate scrutiny to conclude that the constitutional question was "not even a close one."[21]

The set-aside approved in *Fullilove* became the model for other programs, among them Richmond's, which used the federal MBE provision as boilerplate for its own—right down to the inclusion of Eskimos and Aleuts as eligible minorities. Given the similarities, a central question for the Justices in *Croson* (and a crucial problem for conservatives wanting to strike down the set-aside) was whether and in what way their eight-year-old precedent might be distinguished or circumvented.

None of the vote counters at the Court entertained any doubt that a majority of the Justices would find a way around *Fullilove* and declare Richmond's set-aside unconstitutional. After all, Rehnquist had dissented in *Fullilove*, as had Stevens, who objected to Congress's failure to justify specifically its 10 percent quota. Though not on the Court in 1980, O'Connor had an unblemished record of voting against race-based affirmative action programs, and Scalia was even more staunchly opposed. White had been in the *Fullilove* majority but in the interim had become a consistent vote in the other direction. And, given Kennedy's vote to reargue *Patterson*, as well as his generally conservative loyalties, no one expected him to uphold the Richmond program. The critical aspect of *Croson* was not its unsuspenseful outcome but rather the legal reasoning that all sides would employ in defending their positions.

The primary opinion for the Court (six Justices wrote opinions in *Croson*) was delivered by Justice O'Connor, who received the assignment from Rehnquist after the Justices predictably split 6–3 at Conference.[22] The first crucial step in O'Connor's analysis was her ruling, unprecedented in a majority opinion, that the Court must subject affirmative action, so-called benign racial preferences, to the same strict scrutiny standard that it applied to measures discriminating against minorities. As O'Connor put it, "The standard of review under the Equal Protection Clause is not dependent on the race of those burdened or benefitted by a particular [racial] classification." She left open the possibility that, despite past practice, strict scrutiny need not be fatal, at least when applied to affirmative action. Specifically, O'Connor suggested that governments could impose affirmative action remedies if they (as

Richmond had not) compiled a detailed factual record identifying the state's involvement in specific past discriminatory practices or in perpetuating their continuing effects. "Proper findings in this regard," O'Connor concluded, "are necessary to define both the scope of the injury and the extent of the remedy necessary."

O'Connor voiced only contempt for Richmond's asserted justifications for its set-aside. For example, she dismissed statements in the record from proponents of the set-aside recalling discrimination in the local construction industry. She also found irrelevant the disparity between Richmond's black population (roughly 50 percent) and the city construction dollars going to black contractors (0.67 percent). In O'Connor's view, the relevant measure of possible discrimination was the disparity between the actual number of black contractors in Richmond and the percentage of city business they received. The city had compiled no such statistic. She also ruled that the fact the local trade association had no black member did nothing to bolster the city's case. And, finally, O'Connor found that Richmond could not rely on congressional findings of nationwide discrimination in construction contracting that the federal government had compiled in connection with the *Fullilove* set-aside.

In disparaging Richmond's factual basis for enacting its set-aside, O'Connor admitted that she had employed a more stringent analysis than the Court had used to evaluate the federal set-aside in *Fullilove* (which, after all, Congress had enacted without even a hearing). She justified distinguishing *Fullilove* on the ground that a local or state set-aside (such as Richmond's) was categorically different from a federal set-aside program. Specifically, O'Connor argued that Section 5 of the Fourteenth Amendment[23] gave the federal government specific authority to "enforce" the equal protection clause, whereas Section 1 of the amendment (which contained the equal protection clause) explicitly limited state authority to enact racial classifications. In other words, O'Connor parsed the Fourteenth Amendment to mean that states (and their subdivisions) had less power and discretion to enact affirmative action than did the federal Congress.

On first impression, O'Connor's opinion defied easy characterization. It was susceptible to two readings: either as a kind of Powellian dilution of strict scrutiny, allowing affirmative action whenever a state or locality established a "strong basis" for believing that such remedial action was necessary, or as a drastic but cleverly camouflaged prohibition on almost all state-sponsored affirmative action. On the one hand, O'Connor stated that "nothing we say today precludes a state or local entity from taking action to rectify the effects of identified discrimination within its jurisdiction." On the other hand, she seemed to have set such high requirements for identifying such past discrimination (including, for example, extremely exacting standards of statistical proof) that establishing an affirmative action program might be impossible as a practical matter.

Most clerks attributed the ambiguity of O'Connor's opinion to a tension in the Justice herself. In the past, she had demonstrated a strong aversion to affirmative action. Yet she seemed almost self-consciously to be emulating the departed Powell, whose dislike for sweeping doctrinal absolutes (such as banning affirmative action entirely) she shared and whose powerful position as swing Justice she seemed to relish filling.

But whichever way one read her opinion, there was something deeply unsettling about O'Connor's approach. Her presentation of both the facts and the law was skewed by a seemingly calculated omission. Nowhere in the opinion did O'Connor include even a single reference to the historical context behind the Richmond set-aside. Few cities had a stronger symbolic link to the slave economy of the old South, and, perhaps more pertinently, few communities had resisted more persistently the modern legal command of black equality.

In education, rather than comply with Brown v. Board of Education, this former capital of the Confederacy had pursued a policy marked by what a panel of the Fourth Circuit Court of Appeals once called "sordid" efforts to "circumvent, defeat, and nullify" the constitutional right of black children to attend desegregated schools.[24] In social relations, until 1967 Richmond was the capital of a state that prohibited interracial marriage for fear of creating a "mongrel race." In politics, as Richmond's black population neared 50 percent, the city's white elite, determined to thwart growing black political power, decided to dilute black voting strength by annexing part of an all-white neighboring county. Only federal court intervention scotched the plan.[25] And in housing, Richmond's neighborhood development was so rife with bigotry—racially restrictive covenants, race-based redlining, and the like—that one court accused city officials of "tending to perpetuate apartheid of the races in ghetto patterns throughout the city."[26]

This history, much of it recent, was relevant as more than just atmospherics. On behalf of a majority of the Court, Justice O'Connor was ruling that, for the purposes of judicial review, a preference in favor of a black contractor was the legal equivalent of a law discriminating against a black contractor. In the context of Richmond, this bland equivalence rankled. As even one opponent of affirmative action said of such arguments, "To pretend . . . that the issue [of affirmative action] was the same as the issue in *Brown* is to pretend that history never happened and that the present doesn't exist."[27]

In this respect, the problem with Justice O'Connor's opinion was not that it concluded that all racial distinctions, both benign and invidious, must be subjected to the same level of exacting scrutiny. The problem was it reached this conclusion in a manner that ignored and seemed almost to trivialize the suffering of the millions of blacks who had experienced by far the heaviest burden of this country's racism—many of them in the very place from which the *Croson* case arose. If, as O'Connor alleged, the Constitution protected Richmond's whites and blacks equally from the effects of racial preferences, it was not because the races were somehow equal in their victimhood; nor was it (as the tone of O'Connor's opinion sometimes seemed to suggest) because racism against Richmond's blacks was a relic of the past. It was because the oppression of Richmond's blacks and their ancestors throughout the nation had brought into being a principle of constitutional equality won not only for themselves but for everyone, of every color, who came after.*

That O'Connor chose to slight this history suggested to those who held opposing points of view that her stand was grounded not in a high-minded opposition to race discrimination of every kind but in an indifference to the larger issue of racism that formed the legal, moral, and political backdrop to the case. And this suspicion was emphatically confirmed and compounded by the fact that a crucial aspect of her legal analysis fairly reeked of hypocrisy.

The subject of that hypocrisy was *Fullilove*. One could argue sincerely,

---

*Subjecting race-based affirmative action programs to strict scrutiny created some odd anomalies in the law. It meant, for example, that racial preferences designed to help blacks were subjected to a higher degree of judicial scrutiny than laws that overtly discriminated against women (which received only intermediate scrutiny). Likewise, preferences benefiting women received less scrutiny than those benefiting racial minorities. Indeed, of the six cases involving affirmative action that had come before O'Connor, she had approved of only one plan—a hiring preference for women that had been challenged under Title VII. See *Johnson v. Transportation Agency* 480 U.S. 616 (1987). The other five, all race-based preferences, she had voted to strike down—a record that laid her wide open to the charge that she was sensitive to the problem of remedying only the specific variety of discrimination she herself had suffered. See Stuart Taylor, "Swing Vote on the Constitution," *American Lawyer*, June 1989, p. 66.

perhaps even convincingly, that *Croson* was distinguishable from *Fullilove* because the Fourteenth Amendment somehow imposed a heavier burden of justification on states and localities than on the federal government for the purposes of adopting affirmative action programs. Notably, Justice Stevens and Drew Days (a top Justice Department lawyer who had defended the *Fullilove* set-aside and later became President Clinton's solicitor general) concurred. Critics countered that neither history nor precedent compelled O'Connor's interpretation and that it created the irony of reading the Fourteenth Amendment, which Congress had enacted to prevent southern states from discriminating against blacks, as especially inhibiting those states from remedying their own past discrimination.

But whether or not others accepted the interpretation O'Connor advanced, it was practically unimaginable that the Justice subscribed to *her own reasoning*. In the annals of the modern Court, no Justice, with the possible exception of Rehnquist, has been more steadfastly devoted to states' rights—to their autonomy, to the breadth of their powers, to the extreme deference owed the judgments of their officials—than the former Arizona legislator and state court judge Sandra Day O'Connor. She had been weaned on her rancher-father's vehement opposition to the big government social welfare policies of Roosevelt's New Deal, and every station in her professional career—from her first job as a deputy county attorney in San Mateo, California, through her work as a precinct captain for Barry Goldwater in 1964, until her appointment to the Arizona bench—had served only to confirm her inherited bias toward lean government and local autonomy. In every other field of law, from habeas corpus to economic regulation, and in those opinions in which O'Connor herself took the greatest pride, she championed state authority in the face of federal interference and exalted the centrality of state sovereignty in the overall constitutional scheme.[28]

For O'Connor newly to discover that, in the single circumstance of affirmative action, states were suddenly and peculiarly disempowered in comparison to the federal government, was a deeply cynical use of law. The argument she adopted was a favorite of Federalist Society members, developed the previous year by their guru Judge Alex Kozinski (in a Ninth Circuit affirmative action case[29]) and cleverly deployed by O'Connor's cabalist clerk. But her acquiescence in its use was a matter of pure convenience, not conviction. Everyone at the Court understood this at the time; it is no secret now. In 1995, in an opinion striking down a new *federal* construction set-aside (in essence, a replay of *Fullilove*), O'Connor repudiated her *Croson* interpretation of the Fourteenth Amendment and miraculously rediscovered that the provision's constitutional mandate of equality applied "congruently" to the states and the federal government.[30]

Employing whichever legal arguments are necessary and effective to defend a position is part of the craft of being a lawyer. It is not, however, a legitimate part of judging. Judges serve as the law's referees. They cannot declare illegitimate a particular type of reasoning in one case and then use it themselves in another. To do so invites colleagues and the community to suspect their motives, especially when the subject matter is as sensitive as race. In *Croson*, Justice O'Connor brought such charges to her door.

Nor was she alone. Justice Scalia wrote a deeply emotional and undeniably forceful concurrence in *Croson*. Quoting Alexander Bickel, he argued with pure feeling and much force that "the lesson of the great decisions of the Supreme Court and the lesson of contemporary history have been the same for at least a generation: discrimination on the basis of race is illegal, immoral, unconstitutional, inherently wrong, and destructive of democratic society." This truth, in Scalia's view, held for the "benign" racial distinctions of affirmative action no less than for those less well intentioned. Racial preferences, Scalia warned, "appear to 'even the score' . . . only if one embraces the proposition that our society is appropriately viewed as divided into races, making it right that an injustice rendered in the past to a black man should be compensated for by discriminating against a white. Nothing," he concluded, "is worth that embrace."

Only a thoroughgoing skeptic could read what Scalia wrote and question its sincerity, but it raised doubts of another sort. In all other fields of law, Scalia was the nation's most outspoken practitioner of the jurisprudence of original intent and a frequent lecturer, in his opinions and elsewhere, about the illegitimacy of other methods for interpreting the Constitution. Yet when confronting affirmative action, his originalism vanished. Scalia's concurrence makes not a single argument based on the original meaning of the Fourteenth Amendment or what the Framers thought about affirmative action, the idea of race-conscious remedies, or the principle of color blindness to which he would adhere.

Instead, Scalia adopted a methodology he normally deplored: interpreting the Constitution in light of "contemporary history" and morality. For the idea that the equal protection clause required a color-blind Constitution was not native to the clause's authors. They were comfortable with any number of race-based distinctions and even authorized segregated public schools in the District of Columbia. These Framers, moreover, believed and acted upon the assumption that remedial racial preferences and "equal protection of the laws" could coexist. The same Congress that enacted the Fourteenth Amendment initiated a number of social welfare programs administered through the Freedman's Bureau—including land grants, education, job training, and employment set-asides—for the exclusive benefit of blacks.*

Scalia's concept of color blindness originated a full generation after the equal protection clause became law—in the 1896 dissent of the first Justice Harlan from the Court's infamous "separate but equal" ruling, *Plessy v. Ferguson.*[†] Later, the NAACP would adopt the phrase as part of its campaign to erode the moral and legal underpinnings of white supremacy. In other words, the idea of a color-blind Constitution, especially in the sense of prohibiting even remedial race-conscious classifications, was a postframing invention. It was a plausible reading of the equal protection clause but not (as Scalia would normally require) one dictated by history.

Also troubling was the seeming opportunism of Scalia's invocation of the color blindness principle. In theory, it should have led him to disavow forcefully all forms of racial discrimination. Yet, in *Texas v. Tompkins*, he had decisively opposed rigorous measures to root out the use of race-based peremptory challenges in jury selection. And, in *McCleskey v. Kemp*, he had voted to uphold Georgia's death penalty regime even after explicitly acknowledging its infection with racial bias. Such selective

---

*Indeed, such programs gave rise to the complaint common among opponents of Reconstruction that blacks had become the "special favorites of the law." See Eric Foner, *A Short History of Reconstruction: 1863–1877* (New York: Harper & Row, 1988). Perhaps, despite the prevailing view, Justice Scalia could have marshaled an argument that the Framers of the Fourteenth Amendment believed in color blindness. See Michael McConnell, "Originalism in the Desegregation Decisions," 81 *Virginia Law Rev.* 947 (1995). The crucial point here is that he did not even try.

†Nor was this an entirely noble beginning. Harlan's dissent, though often praised, rested on bedrock assumptions of white supremacy. In context, his paean to color blindness reads:

> The white race deems itself to be the dominant race in this country. And so it is, in prestige, in achievements, in education, in wealth and in power. So, I doubt not, it will continue to be for all time, if it remains true to its great heritage and holds fast to the principles of constitutional liberty. But in the view of the Constitution, in the eye of the law, there is in this country no superior, dominant, ruling class of citizens. There is no caste here. Our constitution is color blind.

enforcement of the command of color blindness led critics to wonder why Scalia's (and other conservatives') rigor and emotion seemed reserved for cases in which the racial distinctions in question primarily injured whites.[31]

Integrity is defined, in part, by the strength to adhere to one's principles even when they lead to results one finds personally objectionable. With inspiring rhetoric and a compelling message, Scalia had sought the moral high ground in *Croson*. But an appeal to morality that fails the test of integrity is reduced to hypocrisy in the eyes of those who are looking for it. Scalia's *Croson* concurrence failed in precisely this way.*

On the liberal side, the rejoinder in *Croson* came from Justice Marshall, who no doubt found it ironic to see citations in O'Connor's and Scalia's writings to cases he had won for the NAACP in part by preaching the gospel of color blindness. Of course, in those days the Supreme Court itself maintained segregated bathrooms, and one Justice, Kentuckian Stanley Reed, refused to attend the annual Christmas party when he learned that black staffers had been invited as well. Color blindness, in Marshall's view, had been a powerful image in the days of legal segregation and remained unassailable as an ideal. But, as he had remarked at the 1978 Conference in the *Bakke* case and reiterated at the *Croson* Conference, it was an ideal that would take a hundred years to achieve.

In the meantime, Marshall asserted, Richmond's set-aside was neither immoral nor unconstitutional. It was, on the contrary, "laudable" and "a welcome symbol of racial progress. . . . indistinguishable in all meaningful respects from—and in fact patterned upon—the federal set-aside plan" that the Court had upheld in *Fullilove*. In particular, Marshall (joined by Brennan and Blackmun) argued that Richmond's set-aside was "substantially related" to the important governmental interests of eradicating the effects of past racial discrimination and preventing the city's own spending practices from perpetuating the economic patterns that had resulted from the prior exclusion of minorities from Richmond's construction trades.

---

*Rehnquist did not write in *Croson* but joined O'Connor's opinion. Still, his stance, too, was notable for its apparent inconsistency with his views in other areas of law. During the 1988 Term, the Justices produced nonunanimous rulings in roughly sixty cases involving challenges to various official state actions. In these sixty cases, Rehnquist voted to uphold the challenged state action fifty-nine times. The only exception to this remarkable record of deference was the race-based set-aside in *Croson*.

Marshall's opinion, which purported to apply the seventy-five-watt test of intermediate scrutiny, was a pretense in its own way. With good reason, the Richmond set-aside program was a special target for opponents of affirmative action.[32] Before adopting its set-aside, the Richmond city council had conducted a hearing that was little more than a show. A few elected officials made perfunctory remarks about past discrimination or referred to federal studies discussing discrimination in contracting nationwide. No one suggested, and the city apparently never had attempted, race-neutral measures for remedying the effects of past discrimination in construction (such as simplifying bidding procedures or relaxing bonding requirements).

The council's decision to set aside 30 percent of the city's subcontracting dollars—dramatically higher than the usual set-aside—bore no relation to the actual number of minority subcontractors available in Richmond to do the work. The most that could be said for the number was that it fell roughly halfway between the present percentage of minority subcontractors and the city's total minority population—as if that measure qualified as tailoring a remedy to actual discrimination. And, as a clinching indicator of the city council's cavalier attitude toward the set-aside legislation, the plan made "Eskimos, and Aleuts" eligible for Richmond's racial preference. There may not have been an Eskimo or Aleut subcontractor within a thousand miles of Richmond, much less one that had suffered discrimination in receiving city business.

Marshall's defense of the plan—and the only conceivable one available—was essentially that Richmond was just copying *Fullilove*. Even if true, that was well-nigh damning. The federal set-aside in *Fullilove*—enacted without legislative hearings, committee reports, or debate—was no model. It was as close to the constitutional line as one could sidle without stepping over. As one critic conceded, perhaps the federal program was legitimately saved by the fact that Congress previously had conducted extensive studies of discrimination in construction and because the procedural shortcuts associated with the *Fullilove* set-aside resulted mainly from its attachment to an emergency spending measure.

In at least one crucial respect, though, the Richmond set-aside was much worse than the federal program. The Richmond city council adopting the minority set-aside contained a majority of black members. From the perspective of legal and political theory, one compelling justification for reviewing affirmative action under a more relaxed standard than other race-conscious measures was the fact that, ordinarily, minority preferences were adopted *by the white majority*. Under these circumstances, affirmative action posed no risk that the political majority was acting out of prejudice against so-called discrete and insular minorities—groups that, because of historic discrimination, could not protect themselves in the political process.[33] In other words, if governmental action adversely affected politically handicapped minorities, stringent judicial review of race-conscious measures would be especially appropriate. Not so when the majority—the dominant political group—"discriminated against" itself. Here, there was little risk that the democratic process had misfired and, therefore, less cause for unelected judges to step in to police the system.

In Richmond, however, the political majority had adopted a racial preference *on its own behalf*. Less than a year after the council "tipped" into a 5–4 black majority, it had enacted an unusually high set-aside in an unusually perfunctory manner. The entire enterprise—the size of the set-aside, the failure to consider alternatives, the failure to catalog past discrimination in the construction industry—smacked of racial politics, a kind of "now it's our turn" approach to carving up Richmond's economic pie. Even for someone devoted to the constitutionality of affirmative action as a general matter, this stench of improper motive should have proven too much.

But it did not. It did not because, while the liberal Justices professed to be subjecting affirmative action plans to heightened scrutiny, in fact they were giving such plans a free pass through the system. For to accept uncritically the Richmond set-aside—as Marshall, Brennan, and Blackmun did—was to make a pretense of all their talk that race-based remedies, although constitutional, had to be undertaken with care and specificity to avoid unnecessary injury to those who would pay the price for setting right the past. The point of using heightened scrutiny to evaluate affirmative action plans was to ensure that such plans did not stray from their legitimate objectives and to keep a present-day constitutional promise to *every* citizen that race-conscious remedies would not become race-based entitlements. The dissent in *Croson* broke that promise in all but word.

The Court could have decided *Croson* according to one of two diametrically opposed but legally and morally legitimate theories, theories with which the other side might have strenuously disagreed but which still commanded respect. The conservatives could have fully acknowledged the continuing effects of Richmond's racist past and the fact that the history of the equal protection clause did not necessarily condemn race-conscious remedies. Yet they could have concluded that the best reading of the equal protection clause, the only reading that would give America a real chance at racial justice in the long view, was one that prohibited all (or almost all) racial classifications—and certainly Richmond's.

The liberals could have countered with a spirited defense of the constitutionality of affirmative action as a necessary tool in the ongoing project of establishing truly equal protection of the laws. They could have defended Richmond as the archetypical community where the use of such a tool was especially appropriate. Yet they could have found, precisely in order to preserve the integrity of race-conscious remedies, that Richmond's cavalier redistribution of the city's construction funds simply could not stand.

The Justices failed to make either argument, or, perhaps more accurately, they selected parts of both arguments when those arguments needed to be made as a whole. The result was a multifaceted sham that only confirmed the worst view each side held of the other: that the conservatives didn't give a damn about racial justice and that the liberals lived in a self-righteous haze that warped their vision of morality and law.

The term wore on, and these feelings festered as the liberals, by 5–4 votes, lost one civil rights case after another. Following *Croson*, in *Wards Cove Packing Co.* v. *Antonio*, the conservatives reworked a major piece of Title VII, the most important law prohibiting workplace discrimination.[34] Stripped of technicality, *Wards Cove* made it substantially more difficult to win discrimination cases by adding to the plaintiff's burden of proof. After *Wards Cove*, in *Martin* v. *Wilks*, the conservatives chipped away at civil rights enforcement from the opposite direction: they eased the way for disgruntled whites to challenge judicially approved affirmative action plans, even years after their implementation.[35] The conservatives justified these reforms as necessary corrections of a system out of balance, while, to the liberals, they signaled the ascendance of a Court regime uncaring about or blind to the persistence of discrimination in American life.

Of all the liberals' civil rights defeats that term, however, the cruelest blow came in *Patterson* v. *McLean Credit Union*.[36] Although, as a matter of substantive law, *Patterson* was not a particularly devastating defeat, the way the liberals lost the case was heartbreaking for them and tragic for the Court. It was heartbreaking because for many months it seemed that in *Patterson* the liberals had found one oasis of victory in this Sahara of a term. It was tragic because it exposed how deeply the poison of ideology and faction had corrupted the judgment of individual Justices and the shared mission of the Court.

Patterson had originally presented the Justices with the issue of whether on-the-job harassment constituted discrimination in the "making" of a contract as comprehended by Section 1981. But rather than answer that question, the Justices had ordered reargument to determine whether they should overrule a 1976 decision, *Runyon v. McCrary*, which held that Section 1981 prohibited private as well as official acts of discrimination.[37] At the time, the conservatives' decision to reconsider *Runyon* had outraged the four more liberal Justices—who assumed that the vote for reargument was a mere predicate to *Runyon*'s overruling and a significant retrenchment in antidiscrimination law. The conservatives also had set off a panic among civil rights advocates and many academics who saw the potential reversal of *Runyon* as imperiling a host of legal mechanisms for rooting out discrimination by private actors.[38]

Over the summer, the civil rights community organized an aggressive amicus brief campaign in support of *Runyon*. Of particular note, a group of sympathetic historians, including three Pulitzer Prize winners, wrote to defend the case as having correctly interpreted the intent of the Reconstruction Congress that originally devised Section 1981. Another brief signed by 66 senators and 118 members of the House argued that the Court should reaffirm *Runyon* because it had become an "essential component" of civil rights law that Congress (whose intent was at issue) had accepted and implicitly ratified in the intervening decade.

For the conservatives, this latter argument was especially troubling. As they recognized, to overrule *Runyon* (at least in a principled fashion) they would have to overcome stare decisis—the idea that the Court, in order to foster continuity in the law, should adhere to its precedents *even if wrongly decided*. This principle applies with particular force to statutory cases (such as *Runyon*), in which Congress can readily correct the Court (by passing new legislation) if it feels that the Justices have misconstrued a law.

In ordering reargument, the conservatives had hoped that McLean Credit or an amicus brief on its side would provide an effective counterbalance to the weight of stare decisis, but they were disappointed. As Justice Scalia scolded the lawyer for McLean Credit at one point in the oral argument, "If that's all you have, Mr. Kaplan, I'm afraid it's nothing."

At conference afterward, the conservatives quickly conceded that McLean Credit and its supporters had failed to provide a compelling justification for jettisoning *Runyon*. Rehnquist still floated the idea of overruling *Runyon*, but when his prospective allies proved unenthusiastic, he, too, backed away. As the conference discussion progressed, Rehnquist, White, Scalia, and O'Connor all agreed that while the Court had erred in *Runyon*, the time for correction had passed.

Justice Kennedy went even further. Although he had cast the crucial fifth vote in favor of reargument, Kennedy had since decided, at least tentatively, that *Runyon* was right all along. Having studied the history of Reconstruction during the summer recess, he had concluded that the 1866 Congress probably did intend the Civil Rights Act to reach private conduct and, therefore, that *Runyon* should be reaffirmed. The liberals, of course, were delighted to leave *Runyon* undisturbed, which meant, remarkably, that despite the blowup of the previous spring, in the end, the Justices emerged unanimous to reaffirm *Runyon*'s application of Section 1981 to private acts of discrimination.

This anticlimactic reaffirmance, though, did not settle the *Patterson* case. Reaffirming the application of Section 1981 to private actors meant the Justices now had to decide the question *Patterson* had raised before the Court ordered reargument: was Section 1981's ban on discrimination in the "making" and "enforcement" of contracts broad enough to cover the on-the-job harassment Brenda Patterson claimed to have suffered?

On this point, the Justices' consensus quickly broke apart. Predictably, those Justices who were now only reluctantly accepting *Runyon*'s view that Section 1981 applied to private discrimination were strongly inclined to read the specific terms of the statute narrowly. In particular, they wanted to interpret it as drawing a sharp line between discrimination at the time of making a contract and what they saw as garden-variety racial harassment occurring after an employment contract was fully formed. Speaking first, Rehnquist laid out this distinction and declared that Patterson's claims involved "post-formation" conduct and, thus, were not covered by the statute.

Brennan, next in seniority, countered with a more expansive reading. As he parsed Rehnquist's theory, a racist employer could sign an employment contract with a black woman, then, after she started work, harass her at will because she was black, yet still not have violated Section 1981's requirement that employers make contracts with blacks and whites on equal terms. Looking at the legislative history of the 1866 Civil Rights Act, Brennan assessed the intent of the Reconstruction Congress to have been far more encompassing.

In his view, one evil that Congress sought to counter when it designed Section 1981 was the slaveholder legacy (an "almost irresistible" impulse, according to one legislative report) of subjecting black workers to whippings and other physical compulsion during the course of their employment.[39] Applying this intent to Patterson's claims, Brennan concluded that the pervasive on-the-job racial harassment she alleged was analogous to the postcontractual persecution suffered by black laborers in the post–Civil War South. Both were actionable under Section 1981 as failures to "make" and "enforce" contracts on race-neutral terms.

As the Justices went around the conference table, they reached their familiar 4–4 deadlock, with only Kennedy to speak. And, again, he broke from the conservatives. Kennedy said that Patterson had produced "abundant evidence" of racial harassment, which, in turn, suggested that McLean Credit had not entered into her employment contract in good faith. In Kennedy's view, the failure to make a contract in good faith *did* violate Section 1981, and, accordingly, he cast a fifth vote for holding that Brenda Patterson had stated a valid claim under the statute.

At the time, Kennedy's vote seemed momentous. It was mid-October, only the second week of his first full term on the Court; yet he had been willing not only to strike out from his natural conservative cohorts but to do so in a major case and after rethinking his original position. For the liberals, Kennedy's independent stance delivered both a short-term victory and a glimmer of long-term hope.

In the wake of conference, the liberals' immediate task was to preserve their razor-thin majority by preventing Kennedy from backsliding during the opinion-writing process. This responsibility fell in large part to Brennan, who (as the senior member of the *Patterson* majority) wielded the considerable power of assigning the Court's opinion. Naturally, one strong possibility was for Brennan to keep *Patterson* for himself. Issues of labor and discrimination ran in his blood, a legacy from a father who had risen through the ranks of Irish immigrants from heaving coal in a local brewery to wide acclaim as a union leader. Brennan himself had started practice in labor law and, as a Justice, had been an aggressive champion of employee rights.

At the same time, *Patterson* seemed ideally suited for Earl Warren's favorite opinion assignment strategy of protecting a bare majority by giving the writing assignment to its least certain member. If Brennan harbored doubts about Kennedy's commitment at conference, the surest way to keep Kennedy's vote would be to let him draft the opinion. Even if not, given the Court's deep divisions and the inevitable pressure on Kennedy to return to the conservative fold, prudence alone argued strongly for giving him the assignment. But Brennan had not earned the nickname Piggy by handing off big cases for others to write. He returned from conference enthusiastic about Kennedy's support and decided to write *Patterson* himself.

Nor was Brennan especially cautious about crafting his opinion. Indeed, he felt sure enough of Kennedy to authorize his clerk Tim Bishop to draft an authentically "Brennanesque" interpretation of Section 1981, which, in practical terms, meant reading Section 1981 as including a distinct and broad right not to be subjected to the sort of on-the-job harassment Brenda Patterson had suffered.

Despite these risky choices Brennan recognized at least the possibility of a Kennedy defection and went to special lengths to preempt it. After completing work on his first draft, Brennan took the highly unusual precaution of slipping the opinion to Kennedy for his comment before circulating it to the entire Court.

It was well that Brennan did. His clerks, as liberal as or more liberal than the Justice himself, had a tin ear for phrasing arguments in ways that might appeal to a potential conservative ally. Even when they tried to be cautious and noncontroversial, from the conservative perspective they overreached.[40] And, in *Patterson*, they weren't even trying. The draft was laced with modes of argument and rhetorical flourishes about the Court's commitment to fighting discrimination that were characteristic of Brennan's grand style but sent chills down conservative spines.

Kennedy reacted badly. Although he thought Brennan's draft correctly upheld Brenda Patterson's claims, he felt it adopted an unacceptable method of interpretation and, ultimately, went beyond a fair reading of Section 1981. In particular, he objected to Brennan's extensive reliance on legislative history from 1866 to expand Section 1981's literal terms to include a separate and independent right to be free from pervasive racial harassment on the job.

As a self-proclaimed textualist, Kennedy (while not as dogmatic as Scalia) preferred to interpret the actual language of a statute rather than divine its meaning (as Brennan had) through the use of legislative history. More important, Kennedy's emphasis on text led him to the view that Section 1981 did not prohibit on-the-job racial harassment per se. Rather, the statute prohibited racial harassment only to the extent that such conduct demonstrated that an employer had all along "sought to evade" Section 1981's mandate that contracts be made without regard to race.

In Kennedy's reading, Brennan's draft did not attempt a careful parsing of Section 1981, one that distinguished between on-the-job harassment reflecting an employer's original intent not to "make" a contract on equal terms and other types of on-the-job harassment, not covered by the statute. Instead, as he explained in a detailed four-page reply, the draft threatened to turn Section 1981 into a "generalized proscription of racial discrimination in all aspects of contractual relationships." That interpretation stretched the meaning of the statute's text "past the breaking point" and past where Kennedy could sign on.[41]

The memo miffed Brennan's clerks, who had hoped to lock up Kennedy's vote on the first try and thought he was shifting ground on them. But putting frustration aside, the Brennan Chambers set out to accommodate Kennedy as much as possible. After a few days' work, Brennan sent Kennedy a revised draft with a cover letter acknowledging that his original version "might have been misleading."

The new draft was a finesse job. It went a considerable distance to accommodate Kennedy's concerns without completely abandoning its key premise that pervasive on-the-job harassment in and of itself violated Section 1981. Brennan's tack was to tone down the original draft and paper over his differences with Kennedy's position by borrowing extensively from Kennedy's own phraseology. Thus, for example, the new version stated explicitly that Section 1981 was not a "generalized proscription" of racial harassment and, in particular, did not cover on-the-job racial harassment except insofar as that harassment showed that the employer (using Kennedy's words) "has sought to evade the statute's strictures concerning contract formation."*

This strategy met with considerable success. Ten days after receiving Brennan's redraft, Kennedy responded favorably, thanking him for "accommodating so many of my suggestions." Correctly, Kennedy still perceived some difference in their positions. He read Brennan's draft as continuing to suggest that pervasive on-the-job harassment was itself actionable under Section 1981, while he would treat such harassment solely as strong evidence of a Section 1981 violation at the time of contract formation. By Kennedy's own admission, however, it seemed "unlikely that [these] differences would lead to divergent results in many cases," and, thus, he seemed strongly inclined to join Brennan's opinion. As Kennedy summarized his attitude: "For the sake of having a Court [majority] on this important issue, I believe I can set aside my reservations and join your draft, though I wish to have the benefit of whatever comments and suggestions our colleagues will have after full circulation."

On December 3, one day after receiving Kennedy's encouraging note, Brennan circulated his now revised first draft to the full Court and soon received joinders from Justices Marshall, Blackmun, and Stevens. Six weeks later Justice White's dissent followed.[42]

White's objections were a more extreme version of Kennedy's. In his view, racial harassment alone, no matter how severe, could not amount to discrimination in the making of a contract. Indeed, White found such harassment relevant only when employees of different races were hired under divergent contractual terms (for example, different salaries) for similar jobs. Under those circumstances, on-the-job racial harassment might serve as evidence that this divergence in actual terms resulted from racial discrimination prohibited by Section 1981.

In addition, White suggested that Section 1981 might cover racial harassment so severe as to constitute a formal "breach" of contract under state law. Such a breach might be considered actionable as an impairment of Section 1981's right to enforce contracts on race-neutral terms. In his final analysis, White thought that some of Patterson's allegations against McLean Credit might fit within his categories, but not with nearly the ease that Brennan suggested.

---

*Brennan's accommodation did not include abandoning his discussion of Section 1981's legislative history. He did, however, segregate this material in a subsection, which Kennedy could refuse to join while still endorsing the main body of the draft.

A few days later, Rehnquist joined White's dissent and, soon thereafter, O'Connor and Scalia sent around inconsequential notes suggesting they were near to White's position. Then an ominous silence descended over the case. The rest of January, February, March, and the better part of April passed with no word from Kennedy.

From the liberals' perspective, Kennedy's temporizing could be only bad news. Justices rarely delay their votes as long as Kennedy had and almost never under the cloak of mystery and silence that had come to shroud his deliberations. The time for Kennedy to "benefit" from the "comments and suggestions" of his colleagues (his original reason for not formally joining Brennan's opinion) had long since lapsed. Despite inquiries, the clerk channel remained eerily silent, though, after a while, the liberals picked up rumblings that Kennedy's Chambers was working on a writing of its own. What that might have been—and it might have been many things—they knew not. As the months wore on, Brennan did not ask and Kennedy did not volunteer his intentions. The liberal clerks on the case were left to draw their own conclusions and read the occasional smug look on the face of a conservative counterpart.

Finally, on April 27, Kennedy confirmed the liberals' worst fears. Rather than join Brennan's opinion, he circulated a lengthy dissent that adopted a view of Section 1981 even narrower than the one White had proposed.[43] Specifically, Kennedy rejected White's conclusion (which Brennan shared) that racial harassment on the job severe enough to qualify as a breach of contract might violate Section 1981. Under Kennedy's approach, Section 1981 simply had nothing to do with an employer's conduct after the formation of an employment contract. In his view, Congress had provided a separate remedy for on-the-job harassment when it enacted Title VII—one hundred years after passing Section 1981.

In a private letter to Brennan, Kennedy tried to soften the blow of depriving him of his most important majority of the term. "Dear Bill," Kennedy wrote:

As you must have surmised by now, my remaining doubts about your fine opinion in this case did not go away, though I had hoped to work through them.

I feel quite strongly that since we read the language of Section 1981 literally to apply to private conduct (*Runyon*), we must also read those words precisely in delineating the reach of that statute. This is particularly so given the existence of Title VII.

You are indeed a patient man.

Sincerely,

Tony

In the liberals' Chambers, Brennan's in particular, Kennedy's note brought on the devastation of a suitor tantalized, then spurned. We still remembered the thrill of October and the optimism of January, when it had seemed that Kennedy would join the liberals on a meaningful case. For a little while, we had allowed ourselves to believe that at the end of the term we might look back and laugh at what a bunch of Chicken Littles we had been, cringing at the prospect of seeing our legal ideals destroyed. By the time of Kennedy's defection in *Patterson*, we knew the sky really was falling. This was just another section crashing down on our heads.

Those of us working at the Court identified several causes for the *Patterson* debacle. As an initial matter, we blamed Justice Brennan for assigning himself the *Patterson* opinion rather than giving it to Kennedy and, thereby, ensuring his fidelity. We also recognized that, in *Patterson*, Kennedy was much like a negative ion resisting a positive charge. All the magnetic forces of the Court were pulling him toward his natural conservative pole, and in the sharply divided atmosphere of that spring, every passing day made that invisible tug more difficult to resist.

At the same time, we attributed Kennedy's switch to a much more tangible source: a crucial midterm changeover in his clerk coterie and the machinations of the cabal that followed. In January, three of Kennedy's clerks departed and were replaced by three clerks who had served other Justices during the previous term.* Most important in terms

---

*This unusual shuffling resulted from Kennedy's own midterm ascendance to the Court the previous year and the scramble it had created to put together a group of experienced clerks before the next normal hiring cycle. As it turned out, three clerks from the previous term—Paul Cappuccio, Harry Litman (from Marshall's Chambers), and Richard Cordray (from White's Chambers)—arranged to return to work for Kennedy the second half of the term. This switching of bosses, though once not uncommon, is now rare, and some people were particularly surprised at Litman's move across the Court's ideological divide. Most young lawyers, however, consider clerking such an extraordinary opportunity that they will work for any Justice, regardless of politics or philosophy—and Litman sought Marshall's permission before accepting the job with Kennedy.

of *Patterson*, this incoming trio included Paul Cappuccio, a former clerk and protégé to the Federalist Society heroes Judge Alex Kozinski and Justice Scalia. Cappuccio was so well connected and highly thought of in conservative legal circles that Kenneth Starr, then a prominent Reagan appointee on the D.C. Circuit, jokingly referred to him as Justice Cappuccio. Within the cabal, he was known appropriately as the Don. And from virtually his first day after returning to the Court, Cappuccio latched on to *Patterson* and made it his mission to prevent Kennedy from taking the final step of joining Brennan's draft.

Cappuccio set to work on several levels. First, in discussing *Patterson* with Kennedy, he played to the Justice's strong conservative judicial instincts, his self-image as a judge who understood his limited role as interpreter of the law and repudiated what he saw as the unbounded, result-oriented methodologies of the liberals. Second, he tried to instill in Kennedy a mistrust of Brennan, the liberal master manipulator who supposedly had duped other conservatives in the past. Third, and most important, Cappuccio presented Kennedy with a tangible alternative to joining Brennan's draft. On his own initiative and in collaboration with a cabal colleague in Scalia's Chambers (and perhaps with Scalia himself), Cappuccio put together a draft dissent—a highly textualist interpretation that might appeal to his boss.

The strategy was brilliant. It exploited the very real differences between Kennedy and Brennan and spoon-fed Kennedy an alternative reading of Section 1981. Even before Cappuccio had joined Kennedy's Chambers, he had told Scalia (his former boss) that the new Justice— who in Scalia's view showed distressing Powellian tendencies*—could be worked on and brought around. *Patterson* became his living proof.

Nor were Cappuccio's maneuverings limited to his own Chambers. Through the cabal back channel, he was auditioning drafts of the Kennedy dissent, lining up support. Scalia's endorsement was a given; O'Connor proved receptive, too. Both these Justices, having previewed Kennedy's approach, formally joined his dissent within twenty-four hours after he officially circulated it on April 27. Rehnquist almost cer-

---

*Scalia had no patience for Powell's "balancing" approach to areas of constitutional law or his tendency to trim at the edges of potentially decisive conservative victories. With respect to Kennedy, Scalia was especially disappointed when, in *Croson*, he decided to join O'Connor's rather Powellian approach to affirmative action rather than Scalia's uncompromising view.

tainly would have joined as well, but he already had signed on to White's dissent, and a sudden change in allegiance would have been impolitic.

All these arrangements took place behind the liberals' backs, and they remained in an increasingly nervous oblivion until Kennedy unveiled his dissent. At that point, having lost their majority, the Brennan Chambers started strategizing desperately to see if they could salvage something from the case instead of, as Tim Bishop put it, "simply throw[ing] in the towel."

What Brennan devised—at a clerk's suggestion and in very short order—was a tricky tactical retreat that, if it worked, would sacrifice Brenda Patterson but at least allow Brennan to keep control of the case. Specifically, Brennan decided to rewrite his opinion to rule *against* Patterson because of an alleged deficiency in her original complaint. (As he would now parse the case, Patterson's original complaint was technically deficient for having failed to describe with sufficient accuracy the legal link between on-the-job harassment and a violation of Section 1981.) After thus rejecting her individual claim, Brennan would lay out his broad view of Section 1981 and explain that, if only Patterson had gotten her pleadings right, she would have been entitled to prevail on the facts of her case.[44]

From Brennan's point of view, this rabbit-out-of-a-hat rejection of Patterson's claims presented obvious difficulties. Not a single one of the parties to the case nor any of the sixteen amici who had written briefs had suggested at any stage that Brenda Patterson's pleadings might be defective. Brennan himself did not really think her pleadings fatal to her case, and, in any event, he was hardly one to throw out civil rights suits on grounds the parties themselves had overlooked.

But rejecting Patterson's claims had one overriding virtue. It was a straightforward matter of Court arithmetic. After Kennedy's defection, the Court was split 5–4 against upholding Patterson's claim—with the five-Justice majority split 3–2 between Kennedy and White. Ultimately, that breakdown would mean Brennan would end up in dissent. But once Brennan recast himself as also rejecting Patterson's individual claim, the Justices (assuming Brennan could keep his allies onboard) would be unanimous in rejecting Patterson's claim, and Brennan's view would have more votes (4) than any other single opinion. As a consequence, although Brennan would have no majority, he could still write the lead plurality opinion and lay out an expansive view of Section 1981 even as he refused to apply it to Brenda Patterson.*

Of course, to succeed with this gambit Brennan needed the acquiescence of Marshall, Blackmun, and Stevens. To that end, four days after Kennedy's bombshell, Brennan slipped the liberals a copy of his revised opinion for their preapproval. Marshall and Blackmun quickly responded that they could swallow the move. Stevens kept his peace.†

On May 2, Brennan circulated his new opinion to the Court. The effect was like passing off week-old fish as the catch of the day. It didn't fool anyone and smelled to high heaven.

If Brennan had deluded himself for even a moment that his technical somersault would win back Kennedy simply because they now agreed that Brenda Patterson should lose her case, Kennedy rapidly disabused him. On May 16, Kennedy recirculated his prior opinion, having revised it only to make his criticisms of Brennan's interpretation of Section 1981 harsher and more pointed.

The backlash from Brennan's transparent ploy, moreover, was far more severe. His opinion apparently so miffed Justice White that he decided to withdraw his own *Patterson* opinion and join Kennedy's. Worse yet, White replaced his discarded dissent with a two-page send-up ridiculing Brennan's technical argument for denying Patterson's claim. Brennan's revised view, White wrote, was "as unsatisfying as the conclusion of a bad mystery novel: we learn on the last page that the victim has been done-in by a suspect heretofore unknown, for reasons previously unrevealed."

White's response was not only funny but decisive. By scuttling his own *Patterson* opinion, he freed up Rehnquist to change his allegiance from White to Kennedy—which he did almost instantaneously.‡ And,

---

*In its extensive discussion of *Patterson*, James Simon's *The Center Holds* (New York: Simon & Schuster, 1995) suggests that Brennan hoped to regain Kennedy's support through this tactic. This is inaccurate. Brennan knew at this point that, absent a miracle, Kennedy was lost. I emphasize this only because at least one outstanding scholar has mistakenly relied on Simon's analysis. See Sanford Levinson, "The Rhetoric of the Judicial Opinion," in *Law's Stories: Narrative and Rhetoric in Law*, ed. Peter Brooks and Paul D. Gewirtz, (New Haven: Yale Univ. Press, 1996), p. 199 and n. 55.

†Eventually, Stevens would tell Brennan that he could not go along with denying Patterson's claim, but by this time Stevens's response was irrelevant.

‡The paper record strongly suggests that Kennedy knew White would join him even before circulating his draft of May 16. Kennedy's original dissent had criticized both White and Brennan for suggesting that a breach of contract would state a claim under Section 1981. Kennedy's May 16 draft dropped any mention of White's opinion—a fact that seems to anticipate that White would dispense with his own writing in favor of Kennedy's.

crucially, with both White and Rehnquist joining his opinion, Kennedy now commanded a majority of five for his interpretation of Section 1981. In other words, Kennedy not only had scuttled Brennan's majority opinion but had grabbed the case for himself. The next day, May 18, Rehnquist made Kennedy's triumph official, formally reassigning the opinion for the Court from Brennan to Kennedy. The Kennedy-Cappuccio coup was complete, as was Brennan's humiliation.

By May 22, Kennedy had refashioned his dissent into a majority opinion. In a new (and brief) first section, he tepidly reaffirmed *Runyon* as compelled by stare decisis, while noting that several members of the Court continued to think *Runyon* wrong. In the remainder of the opinion, he restated his view of Section 1981—which continued to get narrower as the months wore on. The latest draft, as the first had not, explicitly concluded that Brenda Patterson's allegations—focused as they were on postformation harassment—could not meet his definition of a valid claim under Section 1981 and should be rejected. Despite this conclusion, Kennedy insisted that his approach was consistent with a full commitment to civil rights. Thus, in his opinion's peroration, Kennedy assured that "neither our words nor our decisions should be interpreted as signaling one inch of retreat from Congress' policy to forbid discrimination in the private, as well as the public, sphere."

The liberals considered Kennedy's pious disclaimer ridiculous and contemptible, a reaction captured succinctly by Justice Marshall's single marginal notation on his copy. On the first page, in enormous letters, he had simply scrawled, "NO!"

As for Brennan, with defeat now assured, he dropped his pretense of denying Patterson's claim on a trumped-up technicality. Instead, he unleashed a sharp attack on Kennedy for using "ahistorical analysis" to construe the crucial safeguards of Section 1981 "as narrowly as possible"—as though this important civil rights law were "a disruptive blot on the legal landscape."

Brennan's criticisms, naturally, triggered a response from Kennedy that Brennan, in turn, escalated. Still reeling from the loss of his *Patterson* majority, and freshly wounded by *Croson*, *Wards Cove*, and *Wilks*, Brennan couldn't bear the thought of Kennedy claiming the moral high ground on civil rights. Adding a new preface to his opinion, Brennan gave full expression to a full term of bitterness by savaging Kennedy's motives:

What the Court declines to snatch away with one hand, it steals with the other. Though the Court today reaffirms Section 1981's applicability to private conduct, it simultaneously gives this landmark civil rights statute a needlessly cramped interpretation. The Court has to strain hard to justify this choice to confine Section 1981 within the narrowest possible scope, selecting the most pinched reading of the phrase "the same right to make a contract. . . ." The Court's fine phrases about our commitment to the eradication of racial discrimination . . . seem to count for little in practice. cf. *Wards Cove Packing Co. v. Antonio* (1989); *City of Richmond v. J. A. Croson Co.* (1989). When it comes to deciding whether a civil rights statute should be construed to further that commitment, the fine phrases disappear, replaced by a formalistic method of interpretation antithetical of Congress' vision of a society in which contractual opportunities are equal.

Not surprisingly, Brennan's insults—which bordered on a charge of racism—infuriated Kennedy. Nor were such charges new. In *Wards Cove*, only a few weeks earlier, Justice Blackmun had published a dissent questioning whether "the majority still believes that race discrimination—or, more accurately, race discrimination against nonwhites—is a problem in our society or even remembers that it ever was."

To Kennedy, such liberal histrionics were bunk, and, on June 13, he circulated to all the Justices a personal note to Brennan threatening to respond. "The 1st, 3rd, and 4th sentences of your first paragraph ought not to go unanswered," Kennedy wrote. "If you wish them to stand, I'll send the enclosed to the printer; but do we really need to do this to each other? Yours, Tony."

Kennedy had attached a one-page zinger he would insert in his opinion as a footnote if Brennan did not yield:

Once again this Term, a dissenter thinks it judicious to bolster his position by questioning the Court's understanding of the necessity to eradicate racial discrimination. See post. at 1. See also *Wards Cove Packing Co. v. Antonio* (1989) (Blackmun, J., dissenting); *City of Richmond v. J. A. Croson Co.* (1989) (Blackmun, J., dissenting). The commitment to equality, fairness, and compassion is not a treasured monopoly of our colleagues in dissent. Those ideals are shared by each member of the Court. We yield to no one in our own deep understanding both of these principles and of the obligations reposed in us by our oath. . . .

Our point of disagreement with the dissenters in this case rests here: Although we loathe private discrimination as much as they, we do not believe this empowers us to construe congressional enactments beyond a fair reading of their terms. . . . Neither analytic precision nor respect for this Court is advanced by barbs about our respective sensitivities.

Brennan was moved by neither Kennedy's personal appeal nor the prospect of airing their respective charges outside the Court. Persuasion had failed with Kennedy; perhaps a public shaming would do better; and, even if not, Brennan would have said what he thought. "This case has sharply divided the Court from the beginning," he responded to Kennedy the same day. "I really think the thought expressed in the first paragraph of my amended [dissent], I should express. I will, however, substitute for the word 'steals' in the second line the word 'takes.' Sincerely, Bill."

Chief Justice Rehnquist and Justice Stevens also responded to the escalating nastiness. The Chief sent Kennedy a one-sentence note of encouragement: "I agree with your response."

Stevens, though, was very distressed and wrote both Brennan and Kennedy saying that he wanted to delay public announcement of *Patterson* for another day "to have time to think the problem through." What he actually had in mind was pressuring Brennan to delete the most offensive sentences of his preamble. In a private note, he urged Brennan to drop his comment about the conservatives' "fine phrases" counting for little in practice and his references to the other race cases from the term. Stevens had joined much of Brennan's *Patterson* dissent, but he'd been with the conservatives in *Croson*, and, in addition to his institutional concerns about the tone of the *Patterson* writings, he no doubt took some personal offense at Brennan's implications.

Though characteristically polite, Stevens wanted to make certain Brennan understood how strongly he felt. "I know I have no standing to make this suggestion because I have not joined this part of your opinion," he wrote of Brennan's accusatory preface, "but I am sufficiently troubled by it to be thinking seriously of joining Tony's footnote response. Respectfully, John."

This bit of arm twisting carried the day. Brennan made the deletions

Stevens suggested, and, in response, Kennedy withdrew his footnote rejoinder.

On June 15, Justice Kennedy announced *Patterson* from the bench. His brief summary of his opinion said much about his self-perception. At some length and in a voice rich in conviction, he dwelled on the Justices' unanimous decision not to overrule *Runyon* and his conviction that *Patterson* signaled not "one inch of retreat" from the Court's commitment to preserve the constitutional ideal of equal justice under law. At the same time, Kennedy downplayed the ugly split over the precise meaning of Section 1981, which he treated as a straightforward question of statutory interpretation. Indeed, that was how he saw the case: as a victory both for civil rights and for conservative canons of judicial construction—in short, a victory for the kind of Justice that Kennedy aspired to be and wanted to be considered.

Outside the Court, reaction was predictable. Paul Kamenar of the conservative Washington Legal Foundation lauded the opinion, despite its reaffirmance of *Runyon*. The Court's narrowing of Section 1981, he remarked, was "a field goal rather than a touchdown," but satisfying nonetheless.[45] Civil rights lawyers, by contrast, quickly branded Kennedy's opinion "a disaster for all those committed to equal employment opportunity," or, as Penda Hair, an NAACP Legal Defense Fund lawyer put it, an "underhanded way to erode a settled civil rights law." They even denigrated the preservation of *Runyon* as (in the words of Julius Chambers, who had argued the case for Patterson) "a victory in a battle that should never have been fought."[46]

As a matter of law, *Patterson* was short-lived. No sooner had the case come down than Sen. Edward Kennedy, reacting not only to *Patterson* but to *Wards Cove* and *Wilks*, declared that "Congress must not let these decisions stand."[47] Two years later, Congress heeded Senator Kennedy's call and, in the Civil Rights Act of 1991, effectively reversed all three cases.

Patterson's legacy inside the Court, however, could not be erased so readily. Although Stevens's intervention with Brennan had spared the Court a full public display of its internecine struggles, *Patterson* exposed and advanced a corruption in the process by which the Justices defined the law.

Certainly, the cabal's role in *Patterson*, Cappuccio's specifically, raised troublesome issues of clerk influence. There is a line, albeit not a bright one, between the usual clerk role of offering one's best advice then carrying out instructions, and the darker realm of scheming into which *Patterson* appeared to have strayed.

Justice Kennedy's decisive switch in the case was engineered in major part by a clerk acting in pursuit of his own legal agenda and that of his former boss, Justice Scalia, with whose Chambers he collaborated. As a substantive matter, the interpretation of Section 1981 that Cappuccio tailored for Kennedy did not even reflect Cappuccio's own conviction about the best or most accurate interpretation of the statute (since he actually believed that *Runyon* should be reversed). But the purpose behind Cappuccio's interpretive efforts was not primarily a search for legal truth. His apparent aim was to find a reading he could sell to Kennedy and, thereby, prevent the Justice from joining Brennan and handing the "dreaded libs" a major victory in a civil rights case. Of course, Kennedy's malleability was a prerequisite for Cappuccio's success and remains the reason, years later, that former clerks consider him one of the more "clerk-driven" Justices.*

On the other side, Brennan's conduct during *Patterson* revealed the desperate lengths to which he would go in trying to salvage his vision of civil rights. In the vain hope of outmaneuvering Kennedy, Brennan had been willing not only to sacrifice the personal interests of Brenda Patterson—a woman he believed to have suffered a series of racist indignities—but also to decide the case on what he knew to be a bogus technicality. No doubt Brennan considered this tactic a kind of judicial triage: let the plaintiff die to save the principle. But the most serious casualty of the Justice's tactics was not Patterson but Brennan himself. The ideological divisions at the Court and the frustration of watching large pieces of his life's work dismantled had overwhelmed Brennan's judgment and subverted his sense of duty as a Justice.

It would be undoubtedly naive and even wrong to suggest that Justices must always act with absolute and complete candor. The Court is an institution performing a highly sensitive, inescapably political role, and, as a consequence, in some cases the full expression of an individual Justice's views must be tempered by statesmanship. A concern for the Court's external authority or for preserving collegiality within the Court inevitably requires Justices, on occasion, to compromise in their respective ju-

---

*An annual ritual among former Kennedy clerks is the scramble between his more conservative and more liberal alumni to see which side can convince the Justice to hire its candidates for the next term.

risprudences. Such compromises may be necessary, for example, to forge a Court majority, or out of a respect for precedent, or to allow the Court, in an unusual case, to speak with a single voice.[48] As Justice Frankfurter once observed, "When you have to have at least five people to agree on something, they can't have that comprehensive completeness of candor which is open to a single man, giving his own reasons untrammeled by what anybody else may do or not do."[49]

Brown v. *Board of Education* is the outstanding example of such statesmanship. From the outset, Chief Justice Warren (thrice governor of California and a man of keen political instincts) resolved that the Court would decide this world-altering case unanimously, without separate concurrences, and in a rhetorical style calculated not to give unnecessary offense to the South. But Warren's drive for unadorned unanimity sacrificed the views of several Justices in the majority as well as a complete or even satisfying discussion of the history and legal principles involved in the outlawing of segregated schools. *Brown* is a short, flat, and almost unexplained opinion because, if Warren had crafted it any other way, he would have lost the grudging concurrence of his colleague from Kentucky, Stanley Reed, who did not think much of the ruling even in its bland form.[50]

In *Patterson*, though, Justice Brennan could make little claim to the mantle of *Brown* or similar cases. He was not merely modulating his judicial beliefs or withholding his complete view of the case. He had predicated an opinion on a legal theory in which he did not believe, based on a reading of the case's history to which he did not subscribe, to reach a result with which he did not agree. And the higher purpose Brennan was advancing was not some institutional need for cohesion or a regard for continuity in the law but simply that his own view of the law should prevail. This was not statecraft; it was subterfuge and more closely resembled the arcane maneuverings of some clever parliamentarian than the deliberations of a judge.

Brennan's maneuvers were especially damning because, as White pointed out, they were so transparently insincere. No one thought Brennan actually believed Patterson's claims to be procedurally flawed—which meant that everyone saw how willing he was to bend the rules to get his way. Such high jinks (much like his unrelenting death penalty abolitionism) destroyed Brennan's ability to make credible arguments from principle in other cases. Simply put, his tactics raised doubts that Brennan still recognized a distinction between principle and expedience.

Of all the distressing aspects of *Patterson*, however, the most disturbing was the factionalism coming to dominate the Court's deliberations. In *Patterson*, as in an increasing number of those difficult cases that define the Court's role in our society, the Justices no longer deliberated as a body of nine. They had split irreparably into two caucuses, each prearranging its own position while scheming against the other.

Such separatism undoubtedly diminished the quality of the Court's work. Neither side seriously concerned itself with the arguments of the other. By the time they shared their respective views, each faction's arguments were essentially set, however serious their logical flaws. The process of deliberation was increasingly a matter of choir preaching and political strategizing within each caucus, and hardly at all a common quest for the most appropriate and just interpretation of law.

More fundamentally, the Justices' descent into faction demonstrated a growing disregard for the interests of the Court as an institution and for the duties of that institution in American public life. As much as any structure in our democracy, the Supreme Court bears the real and visible responsibility of sustaining our political order despite the profound moral and political differences that divide us. Although they are not alone in the task, it is the duty of all courts, the Supreme Court especially, to engage in the enterprise of acknowledging and accommodating even our most passionate differences.

By the time of *Patterson*, the Justices had all but forsaken this obligation to their own community and to the nation at large. Brennan's diatribe against Kennedy was but the latest volley in a cross fire of insults in which both sides had become trigger-happy and indifferent to consequences. It scarcely mattered that the worst of Brennan's comments never saw the light of day. Kennedy and the conservatives knew well that Brennan had, in essence, labeled them racists; that in capital cases he had come close to suggesting their complicity in state-sponsored murder, and that in other cases he had demeaned them as hypocrites and enemies of freedom. The conservatives, of course, had enjoyed their say as well, demonizing the liberals as judicial tyrants, fools and weak sentimentalists, Neville Chamberlains on the bench. In light of these charges, the liberals and conservatives had turned their backs on each other and thus on a vital duty of the Court.

Croson, Wards Cove, Wilks, Patterson were all cases about legal and constitutional methods for addressing our history of slavery and Jim Crow and the legacy that history has left us. On some level, they were all cases about the possibility of reconciliation, of mediating between profound and conflicting claims of right. These cases called for facing uncomfortable truths and aspiring, however unachievably, to see the world through eyes other than one's own. But what the nation received from the Court was neither this candor nor this fraternity. Instead, the Justices surrendered to insincerity and recrimination. They provided not inspiration but another contribution to "the disuniting of America"[51] and a mirror in which we could watch our most divided selves at work.

THE TORTURE OF LAWS

The Right to Privacy

In almost any other term, the civil rights cases would have overshadowed all others and served as its legacy. Even among highly controversial rulings about freedom of speech, the juvenile death penalty, public religious displays, drug testing, separation of powers, the right to counsel, prisoners' rights, habeas corpus, the excessive fines clause, and state sovereign immunity, the civil rights cases stood out. Still, the dominating case of October Term 1988 was *Webster* v. *Reproductive Health Services*, the first post-Powell challenge to *Roe* v. *Wade*. This was our Antietam, the bloodiest battle of our war, and inconclusive but for the certainty that more battles would follow.

Inside the Court, *Webster* began two days after George Bush defeated Michael Dukakis for the presidency. On that day, President Reagan's outgoing solicitor general, Charles Fried, delivered a parting shot to the Court's already reeling liberals. He filed a brief urging the Justices to hear an appeal in this pending Missouri abortion case, which in the administration's view, presented "an appropriate opportunity" for overruling *Roe* v. *Wade*. With that bland phrasing, Fried put forward *Webster* as the vehicle by which the Court's post-Powell conservative majority could expiate what Chief Justice Rehnquist once had described as the "original sin" of judicial usurpation.[1]

Webster was the Reagan administration's third attack on the constitutional right to abortion and the second direct challenge to *Roe*—the latest episode in what Fried, in his memoir, would describe as the conservatives' "obsession" with the abortion issue.[2] In the 1983 case *Akron* v. *Akron Center for Reproductive Health*,[3] Rex Lee, Fried's predecessor as Reagan's solicitor general, had mounted the initial assault. In defense of *Akron's* various limitations on abortion, Lee had stopped short of asking the Justices to overrule *Roe* outright but had urged them to scale it back dramatically.[4] The Justices declined his invitation, pointedly reaffirming *Roe* by a 6–3 vote. (The newly appointed O'Connor joined *Roe's* original opponents, Rehnquist and White, in dissent.)

Despite this setback, in 1986, while serving a trial period as Lee's replacement, Fried raised the *Roe* issue again and upped the stakes. In *Thornburgh* v. *American College of Obstetricians and Gynecologists*,[5] he informed the same set of Justices who had rebuffed Lee's more modest argument that the United States now believed *Roe* had "no moorings in the text of our Constitution or in familiar constitutional doctrine" and should be abandoned. This time, a bare 5–4 majority rejected Fried's suggestion and again explicitly recommitted the Court to *Roe*. (Blackmun wrote the majority; Powell provided the crucial fifth vote; and Burger joined White, Rehnquist, and O'Connor in dissent.)

Given the close vote and the administration's intense legal and political interest in the issue, another *Roe* challenge was inevitable, especially after Reagan (in 1988) appointed Anthony Kennedy to replace the pro-*Roe*, swing-voting Lewis Powell. The administration decided to test *Roe* again as soon as practical and chose *Webster* from among a number of pending abortion cases as the best chance for a potential overruling.*

At issue in *Webster* was a Missouri law, drafted with the assistance of the state's National Right to Life affiliate, that prohibited the use of all public funds and facilities for either abortions or abortion counseling and established certain medical testing requirements before any doctor could perform an abortion on any woman twenty or more weeks into pregnancy. The law also contained a preamble declaring it Missouri's policy that "the life of each human being begins at conception," which appeared to flout *Roe's* caution that a state "may not adopt one theory of when life begins" if the intent is "to justify its regulation of abortion."

As soon as the statute passed, Planned Parenthood and Missouri's chapter of the ACLU (on behalf of Reproductive Health Services) challenged it in federal court as violating *Roe* and other Court rulings based on *Roe*. Applying these precedents, a federal district judge in Missouri had declared most of the Missouri law unconstitutional, and the Eighth Circuit had largely affirmed that decision on appeal.

---

*In the interim, Scalia had also replaced Burger on the Court, but, at least after Burger's defection in *Thornburgh*, this appeared merely to replace one *Roe* critic with another.

In the course of this litigation, Missouri had defended its statute using a variety of arguments (mainly based on precedents establishing the right of states to withhold public assistance to abortion) that stopped short of calling for the overruling of *Roe* itself. As the state prepared an appeal to the Supreme Court, however, Brad Reynolds, Attorney General Meese's chief lieutenant, called the Missouri State's Attorney's Office to urge that it challenge the validity of *Roe* directly. As Reynolds later recalled, "We damn near had to twist their arms," but in the end, under additional pressure from right-to-life groups, Missouri's lawyers reluctantly agreed.[6] The state asked the Court to reconsider *Roe*, which allowed Fried and the administration to pretend to play the secondary role of merely endorsing Missouri's *Roe*-imperiling petition for review.

This behind the scenes maneuvering aside, from the moment the solicitor general singled out *Webster* as an "appropriate opportunity" for reconsidering *Roe*, it became all but a foregone conclusion that the Court would grant review. As Justice Blackmun had complained in numerous speeches, there were "always four votes" to hear abortion cases as the Court's conservatives refused to let the issue rest. The advent of Justice Kennedy's potential fifth vote for overturning *Roe* only gave the conservatives greater incentive.

Even before the term began, Blackmun was anticipating another showdown. That September, in what seemed to have become his annual preterm "state of *Roe*" address, the Justice had added a pessimistic coda to his usual lament about the ceaselessness of *Roe* litigation. "Will *Roe v. Wade* go down the drain?" he had asked a student audience rhetorically. "There's a very distinct possibility that it will, this term. You can count the votes."[7]

In the wake of Fried's brief, the immediate question for those of us clerking at the time was not whether the Court would take the *Webster* case but whether it would do so in time to hear argument in the spring (as opposed to holding it over for the next fall). The answer emerged over the course of a Christmas season memorable primarily for the pall of ill health that hung over a Court already clouded by anxiety and strife.

On October 21, Justice O'Connor had learned during a routine medical checkup that one of her breasts contained a small lump. Within days, she underwent surgery to remove what turned out to be a cancer that had already spread to her lymph nodes. To limit the chance of recurrence, O'Connor would have to undergo chemotherapy, an ordeal she started almost immediately.

Although O'Connor was an active, athletic woman, an enthusiast for golf, skiing, and tennis, the cancer treatments took an inevitable toll. Within weeks, she appeared drawn and weary; walking the halls, she held herself with the unnatural rigidity peculiar to the unwell; for obvious reasons, she donned a wig. Those of us outside her Chambers could only guess at O'Connor's suffering and admire her obvious fortitude as she stoically continued to carry a full load. But we also wondered how the physical and psychological pain of what O'Connor described as "the first major crisis of [her] life" would affect the views of this pivotal Justice. More forebodingly, some even speculated whether she might retire.

In the first week of December, Justice Brennan was rushed to Bethesda Naval Hospital with a high fever and chills. After an original diagnosis of pneumonia, the doctors discovered an infected gallbladder, which they immediately removed. Brennan remained in the hospital for more than a week and did not return to the Court until well after New Year's. In his absence, it was impossible not to worry about the consequences of such major surgery for an eighty-two-year-old man. Those of us in the Chambers of Marshall and Blackmun, the Court's two other octogenarians (neither in perfect health), started watching our own Justices more closely for any signs of trouble.

Christmas itself was an occasion for neither peace nor goodwill. The Court had a tradition of observing the holiday by placing a large, elaborately decorated Christmas tree in the Great Hall and accompanying it with a tape recorder playing Christmas music through tinny speakers. The Court also held a party for the entire staff where singing carols around a grand piano—Justice Scalia usually in the lead—was the primary activity. Justice Marshall made it a practice to absent himself from the party and annually RSVPed with a sarcastic note that he "still believe[d] in the separation of church and state."

A number of clerks shared Marshall's philosophical objections. In a matter of weeks the Court would hear argument on whether the Constitution's First Amendment prohibition on the "establishment" of religion forbade public officials from erecting a holiday display including a tree, a crèche, and a menorah. How could the Justices decide such a case impartially when they played Christmas carols under a huge tree in their own foyer? Some clerks also found the Court's Christian observances exclusionary and personally offensive. Several Jewish clerks, in particular, strongly objected to the Christianizing of their workplace and thought it unconscionable that an institution charged with preserving the secular character of the national government would welcome its countless non-Christian visitors with an overtly religious symbol.

In the Court's hothouse environment, sixteen clerks, all but three from the more liberal Chambers, formally petitioned Chief Justice Rehnquist for a hearing to discuss dispensing with some or all of the Christmas activities. While some conservative clerks mocked their secularist colleagues, Rehnquist met with a representative few. The audience, which lasted mere minutes, served only to embitter the petitioners as the Chief responded to their concerns with a curt "what's-your-problem-it's-Christmas."

Through these illnesses and antagonisms, the Court's processes ground on. Given the time necessary for Reproductive Health Services to respond to Missouri's proposed *Webster* appeal, the initial papers in the case didn't circulate until mid-December. In a painful coincidence, the cert. pool assignment fell to one of my Blackmun co-clerks, Kevin Kearney, who faced the unenviable task of evaluating whether the Court should take a case that might very well destroy the immortalizing opinion of his boss's career.

In the Marshall Chambers, which did not participate in the cert. pool, the clerk on the case recommended a defensive denial. "Taking this case," she warned her boss, "would pose a great threat that the majority on this Court would overrule, or dramatically limit, *Roe*." My co-clerk could not indulge in such strategic thinking. Missouri's various abortion regulations and the Court of Appeals's handling of them raised serious questions about the proper interpretation of *Roe*—in addition to calling that case into question. Kearney tried to walk a line between denying the obvious (that several aspects of *Webster* surely merited the Court's attention) and endorsing the broader suggestion that the case be used as a vehicle for reconsidering *Roe*. While conceding that *Webster* was "adequate" for that purpose, Kearney advised limiting the Court's grant of review to the more specific issues of *Roe* interpretation raised by the case.

On January 9, with only Brennan, Marshall, and Blackmun on record as opposed,* the Justices ignored Kearney's modest proposal and voted

---

*Justice Marshall's tally sheet for this *Webster* vote indicates Rehnquist, White, O'Connor, and Scalia in favor of hearing the appeal, with no notation for Stevens or Kennedy. At least Kennedy, however, also favored taking the case.

to hear all the legal questions posed by *Webster,* including whether to reconsider *Roe.* And they did so just in time to schedule oral argument during the Court's final sitting at the end of April. It was our case now.

I still remember Justice Blackmun telling us about the conference vote, his face impassive, his voice wavering between defiance and resignation. We were in his office. I was sitting but a few feet from where I had sat eleven months before (it seemed much longer), when the Justice, during my job interview, asked me how I would feel about working for the man who had written *Roe.* At the time, my answer, something along the lines of "I'd be honored," had been a reflexive response to a question that felt unreal. On January 9, that question became very real, and that spring I thought about little else. What did I think of *Roe?* The answer depended on where the decision came from and on what it was based.

In one of the numerous ironies that haunt the history of abortion rights, Charles Fried, who as Reagan's solicitor general sought aggressively to overturn *Roe,* was an active participant in the creation of the modern right to privacy on which *Roe* is founded. Fried was a clerk to Justice John Harlan in 1961, when the Court took up *Poe* v. *Ullman,*[8] in which a married couple and their physician challenged the constitutionality of Connecticut's 1879 statute making it a crime for anyone, including married couples, to use a contraceptive drug or device.

After hearing oral argument in *Poe,* a majority of five Justices voted to dismiss the case on technical grounds. In their view, the *Poe* litigation was cooked up, a theoretical exercise designed by Connecticut's chapter of Planned Parenthood and the ACLU to challenge an antiquated law under which no one had been prosecuted for years. The Constitution limits the Court to deciding actual live "cases or controversies," and the majority concluded that *Poe* simply did not qualify.

Four Justices, however—Harlan, Douglas, Stewart, and Black—thought Connecticut's ban on contraceptives (as a result of which not a single family planning clinic operated in the state) had a more than sufficient practical effect to sustain a lawsuit. They wanted to reach the merits of *Poe* and, except for Black, would have struck down what Harlan called in conference "the most egregiously unconstitutional act I have seen since being on the Court."[9]

The bench memo that Fried had written for Harlan laid out the rationale for striking the Connecticut law. According to Fried, it violated the "right to privacy," an aspect of "liberty" that the due process clause of the Fourteenth Amendment protected from unreasonable state intrusion. More specifically, Fried had urged Harlan to declare that "individual married couples have a right to engage in marital relations in the privacy of their own consciences and free of the intrusion of the criminal law."[10]

Justice Harlan shared Fried's thinking and issued a lengthy dissent (that Fried initially drafted) spelling out a due process rationale for overturning Connecticut's law. As Harlan described it, the protections of the due process clause could not be "reduced to any formula" or "determined by reference to any code." The best that could be said, he explained, "is that through the course of this Court's decisions [due process] has represented the balance which our Nation, built upon postulates of respect for the liberty of the individual, has struck between that liberty and the demands of organized society." That balance gained meaning through a "rational process," a weighing of "liberty and the demands of an organized society" based on "the traditions from which [the nation] developed as well as the traditions from which it broke." In sum, due process was "a living thing."

Within this evolving tradition, Harlan went on, the scope of "liberty" could not be "limited by the precise terms of the specific guarantees elsewhere provided in the Constitution." For liberty was "not a series of isolated points." It was "a rational continuum which, broadly speaking, include[d] a freedom from all substantial arbitrary impositions and purposeless restraints."

Connecticut's contraception law, Harlan concluded, clearly abridged interests falling within this "continuum" of due process liberty. The Court had long recognized as much. In search and seizure cases, the Justices consistently had given special protection to the "privacy of the home." Other decisions had guaranteed the right of parents to send their children to private schools[11] and to teach them foreign languages.[12] Drawn together, these (and similar) decisions reflected the Court's understanding, developed case by case over time, that the due process clause protected a "private realm of family life," including "the most intimate details of the marital relation."

In short, "a husband and wife's marital relations" were a "fundamental" aspect of "liberty" that the state could violate only with the most urgent justification. And while Harlan acknowledged that such justification was possible—he volunteered that states could still criminalize traditionally immoral practices such as homosexuality, fornication, and incest—due process prohibited the state from bringing "the whole machinery of the criminal law into the very heart of marital privacy."

In retrospect, Harlan's *Poe* dissent, notable for its eloquence and the much-admired conservatism of its author, was the crucial turning point in the creation of the modern constitutional right to privacy. It became the foundation for almost every subsequent argument in favor of sexual and procreational freedom from contraception and abortion to homosexual rights.

In calling for the recognition of a potentially expansive right to privacy, Harlan's dissent also opened a new chapter in the broader debate over the power of unelected judges to use the Constitution's guarantee of due process to override acts of elected legislators.[13] No legal debate in this century has been more contentious. And none is more conceptually difficult. But to appreciate the origins and merits of *Roe* (as well as related cases), it is essential to try.

At the center of this debate was the doctrine of "substantive due process." This oxymoron is shorthand for the idea that when government impinges on "life, liberty, or property," the judiciary will examine not only the *procedures* by which those regulations were imposed but also the *sufficiency of the justification* underlying the challenged regulations. Despite the due process clause's textual focus on procedural regularity, the Court had employed some version of substantive due process review for more than a century. The question perennially dividing the Court and legal scholars was one of definition: what kinds of human activity fell within the term "liberty" so that legislation affecting those activities would trigger substantive judicial scrutiny?

Over time the Court's answer had varied dramatically. During the late nineteenth and early twentieth centuries, under the sway of laissez-faire economic theory, the Court had concluded that the liberty protected by due process included a broad right to "freedom of contract." During this *Lochner* era (so called after its leading case, *Lochner* v. *New York*), the Court struck down regulations of business, such as maximum hours and minimum wage laws, that conflicted with the free-market ideology to which a majority of Justices subscribed.

In its freewheeling activism, the *Lochner*-era Court also defined due process liberty to include some noneconomic rights, in particular rights related to family and child rearing. As Harlan recalled in his *Poe* dissent, in the 1923 case *Meyer* v. *Nebraska,* the Court had used a due process rationale to vacate a conviction under a Nebraska statute (World War I inspired) making it a crime to teach foreign languages—German was the target—to young children. And two years later (in *Pierce* v. *Society of Sisters*), the Justices struck down an Oregon statute prohibiting parents from sending their children to private schools. (This statute was largely the product of anti-Catholic prejudice.)

The author of both opinions, Justice McReynolds, gave an exceedingly broad definition to due process liberty—the sphere within which the judiciary could scrutinize and override legislative judgments. "Due process," he wrote,

> denotes not merely freedom from bodily restraint but also the right of the individual to contract, to engage in any of the common occupations of life, to acquire useful knowledge, to marry, establish a home and bring up children, to worship God according to the dictates of his own conscience, and generally to enjoy those privileges long recognized at common law as essential to the orderly pursuit of happiness by free men.[14]

Critics within the Court (in particular Justices Brandeis and Holmes) and progressives on the outside (such as then Harvard Law Professor Felix Frankfurter) excoriated the *Lochner* Justices for using an insupportably expansive definition of due process liberty to substitute their own political judgments, especially about economic matters, for those reached by the government's democratic branches. As noted earlier, the Court's *Lochner*-inspired interference with Franklin Roosevelt's efforts to combat the Great Depression precipitated the Court crisis of the mid-1930s and ended only when Justice Roberts made his famous 1937 "switch in time." Once the Court's progressives attained a majority, they emphatically repudiated *Lochner*'s freedom of contract approach to liberty and ushered in a generation of judicial deference to legislative regulation of business. The Constitution, the progressives noted, "does not speak of freedom of contract"[15] and provides the Court with no authority to act as a "superlegislature" and override duly enacted laws merely because they go against the Justices' economic biases.

But while the New Dealers thus agreed on what liberty did not include (and bequeathed to us the modern antipathy to *Lochner*), they split among themselves about a proper definition. The Court majority, led first by Justice Cardozo and later by Justice Frankfurter, adopted a restrained but "flexible" approach to due process liberty. In the view of these Justices, the due process clause protected only those rights "implicit in the concept of ordered liberty" or, as Cardozo once put it, those "principles of justice so rooted in the traditions and conscience of our people as to be ranked as fundamental."[16] Embedded in this flexible approach was a sizable element of judicial discretion, the idea that judges had both the ability and the authority to discern from history and tradition basic standards of justice that government was compelled to recognize and leave inviolate.

The other side, represented most notably by Justice Hugo Black, found this judicial discretion intolerable. While Cardozo and Frankfurter disavowed any similarity between their approach to due process (rooted in long-standing tradition and the English common law) and *Lochner*'s constitutionalization of laissez-faire economics, Black saw them as of a piece. In defining due process liberty according to contemporary assessments about what rights should be deemed "fundamental," Black accused Cardozo and Frankfurter of invoking the very same formula that the *Lochner* Court had used "to roam at large in the broad expanses of policy and morals and to trespass, all too freely, on the legislative domain of the States as well as the Federal Government."[17]

As an alternative, Black espoused a fixed and definite meaning for the liberty protected by due process. According to him, the due process clause provided exactly those protections against state governmental action included in the original Bill of Rights.[18] This was the sum and substance of liberty—no more, no less. Such a definition, Black stated, is what the Framers of the Fourteenth Amendment had intended when they made the states subject to due process, and the Court had no business imposing any different definition.[19]

As a practical matter, during the 1930s, '40s, and '50s, Black's approach to liberty would have given that term a significantly broader definition than Cardozo and Frankfurter's flexible approach. Neither Cardozo nor Frankfurter considered all (or even nearly all) the protections of the Bill of Rights to be "implicit in the concept of ordered liberty" and, therefore, included in due process (as they would be under Black's approach).*

At the same time, because Cardozo and Frankfurter's flexible approach ultimately depended on the judgment of whomever constituted a Court majority at any given time, it was potentially far more *expansive* than an approach, such as Black's, limited by the original Bill of Rights. And this was the other side of Black's critique. Just as, in Black's view, Frankfurter used his discretionary approach to shortchange the Bill of Rights, another group of Justices might use this same approach (as the *Lochner* Court had) to expand due process beyond its legitimate bounds.

Justice Harlan's dissent in *Poe*, while following in the methodological footsteps of Cardozo and Frankfurter, raised precisely this issue of improperly expanding the Constitution (and judicial authority) that so disturbed Black. In the hands of an incrementalist such as Harlan, the practical consequences might be small—a constitutional sheltering of ancient prerogatives of marriage (and little more). But the principle pointed the Court toward a new turn on an old road of expanding judicial power, and the vistas beyond were capacious and alluring.

In 1965, four years after Harlan's *Poe* dissent, the Court enshrined the essence of his views into law.[20] After coming one vote shy of forcing review of Connecticut's anticontraceptive statute, Planned Parenthood challenged the law again, having arranged for the arrest and prosecution of its executive director, Estelle Griswold. (She and a Yale-based obstetrician-gynecologist were fined $100 each after opening a contraception-dispensing clinic in New Haven.)

This time, the Court took up the issue, and, in *Griswold* v. *Connecticut*,[21] a majority of seven Justices, using several theories, struck down the Connecticut statute. In three separate opinions, each of which quoted substantially from Harlan's *Poe* dissent, six Justices (Warren, Douglas, Clark, Brennan, Harlan, and Goldberg) agreed that the Constitution contained a fundamental *unenumerated* right to some sort of family- or marriage-related "privacy" that prevented Connecticut from outlawing

*For example, neither Cardozo nor Frankfurter considered the Fifth Amendment's guarantees against self-incrimination and double jeopardy, or of indictment by a grand jury, sufficiently fundamental to be part of due process. Indeed, part of Black's well-known feud with Frankfurter was based on a conviction that Frankfurter used his discretionary approach to underenforce the Constitution's robust protections of individual liberty. (This was the basis of Black's reputation as—together with Douglas—the Court's leading civil libertarian.) The Court, while never adopting Black's "total incorporation" approach, has applied most of the Bill of Rights to the states.

the use of contraceptives by married adults. (White, the seventh member of the majority, concurred on different grounds.)

Justice Douglas, who wrote the lead opinion, found an overwhelming, albeit implicit, constitutional concern with the notion of privacy in numerous amendments, including the First Amendment's protection of the freedom of association, the Fourth Amendment's protection against personal searches, and the Fifth Amendment's guarantee against self-incrimination. Taken together, these constitutional provisions (and their shadows) created a "zone of privacy" broad enough to encompass the marital relations—"intimate to the degree of being sacred"—into which Connecticut could not intrude.[22]

Harlan, rather than join Douglas's effort, wrote a separate concurrence reiterating the pure due process methodology of his *Poe* dissent. And Goldberg, while expressing support for Douglas's opinion, sought to bolster it with a concurrence (joined by Warren and Brennan) appealing to the open-ended language of the Ninth Amendment, which states: "The enumeration in the Constitution, of certain rights, shall not be construed to deny or disparage others retained by the people."*

According to Goldberg, the Ninth Amendment, although not itself a source of rights, lent "strong support" to the approach Harlan had advocated in *Poe,* namely, that the meaning of due process liberty was open-ended and included all those rights so rooted in the "traditions and conscience of our people . . . as to be ranked as fundamental." Quoting James Madison, the amendment's author, Goldberg argued that its very purpose was to preclude an argument, such as Black's, that the Constitution protects only those fundamental rights specifically provided for in the Bill of Rights. In Goldberg's reading, "To hold that a right so basic and fundamental and so deep-rooted in our society as the right to privacy in marriage may be infringed because that right is not guaranteed in so many words by the first eight amendments to the Constitution is to ignore the Ninth Amendment and to give it no effect whatsoever."[23]

Black answered the *Griswold* majority with a long dissent insistently tying the majority's various methodologies to the discredited *Lochner* line. "I like my privacy as well as the next one," he chided in a memorable statement, "but I am nevertheless compelled to admit that govern-

---

*Like *Poe,* *Griswold* was a case notable for the clerks who worked on it. Just as Fried was Harlan's clerk in *Poe,* the current Justice Stephen Breyer was Goldberg's clerk in *Griswold.* Also, John Hart Ely, now a law professor famous for denouncing *Roe* while defending *Griswold,* worked on the case for Chief Justice Warren.

ment has a right to invade it unless prohibited by some specific constitutional provision." Although Black previously had aimed this argument at the Cardozo-Frankfurter (and now Harlan) approach to due process, he applied the same criticism to Goldberg's newly minted Ninth Amendment argument. Black derided Goldberg for "merely using different words to claim for this Court and the federal judiciary power to invalidate any legislative act which the judges find irrational, unreasonable, or offensive."

The majority, of course, denied that they were deciding the case (as Goldberg put it) "in light of their personal and private notions." Douglas began his opinion for the Court explicitly denying any reliance on *Lochner*-type reasoning.[24] Goldberg and Harlan both emphasized that their search for "fundamental" rights was limited by well-marked "traditions," "the teachings of history," a "solid recognition of the basic values that underlie our society," and principles of judicial "self-restraint."

Such assurances went to the heart of *Griswold*'s legitimacy. Harlan had described the principle of due process liberty as an almost sacred "living thing," the essential embodiment of freedoms handed down to us and enriched since the Magna Carta. He was seeking to apply that principle in a world where a government of unprecedented size enjoyed an equally unprecedented power to intrude on the private side of human life. And as government pushed on the boundary created by the Constitution between the proper realm of government and the private realm of individuals, Harlan, gently but insistently, was pushing back.[25]

Black, for his part, was ordinarily even more aggressive than Harlan in his defense of liberty but confounded expectations when it came to substantive due process. To Black, a New Dealer born into a hatred of *Lochner,* among the foremost enemies of freedom was the power of a judiciary, unconstrained by the Constitution's text, to strike down measures for the general welfare arrived at democratically. And from this perspective, Harlan's "living" tradition of due process liberty was a judicially created Frankenstein monster as dangerous to good as to evil.

In *Griswold,* Harlan had prevailed. Although unable to coalesce around a single opinion, the Court promised that it could be trusted with the power to identify fundamental rights implicit but unenumerated in the Constitution's text and that it would wield this power not to judge legislation in light of the Justices' own prejudices but under the discipline of history and a self-consciousness about the limits of the judicial role.

In this enterprise, *Griswold* was in some sense an easy case, involving an ill-conceived, virtually moribund statute, unique among the fifty states. Striking it, the Court had not so much overridden a legislative judgment as cleansed the statute books of an obvious anachronism. But with the Court now serving as the crucible for resolving society's most difficult social problems, it was inevitable that harder cases would follow.

By the time the Court issued its opinion in *Roe*, both men—Harlan, the conservative patron saint of the common law tradition, and Black, the former Klansman turned champion of the Bill of Rights—would be dead. Yet their competing visions of liberty, the Constitution, and the judicial role would haunt that decision's every word. Theirs is the argument we are having still.

The Price of Good Intentions

Throughout the first half of the twentieth century, the subject of abortion was virtually taboo in America and a movement for abortion rights all but nonexistent. It had not always been so. In Revolutionary times and for the half century after, women could generally obtain legal abortions before "quickening." Doctors and "irregulars" (those without formal medical training) even advertised the service.[1] Starting in the 1850s, however, the American Medical Association launched an aggressive campaign to stamp out what elite doctors viewed as an inherently immoral procedure that also threatened the health of pregnant women.

The campaign succeeded impressively. By 1910, every state in the Union had enacted a statute outlawing abortion. Almost all these laws prohibited the procedure from the moment of conception, except when a woman's life was directly at risk. Although still numbering hundreds of thousands each year, abortions moved into the twilight of back alleys, clandestine weekends in Tijuana, or after-hours visits to doctors willing to operate beyond the margins of the law and their profession. As the number of abortions accelerated during the Depression, by best estimates (closer to guesses actually), somewhere between 8,000 and 15,000 women died from botched operations.[2]

In the 1930s, '40s, and '50s, a few lonely voices in the medical and civil liberties communities called for abortion law reform and tried to lift the blanket of silence smothering the dangerous secret of clandestine abortion practice. Finally, in 1959, they received a receptive hearing from the influential American Law Institute. By a lopsided vote, the ALI decided to endorse an abortion law reform measure allowing for so-called therapeutic abortions. Specifically, the ALI model statute permitted abortion whenever two doctors agreed that there existed a "substantial risk" that continued pregnancy would "gravely impair the physical or mental health of the mother," the fetus had a "grave physical or mental defect," or the pregnancy resulted from rape or incest.[3]

Over the next few years, three independent developments—two public health scares and a rising feminist consciousness—created the first significant public discussion of the abortion issue and dramatically reinforced the ALI's initial impetus toward legal change. In 1962, Sherri Finkbine, a Phoenix, Arizona, TV hostess and pregnant mother of four, realized that she had taken painkillers containing thalidomide, a chemical that when ingested by pregnant women was known to cause very serious birth defects in a high percentage of cases. With the encouragement of their doctor, Finkbine and her husband decided to obtain a therapeutic abortion and made arrangements with a nearby hospital.

Before the scheduled procedure, however, a community newspaper ran a story about the Finkbines' situation and the hospital balked. Concerned about liability under the state's abortion law, the hospital demanded preapproval for the procedure from a state court. Yet, in a classic catch-22, the court refused to render any opinion about the legality of the proposed abortion in the absence of an actual threat of prosecution. In the end, as chronicled daily in all the nation's major newspapers, the Finkbines fled to Sweden to remove a fetus that turned out to be deformed.

This highly publicized ordeal, of a suburban housewife and mother terrified of giving birth to a terribly malformed child, placed the idea of therapeutic abortion in a sympathetic and easily imaginable context and brought home to many Americans the need for abortion law reform. A 1965 national epidemic of rubella (German measles) significantly reinforced that trend. Women who caught rubella in the early stages of pregnancy ran a 50 percent chance of delivering seriously damaged fetuses, and, in response, many hospitals flouted state laws and performed abortions on women with the illness. As actual medical practice and the prevailing legal rules diverged, an increasing segment of the medical community endorsed the concept of abortion law reform.

Changing attitudes in the medical world and in the population generally received a considerable push from women's rights advocates and civil libertarians. For feminists such as Betty Friedan, the right to abortion was not a medical issue but a matter of women controlling their own bodies. Accordingly, the goal for them was the complete repeal of anti-abortion laws. In 1967, the National Organization for Women formally adopted this position while the ACLU endorsed the nearly as expansive principle that "a woman has a right to have an abortion . . . prior to the viability of the fetus."

As the feminists and civil libertarians developed their political positions, lawyers within the abortion rights movement started creating the theoretical basis for a constitutional challenge to bring about a judicially ordered repeal of all the nation's abortion statutes. According to the comprehensive working paper of Roy Lucas, one of the movement's first legal strategists, the springboard for their arguments would be *Griswold*. It was an "altogether reasonable application" of *Griswold*, he argued, to consider abortion "a fundamental right of marital privacy, human dignity, and personal autonomy reserved to the pregnant woman acting on the advice of a licensed physician."[4]

At the end of 1968, the various supporters of abortion law liberalization convened an "International Conference" at Hot Springs, Virginia, to agree on goals and coordinate strategy. By the meeting's end, all talk of ALI-style reform was at an end. A few states (California, Colorado, and North Carolina) had adopted such reform measures, but the results had been "virtually worthless," according to some, counterproductive in the view of others. Prosecution-wary doctors and hospitals performed few abortions as they wrestled with the judgment-laden legal requirement that such procedures be justified by a threat to the pregnant woman's mental or physical "health." In light of this experience, even former advocates of reform agreed that full repeal—the only option giving full expression to a woman's right to choose—was the proper course to pursue.

After Hot Springs, the ever-expanding campaign for abortion rights proceeded rapidly along two tracks. Planned Parenthood, the ACLU, the newly formed National Association for the Repeal of Abortion Laws (NARAL), and other smaller groups pushed hard for legislative repeal. At the same time, they started looking for prospective clients—pregnant women as well as doctors seeking to provide abortion services—to serve as plaintiffs in test cases challenging existing abortion laws as unconstitutional.

The legislative effort soon stalled. Although in 1970 four states, including New York, largely repealed their prohibitions on abortion, the next year thirty-four states considered and rejected repeal proposals.

This legislative failure was partially the consequence of an increasingly well-organized and always passionate anti-abortion opposition. More important, the defeats reflected a profound national ambivalence. In most places, most people simply did not want "abortion on demand" (the practical result of repeal), even as they favored some liberalization of existing laws.

Yet, while state legislatures were rejecting statutory repeal of abortion laws, the litigation campaign to achieve a court-ordered repeal made significant headway. In the four years after Hot Springs, various pro-choice groups initiated nearly thirty cases in lower federal and state courts seeking to strike down various abortion laws as unconstitutional. These included not only suits by pregnant women claiming a *Griswold*-based due process right to obtain abortions but also suits challenging anti-abortion laws as unconstitutionally vague, discriminatory against poor women, and in violation of a physician's right to practice medicine.

Such suits met with mixed results, but the successes were notable. In 1969, the highly regarded California Supreme Court ruled that the state's pre-1967 statute was unconstitutionally vague. (In other words, the statute failed—as required by the principle of *procedural* due process—to give the public sufficiently clear notice about exactly what conduct was being made illegal.) The California court also recognized an abortion-encompassing due process right to privacy "in matters related to marriage, family, and sex."[5] Several other courts followed suit, striking down laws on vagueness or privacy grounds.[6] And every one of these decisions, as well as those that were unfavorable, moved inexorably toward the U.S. Supreme Court. Tommy Emerson, the Yale Law professor who argued *Griswold*, is said to have remarked that the bridge between a privacy right to use contraception and a privacy right to obtain an abortion would take twenty years to build, if it could be built at all. But swept forward on a flood of cases, the lawyers of the abortion rights movement arrived at the Court about fourteen years early.

The case that would become *Roe* v. *Wade* started with two young, inexperienced women lawyers, Sarah Weddington and Linda Coffee, who agreed that they wanted to challenge Texas's highly restrictive abortion law. Weddington had recently graduated from the University of Texas Law School and was active in a women's group centered in the university. Her attachment to the abortion issue was secret and intensely personal. As a terrified third-year law student she had paid $400 cash to end her own unwanted pregnancy at a small clinic in the Mexican border town Pierdas Negras.

Coffee had entered UT Law School as a classmate of Weddington, one of five women who matriculated in 1965. After graduation, she clerked for the state's leading female jurist, Federal District Judge Sarah Hughes. Then Coffee entered private practice, where, mostly by happenstance, she developed some experience in the right-to-privacy area by assisting a close friend who was challenging Texas's antisodomy statute on *Griswold*-related grounds.

Weddington and Coffee had little idea how to find pregnant women who might serve as plaintiffs in their prospective law suit. Norma Nelson McCorvey, soon to become Jane Roe, found them. A high school dropout born of parents who divorced when she was thirteen, McCorvey got married at sixteen to a twice-divorced sheet metal worker, "Woody" McCorvey, who beat her upon learning, soon thereafter, that she was pregnant. After running away, Norma McCorvey had given birth to a daughter in May 1965, then drifted into semiemployment in Dallas-area bars known for their lesbian patronage. By the end of 1966, she was pregnant again, choosing this time to give up the baby (another daughter) for adoption.

McCorvey's third pregnancy followed two and a half years later, and this time she decided to seek an abortion. The first doctor she approached was appalled at the idea. Before seeing a second doctor, the distraught McCorvey decided to embellish her hard luck story by attributing her pregnancy to a vicious gang rape rather than to the brief affair that had produced it. The second doctor gave McCorvey the names of a few sympathetic lawyers she might consult, and eventually she found her way to Linda Coffee.

The rest, as they say, is history. Weddington and Coffee filed suit against Henry Wade in his capacity as Dallas County district attorney (in charge of enforcing the state's abortion law) for a declaratory judgment that Texas's strict abortion law (dating to 1866) was unconstitutional.* Specifically, they charged that the law—which made it a felony for a doctor to perform an abortion except "for the purpose of saving the

---

*Weddington and Coffee also brought suit on behalf of two other plaintiffs: "the Does," a childless couple including a woman unable to take oral contraception and for whom pregnancy posed a significant health risk; and Dr. James Halliford, a doctor under indictment for violating the Texas abortion statute. Because the Supreme Court eventually dismissed the claims of these plaintiffs on technical grounds, I have skirted them in my narrative.

life of the mother"—violated Roe's "right to privacy in the physician-patient relationship" as well as the "fundamental right of all women to choose whether to bear children."

Under special procedures governing declaratory judgment actions challenging the constitutionality of a state law, Roe was first heard by a panel of three federal district court judges, including Judge Hughes, Coffee's former boss. According to the senior judge, Irving Goldberg, they considered Roe an "easy case" and the outcome "almost inevitable," given that Texas did not permit abortion even in the case of rape. "Talk about life, liberty, or anything you want to," Goldberg recounted, "you can't even begin to talk about the constitutional rights if this is prohibited." In a cursory nine-page opinion that ably captured this "it-must-be-so" attitude, on June 17, 1970, the three-judge court struck down Texas's law.

While Coffee and Weddington were waiting for their case to be decided, a group of ACLU lawyers were challenging Georgia's comparatively less restrictive 1968 abortion law, a reform statute roughly patterned on the ALI model code. Under this law, to obtain a legal abortion, a pregnant woman needed to convince three doctors plus a hospital oversight committee (all abortions had to be performed in accredited hospitals) that her pregnancy would endanger her life or health, or that the fetus was very likely to have a serious physical defect, or that her pregnancy resulted from rape.

The lead plaintiff for the ACLU was a twenty-two-year-old, Sandra Bensing (Mary Doe), pregnant for the fourth time by her sometimes estranged husband, a drifter who had been jailed several times for sex crimes. Bensing had tried to obtain hospital approval for an abortion, telling the committee she would be unable to care for the child. The hospital, though, had found this justification inadequate to meet the requirements of Georgia law. Taking up Bensing's case, the ACLU was challenging these requirements as a violation of her "right of privacy or liberty in matters related to marriage, family and sex" as well as "the sacred right of every individual to the possession and control of her own person."*

Another three-judge federal court largely agreed. On July 21, it struck down Georgia's "unduly limiting" restrictions on the reasons a woman

*Ironically, after giving her baby girl up for adoption, Sandra Bensing became an antiabortion activist while her unwanted daughter ended up supporting the right to abortion. John C. Jeffries, Justice Lewis F. Powell, Jr.: A Biography (New York: Scribner's, 1994), p. 332.

could give for seeking an abortion while at the same time upholding the state's regulations providing for hospital committee oversight of abortion candidates. This was the first court decision to find unconstitutional aspects of an ALI-style "reform" law.[7]

The three-judge decisions from Texas and Georgia were eligible for immediate Supreme Court review, but by the time appeals were lodged in the fall of 1970, the Court already was considering another abortion case. Both *Roe* and *Doe* were held in abeyance for *United States* v. *Vuitch*,[8] in which a highly respected federal district judge, Gerhardt Gesell, had thrown out the District of Columbia's abortion law—which limited legal abortions to those necessary to preserve the woman's "health." According to Gesell, this division between legal and illegal abortions was unconstitutionally vague.

In April 1971, the Justices overruled Gesell and resurrected the D.C. law. With Justice Black writing for the majority, they ruled that the statute gave ample guidance to medical practitioners so long as the term *health* was defined broadly to embrace "psychological as well as physical well-being."[9]

At the insistence of Justice Harlan, Black's opinion regarding the D.C. statute's definiteness avoided taking any position on the more fundamental question—unargued by the parties in *Vuitch* but raised by *Roe* and *Doe*—of whether the Constitution included a substantive *right* to obtain an abortion. This sidestepping, however, in no way indicated lack of interest. With the questions they had left open in mind, on April 22, 1971, the day after handing down *Vuitch*, the Justices voted 5–4 (with Douglas, Harlan, Brennan, White, and Marshall in the majority) to schedule the appeals in *Roe* and *Doe* for a hearing early in the fall term.

By the time the Court heard argument on December 13, the Justices had been reduced from nine to seven by the illness-induced September retirements of the *Griswold* antagonists Harlan and Black. The argument itself was notably unenlightening, and, from the outset, the Justices' consideration of the abortion cases was mired in confusion and short-handedness.

By common account, Douglas, Brennan, and Marshall declared themselves to be in favor of some kind of constitutional right to abortion, although none of them was very precise about the scope of such a right. For example, while Douglas was adamant that Texas's law must fall, he was equivocal about Georgia's less stringent regulations. Meanwhile, Marshall expressed concerns about the "time problem," wondering why a state could not prohibit an abortion after a "certain stage" near to birth.

On the other side, Chief Justice Burger criticized the Texas law as "certainly archaic and obsolete" but also seemed to hold the view that both the Texas and Georgia statutes were constitutional. Justice White reached the same conclusion. He saw no firm constitutional basis for trumping the state's interest in fetal life.

The surprises at conference were Justices Stewart and Blackmun. Although Stewart had dissented in *Griswold* and although Blackmun was seen as the unswerving ally of the Chief Justice (his "Minnesota Twin"), each thought some or all of both statutes might be unconstitutional. Neither seemed inclined to write a broad opinion, and both expressed concern about the state's interest in the fetus. Nonetheless, they recognized some measure of constitutional protection for a woman seeking an abortion, and Blackmun, harkening to Goldberg's *Griswold* concurrence, even stated specifically that he thought Texas's law "impinge[d] too far" on a woman's "Ninth Amendment rights."[10]

Immediately after conference, the Justices themselves fell into sharp disagreement about how they had resolved the cases. The argument started when Burger, despite having endorsed the *minority* view that both abortion statutes were constitutional, assigned the cases to Blackmun. The other Justices had fumed over past instances where the Chief had usurped the assignment power, but never in such an important set of cases. Douglas, who thought he should rightfully have assigned *Roe* and *Doe*, became enraged and protested Burger's presumption.* But the Chief stood his ground. The conference discussion had been inconclusive, he replied. In the end, he had "marked down no votes and said this was a case that would have to stand or fall on the writing, when it was done." Pursuant to that view, he had assigned the cases.

As for the assignee, Blackmun agreed with the Chief in a backhanded sort of way. Confusion at conference, he would later recall, "was, unfortunately, symptomatic of pervasive problems during the Burger Court era." A frequent solution was for one Justice to be assigned to draft a pre-

---

*It is interesting that, in his memo of protest, Douglas counted Blackmun in the Chief's camp, leaving the Court split 4–3 in favor of striking down some or all of both abortion laws. Blackmun himself recalls being in the majority—making the vote 5–2.

liminary memorandum on a case rather than a full-fledged majority opinion. And this was exactly how Blackmun viewed his task in *Roe* and *Doe*.

Douglas and the other liberals, however, were hardly mollified, and abortion rights sympathizers around the building dreamed up a number of conspiracy theories to explain the Chief's power play. In his response to Douglas's original complaint, Burger had noted that he considered these two "sensitive cases . . . probable candidates for reargument" before a full Court of nine—including the two impending Nixon appointees (Powell and Rehnquist), who might swing the cases in Burger's favor. Some suspected that the Chief gave Blackmun the assignment because he was slow to draft and every day's delay would strengthen the reasons for letting the new Justices participate. Others thought that Burger hoped to detach Blackmun from the liberals or that his draft would prove divisive and split the majority.

In any event, the assignment stood; and Douglas simply ignored it. In his usual rapid-fire fashion, Douglas banged out a draft opinion extending *Griswold* to recognize as a "species" of due process liberty a "fundamental right" to privacy, including abortion, that the state could limit only for the most compelling reasons. He forwarded his handiwork to Brennan, who convinced his frequently rash colleague not to circulate the draft and thereby risk alienating Blackmun. To keep Douglas busy, Brennan sent him eleven pages of suggested revisions.

Blackmun, meanwhile, labored through winter and into spring. His days were spent alone in the relatively spare quarters of the Justices' Library, surrounded by neatly stacked piles of books. An agonizer by nature, Blackmun felt keenly the burden of what was by far the most awesome assignment of his short tenure on the Court. Not only were the legal issues intrinsically difficult but his life experience led him in conflicting directions. On the one hand, Blackmun, who'd once dreamed of a medical career, had developed great respect for hospital review committees (such as those mandated by the Georgia law) during his time as general counsel of the Mayo Clinic. On the other hand, that same job had brought him face-to-face with "the general misery" caused by what he referred to as unsanctioned "abortion mills." Compounding his dilemma, Blackmun felt certain that, regardless of how the Justices decided *Roe* and *Doe*, the rulings would draw fire to the Court.

In short, all Blackmun's instincts cried out for caution. And he heeded them. After Powell and Rehnquist had joined the Court in January, Burger had asked each of the Justices to suggest possible cases for reargument. Noting "the importance of the issue," Blackmun immediately had nominated the two abortion cases. But his colleagues kept him on the hook. They deferred the reargument question, and Blackmun went back to work.

Four months later, on May 18, Blackmun produced a seventeen-page draft in *Roe*. For those like Douglas and Brennan looking to expand the right to privacy, it was an absolute dud. As Blackmun explained in his cover memo, he had found the Texas statute unconstitutional not on privacy grounds but on the much narrower ground of vagueness. That ground was sufficient, he suggested, and the Court could then sidestep the "more complex Ninth Amendment issue." Blackmun recognized that his approach might not appeal to everyone and emphasized that he remained "flexible." What his note made most clear was his hope that the Justices, in a rough emulation of *Brown*, could all "come together on something" and present a united front to the public. He also promised that his work on the Georgia case would be forthcoming but reiterated his view that this case especially should be reargued before a full bench.

Brennan and Douglas wasted no time telling Blackmun in separate memos that they found his avoidance of what Brennan called the "core constitutional question" totally unsatisfactory. As Brennan reminded Blackmun, a majority at conference had agreed that "the constitution required the invalidation of abortion statutes save to the extent that they required that an abortion be performed by a licensed physician within some limited time after conception." Both he and Douglas wanted a majority opinion reflecting that view.

A week later, Blackmun circulated his draft in the Georgia case. It was much more substantial than the *Roe* draft and did confront the "core" issue directly. Citing privacy-related cases dating to *Meyer* and *Pierce* from the 1920s, Blackmun stated that "a woman's interest in making the fundamental personal decision whether or not to bear an unwanted child is within the scope of personal rights protected by the Ninth and Fourteenth Amendments." That right was not absolute, however. Abortion, Blackmun stressed, was different from child rearing or contraception. In the case of fetal life, the woman was "not isolated in her privacy." The state's interest in that life "grows stronger as the woman approaches term" and "the woman's right to privacy must be measured accordingly." Despite these qualifications, Blackmun considered most but not all of Georgia's elaborate scheme for abortion approval to be "unduly restrictive of the patient's rights and needs" and, therefore, unconstitutional.

Brennan and Douglas wanted the Court to go still further and hold the entire Georgia statute invalid, but they were restrained by a continuing concern that too much debate would rekindle talk of reargument and potentially deprive them of an incomplete but still substantial victory. After a quick caucus with Marshall and Stewart, they decided to join Blackmun's *Doe* opinion immediately (thereby creating a majority) and work for improvements afterward. Indeed, before the day was over, Brennan, Douglas, and Marshall all had sent Blackmun their official joinders, and, a few days later, Stewart phoned Blackmun to indicate his "basic agreement."

These best laid plans immediately went awry. The same day as Stewart's call, White circulated a dissent from Blackmun's *Roe* draft. In a mere three pages he pointed out a significant potential problem. The Court really couldn't strike down Texas's statute as vague without implicitly overruling its decision the previous term in *Vuitch*. After all, in *Vuitch* the Court had held that the language in the D.C. statute referring to the "health" of the mother was not unconstitutionally vague. Surely, then, a statutory provision (such as Texas's) referring to the seemingly more definite concept of "saving the life" of the mother must be acceptably clear.

Whether in direct response to White's criticism or simply as a consequence of strong lingering concerns, two days later Blackmun circulated a formal appeal for reargument in both abortion cases. "The country deserves the conclusion of a nine-man, not a seven-man court," he urged—"whatever the ultimate decision may be." In addition, he still was not "certain about all the details," including basic issues such as which of the two opinions, *Roe* or *Doe*, should be "primary" and whether the Court should "emasculate" the Georgia statute by carving out its unconstitutional parts or strike it entirely (as Brennan and Douglas wanted) and let the state legislature start over. All things considered, Blackmun had concluded "somewhat reluctantly" that, despite his long labors, reargument early in the next term was advisable.

Not surprisingly, within hours Douglas shot back that neither case should be reargued. He commended Blackmun for his "yeoman service" and the creation of two opinions both of which had commanded majorities of five. These "creditable jobs of craftsmanship" would "stand the test of time," Douglas predicted. In his view, the "important thing [was] to get them down." Brennan called Blackmun to express similar sentiments, and both he and Marshall wrote official notes opposing reargument.

Blackmun's self-abnegation, though, provided Burger an opening for putting off the cases. "This is as sensitive and difficult an issue as any in this Court in my time," the Chief wrote his brethren on May 31, "and I want to hear more and think more when I am not trying to sort out several dozen other difficult cases. Hence, I vote to reargue early in the next Term."

Burger's memo set off a fury in the Chambers of all four Justices who had joined Blackmun's drafts (in part to avoid reargument) and made Douglas so furious that he sent the Chief a note threatening to expose publicly "what is happening to us and the tragedy it entails" if he persisted in putting off the abortion cases. Douglas's threats notwithstanding, Burger received crucial support from Powell, who stated that, after half a term on the Court, he had begun to feel a duty to participate in the abortion cases and, in light of Blackmun's own doubts, had become "persuaded to favor reargument." Rehnquist followed with a memo simply agreeing with Powell, which meant Burger now commanded five votes for reargument: his own plus those of Blackmun, Powell, Rehnquist, and White (the one certain dissenter from both Blackmun drafts).

In response, Douglas prepared to carry out his threat. He drafted a scorching dissent accusing Burger of trying to "bend the court to his will" first by "manipulating assignments" and then by "suppress[ing] the majority view with the hope that exigencies of time will change the result." As Douglas saw it, Burger's motive was transparent: to delay the abortion cases past November's presidential election—presumably to help Nixon, who actively opposed abortion rights. Burger's strategy, Douglas complained, "dilutes the integrity of the Court and makes the decisions here depend on the manipulative skills of a Chief Justice."

As Blackmun would later recall, after Douglas circulated his proposed exposé, things became "rather ugly."[11] Brennan tried to achieve some measure of damage control by proposing numerous deletions from Douglas's screed. Blackmun tried a more direct approach. He went to see Douglas and promised that, whatever Burger's hope, his votes were firm in both abortion cases and would not change with reargument. The visit was successful. After circulating six versions of his intended dissent, Douglas never published it. Instead, on June 26, the Court issued a non-descript order setting *Roe* and *Doe* for reargument the next fall.

Events moved swiftly when the Court reconvened. At the Justices' conference after the October 11 reargument, the result was even more definitive than that of the previous term. Douglas, Brennan, Marshall, and Stewart all restated their previous position to strike both the Texas and Georgia laws. Blackmun remained true to his promise to Douglas. Having spent much of the summer isolated in Minnesota at the Mayo Clinic library researching the history of moral, medical, and legal attitudes toward abortion, he announced emphatically that he stood "where he was last spring."

In addition, this majority picked up two new allies. Burger, who had waffled before, now stated definitively that the Texas law was "too restrictive," although he still was not certain about Georgia's more modest restrictions.

More resolutely, Powell weighed in for striking both laws. He found the issues sufficiently straightforward that he had declared his intentions to his clerk a full month before oral argument. As he now shared with his colleagues, Powell generally agreed with Blackmun's views, though with two significant caveats. He thought *Roe*, the Texas case, should take precedence over *Doe*, and he felt (as had Douglas, Brennan, Marshall, and Stewart in the spring) that the Court should decide both cases on the core issue of privacy rather than striking the Texas law as excessively vague. Blackmun immediately responded by volunteering to adopt both suggestions.

Powell's fellow newcomer, Rehnquist, joined White on the other side, though he limited his comments to an endorsement of White's position that the Court should not "second-guess state legislatures in striking the balance in favor of abortion laws." All told, that made at least six and probably seven votes for a decision that would effectively invalidate most or all of every abortion statute in the country.

Blackmun wasted no time reworking his opinions. On November 22, he circulated drafts that, with one major revision, would become the law of the land in January. After dispensing with the jurisdictional issues in the case, Blackmun's much-revised *Roe* opinion (now the lead) started with a lengthy history of ancient and modern attitudes toward abortion. It canvassed the pre-Socratic Greek philosophers (with special concern for the Hippocratic oath's denunciation of abortion), then moved forward through canon law, English common law, and later English statutes, until finally considering the statutes of American states. The purpose of this investigation was to show that historically abortion had by no means been universally condemned and that "at common law, at the time of the adoption of our Constitution, and throughout the major portion of the 19th century, abortion was viewed with less disfavor than under most statutes currently in effect."

Blackmun then considered the purposes underlying the mid to late nineteenth-century shift toward criminalizing abortion throughout pregnancy rather than—as under the common law—only after "quickening." The first concern was the health of pregnant women subjecting themselves to what, before the development of antisepsis, was an inherently hazardous medical procedure often performed by less than expert hands. Second, the new laws recognized a state interest "in protecting prenatal life."

Only at this point did Blackmun turn to the legal crux of the abortion cases: whether the Constitution addressed the right of women to obtain abortions. And his discussion was brief, just a few paragraphs. He began by noting that as early as 1891 the Court had recognized "a right of personal privacy" and had found "the roots of that right" in the First, Fourth, and Fifth Amendments, in the "penumbras of the Bill of Rights," in the Ninth Amendment, or in the concept of liberty protected by the due process clause.

Following Harlan (and quoting Cardozo), Blackmun emphasized that the constitutional right to privacy protected only those personal rights deemed "fundamental" or "implicit in the concept of ordered liberty." Then, citing cases from the *Lochner* era through recent precedents based on *Griswold,* he pointed out that the Court already had determined that the right extended to "activities relating to marriage, procreation, contraception, and child rearing and education." On this basis, in the opinion's most crucial sentence, Blackmun concluded: "This right of privacy, whether it be founded in the Fourteenth Amendment's concept of personal liberty and restrictions upon state action, as we feel it is, or, as the District Court determined, in the Ninth Amendment's reservation of rights to the people, is broad enough to encompass a woman's decision whether or not to terminate her pregnancy."

Finally, Blackmun sought to reconcile this right with the state's "important" interests in maternal health and fetal life. He began by rejecting the notion that a fetus was a "person" as contemplated by the Constitution and, therefore, entitled to its full protections. But having rejected fetal personhood (which would presumably have made every abortion, even one to save the mother's life, a homicide), Blackmun nonetheless concluded that at some point in pregnancy the state's "interest in the potentiality of human life" became sufficiently "compelling" to override the woman's fundamental right to privacy. (Here he was applying essentially the same strict scrutiny—the 100-watt illumination light—used in equal protection jurisprudence. This test required that the state present not merely a rational or important justification for its actions but a "compelling" one.)

Under this approach, the crucial question was when in pregnancy (at conception, after a certain number of weeks, at quickening, or at viability) did the tipping point occur? And Blackmun—admitting to his colleagues that the choice was as "arbitrary" as any other—chose the end of the first trimester. Before this point, he asserted, a state "must do no more than to leave the abortion decision to the best medical judgment of the pregnant woman's attending physician." Afterward, the state could restrict abortion to "reasonable therapeutic categories," presumably circumstances involving the woman's life or health.

Because Blackmun had made *Roe* the lead case, his draft in *Doe* was essentially an application of the principles he had laid out in *Roe*. The result was to nullify all the major provisions of the Georgia law, including its mandate of hospital committee preapproval of all abortions.

In general, Blackmun's colleagues reacted warmly to his new efforts. Douglas, Stewart, and Powell each wrote to commend him for an "excellent," "admirably thorough," and "fine" job. Powell, Brennan, and Marshall, however, shared reservations about Blackmun's choice of the end of the first trimester as the "critical" point for balancing the competing interests of the woman and the state. Powell raised this objection first, privately urging Blackmun to extend the woman's unfettered right to abortion through viability, the point at which the fetus could survive outside the womb.* At viability, Powell argued, "the interest of the state

---

*In advocating the use of viability as the point when the state's interest in fetal life becomes compelling, Powell was following the lead of Judge Jon Newman (now the chief judge of the Second Circuit), who wrote the most persuasive of the lower court opinions striking down an abortion statute. See *Abele v. Markle*, 351 F. Supp. 224 (1972).

becomes clearly identifiable, in a manner which would be generally understood."*

Through the clerk back channel, Brennan and Marshall expressed similar concerns, and Blackmun—who had chosen the end of the first trimester mainly because he thought other Justices would prefer it—expressed his willingness to revise. In a letter airing the issue, Blackmun acknowledged the "logical and biological justifications" for focusing on viability. He also admitted that a first trimester cutoff point raised the practical problem that "many pregnant women, particularly young girls," might "refuse to face the fact of pregnancy" and fail to seek medical advice until after their first trimester had passed.

After some additional back-and-forthing, Blackmun ultimately followed a path charted in memos from both Justices Marshall and Brennan observing that the state's separate interests—first in maternal health and second in fetal life—did not necessarily become compelling at the same time. Specifically, the state might have a "compelling" interest in mandating particular medical safeguards for abortion *before* it could assert a compelling interest in the fetus. Pursuing this logic, they suggested that Blackmun differentiate between these distinct state interests when determining the all-important "cut-off point" for state regulation.

The result, which Blackmun unveiled in mid-December, was the formula that has become known as *Roe*'s "trimester framework." As Blackmun explained:

> With respect to the State's important and legitimate interest in the health of the mother, the "compelling" point . . . is at approximately the end of the first trimester. This is so because of the now-established medical fact . . . that until the end of the first trimester mortality in abortion is less than mortality in childbirth. It follows that, from and after this point, a State may regulate the abortion procedure to the extent that the regulation reasonably relates to the preservation and protection of maternal health.

Conversely, Blackmun emphasized that, before the end of the first trimester, "the attending physician, in consultation with his patient, is

---

*Jeffries, *Justice Powell*, 342. Other accounts have credited Marshall or Brennan with originally questioning Blackmun's focus on the end of the first trimester, but Jeffries (who had access to private correspondence between Powell and Blackmun) is convincing in arguing that Powell raised the issue first.

free to determine, without regulation by the State, that in his medical judgment the patient's pregnancy should be terminated."

In assessing the state's interest in "potential life," Blackmun shifted the "compelling point" to viability. Before viability (then estimated at between twenty-four and twenty-eight weeks), the state was barred from regulating abortion in the interest of fetal life. After viability, however, "if the state is interested in protecting fetal life . . . it may go so far as to proscribe abortion during that period, except when it is necessary to preserve the life or health of the mother."*

After this latest revision, *Roe* and *Doe* moved swiftly toward publication. Douglas added a concurrence insisting that neither *Griswold* nor *Roe* depended on substantive due process (that doctrine pertained to economic not personal rights, he claimed). Stewart, meanwhile, wrote a concurrence candidly admitting that both opinions relied on exactly that doctrine. Burger, the last to join Blackmun's drafts, also wrote separately to emphasize that the Court had by no means endorsed "abortion on demand."

White authored the principal dissent and stepped into the shoes Justice Black had formerly filled. He found "nothing in the language or history of the Constitution to support the Court's judgment" and, in his characteristically sharp style, accused the majority of simply fashioning "a new constitutional right for pregnant mothers and with scarcely any reason or authority for its actions." Rehnquist's dissent was somewhat less biting, even conceding that Blackmun's opinion commanded his "respect." But he doubted that abortion was in any real sense "private" or specially protected as such and denounced the trimester framework's elaborate balancing of competing interests as "far more appropriate to a legislative judgment than a judicial one."

With the announcement of *Roe* set for January 22, 1973, Blackmun circulated an eight-page statement that he proposed to distribute to the media the morning of the decision. As his actions had done from the outset, Blackmun's proposed press release reflected deep apprehension about the Court's resolution of an issue he recognized to be "perhaps one of the most emotional that has reached the Court for some time." Bren-

---

*It is commonly misperceived that under Blackmun's approach the state can proscribe abortion after viability except where necessary to save the mother's life. Actually, even after viability, *Roe* preserves the right to abortion where the life *or health* of the mother is at stake. Given that in both *Vuitch* and *Doe* the Court defined *health* as including the pregnant woman's psychological well-being, this limitation on the state's regulatory power is potentially quite broad and remains a source of great consternation for anti-abortionists.

nan, though, prevailed on him not to release any additional writing; he feared any written statement would be taken as an extension of the Court's actual opinions.

It didn't matter. Blackmun's sentiments were evident from the opinion's second paragraph, where he candidly acknowledged "the sensitive and emotional nature of the abortion controversy, the vigorous opposing views, even among physicians, and . . . the deep and seemingly absolute convictions that the subject inspires." "However the Court decides these cases," he observed, "the controversy will continue."

Blackmun's words were, of course, prophetic. The abortion controversy not only continued but sharpened and exponentially intensified around *Roe* itself. Before the decision, the passion and commitment underlying the debate had been spread across dozens of legislative and legal contests. With its definitive balancing of competing rights and interests, *Roe* drew to itself the full fury of both sides and became the single focus for their clash of moral absolutes.

In its aftermath, *Roe* played a significant role in creating the modern mass movement of social conservatism and remains its motivating symbol: the embodiment of our cultural degradation and a legal charter for what some believe to be the mass murder of innocent unborn children. With equal passion, liberals, especially women, embraced *Roe* as an emancipation proclamation, a liberation from the cold fear of unwanted pregnancy and an inalienable part of the emerging ideal of female autonomy. To control one's body, to decide for oneself when and if to become a mother, was to control one's destiny and be truly free.

In addition to such broad ramifications, still an urgent part of our national politics, *Roe* also had a profound impact on the narrower world of our legal culture. For legal scholars, the Court's declaration of a right to abortion polarized an already existing debate over the nature of the Constitution. Beforehand, scholars generally agreed that defining constitutional law required "interpretation," by which they meant an assessment of text, history, and governmental structure using a variety of traditional methods of legal reasoning. Afterward, many of *Roe*'s most dedicated opponents abandoned interpretive methods, such as Justice Harlan's, that left room for contemporary judgment or discretion. They retreated into the mechanistic formalism of originalism and the pretense that judging could somehow be divorced from the value-laden exercise of reason.

For their part, *Roe*'s defenders threw off the shackles of text and history and turned to sources external to the Constitution, such as moral philosophy and political theory, to justify an expanding list of nontextual "fundamental rights," including the right to abortion. And on both sides the tone of argument absorbed the savage intensity of the street fights and political battles raging outside the ivory tower.

All of which is to say that in the twenty-three years since the Court announced *Roe v. Wade*, the ruling's merits have become shrouded in webs of conflicting moral passion, political expediency, and the hindsight of scholarly debate. Rendering a balanced assessment of the decision is difficult, if not impossible. The feelings are too intense on both sides, the competing values too deeply contested. Yet it is essential to try.

The most strident critics of *Roe* and *Doe* assailed them as "the most radical decisions ever issued by the Supreme Court" and the twentieth-century equivalents of *Dred Scott* (the decision upholding slavery).[12] The most influential scholarly critique came from John Hart Ely, the prominent liberal law professor and former Warren clerk who denounced *Roe* as a "very bad decision"—"bad because it is bad constitutional law, or rather because it is *not* constitutional law and gives almost no sense of an obligation to try to be."[13] According to Ely, the Justices had not found the right to abortion in the Constitution. They had put it there.

On the other side, many leading newspapers lauded the decision. *The New York Times*, for example, welcomed *Roe* as "a major contribution to the preservation of individual liberties" that offered "a sound foundation for final and reasonable resolution" of the abortion debate.[14] Academic supporters were somewhat less certain. Although many defended *Roe* on its own terms as a natural and legitimate outgrowth of the Court's line of privacy decisions,[15] others tried to rewrite the decision and discover a right to abortion elsewhere in the Constitution. Some traced the right to the equal protection clause and its guarantee of women's rights.[16] A few scholars even sought support in the First Amendment's prohibition on the establishment of religion and the Thirteenth Amendment's abolition of involuntary servitude.[17] Indeed, academics defended *Roe* on so many bases other than its own that one particularly caustic critic described the decision as the "Wandering Jew of constitutional law"—a right constantly in search of a home.[18]

Naturally, *Roe* is anathema to anyone who considers every fertilized egg, from the moment of conception, to be the equivalent of a living person. Nor can *Roe* be defended to someone, such as Robert Bork, who rejects the very idea of substantive due process and believes instead that the due process clause requires only that government employ "fair procedures" when imposing on individual liberty.[19] Similarly, an adherent of Justice Black's approach to due process would automatically reject *Roe*'s recognition of an unenumerated right to privacy untethered to a provision of the original Bill of Rights.

In my view, little is gained by approaching *Roe* from a position that, as a matter of first principle, rejects outright the possible legitimacy of legal abortion, substantive due process, or unenumerated constitutional rights. As a matter of history and practice, all three of these concepts are familiar to American law. Fetuses have not been considered persons, nor has a single Justice of the Supreme Court, even those who despise *Roe*, suggested that a fetus must (or even may) be considered a "person" for the purposes of constitutional protection. To do so would not only make all abortion a homicide but would require a substantial revamping of long-standing legal traditions about the entitlements of unborn children and society's relationship to them. Substantive due process, in one form or another, has been an established doctrine for one hundred years. And some constitutional rights that all of us take for granted—such as the right to travel between states and even the right to vote—while implicit in the structure of the constitutional blueprint, are unenumerated in the actual text.

A better question to ask is whether *Roe* succeeds in the task it set for itself. The decision claims for its pedigree the Cardozo-Frankfurter-Harlan flexible approach to due process—defining that clause as protecting all those personal rights "implicit in the concept of ordered liberty" or "so rooted in the traditions and conscience of our people as to be ranked as fundamental." The fairest test of *Roe* is to accept this admittedly controversial approach and its corollary that the scope of the due process clause is not limited to those rights specifically enumerated in the Constitution. The question then becomes whether *Roe*'s privacy-based right to abortion fits legitimately in this line. And it is here that the decision's shortcomings arise and multiply.

Under the Harlan approach, whether the right to abortion should qualify as a fundamental aspect of liberty was an ever-evolving but essentially retrospective inquiry. The process was one of asking whether society, in time-honored practices or through judicial decision, had carved out a sphere of private life that logically would include a woman's right to obtain an abortion. In many respects, this process resembles the childhood game of connect the dots. Constitutional provisions, common law traditions, the Court's own precedents: these were dots or reference points that when connected created the rough outline—what Harlan called the "continuum"—of due process liberty. And the issue was whether a right to abortion fell inside the boundary created by the line.

In *Poe* and *Griswold*, Harlan had found his points of reference in the First and Fourth Amendments as well as the Court's own decisions limiting intrusions on marriage and family life. Plotting these points, and generalizing among them, Harlan had found that the realm of privacy they delineated included the right of married persons to use birth control.

In *Roe*, the Court asserted that essentially these same reference points (plus the birth control cases) also embraced a right to abortion. But several of the boundary markers crucial to *Griswold* did not easily fit a comparable right to abortion. For example, unlike the right to use contraception at stake in *Griswold*, the right to abortion did not implicate the privacy of the home (at least not in the sense of physical intrusion into "marital bedrooms" central to *Griswold*),[20] nor was it necessarily linked to marriage.

Also, *Griswold* had placed particular reliance on *Meyer* and *Pierce*, two *Lochner*-era decisions involving the teaching of foreign languages and private schooling. By extending the right of privacy to matters associated with family and child rearing, these decisions lent some support to including a right to abortion within due process liberty. But a close look suggests that *Meyer* and *Pierce*, already suspect because of their *Lochner* ancestry, fit within Harlan's due process approach in ways that an abortion case did not.

At the heart of Harlan's approach was the idea of protecting time-honored freedoms from legislative acts notably out of step with the best traditions of the nation. The statutes at issue in *Meyer* and *Pierce* fit this profile precisely. *Meyer*'s prohibition against teaching foreign language was a World War I–inspired targeting of German immigrants. Similarly, *Pierce*'s prohibition on private schooling grew from a local prejudice against Catholics. These laws were aberrational, the work of temporarily inflamed nativist majorities seeking to impose a uniformity of thought on unpopular minorities. The prohibition on the use of contraception that *Griswold* struck down suffered from a related flaw. It was a pure anachronism, unique in the nation, almost never invoked, and ineffectual except to preclude birth control clinics from distributing contraceptives to the poor.

The right to abortion presented a very different case. At the time of *Roe*, almost every state regulated abortion in some fashion, some quite strictly, and had done so for a century or more. In many places these laws were the subject of debate, but by and large they were still enforced.

Recognizing this, Blackmun's *Roe* opinion went to some lengths to demonstrate that modern laws were considerably harsher than the English and colonial common law as well as most ancient practices. His opinion also stated that the modern laws, dating to the midnineteenth century, arose in significant part from social and medical concerns with little contemporary validity. Blackmun's version of this history was not without sharp critics. But even granting all Blackmun's conclusions, the history of abortion and its regulation did not seem to demonstrate a right to abortion "so rooted in the traditions and conscience of our people as to be ranked as fundamental." Nor did his history show that antiabortion statutes, still fairly robust after a century, were aberrational or anachronistic.

Roe did have some foundation in case law. In a few cases the Court had linked procreation and due process liberty, most directly in *Eisenstadt v. Baird*, a post-*Griswold* (1972) decision striking down Massachusetts's ban on distributing contraceptives to unmarried persons.[21] There, in a Brennan opinion, the Court had stated directly that "if the right of privacy means anything, it is the right of the *individual*, married or single, to be free from unwarranted governmental intrusion into matters so fundamentally affecting a person as *the decision whether to bear or beget a child.*"[22]

But even *Eisenstadt's* endorsement of a privacy-related abortion right (on which most *Roe* defenders heavily depend) is less persuasive than it first appears. As an initial matter, *Eisenstadt* was an equal protection case. The Court struck down the Massachusetts law as improperly distinguishing between married and unmarried persons for the purpose of obtaining birth control (thereby liberating *Griswold* from the confines of marriage). Brennan's comments about the right to privacy were gratuitous dicta.

More important, Brennan added the crucial "bear or beget" language in *Eisenstadt* precisely because, while he was working on his *Eisenstadt* draft, the Court already was considering *Roe*. Brennan knew well the tactic of "burying bones"—secreting language in one opinion to be dug up and put to use in another down the road. *Eisenstadt* provided the ideal opportunity to build a rhetorical bridge between the right to use contraception and the abortion issue pending in *Roe*.* And taking full advantage, Brennan slipped into *Eisenstadt* the tendentious statement explicitly linking privacy to the decision whether to have an abortion. As one clerk from that term recalled, "We all saw that sentence, and we smiled about it. Everyone understood what that sentence was doing."[23] It was papering over holes in the doctrine.

When evaluating *Roe*, it must also be remembered that even if one could adequately defend the proposition that due process liberty included a right to abortion, that still would satisfy only one-half of Harlan's equation for invalidating state abortion laws. Harlan recognized that the state could infringe even a fundamental right if its justification was sufficiently important or "compelling." For that reason, in *Poe*, he acknowledged the state's authority to criminalize homosexuality, incest, or fornication, even though such activity was undeniably private.

In this regard, abortion raised the question of why the state's interest in fetal life is not sufficiently important to support abortion regulation throughout pregnancy rather than only after viability. *Roe* answered by stating that fetuses are not constitutional persons "in the whole sense" and do not possess constitutional rights. But surely a state may have a strong interest, even a compelling interest, in restraining individual action even where the life or rights of another person are not involved. As Professor Ely put it sharply in his critique of *Roe*: "Dogs are not 'persons in the whole sense' nor have they constitutional rights, but that does not mean the state cannot prohibit killing them."[24]

In short, creating a due process–based right to abortion, even using Justice Harlan's flexible approach, required an extralong logical and doctrinal stretch, much longer than that required for *Griswold*. Worse yet, *Roe* compounded this intrinsic difficulty by failing to present a full argument. A clerk at the time tells a story about the day Blackmun's opinion first circulated. The draft was much awaited, of course, and this clerk started looking at it right away. But because the opinion was quite

---

*Notably, Brennan's *Eisenstadt* opinion commanded only four votes and was a "majority" only because the Court was shorthanded at the time.

lengthy, he decided to call the *Roe* clerk in Blackmun's Chambers and ask where he should look for the crux of its legal analysis. The clerk directed him to a particular section, and they hung up. The other clerk read the indicated pages and called the Blackmun clerk again. "I read what you suggested," he said. "So where's the analysis?"

The story captures much of what is wrong with *Roe*. The opinion's actual legal argument is stunningly brief. Presented with the challenge of extending the right to privacy from contraception to abortion, the Court largely skipped the process of interpretation and moved on to announcing its conclusions. While the Court decorated the fringes of its opinion with historical details, it left the center barren. *Roe* makes no attempt to define the contours of the right to privacy or its underlying principles. Rather than discuss the traditions or decisions supporting the right to abortion as a fundamental aspect of liberty, the opinion simply lists precedents bearing some relation to the idea of privacy. The entire section runs but a paragraph, as if the connection between the Court's prior cases (whether involving search and seizure, marriage, or contraception) and abortion was self-evident. Then, in the critical culminating sentence, the opinion equivocates even on the basic question of whether the right is properly located in the Ninth Amendment or the Fourteenth Amendment's due process clause. And its discussion of the state's competing interest in fetal life is scarcely more elaborate.

It was not that potential arguments were nonexistent. One could have argued (as some have since tried)[25] that the Court's several decisions about marriage, contraception, child rearing, and preserving bodily integrity supported a more general privacy right to make certain intrinsically personal, family-oriented, and life-determining decisions free from government compulsion. Or the Court might have argued that a right to abortion was only the slightest step past *Griswold*, especially as broadened in *Eisenstadt*. After all, the line between contraception and abortion blurs at the edges. Indeed, many common forms of contraception are actually abortifacients: they prevent implantation in the uterus of already fertilized eggs. In any event, surely the choice about whether to have a child is no less fundamental the day after conception than the day before.[26]

Yet these arguments could never have been completely persuasive. For even if one could argue that the basic rights at stake in *Griswold* and *Roe* are identical—that the choice whether to have a child is if anything more fundamental the day after conception than the day before—the state interest at stake in *Roe*, the existence of potential life, still sets the cases substantially apart.

But at a minimum, given that the Court was nullifying dozens of state laws not on the basis of constitutional text but according to its own judge-made doctrines, the Justices were under a powerful obligation to explain their logic. And the Court in *Roe* must be doubly faulted for the hollowness of its effort. Such failings raise an obvious question: how, especially in such a monumental case, could the Court have so failed in its responsibility to justify its ruling or even clarify the source of its authority? The explanation is remarkably straightforward. More than anything, it appears, the Justices were swept away on a current of their own good intentions. Like the vast majority of well-educated, non-Catholic, professionally successful males, the Justices in the *Roe* majority thought the nation's abortion laws excessively restrictive, ineffective, and potentially highly dangerous. To them, abortion was a private tragedy to be handled discreetly between a woman and her doctor, not a matter for political decision or the business of the criminal law. In this assessment, the Court's sole Catholic, Justice Brennan, certainly concurred.* And even White and Rehnquist, the Justices who dissented, confined their objections to issues of pure law and showed no particular sympathy for the anti-abortion cause.

The personal experience of several Justices confirmed general sentiments in favor of a woman's right to choose. While senior partner at Richmond's leading law firm, Justice Powell had received a late-night call from a nineteen-year-old office assistant who confessed that the older woman he had been seeing had become pregnant. Weeping, the caller told Powell that the woman had decided on an abortion and had asked for his help. The young man had tried to follow his lover's instructions, but she had hemorrhaged to death. Powell calmed down his employee and interceded with the authorities, who, after ascertaining the facts, decided against pressing charges.

The incident convinced Powell that women would seek abortions regardless of the law. Criminal sanctions ensured only that many women would suffer serious injury or death in the terrifying ordeal.[27] Justice Blackmun had reached similar conclusions from his years of observation

---

*Indeed, Blackmun was especially reassured by Brennan's active support for *Roe*.

at the Mayo Clinic. And with each man such inclinations were significantly reinforced by their circle of intimates. Both Justices enjoyed close friendships in the medical profession and believed its members could be relied on to guide women in their decisions about childbearing. Both also shared the experience of outspoken daughters who brought home the danger and invasiveness of current abortion laws.

From this perspective, *Roe* was simply the right and decent thing to do. It would end the horror and humiliation of self-induced or underground abortions and return the abortion decision to safe and responsible hands. As a legal matter, the Court took this step in the noble cause of what the much-revered Justice Brandeis had once called "the right to be let alone—the most comprehensive of rights and the right most valued by civilized men."[28] At the same time, *Roe* rejected the "extreme" of abortion on demand. It struck a balance between a shared rational judgment that a woman's rights were more compelling than the interests of a zygote and the emotional and biological truth that at some point in pregnancy abortion too closely resembled infanticide to preclude its regulation.

Thus, while Blackmun's *Roe* opinion acknowledged that abortion was a subject marked by fierce division, this was an intellectual observation divorced from the Court itself. There, sentiment was basically uniform. No one declared that abortion was outright murder or intrinsically wrong, or otherwise injected a note of moral caution (much less outrage) into the Justices' deliberations. No one's passionate objection slowed the collective momentum to place the Constitution and the Court's enormous prestige on the side of what was a seemingly unanimous view of social progress.

Who can say whether the presence of an anti-abortion perspective at the Court would have made any difference? Powell's well-informed and insightful biographer thinks it might have in his Chambers.[29] Notably, Blackmun originally proposed a modest "vagueness"-based decision that would have left much greater room for continued abortion regulation. He reached his final disposition only haltingly and never free from agonized reservation. Perhaps under different circumstances, the ultimate result would have hewn closer to his original.

The climate at the Court, however, was not one that appreciated or fostered doubts. Despite the presence of four Nixon appointees, the strongest influence remained Brennan, the ever-confident master tactician of the Warren years. With his once-certain liberal majority withered to only Douglas and Marshall, he seemingly had resolved to exploit every opportunity for a liberal victory to its limit or beyond. True to his mantra of "five votes can do anything here," whenever possible—as in *Roe*—Brennan goaded the Court in spasmodic leaps toward his vision of the Constitution as an ever-expanding charter for achieving social justice.

It is no coincidence that *Roe* was separated by less than a year from *Furman* v. *Georgia*, the decision voiding the nation's death penalty laws. Both were thunderbolts from an Olympian Court, obliterating dozens of statutes, despite little warning in past decisions. Both shared the flaw of exercising the greatest measure of judicial power on the least defensible justification.[30] This was Justice Black's nightmare come to life: a Court unrestrained by constitutional text, history, or Harlan's promised discipline of legal reasoning and judicial self-restraint.

And as in *Furman*, where a bare majority preempted powerful race-based arguments against the death penalty, the Court's rushed efforts to forge a social consensus on abortion precluded the development of stronger constitutional arguments for the same result. From the outset, Planned Parenthood, the ACLU, and others had argued for a right to abortion mainly in terms of *Griswold* and its unenumerated right to privacy. Lower courts in their decisions followed suit. But that categorization was not entirely apt. The right to privacy drew much of its force from the Constitution's protection of particular places, especially the home. What was at stake in attacking abortion regulations was not so much privacy as equality, specifically, an equal right between men and women to individual autonomy—the power to decide for oneself how to use one's body and direct one's life. And, in contrast to privacy, this principle was an explicit constitutional command.

It is beyond the scope of this book to fully elaborate an equality-based justification for the right to abortion; others have done so fairly compellingly.[31] The basics of the argument, however, stem from the simple fact that restrictive abortion laws impose solely on women a burden unique to law. At the price of months of pain, exhaustion, and anxiety as well as, potentially, a lifetime's responsibility, such laws compel women to sacrifice themselves for the benefit of fetal life. Nowhere does the law require men involuntarily to donate their bodies, endure months of unwanted physical hardship, risk permanent illness, or curtail their desires and ambitions as means of furthering a similar interest of the state.* Even when such a sacrifice might save the life of an independent living person—say, a father giving a kidney to save the life of a daughter—we do not require it.[32] Only in the context of abortion, only of women, is such a duty called.

The evidence is overwhelming, moreover, that states adopted their harsh late nineteenth-century abortion laws in significant part as a method of keeping women in their traditional place.[33] As "respectable" women of the day increasingly sought abortions to limit family size and break out of the homemakers' role to which society had relegated them, men responded with criminal sanctions reinforcing Victorian ideas about the proper aspirations of the sexes. Still on the books a century later, these laws—in essence forced conscription into motherhood—perpetuated outmoded attitudes and continued to deny women the right to equal participation in the nation's social, economic, and political life.

In short, the true constitutional choice raised by abortion is whether the state has an unfettered right to subordinate women and impose on them unique risks and burdens in order to protect fetuses before they become viable human beings in their own right. And an appropriate constitutional answer is that while the existence of an emerging organism inside a woman is a compelling moral fact, society may not require a woman to sacrifice her inalienable right of equality for the still contingent life within her.

To a person convinced that every fertilized egg is the moral and legal equivalent of a living person, such an answer would have been as reprehensible as *Roe*. But the certainty of that opposition, while tragic, is unavailing. The law has never recognized fetal personhood, and, in the absence of that recognition, constitutionalizing the right to abortion would force the procedure on no one and only prohibit the majority from taking for itself the power to direct the course of every pregnant woman's life.

Such tragic choices to subordinate one interest (the fetus's) to another (the woman's) are an inevitable part of law, as are other constitu-

---

*The closest analogue for men would be the wartime draft. Strictly speaking, though, the draft (unlike abortion) is not a burden that can be imposed only on men. Other countries, such as Israel, draft women as well—and the United States could do the same. Also, from the standpoint of current legal doctrine, courts would not evaluate an equal protection challenge to abortion and an equal protection challenge to an all-male draft in the same light. Because women are a historically disadvantaged group, courts would look more skeptically on legislation affecting them.

tional decisions (such as *Brown* or *Engle* v. *Vitale*, prohibiting prayer in public school) in which the Court must resolve constitutional questions over which the nation seems irreconcilably split. In such situations, whatever the Court does is sure to be contested. Ultimately, the Court's obligation is to determine what the best reading of the Constitution commands, even if many people cannot be so persuaded.

That said, to those uncommitted to the principle of fetal personhood, the arguments derived from equality and privacy are importantly different. By locating the right to abortion in the due process clause's protection of privacy, *Roe* skewed the terms of the debate away from the strongest (and textually supported) pro-choice legal arguments as well as from what was really at stake socially and morally for women. And by writing a broad opinion establishing definitive ground rules for abortion regulation, the Court lost the benefit of time.[34]

The argument from equality was not yet developed in 1973. At that point, the Court was only beginning to turn its attention to issues of gender equality. In a perfect world, the Court would have waited for the equality arguments to ripen. And it would have decided abortion challenges incrementally, in the way calculated to build the greatest possible social consensus, starting, for example, by striking down those statutes so restrictive that they prohibited abortion even in cases of rape and incest. Simply put, the Court built the right house on the wrong land and put it up too quickly.

Who knows to what degree proper timing and an enhanced legal foundation would have inhibited the social civil war that *Roe* unleashed? Certainly, though, in the legal community, grounding the right to abortion in the Constitution's mandate of equality would have saved liberals—anxious to support the Court's expansion of civil liberties—from ignoring their better judgment in a stampede to defend a terribly vulnerable decision. And it would have avoided the incalculable damage that *Roe* inflicted on the idea that there is such a thing as constitutional law ruled by neither the hands of long-dead Framers nor the personal biases of sitting Justices. Soft but essential notions such as trusting in discretion and reasoned judgment melt away quickly, and *Roe* was a very hot flame.

By the time of *Webster*, these historical what-ifs were mere idle speculation. Sixteen years before, the Justices' best intentions had unleashed the law of unintended consequences. The Court's effort to end the abortion debate cleanly and with a minimum of conflict had led to bruising confrontations both in the academy and on the nation's streets. And the Justices' effort to remove the issue from politics had resulted only in bringing politics directly to the Court's front door. In the wake of annual demonstrations, furious lobbying, countless political speeches, and televised nomination hearings, the nation's conception of the Court, of the Constitution, and of judicial nominees all were reduced almost entirely to the merits of *Roe*.

The decision had come to stand for something much larger than itself. Conservatives held up *Roe* as symptomatic of everything wrong with the Warren Court's legacy of social intervention, from banning school prayer to imposing *Miranda*. On the other side, liberals defended *Roe* as though on its fate hinged the Court's entire post-*Brown* crusade to redeem the Constitution's promises of liberty and equality and make the nation fairer and more free. *Roe* should never have been positioned to carry such weight. But as *Webster* came before the Court, with *Roe* truly imperiled for the first time, one was either for it or against it, and on that rancor-filled choice the whole world of law seemed to spin.

The Triumph of Politics

From the moment the Justices granted review in *Webster*, the political and legal armies that for sixteen years had squared off over *Roe* subjected the Court to an unprecedented siege. On January 23, 1989, the day after *Roe*'s anniversary and two days into the Bush administration, 70,000 anti-abortion protesters gathered on the Ellipse near the Washington Monument. After receiving a message of support from the new president, they streamed toward the Court in the largest of what had become their annual marches against *Roe*.

On April 9, the pro-choice movement responded in kind. Aroused from years of *Roe*-induced complacency, 300,000 abortion rights supporters rallied on the same grounds that the right-to-lifers had occupied three months earlier, then made their way to the Court. Where anti-abortionists had carried graphic photographs of aborted fetuses, pro-choicers draped coat hangers around their necks as reminders of pre-*Roe* self-mutilations.

Between competing demonstrations, both sides sought to breach the Court's outer walls through a barrage of letters. NARAL campaigned to send the Justices a million pro-choice postcards, while, on the other side, evangelists exhorted their followers to give voice to the souls of *Roe*'s innocent victims, another million each year.[1] At the height of the pre-*Webster* frenzy, the Court's mail room handled a daily inundation of 45,000 letters, about forty-five times its usual load.

The pro-life and pro-choice movements engineered an equally prodigious influx of legal briefs. The Court received seventy-eight amicus briefs in *Webster*, far surpassing the previous record of fifty-seven, which the Court had received when considering *Bakke,* the first challenge to affirmative action. On the pro-choice side, Planned Parenthood and the ACLU orchestrated the submission of thirty-two briefs designed to show the depth and diversity of *Roe*'s support. Two hundred eighty-one historians, 885 law professors, 608 state legislators, 140 members of Congress, 167 scientists and physicians, as well as a number of prominent medical, labor, religious, and feminist organizations submitted briefs laying out their grounds for reaffirming *Roe.* Then, as a dramatic finale, "2,887 Women Who Had Abortions and 627 Friends" shared with the Justices intimate recollections of their harrowing experiences with underground abortion and their gratitude for the safe haven *Roe* subsequently had provided.

The pro-lifers could count very few big institutional guns on their side, but what they lacked in tonnage they made up in numbers. They delivered briefs from a dozen groups that specialized in fighting abortion and an equal number from church groups (ranging from Catholic to Orthodox Jewish), as well as from their own set of nurses, doctors, and state legislators.

Many of the briefs were numbingly redundant. For the most part, neither side intended them as traditional "friend of the court" briefs, bringing to the Justices' attention legal arguments, technical data, or social perspectives that the parties themselves might neglect. Rather, the brief writing campaigns, like the mass demonstrations, the letters, and the millions spent on media advertisements, were mainly political lobbying—an attempt to make the Justices think in terms of constituencies and then to bring constituent pressure to bear. As Faye Wattleton (the president of Planned Parenthood) explained, "The Court is not sequestered on another planet. It does hear the voices of the American people."[2] And in that belief, she and her opponents cranked the volume to full.

On a less sensational level, the Court had been the target of such abortion politics for every moment of *Roe*'s existence. The same scenario had played out over and over again. Pushed by right-to-life activists, state and local legislatures would adopt new abortion codes to test the limits of *Roe.* And every time they did so, Planned Parenthood or the ACLU would protest the regulations in court while urging the broadest possible definition of a woman's right to choose.

In the first years after *Roe,* litigation over abortion arose almost haphazardly. For a right-to-life movement preoccupied with overturning *Roe* through a "Human Life Amendment" to the Constitution, pushing for new local abortion laws was a second-tier concern. At this level, anti-abortionists followed what one expert dubbed a "spaghetti against the wall" approach. They cooked up as many new abortion restrictions as they could devise, threw them at the Court, and hoped that at least some would stick—or, better yet, that the Justices would see the error of their ways and overrule *Roe* outright.[3]

The regulations produced by this process fell into a few general categories. Many state legislatures passed funding limitations, which banned the use of state money (such as medicaid dollars) to pay for some or all types of abortions. These were matched on the federal level by the 1976 Hyde Amendment, a statutory provision that barred federal funding for any abortion not required to save the pregnant woman's life.

In addition, more than a dozen states passed "consent" laws. These delegated to someone other than the pregnant woman—such as a spouse or the parents of a minor—the power to veto her choice of abortion. (More modest versions of such laws required only "notification" rather than actual consent.) States also adopted a host of measures—mandatory waiting periods, hospitalization requirements, two-doctor requirements, patient information requirements, extra record-keeping requirements—designed to discourage abortion by making it more inconvenient, unpleasant, or expensive.

After challenge by pro-choice litigators, the question of whether any or all of these restrictions were constitutional under *Roe* moved inexorably through the funnel of the federal judicial system toward the Supreme Court. As a consequence, the Justices ruled on eighteen abortion cases between *Roe* and *Webster*. And the results were decidedly mixed.

The right-to-life movement scored significant victories on the issue of abortion funding. In a series of especially contentious cases, Justices Powell and Stewart (though firm members of the original *Roe* majority) joined with Justices Burger, White, and Rehnquist to hold that both states and the federal government could refuse to provide medicaid funding for abortions, even when they paid the costs associated with live births.[4] Powell and Stewart justified the funding decisions as reflecting an important distinction between a constitutional limit on government's power to outlaw abortion and a constitutional requirement that government spend tax dollars to support it. In their view (and the majority's), nothing in the Constitution prohibited government from refusing to pay for the abortions of poor women or from using the power of the purse to favor childbirth over abortion.[5]

At the same time, Powell and Stewart insisted that the funding decisions "signal[ed] no retreat from *Roe*,"[6] and, in keeping with that assurance, they joined with Justices Blackmun, Brennan, Marshall, and usually Stevens to void spousal consent laws and consent laws aimed at minors as well as a host of regulatory schemes imposing medically unnecessary or otherwise superfluous regulations.

Of broader significance, beginning in the early 1980s, a majority of the Justices (including Powell but not Stewart, who had been replaced by O'Connor), directly rebuked those who sought to overturn *Roe*. In response to the Reagan administration's attacks on *Roe*, the majority both explicitly reaffirmed the decision and admonished that the reasons for doing so were "especially compelling." As Justice Powell pointed out in a major 1983 opinion, the Court—having considered *Roe* over the course of two separate terms—had reached its decision "with unusual care" and then had accepted and applied *Roe* in numerous subsequent cases. In light of that history, *Roe* was supported not only by its intrinsic merits but by the doctrine of stare decisis, which counseled decisively in favor of adhering to this precedent.[7]

The right-to-life movement responded to such active discouragement simply by regrouping and trying even harder. They saw themselves as soldiers in a righteous cause, likening their struggle to save unborn life to the abolitionist struggle against the sin of slavery more than a century before. From modern-day John Browns firebombing abortion clinics to Frederick Douglasses decrying the moral repugnance of fetal murder, they held up *Roe* as their *Dred Scott* and vowed to fight it in court, in Congress, or in the streets until they succeeded in its overturning.

By the mid-1980s, as hope for a Human Life Amendment faded, leading anti-abortionists concluded that, despite short-term setbacks, the federal judiciary still offered the best prospect for undoing *Roe*. In particular, the right-to-lifers counted on President Reagan's pledge to appoint only anti-*Roe* judges to the bench and, looking ahead, tried to coordinate a long-term strategy for achieving a judicial overruling. In March 1984, Americans United for Life convened a national anti-abortion conference and held up to the assembled activists the model of the NAACP's step-by-step assault on *Plessy* v. *Ferguson* and the principle of "separate but equal." Much as the NAACP had spent twenty-five years chipping away at the foundations of segregation before the ultimate triumph of *Brown*, leading right-to-lifers proposed attacking *Roe* in a lawyerly way, patiently hammering at its central pillars—the trimester system, the dividing line of viability, its refusal to define when life begins—until the whole edifice came crashing down.

What the new campaign called for was more state legislation, containing innovative restrictions that targeted what the anti-abortionists considered particularly vulnerable aspects of *Roe*. The Missouri law at issue in *Webster* was the imperfect offspring of this idea.

The statute opened with a "preamble" setting forth the legislature's "findings" that "the life of each human being begins at conception" and that "unborn children have protectable interests in life, health, and well-being." Deciding the practical legal effect of that language would be a matter for the courts. But however they construed the preamble, the right-to-lifers meant it as a challenge to what they considered *Roe*'s morally and legally untenable view that fetuses were not persons and that states could not adopt "one theory of life" in order to "override" a woman's right to choose.

Other provisions sought to push beyond the boundaries of the Supreme Court's already favorable abortion funding decisions and to sever all ties between the state and the process of abortion. To that end, the law prohibited public employees from performing or assisting in abortions except when necessary to save the mother's life. It also prohibited the use of any public facility for nonlifesaving abortions—even when the abortions were to be performed by private doctors with private financing. In addition, the statute barred state employees from engaging in speech encouraging or counseling a woman to have an abortion not medically necessary to save her life. And it directed that no public funds could be expended for such encouragement or counseling.

Finally, in an effort to break down *Roe*'s trimester framework, the statute commanded that when a doctor had reason to believe a fetus was twenty weeks into gestation (well before the third trimester), that doctor must perform tests to determine whether the fetus was viable. In making this determination, the doctor was instructed specifically to make findings as to age, weight, and lung maturity—an instruction seemingly in conflict with the command of a post-*Roe* case (*Colautti* v. *Franklin*)[8] that states must leave the all-important determination of viability entirely to the best judgment of the attending physician.

Taken as a whole, the Missouri law emerged from the legislature as too much a grab bag (even called the Kitchen Sink Bill by Missouri right-to-lifers) to fit a *Brown*-style incrementalist litigation strategy.* Some national anti-abortion groups, finding the law messy and overly confrontational, responded tepidly to the idea of making it the subject of a test case. But litigation, once begun, takes on a life and significance of its own. And after immediate challenge by *Roe*'s ever-vigilant courtroom defenders, the new Missouri abortion code became a nuclear missile directed straight at the Court.

Inside the building, the pressure of *Webster* was monumental. It was not only that the Justices and those of us who worked for them had been called upon to redecide the most divisive legal and political issue of our time. It was also that *Webster*, uniquely, felt personal. Unlike the abstract issues surrounding the death penalty, criminal procedure, the right to burn a flag, or protections against search and seizure, the right to abortion was meaningful to us—for our own sakes. Perhaps some in our group had availed themselves of *Roe*'s protections. Most of us knew friends who had. And all of us had come of age assuming the existence of a right to abortion, perhaps counting on it at times. Some of us were parents already. The rest were old enough to have thought hard about parenthood. This was true both for the most zealous advocates of choice and for those who thought abortion morally wrong or even murder. We were the first generation to grow up with *Roe*, and, in a palpable way, its fate felt intertwined with our own.

In Blackmun's Chambers, the psychological burden of *Webster* was so heavy it seemed to take on a physical aspect. As the abortion mail piled up in odd corners of the offices, it was as though the walls were slowly closing in. Here the case was personal in a second sense. Whatever thoughts we clerks had for ourselves were many times compounded by what *Webster* meant to our boss. Few people think about famous cases in terms of their authors. Who wrote *Miranda? Engle* v. *Vitale? United States* v. *Nixon?* But Justice Blackmun's name was fused to *Roe* with a solder of unbreakable strength. To most of the world, *Roe* was Harry Blackmun, and Blackmun was *Roe*. *Webster* was a referendum on him, however unfair or unasked for.

---

*The statute also contained at least one paradox: the preamble promised complete protection of fetal life from the moment of conception, yet other parts of the law were premised on the underlying legality of abortion.

Blackmun made no attempt to shield himself from the stakes of the case. While some Justices ordered their cartloads of *Webster* mail discarded unseen and unopened, Blackmun waded into the correspondence and, when the sheer volume overwhelmed him, ordered the remainder saved to be caught up on later. His secretaries claimed that through sixteen years of *Roe*-inspired correspondence he had read every note and postcard. During *Webster,* I realized they were not kidding.

The written assaults were the cross Blackmun chose to bear. Many of the letters were vicious. They called him a butcher, a baby killer, compared him unfavorably with Hitler, included graphic pictures of aborted fetuses, and wished him dead. Still, year after year, thousand after thousand, he sat alone at his desk and read through them. Serving on what he liked to call "the people's Supreme Court," Blackmun considered it an unshirkable duty to "know what people are thinking and what they're worried about."[9] Absorbing the anger of his critics came with the job.

By the same token, the letters were also a source of deep satisfaction. In the eyes of millions of women, Blackmun was a national hero, one of history's great champions of freedom. Some of these also wrote, pouring out adulation as on a savior or simply thanking him for taking from the government dominion over their wombs. He read these letters, too, and although I never saw them penetrate his thick armor of self-effacement, never heard him so much as mention a tribute paid, watching him I sensed that they nurtured a fierce pride in what he had done.

From Blackmun's perspective, *Webster* had been a long time coming. As first Stewart and then Burger resigned, he had seen the original *Roe* majority dwindle from seven to five. Now Powell, too, was gone. Throughout, Blackmun had faced recalcitrance from states such as Pennsylvania and Missouri, with large Catholic populations, aggressive right-to-life leadership, and elected state officials who would enact, sign, and defend a constant stream of anti-*Roe* legislation. Then, for the last eight years, he had watched as the president joined their resistance and, for the first time in more than a century, sought to condition judicial appointment on a willingness to overrule a single specific decision of the Court—his decision, *Roe.**

This war of attrition had worked changes in Blackmun. The man who

---

*The last instance was in 1870, when President Ulysses Grant made two appointments (Joseph Bradley and William Strong) aimed specifically at heading off the Court's impending decision to invalidate the Legal Tender Act.

prepared for *Webster* was not the same as the one who had written *Roe*. Nor was his view of the right to abortion the same. Through the intervening years, Blackmun's pro-choice convictions had only grown stronger, his commitment to a woman's right to direct her own life more pure, and his appreciation of *Roe* as an engine for social equality more fully considered and expressed. It was as though Blackmun had internalized the voices of the women whose distresses *Roe* had eased and made them his own.*

Nowhere was this more true than in the funding cases, where Blackmun denounced the Court's decisions as "punitive and tragic." In their granting poor women an abstract right to abortion while depriving them of the means to make that right attainable, Blackmun accused the majority of sinking to a level of coldhearted condescension "almost reminiscent of: 'Let them eat cake.' " "There is another world 'out there,' " he lamented, "the existence of which the Court, I suspect, either chooses to ignore or fears to recognize."[10]

Defending *Roe*, Blackmun accepted no compromise. With the exception of a few innocuous regulations that the Justices accepted unanimously, he voted to strike every abortion restriction that came before the Court. Increasingly, Blackmun came to view the drive to circumvent and overturn *Roe* in terms of the South's resistance to *Brown*. Indeed, he alluded to this similarity in *Thornburgh*, where Charles Fried, Reagan's solicitor general, first had suggested that the Court overrule *Roe*. Rejecting Fried's invitation, Blackmun included in his 1986 majority opinion a pointed citation to *Cooper* v. *Aaron*, in which the unanimous Court had demanded that Arkansas's obstructionist governor yield to its authority and obey the mandate of *Brown*. Blackmun's message was unmistakable.

---

*A leading scholar has suggested that Blackmun's perceived drift from moderate conservative to outspoken liberal resulted from an extreme defensiveness of *Roe* in the face of harsh and sometimes ridiculing criticism. By this account, "Blackmun's turn to the left was . . . not intellectual but psychological" and took the form of a personal bond with those, like Brennan and Marshall, who defended *Roe* and a distancing from others who assailed it. John C. Jeffries, *Justice Lewis F. Powell, Jr.: A Biography* (New York: Scribner's, 1994), pp. 364–69.

I think it easy to overestimate the extent of Blackmun's philosophical conversion. To some degree, the politics of the Court moved (rightward) around him. And to some degree, his original labeling as a bland conservative was overplayed. Still, I expect there is some truth to the alleged explanatory power of *Roe*. No person could suffer such ugly assaults on his character and intelligence over such a long period without accumulating emotional scar tissue. But I would venture that this was only one side of the psychological calculus. For every brutal insult, for every protester shadowing Blackmun's public appearances, there was someone, usually a woman, telling the Justice he had saved her life, preserved her family, or allowed her to realize the life she sought for herself. To the extent that the experience of *Roe* moved Blackmun leftward over the years, I would say he was not only pushed by criticism but pulled by a certain kind of praise.

The anti-abortionist campaign against *Roe*, whether emanating from the states or from the executive branch, defied not only that decision but the authority of the Court and the rule of law.[11]

Charles Fried and the anti-abortionists, of course, thought this duty ran the other way—that the Court was obligated to disgorge the power it had illegitimately seized in *Roe*. And on both sides, as *Webster* moved forward, the careful counting of votes began.

Seven votes seemed certain. Blackmun, Brennan, Marshall, and Stevens had voted to uphold *Roe* many times, and Stevens, the only one not part of the original *Roe* majority, had defended the decision as recently as 1986.[12] On the other side, White had written a dissent in *Thornburgh* arguing at length for *Roe*'s overruling in which Rehnquist, his fellow naysayer from 1973, had joined. Although Scalia had yet to vote in an abortion case, he made no secret that, like Bork, he considered *Roe* a legal and moral abomination.

This split meant that, as with so many issues, the decisive votes belonged to Kennedy and O'Connor. Of these two, Kennedy's views were as yet unrecorded. At his confirmation hearings, he had given a general endorsement to Harlan's flexible approach to due process liberty and also stated that the due process clause protected "the values of privacy that Americans legitimately think are part of their constitutional heritage." With respect to specific due process cases, Kennedy had expressed a favorable view of *Griswold*.[13] But nothing in either his testimony or his previous writings hinted at whether Kennedy's conception of due process would encompass *Roe*'s right to abortion.

Most of us guessed that it would not. When Kennedy's appointment was being considered, his close confidants had assured Reagan hardliners that he could be trusted to repudiate *Roe*. Voting against *Roe*, moreover, would be consistent with Kennedy's political allegiances, deeply felt Catholicism, and evident intellectual admiration for Scalia. Blackmun had observed at the start of the term, "One never knows what a new justice's attitude toward *stare decisis* is."[14] But if Kennedy's ultimate verdict remained a question mark, in the eyes of many people around the Court, it was a relatively faint one.

O'Connor was an enigma of a different sort. Evidence abounded regarding her views on abortion and *Roe*. Still, the record was not entirely conclusive. By upbringing and public affiliation she subscribed to Barry Goldwater's brand of conservative Republicanism, yet her record during three terms as an Arizona state senator suggested some sympathy for the idea of legal abortion. On one occasion, she voted against a resolution calling for a Human Life Amendment; on another, she opposed a provision banning abortions at some state-run hospitals. She also cast a preliminary vote for a bill repealing Arizona's criminal abortion statute and, on the related subject of birth control, sponsored a bill making family planning information more widely available.

During her screening interview with President Reagan and during her confirmation hearings, O'Connor had tried to distance herself from these votes and had expressed a personal aversion to abortion. Nonetheless, the head of the National Coalition for the Right to Life opposed her nomination, as did the Moral Majority's Jerry Falwell, who called it "a disaster." They were suspicious of both O'Connor's record and her personal history. She was a victim of gender discrimination, a woman who still smoldered at the memory of being offered only secretarial jobs after graduating third in her class from Stanford Law. And O'Connor was a trailblazer, the first woman to become leader of the Arizona Senate and then the state's leading female judge. To Howard Phillips, director of the Conservative Caucus, that background—as well as O'Connor's support for the Equal Rights Amendment—smelled of "radical feminism" and added to already strong suspicions on the litmus test issue of *Roe*.[15]

Once on the Court, however, O'Connor confounded both the pessimism of conservative critics and the extravagant hopes of feminist supporters. At the first opportunity (dissenting from Powell's 1983 majority in *Akron v. Akron Center for Reproductive Health*), she fixed *Roe* in her judicial crosshairs and fired. Although O'Connor stopped just shy of calling for *Roe*'s overruling, she denounced its essential aspects and proposed her own judicial standard—far more regulation friendly than *Roe*'s—for evaluating state abortion laws.

O'Connor's first target was *Roe*'s trimester framework—the idea that the state's interests in regulating abortion varied, from nonexistent to "compelling," depending on the stage of pregnancy. In O'Connor's view, this structure was "outmoded" and "completely unworkable." New techniques had made abortion safer than childbirth well into the second trimester, making a hash of *Roe*'s distinction between the first and second trimester for allowing state regulations based on a concern for maternal health. On the other end, medical technology was pushing earliest potential viability—the moment under *Roe* when the state's interest in fetal life became compelling—well back into the second trimester. These compacting trends, O'Connor asserted, were certain to continue, which meant, as she suggested in a memorable phrase, that *Roe*'s trimester framework was "on a collision course with itself."[16]

Aside from this fatal scientific flaw, in O'Connor's view, *Roe*'s premise that the state's regulatory interests varied as a woman's pregnancy progressed had been wrong from the start. "Potential life is no less potential in the first weeks of pregnancy than it is at viability or afterward," she reasoned. "At any stage in pregnancy, there is the *potential* for human life." And the same was true of the state's interest in maternal health. Both interests existed "*throughout* pregnancy" and, more important, were "compelling"—that is, sufficiently important to override even a fundamental right—from the moment of conception onward.

Applying this view, O'Connor argued that the appropriate method for evaluating abortion regulations was something she called the "unduly burdensome" standard. Under this two-tier system, the Justice would apply "strict scrutiny" (requiring a state to narrowly tailor its regulations to a compelling interest) only to those regulations that "unduly burdened" a woman's right to abortion. She then defined these as "situations involving absolute obstacles or severe limitations on the abortion decision." To all other regulations (such as hospitalization or consent requirements), O'Connor would apply only rational relations review, the lowest level, everything-passes test.

Justice Powell described O'Connor's analysis as "wholly incompatible with the existence of the fundamental right recognized in *Roe v. Wade*." As he noted, regardless of which test O'Connor applied, virtually every regulation would pass. Given that O'Connor considered the state's interests in regulating abortion "compelling" from the moment of conception, even where she would apply strict scrutiny she had preordained that the state's justification met the required mark.

Still, whether O'Connor agreed with Powell's assessment of her approach or favored actually overruling *Roe* was not entirely clear. However implausibly, O'Connor seemed to suggest that she considered her approach somehow consistent with the spirit (if not the details) of *Roe*. Indeed, she claimed to have derived her test from several Court decisions applying *Roe*, which stated that *Roe* "protect[ed] the woman from unduly burdensome interference with her freedom to decide whether to terminate her pregnancy."[17] (Here, she seemed to convert a *description* of *Roe*'s purpose into a standard of review.) More tellingly, three years after *Akron*, in *Thornburgh*, she did not join White's dissent calling for *Roe*'s overruling and, instead, wrote separately to reiterate her undue burden test.

In short, O'Connor had savaged crucial aspects of *Roe* without repudiating the decision entirely and even seemed to suggest that her own approach, which others thought fatal to *Roe*, was in fact descended from it. What this tightrope walk would mean for *Webster*, where O'Connor's vote might for the first time actually decide *Roe*'s fate, was anybody's guess.

One thing was certain, though: few people at the Court seemed to think her answer would be solely a matter of doctrine or past declarations. O'Connor was the first woman to serve as a Supreme Court Justice; the only one to have gone through pregnancy and childbirth, to have considered firsthand the importance of choice to personal identity and fulfillment, to have felt the burn of gender discrimination, and to be revered as a role model by countless women's groups. She was also mother to a pregnant daughter and suffering from the predominantly female illness of breast cancer.

Simply put, many of us thought O'Connor's decision would depend at least in part on her reflections about womanhood. And in the crazed vortex of *Webster*, that hunch even led a few pro-choice female clerks to consider fanciful schemes for reminding O'Connor of *Roe*'s value to their shared sex. One I recall was to take place after the all-female aerobics class that O'Connor hosted three mornings a week upstairs on the basketball court. The idea was to have one of the clerks fake an unwanted pregnancy and break down in the locker room when the Justice was sure to overhear. The notion quickly passed, but the warping emotion and the desperate attention to O'Connor's vote—those lasted until the end.

As the Court geared up for *Webster*, another case, argued much earlier in the term, suddenly intruded on our collective preparations. Some attacks on *Roe* came not from the front but from the side and took the form of opinions in cases that had nothing to do with abortion yet involved the doctrine of substantive due process, on which *Roe* was based.

One such case was *Michael H. v. Gerald D.*,[18] a paternity dispute of seemingly small significance, except that it very nearly predetermined the outcome of *Webster* and the fate of *Roe*. Indeed, though *Michael H.* is little noted in the literature of abortion rights, neither *Webster* nor the subsequent history of *Roe* can be understood without appreciating what happened in this obscure case.

To complicate matters even further, to understand *Michael H.* it is necessary first to know something about yet another substantive due process case, *Bowers v. Hardwick*.[19] This is the lightning rod 1986 decision in which a bare majority of five ruled that the due process clause did not prohibit states from punishing homosexuals for engaging in private and consensual acts of sodomy.

The plaintiff in *Bowers*, Michael Hardwick, had been arrested when a police officer, let into his home by a houseguest, burst into his bedroom, found him having sex with another man, and charged him under the Georgia law making the act of sodomy a crime. In response, Hardwick challenged that law as violating his right to privacy protected by the due process clause.

Bowers was a referendum on exactly the line of cases on which *Roe v. Wade* had relied. Indeed, arguably, private homosexual conduct presented a stronger case than abortion for protection under the right to privacy. Unlike a woman seeking an abortion, a homosexual engaged in consensual sex inside his own home could invoke two separate strands of due process precedents: first, those decisions crucial to (and including) *Roe* that protected the privacy of intimate personal choices associated with sex; and second, those numerous precedents (tangential to *Roe*) protecting the privacy of the home against physical invasion. Furthermore, on the other side of the due process scale, the government's interests in limiting abortion (protecting maternal health and fetal life) were surely more "compelling" than the government's purely moral interest in prohibiting homosexual sodomy.

In the view of many scholars, even critics of *Roe*, the logic of *Roe* essentially compelled the outcome in *Bowers*. If *Roe* was still good law, then the Court—to be consistent in applying the right to privacy—had to strike down Georgia's sodomy statute. Yet, despite explicitly reaffirming *Roe* that term (in *Thornburgh*), the Court upheld Georgia's anti-sodomy law.*

---

*Although it was neither argued by his counsel, Harvard Professor Laurence Tribe, nor passed on by the Court, Hardwick also could have presented a strong equal protection argument. The Georgia statute at issue criminalized all acts of sodomy, whether heterosexual or homosexual, yet from every indication Georgia had no intent to enforce the law evenhandedly. Even in terms of the Court's due process analysis, Justice White's opinion clearly erred (and demonstrated an antigay bias) in characterizing the constitutional question as one of whether the Constitution protected a right to engage in homosexual sodomy. One can only speculate how the Justices would have responded had they dealt with the law as written, and conducted their inquiry in a context involving common heterosexual practices.

The key to this seeming contradiction was the swing-voting Justice Powell, and the decisive factor explaining his irreconcilable votes was a matter of personal experience and empathy. As discussed earlier, Powell was politically and temperamentally opposed to strict abortion laws and, through one of his former employees, had experienced directly the tragic consequences of underground abortion. To say the least, he had no corresponding understanding of homosexuality. At the *Bowers* conference, Powell told his colleagues that he had "never met a homosexual." He made the same comment to one of his clerks, oblivious to the fact that this clerk (as well as others in the past) was gay. As Powell engaged him in presumably hypothetical discourse on gay sexual attraction, the clerk considered revealing his sexual orientation but ultimately chose instead merely to plead Hardwick's case with unusual emotion.*

From the outset, Powell was of two minds about *Bowers*. He could not bring himself to include conduct he found so personally remote and distasteful within the nearly sacred ambit of due process liberty. Yet neither was he comfortable accepting the idea of criminalizing sexual acts between consenting adults within the privacy of a home.

By the time of conference, Powell had reached an awkward compromise, one that involved a considerable doctrinal stretch. He wanted to avoid the due process issue altogether. As an alternative, he advanced a novel theory: that imprisonment for the crime of sodomy (as Georgia provided) violated the Eighth Amendment's prohibition on cruel and unusual punishments.† By so arguing, Powell provided Justices Brennan, Marshall, Blackmun, and Stevens a fifth vote for striking Georgia's antisodomy statute (though the others would do so on privacy grounds).

This alignment, however, proved short-lived. On the day after Conference, Chief Justice Burger, who had been the most vociferous defender of the Georgia law at Conference, sent Powell a long private

---

*A reconstructed version of their conversation appears in Jeffries, *Justice Powell*, p. 521. Among the exchanges was the following:

Powell:	Are gay men not attracted to women at all?
Clerk:	They are attracted to women, but there is no sexual excitement.
Powell:	None at all?
Clerk:	Justice Powell, a gay man could not get an erection to have sex with a woman.

†Powell based his argument on *Robinson v. California*, an unusual case that seemed to say a person could be held criminally liable for his *acts* but not solely for his *status*. (In *Robinson*, the "status" at issue was that of being a drug addict—which the Court held could not be made a crime.) The key to using this precedent in *Bowers* was to argue that by criminalizing sodomy Georgia was criminalizing the status of homosexuality.

letter imploring that he switch sides. Part of Burger's letter tried (with some success) to debunk Powell's Eighth Amendment theory. Much of the letter, however, railed at the catastrophic consequences for Western civilization if the Court were to cast aside a millennium of moral teaching and decriminalize homosexual sex. "This case presents for me the most far reaching issue of [the last] 30 years," Burger closed on a particularly personal note. "I hope you will excuse the energy with which I have stated my views, and I hope you will give them earnest consideration."

Powell had a mixed reaction to Burger's letter, noting on the top page: "There is both sense and non-sense in this letter—mostly the latter." But Burger's criticisms of Powell's Eighth Amendment theory struck home and were importantly reinforced by a skeptical memo he received from the most conservative clerk in his own Chambers.[20]

A week after conference, Powell informed his colleagues that he had changed his mind and would vote to affirm the Georgia statute. A delighted Burger, now in the majority (with White, O'Connor, and Rehnquist), assigned the opinion to White. And White, in turn, churned out a draft in just over a week.

The general approach of White's opinion was standard enough. He appeared to embrace the familiar Cardozo-Frankfurter-Harlan discretionary approach to due process. By its very terms, the Harlan formula required the Court to decide the following initial question: what "right" was at issue in a case that might be so "deeply rooted in" national tradition that it would be protected under due process? In *Bowers*, White might have answered in a number of ways. He might, for example, have characterized Michael Hardwick as claiming a right to intimate association or intimate association within his home—and then have assessed whether such a right was sufficiently rooted in tradition to be protected under due process.

White, however, choose to cast the right at issue much more narrowly. He characterized Hardwick as claiming a constitutional right of "homosexuals to engage in sodomy," then considered whether such a right was "deeply rooted in the nation's history and tradition." Framed this way—focusing on the issue of homosexual sex—the question answered itself. And, unsurprisingly, White dismissed the notion that tradition recognized a right to commit homosexual sodomy as "at best, facetious."

In dissent, Blackmun immediately attacked White's methodology, accusing him of "distort[ing] the question this case presents" in order to predetermine its outcome. In Blackmun's view, *Bowers* was "no more about 'a fundamental right to engage in homosexual sodomy' . . . than *Stanley* . . . was about a fundamental right to watch obscene movies, or *Katz*," a 1967 decision extending Fourth Amendment protection to electronic surveillance, "was about a fundamental right to place interstate bets from a telephone booth." Rather, *Bowers* was about the broader right to conduct consensual intimate associations in the privacy of one's home, a right the dissenters believed fit readily within the Court's established line of privacy cases.

In *Bowers*, White and Blackmun conducted their debate over how narrowly or broadly to frame due process inquiries strictly within the confines of the facts of that case. But, in *Michael H.*, as the Court returned to the issue of substantive due process, it became apparent that Justice White's methodology in *Bowers*, if elevated to a general rule, held the potential for substantially undercutting *Roe*. And, as *Michael H.* developed, with *Webster* on the immediate horizon, that is precisely what Justice Scalia tried to do.

At issue in *Michael H.*, which was argued in October 1988, was the constitutionality of an obscure California statute declaring that when a married woman living with her husband gives birth, the resulting child is conclusively presumed to be a child of the marriage. The facts behind *Michael H.* read like an excerpt from *Valley of the Dolls*, but the essentials were simple enough. A married woman, an international model named Carole, had entered into an adulterous affair with her neighbor, Michael H. Carole had become pregnant and given birth to a daughter, Victoria, whom blood tests suggested (to a 98 percent certainty) was Michael's biological child. After some years of acting informally as Victoria's father, Michael sought to have his parental status legally recognized and to obtain certain parental rights. The California courts, however, had ruled against him on the basis of the state's paternity statute. Michael H. then challenged that statute as depriving him of an aspect of liberty in violation of substantive due process.

At Conference, the Justices voted 5–4 to reject Michael H.'s claim, and Rehnquist assigned the opinion to Scalia, the Court's most ardent critic of using the due process clause to second-guess legislative judgments. Although Scalia had not been on the Court when it decided

Bowers, he hoped to use *Michael H.* to bolster White's highly controversial approach.

In a draft of *Michael H.* circulated close to Thanksgiving, Scalia followed directly in White's *Bowers* footsteps. He began by endorsing the familiar Cardozo-Frankfurter-Harlan idea that the due process clause gave substantive protection to those rights "so rooted in the traditions and conscience of our people as to be ranked as fundamental." Then, again like White, Scalia framed his inquiry into tradition extremely specifically.

He chose to characterize Michael H. as claiming the parental rights of an *adulterous* natural father, then asked whether tradition recognized any such rights. Of course there was no such tradition.

In a draft dissent circulated in January, Brennan complained (as Blackmun had in *Bowers*) that Scalia was manipulating his inquiry— making it unnecessarily narrow—in order to preordain the case's outcome. According to Brennan, instead of asking whether tradition recognized the rights of adulterous natural fathers, Scalia should have asked "whether *parenthood* is an interest that historically has received our attention and protection." And, in Brennan's view, under the Court's precedents, the answer to that question was clearly yes.

At this point, the Court's handling of *Michael H.* might have ended as simply a replay of *Bowers* in a much less dramatic setting. But Scalia decided to respond to Brennan's dissent. And he decided to do so in way that would narrow the scope of substantive due process much more comprehensively and have the practical effect of severing *Roe* (and several other due process landmarks) from their jurisprudential moorings.

In a new *Michael H.* draft circulated April 12, two weeks before the looming oral argument in *Webster*, Scalia added a lengthy footnote that not only defended his framing of the issue in *Michael H.* as proper for that case but argued that to avoid the danger of "arbitrary" judicial decision making, the Court should *always* conduct its inquiry into tradition in the narrowest possible manner. According to Scalia, Brennan's choice of what societal tradition to look for (like Blackmun's in *Bowers*) was ad hoc and standardless; he, by contrast, would adhere to a consistent rule. As Scalia put it: "Though the dissent has no basis for the level of generality it would select [in defining the right at issue], we do: We refer to the most specific level at which a relevant tradition protecting, or denying protection to, the asserted right can be identified."

Although it was somewhat confusingly expressed, the practical rami-fications of Scalia's due process methodology were enormous, and they instantly transformed *Michael H.* into a winner-take-all referendum on what he considered the liberals' illegitimate use of the doctrine to ex-pand individual liberties. Gone from Scalia's approach was Harlan's no-tion of an evolving continuum of liberty—that judicial game of connect the dots, generalizing from past practice, precedent, and current under-standings to create a shaded area of due process protection. As Scalia played the game, due process contained only dots—highly specific and narrowly defined points of constitutional protection—and no fluidity or shading at all.[21]

Under Scalia's methodology, many of the Court's due process decisions were clearly wrong. In a much-heralded 1967 case (*Loving* v. *Virginia*), for example, the Court had struck down Virginia's anti-miscegenation statute in part because it violated the due process clause's protection of the right to marry. But under Scalia's methodology, the Court should have considered *Loving* as raising only a right to *interracial* marriage. And if the Court had asked whether there was a historical tra-dition recognizing a right to interracial marriage, the answer would have been no.

Scalia's approach would also (and more pertinently) doom *Roe*. After all, it could hardly be said that a country where most states had crimi-nalized abortion for a century enjoyed a tradition of recognizing the right to abortion.[22] *Griswold, Loving, Roe*, and other cases like them depended on the shading between traditions, on generalizing (sometimes perhaps too much) from specific precedents to create protections for broader cat-egories of liberty, such as marriage, procreation, child rearing, or sexual intimacy. This was the process of contemporary judicial discretion and judgment that Scalia would deny.

The strategy behind Scalia's footnote was especially clever. Both O'Connor and Kennedy had formally joined his draft *Michael H.* opin-ion back in November, when it first circulated. It was highly unusual for a Justice who already had signed on to an opinion to qualify that en-dorsement during the subsequent almost obligatory footnote battle with the dissent. By using his footnotes to write into law a due process theory aimed at *Roe* and fatal to it, Scalia had laid something of a trap for his cosigners. If O'Connor and Kennedy stood by their joinders, they would either have to vote to overturn *Roe* in *Webster* or find themselves having subscribed almost simultaneously to blatantly contradictory positions.

A clerk for O'Connor spotted Scalia's stratagem and flagged its intended consequences. The message quickly found its way to the Kennedy Chambers. And, thus, while the Court geared up for the biggest oral argument of the term, in the Chambers that would undoubtedly prove decisive, the first front in the *Webster* war was already open and being fought in the small type at the bottom of the page of an otherwise unremarkable opinion.

In the O'Connor Chambers, it was ordinary practice for one clerk to prepare a detailed bench memo for the Justice in every case. Then, on the weekend before oral argument, O'Connor would conduct a freewheeling discussion with all her clerks on the merits of the issues raised. In *Webster*, however, although one clerk (Daniel Mandil) had primary responsibility for the case, two of his co-clerks felt so strongly about the outcome they submitted their own long and passionate memoranda to the Justice.

Andrew McBride, the exceptionally smart and tireless former Bork clerk who presided over the cabal, mounted a carefully plotted and sustained attack on *Roe*. According to his parsing of the Missouri statute, its viability testing provision raised a direct conflict with *Roe*'s trimester system and provided an ideal opportunity to overturn a decision that was profoundly wrong from the outset and had proven unworkable and divisive in practice.

To replace *Roe*, McBride urged O'Connor in the strongest possible terms to adopt Scalia's due process methodology from the still pending footnote in *Michael H.* As McBride reminded the Justice, she had signed on to *Bowers*, the case from which Scalia derived his approach. At the same time, recognizing O'Connor's propensity for Powellian moderation, McBride tried to soften the impact of his proposal. As he explained Scalia's *Michael H.* approach, it would excise the cancer of *Roe* yet leave intact other precedents, such as *Griswold*, whose results (if not their due process reasoning) could be defended on other grounds.

From the other side, O'Connor's most liberal clerk, Jane Stromseth, yearned to defend *Roe* on its own terms but thought better of squandering her potential influence as the Chambers's only other woman by defending a position the Justice previously had condemned. The strategic compromise Stromseth reached with herself was to advocate that the Justice reaffirm the core innovation of *Roe*—that the right to abortion was fundamental under the Constitution—while abandoning the trimester system O'Connor previously had maligned.

In lieu of the *Roe* framework, Stromseth urged O'Connor to stand by her "undue burden" test and to center it on viability, a concept she described as a scientifically stable, morally sound, and traditionally recognized line for assessing fetal rights.* Under Stromseth's version of the undue burden test, viability would remain (as in *Roe*) the point before which states could not prohibit or seriously obstruct women from obtaining abortions. The only practical difference between Stromseth's undue burden standard and *Roe* would be that before viability Stromseth would permit (as the cases following up on *Roe* had not) regulations such as twenty-four-hour waiting periods and informed consent rules that reflected a state's interest in fetal life or maternal health without excessively inhibiting a woman from obtaining an abortion.

Mandil adopted an approach decidedly different from his colleagues'. While the others assumed that Missouri's abortion law conflicted with *Roe* and, hence, advocated dramatic steps one way or the other, Mandil advised O'Connor that the Missouri law did not necessarily conflict with *Roe* and that she should do essentially nothing in *Webster*. The key to this approach was to carefully parse the details of the Missouri statute and evaluate it section by section in terms of both the Court's abortion precedents and its many precedents counseling that, where possible, the Court should construe statutes to avoid raising serious constitutional questions. Viewed this way, Mandil urged, O'Connor could uphold all the challenged sections of Missouri's law under the Court's current precedents without passing any judgment on *Roe* itself.

Mandil was considerably helped in his analysis by the brief the state of Missouri had submitted defending its statute. Although Missouri had asked the Court to overrule *Roe*, it delegated the argument on this point to Charles Fried's brief on behalf of the United States. Most of Missouri's brief was devoted to defending its statute in the event the Court reaffirmed *Roe* or, at least, preserved the idea of abortion as a fundamental right. In so doing, William Webster, the Missouri attorney general, had

---

*Given O'Connor's previous statements that the trimester system was "on a collision course with itself," considerable argument in *Webster* focused on whether science was still pushing back the earliest point of potential viability or whether the timetable for fetal lung development made viability before roughly twenty-three weeks a medical impossibility. In their various amicus briefs, the medical community had taken the position that significant new progress in pushing back viability was exceedingly unlikely, and Stromseth predicated her argument on this view.

taken a statute that right-to-lifers had designed to be fiercely antagonistic to *Roe* and either given its various provisions their most innocuous meaning or, in some cases, conceded their unconstitutionality.

Webster, for example, argued that the statute's *Roe*-baiting "life begins at conception" preamble was essentially rhetorical and had no substantive meaning in the context of abortion. Similarly, he declawed the viability testing provision by claiming the specific medical findings it mandated were in fact discretionary and only had to be made if deemed appropriate by a woman's doctor. Webster did not even contest the lower court's decision striking down the provisions prohibiting employees from "encouraging and counseling" about abortion or prohibiting the use of public facilities for these purposes. And he defended the statute's ban on the use of public funding or facilities for abortions as constitutional under the principles of the abortion funding cases the Court already had decided.

Although some of Webster's ducking and dodging was at odds with the statute's plain language, for someone inclined to chart a path that would leave both *Roe* and the current state of law entirely untouched, the state's many tactical concessions pointed the way. Mandil followed these signposts while adding a few innovations of his own. The result was to bring his recommendation in line with two relevant aspects of his boss's record: she had never voted to strike down an abortion regulation, and she had been known, when it suited her, to avoid broad pronouncements and decide cases on their narrowest possible grounds. In other words, if O'Connor wanted off the hot seat of deciding *Roe*'s fate, Mandil held out a cool and relatively comfortable alternative.

Mandil, however, recognized that O'Connor might reject his strategy of avoidance, and, accordingly, he offered her substantive advice as well. In particular, he sought to counter McBride's suggested endorsement of Scalia's *Michael H.* approach to due process. As Mandil emphasized, Scalia's narrowest tradition approach to defining due process liberty was diametrically opposed not only to *Roe* but to the entire flexible approach to due process espoused by Harlan, the former Justice whom O'Connor most revered. Scalia would adopt exactly the "mechanistic yardstick" to define due process that Harlan had rejected and would, in the measuring, cast serious doubt on *Griswold, Loving,* and other important precedents. That was an uncharted path, Mandil suggested, that the Justice should leave untrod.

At O'Connor's weekend conclave, often the site of strong arguments, the clerks advanced their radically divergent positions with a rawness of emotion that reflected an exhausting year of almost constant infighting to sway the Court's most frequently decisive vote. Over time, antagonists within a single Chambers learn each other's passions and insecurities—and how to wound most deeply. The *Webster* meeting was the year's most bruising and ended in barely contained fury among the clerks. The Justice, meanwhile, did not reveal her intentions.

The situation was fairly similar in the Kennedy Chambers, although his style was somewhat different from O'Connor's. Kennedy did not ask for much in the way of written briefings on the cases, but, while driving, he sometimes listened to audiotapes his clerks prepared summarizing the essentials. Like O'Connor, he usually convened the Chambers for a lengthy face-to-face discussion of competing positions, even using a white board mounted on an easel to chart various lines of argument. Though not a dazzling intellect, Kennedy enjoyed turning a legal problem around and around, trying on various approaches for size before choosing the one with which he was most comfortable.[23] Far more often than not, his final selection would be governed by his deeply ingrained conservative instincts. Still, in the minds of his clerks, he always held out at least the possibility of being persuaded—which meant that in *Webster* Kennedy's clerks vied for his critical vote with absolute abandon.

The main protagonists were both retread clerks from the previous term, Paul Cappuccio, Scalia's protégé, and Harry Litman, who had worked originally for Justice Marshall. Cappuccio, much like McBride in O'Connor's Chambers, pressed for Kennedy to overturn *Roe* and adopt Scalia's *Michael H.* approach to due process. Over and over, Cappuccio reminded Kennedy that the Court's foray into *Roe*-style substantive due process had originated in the abomination of *Dred Scott,* in which Chief Justice Taney had invoked the due process clause to strike down the Missouri Compromise as violating the property rights of slave owners.[24] Echoing a line of thinking that Scalia shared with Bork and other leading conservative legal theorists, Cappuccio insisted that substantive due process—as evident from both *Dred Scott* and *Roe*—was a doctrine that corrupted law with political judgment. Accordingly, overturning *Roe* was not only proper but imperative.

On the other side, Litman's argument focused on the consequences of overruling *Roe.* As a jurisprudential matter, Litman suggested that there could be no meaningful line drawn between *Roe* and *Griswold*, the contraception case Kennedy had referred to approvingly at his confirmation hearings. Both decisions were based on the same elastic Harlanesque concept of due process and, indeed, relied on many of the same precedents. Both dealt with the same basic right—the right to avoid having a child—and it was difficult to see how, in that context, Kennedy could draw a magic line distinguishing one second before contraception from one second after. In other words, logically, dumping *Roe* meant dumping *Griswold* and everything in between.

The likely result of such a purge, Litman continued, would not be to end public division over abortion but to unleash a new and deeper level of social strife as hundreds of thousands of women, having once counted on *Roe*, flouted the law and, despite enormous risks, resorted to criminal abortions. This, he argued, would be unfortunate for the law, the country, and, most particularly, the Court.

The meeting was among the most dramatic of the term, a tug-of-war for Kennedy's mind, conducted by two of the Court's smartest and fastest-thinking clerks (who, notably, were also good friends). Still, with oral argument upon them, the discussion ended inconclusively. Kennedy had decided that he wanted to uphold Missouri's abortion regulations, but whether, in his view, that also meant overturning *Roe* remained uncertain.

In the Blackmun Chambers, I remember having only a relatively vague sense of the tempest brewing in these decisive quarters. I was writing my own bench memo in *Webster*, though for obvious reasons one intended to provide strategy and encouragement to *Roe*'s author, not an evaluation of its merits.

Looking back at what I wrote, I can see how convinced I was of at least three points of note. First, in the sixteen years since *Roe*, the decision, while still formally resting on substantive due process, had come to be a case about women's autonomy and equality, and properly so. Second, given the settled expectations of millions of women—and the prospect of turning them into potential criminals—the principle of stare decisis weighed heavily in favor of retaining *Roe*. Unless the Court was willing either to commit itself to the idea that fetuses were living persons (whereby abortion was homicide) or to repudiate entirely the doctrine of substantive due process on which *Roe* was based, the error in *Roe* was not so irredeemable as to justify the massive social and legal upheaval that scrapping the decision would entail. And, third, from where I sat, reading the tea leaves about O'Connor and Kennedy, there appeared to be every chance the Court would overrule *Roe*.

As well as anything I could write now, the words I wrote then, at the end of my bench memo on the eve of oral argument, capture how freighted that time was and what it meant personally to be clerking for that man at that moment. "Whatever happens at Conference on Friday, April 28, however the final opinion reads, *Roe* will endure. Emancipation proclamations always do, even when the freedoms they announce are temporarily eclipsed. In his book *Modern Times*, Paul Johnson remarks that perhaps the most stunning development of this century across the continents has been the growing power of the State to control, coerce, and extinguish the lives of the citizenry. At the risk of sounding trite, it seems to me that *Roe* stands nicely against that tide."

Oral argument in big cases is often more spectacle than substance, and *Webster* was no exception. The buildup began the night before as members of the public, keen to guarantee themselves one of the hundred or so unreserved courtroom seats, lined up for an all-night vigil. When I arrived early the next morning, competing anti-abortion and pro-choice demonstrators already were shouting each other down on the Court's front sidewalk as numerous camera crews—connected to their minivans by a spider's web of black cables—filmed the scene.

Inside the Court, a reverberating nervous chatter had replaced the usual monastic hush. My co-clerks and I breakfasted with Justice Blackmun in the cafeteria, precisely at 8:10 as we always did, except that the room, usually half empty, was teeming—and an unusual number of eyes were directed unmovingly at us. These observers included several police officers on general alert for an anti-*Roe* fanatic trying to carry out one of the bodily threats Blackmun commonly received.

By 9:30, a half hour before argument, some of us went to the courtroom to claim front seats in the obstructed-view section that is reserved for clerks. From there, we watched with feigned nonchalance as the chamber filled. A host of anti-abortion and pro-choice luminaries filed in with the crowd, faces one recognized from *Nightline* or the national news, including Norma McCorvey, the original "Jane Roe." As rarely happened, most of the Solicitor General's Office staff had ventured from the Justice Department and took seats behind the former solicitor general Charles Fried, whom the Bush administration had recalled specially to deliver its argument against *Roe*. Even the recessed corridors running along each side of the public chamber overflowed with Court staff eager for a peek at history making.

The argument itself was predictably anticlimactic. Missouri Attorney General William Webster spoke first. He had arranged with Fried beforehand to defend the statute within the confines of *Roe* while Fried attacked *Roe* itself. That division of labor relegated Webster to a fairly detailed parsing of the statute, during which, as in his brief, he tried mightily to run away from the most confrontational language in his state's law.

Following Webster, Fried tried to minimize what was at stake in a different way. While calling emphatically for *Roe*'s overruling, he emphasized that "we [the United States] are not asking the Court to unravel the fabric of unenumerated and privacy rights which this court has woven in cases like *Meyer* and *Pierce* and *Moore* and *Griswold*. Rather we are asking the Court to pull this one thread." Far from repudiating substantive due process, Fried explicitly endorsed the Harlan approach from *Poe* that he had helped to formulate and, hence, condemned *Roe* merely as an overly "abstract" application of his own most important idea.

When his turn arrived, Frank Susman, the lawyer for Reproductive Health Services, immediately attacked Fried's one thread analogy. In the most memorable moment of the morning, he derided as disingenuous Fried's claim not to be unraveling "the whole cloth of procreational rights." "It has always been my experience that when I pull a thread, my sleeve falls off," Susman began. "There is no stopping. It is not the thread he is after. It is the full range of procreational rights and choices that constitute the fundamental right that has been recognized by this Court." The inspired moment passed, however, and within moments Susman found himself treading in deep water as Justice Scalia pressed him to defend *Roe*'s trimester line drawing as well as the decision's unexplained conclusion that a right to abortion was so "deeply rooted" in tradition that it assumed a constitutional proportion.

Despite the high drama, there was something desultory about the whole event. The three lawyers were, to varying degrees, ineffective. Webster, like most state attorneys general, proved more politician than advocate and was uninspired in his backpedaling defense of Missouri's statute. Susman, except for his well-put "thread-pulling" ad lib, confirmed his reputation as a professional abortion rights advocate who, despite having argued several previous cases before the Court, remained long on commitment but short on persuasive advocacy.

Fried's presentation was the most interesting psychologically. Although his European-émigré accent and professorial style gave his presentation a formal quality, there was no mistaking the ferocity with which he went after *Roe*. Fried directed much of his argument straight at Blackmun's spot on the bench, as though settling a personal score. And in a way he was. From Fried's perspective, Blackmun's *Roe* opinion had substantially discredited the self-restrained yet flexible approach to due process liberty that he had helped Harlan fashion in *Poe*. In a sense, *Roe* was the Frankenstein's monster Fried had helped to create and, in *Webster*, felt compelled to destroy.

This personal byplay did not make Fried's argument any more compelling. After all, if, as he suggested, *Roe* was no worse than a misapplication of fundamentally sound legal principles, why should the Court take the drastic step of setting aside stare decisis and overruling it?

The faults with the oral argument, however, did not lie entirely with counsel. Over the years, commentators had so thoroughly picked over *Roe* that there was really nothing new or surprising for the lawyers to say. After dissection in some eighty briefs, much the same was true of Missouri's statute.*

I found the most striking aspect of the *Webster* argument to be the dog that did not bark. In the entire hour, the author of *Roe* said not a word, even as Fried frequently pitched his anti-*Roe* diatribe directly at him. Blackmun just kept rocking, his face impassive, almost swallowed up against the unnaturally high back of his chair. His fellow cosigners from *Roe* were no more active. Cumulatively, Blackmun, Brennan, and Marshall asked a single question, one Brennan put to Fried.[†] Their virtual silence, though common that term, seemed terribly foreboding, a white flag of surrender. Walking out, I thought *Roe* was lost.

---

*One indication that most of the Justices did not think oral argument would prove especially enlightening in *Webster* is their rejection of a suggestion by Justice Stevens that, because of the many statutory provisions involved, argument be lengthened beyond the usual one-hour limit.

[†]Brennan's question raised an interesting side issue. In his brief to the Court, Fried had characterized *Griswold* not as a due process case but as a Fourth Amendment case involving the potential search of a home to prove the use of contraception. He used this characterization as part of his effort to distinguish *Griswold* from *Roe*. As Fried knew, however, *Griswold* was certainly not a Fourth Amendment case, although it drew on that amendment as well as others. To the liberals, Fried's mistake was typical of a Reagan-Bush Solicitor General's Office that played fast and loose in its use of precedents. Brennan called Fried on the point, and Fried tacitly admitted his error.

* * *

The Justices met in conference two days later, on April 28. As always, Rehnquist spoke first. Next to the assignment power, this prerogative of initially framing the discussion of every case is perhaps the most powerful tool associated with being Chief Justice. And, in *Webster*, Rehnquist wielded his agenda-setting authority to considerable effect.

The Chief opened the discussion with a shocker. Instead of reiterating his previous opposition to *Roe*, he stated that he now thought *Roe* v. *Wade* had reached the right result given the specific facts of that case. Texas had banned all abortions except in the narrow circumstance where the life of the mother was at stake. In Rehnquist's revised view, that was too restrictive. Although he remained sharply critical of *Roe*'s trimester framework, he said that Missouri's law, much less stringent than Texas's had been, could be upheld in every aspect without explicitly overruling *Roe* itself.

Brennan spoke next and delivered the liberal verdict. Eighty-two years old, he was still terribly weak from his pre-Christmas gallbladder removal. During the spring his voice had faded in and out, and at the conference he read slowly, in a barely audible whisper, from a long, prepared text. Naturally, he favored striking the Missouri statute in all its particulars.

White followed Rehnquist's lead. And Marshall said ditto to Brennan. Blackmun advanced some minor variations on Brennan's basic theme. Then, Stevens declared that while he was for striking most of the Missouri statute (and certainly for retaining *Roe*), he thought some of the law might be constitutional under the abortion funding cases.

O'Connor hewed close to Mandil's recommendations. Rather than address *Roe*, she confined her discussion to the specific provisions of the Missouri statute—which she would either abstain from considering or uphold under current precedents. In her only general remarks, she said that she would adhere to her previous views, presumably a reference to the unduly burdensome approach sketched out in *Akron* and *Thornburgh*.

Scalia made no bones about where he stood on *Roe*. It was dead wrong, a self-inflicted wound on the Court, and he was for overturning it, now. In that event, of course, the Missouri statute was certainly valid.

Justice Kennedy was nearly as vehement. He, too, favored overturning *Roe*, which he specifically denounced (picking up the right-to-lifers' preferred analogy) as a contemporary *Dred Scott*. He thought the entire Missouri law constitutional.*

As the Justices finished stating their points of view, it was evident that a majority of five (Rehnquist, White, O'Connor, Scalia, and Kennedy) favored upholding all the challenged provisions of Missouri's law. Within this majority, however, there was no firm consensus as to approach, but rather a spectrum of views, running from Scalia's eager call for *Roe*'s overturning to O'Connor's tiptoeing through the various constitutional questions posed by the statute.

As happened with some frequency at the end of the truncated conference "discussions" that Rehnquist enforced, he announced a bottom-line judgment in *Webster* (to uphold the Missouri law) but deferred the all-important details to be "worked out in the writing." And that job, of crafting an opinion satisfactory to all five members of the majority, Rehnquist took for himself.[†]

With little doubt, this was exactly the goal the Chief had set for himself. In his surprise opening statement, Rehnquist had reoriented *Webster* from an up-or-down referendum on *Roe* to something much muddier—a matter of how much *Roe* should be trimmed. From a strategic perspective, this was the safe bet. By taking *Roe* off the table, Rehnquist had put aside the need to get both O'Connor's and Kennedy's assent for *Roe*'s overturning and, thereby, had maximized the chance for achieving a unified majority for some sort of *Roe* cutback that also upheld Missouri's law. In other words, Rehnquist had given up on going for the home run to pursue the higher percentage play of trying for a solid double. Having secured the *Webster* writing assignment, that chance was now his.

---

*Other commentators have suggested that Kennedy's position was less firm in rejecting *Roe*: for example, that while disapproving of *Roe* he favored standing by the decision because of stare decisis concerns. See James Simon, *The Center Holds: The Power Struggle Inside the Rehnquist Court* (New York: Simon & Schuster, 1995), pp. 135–36. This is an error, and an important one given the key role Kennedy subsequently played in preserving *Roe* in *Planned Parenthood* v. *Casey*. As Kennedy characterized his own view in a postconference letter to Rehnquist, he explicitly favored overturning *Roe*. Past commentators have been misled at least in part by the fact that the confirming Kennedy letter does not appear in the Thurgood Marshall Papers because, as with other telling correspondence, it was circulated only to the Court's conservatives.

[†]It has been suggested that Rehnquist initially offered the *Webster* assignment to Scalia. Supposedly, Scalia responded that while he would join any majority opinion upholding the Missouri law, he would only write that opinion if it overruled *Roe*. Given that O'Connor appeared disinclined to reverse *Roe*, Rehnquist decided to write *Webster* himself and attempt to craft an opinion satisfactory to all five members of his tentative majority.

When the bell went off signaling the end of Conference, I remember suppressing an urge to race down the hall to watch the Justices emerge from their inner sanctum. Of all the images I carry from the term, the one that remains most vivid is of that weekly recessional. Blackmun and Brennan would walk slowly, side by side, toward their Chambers, with Marshall a half step behind, his arms spread, appearing almost to engulf his diminutive brethren. It always seemed as though they were pooling their energy, although I was never sure whether Marshall's arms were draping Blackmun and Brennan in a protective embrace or whether they were supporting him.

In any event, I stayed in my office and waited for Blackmun to come through my door on the way to his own. I caught his eye as he slipped quietly by, and he gave a little shake of his head, then whispered, "We'll see."

In the wake of conference, a silence descended over the liberal Chambers as we waited to assess the damage Rehnquist would do. In our vacuum, we tried to guess what the Chief had really meant when he disavowed overturning *Roe*. All we knew for certain was that he would still be upholding Missouri's restrictions on abortion, and we assumed that meant a significant retreat from the current state of law. Beyond that was a terrible, depressing mystery.

On May 1, the Monday after the conference, the liberals received their first encouraging sign. Justice O'Connor circulated a concurrence in *Michael H.* announcing that she was separating herself from Scalia's controversial footnote. She expressed concern about the footnote's apparent inconsistency with *Griswold* and other cases, including *Loving*. More generally, O'Connor (in a seeming echo of Harlan's aversion to "mechanical yardsticks") stated her reluctance to tie the Court to "a single mode of historical analysis" when deciding substantive due process cases. She wanted to maintain at least some of the flexibility Harlan had championed.

O'Connor's concurrence touched off another dramatic meeting in Kennedy's Chambers. Harry Litman encouraged his Justice to follow O'Connor's lead. He pushed hard on the *Loving* point—that the decision was a noble blow against bigotry not to be kicked unceremoniously out the back door. And, echoing O'Connor, he advised Kennedy against wedding himself to a single approach that might be ill suited to unanticipated cases in the future. Paul Cappuccio, of course, had counterarguments ready, not least that Scalia's approach possessed the virtue, always considerable to conservatives such as Kennedy, of avoiding the sort of indeterminacy that liberal Justices had exploited illegitimately in the past. Kennedy also had to weigh the intangible factor of snubbing Scalia, his closest ally throughout the term. The meeting ended indecisively.

On May 18, Rehnquist circulated a first *Webster* draft to his conservative colleagues while keeping the prospective dissenters in the dark.* In a cover letter to White, O'Connor, Scalia, and Kennedy, he also took the unusual step of lobbying openly for unanimity among themselves. "Because of the 'media hype' that this case has received," he wrote, "and because we are cutting back on previous doctrine in this area, I think it more than usually desirable to have an opinion of the Court if we possibly can."

In the body of the draft, Rehnquist marched one at a time through the challenged provisions of the Missouri law. He started with the life-begins-at-conception preamble, which he dispensed with on the *Roe*-avoiding ground that it had no clear substantive effect in the area of abortion and, thus, presented no active legal controversy for the Court to decide.

Next, he turned to the ban on public employees performing or assisting in abortions and the ban on the use of public facilities for those purposes. Here, too, he avoided doctrinal innovation. Rehnquist upheld these provisions as appropriate under the Court's abortion funding precedents, which, as he read them, allowed government to absent itself entirely from "the business of performing abortions."

Third, Rehnquist turned to Missouri's ban on funding for encouraging or counseling with respect to abortion—a provision that had received considerable attention from both Scalia and Stevens at oral argument. The court of appeals had struck down this provision both as unconstitutionally vague and as violating the doctor-patient relationship protected by *Roe* and subsequent cases. A number of briefs further challenged the ban as violating the First Amendment free speech rights of medical personnel. They argued that the ban would impermissibly force nurses and

---

*Previous "insider" accounts of *Webster* have made no mention of this draft or the crucial correspondence that followed it. They pieced together their versions of the story based mainly on the Thurgood Marshall or William Brennan Papers, neither of which, for obvious reasons, contain the private letters sent within the conservative caucus of the Rehnquist Court. *Webster* is only one example, albeit a glaring one, of how dramatically the presently available paper trail can seriously mislead students of the Court.

doctors to distort their professional advice-giving by remaining silent about the alternative of abortion.

The first problem Rehnquist addressed was to define exactly what practical effect the ban might have. Despite all the briefing, it remained unclear whether the provision was merely an instruction to hospital funding administrators not to spend money promoting abortion or whether, more harshly, it subjected doctors and nurses to discipline or even criminal penalties for advising patients about abortion. Rehnquist gave the statute a fairly tough construction. In his view, it required hospital funding officers to issue regulations implementing the ban. And, presumably, medical personnel could be disciplined for violations.

The Chief found no constitutional problem with this arrangement. In his view, under the Court's abortion funding precedents, the state could favor childbirth over abortion by "prohibiting [state-employed] physicians from advising a patient to have an abortion." Also, prior cases limiting the free speech rights of state employees answered whatever First Amendment questions the provision raised. Simply stated, according to Rehnquist, when the state paid the piper, it could call the tune.

Finally, in the last few pages of his draft, Rehnquist turned to Missouri's requirement that certain tests be performed on any woman suspected to be twenty or more weeks pregnant in order to determine potential fetal viability. And, here, at the very end, the Chief launched his attack on *Roe*.

As an initial matter, he had to define what the viability-testing provision actually required. The provision's first section directed physicians to determine viability using an ordinary "degree of care, skill, and proficiency." Yet the second section instructed that physicians "shall" perform tests "necessary to determine gestational age, weight, and lung maturity of the unborn child" and to make records of these specific findings. If taken literally, this section required physicians to perform dangerous and intrusive procedures, in particular amniocentesis (to determine lung maturity), even though these procedures would be contrary to sound medical practice and often irrelevant to determining viability. Rehnquist solved this problem by reading the provision's first section as overriding the second—that is, as requiring only those tests consistent with sound medical practice and "useful to making subsidiary findings as to viability."

After giving the testing provision this relatively benign definition, however, Rehnquist nonetheless concluded that it posed a direct conflict with *Roe*'s trimester framework. He presented the following syllogism: Under *Roe*'s trimester framework, the state may regulate to protect fetal life only after viability. Scientifically, viability occurs no sooner than twenty-three and a half weeks into pregnancy. The viability-testing provision regulates and imposes costs on the right to abortion at twenty weeks—before viability. Therefore, the provision is incompatible with the trimester framework.

Rehnquist resolved this alleged conflict in a few short paragraphs. The "flaw," he wrote, was not in the statute but in the "virtual Procrustean bed" of *Roe*'s "rigid trimester analysis," which had proven "unsound in principle and unworkable in practice." Despite the force of stare decisis (which Rehnquist emphasized was less significant in constitutional cases), this aspect of *Roe* could not stand.[25]

"In the first place," Rehnquist explained, "the rigid *Roe* framework is hardly consistent with the notion of a Constitution cast in general terms. . . . The key elements of the *Roe* framework—trimesters and viability—are not found in the text of the Constitution or in any place else one would expect to find a constitutional principle."

Rehnquist cribbed his second argument directly from O'Connor's *Akron* dissent. As she had noted, the state's interests in regulating abortion did not vary with the stages of pregnancy but were constant throughout. Applying that principle, he concluded that "we do not see why the state's interest in protecting maternal health should change dramatically at the close of the first trimester. . . . [and] we do not think the state's interest in protecting potential human life should undergo a constitutionally relevant change at the point of viability."

Having thus dispensed with *Roe*'s trimester approach, Rehnquist was oblique about what method he would use for assessing abortion regulations. Without any elaboration, he concluded that "we think it clear that the tests at issue reasonably further the state's interest in protecting potential human life. We therefore hold [them] to be constitutional."

Rehnquist added a one-paragraph coda about *Roe* itself. "The facts of the present case . . . differ from those at issue in *Roe*," he stated. Missouri, in contrast to Texas, had not banned all abortions except when the life of the mother was at stake. "This case therefore affords us no occasion to revisit the holding of *Roe*, which was that the Texas statute unconstitutionally infringed the right to an abortion derived from the Due Process Clause, and we leave it undisturbed."

In part, Rehnquist's opinion was an obvious play for O'Connor, the weakest link in his coalition. Consistent with her views at Conference, the draft professed not to be overruling *Roe*. Indeed, it stayed remarkably silent on the entire political, moral, and jurisprudential firestorm that *Roe* had touched off. At the same time, Rehnquist buried the trimester system to which O'Connor previously had taken such strong exception. And, to a significant degree, he relied on her past writings as the basis for his decision.

Rehnquist's one notable departure from O'Connor's past views was in not replacing the trimester framework with her unduly burdensome standard of review. Instead, he erased the notion of viability as "constitutionally relevant" and described the viability-testing provision as "reasonably" furthering the state's interest in potential life.

Both innovations seemed implicitly to overrule *Roe*. First, if viability was no longer "constitutionally relevant" in assessing the state's interest in fetal life, and if, even under *Roe*, states could further their interest in fetal life by prohibiting all nontherapeutic abortions after viability, then, presumably, under Rehnquist's approach, states could prohibit all non-therapeutic abortions throughout pregnancy. In that case, *Roe* was gone.

Second, and equally important, the Court generally employed the language of "reasonableness" only when applying its *lowest* level of judicial scrutiny—otherwise known as rational relations review, the lowest wattage test. By harkening to that standard of review, Rehnquist was repudiating *Roe*'s central premise: that the right to abortion was fundamental and that, therefore, the Court would apply strict scrutiny to its regulation. This hint, clear but still not explicit, was carefully planned. In fact, the reasonableness phrasing was cooked up by cabal members in other Chambers and fed to Rehnquist's clerk for incorporation in his draft. They were banking that O'Connor either would not appreciate its significance or, assuming she did, would go along.

O'Connor quickly dashed these hopes. In a reply to Rehnquist delivered on May 22, she showed a clear understanding of what his draft would accomplish—and no desire to join in its mission. Your draft "effectively overrules *Roe*," she told him, "despite the disclaimer." And she balked at that, as well as other aspects of the draft.

O'Connor did not see the need to call into question *Roe*'s trimester framework. In her view, Rehnquist's supposed conflict between the framework and Missouri's viability testing provision was contrived. Even under *Roe*'s trimesters, the testing provision was constitutional. *Roe* recognized the state's right to regulate abortion to protect viable fetuses. Although viability could not occur before twenty-three and a half weeks, there was a four-week margin of error for estimating gestational age. That meant a fetus thought to be twenty weeks old might actually be twenty-four weeks—and, therefore, potentially viable. Seen this way, testing at twenty weeks was nothing more than a way for the state to ensure that its *Roe*-permitted postviability restrictions on abortion extended to every viable fetus. In other words, in O'Connor's assessment, the testing was simply a necessary incident to the state's exercising its legitimate rights under *Roe*.

As O'Connor summarized her current view, "I have previously indicated that I would reject the trimester framework, and would recognize the State's interest in potential life at all stages of pregnancy. I see no reason to go further than that in this case and to hold that the point of viability has no relevance at all."

O'Connor also disagreed with the Chief's treatment of Missouri's ban on funding for "encouraging or counseling" with regard to abortion. As she had stated at Conference, O'Connor still considered the actual impact of the ban too speculative to support a lawsuit. In her assessment, the Court should simply dismiss this part of the case entirely.

That said, O'Connor volunteered that if her colleagues insisted on evaluating the ban, she thought it violated the First Amendment by forcing doctors to "mislead" their patients. She disagreed with Rehnquist that the fact of employment empowered the state to limit the kind of advice doctors could give within the scope of their professional responsibilities.

The Chief's draft fared better in other quarters. Justice Kennedy thought Rehnquist had done a fine job and was basically ready to sign on. Still, Harry Litman, the clerk assigned to *Webster*, suggested certain changes. He believed that the "reasonableness" language in Rehnquist's draft effectively overruled *Roe* without saying so. And, as Litman forcefully argued to Kennedy, if the Court sought that world-altering result, it should say so openly and with its reasons fully expressed. To do otherwise would be duplicitous and damaging to the Court as an institution.

Within hours of O'Connor's response, Kennedy sent Rehnquist a note expressing "substantial agreement with your excellent opinion" but including a few reservations. He opened by asserting explicitly that he thought *Webster* presented an opportunity to reconsider *Roe* and that he "would have used the occasion to overrule that case and return this difficult issue to the political systems of the states."

But, given that Rehnquist had chosen not to address *Roe* directly, Kennedy stated his "preference" that the crucial draft language okaying the viability-testing provision as "reasonably" furthering the state's interest in fetal life be changed to say "permissibly" furthering. "Permissibly" was a fudge—it was an empty, question-begging standard. But the substitution would avoid conveying the impression that the Court had surreptitiously replaced *Roe* with its everything-goes rational relations test.

Secondarily, Kennedy expressed "real concerns" about Rehnquist's treatment of Missouri's funding ban on encouraging and counseling with respect to abortion. He was uneasy about answering "untested First Amendment questions" in a case where the facts were so poorly developed. And he was concerned about cluttering "a decision of this import and moment" with extraneous issues. He urged Rehnquist to read Missouri's statute more narrowly. All in all, however, Kennedy said that he "admire[d] this powerful piece of work."

After White indicated his support for Rehnquist's draft, Scalia weighed in. In contrast to Kennedy, but like most of the clerks who read Rehnquist's draft, Scalia thought the Chief had done a "crummy" job. Although early in his tenure Rehnquist had enjoyed a reputation for well and stylishly argued opinions, in more recent years he had become notorious for opinions that gave conclusory and unpersuasive answers to difficult and complex questions. In legal argot, the Chief's method was known as ipse dixit, the making of arbitrary and dogmatic statements. And many believed that his *Webster* draft—shiftily skirting the jurisprudential debate of the decade while making huge and unexplained changes in settled law—fit in this vein.

Scalia certainly chafed at Rehnquist's poor craftsmanship and his refusal to discuss the profound error of *Roe*. But he had decided beforehand to support any majority opinion, regardless of quality, that inflicted real damage to *Roe*. Rehnquist's draft certainly did that. Accordingly, he endorsed it and even defended Rehnquist against O'Connor's and Kennedy's suggested revisions.

Taking on the smaller issue first, Scalia saw no First Amendment problem with Missouri's "encouraging or counseling" prohibitions. In his view, Missouri's instruction to its medical personnel was similar to the solicitor general telling one of his deputies not to make a certain legal argument before the Court. What was wrong with that? As Scalia put it, the First Amendment arguments—which would perpetuate the wrong-headed idea that abortion deserved some special constitutional consideration—were "really *Roe v. Wade* in bad disguise."

Next, Scalia said, without elaboration, that he preferred Rehnquist's "reasonably furthers" language to Kennedy's less definitive "permissibly furthers."

But the balance of Scalia's response was reserved for a particularly barbed answer to O'Connor. He professed not to "know what to make" of her hesitation about Rehnquist's "restructuring of *Roe*." After all, Scalia pointed out, Rehnquist's disposal of the trimester framework was based in large part on O'Connor's own prior critique. "If what Sandra now proposes," he continued, "is merely replacing the rigid 'third trimester' test (*Roe I*) with a more medically flexible 'viability' test (*Roe II*), I cannot possibly go along. *Roe I* has the great advantage, as far as I am concerned, of being more obviously (though no more truly) made up."

The problem with *Roe*, Scalia fumed, was not some flaw in specific design but that the decision was "*without constitutional legitimacy*"—ungrounded in text, theory, or tradition. Until that error was corrected, he concluded, "the public perception of this Court as an institution will continue to be grotesquely distorted as we have seen in the past year. If it comes to a choice, I will go along with Bill Brennan in applying *Roe I*, until such time as the Court can muster sufficient resolve to overrule it, rather than heap error upon error with *Roe II*."

On May 25, two days later, Rehnquist circulated his already imperiled draft to the rest of the Court. He had made two significant changes from the original, both seemingly directed at O'Connor. First, with respect to the still problematic encouraging and counseling provision, Rehnquist abandoned his prior interpretation in favor of a much narrower one that Kennedy had suggested. His new draft interpreted the statute as having no direct effect on medical personnel. As reconstrued, it was aimed "solely at those persons responsible for expending public funds" and merely prohibited expenditures of public money for "the *purpose* of encouraging a woman to have a non-therapeutic abortion." Given this more benign reading, Rehnquist upheld the provision as consistent with the abortion funding cases and omitted entirely the once lengthy discussion of the First Amendment to which O'Connor had objected.

Rehnquist also revamped his discussion of the viability testing provision, though most of the changes were more structural than substantive. The thrust of the section remained constant: the requirement of viability testing conflicted with *Roe*'s "rigid," "unsound," and "unworkable" trimester framework, which the Court was now abandoning. Notably, Rehnquist did not honor Kennedy's request to modify the arguably *Roe*-reversing "reasonably furthers" language.

Still, the Chief did somewhat alter (and soften) the discussion of viability that O'Connor had specifically rejected. Instead of describing viability as having no "constitutional relevance," the new draft said more elaborately, "We do not see why the State's interest in protecting human life should come into existence only at the point of viability, and that there should therefore be a rigid line allowing state regulation after viability, but prohibiting it before viability." Apparently, Rehnquist hoped that this formulation, which left open the possibility that viability might have some constitutional significance other than the one *Roe* ascribed to it, would placate O'Connor and garner her all-important fifth vote for his draft.

Meanwhile, Blackmun, Brennan, Marshall, and Stevens were seeing Rehnquist's handiwork for the first time. From their perspective, the draft was a cowardly shot in *Roe*'s back, compounded by Rehnquist's disingenuous disclaimer. As seemed appropriate to the occasion, Justice Brennan assigned the dissent to Blackmun, but before he started work, Stevens circulated a letter to the Chief that captured common sentiment in the more liberal Chambers.

Stevens's principal target was Rehnquist's "newly minted" reasonableness test for evaluating abortion regulations. "You make no attempt to explain or justify your new standard," he wrote. "If a simple showing that a state regulation 'reasonably furthers the state interest in protecting potential human life' is enough to justify an abortion regulation, the woman's interest in making the abortion decision apparently is given no weight at all. A tax on abortions, a requirement that the pregnant woman must be able to stand on her head for fifteen minutes before she can have an abortion, or a criminal prohibition would each pass your test."

Stevens had no doubt that Rehnquist was shelving *Roe* and warned the Chief "that it would be much better for the Court, as an institution, to do so forthrightly rather than indirectly with a bombshell first introduced at the end of its opinion. . . . As you know," he closed, "I am not in favor of overruling *Roe* v. *Wade*, but if the deed is to be done I would rather see the Court give the case a decent burial instead of tossing it out the window of a fast-moving caboose."

Though it was addressed to the Chief, the secondary target of Stevens's memo was O'Connor, who he hoped would pause before giving her majority-producing assent to such a dishonorable enterprise. With regard to her, the memo was more than a caution; it was an overture. Before chastising Rehnquist, Stevens indicated that he might actually be willing to uphold portions of the Missouri statute and even join other sections of Rehnquist's opinion (although he expressed "some doubts" about the handling of the preamble and the ban on encouraging or counseling). In so doing, his motive was not to assuage the Chief but to signal O'Connor that they might be able to find common middle ground. And coming from Stevens, universally admired for his intellect and untainted by the old guard's doctrinaire liberalism, the prospect of some companionship was likely to appeal.

The irony, of course, was that Stevens wrote his memo unaware that O'Connor already had rejected a slightly different version of the Chief's unceremonious *Roe* dumping. Indeed, none of the prospective dissenters knew what O'Connor thought about the Chief's draft and, given her previous criticisms of *Roe*, they took very seriously the possibility that she would give the Chief his majority.

As days passed, word filtered out that O'Connor was writing some variety of concurrence to the Chief's draft, but in the liberal Chambers we remained excruciatingly ignorant of the details that promised to make all the difference. For us, anticipating O'Connor was akin to waiting for an earthquake, knowing one was coming within days or weeks but having no idea whether it would turn out to be a minor shaker or the world-destroying Big One. The anxiety was paralyzing. I recall more than one afternoon sitting alone with Justice Blackmun in his office. Neither of us said a word. We just sat there, subdued, in a half-light filtering through the blinds, wondering which way the pendulum would swing, and how far.

As a practical matter, the direction of Blackmun's dissent in *Webster* depended entirely on knowing where O'Connor stood. If she joined the viability testing section of Rehnquist's draft, Blackmun would be writing a requiem for *Roe*. If she did not, the dissent might vary considerably depending on the degree to which O'Connor separated herself from the

Chief. But O'Connor, despite inquiries, revealed nothing, so Blackmun started his own labors while assuming the worst—that Rehnquist's opinion would stand and that *Roe* would disappear in all but name.

Blackmun's dissent, which circulated on June 21, was pure fury. "Today," he opened,

> a bare majority of this Court disserves the people of this Nation, and especially the millions of women who have lived and come of age in the 16 years since the decision in *Roe v. Wade.* . . . To those women, and to all others, this Court owes an essential duty of explanation—a duty of candor and forthrightness, a duty to interpret the Constitution and our past decisions in a reasoned and honest fashion. The majority mocks this duty.
>
> Let there be no misunderstanding: the two isolated dissenters in *Roe* [Rehnquist and White], after all these years, now have prevailed, with the assent of the Court's newest Members, in rolling back that case and in returning the law of procreative freedom to the severe limitations that generally prevailed before January 22, 1973. . . .
>
> I rue this day. I rue the violence that has been done to the liberty and equality of women. I rue the violence that has been done to our legal fabric and to the integrity of this Court. I rue the inevitable loss of public esteem for this Court that is so essential. I dissent.

In its particulars, Blackmun's draft focused almost exclusively on Rehnquist's treatment of Missouri's viability testing provision, the only section of the proposed majority opinion that explicitly cut back on *Roe*.[26] Like O'Connor, but for different reasons, Blackmun thought Rehnquist had cooked up the conflict between the testing provision and *Roe's* trimester framework. In Blackmun's view, the statute plainly ordered that "physicians *shall* perform" those tests necessary to determine fetal weight and lung maturity or, in other words, that doctors had no choice under the law but to undertake procedures, such as amniocentesis, that had no medical justification and were potentially dangerous. So construed, the testing provision was patently irrational and, thus, flunked even the Court's rational relations level of constitutional scrutiny—regardless of *Roe*. (Blackmun also agreed with O'Connor that, under the Chief's more benign reading of the testing provision, it did not conflict with *Roe*.)

Blackmun's critique of Rehnquist's interpretive methods, however, was mere prelude to his dismembering of the Chief's proffered reasons for jettisoning the trimester framework. One by one, Blackmun showed how Rehnquist, in refusing to join the fundamental argument over the legitimacy of substantive due process, had offered up reasons for shelving the trimester framework that on inspection proved either fatuous or insubstantial.

Typical was Rehnquist's initial objection that the key elements of the *Roe* framework—trimesters and viability—did not appear in the Constitution. As Blackmun pointed out, that was true of any number of settled constitutional doctrines, such as the "actual malice" standard for evaluating libel claims or the various standards of review—rational relations, intermediate, and strict scrutiny—that the Court used to evaluate equal protection claims. All these were merely "judge-made methods for evaluating and measuring the strength and scope of constitutional rights" and, of course, were not themselves "rights protected by the Constitution." If taken seriously, Rehnquist's objection would make a shambles of most fields of constitutional law.

The point of Blackmun's critique was not only to undermine Rehnquist's specific contentions but to demonstrate that he had abandoned any semblance of serious argument precisely when it was most called for—as the Court, for the first time in its history, overturned a constitutional decision that secured a fundamental personal right for millions of individuals. "Today's decision involves the most politically divisive domestic legal issue of our time," Blackmun wrote. "By refusing to explain or to justify its revolutionary revision in the law of abortion, and by refusing to abide not only by our precedents, but also by our canons for reconsidering those precedents, the majority invites charges of cowardice and illegitimacy to our door. I cannot say that these are undeserved."

The circulation of Blackmun's counterattack provided a psychological lift for the liberals. Even Scalia was heard acknowledging that, however misguided, Blackmun's dissent demolished the Chief's tissue-thin arguments. A few Pollyannas went so far as to suggest that the dissent's discrediting of Rehnquist's draft might influence O'Connor not to join it.

Such speculation, though, was absurd. By the time Blackmun's dissent circulated, O'Connor had all but finished her own writing, and, one day after Blackmun, she sent around a draft. The sixteen pages were styled: "JUSTICE O'CONNOR, concurring in part and concurring in the judgment," which indicated in legal parlance that she had reached the same bottom-line conclusions as Rehnquist with respect to Missouri's statute but in part for significantly different reasons.

The body of the draft made clear that Rehnquist's minor revisions had done nothing to alleviate O'Connor's concerns. She had parted company with him over both the encouraging and counseling ban and the *Roe*-modifying analysis of the viability testing provision.

On the encouraging and counseling provision, O'Connor agreed with Rehnquist's revised view that the section was "directed solely at those persons responsible for expending public funds." But, in her view, the original plaintiffs in *Webster* had only challenged the provision to the extent that it directed medical personnel to skew the advice they gave to patients. In other words, under Rehnquist's reading of the statute, the argument between the parties was over (technically moot) and therefore no longer subject to decision by the Court. In short, O'Connor still thought this part of the case should be dismissed and the potentially tough issues it raised avoided.*

O'Connor continued to agree with Rehnquist's interpretation of the viability testing provision as requiring only those tests prudent and appropriate given the particular medical situation. "Unlike the Court," though, she did "not understand these viability testing requirements to conflict with any of the Court's past decisions." Accordingly, she saw no reason to depart from the "fundamental rule of judicial restraint" and (quoting the much-revered Brandeis) "anticipate a question of constitutional law in advance of the necessity of deciding it." When "the constitutional invalidity of a State's abortion statute actually turns on the constitutional validity of *Roe v. Wade*," she asserted, "there will be time enough to reexamine *Roe*. And to do so carefully."

For the conservatives, O'Connor's ode to restraint crushed decisively what had been a bright hope for doing away with *Roe*. Bearing in mind Brennan's timeworn adage that it takes five votes to change the law, O'Connor's partial defection meant that the constitutional protection of a woman's right to abortion would move not an inch in *Webster*. Although the Court would uphold each provision of Missouri's statute, it would do so by rendering some provisions essentially meaningless and by upholding the others under principles previously established in the abortion funding cases.

---

*At the end of her discussion, O'Connor noted that her position might leave the Court split 4–4 on the merits of Missouri's encouraging or counseling provision. In that case, rather than leave intact the lower court ruling striking down the law, O'Connor said that she would break the tie by concurring with the Chief.

The liberals were almost giddy with relief, though they still feared that O'Connor might change her mind as the conservatives, especially Scalia, reacted to her opinion. To reinforce O'Connor's separate stance, the liberals moved quickly to join those portions of her concurrence with which they could plausibly agree. On the same day O'Connor's draft circulated, Stevens wrote to endorse her analysis dismissing the challenge to the encouraging and counseling provision as moot. Within days, Blackmun, Brennan, and Marshall followed suit—which meant that O'Connor rather than Rehnquist commanded a majority for that portion of the case.*

Rehnquist parried in turn. He certainly did not want to lose control over any portion of the opinion or, worse yet, to have O'Connor end up announcing the now sure to be fractured judgment of the Court. Accordingly, he circulated a new draft, yet again revising his handling of the encouraging and counseling provision. This time, he coopted O'Connor's approach while, in his cover note, graciously thanking her for permitting some plagiarism.

Rehnquist's coalition was also hemorrhaging from the other side. At the outset of Rehnquist's drafting, Scalia had agreed to join any opinion the Chief wrote so long as it commanded a majority. For the sake of having an Opinion of the Court, it was worth squelching his own extremely strong preference for overruling Roe explicitly. But O'Connor's refusal to join the all-important viability testing section of Rehnquist's opinion changed Scalia's calculus. There would be no majority for undercutting Roe and, thus, no reason to check his pen.

After O'Connor's concurrence circulated, Scalia met with his clerks to decide how to handle her now official apostasy. They debated whether to concentrate their fire on the unsurpassed errors of Roe or, instead, on what they considered O'Connor's grossly improper and hypocritical sidestepping of the issues presented. Scalia recognized that if he targeted O'Connor, he ran the risk of alienating an important potential ally in many other fields of law. But her pretended coyness with respect to Roe disgusted Scalia and promised to continue indefinitely what he viewed

---

*Regarding the liberals' continuing worries about an O'Connor change of heart, on June 23, the day after O'Connor circulated her first draft, she sent around a new version that contained only one change—a single word—that greatly encouraged the liberals. In describing her current view of the Roe trimester framework, O'Connor had replaced the adjective *outmoded* with the adjective *problematic*. The liberals invested this supposed softening of word choice with huge significance, undoubtedly more than it deserved.

as a disastrous course for the Court. After three years as O'Connor's colleague, moreover, Scalia had decided that she never was swayed by friendly advice anyway. Perhaps she would listen to comments of a very different sort, and, in any event, he would have had his say.

On June 26, Scalia circulated a brutal attack on O'Connor's professed devotion to "judicial restraint." For page after page, citing case after case, he demolished the idea that O'Connor, as she claimed in *Webster,* was a principled advocate for addressing only those constitutional questions necessarily raised in a case. Over and over, O'Connor had either written or joined opinions that had reached more broadly than required when good reasons existed. And there could be no better reason, in Scalia's view, than to undo the untold harm of *Roe.*

"The result of our vote today," he complained, "is that we will not reconsider [*Roe*], even if most of the Justices think it is wrong, unless we have before us a statute that in fact contradicts it—and even then (under our newly discovered 'no-broader-than-necessary' requirement) only minor problematical aspects of *Roe* will be reconsidered, unless one expects State legislatures to adopt provisions whose compliance with *Roe* cannot even be argued with a straight face. It thus appears that the mansion of constitutionalized abortion-law, constructed overnight in *Roe v. Wade,* must be disassembled door-jamb by door-jamb, and never entirely brought down, no matter how wrong it may be."

And as if that criticism were not pointed enough, Scalia concluded: "Of the four courses we might have chosen today—to reaffirm *Roe,* to overrule it explicitly, to overrule it *sub silentio,* or to avoid the question—the last, the one we have chosen, is the least responsible."

With the term scheduled to end in less than a week, the Justices scrambled to revise their respective opinions in response to Blackmun's dissent, O'Connor's end run, and Scalia's reaction. Rehnquist added two paragraphs defending his opinion against Blackmun's charge of avoiding the real issue in the case while casting women back into the pre-*Roe* "dark ages."* More important, Rehnquist adopted Kennedy's suggestion to change his "reasonably furthers" standard for assessing the viability testing provision to the circular and meaningless "permissibly furthers."

Blackmun, for his part, faced the choice of toning down his apocalyp-

---

*That Rehnquist would use the phrase "dark ages" to describe the pre-*Roe* world in which most abortion occurred underground was telling. It confirmed that his opposition to *Roe* continued to stem from legal philosophy, not sympathy for the idea of fetal life.

tic rhetoric (given that O'Connor's stance effectively neutralized Rehnquist's opinion) or of publishing a slightly revised version as a caution
about how close a call *Roe* had suffered and how the same crisis would
surely soon arise again. He opted for the latter. "Although today, no less
than yesterday, the Constitution and the decisions of this Court prohibit
a State from enacting laws that inhibit women from the meaningful exercise of [the right to abortion]," Blackmun warned, "a plurality of this
Court implicitly invites every state legislature to enact more and more
restrictive abortion regulations in order to provoke more and more test
cases, in the hope that sometime down the line the Court will return the
law of procreative freedom to the severe limitations that generally prevailed in this country before January 22, 1973. Never in my memory has
a plurality announced a judgment of this Court that so foments disregard
for the law and for our standing decisions."

O'Connor, meanwhile, had to decide whether to respond to Scalia's
smear on her integrity and judgment. His charges smarted. O'Connor
was far from the most intellectually secure Justice. By common account,
she admired the sheer power of Scalia's brain and coveted his approval.
But she also had a certain patrician pride, a self-image that placed her
above the nastiness in which Scalia seemed to revel. And so, although
Daniel Mandil prepared a retort to Scalia's invective, O'Connor chose
to walk the high road in a principled silence.

Justice Stevens considered responding in her stead. There existed a
certain natural affinity between their positions. Although Stevens supported *Roe* and (in *Thornburgh*) had written its most articulate defense,
he wasn't a true believer like Blackmun, Brennan, and Marshall, who
saw almost every abortion regulation as an unprincipled attack on *Roe*.
He had voted with the conservatives in some of the funding cases and
was willing to accept even those with which he had disagreed. Unlike
Brennan, who celebrated Blackmun's strident dissent as "magnificent,"
Stevens thought it overheated. And he had even greater antipathy for
Scalia's rhetorical bludgeon. More strategically, Stevens recognized that
in the cases sure to come O'Connor would hold the key to *Roe*'s future.
In his view, she both needed and deserved some applause for standing up
to Rehnquist and suffering Scalia's scorn.

Stevens already had drafted his own dissent, which, uniquely, asserted
that Missouri's "life begins at conception" preamble violated the First
Amendment's prohibition on state establishment of religion. At Conference on June 29, the last planned for the term, Stevens announced

rather cryptically that he was thinking about adding another paragraph to his opinion. On further reflection, he changed his mind, but in a private note to O'Connor he shared what he would have said:

> The greats who sat on this Court consistently sought to avoid unnecessary or premature adjudication of constitutional questions. . . . For them it would have been a cardinal sin to discuss an important and divisive constitutional question that need not be answered in order to decide the case before the Court. Unfortunately, today three of the opinions issued by my colleagues fail to observe this bedrock rule of restraint that has been one of the bulwarks of the Court's institutional strength. . . . Although I disagree with Justice O'Connor's view on the merits of the issues discussed in my opinion, I wholeheartedly endorse her wise decision to adhere to the best tradition of this Court in its constitutional adjudication.

Stevens's defense of O'Connor was not the only *Webster* writing never to see the light of day. Justice Kennedy, too, tried his hand at a brief statement. Despite his decision to join Rehnquist's entire opinion, and despite his avowed desire to overturn *Roe* explicitly, Kennedy was struggling to reconcile his aversion to *Roe* with a visceral sympathy for other substantive due process decisions, such as *Griswold* and *Loving*, as well as an almost romantic attachment to the idea of liberty as the Constitution's organizing principle. In mid-June, he had joined O'Connor in *Michael H.* and distanced himself from Scalia's narrow theory of how to define the scope of liberty protected under due process. And in the waning days of the term, he tried to craft a public explanation for how one could, like Harlan, be devoted to an exalted view of liberty (and the Court's role in protecting it) while feeling duty bound to scuttle *Roe*.

Kennedy managed a page or two, but in the end he abandoned the task. Rather than write separately, Kennedy preserved for himself a degree of public uncommittedness with respect to due process and even (despite his privately stated position) on *Roe* itself. Although he signed on to Rehnquist's opinion, Kennedy had diluted its ultimate judgment of *Roe* by prevailing on the Chief to use the vacuous "permissibly furthers" standard in place of the Chief's *Roe*-antagonistic reference to reasonableness. And Kennedy separated himself from Scalia's methodology in *Michael H.*[27] In short, he preserved his every option for the future.

The Court handed down *Webster* on July 3, the preannounced last day of the term. The whole world knew it was coming. Along with one other case, *Webster* was the Court's only unfinished business before adjourning for the summer.* As at the *Webster* oral argument, the media and the superstars of the abortion debate flocked to hear the Court's ruling and to provide their instant spin on the decision. Once again, as the Justices took the bench, the courtroom was jammed, mostly by women. This time, I remember it as being unusually quiet, as though people were too anxious even to chatter.

By custom, the Chief Justice starts the process of handing down a decision by turning over the proceedings to whichever Justice wrote the controlling opinion. When Rehnquist declared that he would be announcing *Webster*, there was an audible gasp as abortion rights activists braced themselves for the worst. In a flat voice, as though reading a laundry list, Rehnquist briefly described how the Court had upheld each challenged provision of the Missouri abortion law. Then he stated that Justice O'Connor had concurred in part and concurred in the judgment—which meant to knowledgeable observers that she had in some manner qualified her support for Rehnquist's opinion. The Chief did not explain how completely nullifying her qualification was. Nor did O'Connor speak for herself. Indeed, her chair was empty. Both she and Kennedy had left town for the summer.

Ordinarily, the Chief's statement would have ended the proceedings, but Justice Blackmun was so outraged at what Rehnquist had tried to accomplish that he decided, for the first time that term, to read portions of his dissent from the bench. As Blackmun knew, the Court would announce later in the day that, at the insistence of Rehnquist, White, Scalia, and Kennedy, it would be hearing three more abortion cases the next term. For Blackmun, the stalemate of *Webster* was but a momentary lull in the country's anguish, and his own.

For ten minutes, by turns grave, angry, and distressed, Blackmun addressed a crowd that seemed not even to breathe as he spoke. I remember watching Justice White squirm in his chair as Blackmun delivered his message that, for the moment, by the narrowest of margins, *Roe* had been saved. I remember thinking that the sadness in Blackmun's voice

---

*Some reports have suggested that the *Webster* ruling was held up several days because of last-minute redrafting by one or more of the Justices. As I recall, both *Webster* and *Allegheny County* were held over the weekend before the July 4 holiday in part because of late changes in *Allegheny* (no small case in its own right) but mostly because the Court's print shop was simply overwhelmed by the myriad opinions generated by the two cases.

was so deep it would crack. But it did not. "For today," he cautioned, "the women of this Nation still retain the liberty to control their destinies. But the signs are evident and ominous and a chill wind blows." Then, he looked down. The case, the term, was over.

From the courtroom the crowd flooded onto the marble apron in front of the building, where anti-abortion and pro-choice advocates convened competing news conferences. Self-interest prompted both sides to misrepresent what the Court actually had done. The right-to-lifers, anxious to energize their constituents and spur new state abortion restrictions, declared near total victory. "*Roe* is dead," asserted James Bopp, Jr., the general counsel of the National Right to Life Committee. "*Roe* and its progeny are de facto overruled."

Pro-choicers very nearly agreed. Theirs was a political calculation. The more precarious *Roe* appeared, the more scared women became, the better their prospects. "Today's opinion," a leading ACLU lawyer proclaimed, "strikes a blow to all Americans who look to the Constitution and to the United States Supreme Court to safeguard privacy and freedom." Blackmun's solemn "A Chill Wind Blows" became ad copy as the pro-choice movement adopted it as a slogan. And lost in these competing misrepresentations was the simple truth that in *Webster* the Court had done nothing.

For the clerks, the announcement of *Webster* ended a year of plotting, maneuvering, and warfare. The previous Thursday, in one of the building's lovely stone courtyards, we had held the last of our afternoon happy hours. The original idea had been to reserve a little time each week for setting aside our workloads and building camaraderie across the nine Chambers. That theory, of course, had long since fizzled. Thursday afternoons had become just another exercise in cliquish hostility, albeit one slightly leavened by alcohol. On that final Thursday, after most of the clerks had dispersed, a shouting match started between a Brennan clerk, Tim Bishop, and Andrew McBride, the mastermind of the cabal. Not entirely sober, they traded taunts and epithets before graduating to shoves and swings that drove them into the courtyard fountain. It was a fitting end to the term, a mismatch of vaguely pathetic liberal rage against the bullyboy swagger of ascendant conservatism.

Looking back, I see *Webster* as a snapshot that captured much of the damage we have inflicted on the Court and the Court has inflicted on itself.

And although four of the Justices who participated in *Webster* have since retired, the case still speaks volumes about the Court that sits today.

As a matter of pure vote counting, the Court of *Webster* has changed little in the last seven years. Today, as then, in crucial areas of law, the Court is split evenly between an aggressive conservative faction and a more liberal group seeking to protect the status quo. On abortion, race, religion, federalism, voting rights, a single Justice—often O'Connor (as in *Webster*) but now also frequently Kennedy, depending on the area of law—holds the decisive balance of power. Today, as then, it is a Court divided 4–1–4 (or broken into even smaller pieces). And with this splintering, the act of defining many of the furthest-reaching aspects of constitutional law falls not to a majority but to one essentially omnipotent Justice, whose often inscrutable views must be parsed by those among us, whether judges, lawyers, or laypeople, who would seek to know the law.*

"The business of the Court," the late Justice Potter Stewart once commented, "is to give institutional opinions for its decisions"[28]—institutional because it is the Court's role, above all, to give coherent and persuasive definition to our fundamental laws. By the time of *Webster*, with the Court riven by faction and dominated by a narrow and ballastless "center" of either Kennedy or O'Connor, the institutional opinion had started to disappear under a blizzard of separate concurrences. The result was neither coherence nor persuasion, but rather the reduction of a Supreme Court of nine to the idiosyncrasy of one.

On another level, the *Webster* saga dramatized the expanding and inappropriate politicization of the Court and the judicial process. There is

---

*The 1995 Term demonstrates the point. Six cases from that year stand out as especially significant. For the first time in fifty years, the Court invalidated a federal law (the Gun-Free School Zones Act) as beyond the scope of Congress's previously elastic authority under the Constitution's commerce clause. A majority of the Justices demanded stricter judicial scrutiny of federal affirmative action programs while, in another case, ordering less zealous judicial intervention to preserve integrated schools. In the related field of voting rights, the Court overturned a redistricting plan intended to increase minority representation and even threatened to declare unconstitutional the Voting Rights Act of 1965. For the first time, the Court approved government financing of an explicitly religious undertaking—in this case a student religious magazine. And the Court declared term limits for elected federal representatives unconstitutional.

Quite apart from the far-reaching ramifications of these decisions, they are remarkable in that the Court split 5–4 over every one—with Rehnquist, O'Connor, Scalia, Kennedy, and Thomas as the majority in all but the term limits case (in which Kennedy defected to the other side). Even more remarkably, either Justice Kennedy or Justice O'Connor (or in one case both) provided the crucial fifth vote for a Court majority. And more remarkably still, in almost every case, either Kennedy or O'Connor refused wholeheartedly to endorse the majority position and instead wrote a separate concurring opinion, deliberately and effectively limiting the Court's various rulings.

no wall separating politics and the judiciary. The two are inevitably and properly linked. The nomination and confirmation of judges, for example, are appropriately informed by politics. We elect presidents and senators in the expectation that they will make political (or ideological) choices about who should sit on the federal judiciary, especially the Supreme Court.*

We also know that the Court's responsibility for constitutional adjudication will draw it deeply into many of our most intractable political and social debates. Moreover, in dealing with such issues—when choosing among competing interpretations of the Constitution's more open-ended phrases—the Justices, even the most conscientious, will be making what some people would call political decisions: ones influenced in part by subjective judgments based on personal outlook about what the Constitution fairly and sensibly should mean.

But, as was manifest in *Webster*, the reach of politics into the province of the Court had jumped these natural bounds. In our many political factions outside the Court, we have come to see and to treat the Court as but yet another purely political, indeed, quasi-legislative institution for forwarding our respective agendas. We conduct litigation through street demonstrations, letter-writing campaigns, and special interest testimony submitted in the form of amicus briefs. We use the Court's opinions, or distorted versions of them, as propaganda, the stuff of stump speeches and advertising campaigns. We seek to seduce the Justices into believing they have constituencies and to wield the influence that brings.

The Justices, for their part, have become complicit in this sort of thinking. Their rancorous opinions, charges and countercharges of illegitimacy and hypocrisy sound less and less like legal arguments responding to one another and more and more like political speeches seeking to affect the debate outside the Court over its future and that of the law. Certainly Blackmun's dissent, as well as embarrassing Rehnquist's plurality, read as a call to arms for the defenders of *Roe*. Scalia's attack on

---

*This is not to say that the president and Senate cannot give too great a role to political considerations or that making nominations contingent on a candidate's views of a single case, such as *Roe*, is any healthier than single-issue politics generally. In the wake of the Bork hearings, some commentators argued that Senate confirmation should be limited to evaluating a nominee's character and qualifications, not substantive views. I am unconvinced, however, that the Senate should abdicate to the president's ideological selection. If the president and Senate are at odds politically, as in the Bork situation, the appropriate solution is not a Senate rubber stamp but meaningful consultation between the president and the Senate to locate a mutually acceptable nominee.

O'Connor gave similar encouragement to the other side. It is hardly surprising, then, that others—the audience—should put these statements
to their most obvious use.

The Court's best defense against this political encroachment was the
one the Justices most assiduously refused to employ. That was to do their
jobs well—to exercise self-discipline over their personal views, to deliberate carefully and sincerely, and then to articulate well-reasoned and
persuasive explanations for their decisions. These are the attitudes and
processes that distinguish judging, especially in politically charged cases,
from the wielding of raw power—the ingredients that make a Court peculiarly a Court and not just another political institution.

In *Webster*, what passed for judging was mostly pretense. Justice
O'Connor wrapped her decisive opinion in the Brandeisian vestments of
judicial self-restraint. The fit, however, was poor. In the first place, judicial restraint (in the aspect O'Connor invoked) was a philosophy that
cautioned strongly against the premature or unnecessary decision of constitutional questions. But in sidestepping a reevaluation of *Roe*, O'Connor did no such thing. When *Webster* was under consideration, the
Court *already* had decided the key constitutional question sixteen years
before, in *Roe*, when it created the right to abortion. At issue in *Webster*
was whether the answer the Court had given in 1973 was the correct
one. And, in refusing to consider this issue, O'Connor did not (as restraint would have it) leave a constitutional question unanswered; she
merely left the current answer—which critics claimed was the most unrestrained answer in a hundred years—in place.

Even on her own terms, moreover, O'Connor's actions were not
nearly so modest as she professed. She had predetermined that she
wanted to uphold Missouri's statute under the Court's current precedents
without revisiting *Roe*, and she did whatever was necessary to reach that
goal. Mangling a statute virtually beyond recognition in order to manufacture a jurisprudential tie may have been a clever way for O'Connor to
postpone giving a definitive verdict on *Roe*; it may even have been a
courageous break from her accustomed allies; but it was an act of restraint only in the narrowest sense of its outcome.

For O'Connor, the recourse to judicial restraint was mere con-
trivance. As Scalia elaborated in excruciating detail, O'Connor was
hardly consistent in her jurisprudential forbearance. When it suited her,
especially in her favored field of states' rights, she rivaled Brennan in her
zeal to write broad and unnecessary pronouncements on constitutional

questions. In our term, O'Connor had seized on a case ostensibly about the Sixth Amendment's right to an impartial jury and used it to rewrite a huge swath of federal habeas law, even though the habeas issues had nothing to do with why the Court had granted review in the case and were neither argued nor briefed by the parties.[29]

The problem here was more than one of inconsistency. A crucial aspect of judicial restraint is not debasing that vital and fragile principle by invoking it only when convenient or self-serving. O'Connor broke that rule and, in so doing, contributed once again to the perception, fostered by other Justices as well, that fundamental canons such as judicial restraint or stare decisis could be used or discarded, depending on circumstance, like cards in a hand of draw poker.

Whatever O'Connor's sins, however, they paled before Rehnquist's. Inevitably, a Court is shaped by the Chief Justice who leads it. That Justice sets a tone, controls the conference, assigns the most opinions, and, usually, takes the most important, nation-changing decisions for himself. The Chief is not always the most influential Justice in terms of result. That role drifts toward the Court's ideological center, as it did to Powell during Burger's time, and as it has now to O'Connor and Kennedy. But the Chief Justice remains first among equals, the individual who gives a period in Court history its name, and who is responsible for the institution's character.

In *Webster*, Chief Justice Rehnquist sought deceitfully and surreptitiously to overturn the most significant decision of the previous generation. In an opinion that ignored the monumental legal issues at stake (issues essential to defining the Court's proper constitutional role) and that offered transparently silly or undefended justifications for its unprecedented conclusions, he proposed to take back a personal liberty cherished and counted on by millions of women. Inside the Court, Rehnquist tried to engineer this legal revolution in a secret caucus behind the backs of those Justices who would most strenuously oppose his plan.

Roe's most ardent critics frequently likened the decision to *Dred Scott* for their shared reliance on substantive due process. But whatever the merits of that comparison, Rehnquist's effort in *Webster* certainly harkened to *Dred Scott* in another way. The leading historian of the pre–Civil War Court described Chief Justice Taney's majority opinion as "a work of unmitigated partisanship, polemical in spirit [with an] extraordinary cumulation of error, inconsistency, and misrepresentation."[30]

Blackmun's dissent leveled many of the same charges against Rehnquist's *Webster* plurality, which, it concluded, embodied "nothing other than an attempted exercise of brute force [where] reason, much less persuasion, has no place." *Webster* was simply a glaring example of a decisional style that—from conference to final draft—virtually prohibited intellectual engagement, deliberation, or open-mindedness and seemingly denied any responsibility to articulate honest and coherent rationales for exercising the Court's enormous authority.

It was as though Rehnquist sought to impose on the Court the advice he once gave another Justice, who, in Rehnquist's view, was struggling too long over an opinion: "Don't bother so much with the reasoning," the Chief told him, "it will only trip you up."

A COURT DIVIDED

Transitions

On the afternoon the Court handed down *Webster*, as the lawyers and spectators dispersed and the reporters scrambled to file their stories, Paul Cappuccio and Andrew McBride commiserated over a beer. They were certainly disappointed with the Court's splintered nonverdict in *Webster*, but more troubling for the long term were the decision's implications for the conservative counterrevolution in law.

In that enterprise, Justice O'Connor had always been too self-conscious a mimic of the "centrist" Powell to be counted a reliable ally. While some dismissed her do-nothing concurrence as the vacillation of a judicial Hamlet paralyzed by indecision, insiders knew better. O'Connor had employed more than a little creative interpretation to weave her way through the minefield of Missouri's abortion law. Such careful plotting, point by point, implemented a decision—a fundamental one—that hers was never going to be the vote that overturned *Roe*. O'Connor's *Webster* temporizing may have left that decision implicit, but it was made nonetheless.

Though distressed by this development, Cappuccio and McBride focused less on O'Connor than on Justice Kennedy, whom they now saw as potentially (and perhaps inevitably) drifting from Scalia's camp. The problem, as such hard-liners saw it, lay with Kennedy's apparent preoccupation with being liked and thought of as "judicious" and "reasonable," a tender sensibility that they perceived both in his private reactions to negative publicity and in the content of his public writings.

A prime example was Kennedy's response when civil rights groups and the mainstream press lambasted his opinion in *Patterson* v. *McLean*

Credit Union. While the Court's true hard-liners ignored such criticism (or reveled in it), Kennedy was visibly upset and disappointed. Having convinced himself that he had crafted a Solomonic compromise in not overruling *Runyon*, he felt crushed that civil rights leaders and journalists echoed the dissenters' charges of racial insensitivity.

In the aftermath, Kennedy seemed at pains to protect his public image. In *Texas* v. *Johnson*, for example, he joined Brennan's 5–4 majority giving First Amendment protection to the odious act of flag burning, but not without writing a separate concurrence distancing himself from the ruling's unpopular result. "Sometimes we must make decisions we do not like," he justified himself; or as others rephrased Kennedy's point, "I'm really not a bad guy, honest."

From the conservatives' perspective, Kennedy's craving for approval—what they would come to call the Greenhouse Effect, after *The New York Times*'s left-leaning Supreme Court correspondent, Linda Greenhouse[1]—was incompatible with the essential but largely thankless task of slaying the sacred cows of the Warren era. *The New York Times* was never going to applaud their efforts to overturn *Roe*, prohibit affirmative action, allow voluntary school prayer, and cut back on the exclusionary rule or habeas corpus. This agenda was not "reasonable," at least in the sense that the liberal editorialists would apply the term. And its success depended on maintaining precisely the thick skin and firm resolve that Kennedy increasingly appeared to lack.

The liberalizing potential of Kennedy's craving for popularity was compounded by a second factor: his underlying Jimmy Stewart idealism about the Court and its role in shaping American society. In its innocuous form, Kennedy's romanticism expressed itself in his love of Court lore and in wide-eyed lectures delivered to student groups about the high points in the institution's history. Of greater import, his Olympian sense of the Court seeped into his opinions through the grand style of his separate writings and their tendency toward the panegyric. Kennedy yearned to be a phrasemaker, an articulator of timeless and profound truths—so much so, in fact, that with no apparent irony he implored one law school professor to find him a clerk "who could write like Oliver Wendell Holmes," the Court's most accomplished rhetorician.

Kennedy's attempts at eloquence (his own or those borrowed) were not simply for show. They reflected his intention that the Court serve as more than merely an interpreter of laws, that it act as a repository of

American virtue. As he would tell the American Bar Association, in his vision, the Justices were bound not only by the force of logic and precedent but "by our own sense of morality and decency." We must never lose sight, he declared, "of the fact that the law has a moral foundation and we must never fail to ask ourselves not only what the law is, but what it should be."[2] In other words, while Kennedy remained critical of many specific decisions of the Warren era, he cherished beneath his conservative political views an essentially Warrenesque image of the Court as charged with ensuring fairness and decency in the nation at large.

Much like Kennedy's preoccupation with self-image, this expansive view of the Court's role contained a latent incompatibility with the conservative counterrevolution. The nucleus of this Scalia-led enterprise was a philosophical commitment to judicial self-abnegation, a belief that the Court was an institution of strictly limited purposes enforcing an "imperfect" Constitution that remained silent on many of the pressing moral questions of the day.[3] One side of Kennedy, the one that identified himself as a loyal conservative, no doubt shared these principles, but another side, one perhaps closer to his heart, was beguiled by the idea of broader judicial mission.

Evaluating *Webster* in this light, shrewd hard-liners, such as Cappuccio and McBride, realized the case was nothing short of a disaster for the long-term project of keeping Kennedy in the counterrevolutionary fold. True, he had joined Rehnquist's plurality and even stated privately that he supported overturning *Roe*. But as a legal matter, Rehnquist's opinion had accomplished nothing. And, in its wake, with everyone from right-to-life groups to abortion activists portraying the case as imperiling *Roe*, Kennedy was going to take a brutal licking in the papers for joining the Chief's failed enterprise.

In short, Kennedy was going to come under just the sort of public pressure to which he appeared particularly susceptible. And that pressure would come in an area of law—the Constitution's promise of "liberty"—where his underlying idealism was most likely to be tapped. Thus, although Kennedy's voting record during his first full term on the Court was nearly indistinguishable from Scalia's, there were deep cracks hidden beneath the smooth surface of Kennedy's conservatism. In the aftermath of *Webster*, with the chance for a quick conservative victory gone, it seemed almost certain that over time these fissures would gradually but inexorably emerge.

* * *

The immediate political fallout from *Webster* was dramatic. Pro-choice forces used the scare of *Webster* as a motivational tool in two interim gubernatorial races. The candidates endorsing *Roe*—Jim Florio (in New Jersey) and Douglas Wilder (in Virginia)—won both. Anti-abortionists, for their part, responded enthusiastically to Rehnquist's tacit invitation to draft new laws tightening the restrictions on abortion and taking aim yet again at *Roe*. The governors of Louisiana and Idaho vetoed the anti-abortion bills emanating from their state legislatures, but most of the new statutes made their way onto the books. From Pennsylvania to the protectorate of Guam, pro-choice litigators once again leapt to the *Roe* barricades and mounted a myriad of new test cases. And, as ever, these moved steadily through the judicial system toward the Court.

While the lower courts considered these new challenges, the Justices turned their attention to the abortion cases already on their docket. Of the three accepted for review, the most comprehensive challenge, the only one seriously implicating *Roe,* involved a number of Illinois regulations that, among other effects, pushed most abortions out of clinics and into more expensive full-service hospitals.[4] Liberal clerks at the Court fretted about how Justice O'Connor would respond to the Illinois law, but to their relief, one week before oral argument, pro-choice litigators agreed to settle the case with Illinois Attorney General Neil Hartigan, and it disappeared from the Court's docket.

Neither of the remaining two cases, *Hodgson* v. *Minnesota* and *Ohio* v. *Akron Center for Reproductive Health*, presented a direct threat to *Roe* itself. Instead, they raised the discrete and difficult issue of parental notification: the degree to which states could give parents a right to know before their daughters obtained abortions. This limited scope, however, did not make *Hodgson* and *Akron* inconsequential. These cases were tests of attitude, probes of whether, after *Webster,* a Court majority—and, specifically, the balance-of-power-wielding Justice O'Connor—would confirm that the right to abortion (in terms of *Roe* or otherwise) remained more than a meaningless vestige.

Hodgson, the Minnesota case, involved the country's most rigid notification statute. It prohibited any abortion on a woman under eighteen years old until at least forty-eight hours after notice to *both* her parents. The law made exceptions only for dire medical emergencies and for girls who claimed to be victims of parental abuse.

In a highly unusual feature, the Minnesota law also contained a built-in contingency plan in case it was found to be unconstitutional. The statute's pro-life architects had provided that, if any court blocked enforcement of the original statute, the block would trigger an automatic change in the law. Under the backup system, the two-parent notification requirement would remain in force, but every minor seeking an abortion would also have the option of "bypassing" the requirement by going before a local judge and convincing him to grant an exemption. The idea was that this loosening of the rules would cure whatever constitutional flaw a court had found in the original statute; the law could then continue in effect without having to go back to the legislature for revision.

Pro-choice attorneys immediately brought suit against both the "pure" two-parent notification rule and the backup plan. The crux of their argument was simple: the notification rule was largely superfluous in healthy family situations but would foment abuse in unhealthy ones. To support this claim, during a five-week trial, they put on extensive testimony from counselors, psychologists, and juvenile court judges that notifying both parents in divided or dysfunctional families often resulted in recriminations or violence.

The district judge agreed and struck down both the law's original formulation and the backup provision. The Eighth Circuit Court of Appeals, however, while agreeing that the pure form of the statute was unconstitutional, ruled that the law did pass muster once the contingency of judicial bypass kicked in.

The Ohio case, *Akron*, presented similar issues. In contrast to Minnesota, though, Ohio required notification of only one parent and, from the outset, provided for judicial bypass in some circumstances. Still, both a federal district court and the Sixth Circuit Court of Appeals had found Ohio's law unconstitutional because its bypass system failed adequately to protect the interests of the pregnant minor.

The Court heard oral argument in both cases on November 29 and took them up at Conference on December 1. At argument, Justice O'Connor had expressed strong concern about the practical effect of parental notification on young women from broken homes. But the crucial question remained whether that concern would, for the first time in O'Connor's tenure, translate into a vote actually to strike down a state abortion law.

The Justices entered Conference fully aware of O'Connor's centrality. On one side of her, the anti-*Roe* coalition from *Webster*—Rehnquist,

White, Scalia, and Kennedy—naturally saw no constitutional problem with parental notification through Minnesota's two-parent law or through Ohio's somewhat more lenient statute. On O'Connor's other flank, the three Justices remaining from the *Roe* majority (Brennan, Marshall, and Blackmun) considered both state laws misguided anti-abortion obstructionism and wanted to void them using *Roe*'s strict scrutiny approach.

Anticipating this predictable breakdown, Justice Stevens decided to intensify his project, started during *Webster*, of reaching out to the otherwise isolated O'Connor. His goal was to lure her off her strictly neutral position in *Webster* and convince her to affirm (by voting to strike down a state statute) that the constitutional right to abortion had some actual, enforceable content.

He knew from O'Connor's record that she would have no truck with *Roe*'s strict scrutiny standard, to which Brennan, Blackmun, and Marshall adhered. Accordingly, he proposed an alternative. Generally speaking, the Court did not use its lowest level, dim-wattage "rational relations" standard of review to strike down legislation; after all, state legislatures rarely act in ways that are truly "irrational." But on a few occasions, in a brief line of cases that O'Connor herself had helped pioneer, the Court had invoked the language of rational relations review while actually conducting a somewhat more severe assessment of the legislation at issue.[5]

Law clerks commonly referred to the standard of review in these cases as "rational relations with teeth." It came in handy when the Court wanted to strike down what it saw as obnoxious legislation without taking the precedent-setting step of recognizing some new interest as "fundamental"—and therefore permanently deserving of heightened judicial scrutiny. (In 1996, for example, the Justices used rational relations with teeth to strike down Colorado's antihomosexual ballot initiative. In this way, they voided a bigoted law without recognizing homosexuality as a class routinely entitled to special judicial protection.)[6]

In Stevens's view, rational relations with teeth was exactly the treatment the Minnesota statute called for and, at Conference, he proposed voiding it on that ground. Minnesota's requirement of notifying *both* parents did not reasonably further any legitimate state interest. On the contrary, although ostensibly passed to protect the interests of minors and their parents, in thousands of instances involving dysfunctional families the law (as shown at trial) had proven distinctly harmful to its intended beneficiaries. Nor, Stevens asserted, could Minnesota redeem such a wrongheaded scheme simply by tacking on a still burdensome judicial bypass provision.

From the inception of the case, Stevens had been working through the clerk back channel to promote his views in O'Connor's Chambers and to provide intellectual support should she agree with his assessment. At conference this strategy seemed partially to pay off. While (as in many close cases) O'Connor insisted that her views were "tentative," she agreed with Stevens that Minnesota's pure two-parent notification requirement was irrational. At the same time she stopped short of condemning the law altogether. As had the court of appeals, she added that Minnesota's judicial bypass plan saved the statute from total condemnation. O'Connor also expressed some concerns, though probably not fatal ones, about Ohio's notification scheme.

Conference, then, ended in a muddle. There were four votes to uphold Minnesota's regime in its entirety, four votes to strike it down, and O'Connor to uphold it but only as modified with the judicial bypass provision. In the Ohio case, there were four votes to uphold the statute without reservation, Stevens's vote to uphold the statute with certain provisos, three votes to strike down the statute, and O'Connor expressing some concerns.

Matters became even more complicated in the days immediately following, as it emerged that O'Connor's views were not entirely at rest. The cause was Stevens's persistent effort, both by letter and in person, to convince her that Minnesota's law simply could not be saved. Judicial bypass might save a statute (such as Ohio's) that involved only one parent and thus was sensible in most cases, Stevens reasoned. But "a child . . . should not be compelled to go to court to obtain relief from a statute [such as Minnesota's] that is unconstitutional because it is irrational as applied in most cases."[7]

In the end, she was persuaded—to a degree. On December 8, O'Connor circulated a letter to the Chief explaining that she had revised her position after talking to Stevens. "I am presently in the unhappy position of adopting a disposition which is supported by no other Justice," she wrote. "John's views are close to my own in these two cases, and, if I understand his approach correctly, I think I can agree with it." Accordingly, she now voted to strike down the Minnesota statute in its entirety—a change that shifted the assignment of the opinion from Rehnquist to Brennan, who, in turn, wisely gave the case to Stevens.

On the same day, O'Connor announced that she'd resolved her concerns about the constitutionality of Ohio's statute. That meant six votes in *Akron* (including Stevens's qualified one) to uphold the single-parent-with-bypass notification scheme. Rehnquist assigned the opinion to Kennedy, who set to work on a fairly narrow, precedent-based opinion that, with O'Connor firmly onboard, easily garnered a majority.

Stevens's task in *Hodgson* was much more delicate. To hold on to the skittish O'Connor, he had to write the opinion as narrowly as possible, using the rational relations standard of review. At the same time, to obtain a working majority, he had to convince Brennan, Blackmun, and Marshall to go along with a methodology that in their view gave short shrift to the fundamental rights at issue.

Stevens's first priority was to lock in O'Connor, for without her vote he would have no majority even for the opinion's basic result, much less its reasoning. To this end, he circulated three drafts over the course of four months, all devised with the intent of calming O'Connor's anxiety at taking what she apparently considered an enormous step. But for reasons never really expressed, O'Connor continued to feel that Stevens was seeking to push her just a bit too far in striking down the entire Minnesota law. Finally, on June 11, she circulated a memo informing her colleagues that "at the end of the day" she was "back where [she] started": the Minnesota statute was invalid in its pure form but acceptable once the safety valve of judicial bypass was added.

O'Connor stated her own views in a brief partial concurrence to Stevens's opinion. There, she agreed with the "central points" of his framework for analyzing Minnesota's law but said that she could not join its "broader discussion" (which perhaps seemed a little too abortion-rights friendly) or its invalidation of Minnesota's contingency plan. With this backtracking, Minnesota's notification law would still be standing, albeit in its modified form.

On the brighter side, and to Stevens's considerable satisfaction, O'Connor did unreservedly join the section of his opinion striking down Minnesota's pure form of two-parent notification. That, in itself, was precedent setting. O'Connor finally had declared an abortion regulation invalid and set herself even further apart from the anti-*Roe* wing of the Court.

The significance of this development was certainly not lost on the liberals, who had held their own views in abeyance while Stevens made his overtures to O'Connor. On June 13, Brennan sent a private note to Marshall, who was drafting a more definitive repudiation of the Minnesota law. Although he preferred the straight-*Roe* approach Marshall was taking, Brennan informed Marshall that he would be joining almost all of Stevens's opinion. "I think it is important for John to get as much support as possible," he explained, "now that Sandra has for the first time joined us in holding invalid a law regulating abortion."

On June 18, Blackmun sent a letter to Stevens, Brennan, and Marshall expressing much the same view; and Brennan wrote yet another note (this time to Blackmun and Stevens as well as Marshall) repeating that they should seek the greatest possible unanimity with Stevens. But this ring of solidarity was quickly severed by ideology. In important sections of his opinion, Stevens had relied on past decisions, in particular abortion funding cases, that the liberals despised. While Brennan was willing to stomach the citations, Blackmun and Marshall balked at endorsing anything that might suggest tacit approval of decisions they thought antithetical to *Roe*.

After considerable back-and-forth, and some minor revisions by Stevens, Brennan joined most of the opinion while Blackmun and Marshall joined one section fewer. All three, however, fully endorsed the crucial section discussing why Minnesota's pure two-parent notification scheme did not reasonably advance any legitimate state interest. Because O'Connor also had joined that section of the opinion, Stevens obtained his much sought majority on this point.

Even so, Stevens ended up with a scrambled egg of an opinion. He commanded a full majority in only four of its eight subsections. Brennan supported him in a fifth, O'Connor in two others. The last section, that dealing with the bypass provision, was actually a dissent, because O'Connor had switched sides, giving a majority to Justice Kennedy's opinion (also joined by Rehnquist, White, and Scalia) approving the bypass contingency plan.

The mess of writings was increasingly characteristic of how the Rehnquist Court decided the numerous close and divisive cases on its docket. Each Justice, driven by ideology, strategy, uncertainty, or some combination, acted solely as an unyielding independent agent and produced collectively a blizzard of writings, utterly blinding those who were supposed to follow them. Although *Hodgson* decided the fate of Minnesota's notification law, it produced four conflicting views (strict scrutiny, rational relations, rational relations with teeth, and undue burden) of how lower courts, elected representatives, or anyone else should regard similar regulations in the future. This was not performing the Court's essential task of delineating rights.[8] It was just creating confusion.

The profusion of theories in *Hodgson* inspired Justice Scalia to write a brief mocking concurrence that emphasized what he deemed to be the root cause of the problem. "The random and unpredictable results . . . make it increasingly evident, term after term," he observed, "that the tools for this job are not to be found in the lawyer's—and hence not the judge's—workbox. I continue to dissent from this enterprise of devising an Abortion Code, and from the illusion that we have the authority to do so."

Unlike his passionate appeal in *Webster,* this time Scalia's comments wore an air of resignation. In *Hodgson,* O'Connor had whispered, however quietly, that she had crossed over, however minimally, into what Scalia considered the dream garden of abortion rights creation. And with her now explicit defection, it would take more than just an appropriate new case to bring down a killing frost.

A few days after the Court recessed for the summer, Justice Brennan boarded the *Q.E. II* for a luxury cruise to England. During the crossing, he suffered what was later determined to have been a minor stroke (his second), which left him ill though not incapacitated for the remainder of his two-week trip. On his return to Washington, Brennan's doctors urged him in the strongest terms to retire immediately for the sake of his health. Some hurried consultations with his family followed. Then, on July 20, he acquiesced.

Brennan's departure came out of nowhere. During the term, he had given no apparent thought to retiring. On the contrary, the Justice had rallied somewhat from the infirmities that had dogged him the previous year. Brennan also had won some surprising and gratifying victories, in particular a 5–4 decision upholding federal affirmative action in the allocation of broadcast licenses. (Here, Justice White, who tended to give wide latitude to *federal* legislation, deserted the conservatives' anti–affirmative action majority from *Croson.*)[9] Even Brennan's clerks learned of their boss's decision to retire only a few hours before the news leaked to the press.

The unexpectedness of losing Justice Brennan turned what ordinarily would have been a momentous and sad event into something incomprehensible and devastating to the liberal community. In historical terms,

Brennan belonged to the small company of this century's truly towering legal figures. In the course of more than three decades, he had authored over 1,300 opinions. Many, such as *Baker* v. *Carr, Cooper* v. *Aaron, Fay* v. *Noia, New York Times* v. *Sullivan, Goldberg* v. *Kelly,* and *Craig* v. *Boren,* had led the Court and country across new thresholds in striving for race and gender equality, equal voting rights, a free press, fair trials, and protection from the bureaucratic power of an ever-expanding government. If late in the day some of Brennan's views were eclipsed and his influence on the wane, he was still the Justice most responsible for shaping the Court's modern mission of protecting individual liberty and equality, and of interpreting the Constitution as a "living" document to be made responsive to a changing time.

In personal terms, Brennan was unique. Even into his eighties he retained a head-turning movie star quality. Equipped with a bottomless reserve of anecdotes and Irish charm, he commanded the largest audience at every Court event. Clerks unabashedly sought his autograph. Brennan was the closest thing the law knew to a living demigod, and now he was gone.

Hearing the news, I became light-headed. It was as though the physics of the legal world had suddenly changed, a source of gravity vanished, the whole calculus of law upended. A profound sense of mourning descended over the liberals, and behind that mourning, fear. Without Brennan, how much more would the Court's balance shift? And without his soul mate and support, how much longer could Marshall hold on? And what of Blackmun beyond that? Such questions danced in our heads, though we dared not answer them.

The Bush White House moved swiftly to fill Brennan's seat. Borrowing heavily from evaluations made during the Reagan years, within twenty-four hours of Brennan's announcement, Bush's advisers had narrowed the field to five.

Bush's own favorite was Clarence Thomas, a black conservative and former chair of the Equal Employment Opportunity Commission, whom Bush had recently named to the D.C. Court of Appeals. Thomas, though, had yet to publish a single judicial opinion, and the president's advisers quickly convinced him that the judge lacked sufficient experience for elevation to the Court.

Two other finalists failed on grounds of ideology. Both Bush and his chief of staff, John Sununu, were anxious to avoid a summer-long repeat of the Bork fiasco and, in particular, a confirmation bloodletting over abortion. That disqualified Kenneth Starr, the solicitor general, who was well liked but had signed several controversial abortion-related briefs since taking over from Charles Fried. The other early loser was Lawrence Silberman, a Reagan appointee to the D.C. Circuit, who had inherited Bork's and Scalia's mantle as the leading conservative on the nation's second most prestigious Court. During an extensive political career, Silberman's hard-nosed views and explosive temper had earned him too many enemies to guarantee safe passage through the Senate.

The remaining two candidates were a study in contrast. Edith Jones fit the mold of the Reagan counterrevolutionary. Once a member of James Baker's Houston law firm, she had been a Texas GOP activist before Reagan named her to the Fifth Circuit. There, she had written several notably conservative opinions and had become a regular at the gatherings of prominent conservative legal organizations such as the Federalist Society. Despite lacking strong personal contacts within the Bush White House, Jones was one of the "usual suspects" mentioned for elevation to the Court.

The final possibility was much further from convention. David Souter was a former New Hampshire attorney general and state court judge whom Bush had newly placed on the federal court of appeals for the First Circuit. In his home state, Souter had earned a reputation as a highly intelligent and conscientious jurist. He was also a self-described conservative, a depiction consistent with his state law opinions.

On the national level, Souter was an unknown and, as a new appointee to the federal bench, had no record on the types of issues he would face if elevated to fill Brennan's empty chair. But what Souter lacked in profile he made up for with the backing of two powerful fellow New Hampshirites, Sununu and Sen. Warren Rudman. As governor of New Hampshire, Sununu had passed over Souter when choosing a chief justice for the state supreme court. That slight, however, did not stop Sununu from promoting Souter now. Rudman was even more enthusiastic. Souter had been his protégé ever since serving as Rudman's deputy in the New Hampshire Attorney General's Office. Rudman considered Souter a sensational choice for the Court and had been promoting him in Washington for some time.

On the Sunday after Brennan's resignation, the White House asked Souter and Jones to come to Washington for personal interviews the next day. That evening, Bush divided his advisers into two teams and asked each to make the case for one of the candidates. Vice President Dan Quayle and Sununu argued on Jones's behalf that she would make an excellent "in your face," unabashedly conservative appointee and that, as a woman, she might be immune to *Roe*-based attacks. C. Boyden Gray and Richard Thornburgh presented Souter as the better choice for exactly opposite reasons. In addition to being unimpeachably smart, he could be confirmed without a significant fight.

The next day, the tide turned against Jones. Bush met with both candidates and was especially impressed with Souter, whose humble, life-long devotion to the law elevated him in the president's eyes. After one more go with his advisers, Bush made his final selection. In the end, he opted for ease of confirmation over ideological purity, and, at 5:00 P.M. only three days after Brennan's decision, he named an obscure New Englander to the nation's highest Court.[10]

Souter's nomination immediately became the subject of some ridicule. On first glance (especially from the Beltway perspective), he seemed like an oddball, a confirmed bachelor who lived with his mother in the semiseclusion of small-town New Hampshire. Wags conjured up images of Norman Bates, the demented motel manager from Hitchcock's *Psycho*. Even Souter's local newspaper, the *Concord Monitor*, voiced concern that his "cloistered life, devoted exclusively to the law, in one of the nation's most homogeneous states" had "limited his grasp of the human complexities" and left him without "empathy for groups of people with whom he has had little or no contact."[11]

Although the ambit of Souter's life experience was rather limited, he was hardly the grim recluse of early portraits. True, he did seem plucked from another century. He collected books and antiques, pursued long hikes in the New Hampshire hills, lived in the austere surroundings of a small farmhouse in the town of his childhood, and still put pen to paper in the computer age. But Souter was strange only in the sense that old-fashioned virtues have come to feel foreign. By common account, his life had been a model of hard work, frugality, modesty, and graciousness. At the same time, he kept a warm circle of friends and was known as a witty raconteur, especially over a bottle of good port. At Harvard College he had written his thesis about a particular judicial favorite, Oliver Wendell Holmes. Souter's dominant trait was one shared with that hero. They were pure Yankee, bred to the bone.

The misperceptions were simply a factor of ignorance, which, in turn, was the product of post-Bork warping in the nomination process. Having created a system that turned obscurity from a vice into a virtue, liberals and conservatives alike wondered about the allegiances of a man with no paper record on the many issues of surefire controversy, especially *Roe*. The Bush White House placated nervous conservatives, assuring them, as Sununu put it, that Souter was a "home run." This promise was based in part on confidential information Sununu had received from one of Souter's former state court colleagues that he would vote against *Roe*.[12] (The White House had not asked Souter directly about his attitude toward *Roe*, and Souter had signaled in advance that he would not answer.) Liberals had no such sources and were left to guess at the views of this "stealth" nominee—and to expect the worst.

At his confirmation hearings in September 1990, Souter followed much the same script Kennedy had used successfully: to avoid particularly contentious areas and, most important, to remain agnostic on the subject of *Roe*. But, that said, to those who paid close attention, Souter's testimony was extremely revealing and should have been mortifying to the Reagan-style hard-liners.

His testimony showed first and foremost that his confirmation would place a sterling intelligence on the Court. His credentials made this no particular surprise. He was a former Rhodes Scholar and graduate of Harvard Law School. But Souter's responses to the Judiciary Committee, delivered without the benefit of notes, revealed more than just smarts. His choices of phrasing, his apt historical asides, and the ease with which he discussed complex cases and doctrines suggested a deep appreciation of legal method and culture. As Walter Dellinger, a noted constitutional scholar (and later President Clinton's acting solicitor general) commented, Souter was "the most intellectually impressive nominee I've ever seen."[13]

His answers—assuming them to be truthful—also revealed a judicial philosophy that would inevitably put him at odds with Scalia and the counterrevolutionary agenda at the Court. Time and again Souter invoked the work of Justice Harlan as the model for his legal reasoning. Two points stood out particularly. First, Souter firmly and explicitly endorsed Harlan's flexible approach to interpreting the due process clause. In his initial exchange with Committee Chairman Joseph Biden, he specifically stated his agreement with Harlan's opinion in *Griswold* as well as with the broader proposition that "the Due Process Clause of the

Fourteenth Amendment does recognize and does protect an unenumerated right to privacy."

Even more telling, Souter did not hesitate to take sides in the dispute over Scalia's crucial and *Roe*-imperiling *Michael H.* footnote limiting the Harlan approach to due process. Again in response to questioning from Biden, Souter said that he "could not accept" Scalia's notion that due process inquiries into historical tradition be framed as narrowly as possible—and that he did "not think that Justice Harlan would have done so either." We cannot, Souter continued, "as a matter of definition at the beginning of our inquiry, narrow the acceptable evidence to the most narrow evidence possible."

Second, Souter spoke approvingly of Harlan's exceedingly high regard for stare decisis—a regard that had led Harlan to accept and apply numerous Warren Court precedents, such as *Miranda,* from which he originally had dissented. Notably, Souter expressed his appreciation for Harlan's viewpoint both in general terms and in the specific context of *Roe.* While gracefully dodging the committee's obsessive curiosity about his views on *Roe,* Souter volunteered that his decision, should the occasion arise, would depend not only on the correctness of the earlier decision but also on "extremely significant issues of precedent."

Souter's allegiance to Harlan did not necessarily preordain how he would vote in the next challenge to *Roe.* It was possible to believe in Harlan's flexible due process approach and also to value stare decisis, yet still to conclude that the Court must overrule *Roe.* But Souter's stance did suggest that his decision would be a close one and that he would approach *Roe,* at worst, as a misapplication of sound principles rather than (following Scalia) as a basic betrayal of the Court's role.

And Souter's self-linkage to Harlan had relevance far beyond the context of abortion and due process. The association, indeed all his testimony, marked Souter as a "true" judicial conservative—an incrementalist with strong allegiance to existing law and an abiding faith in the traditional ability and discretion of judges to reason from text, history, and precedent to apply the Constitution to the present day. Just as Harlan's traditionalism had placed him in opposition to much of the activism of the Warren Court, Souter's open embrace of Harlan made him an unlikely candidate to join the aggressive rollback to which Rehnquist and Scalia aspired.

At the time, liberals were too obsessed with Souter's refusal to discuss

Roe to appreciate fully the import of his testimony. On the other side, right-wing GOP activists were getting increasingly nervous that Bush, whom they had never trusted anyway, had sold them out in choosing Souter. They downgraded their expectations from the home run Sununu promised to a "bloop single." None of this jeopardized Souter's nomination. Neither his scant record nor his erudite answers offered grounds for rejection. On October 2, the Senate confirmed him 90–9.

The timing of Souter's installation at the Court, just before the first round of oral arguments, placed him at a significant disadvantage. While coping with the personal adjustment of moving from Weare, New Hampshire, to the nation's capital, Souter faced the daunting task of setting up his Chambers inside the Court and playing catch-up on what he described as a "tidal wave" of legal issues that, even in small cases, were different in kind and far more momentous than those he had faced as a state court judge. According to friends, Souter came to the Court "in awe of the challenge," and his self-described "reverence" for the place ended up paralyzing him. In "trying to satisfy himself that he was worthy" of the job, he fell further and further behind in his writing, producing only a single opinion before late May 1991, near the end of the term.[14]

While scrambling to keep pace, Souter usually cast his lot with Rehnquist and, in several important cases, proved the decisive vote in conservative victories. To the dismay of the pro-choice movement, one such case was *Rust v. Sullivan*, the term's only abortion-related decision.[15]

At issue in *Rust* was the so-called gag rule, a federal regulation that barred doctors at facilities receiving federal funds from counseling patients about abortion. Replaying an argument the Justices had left unresolved in *Webster,* opponents challenged the gag rule as violating the First Amendment rights of doctors to give full medical information to their patients. The administration, in the person of Solicitor General Kenneth Starr, defended the rule as a permissible precondition on the receipt of federal funding.

At oral argument, Souter expressed concern that the ban would prohibit doctors from giving appropriate advice even when the pregnant woman's health was at risk if the fetus were carried to term. Nonetheless, at conference, with the other Justices split 4–4 (O'Connor joined Marshall, Blackmun, and Stevens in voting to strike down the counseling ban),* Souter cast the crucial fifth vote to uphold the gag rule. Before joining Rehnquist's draft majority, he did prevail on the Chief to include in his opinion an exception for cases of medical emergency. But this mild qualification did nothing to quell liberal fears that Souter's position in *Rust* (notwithstanding his confirmation testimony) presaged a general hostility to the right to abortion and, by extension, *Roe*.

Souter himself recognized no such implication. To him, *Rust* was a case involving the First Amendment in the context of government funding, not abortion. As for *Roe*, he considered himself genuinely undecided. And he had no intention of facing that issue, as he had so many others during his first year, without adequate preparation. Like everyone else at the Court, Souter knew another direct challenge to *Roe* was almost certain to arrive during the next year. Hence, as October Term '90 wound down, he gave each of his outgoing clerks a final assignment: to write a memo on whether *Roe* should be overruled. For the Court's newest Justice, those memos, getting himself ready for the inevitable, were the newfound purpose to fill the much-missed tranquillity of New Hampshire's summer.

The biggest news of Souter's first term came not in abortion rights but in criminal law, where Rehnquist pushed his activist agenda along a broad front. In several important cases Rehnquist succeeded in severely limiting federal habeas corpus. Several other decisions departed sharply from precedent and demonstrated the Court's increasingly conservative tilt.

In one closely watched case, the conservatives cut back drastically on the Eighth Amendment's protection against cruel and unusual punishments while upholding a life sentence without parole given to a man convicted on a first offense of cocaine possession.[16] In another, the conservatives reversed forty years of precedent to change the rule for dealing with confessions "coerced" in violation of the Fifth Amendment. Previously, a prosecutor's use of such a confession at trial required an automatic reversal of the defendant's conviction. Under the new ruling,

---

*O'Connor's vote here was not surprising. Although in *Webster* the Court ultimately did not rule on the constitutionality of Missouri's counseling ban, O'Connor was already on record inside the Court that such skewing of professional speech presented serious First Amendment concerns.

courts could uphold the conviction so long as admission of the tainted confession was "harmless error"—that is, if the outcome of the trial would have been the same even if the confession had not been used.*

For the liberals, such backsliding, indeed the entire disastrous, Brennanless year culminated in the term's final case, *Payne* v. *Tennessee*.[17] The petitioner, Pervis Payne, had been sentenced to death for the vicious murder of Charisse Christopher and her two-year-old daughter. At his sentencing hearing, Payne had called his parents and a family friend to testify to his good character. The prosecutor had countered by putting Ms. Christopher's mother on the stand and having her discuss the impact of the murders on her surviving three-year-old grandson. The prosecutor, in her closing remarks, also had stressed the devastating effect of the murders on the little boy.

Payne appealed his conviction and sentence on a number of grounds, among them that the testimony of the victim's mother and the prosecutor's closing remarks violated *Booth* v. *Maryland*, the controversial 5–4 Powell decision of 1987 that banned the use of "victim impact evidence" in capital sentencing. The Tennessee Supreme Court rejected Payne's claims. After disparaging the rule of *Booth* as "an affront to the civilized members of the human race," the state judges ruled that, even under *Booth*, the use of victim impact evidence in Payne's case had been "harmless error . . . beyond a reasonable doubt."[18]

At the Court, *Payne* was controversial from the outset. Normally, the conservatives would never have voted to grant cert. in a capital case in which the convicted murderer had *lost* below. (This was the outcome they favored, so why tinker with it?) More generally, the Court routinely denied cert. when the lower court decision was "factbound"—that is, based on a case-specific factual determination, such as the Tennessee courts' ruling that the *Booth* violation in Payne's case had been harmless error.

But at Rehnquist's urging, in *Payne* the conservatives made an excep-

---

Arizona v. *Fulminante*, 499 U.S. 279 (1991). For Rehnquist, who wrote the opinion, this was a particularly cherished victory. Back in 1952, when clerking for Justice Jackson, he had urged unsuccessfully that the Court adopt the harmless error rule for coerced confessions. Automatically reversing convictions, he had then complained, was "ivory tower jurisprudence" that "weakened local law enforcement" and "a boon to smart criminal lawyers." Thirty-nine years later, Rehnquist's view finally had prevailed, although Kennedy robbed him of a complete victory. Writing separately in his capacity as the "reasonable" conservative, Kennedy emphasized that, given the powerful impact of confessions on juries, the introduction of coerced confessions would rarely prove harmless.

tion. Reversing *Booth* had been a Rehnquist priority from the day the case was decided, and Payne's case, for somewhat complicated reasons, became his chosen vehicle.

Rehnquist had thought he could overrule *Booth* back in 1989. After Justice Kennedy replaced Powell (*Booth*'s author), the conservatives had granted cert. in *South Carolina v. Gathers*,[19] in which the lower court had thrown out Gathers's death sentence on *Booth* grounds. The plan was to reverse the lower court and overrule *Booth* in the process. It backfired, though. As Rehnquist had hoped, Kennedy voted to scuttle *Booth*; but, unpredictably, Justice White, despite having written a dissent in *Booth*, voted to stand by the precedent. Instead of being the occasion for overturning *Booth*, *Gathers* became a 5–4 liberal victory reaffirming it.

In the fall of 1990, with Souter having replaced Brennan, Rehnquist thought the time was ripe to go after *Booth* again. To that end, the conservatives granted cert. in an Ohio case in which the death row defendant had prevailed on a *Booth* claim. But, in February '91, the Justices belatedly realized that the Ohio case contained a fatal jurisdictional flaw and they had to drop it from the docket. As a result, Rehnquist had to find yet another case to scuttle *Booth*, and the best he could come up with on such short notice was *Payne*—which had been a hold for the just-dismissed Ohio case.

On Rehnquist's suggestion, O'Connor, Scalia, and Kennedy joined to grant cert. in *Payne* (even though the defendant's *Booth* claim had failed) and directed the parties to brief the issue of whether *Booth* and *Gathers* should now be overruled. In addition, the conservatives specially expedited the Court's review. According to the Court's usual briefing schedule, a case granted in mid-February would go on the fall calendar. That was too long a delay for Rehnquist. He ordered the parties to file their briefs in half the usual time and set the case for argument on the last day of the final spring sitting.[20]

For the liberals, the handwriting was on the wall. Stevens, joined by Marshall and Blackmun, dissented from the cert. grant, calling it "unnecessary and unwise." They also complained about rushing the case to judgment. But for *Booth* and *Gathers* it was all over but the shouting.

Rehnquist's majority opinion was blunt. By preventing prosecutors from introducing victim impact evidence at sentencing, *Booth* and *Gathers* had deprived "the state of the full moral force of its evidence" and turned the "victim into a faceless stranger." The state had every right to punish murderers according to the "specific harm" they had caused, and victim impact evidence was a useful tool for bringing that harm to the attention of the sentencing jury.

As for overturning a rule of law reaffirmed only two years earlier, Rehnquist responded with the usual collection of citations about stare decisis not being an "inexorable command," especially in constitutional cases. The Court had many times reversed decisions that had proven "unworkable and badly reasoned." According to Rehnquist, *Booth* and *Gathers*—both subjects of "spirited dissents" when decided—had proven precisely that and deserved to be overruled. White, O'Connor, Scalia, Kennedy, and Souter all agreed.

Justice Stevens was so upset by the Court's decisions in *Payne* that he read his dissent from the bench. In Stevens's view, the Court had no business granting cert. in *Payne,* much less rushing its consideration. He also disagreed with Rehnquist's rather cavalier treatment of stare decisis. But what especially provoked Stevens was the idea of overruling *Booth* in particular, a precedent that he considered unequivocally right.

Victim impact evidence, Stevens insisted, was "irrelevant to the defendant's moral culpability." Its use, moreover, threatened to divert the focus of capital sentencing away from a rational evaluation of the nature of the crime and the character of the criminal toward an emotional evaluation of the relative "worth" of the victim in each case. In Stevens's assessment, the Court majority had caved to the " 'hydraulic pressure' of public opinion" and was simply pandering to the ascendant movement promoting victims' rights. "Today," he closed, "is a sad day for a great institution."

Justice Marshall looked on grimly as Rehnquist and Stevens described their competing visions to the full house attending the term's last day. Sitting before him, in the front section reserved for Court officers, was his missing comrade, Justice Brennan, who had come down from his office to observe the proceedings. Brennan's presence added considerable poignancy to the moment and punctuated what had been a long and trying year for Marshall. Marshall's health, deteriorating for many years, had continued to slip. His eyes were failing, his breathing ever more labored, and he had taken a nasty fall that put him in the hospital for several days.

In truth, Marshall was no longer up to his responsibilities, or even the appearance of being up to them. Without Brennan's lead to follow he made mistakes, some embarrassing. In one argued capital case, *Lankford*

v. *Idaho*,[21] Marshall became so confused that, for the first time in his career, he voted at conference to uphold a defendant's death sentence. Worse yet, the error gave the conservatives a 5–4 majority. Marshall's clerk, in a tactful though slightly panicked memo, had to point out her boss's obvious blunder. Then Marshall had to write his colleagues to recant.

Such embarrassments for a fiercely proud man were naturally compounded by the bitterness of watching Rehnquist dismantle brick by brick the edifice of liberal precedents that he had helped Brennan to build. And, in his own *Payne* dissent, Marshall vented the frustrations of a Justice outmanned, outgunned, and feeling very much alone.

"Power, not reason," he declared in his opening sentence, "is the new currency of this Court's decisionmaking. . . . Neither the law nor the facts supporting *Booth* and *Gathers* underwent any change in the last four years. Only the personnel of this Court did." And, in Marshall's view, those new personnel had declared themselves exempt from the usual rules of stare decisis and, therefore, free to reverse every decision with which they disagreed. "In dispatching *Booth* and *Gathers* to their graves," he warned, "today's majority ominously suggests that an even more extensive upheaval of this Court's precedents may be in store."

There was considerable irony in Marshall's dissent. The liberal legacy he was defending owed its very existence to the Court's willingness, especially during Chief Justice Warren's day, to rethink and overrule established precedents, sometimes abruptly. Indeed, it was Brennan (not Rehnquist) who commonly received credit for turning what should have been the caution "five votes can doing anything around here" into a precedent-dispensing credo. And, in the death penalty debate of which *Payne* was a part, it was Brennan and Marshall together who for twenty years had adamantly refused to follow stare decisis and accommodate themselves to the constitutionality of capital punishment.* (In a gleeful concurrence, Scalia skewered Marshall with his own previous statements setting aside stare decisis.)

---

*Marshall's death penalty abolitionism not only undermined his reliance on stare decisis but also created inconsistencies in his substantive defense of *Booth*'s ban on victim impact evidence. Part of *Booth*'s objection to victim impact evidence was the way it introduced "emotion" (as opposed to pure reason) into the jury's sentencing deliberations. But Marshall did not always object to the infusion of emotion into capital sentencing. When the issue was turned around, when it was a question of whether a *defendant* could appeal to emotion when seeking mercy from a sentencing jury, Marshall and Brennan argued strongly that "sympathy" and "compassion" had their place. See *Saffle* v. *Parks*, 494 U.S. 484 (1990). Also, Paul D. Gewirtz, "Victims and Voyeurs at the Capital Trial," 90 *Northwestern Univ. Law Rev.* 863 (1996).

Marshall's evident inconsistency did not mean, of course, that Rehnquist was justified in overruling *Booth* and *Gathers* or in his rush to do so. The test of a decision such as *Payne* is not the *fact* of overruling precedent (which is not and should not be sacred) but the persuasiveness of the reasons given.

Booth was supported by a powerful logic. As Stevens pointed out, victim impact evidence is inherently inflammatory; it raises the specter of race and class bias in the valuing of a human life; and it is unrebuttable unless, bizarrely, the defendant turns his sentencing hearing into a trial on the victim's life.

The conservatives, however, were not without reasonable counterarguments. As Justice Souter pointed out in a separate concurrence, every mentally competent defendant knows that his crime will impose specific and terrible harm on certain survivors. The legitimate purpose of victim impact evidence is simply to ensure that a defendant's sentence reflects the predictable and foreseeable injuries that he has caused. Also, stripped of legalism, victim impact evidence gives the oft-neglected victim a voice in the criminal process and fills a silence that, in this apprehensive time, has threatened to erode public confidence in our system of law.

In short, *Payne* was not an easy case on the merits. Nor was the pull of stare decisis that compelling. *Booth* and *Gathers* were hotly debated 5–4 decisions of recent vintage on which few societal expectations had yet come to rest. Their passing would work no great upheaval in the law.

The importance of *Payne*, and the root cause of the dissenters' hyperventilation, was a matter less of merit than of symbolism. *Payne* marked Rehnquist's ever more obvious determination to push his conservative majority as far and as fast as he could. And, with Brennan looking on from the bleachers, *Payne* also marked the dwindling of a liberal judicial vision whose architects now reviled in others the disregard for process and precedent that they had come to excuse in themselves.

As Stevens came to the close of his dissent, Blackmun gazed down to where Brennan was seated. He suddenly looked terribly small and old, as though the life were slipping out of him. When the gavel banged, adjourning the Court for the summer, Blackmun decided not to retreat behind the velvet curtains as was customary. Still in his robe, he hurried down around the front of the dais to visit with his friend. He laid his hand on Brennan's shoulder and shared a few moments of comfort and commiseration.

To Rehnquist's consternation, the brief exchange made Blackmun late for the Justices' final conference of the term. But Blackmun arrived in time for the news: Marshall had endured enough. Although he liked to joke that he would never leave the Court until carried out shot dead by a jealous husband, Marshall was by his own admission "falling apart."[22] The time had come for him, too, to step down—effective as soon as his replacement was confirmed.

At a final news conference the next day, Marshall offered some gratu-itous advice to President Bush about choosing his successor. A reporter had asked whether Bush had an obligation to appoint another minority to replace him. That shouldn't be an "excuse" for "picking the wrong kind of negro," Marshall responded. "My dad told me way back . . . that there's no difference between a white snake and a black snake. They both bite."

Marshall hadn't named names, but everyone understood who he was talking about: Judge Clarence Thomas, the black D.C. Circuit judge whom Bush had considered when Brennan retired. From Marshall's per-spective he was distinctly "the wrong kind of Negro." During eight years as Reagan's choice to head the Equal Employment Opportunity Com-mission (the governmental watchdog for discrimination in the work-place), Thomas had skewered liberal orthodoxies and accused the mainstream civil rights leadership of doing little more than "bitch, bitch, moan, moan, and whine." He had even criticized *Brown* v. *Board of Education*, Marshall's signal triumph, as a source of condescension toward blacks, a charter for integration based on the insulting belief that in order to excel blacks needed to be placed in proximity to whites.

For similar reasons, Thomas had denounced affirmative action and declared himself "unalterably opposed to programs that force or even ca-jole people to hire a certain percentage of minorities." Instead of such group-based remedies—which he considered both stigmatizing and counterproductive—Thomas preached the gospel of color blindness, in-dividual merit, and black "self-sufficiency."

Nor were his conservative opinions confined to matters of race. As a favorite on the conservative after-dinner circuit, he had endorsed Oliver North and expressed a philosophical attraction to several libertarian thinkers devoted to greater protection of property rights from government regulation. Although he did not speak to the issue of *Roe* directly, in a much-noted speech before the conservative Heritage Foundation, Thomas also praised as "splendid" an article by the conservative business tycoon Lewis Lehrman that called abortion a "holocaust" and asserted that fetuses enjoyed an inalienable right to life.

Marshall's commentary notwithstanding, within the Bush White House, Thomas quickly emerged as the consensus choice. He fit the three main criteria the administration needed. First, Thomas was black. For obvious reasons, Bush did not want to be seen as returning the Court to its pre-Marshall, lily-white composition. As a practical matter, though, on the Republican side there were few minority jurists sufficiently distinguished to merit consideration. Bush told his advisers to look closely at Hispanic candidates, and they talked to one, Emilio Garza, a Texan recently named to the Fifth Circuit Court of Appeals. But Garza had yet to write a single judicial opinion and was eliminated for lack of experience.

Second, Thomas was a committed conservative. With the presidential primary season fast approaching, Bush was anxious to placate the right-wing GOP activists who posed the only realistic threat to his renomination. These hard-core Reaganites and religious conservatives distrusted Bush for many reasons (such as the breaking of his "no new taxes" pledge), and they already felt betrayed by his selection of Souter to replace Brennan.

Thomas was the Republican right's first choice for Marshall's empty seat. Outspokenly conservative and a member of a fundamentalist church, Thomas appeared a safe bet on the issues that mattered, including *Roe*. As Thomas Jipping (a point man for the religious right on legal issues) faxed the president in the wake of Marshall's retirement, "The entire conservative movement not only supports [Thomas] but believes in him."[23] At the Bush White House, that endorsement carried enormous weight.

Third, Thomas seemed confirmable. His personal history, that of a black man born into crushing southern poverty and the indignities of Jim Crow, would automatically make him a formidable nominee. Thomas's first home, buried in the marshland of Pin Point, Georgia, was a wood shanty with a dirt floor and newspaper for insulation. His mother plucked crabmeat at five cents a pound and served as a maid in white-owned houses for pittance wages.

Yet Thomas had overcome it all. Under the stern guidance of his grandfather, he had weathered racist insults while earning a strong Catholic school education. Eventually hard work, his own aptitude, and affirmative action had carried him to Yale Law School. Yale, in turn, had led to the office of then Missouri Attorney General John Danforth. And Danforth, for his part, had given Thomas entrée into the Republican political circles where he would come to thrive.

In light of this background, the administration saw Thomas as largely immune from a Bork-style attack from the left. However stridently he had denounced affirmative action, criticized *Brown* v. *Board of Education*, or frustrated civil rights lawyers, the black leadership of organizations such as NAACP, who had so devastated Bork, would surely hesitate before torpedoing the nomination of one of their own. Similarly, Thomas was not someone that Ted Kennedy or Joe Biden could lecture about sensitivity to racism and inequality. Thomas knew these evils first hand and could defend himself on the moral high ground of his life experience against anyone who challenged his unorthodox views.

If Thomas seemed to have an Achilles' heel, it was his lack of experience with or demonstrated thought about constitutional issues. His entire litigation career consisted of two and one half years as an entry-level lawyer in the Missouri Attorney General's Office, during which he never argued a case in federal court. As a D.C. Circuit judge for barely more than a year, Thomas had written only twenty opinions, none noteworthy. As Boyden Gray observed, ideally Thomas "could use two or three more years" seasoning on the D.C. Circuit. Nonetheless, Gray deemed him "ready,"[24] and Bush concurred. On July 1, the president announced Thomas's nomination at a Kennebunkport press conference, where, in a show of reflexive defensiveness, he insisted that Thomas was not only the "best person" for the Court but "the best qualified," and that race had played no part in his selection.[25]

The White House strategy for promoting Thomas's nomination might best be described as "reverse Bork." The Reagan administration and Bork himself had staked their case on competence and constitutional theory—the idea that Bork's superb résumé and interpretive vision qualified him for the Court, whatever his personal background or character.

The Bush administration, by contrast, orchestrated a confirmation campaign for Thomas designed to bury the issues of competence and ideology, and to sell Thomas almost exclusively on the basis of his character. As a Justice Department lobbyist instructed the group assigned to coach and handle the nominee, "just keep getting his personal story out. Tell the Pin Point story."[26]

At his confirmation hearing, Thomas stuck closely to the White House strategy, opening his testimony with what would become the incessant refrain of his Senate defenders. "My earliest memories are those of Pin Point, Georgia," he began, "a life far removed in space and time from this room, this day, this moment." But Thomas could not deflect every question with this shield of personal experience, and, in what would become the substantive crux of the hearings, Democratic skeptics bored in on the controversial statements Thomas had made during his tenure in the Reagan administration.

In response, Thomas adopted a strategy of disassociating himself from his record. As an initial gambit, he suggested that his past views were essentially irrelevant. He had made them in his capacity as a bureaucrat and policy maker—before he "changed roles" to that of an impartial judge. As judges, he continued, we "shed the personal opinions that we have." Thus, whatever his previous political opinions, and however strongly expressed, they simply had no bearing on his prospective jurisprudence.

As unpersuaded Democrats continued to press, Thomas sought to minimize the importance of his record in another way: by disavowing or trivializing any potentially controversial or revealing statement. When asked about his Heritage Foundation speech lavishing praise on Lew Lehrman's anti-*Roe* article about natural law, Thomas now professed only to have "skimmed" it and to have intended no meaningful endorsement. When asked about the report of a White House working group of which he was a member that called for denying welfare benefits to unwed mothers, Thomas said he had never read what he signed. When asked about his stated attraction to the theories of the libertarian philosopher Stephen Macedo—who would place property rights on an equal constitutional footing with personal rights—Thomas admitted to reading Macedo but dismissed his interest in the man's theories as a purely academic exercise.

From the Democrats on the committee, Thomas's "out to lunch" defense[27] met with an initial skepticism that ripened into total incredulity as he avoided every substantive matter by pleading disengagement or ignorance. The most troubling testimony came in Thomas's exchanges with Vermont Senator Patrick Leahy. There, Thomas took the now standard avoidance of the *Roe* question to new heights of disingenuousness. Although *Roe* was decided while Thomas was a student at Yale Law School, in response to Leahy's inquiry, he could not "remember personally engaging" in any discussion of it at the time. Nor, Thomas claimed, had he once "debated the contents of it" in the intervening eighteen years.

In a second round of questions, Leahy asked Thomas to tell him which cases of the last twenty years he considered the most important. Thomas responded that he would "have to go back and give it some thought." Then, haltingly, he cited *Roe* v. *Wade* and *Griggs* v. *Duke Power* (a significant employment discrimination case). Leahy persisted, suggesting that his question was akin to asking a baseball fan to name his all-time favorite teams. One would have thought Thomas, who presumably cared deeply about the subject matter, would have been brimming with possibilities. But again he balked. He said that he couldn't list any "off the top of his head." Finally, after Leahy pressed him about cases that might have influenced his thinking, Thomas added *Brown* to his list.

Outside the hearing room, Ken Duberstein, the political consultant in charge of shepherding Thomas through the Senate, accounted for his candidate's apparent paralysis on the subject of constitutional case law by saying that Thomas had thought Leahy's question limited to cases the Court had decided from 1971 to 1974—while Thomas was in law school. But that explanation was hardly convincing. Even during those three years the Court had handed down any number of blockbusters, including the Pentagon Papers case, the Nixon tapes case, *Furman* v. *Georgia* abolishing the death penalty, and standard setters in the controversial areas of religion, obscenity, and busing.

Thomas's performance, which even his White House advisers found "terrible, wooden,"[28] hardened Democratic opposition to his nomination within the committee, which deadlocked 7–7 over whether to recommend confirmation. As a result, his candidacy went to the full Senate with no recommendation, although most observers expected that he would prevail by a comfortable margin.

One day before the scheduled vote, after much behind-the-scenes machination, Anita Hill went public with her charges of inappropriate sexual advances; the Judiciary Committee reopened its hearings; Hill recounted the lurid details of her encounters with Thomas; and Thomas responded with a blanket denial and by denouncing the entire proceedings as "a high tech lynching for uppity blacks."

The charge, which Thomas leveled from his "standpoint as a black American," saved his nomination. Though the lynching metaphor hardly fit—after all, Thomas's accuser and many of his critics were black—it froze the committee's liberals, who seemed not to know how to proceed when faced with a charge of racism. While the committee's Republicans ripped into Hill, hour after televised hour, Biden, Kennedy and Co. tiptoed gingerly around the edges of Thomas's testimony and never pressed him about its details.[29]

In the end, the Senate confirmed Thomas by a vote of 52–48, the narrowest margin in the history of Court confirmations.

The process by which Thomas was ultimately confirmed, especially the yes-he-did, no-he-didn't confrontation with Anita Hill, has been the source of exhaustive investigation and analysis. We are now party to revelations (by Thomas partisans no less) of a confirmation-at-all-costs nominee reduced to incoherent mutterings delivered from a fetal crouch and allegations (also by Thomas partisans) of a sexual accuser "a little bit nutty, a little bit slutty."[30]

It is not my intent here to rehash the evidence surrounding Anita Hill's charges. (Although, in candor, my own appraisal of the voluminous literature suggests that the truth lies closer to Hill's version of events than to Thomas's blanket denials.) Nor am I concerned with every ramification of the Thomas hearings, even important ones, such as riveting public attention on the problem of sexual harassment, widening the "gender gap" in national politics, and contributing to the election of an unprecedented number of women representatives in 1992. What matters here is what the Thomas nomination meant for the Court and, specifically, the way it became a permutation of the Bork debacle, another political war with the Court as the prize and honest conviction as the immediate casualty.

To conservatives and to Thomas himself, the handling of Anita Hill's charges was a meaner and dirtier extension of the smearing of Bork, a conspiracy cooked up in the shadow world of liberal Senate staffers and their sympathetic partners in the press.[31] These were, as Thomas put it, "evil people . . . who were going to destroy the whole country," manipulating senators who lay in wait like a group of "petty thieves." For Thomas and his partisans, such as his mentor, the usually levelheaded and later repentant Sen. John Danforth, these conspirators had to be defeated, no matter the cost to ordinary rules of fair play or personal dignity.[32]

To liberals the Thomas nomination originated in hypocrisy, was sustained by connivance, and ended with the nominee's blatant perjury. The hypocrisy, of course, concerned the issue of race and, specifically, the role of affirmative action in Thomas's career and nomination. Here was a nominee who owed his door-opening education to affirmative action, who was selected for the Court (despite Bush's denial) in significant part because of his race, and who salvaged confirmation by playing the race card in his testimony, yet who preached the gospel of a colorblind world and sought to deny other minorities the very preferences that had sustained his career.

The connivance was the way Thomas's supporters stole the liberals' script from their success in beating Bork and mounted a huge campaign of backroom arm-twisting, grassroots mobilization, and media spin to pave the way for Thomas's move to the Court. As the vote count tightened, and then as the Hill charges broke, the conservatives' campaign grew increasingly nasty and inattentive to the truth, a trend that, in the liberal view, culminated in Arlen Specter's brutal attack on Hill's character.

The perjury centered not only in Thomas's categorical denial of Hill's charges but in his pre-Hill testimony about never having discussed *Roe*. In the eyes of his opponents, the Senate had confirmed a felon, and they tried to comfort themselves with dark but faintly ridiculous talk about the prospect of indictments and impeachment.

Most bitter of all, in some sense, were the denizens of the civil rights establishment, who, while on record against Thomas, were largely to blame for his ultimate triumph. As the administration had hoped, concerns about racial solidarity and the delusion that any black Justice would prove better than none delayed their opposition and kept muted what belatedly arrived.

Afterward, these pillars of liberal black rectitude, having tried to convince themselves that Thomas's race would ultimately triumph over his ideology, took to lecturing the new Justice about why it should. In a much hyped and celebrated open letter, Leon Higgenbotham, a distinguished black federal appeals judge,[33] told Thomas that he was "con-

cerned" about his appointment and thus had decided to refresh
Thomas's memory about the history of the civil rights movement's accomplishments—a history that he had "no right to forget."[34] Why
Higgenbotham thought his civics lesson might be welcomed by a nomi-
nee-cum-Justice who despised the civil rights establishment precisely
because it sought to strip nonconforming blacks of their racial identity is
beyond comprehension.[35] This was an act not of education but of stunning presumption, which served only to add another layer of mutual resentment to the many that had come before.

As with the extreme rancor surrounding Bork's nomination, the replay involving Thomas exacted a high toll on both the Court's public
image and its much-abused internal culture. The Thomas affair powerfully reinforced the idea that Supreme Court confirmations were not occasions for seriously evaluating the nominee's legal thinking and
qualifications but rather election campaigns for political control of the
Court, to be waged by any means necessary. At a minimum, the gross
and distortive process revealed an attitude on both sides of official Washington that treated the Court as simply another power center and placed
no value on its special role in the nation's political architecture. Regardless of Anita Hill, the president had nominated and the Senate had confirmed someone who either had lied to cover up his record and opinions
or, almost as bad, was largely ignorant about the vital constitutional issues of his time and had professed to opinions merely to curry favor with
the political operatives who could advance his career.[36]

This corruption of the appointment process was not trivial. It was a
breakdown in the essential democratic link between the Court and the
people, the channel by which the nation gradually and over time re-
makes the composition of the Court to reflect changes in social judgments and values. A failure in the integrity of that system, a disregard by
both the president and Senate for who should serve on the Court, inevitably jeopardizes the institution itself and the legitimacy of the great
authority we have yielded to it. For if the executive branch, the Senate,
and the partisans on both sides show nothing but contempt for the
Court, how long will it be before that toxic cynicism poisons the main
arteries of our body politic?

The Justices themselves certainly felt such concerns about the Court's
reputation and authority. Inside the Court, however, Thomas's confirmation created a more immediate problem. It brought to an institution

already severely divided the very opposite of the Court citizen whose services were so desperately required.

From the moment Thomas crossed the Court's threshold, he carried an aura of partisanship as well as indifference to the institutional culture to which he had ascended. Some of this was a matter of style or taste. For example, Thomas offended some Justices with an unusually political guest list for his installation, and shocked almost everyone by posing for the cover of *People* magazine with his wife and a Bible.

More substantively, at oral argument, Thomas not only remained unvaryingly silent but looked uninterested, often not even bothering to remove the rubber band from his stack of briefs. He also surrounded himself with uniformly archconservative clerks—including Chris Landau, a hand-me-down from Scalia who had found even his first boss insufficiently pure ideologically. Thomas gave these clerks enormous latitude, and they, with typical narrow-gauged zeal, created drafts remarkably provocative in result and dismissive of any point of view other than their own.*

Thomas's Chambers exuded a sense of score settling. His wife spoke ominously about the Justice feeling that he "doesn't owe any of the groups who opposed him anything." Thomas himself reveled in distinguishing himself from prior appointees, such as Blackmun, who disappointed their political patrons by moderating their views once on the Court. As Thomas likes to tell his clerks, "I ain't evolving."[37] And, as if to prove the point, he flouted convention (as well as the Code of Judicial Conduct from which the Justices exempt themselves) by making public appearances on behalf of right-wing organizations that had backed his nomination. All in all, he presented a figure very different from the one who had assured the Senate, almost meekly, that "I have no agenda."

---

*Thomas's best-known opinion remains his dissent in *Hudson* v. *McMillian*, a prison brutality case in which he argued that the Court had expanded the cruel and unusual punishments clause "beyond all bounds of history and precedent" in applying it to deprivations suffered in prison, including the brutality of guards. Thomas wanted to limit the clause to officially imposed punishments. He also characterized as "minor" Hudson's injuries, which included a bruised and swollen face and mouth, loosened teeth, and a cracked dental plate. 503 U.S. 1 (1992).

Critics noted that Thomas's view seemed to conflict with his poignant confirmation hearing testimony about watching busloads of prisoners from his window and saying to himself "almost every day, there but for the grace of God go I." Less remarked on is the fact that Thomas's opinion not only was drafted by Landau but was nothing more than a warmed over version of a memo Landau had written for his former boss, Scalia.

None of this should have been terribly surprising. Thomas was chosen because of his sharp-edged politics, an edge since tempered in the flame of public trial. According to his own mentor, Senator Danforth, during the confirmation nightmare Thomas was reduced to uncontrollable fits of weeping, vomiting, hyperventilating, and writhing on the floor. Even before Anita Hill, he suffered visions of people trying to kill him. After, he envisioned his guts being pulled out and his life and family destroyed.[38] What such man wouldn't be bitter, wouldn't surround himself with aggressive and loyal foot soldiers, wouldn't try to help out those who had stood by him in his hour of need? If Anita Hill told the truth, Thomas's enemies had humiliated him, exposed him, forced him into lying. If she lied, all the worse.

Either way, the cost to the Court was substantial. To an institution already desperately short on mutual trust, self-restraint, and intellectual integrity, Thomas brought not only ideology but an inner rage, a willingness to sacrifice every inch of his personal dignity to satisfy his own ambition, and the deep scars of one who thinks himself grievously wronged. These are not ingredients that make for balanced, impartial, collegial judgment, and they ensured that Thomas's wounds would only add to those the Court already had inflicted on itself.

A Fragile Peace

O n October 21, 1991, two days before Clarence Thomas officially
assumed his duties at the Court, the Third Circuit Court of Appeals (which covers Pennsylvania, New Jersey, and Delaware) handed
down a decision saying, in effect, that *Roe* v. *Wade* was no longer the law
of the land. The occasion was the appeals court's ruling in *Planned Parenthood of Southeastern Pennsylvania* v. *Casey,* the pro-choice challenge
to the abortion regulations Pennsylvania had adopted in the wake of
Webster.[1] In an extraordinary 103-page decision, the Third Circuit announced that, because *Roe*'s central premise—its high-wattage "strict"
judicial scrutiny test for abortion regulations—no longer commanded a
Court majority, it should no longer be applied.

In the appeals court's view, the Justices were hopelessly splintered
over how to evaluate abortion laws, and thus its obligation was to engage
in a prediction about which of the Justices' various approaches to abortion would be decisive in the next case to reach the Court. The appeals
court would then apply that approach to Pennsylvania's abortion law.
This prognostication was easy. Justice O'Connor had been the swing
vote in *Webster, Hodgson,* and *Akron.* Accordingly, the Third Circuit
substituted her "undue burden" standard for *Roe*'s strict scrutiny test and
tried to guess how she would evaluate Pennsylvania's new abortion regulations. As a result, even though the Court itself had never overruled
Roe, the Third Circuit replaced the core of *Roe* with the jurisprudence of
a single isolated Justice.[2]

The Third Circuit's shift in standard of review had a dramatic effect.
Although Pennsylvania's new abortion law was not as stringent as some
others adopted after *Webster* (including outright bans), it was still con-

sciously designed to test the outer boundary of what regulations the Court might allow after *Webster*.[3]

Among the new restrictions imposed by Pennsylvania's law was an "informed consent" requirement. Under penalty of prosecution, doctors planning to perform abortions now had to give their patients a specified package of information, including a discussion of abortion's risks and alternatives as well as printed materials describing the human features of the fetuses that would be destroyed if their patients went forward. After receiving this information, women seeking abortions were required to wait twenty-four hours before having their abortions. Pennsylvania also insisted that these women notify their husbands, except in very limited circumstances. Finally, in cases of minors seeking abortions, Pennsylvania added a strict parental notification regime.*

Had the Third Circuit evaluated these restrictions under *Roe*'s strict scrutiny test, all would have failed. The regulations reflected a deliberate effort to make abortion more difficult and unpleasant, an apparent contradiction of Justice Blackmun's admonition that "states are not free . . . to intimidate women into continuing pregnancies."[4] Also, in many respects, they resembled regulations the Court had declared unconstitutional in the *Akron* and *Thornburgh* decisions of 1983 and 1986 respectively—before Justice Powell's retirement put *Roe* in limbo.

But, applying Justice O'Connor's "undue burden" standard, the Third Circuit reached a very different result. Despite the obstacles to abortion created by Pennsylvania's new regulations, the appellate court struck down only the requirement that adult women give advance notice to their husbands.

For the lawyers at Planned Parenthood and the ACLU, the Third Circuit's decision—the front-page headline-grabbing presumption of an appellate court that *Roe* no longer held sway—came as a bolt from the blue and was "as bad as it gets," a leading pro-choice lawyer said.[5] The ruling presented pro-choice advocates with three options, none hopeful. They could ask the Third Circuit to reconsider its decision en banc, hoping that the full circuit would reject the three-judge panel's handling of *Casey*. They could give up, accept the Third Circuit's ruling, and live with what they considered the severe obstacles and humiliations of the

---

*The statute made exceptions regarding spousal notification for spousal rape and where notification was likely to result in actual violence. Pennsylvania's law also outlawed abortions for selecting the sex of the child as well as certain very late-term abortions. Planned Parenthood decided not to challenge these provisions, however.

Pennsylvania law. Or they could appeal immediately to the Supreme Court, where one of the post-*Webster* appointees (Souter or Thomas) might give Rehnquist the fifth vote to bury *Roe*.

For Kathryn Kolbert, the ACLU lawyer who had won *Thornburgh* (the last big Pennsylvania abortion case) and who was in charge of *Casey*, the decision boiled down to a political calculation. Counting votes at the Supreme Court, she and other prominent pro-choice advocates felt certain that *Roe* would not survive another challenge. Kolbert also knew that, if *Casey* did not go to the Court, another case, involving some other state's post-*Webster* abortion law, would. Challenges to new abortion laws in Louisiana, Utah, Guam, and elsewhere were already far advanced in what ACLU and NARAL monitors called "the pipeline"— the judicial conduits funneling abortion cases from the statehouses in anti-abortion country through the lower federal courts toward the Justices in Washington.

The question looming over the pro-choice leaders was not whether *Roe* would fall, but when. And from their perspective, the answer, strangely enough, was the sooner the better. The decisive factor in their thinking was the upcoming presidential election. As abortion rights leaders assessed public opinion, a strong majority of Americans supported a woman's right to choose. This popular support meant that the seemingly inevitable legal disaster of losing *Roe* might at least be counterbalanced by an election-time backlash. In the most hopeful scenario, if the Court issued an anti-*Roe* opinion before the November 1992 election, it would touch off a reaction powerful enough to sweep pro-choice candidates into control of the White House, Congress, even state legislatures.

The key to this political strategy was speed. Unless Kolbert immediately appealed the Third Circuit's decision to the Supreme Court, none of the cases in the pipeline would arrive at the Court in time to be decided before the election. Eventually one of the abortion cases, perhaps even Pennsylvania's, would reach the Court, and the Justices would take another swing at *Roe*. But it would come too late to do any good.

One week after the Third Circuit's decision, Kolbert obtained the consent of her clients (Pennsylvania abortion clinic directors) to pursue the risky strategy of immediate appeal to the Supreme Court. And ten days after that, on November 7, more than two months before their filing deadline, Kolbert and her legal team submitted their cert. petition asking the Justices to decide a single question: "Has the Supreme Court overruled *Roe* v. *Wade*, holding that a woman's right to choose abortion is a fundamental right protected by the United States Constitution?"

The phrasing was carefully selected. Not only did the pro-choice advocates want a Court decision before the election, they wanted a clear and decisive referendum on *Roe*. If they were going to lose, they wanted to lose big—big enough to tilt national politics in their favor. They weren't just gambling; they were betting everything in the hope of avoiding another *Webster*-like muddle full of undramatic half-measures and confusing obfuscations.

In early December, Pennsylvania responded. The state agreed that the Court should hear *Casey*. It also cross-petitioned, asking the Justices to review as well the one aspect of the case it had lost— the Third Circuit's decision to strike down the spousal notification requirement.

The timing of Pennsylvania's response meant that, in the normal run of things, the Justices would consider whether to hear *Casey* at a Conference in late December. This left ample time for scheduling a spring argument and deciding the case before the 1992 summer adjournment, four months before the election.

Inside the Court, the cert. pool memo treated *Casey* diplomatically. Recognizing that the case's fate was not likely to hinge on a clerk's advice, the memo's author (from Justice Thomas's Chambers) filled in the bottom line with an unusual and tactful "No Recommendation" about whether to grant review.

Few doubted that the Court would hear the case. The Third Circuit's decision to trade in *Roe*'s strict scrutiny standard for O'Connor's undue burden model certainly warranted the Court's attention. In any event, the four anti-*Roe* Justices from *Webster* had enough votes to force another *Roe* referendum and, with Souter and Thomas having replaced Brennan and Marshall, they had every reason to do so.

Chief Justice Rehnquist (a consistent vote for hearing abortion cases) no doubt welcomed the very strong likelihood that either Souter or Thomas would give him the fifth vote to complete the job left unfinished in *Webster*. Yet he fumed at the pro-choicers' litigation strategy of using the Court—and his potential victory in *Casey*—as a pawn in their larger political game.

In response, the Chief may have decided to make some political chess moves of his own. He started "relisting" *Casey*—Court jargon for having

consideration of a pending cert. petition deferred until the next conference. Occasionally, a Justice will relist a case when the cert. vote is close
and he or she wants a little more time to review the pertinent issues. At
other times, a Justice will relist a case in order to complete work on a dissent from the denial of cert. Neither of these customary reasons applied
to the Chief's relisting of *Casey*.

In any event, after Rehnquist relisted *Casey* on January 10, 1992,
some inside the Court began to think that the Chief was deliberately
stalling the *Casey* cert. vote for long enough (about one month) that,
given the time necessary for briefing, the Court would have to push off
oral argument until the fall. This, of course, would delay a final ruling
until sometime in 1993, long after the election.

Apparently, this is exactly what almost came to pass. Although the
true motive of Rehnquist's relisting remains uncertain, Justice Blackmun
(reportedly joined by Justice Stevens) confronted the Chief and demanded that he let the *Casey* petition come to a vote. Rehnquist acquiesced and, on January 21, 1992, the day before *Roe's* nineteenth
anniversary, the Court announced it was accepting *Casey* for review. It
scheduled oral argument for April 22 — the very last argument day of the
term.

The Justices' action guaranteed that once again the Court would draw
to itself the full fury of the ever-escalating abortion debate. As the Court
braced for another bruising battle over *Roe*, abortion clinics suffered a
series of firebombings, and an anti-abortion zealot shot two clinic workers in Springfield, Missouri. Meanwhile, the "baby-does" of Randall
Terry's Operation Rescue moved from city to city blocking clinic en-
trances, stalking clinic workers, shouting at potential patients, and
wrestling with police—all on TV. For abortion workers, a fear of violence accompanied every trip to work, every stranger met on the street.
For their most determined opponents, that was the price for participating in mass murder.

As the street war flared, both sides in *Casey* orchestrated yet another
brief-writing campaign. A now familiar collection of right-to-life and religious groups submitted twenty-three briefs in defense of Pennsylvania's
law, most of them calling for *Roe's* overruling. In something of a surprise,
pro-choice organizations added only eleven amicus briefs on their side as
Kolbert—who had coordinated the slew of *Webster* amicus briefs—
changed tactics. Instead of overwhelming the Justices with the sheer

number and volume of pro-choice briefs, Planned Parenthood and the ACLU consolidated all their backers into eleven briefs, many of them signed by dozens of separate groups.

The purpose behind reducing the numbers was for Kolbert and her staff to keep a tight rein on what every brief said. Arguing *Casey* with an eye to the November elections meant framing the case exclusively as an up-or-down decision on *Roe*. Kolbert and the pro-choice brain trust wanted to make sure no well-meaning amicus spoiled their political strategy by making compromise arguments aimed at convincing Justice O'Connor, Kennedy, or perhaps Souter to strike down all or part of Pennsylvania's abortion law under some sort of watered-down version of *Roe*.

In her own brief, Kolbert certainly presented the Justices no such option. As she put it, *Casey* called on the Court either to "resoundingly reaffirm *Roe*" or else to "forsake its historic role as guardian of constitutional liberties." More specifically, the Court could either stand by *Roe's* strict scrutiny test for abortion regulations or it could scrap the right to reproductive privacy, apply the low-wattage rational relations test to these issues, and thus open the door (theoretically) to such horrible abuses of women's rights as forced sterilization. Kolbert made no effort to woo the fence-sitting, swing-voting O'Connor. To the contrary, while mounting a spirited defense of *Roe*, she derided O'Connor's "undue burden" approach as "vague," "unworkable," and "wholly inadequate" to protect women's fundamental rights.

On the other side, Pennsylvania took the opposite tack and tried to sidestep the *Roe* issue entirely. The state's logic closely followed the tortured path O'Connor had laid out in her early abortion dissents: the precedents interpreting *Roe* as requiring strict scrutiny were wrong; actually, *Roe* had established an undue burden approach to abortion regulation. Pitching its argument directly at O'Connor, Pennsylvania claimed that its new regulations were wholly consistent with *Roe*—at least as she read it.*

As in *Webster*, it was left to the solicitor general, now Kenneth Starr (currently Whitewater special prosecutor), to argue aggressively for *Roe's* overruling. In a brief relying heavily on Rehnquist's plurality opinion in

---

*This was the same tactic Missouri had used in *Webster*, where the state strained to reconcile its law with *Roe* while letting the United States argue that *Roe* should be overruled.

Webster and on Scalia's *Michael H.* view of due process, Starr asserted that "no credible foundation exists for the claim that a woman enjoys a fundamental right to abortion." Abortion regulations, he submitted, should have to be no more than "reasonably designed to advance a legitimate state interest"—the old low-wattage test.

At oral argument, on April 22, the respective parties stuck closely to their briefing strategies. In one practice session after another, Kolbert had steeled herself not to let the Justices' questions distract her from presenting *Casey* as a stark choice between reaffirming *Roe* or abandoning it. Two weeks earlier, the abortion rights movement had turned out more than 500,000 participants—by far the most ever—for a pro-choice march on Washington. Kolbert was determined to make it as hard as possible for the Court to undermine that political momentum.

The preparation proved well-advised. Kolbert's opening remarks met with a stony silence. For a remarkable seven minutes, the Justices let Kolbert lecture them on the "genius of *Roe*" and how any attempt to tinker with its strict scrutiny standard would be tantamount to overruling the entire case. Finally, Justice O'Connor broke in. "You're arguing the case as though all we have before us is whether to apply stare decisis and preserve *Roe* in all its aspects," she observed with undisguised annoyance. "Nevertheless, we granted certiorari on some specific questions in this case. Do you plan to address any of those in your argument?"

As became apparent over the remainder of the argument, Kolbert's answer was basically no, even after Justice Kennedy joined O'Connor in suggesting that Kolbert compromise on her strict scrutiny reading of *Roe*. Kolbert's insistence annoyed Kennedy especially. Glaring at her over the bench, he practically accused her of irresponsible lawyering— alienating her potential swing votes. "If you are going to argue that *Roe* can survive only in its most rigid formulation, that is an election you can make as counsel," Kennedy said with obvious disapproval. "I am suggesting to you that is not the only logical possibility in this case." Still, Kolbert refused to budge.

Neither Ernest Preate, Jr., the lawyer representing Pennsylvania, nor Kenneth Starr, on behalf of the United States, received a friendlier reception. Preate had barely opened his mouth when Justice Blackmun asked contemptuously whether he had even read *Roe*. O'Connor followed Blackmun's outburst with half a dozen extremely skeptical questions trying to pinpoint what state interest could possibly be served by forcing a woman to notify her husband before having an abortion. Was it "to try to preserve the marriage?" she asked sarcastically. "It's a curious sort of provision, isn't it?" Preate spent almost his entire twenty minutes trying to defend this aspect of the statute.

The final ten minutes belonged to the solicitor general, and Starr spent nearly all of them trying to dodge the potential implications of his argument for overturning *Roe*. He refused to answer a series of questions from Justices Stevens and O'Connor about whether the United States was now endorsing the right-to-life position (explicitly rejected in *Roe*) that a fetus is a constitutional "person within the meaning of the Fourteenth Amendment."*

Later, Starr also tried to sidestep when Justice Souter pressed him about what sorts of regulations would be permissible under the rational basis test Starr touted. But Souter insisted on an answer. After all, the Justice observed, "you're asking the Court to adopt a standard and I think we ought to know where the standard would take us." Finally, Starr conceded that "the rational basis standard would, in fact, allow considerable leeway to the States, if it saw fit"—indeed, any regulation that was not "arbitrary or capricious."

Overall, the *Casey* argument was testy but not surprising. Liberal clerks took some solace from O'Connor's obviously substantial concerns about Pennsylvania's spousal notification requirement. Souter apparently shared those concerns and also seemed uneasy about the sweeping implications of switching to Starr's low-wattage standard of review.

But nothing in the argument changed the air of inevitability that hung over the case. On the eve of the all-important *Casey* conference, clerk calculations varied little from those of the pro-choice strategists. O'Connor and Souter were superfluous. With Thomas (who sat sphinxlike during the argument) added to Rehnquist's four votes from *Webster*, *Roe* was doomed. The only question was whether the conservative majority would do away with *Roe* openly or, instead, quietly eviscerate it as the Chief had attempted in *Webster*.

Exactly where each Justice stood at the *Casey* conference on Friday, April 24, is not fully known—and may never be known definitively. This is largely because the *Casey* "discussion" was perfunctory, even by the

---

*If fetuses were such "persons," most abortions would have to be considered homicides and presumably would make abortion-seeking women and their doctors subject to criminal prosecution.

low standards of Rehnquist Court discourse. One well-informed clerk doubted that any Justice "said more than two sentences." And, thus, when they were initially deciding one of the most important cases in a generation, what the Justices were actually thinking—either about Pennsylvania's regulations or about whether to overrule *Roe*—was left mostly unstated.

In a 1976 essay, Rehnquist had observed that the Chief Justice has a "notable advantage over his brethren" in the power to frame each case at conference.[6] In *Casey*, Rehnquist used that advantage to steer the discussion away from *Roe* and toward a relative silence. Focusing on outcome rather than theory, he said simply that he would uphold all Pennsylvania's regulations. Reaching this result, Rehnquist continued, would require overruling two long-standing abortion precedents (*Akron* and *Thornburgh*), which had struck down similar regulations in the past. Yet, despite having five likely votes for overruling *Roe*, Rehnquist claimed (as in *Webster*) that overruling *Roe* itself was not necessary.

The Justices' comments following Rehnquist's opening, cryptic as most were, fell into three general categories. Justices White, Scalia, Kennedy, and Thomas agreed with the Chief that the Court should uphold the entire Pennsylvania statute. Scalia stated specifically that they should do so using the rational relations standard—code for overturning *Roe*.

Justice Blackmun "passed" when his turn came to speak at the conference, although his antipathy to Pennsylvania's regulations was a given. Justice Stevens stated specifically that he would strike down the state's twenty-four-hour waiting period and the spousal notification provision. Both Justices, of course, were also for maintaining *Roe*.

Justices O'Connor and Souter were in the middle. O'Connor (as at oral argument) was troubled by at least Pennsylvania's spousal notification requirement. Souter had even deeper and broader concerns about the statute and volunteered that the spousal notification provision flunked even the undue burden test.[7]

One Conference tally put the vote at 5–4, meaning five votes to uphold Pennsylvania's law, presumably by either overruling *Roe* explicitly or "pulling a *Webster*" and adopting a rational relations standard without addressing *Roe* explicitly. What the opposing four Justices shared in common was a belief that at least one aspect of Pennsylvania's law was (or in O'Connor's case, probably was) unconstitutional. Beyond that, they were divided.

In deciding who would write the majority opinion, Rehnquist again followed his script from *Webster*. After virtually ensuring that the Conference itself would reach no firm rationale for upholding Pennsylvania's law, the Chief kept the writing assignment for himself and, with it, the all-important power to draft the majority's approach to *Roe*.

Almost immediately after conference, however, the process for deciding *Casey* took a stunning and momentous turn. The catalyst was Justice Souter.

Souter had come to the case with a still open mind. As late as oral argument he had not firmly decided how to vote. Then, late in the afternoon of the day before conference, pondering the case in his office, he settled on an answer.[8]

Among the last items Souter considered was one of the memos he had received the previous July from his outgoing clerks presenting their individual views about whether he should vote to overrule *Roe*. Only one of those four memos made the case for reaffirming *Roe*, and Souter turned to it now.

In two respects, the memo carefully tracked the thinking of Souter's judicial hero, the patron saint of the incrementalist common law method of judging, Justice Harlan. First, it emphasized that *Roe* was simply an extension of the idea—originally set forth in Harlan's *Poe* v. *Ullman* dissent—that the flexible, "living" principle of due process liberty protected a couple's intimate decisions about reproduction against intrusion by the state. In other words, *Roe* was not revolutionary or the illegitimate offspring of liberal judicial activists. Rather, it was the natural product of Harlan's much admired approach to due process.

Second, the memo relied on a Harlanesque approach to stare decisis. True to his conservative principles, Harlan demanded especially compelling reasons before voting to overrule precedents, even ones with which he strongly disagreed. If *Roe* was, at worst, a misapplication of Harlan's own flexible approach to due process, then shouldn't it be reaffirmed? The ruling was nearly twenty years old, and in the interim a world of expectations had built up around it. In the absence of some truly fundamental error, surely it should stand.

Related to the issue of stare decisis was that of the Court's own legitimacy. Thirty years earlier Harlan had written: "A basic change in the law upon a ground no firmer than a change in our membership invites the popular misconception that this institution is little different from the two political branches of the Government. No misconception could do more lasting injury to this Court and to the system which it is our abiding mission to serve."⁹

For a decade, two successive Republican presidents, through five separate appointments (including Souter's own), had tried to change the Court's membership with the nearly single-minded intention of overturning *Roe*. In the view of Souter's clerk, to acquiesce in this targeting, to contribute to its success, would be to advance the very thinking that so troubled Harlan: that law is not a matter of enduring principle but simply a creature of which presidential appointees sit on the Court at any given time.

Such arguments had an obvious appeal for Souter. Harlan was his self-proclaimed judicial hero and, at his confirmation hearings, Souter had specifically endorsed Harlan's view of both due process and stare decisis. He especially shared Harlan's concern for the Court's institutional integrity. As a law student, Souter had trained in Harvard's "legal process" school of constitutional interpretation—one that put a premium on the Court's role as a "forum of principle," an anchor against the pull of politics. To the extent that overruling *Roe* undermined the integrity of that forum, it ran hard against Souter's grain.

The memo's pro-*Roe* arguments also fit with Souter's personal inclinations. He possessed a powerful regard for legal tradition and a particular reverence for the judgments of those who had preceded him at the Court. Unlike the other conservatives, Souter openly admired Justice Brennan (whom he had replaced) and cultivated warm friendships with both Brennan and Blackmun. Souter never felt the broad contempt either for them or for the liberal decisions of the Warren and Burger eras that fueled many of the attacks on *Roe*. Counterrevolution simply wasn't in his nature.

On the day before the *Casey* conference, these factors led Souter to conclude that he could not support overruling *Roe* and its recognition of a constitutional right to abortion. Then, shortly after conference, he reached an even more important decision. Uneasy about the results of the conference, Souter decided to sound out Justice O'Connor (whose view of *Casey* seemed potentially compatible with his own) about working together to steer the Court toward some compromise resolution of the abortion debate.

Justice O'Connor welcomed his approach. She hated the abortion cases and considered them destructive for both the Court and the country. From a personal standpoint, as her brother described it, the abortion issue put O'Connor in a "no-win situation" where "half the people will hate her no matter what she does."[10] Like Souter, O'Connor revered Justice Harlan and fancied herself a disciple of his "restrained," precedent-honoring approach to law. In *Hodgson* (the Minnesota parental notification case of 1990), she already had struck down one state regulation as violating a woman's right to obtain an abortion. Standing by some revised version of *Roe*—and striking down part of Pennsylvania's abortion code in the process—was something she could reconcile with her long-stated views. If somehow that compromise could become the basis of a truce in the war over abortion law, she was willing to promote it.

The key, as O'Connor recognized, was Justice Kennedy. To be successful, any centrist coalition would need his third vote to secure the balance of power between Blackmun and Stevens (on one side) and Rehnquist, White, Scalia, and Thomas (on the other). Although O'Connor (who had seen Kennedy's anti-*Roe* letter to Rehnquist in *Webster*) was not sanguine about getting his support, both she and Souter agreed that Kennedy's comments at the *Casey* conference left him presently uncommitted on the issue of *Roe*.

Kennedy, for his part, was apparently open to persuasion. From the outset of *Casey*, he had broken his usual practice of having all his clerks participate in every case and had assigned *Casey* exclusively to only one: Michael Dorf, an intense and gifted disciple of Harvard Law Professor Laurence Tribe, a leading academic defender of *Roe*. Kennedy could be sure Dorf would make the strongest possible case for *Roe* and, in selecting him, the Justice seemed almost to be signaling a willingness to rethink his views from the ground up.

In many ways, *Casey* forced Kennedy to confront a conflict within himself. One side of the Justice was a devout practicing Catholic with a deep personal aversion to abortion who also had honed an intellectual opposition to *Roe* over many semesters teaching constitutional law as an adjunct professor in Sacramento.

On the other side, however, was the Kennedy that hard-nosed conservatives feared and mocked—the one who liked to be liked, thought of himself as reasonable and judicious, and showed flashes of attachment to the idealistic judicial pronouncements of the Warren era. This Justice

Kennedy seemed increasingly to view the judiciary as an oasis of rectitude within a regrettably fractious and partisan society. And, within that oasis, he seemed to define the essence of principled "judging" as a self-conscious separation of his own personal morality from the interpretation of law. "The hard fact is that sometimes we must make decisions we do not like," Kennedy had written in the flag-burning case. To the conservatives' dismay, that declaration was very nearly becoming his credo.[11]

Kennedy's penchant for self-denial had already played a decisive role in another potentially watershed 1992 case. The issue in *Lee* v. *Weisman* was whether the use of a nondenominational prayer at a public junior-high school graduation ceremony violated the Constitution's ban on "establishment" of religion. Previously, Kennedy had joined other conservatives in attacking the Court's establishment clause precedents as "hostile" to religion and suggested their "substantial revision."[12] At conference in *Weisman*, he followed up those views, forming a narrow majority with Rehnquist, White, Scalia, and Thomas to permit the graduation prayer despite thirty years of precedent to the contrary.

But after Rehnquist assigned Kennedy the opinion, he experienced a change of heart. Despite strong personal religious convictions, Kennedy couldn't bring himself to write an opinion overturning Warren era landmarks enforcing a strict separation of church and state. Kennedy went back to the Chief, told him that an opinion upholding the graduation prayer "just wouldn't write," and switched sides. Indeed, as the Court heard argument in *Casey*, Kennedy was working on the majority opinion in *Weisman*, coming out the opposite way from how he originally had voted and leaving untouched the Warren Court rulings he had criticized in the past.

O'Connor and Souter were appealing to much the same qualities in Kennedy that had led to his *Weisman* switch. Reaffirming a modified version of *Roe* would confirm Kennedy as a "principled" jurist. He would be standing by precedent despite his personal views. And he would be contributing to his perception of the Court's proper role as a mediator in society's most divisive disputes. In short, joining O'Connor and Souter in finding some stable, defensible middle ground on *Roe* was an endeavor Kennedy could sell to himself as truly judicious and advancing the country's welfare.

Together, Souter, O'Connor, and Kennedy mapped out a plan for a joint separate opinion. First, they agreed to reaffirm what they deemed to be "the essential holding of *Roe* v. *Wade*": the idea that women possess a constitutionally protected right to abortion. At the same time, they decided to replace *Roe's* strict scrutiny standard with a version of O'Connor's undue burden test and, thereby, give states greater latitude in advancing their legitimate interests in maternal health and fetal life. Applying that standard to Pennsylvania's abortion regulations, they agreed to strike down only the spousal notification requirement.*

The trio also decided to keep their venture a closely guarded secret from the other Justices, including the Chief—who was drafting what he presumed would be the majority opinion. Fearing the pressure that would surely follow the revelation of his defection, Kennedy went so far as to instruct Dorf to conceal their *Casey* work even from his own co-clerks. According to one reliable source, Dorf encrypted his computer to avoid the possibility of spying by more conservative colleagues in the Chambers. (They, not surprisingly, were furious and frustrated at being cut out of what seemed a history-making case.)

As Rehnquist was expected to circulate his draft before the end of May, the three Justices and their clerks worked furiously to prepare their silent coup. Kennedy was assigned to write the opening section, which included their explicit endorsement of the *Roe*-based idea that due process "liberty" included a right to abortion. Souter's job was to craft their explanation for why the principles of stare decisis argued, almost irrefutably, for reaffirming *Roe*. And O'Connor took on the section most natural to her—setting out a definitive version of the "undue burden" standard and applying that standard to Pennsylvania's law.

As the writing process unfolded, the trio visited with each other almost every day, discussing their respective progress, assembling the various pieces, and keeping the enterprise on track.† Kennedy, the most skittish of the three, needed almost constant reassurance that he was doing the right thing. Many days, he could be seen standing alone in the flagstone courtyard outside his Chambers rubbing his face and arms in a

---

*This result was the same as the Third Circuit's, but the trio's approach would differ in important details.

†Some press reports have suggested that the joint opinion was largely the handiwork of Kennedy's clerk (Dorf) and another Laurence Tribe disciple, Peter Rubin, who worked on the case for Souter. No doubt these liberal clerks provided enthusiastic and effective support for their bosses' decision to reaffirm the essence of *Roe*. In both Chambers, however, the Justices themselves did an unusually large share of the actual opinion drafting.

very public display of agonizing. Kennedy seemed to be wrestling with an internal paradox. He continued to doubt the wisdom of retaining a right to abortion; yet he believed that if it was to be done, it must be done boldly and in broad strokes. Out in the courtyard the bold side was winning, while others at the Court were left to speculate about the subject of Kennedy's ruminations.

The Chief, meanwhile, finished his draft majority and circulated it on May 27. It was a *Webster* repeat, the worst nightmare of pro-choice forces outside the Court. Using the low-wattage rational relations test, Rehnquist upheld all Pennsylvania's abortion restrictions. But while replacing *Roe*'s legal mainspring, he said nothing about overruling it. As one clerk remarked, Rehnquist treated *Roe* like "a dead dog" while pretending it was still alive.

Rehnquist's draft infuriated the liberals in the building. Blackmun's Chambers, in particular, saw the Chief's covert burial of *Roe* as conceived purely for the benefit of Republican candidates, including President Bush, in the November election.* Blackmun and his clerks set to work on their own political countermeasure: a dissent (much as in *Webster*) that proclaimed the death of *Roe* from the rooftops while decrying Rehnquist's "hypocrisy" for pretending otherwise.

Justice O'Connor was also disappointed in the Chief's opinion. Perhaps from friendship, she had held out a small hope, however unrealistic, that he would produce an opinion she would find palatable and render her joint opinion unnecessary. Rehnquist's circulation buried those thoughts, and the troika quickly moved forward with plans to circulate their own nearly ready draft.

The trio dropped their bombshell on June 3.† It was a stunning document. The woman Justice who had once been among *Roe*'s harshest critics had combined with a Justice previously on record favoring *Roe*'s overruling and an ascetic New England bachelor nominated to the Court for his conservative reputation to produce a sweeping endorse-

---

*There was also wide speculation at the time, amplified by some former Rehnquist clerks, that the Chief intended to retire if Bush were reelected. If that was true, Rehnquist's *Casey* tactics also served this personal goal.

†Contrary to some reports, the three-justice opinion was not a complete surprise. A few days before its circulation, Kennedy had visited Blackmun's lonely perch in the upstairs Justices' library to inform him that a centrist opinion was in the works. He may also have given advance notice to Rehnquist. Otherwise, though, and certainly in its details, the three-Justice opinion did come as a shock.

ment of *Roe*'s basic premises and a dramatic plea for both the Court and country to accept the right to abortion as settled law.

The Justices' monumental aspirations appeared boldly on their opinion's first page, where, in an obvious break from practice, they declared the entire document to be coauthored. While this byline reflected the Justices' unusual collaboration, it also self-consciously echoed the legendary coauthorship of *Cooper* v. *Aaron*. Just as the Court spoke unanimously in trying to quell resistance to *Brown,* the centrist trio called in unison for acceptance of their version of *Roe.**

Beneath the byline, the opinion's opening line confirmed the breadth of the trio's intentions. "Liberty finds no refuge in a jurisprudence of doubt," it declared in a line Kennedy had crafted with characteristic grandiloquence.[13] The trio meant to dispel such doubts, both the doubts that had clouded its due process doctrine and those *Roe* had cast upon the Court's own reputation and legitimacy.

The trio began (in a section Kennedy drafted) by announcing their shared—and grand—vision for due process liberty. It was a full, almost passionate, embrace of all *Roe*'s underlying principles, starting with Justice Harlan's flexible approach to due process liberty and including the entire range of cases that collectively made up the modern right to privacy. The authors discounted the fears of Scalia and other critics of substantive due process who saw the doctrine as a potentially limitless warrant for judges to impose their personal values on the Constitution. In the trio's view, interpreting the due process clause—defining its "realm of personal liberty which the government may not enter"— merely called upon judges to exercise the time-honed faculty of "reasoned judgment." And in their reasoned judgment, the Constitution's protection of liberty was broad enough to include the right to abortion.

The opinion's rhetoric soared. At the heart of the zone of privacy that due process protected, Kennedy waxed on, stood "the right to define one's own concept of existence, of meaning, of the universe, and of the mystery of life." A woman's choice whether to have an abortion—a choice "unique to the human condition and so unique to the law"—fit

---

*Actually, the analogy to *Cooper,* much ballyhooed in the press, was deeply flawed. There is a considerable distance between three Justices pleading for acceptance and nine Justices unanimously demanding obedience. The joint opinion in *Casey* much more closely resembled the coalition of Stewart, Powell, and Stevens in *Gregg* v. *Georgia,* the 1976 decision reallowing the death penalty in limited circumstances. In both *Gregg* and *Casey,* a surprise centrist coalition emerged after Conference and sought to force the Court toward a compromise position on a highly polarized issue.

readily within this construct. A pregnant woman's "suffering," Kennedy concluded, "is too intimate and personal for the State to insist" on child-birth out of "its own vision of the woman's role." Thus, while "some of us as individuals find abortion offensive to our most basic principles of morality," ultimately whatever "reservations any of us may have in reaf-firming the central holding of *Roe* are outweighed by the explication of personal liberty we have given combined with the force of *stare decisis*."

With that transition, it was left to Justice Souter to explain next why "principles of institutional integrity and the rule of *stare decisis*" com-manded adherence to *Roe*. This section began unremarkably, explaining the various factors to be considered before overruling a prior opinion. Had that opinion become "unworkable"? Would overruling the prece-dent create a "special hardship" for those who had relied on it? Had the factual understandings justifying the precedent so changed or come to be seen so differently as to render the old rule obsolete or clearly mistaken?

One by one, Souter addressed these factors and concluded, as *Roe* sup-porters had argued for years, that none weighed in favor of overruling *Roe*. No factual or legal developments had undermined the soundness of the decision, and although a few changes in medical technology had un-dermined some aspects of the trimester framework, these changes had "no bearing on the validity of *Roe*'s central holding."

According to Souter, far from eroding *Roe*'s premises, time had deeply ingrained its assumptions into the nation's social fabric. "For two decades of economic and social developments," he wrote, "people have organized intimate relationships and made choices that define their views of themselves and their places in society, in reliance on the avail-ability of abortion in the event that contraception should fail." In that light, as liberals had argued for years, the trio concluded that "the stronger argument is for affirming *Roe*'s central holding, with whatever degree of personal reluctance any of us may have, not for overruling it."*

For Souter, however, this balancing of the appropriate factors was mere prologue for a more fundamental discussion of how overruling *Roe*

---

*Souter tried at length to distinguish *Roe* from the Court's two great twentieth-century overrul-ings: the overruling of the right to freedom of contract in the mid-1930s (the famous "switch in time") and the overruling of *Plessy* v. *Ferguson* in *Brown*. According to Souter, both overrulings could be explained as judicial reevaluations in light of new factual understandings—a new under-standing of economics in the 1930s and a new understanding of the stigmatizing effect of segrega-tion by 1954. This revisionist history drew criticism both from conservative dissenters on the Court and from academics. See, e.g., Morton J. Horwitz, "The Constitution of Change: Legal Fundamen-tality without Legal Fundamentalism," 107 *Harvard Law Rev.* 32 (1993).

would exact a "terrible price" from the Court's own power and legitimacy. The Court's authority flowed from its reputation for making rulings "grounded truly in principle, not . . . compromises with social and political pressures." Overruling *Roe*, he argued, would destroy this essential claim to principled action.

As Souter explained in the most remarkable paragraphs of the joint opinion:

> Where, in the performance of its judicial duties, the Court decides a case in such a way as to resolve the sort of intensely divisive controversy reflected in *Roe* and those rare, comparable cases, its decision has a dimension that the resolution of the normal case does not carry. It is the dimension present whenever the Court's interpretation of the Constitution calls the contending sides of a national controversy to end their national division by accepting a common mandate rooted in the Constitution.
>
> The Court is not asked to do this very often, having thus addressed the Nation only twice in our lifetime, in the decisions of *Brown* and *Roe*. But when the Court does act in this way, its decision requires an equally rare precedential force to counter the inevitable efforts to overturn it and to thwart its implementation. Some of those efforts may be mere unprincipled emotional reactions; others may proceed from principles worthy of profound respect. But whatever the premises of opposition may be, only the most convincing justification under accepted standards of precedent could suffice to demonstrate that a later decision overruling the first was anything but a surrender to political pressure, and an unjustified repudiation of the principle on which the Court staked its authority in the first instance. So to overrule under fire in the absence of the most compelling reason to reexamine a watershed decision would subvert the Court's legitimacy beyond any serious question.

In the trio's view, the opponents of *Roe* had failed to advance the "most compelling" reasons for overruling, and thus "a decision to overrule *Roe*'s essential holding under the existing circumstances would address error, if error there was, at the cost of both profound and unnecessary damage to the Court's legitimacy and the Nation's commitment to the rule of law."

The final sections of the joint opinion were devoted to explaining exactly what the three authors meant in reaffirming "*Roe*'s essential holding" and the consequences of that definition for the specific abortion regulations under challenge in *Casey*. As the opinion made clear, the trio's view of *Roe*'s "essential holding" differed substantially from the Court's own prior interpretations of *Roe*. According to the joint opinion, the Court's post-*Roe* precedents had given too little weight to the State's interests in maternal health and fetal life. For that reason, the trio "reject[ed] the trimester framework" and replaced that scheme for balancing the competing interests of the pregnant woman and the State with a modified version of O'Connor's undue burden standard.

As the trio now described their new undue burden test, the crucial tipping point would be viability.* Before viability, states were barred from imposing undue burdens on abortion, which the trio further defined as all state regulations that had "the purpose or effect of placing a substantial obstacle in the path of a woman seeking an abortion of a non-viable fetus." After viability, as in *Roe*, the state could regulate abortion, even ban it, as long as exceptions were made where the life or health of the pregnant mother was at risk.†

Turning to the specifics of Pennsylvania's abortion law, the trio concluded that only the spousal notification provision—which they described as "repugnant to our present understanding of marriage and of the nature of the rights secured by the Constitution"—in fact imposed an undue burden. They also thought it a "close question" whether the mandatory twenty-four-hour waiting period passed this test. While recognizing the significant costs and inconveniences imposed by the waiting period, the trio decided that "the record before us" did not contain sufficient evidence to prove that the twenty-four-hour wait was sufficiently onerous to qualify as a "substantial obstacle." They let it stand, pending further proof of its actual effects. With less reservation, the trio also okayed the state's various informed consent requirements, even though doing so meant overruling those parts of two prior decisions (*Akron* and *Thornburgh*) that had invalidated similar provisions in the past. And finally, the trio upheld the state's parental notification scheme.

---

*Viability, of course, was also crucial to *Roe*. Thus, the trio's revision of the trimester framework was limited to doing away with *Roe*'s distinction between the first and second trimesters in evaluating state regulations designed to protect maternal health.

†It is interesting that this formulation of the undue burden standard, certainly more abortion friendly than O'Connor's previous formulations, closely resembled the proposal her clerk Jane Stromseth had suggested in *Webster*. Whether her suggestion was the model for O'Connor's reformulation in *Casey* I do not know.

The circulation of the joint opinion devastated *Roe*'s strongest opponents and, despite its approval of almost all Pennsylvania's regulations, was received as a virtual miracle by most of the liberals. Both Rehnquist and Scalia scrambled to undo the damage. The Chief invited Kennedy for one of his periodic walks around the Court building in the hope of wooing him back into the anti-*Roe* fold. Scalia reportedly visited Kennedy at home to plead with him to change his mind, again. As liberals gathered secondhand, Scalia initially appealed to his and Kennedy's shared anti-abortion Catholic beliefs and, failing in that, warned Kennedy that he was destined to become another Blackmun—a sentimentalist scorned by both conservatives and serious legal thinkers generally.*

The liberals certainly feared that these importunings would pry the ambivalent Kennedy away from the grand venture on which he had embarked.† But they did not, and the process of reaction to the joint opinion quickly set in.

On June 17, two weeks after the three Justices' circulation, Rehnquist produced a response. His main line of attack was to ridicule the notion that the trio actually had adhered to their much vaunted principle of stare decisis. Hadn't they replaced *Roe*'s strict scrutiny with an undue burden test, jettisoned the trimester framework, and overruled much of two decisions that purported to implement *Roe*? In light of the joint opinion, Rehnquist concluded, "*Roe* continues to exist, but only in the way a storefront on a western movie set exists: a mere facade to give the illusion of reality."

A far more vicious critique arrived six days later from Scalia, who (as in *Webster*) felt free to speak his mind now that Rehnquist had failed again to achieve a majority for his plan to scuttle *Roe* indirectly. Two aspects of the joint opinion received especially harsh treatment. First, Scalia mocked Kennedy's much labored over opening line, "Liberty finds no refuge in a jurisprudence of doubt." To read this sentence in an opinion "which calls upon federal district judges to apply an 'undue burden' standard as doubtful in application as it is unprincipled in origin . . . is

---

*Reportedly, at least some members of the trio did fear opening themselves up to the incessant protests that had dogged Blackmun since he authored *Roe*. Some have speculated, reasonably I believe, that the idea of jointly authoring *Casey* stemmed in part from a desire to avoid having a single author-Justice suffer the consequences that were sure to follow reaffirming the right to abortion.

†According to one published report, Blackmun sought to reassure Kennedy by showing him some of the passionate pro-*Roe* letters he had received from Catholics. While unconfirmed, this story rings true.

really more than one should have to bear," he fumed. The new standard is "inherently manipulable and will prove hopelessly unworkable in practice." Reason, Scalia taunted, "finds no refuge in this jurisprudence of confusion."

Scalia was equally derisive of Souter's essay on the necessity of not overruling *Roe* "under fire" in order to preserve the Court's legitimacy. "I cannot agree with, indeed I am appalled by, the Court's suggestion that the decision whether to stand by an erroneous decision must be strongly influenced—*against* overruling, no less—by the substantial and continuing public opposition the decision has generated." The Court's real focus, Scalia continued, should be not on "the hopeless task of predicting public perception—a job not for lawyers but for political campaign managers" but on ending the real threat to its legitimacy, exemplified by *Roe*, of abandoning proper constitutional interpretation in favor of imposing the "value judgments" of individual Justices on the American people.

A recurrent theme of Scalia's opinion was the comparison, a favorite of *Roe* critics (especially right-to-lifers), between *Roe* and *Dred Scott*. In the 1850s, Scalia claimed, Chief Justice Taney had presumed the Court could somehow settle the national debate over slavery by (as the joint opinion described its own aspiration) "calling the contending sides of national controversy to end their national division." The Court's arrogation of power in *Dred Scott* had only hastened the tragedy of Civil War, and Scalia saw a similar disaster and "dishonor" in its current endeavor. He ended with a poignant description of the Taney portrait that hangs prominently at the Harvard Law School, "an expression of profound sadness and disillusionment" on his face. Taney, too, had thought he was (as the joint opinion put it) calling opposing sides to accept "a common mandate rooted in the Constitution." Yet, within two years, his once great reputation lay shattered, and he posed, his "right hand hanging limply, almost lifelessly, beside the inner arm of the chair."

Aside from its poetic qualities, the image was a subtle personal jibe at Kennedy, the former ally who had now deserted Scalia in the two most important cases of the term—*Casey* and *Weisman*. At the *Webster* conference, it had been Kennedy who forcefully drew the analogy between *Roe* and the nightmare of *Dred Scott*. Scalia wanted Kennedy to feel the ghost of Taney—broken and reviled—over his shoulder now.

During the next two days, the trio received gentler replies from Justices Stevens and Blackmun. Stevens circulated an opinion commending the three for reaffirming the basic right to abortion and recognizing the "enormous" social costs of overruling *Roe* "at this late date." He limited his criticism mainly to the joint opinion's acceptance (albeit provisional) of Pennsylvania's twenty-four-hour waiting period—which, in Stevens's view, should not have passed the trio's own undue burden test.

Blackmun's opinion exuded a powerful sense of vindication. After *Webster,* he recalled, "all that remained between the promise of *Roe* and the darkness of the plurality was a single, flickering flame. . . . But now, just when so many expected the darkness to fall, the flame has grown bright." The trio's "fervent view of individual liberty and the force of *stare decisis,*" he declared triumphantly, was "an act of personal courage and constitutional principle."* Naturally, Blackmun still defended *Roe* in its entirety and chastened O'Connor, Kennedy, and Souter for not striking down more of Pennsylvania's onerous regulations. Overall, though, he tried to minimize their differences.[14]

The real target of Blackmun's opinion was Rehnquist. In Blackmun's view, the Chief's continued pretense that his own opinion would not overrule *Roe*—like his earlier efforts to push *Casey* off until the next term—was an outrageous political ploy. As he had in *Webster,* Blackmun lambasted Rehnquist for the dishonesty of his position. This time, however, he went considerably further, countering the Chief with his own overtly partisan message. "I am eighty-three years old," Blackmun reminded prospective voters. "I cannot remain on this Court forever, and when I do step down, the confirmation process for my successor well may focus on the issue before us today. That, I regret, may be exactly where the choice between the two worlds [of a Court that protects fundamental liberties, or not] will be made."

The authors of the joint opinion agreed not to respond to any of the other opinions. The overriding purpose of their enterprise was to move beyond the terrible divisions that the abortion cases had caused both inside and outside the Court. They would only undermine that purpose by trading footnote sniper fire with their critics.

Rehnquist, though, decided to make a major change to his opinion (which White, Scalia, and Thomas joined).† On June 26, he circulated

---

*It was important that both Blackmun and Stevens joined the sections of the three-Justice opinion endorsing Harlan's view of due process and defending *Roe* on stare decisis grounds. Thus, these sections of the joint opinion carried the weight of a Court majority.

†Kennedy had held some hope that Thomas would join the centrist opinion, but discussions with Thomas proved unavailing.

a new draft definitively stating, "We believe that Roe was wrongly decided and that it can and should be overruled."

Rehnquist's about-face called for an equal revision in Blackmun's opinion, yet as his Chambers raced to rework their draft, the Chief declared that Casey would be announced and the term would end three days later, on June 29. That schedule gave Blackmun little more than a day to revamp his largely obsolete criticisms of Rehnquist's old draft.

On the twenty-seventh, Blackmun circulated a new version that replaced his charges of intellectual dishonesty with a section that began, "At long last, THE CHIEF JUSTICE admits it." Notably, Blackmun did not expunge the electioneering reference to his own age and approaching retirement, despite Rehnquist's having ended his political gambit. Even a rare personal appeal from Justice Stevens failed to convince Blackmun to make the change. The residue of anger was too great, the time for reconsideration too short, and the reference—originally a clerk's flourish—remained.

The morning of June 29, preannounced as the Court's last sitting, was sheer pandemonium. By 9:30 the stage was set for what everyone expected to be among the most important rulings in a generation. On the Court's marble apron, clusters of television lights trained on unattended microphones intensified the glare of an already sunny morning. A dozen or so police officers from the Court's own force milled about, casting occasional glances at the growing crowd of pro-choice and right-to-life activists shouting and waving signs: ABORTION STOPS A BEATING HEART 4400 TIMES A DAY; KEEP ABORTION SAFE & LEGAL.

Inside, past the massive bronze doors, through the metal detectors that had come to grace the Great Hall, in the intimate grandeur of the courtroom, every seat was filled. Justice Blackmun's four clerks had arrived a full hour ahead to capture the choicest spots in the clerk section. Kennedy's clerk Michael Dorf, raccoon eyed from sleeplessness, flitted nervously from conversation to conversation. In the pews reserved for special guests of the Justices, Mrs. Byron White exchanged a few forced-looking pleasantries with Dottie Blackmun.

Amid the sea of dark blue or gray suits, retired Justice William Brennan, eighty-five, frail from a stroke, announced his presence with a brassy sport coat. Those in the audience fell to speculating whether he had come because another of his cherished legal castles was about to fall.

Resting his cane between his legs, Brennan received effusive greetings, most notably from Solicitor General Starr, whose avowed purpose in office was to nullify the whole of Brennan's lifework on the bench. As he had in more active days, Brennan handled the business with a politician's bonhomie.

The audience was filled with ex-clerks of recent vintage. Three former Blackmun clerks, three more of Scalia's, one of Kennedy's eyed one another warily. Lawyers and activists from both sides of the abortion debate nodded greetings to their allies and fidgeted nervously. Randall Terry, the head of Operation Rescue, sat at the end of a pew of high schoolers.

Behind the scenes, the trio prepared to make public their stunning alliance. Swept up in the epochal feeling of the moment, in an amazing act of self-promotion, Justice Kennedy invited a reporter to shadow him for the morning. Looking out at the gathered crowd from his Chambers' window, Kennedy became wistful: "Sometimes you don't know if you're Caesar about to cross the Rubicon," he mused almost in a whisper, "or Captain Queeg cutting your own tow line." At 9:50, Kennedy excused himself. "I generally brood . . . just before we go on," he explained. "It's a moment of quiet around here to search your soul and your conscience."[15]

At 10:00 sharp, the marshal of the Court, Al Wong, announced the ascension of the Justices to the bench, and, after ruling in another case, Chief Justice Rehnquist announced that the judgment of the Court in *Casey* would be delivered by Justices O'Connor, Kennedy, and Souter. The crowd stirred, surprised that Rehnquist had not commanded the majority, confused that three Justices were to announce this opinion (or any opinion) jointly.

Then O'Connor began, her face pressed into one hand, a small tremor in her voice, "We conclude the central holding of *Roe* should be affirmed." Kennedy picked up the thread, reading parts of the section he wrote, leaning forward, beseeching with his voice that the audience— the leaders of both sides—accept their compromise judgment. Then Souter, with his sharp New England accent, he too imploring, delivered their lecture on precedent and the Court's fragile authority.

In the lawyers' section, the pro-choice advocates looked at one another, trying to make sense of the ruling from these snippets, wondering whether the Court had confounded them again or whether, incredibly, they had won. Closer to the back, Randall Terry looked near to explosion. Straight before him, Justice Blackmun was rocking, a slight smile on his face.

With the trio's plea for reconciliation and acceptance still hanging in the air, Rehnquist starting reading excerpts from his dissent, deriding the joint opinion as a "judicial Potemkin Village," nothing but a facade of *Roe*, "which may be pointed out to passers by as a monument to the importance of adhering to precedent." Within moments he banged the gavel ending the Term, and the press corps rushed for the exit.

Judging by the reaction of partisans in the courtroom, the trio's plea for peace had fallen on deaf ears. Exiting, a lawyer from Kenneth Starr's Solicitor General's Office mumbled angrily, "One more vote, we need one more fucking vote." Meanwhile, someone turned to Kathryn Kolbert to offer congratulations. "This was no victory," she snapped.

Outside on the steps, the spinning began immediately. Most of the commentators had not even seen the opinion. None had sufficient time for more than the most cursory skim. It did not matter. For right-to-lifers, anything short of *Roe*'s interment was totally unacceptable, and their spokesmen vehemently denounced the Court's betrayal of the unborn. "Three Reagan-Bush appointees have stabbed Justice in the back," Terry shouted into a cluster of microphones.

On the pro-choice side, press strategy had been established in advance, regardless of how the Justices ruled. "Even if the court retains *Roe* and strikes down the spousal notification requirement," the pro-choice media response instructions read, "the abortion rights message should be: 'Don't be fooled . . . the Court has gutted the core holding of *Roe*."[16] Out on the Court's plaza, with clerks watching in dismay and astonishment, the trio's opinion took a backseat to election strategy as Kolbert and others followed their preset line.

Inside the Court, a small scene captured what really had happened. In the hall behind the courtroom, William Brennan, the law's great liberal icon, intercepted Harry Blackmun, the last of the Court's liberal guard. Wordlessly, the two octogenarians shook hands and exchanged a smile of exhausted relief.

It is easy to malign O'Connor, Kennedy, and Souter's opinion in *Casey*. The conservative dissenters were certainly right that the joint opinion's "undue burden" test was inherently circular and infinitely malleable.[17] Also, the trio's claim to be following the command of stare decisis (at least in a traditional sense) was difficult if not impossible to square with their substantial rewriting of abortion law.

Furthermore, the dissents presented a serious challenge to Souter's argument that the nation would lose confidence in the Court if it failed to "remain steadfast" and overruled *Roe* "under fire." The validity of that claim depended entirely on one's assessment of *Roe*. If, as Scalia and others believed, *Roe* was profoundly wrong—an unjustifiable usurpation of the people's democratic right to preserve fetal life—then the Court would only enhance its reputation and authority by admitting error and restoring the Court to its proper role. Indeed, from the conservative point of view, overruling *Roe* was an absolute prerequisite for the Court to reclaim a legitimacy lost in the Warren era.*

It is thus a measure of the terrible predicament the Court had placed itself in that such an unconvincing opinion, produced in cliquish secrecy and (at least in Kennedy's case) for rather suspect reasons, nonetheless achieved a highly valuable result. For all its flaws, *Casey* was a not-to-be-emulated but much-needed act of judicial statesmanship. By the time of *Casey*, the Court had worked itself into an impossible bind. *Roe* already had poisoned the nomination and confirmation process for the Court, already grossly distorted the debate over constitutional interpretation, already further polarized the Court and pushed Justices into adopting dishonest or overtly political strategies such as Rehnquist's and Blackmun's in *Casey*.

These were not ills that could be stopped or reversed with either a pure affirmance or an overruling of *Roe*. True, *Roe* was difficult if not impossible to defend on its own terms—a far stretch of the already thin doctrine of substantive due process. But it was equally true that, after nineteen years, stare decisis supported its retention, and in any case *Roe*'s basic result could be effectively defended on the firmer ground of gender equality.†

---

*The joint opinion was also subject to obvious criticism from the left. Particularly vulnerable (as Justice Stevens showed) was the trio's conclusion that the twenty-four-hour, mandatory waiting period—making abortion much more difficult for working women and women from communities with no abortion clinics—did not constitute an undue burden.

†The joint opinion, though never explicitly invoking the constitutional command of equality, several times discussed the right to abortion in terms of a woman's ability to break out of traditional gender roles and participate equally in society. Also, Justice Blackmun stated definitively for the first time that he believed that the equal protection clause guaranteed a right to abortion. These references reflected both an evolution in thinking about the right to abortion and an equal resistance to abandoning the original grounds for the decision.

The Court was stuck. Both a decision to affirm *Roe* and one overruling it would have led to the same practical result. One side or the other would have denounced the Court as "illegitimate"—for the reasons stated by Souter or for those stated by Scalia, depending on who won. Either way, the war over the right to abortion would have continued, erupting volcanically with every future nomination to the Court or new abortion case slated for review.

What the Court needed, to borrow the argot of politics, was an "exit strategy." It needed a peace imposed from the center: a plausible legal formulation supported by enough Justices to show both sides that this was, at least for the foreseeable future, the Court's last word on abortion. Here, O'Connor, Kennedy, and Souter succeeded, perhaps unwittingly. The joint opinion did not solve the problem of the Court's endangered reputation (as it professed) by reaffirming the essence of *Roe*. It solved the problem by creating a mushy, let-the-details-be-worked-out-later legal standard that reflected the views of the vast majority of Americans: abortion should be available, especially early in pregnancy, but it should be a rare, considered, even discouraged choice.

There was no beauty in such a peace. At its core, the joint opinion was the opposite of the coherent, principled decision making to which the Court should regularly aspire. Although Blackmun had praised the joint opinion as an act of "courage," it was really the opposite—a careful move to the mainstream. And, ironically, that was its strength. In creating a position politically tenable outside the Court and strategically tenable within, the trio had cauterized a terrible wound and given the Court a real chance to move past this generation-long obsession.[18]

The joint opinion left the partisans of both sides ample opportunity to vent the frustrations so evident in their immediate reactions to the ruling. While antithetical to right-to-lifers, *Casey* gave them considerable leeway to discourage the procedure through legislation. And while ardent abortion rights advocates chafed under the new regulations *Casey* allowed, the opinion guaranteed the basic right they cherished and provided legal grounds for attacking especially restrictive laws.

But as these battles raged, the Court itself could remain—for the first time in nineteen years—outside the fray. Although the trio could not stop the four anti-*Roe* Justices from granting cert. in future abortion cases, still, by controlling the outcome of such cases, they had rendered cert. grants futile. The conservatives recognized as much. In the five years since *Casey*, while occasionally skirmishing over side issues, the Court has not granted full review in a single pure abortion case.*

As it has turned out, *Casey* also marked the end of the broad view of due process that originally led to *Roe*. Despite the joint opinion's high-flown rhetoric—in particular Kennedy's claim that due process liberty included "the right to define one's own concept of existence, of meaning, of the universe, and of the mystery of human life"—the Court has since rejected litigant claims and lower court rulings further expanding due process. The most important of these cases was the definitive denial in 1997 of a right to physician-assisted suicide, a right premised on exactly the same due process–privacy logic as *Roe*.[19] When read together with *Casey*, the right-to-die decision makes clear that a majority of the Court (including Kennedy) are now committed to a truce of the status quo: the *Roe*-based right to abortion will stand, but it will have no heirs.

Yet while *Casey* successfully brought some closure to the Court on the terribly divisive issues of abortion and due process, the question still remained what this turning point would mean for the Court more generally. Some speculated at the time that the joint opinion heralded the appearance of a new center at the Court, an oasis of what the trio had called "reasoned judgment" within that desert of extremes. This was too hopeful by far. Abandoning the abortion battlefield only revealed an older, deeper rift—the rift of race and states' rights that had been the true dividing line of the Warren era. Here, as along an active fault line, the pressure had been building continually, and was now ready to explode.

---

*The turning point came the term after *Casey*, when the Court denied cert. in a major abortion case involving Guam's anti-abortion law. Although Rehnquist, White, and Scalia wanted to grant cert., Thomas voted against forcing a *Casey* rerun on the Court. *Ada v. Guam Society of Obstetricians and Gynecologists*, 506 U.S. 1011 (1992).

In particular, the Justices have argued, sometimes vehemently, over the rights of anti-abortion demonstrators and the power of federal authorities to prosecute certain anti-abortion protesters under federal civil rights laws. But these were free speech cases or cases about statutory interpretation, not about abortion per se. See *Bray v. Alexandria Women's Health Clinic*, 506 U.S. 1013 (1993); *Madsen v. Women's Health Center, Inc.*, 512 U.S. 753 (1994).

The centrist trio from *Casey* did split over the handling of one abortion case in the context of an emergency stay. In 1993 a federal district court in North Dakota, allegedly applying *Casey*, threw out a "facial" (generalized) challenge to that state's abortion law because the plaintiffs had failed to show that "no set of circumstances exists under which the law would be valid." The pro-choice litigants asked the Supreme Court to stay this ruling while they appealed it, but the Justices (7–2, with Blackmun and Stevens dissenting) turned them down. O'Connor and Souter wrote separately to emphasize that, although they did not think a stay was in order, they considered the district court's decision "inconsistent" with *Casey* as it imposed too heavy a burden on the plaintiffs. Behind the scenes, O'Connor and Souter were deeply disappointed that Kennedy broke from the solidarity of the joint opinion and refused to join their clarification of *Casey*'s meaning.

Old Battles, New Wounds

In the spring of 1987, after the Supreme Court decision in *McCleskey v. Kemp* (the NAACP Legal Defense Fund's race discrimination challenge to the death penalty), Warren McCleskey's lawyers, Robert Stroup and Jack Boger, started investigating potential new legal claims to raise in a second federal habeas petition. They didn't have much to go on—a possible *Batson* jury selection argument, perhaps a claim that the jury had been too thoroughly cleansed of death penalty opponents. They did receive one break. In an unrelated case, a Georgia court had held that police investigative files could be obtained under the state's Open Records Act. Although the decision was being appealed, Stroup viewed McCleskey's police file as perhaps his last real hope to avoid execution, and the lawyer begged and favor-traded with contacts in the department to get something, anything, turned over.

What he eventually received was stunning. The file contained a previously unrevealed twenty-one-page typed statement that had been given to the police by Offie Evans, the jailhouse informant whose testimony had solved all the prosecution's evidentiary problems in identifying McCleskey as the killer of Officer Frank Schlatt. Evans had been the focus of defense scrutiny before. In 1985 Judge Owen Forrester had granted McCleskey's first petition for habeas relief because, in his view, the state had made an undisclosed deal with Evans in exchange for his testimony. The Eleventh Circuit, though, had revoked the writ on the ground that a police officer's suggestion that he would "speak a word" for Evans was not the kind of deal that had to be revealed.

Now, Evans's previously unknown statement suggested another constitutional violation. Recounting repeated conversations with

McCleskey, Evans revealed himself as a relentless interlocutor, who had pretended to be a relative of Ben Wright (one of McCleskey's accomplices), and tried through a series of clever lies to obtain exactly the information (such as the location of the murder weapon) that the police were missing. The statement, given to the prosecutor, Russ Parker, and two detectives, did not make clear exactly what Evans was up to, but it strongly suggested that he was not a casual recipient of McCleskey's loose prison cell talk, but rather a police plant deliberately seeking incriminating information.

Such arrangements are unlawful. Under *Massiah* v. *United States*,[1] the police may not circumvent a defendant's right to counsel by having an informant elicit information on the state's behalf. Having seen Evans's statement, Stroup and Boger were virtually certain this was what had happened. Now they had to prove it to Judge Forrester, as well as convince him that they had not been remiss in failing to discover and present such a *Massiah* claim in McCleskey's first federal habeas petition four years before.

In July 1987, Judge Forrester held a hearing at which Boger and Stroup called a series of witnesses to prove the state had used Evans illegally. Parker, the prosecutor, denied he'd had any relationship with Evans until after the prisoner's conversations with McCleskey. So did the two lead investigators on the case, Welcome Harris and W. K. Jowers. A third officer, Sidney Dorsey, admitted knowing Evans, and even using him as an informant in past cases. Yet Dorsey suffered amnesia about whether he had dealt with Evans in connection with the Schlatt killing. He didn't deny the possibility of having met with Evans about the case; "in all honesty," he just couldn't remember.

Late on the hearing's second day, Stroup and Boger called Ulysses Worthy, a correctional officer they had subpoenaed because (according to Evans's statement) Evans and the Schlatt case detectives had met in Worthy's office at the Fulton County Jail. To Stroup and Boger's astonishment, Worthy confirmed their worst suspicions. A reluctant witness, he gradually admitted that one of the detectives (Dorsey, he thought) had asked him to transfer Evans to the cell adjoining McCleskey's and then instructed Evans "to engage in conversations with McCleskey."

This was a clear admission of a *Massiah* violation, and the state's lawyers requested a recess to find new evidence to rebut Worthy's testimony. They didn't find any. When the hearing resumed a month later, the state put Worthy back on the stand, and he backtracked a bit from his earlier recollection. Still, he continued to admit the crucial facts: having been asked to move Evans next to McCleskey and having overheard Evans being asked to elicit information from McCleskey.

From Stroup and Boger's perspective, that was good enough. And Judge Forrester agreed. After weighing the evidence, he concluded that the police, "determined to avenge [Schlatt's] death, . . . had violated clearly established case-law." Forrester granted McCleskey habeas relief, specifically, a new trial—for a second time.

Georgia—which had a policy of never confessing error, even when facing strong evidence of unconstitutional conduct—appealed to the Eleventh Circuit. Here, the state's main argument was not that Forrester was wrong in finding that the Atlanta police had violated McCleskey's rights, but that McCleskey should have raised this claim in his first federal habeas petition and that his doing so now was a disqualifying "abuse of the writ."

Stroup and Boger thought this suggestion absurd. Under the governing standard, they were not guilty of abusing the writ unless they had "deliberately bypassed" the *Massiah* claim on first federal habeas as a strategy for manipulating the process.[2] As far as the two lawyers were concerned, the reason they hadn't included a *Massiah* claim the first time had nothing to do with bad faith on their part. It was caused by the police and prosecutor having played hide-and-seek with Evans's smoking gun statement. The *Massiah* claim was all but a sure winner for their client. Why on earth would they have deliberately withheld it?

It was true that, in 1981, Stroup had included a *Massiah* claim among the two dozen arguments in his first *state* habeas petition, then had dropped it (and several others) when initially filing for federal habeas. The problem had been no evidence. Stroup had talked to a few correctional officers about whether Evans was a police informant, but he had found out nothing. Nor did anything emerge at a 1981 state habeas hearing, where Parker denied knowing Evans beforehand.

The key to uncovering the misconduct had been finding Evans's statement, which, Stroup and Boger now argued to the court of appeals, the state had "sought for a decade to hide . . . and avoid its production to defense counsel."[3] Initially, Parker had not shown it to John Turner, McCleskey's lawyer, before trial. Then, during trial, the judge had further obscured the statement's existence when Parker started crossexamining McCleskey using information he'd gotten from Evans. Turner had objected and renewed his request to see any statements the prosecution had obtained from McCleskey. After a very confusing exchange (confusing because Turner thought Parker was using a statement of McCleskey's, while Parker and the judge knew the statement was made by Evans), the judge threw Turner—and later Stroup and Boger—off the scent by saying, "I don't know that we are talking about any written statement." Next, years later, during the first go-round of habeas, the Attorney General's Office had sent Stroup what it described as "a complete copy of the prosecutor's file"—complete, that is, except for Evans's incriminating statement. And finally, Detective Dorsey had claimed not to remember the crucial meeting where he arranged for his snitch to move cells and befriend McCleskey.*

Under the circumstances, Judge Forrester had concluded that Stroup and Boger had made a reasonable effort to investigate the Evans situation and had dropped the *Massiah* claim not for tactical reasons but for a lack of evidence—evidence, he said, "that state officials were in fact actively concealing from the defense." Once again, though, the Eleventh Circuit disagreed. The appeals court gave the term "deliberate bypass" an oddly literal interpretation. There was no dispute that Stroup and Boger had dropped the *Massiah* claim: their state habeas petition contained it; their first federal petition did not. Moreover, the defense lawyers were not claiming to have "accidentally failed" to include the claim. It followed, then, so the appeals court reasoned, that they had "knowingly," and thus "deliberately," bypassed it. As a backup theory, the Eleventh Circuit also ruled that, even if the state had violated *Massiah*, the error was "harmless." Although Evans had destroyed McCleskey's alibi and was the only witness other than Ben Wright (McCleskey's coconspirator) to tag McCleskey as Schlatt's killer, the appeals court ruled that removing Evans's testimony from the trial would not have affected the verdict. Accordingly, it again revoked McCleskey's writ and returned him to the netherworld of death row.[4]

---

*Brief for Petitioner, *McCleskey* v. *Zant*, pp. 7–13, 25. McCleskey's lawyers had made one error. At the first state habeas hearing in 1981, Stroup had questioned Parker about Evans's trial testimony, introducing the subject by saying, "Now, I want to direct your attention to a statement from Offie Evans that was introduced at Warren McCleskey's trial and ask you a few questions about that statement." Stroup was referring to Evans's actual live testimony, but Parker's mind went to the twenty-one-page written statement. "Okay," he responded. "When you referred to a statement, Offie Evans gave his statement but it was not introduced at the trial. It was part of that matter that was made *in camera* inspection by the judge prior to trial."

Stroup thought Parker had misunderstood him and rephrased his question to focus more clearly on Evans's trial testimony. Parker's mention of Evans's written statement went right by Stroup, and the prosecutor didn't volunteer further clarification. The moment passed.

Furiously disappointed, Stroup and Boger naturally asked the Supreme Court to review and reverse the Eleventh Circuit's ruling. The theme of their cert. petition, filed in spring 1990, was blunt. The appellate court's definition of abuse of the writ let Georgia get away with a ten-year pattern of "secrecy and deception." That, they thought, just couldn't be the law. Boger, for one, was optimistic about McCleskey's chances at the Court. But he had been optimistic the last time, too, and once again, apparently failed to see the tidal wave of conservative lawmaking about to swamp his client and sweep his claims into the deep blue sea.

Inside the Court, the liberal Justices expressed immediate interest in granting McCleskey's cert. petition. In truth, it was a borderline case for review. Even if McCleskey were not disqualified for abusing the writ, the Eleventh Circuit had found any error resulting from the violation of *Massiah* to have been harmless. This alternative ground for denying McCleskey relief clouded the Court's consideration of the potentially certworthy issue of whether the appeals court had misconstrued the standard for finding abuse of the writ. But McCleskey's case defied such logic. For death penalty critics, McCleskey had come to symbolize the very deepest flaws in the capital punishment system, and here he was, back again, having suffered yet another injustice. It was April 1990, and Justices Brennan and Marshall were still on the Court, voting to grant every capital case. With the agreement of Justice Stevens and Blackmun, vocal dissenters in *McCleskey I*, they granted McCleskey another chance at salvation.

But the liberals were courting disaster. The conservatives now regularly defeated new efforts to limit the death penalty, and in places had started stripping down the process. At the same time, they remained deeply frustrated, even angry, at continued delays in carrying out death sentences. Nationwide, there were only sixteen executions in 1990, down from a 1987 high of twenty-five; and the expectation for 1990 was only slightly higher. The Court's pending docket included a slew of capital cases, all of which would end in conservative victories, but which were freezing executions in many big death penalty states until the rulings came down. Chief Justice Rehnquist was convinced that the liberals were stalling on completing their written dissents to keep these mini-moratoriums in place. And all the while the Court continued to receive its near-weekly dose of emergency stay applications, each one resentment-spreading.

For the last sixth months the conservatives, especially Rehnquist, had been hoping to enlist Congress in relieving the paralysis of capital case judicial review. In 1988 the Chief had appointed an ad hoc committee of the Judicial Conference (the policy-making body for the federal judiciary, presided over by the Chief Justice) to suggest reforms for the capital appeals process. As chair, Rehnquist appointed retired Justice Lewis Powell, a long-standing critic of death penalty delays and, particularly, of habeas redundancy. In August 1989 the Powell Committee, as it was known, produced a report recommending a substantial streamlining of federal habeas, with special emphasis on curbing "successive" federal habeas petitions—such as McCleskey's.

Rehnquist immediately pushed for the circuit court chief judges who make up the Judicial Conference to endorse Powell's report and forward it to the Senate Judiciary Committee—which was waiting for the conference's recommendations. But a majority of the judges, concerned about the severity of Powell's proposal, voted to table the report for more considered evaluation at their next scheduled meeting in March 1990.* Rehnquist simply went around them. He submitted the report to the Senate without the conference's approval, igniting a public spitting match with the spurned chief judges, but also triggering a standing agreement with the Judiciary Committee that the report would be considered directly upon its delivery.[5]

The judges got their revenge the following March. Belatedly addressing Powell's report, they approved several amendments, including one directly pertinent to McCleskey that watered down Powell's suggested limits on successive federal habeas petitions. In so doing, the judges helped kill congressional habeas reform in the near term, infuriating Rehnquist and other conservatives—just as McCleskey's cert. petition arrived at the Court.

At the Justices' conference in mid-May, the conservatives were willing to let McCleskey's case slide quietly into the night. They were content with the result reached by the Eleventh Circuit. But once the liberals forced the case upon them, it became a lightning rod for their

---

*The thrust of the Powell report was to create a system where every capital defendant received one "full and fair" chance at federal habeas review, including the mandatory appointment of counsel. Critics challenged the report for failing to provide counsel to capital defendants during crucial state court proceedings and for recommending excessively rigid timetables for capital litigation.

frustrations. After the vote to grant, Justice Kennedy circulated a memo complaining about the "inflammatory" manner in which Boger's cert. petition had framed the questions presented for the Court's consideration. Kennedy proposed that the Court throw out Boger's characterization of the case and "reformulate" more neutrally the questions to be briefed by the parties.

Justice Brennan countered that most cert. petitions used inflammatory language—it was part of advocacy—and he seemed on his way to heading off Kennedy's proposal. Then Justice Scalia weighed in. He didn't mind the argumentative tone in which Boger presented the questions in the case. Instead, Scalia complained that they were incomplete. Boger's questions *assumed*, following precedent, that the appropriate standard for determining abuse of the writ was "deliberate bypass." For Scalia, the better (and predicate) question was whether the Court should adopt a stricter standard for successive petitions—and he suggested putting that additional question to the parties. In short order, the other conservatives agreed. And, thus, while the liberals granted *McCleskey* in order to correct what they saw as a manifest injustice, within days the conservatives had hijacked the case for the purpose of making another substantial cutback on federal habeas.*

The actual deciding of *McCleskey* proceeded with the debate-free efficiency so characteristic of the Rehnquist Court. With Justice Souter having replaced Justice Brennan after his summer retirement, the Justices voted 6–3 at Conference that McCleskey had abused the writ in failing to include the meritorious *Massiah* claim in his first federal habeas petition. Rehnquist gave Kennedy the honor of deciding exactly what standard to use in reaching that result.

---

*Events between the granting of cert. and oral argument in the fall of 1990 only made the outcome of *McCleskey* more certain. Just before the summer recess, in the case of James Edward Smith, the Court faced the problem, narrowly averted in 1986, of what to do when four Justices vote to grant cert., but no fifth Justice is willing to grant a stay of execution to keep the petitioner (and his case) alive. For several years after the crisis of the Willie Darden case, Justice Powell had lent a "gentleman's fifth" to preserve the integrity of the Court's cert. grant rule. But Powell, almost cadaverous in his gauntness, now functioned at the Court as little more than a ghost calling from the shadows in remembrance of a kinder, gentler time. In his absence, none of the remaining conservatives would budge, and, to the anguish of liberals in the building, Smith went to his appointed fate on time.

Circumstances such as the Smith stay application were gradually convincing Justice Powell that the death penalty had become so corrupting of the judicial process—and so resistant to effective regulation—that it should be abolished. In 1991, he began saying as much openly. See Jeffries, *Justice Powell*, p. 452. In the meantime, after Smith's execution, Justice White reluctantly agreed to take Powell's place as an automatic fifth vote for a stay when four Justices voted to grant cert.

As Kennedy concluded for the majority, by potentially upsetting the "finality" of state court criminal convictions, federal habeas review presented a serious threat to "the States' sovereign power to punish offenders." That threat was too severe to allow petitioners to include in successive petitions all claims they had not deliberately bypassed. Instead, Kennedy held petitioners to a much tougher standard—tougher even than the one Georgia had advocated in its briefs. Henceforth, before a federal court would entertain a second or successive petition, the petitioner would have to show "cause" why a new claim had not been raised previously and "actual prejudice" from the constitutional error being alleged.*

The Court had used this cause and prejudice requirement in other areas of law, and it was exacting. To meet the cause requirement, a petitioner would have to show that "some external impediment," such as actual governmental interference, had prevented him from raising a claim in his original petition.[6] And to meet the additional requirement of prejudice, a petitioner would have to show that a pervasive constitutional error at his trial had "worked to his actual and substantial disadvantage."[7]

Ordinarily, the Court's next step after fashioning such a new test would have been to remand the case to the district court for application to the specific facts of the case at hand. The district court has heard the evidence, seen the witness, and generally knows best what really happened. But the conservatives had no intention of giving Judge Forrester (despite his pedigree as a Reagan appointee and former prosecutor) a third chance to grant McCleskey relief. Instead, Justice Kennedy concluded on his own, in direct contradiction of Forrester's factual findings, and without allowing argument from Stroup and Boger, that McCleskey had failed to show proper cause for omitting his Massiah claim on first federal habeas.[8]

As Kennedy parsed the evidence, McCleskey's lawyers knew everything they needed to know to pursue a Massiah claim from the start. McCleskey himself, Kennedy suggested, could have told his lawyers

---

*Kennedy also made an exception for cases where a finding of abuse of the writ would work a "manifest injustice"—presumably a reference to a case where the constitutional error in question made it highly doubtful that the petitioner had committed the crime for which he was convicted. The Court has yet to find such a case, and this exception certainly was not relevant to McCleskey— who, while in prison, admitted to participating in the furniture store robbery, but not to killing Officer Schlatt.

about the circumstances of his conversations with Offie Evans. The newly discovered statement confirmed but did not add to that pool of knowledge. In general, Kennedy decided, Stroup and Boger had simply failed to conduct a "reasonable and diligent" investigation into Mc-Cleskey's potential *Massiah* claim. He rejected out of hand McCleskey's argument that Georgia officials had concealed the evidence they needed to make the case—and with that rejection Kennedy sealed McCleskey's fate.

In dissent, Justice Marshall (writing for Blackmun and Stevens) attacked Kennedy's twenty-twenty-hindsight reconstruction of events. For Marshall, Kennedy was being either naive or disingenuous in excusing the "disinformation strategy" of the Schlatt case prosecutors and detectives. But for Marshall, this "dangerous" error in Kennedy's opinion was dwarfed by the gross inappropriateness of his entire enterprise. In 1966 Congress had amended the statute governing federal habeas specifically to codify the deliberate bypass standard the Court had set up in 1963 to govern new claims in successive petitions. In 1989 and 1990, following the Powell report, conservatives in Congress had tried and failed to tighten that standard. (They wanted to require the dismissal of any new claims that could have been discovered through the exercise of "reasonable diligence" when the first petition was filed.) Yet "unfazed by Congress' rejection of this legislation," Kennedy and his supposedly conservative cosigners had arrogated to themselves the power to adopt an even tougher standard than the one Congress had spurned. That was pure judicial legislation.

The result of this judicial lawmaking, moreover, was a classic catch-22 for every potential habeas petitioner. If he chose (as McCleskey had) to forgo a potential claim because of a lack of hard evidence, he would almost surely forfeit the claim under Kennedy's cause and prejudice scheme. Yet if (as Kennedy demanded) he included the unsubstantiated claim in his first petition, it would be permanently lost when the federal district court rejected it for lack of evidence.

The cruelty of this court-built trap so incensed Marshall that he began the first draft of his dissent by declaring Kennedy's opinion "lawless." It fell to Stevens to suggest the description be changed. Although he agreed Kennedy's opinion was "outrageous," Stevens felt duty bound to remind Marshall that, however much he might regret it, "when five members of the Court agree on a proposition, it does become law."

* * *

Five months later, on September 24, 1991, the Court's new law sent Warren McCleskey to his death. That morning the Georgia Board of Pardons and Parole voted 3–2 (split down racial lines) not to forgive his death sentence. During the day new lawyers mounted a last-ditch legal challenge. The previous week, Georgia's attorney general, Michael Bowers, reportedly had threatened to "wage a full scale campaign to overhaul the pardons and paroles board" if it granted McCleskey clemency.[9] And days before McCleskey's hearing, the chairman of the pardon board allegedly had been overheard in an elevator guaranteeing that the board would deny McCleskey relief. Based on these facts, McCleskey had started another round of habeas, charging that he had been deprived of a fair chance at clemency.

In Atlanta, Judge Forrester was troubled by the story of the elevator conversation—the possibility that the clemency hearing in McCleskey's prominent and politically charged case had been a sham. As execution hour approached, Forrester issued a temporary stay while he called in witnesses to clarify what, if anything, the pardon board chairman had said.

Up the judicial ladder at the Supreme Court, the clerk's office started its procedures for handling execution night emergency stay applications. While Judge Forrester sifted the evidence, both sides were faxing their arguments to the Court, expecting that the case would arrive there before the night ended. About 7:00 P.M., Justice Kennedy, as circuit justice for the Eleventh Circuit, sent around a memo (signed in his absence by a clerk) indicating that, while Forrester had issued a temporary stay until 7:30, McCleskey's lawyers were asking the Court to issue its own emergency stay. If Forrester lifted his stay or it expired, McCleskey's new lawyers wanted time to present their client's undue influence claims to a state court or to the Eleventh Circuit.

Kennedy considered McCleskey's claims so flimsy he simply announced that "there is no substantial factual showing and no substantial legal basis for [McCleskey's undue influence] claim." In closing, he not only voted to deny McCleskey an emergency stay to allow further consideration of his allegations but he added that, unless circumstances changed dramatically, he would "vote to deny relief based on any further filings" McCleskey might make.

Back in Atlanta, after having several times extended his stay, Judge

Forrester ultimately denied McCleskey relief when the evidence to support his claims against the pardon board chairman proved equivocal. The execution process resumed its forward march as McCleskey's lawyers frantically appealed. Within minutes the Eleventh Circuit had denied McCleskey relief. His stay application, together with a grabbing-at-straws cert. petition, moved on to the Supreme Court.

As Kennedy's memo reflected, McCleskey stood no chance of getting a reprieve from the Court. Still, in Justice Marshall's Chambers, a clerk prepared a dissent. By this time Marshall had tendered his resignation from the Court, and he continued to participate in the emergency stay process only because the Senate had yet to confirm his successor. In what would prove the final chapter in his and Brennan's long-standing abolitionist documentary, Marshall excoriated his colleagues for refusing to grant a stay so that McCleskey's new claims might be investigated fully. Having accused the Court majority of "valu[ing] finality over justice" and "expediency over human life," he distilled the essence of McCleskey's odyssey through the system. "Repeatedly denying Warren McCleskey his constitutional rights is unacceptable," Marshall closed. "Executing him is inexcusable."

In all likelihood, none of the other Justices would even see Marshall's dissent until the next day. Such writings had long since become futile or annoying, depending on the reader's views. Nonetheless, for many of the clerks working the case, newcomers to the ritual scramble of the death watch, McCleskey's death felt particularly momentous. They gathered down in the clerk's office as the final papers and final votes trickled in.

Down in Georgia, around 2:00 A.M., prison officials escorted Jack Boger to the building that housed the electric chair. Lights ablaze amid a pounding rain, the pavilion of death sparkled eerily in the night. Behind a glass wall, guards placed McCleskey in the chair and strapped in his legs, waist, and arms. Speaking deliberately, McCleskey began his final statement. He asked forgiveness of Officer Schlatt's family, though implicitly he continued to deny even now that he had fired the fatal shots. He thanked his attorneys for all the years of work on his behalf and asked his family to go on with their lives without bitterness. "Keep God at the center," he told them. McCleskey said good-bye to the "fellow men and brothers" he was leaving behind and had started a concluding prayer when, literally seconds before he would die, the warden, Walter Zant, interrupted to announce that McCleskey had been granted a fifteen-minute stay.

Boger watched as the execution team removed McCleskey from the chair. He had no idea what had happened, and it would turn out that not much had. Somewhere communications had broken down between McCleskey's new lawyers, the prison, and the Court. Everything had to wait while this was sorted out.

Twenty minutes later the execution team placed McCleskey back in the chair. Still composed, he tried to reweave some of his thoughts. He addressed himself again to his victim's family, counseling them not to expect satisfaction from his death. Then, with his very last words, Mc-Cleskey prayed "that one day this country, supposedly a civilized society, would abolish barbaric acts such as the death penalty." Moments later, at 3:13 A.M., Superintendent Zant pulled the switch and McCleskey, age forty-three, was dead.

As I was reading the next day about McCleskey's execution, my mind immediately jumped to two other cases. The first was *Coleman v. Thompson*,[10] in which the lawyer for a death-sentenced murderer had missed the deadline for filing a state habeas appeal by two days. The question facing the Justices was whether this inadvertent error should cost Roger Coleman the right to present his constitutional claims to a federal court. With Justice O'Connor writing, the conservatives answered yes—a default that would send Coleman to the electric chair eight months after McCleskey. "This is a case about federalism," O'Connor had begun her opinion. "It concerns the respect that federal courts owe the States. . . ."*

The second case was one from my term, *Teague v. Lane*, decided on February 22, 1989. Surrounded by the year's many headline-grabbing cases, no one paid much attention to this complicated habeas case. Even inside the Court, many of us missed *Teague*'s implications and the case remains obscure. Yet when one looks back from the high hill of *McCleskey* and *Coleman*, it must rank among the more important rulings of the last decade and a harbinger of things to come.

---

*O'Connor's choice to characterize a ruling that would send Coleman to virtually immediate execution because of the minor blunder of his lawyer as "a case about federalism" became the target of much mordant Court humor. "This is an e-mail about federalism," jokers prefaced casual internal exchanges. But O'Connor's obvious overstatement reflected the status of federalism as a main article of conservative faith.

Frank Teague was a black man who had been convicted by an all-white jury of attempted murder, armed robbery, and aggravated battery. Having unsuccessfully appealed these convictions through the Illinois state courts, he was now petitioning in federal court for a writ of habeas corpus. Teague's central argument—and the one that had prompted the Justices to grant cert.—stemmed from the fact that the prosecutor at trial had used all his peremptory challenges to remove blacks from the jury. Teague claimed that these race-based strikes had deprived him of the "impartial jury" the Sixth Amendment guarantees.*

In Justice O'Connor's Chambers, Andrew McBride, the clerk responsible for *Teague,* had only a secondary interest in this issue of potential jury bias. McBride saw the case in grander terms. Embedded in *Teague,* he realized, was an ideal opportunity to further carve away at federal habeas corpus and thereby sharply reduce the prospects of capital defendants at the Court.

What McBride had in mind was a dramatic revision in the Court's "retroactivity" doctrine. This was another arcane area of law, little thought about or understood, yet freighted with importance. Say the Court changes its approach to some aspect of criminal procedure, as, for example, in *Miranda,* where for the first time it required police officers to warn suspects of their right to have counsel and to remain silent before starting an interrogation. Should this decision apply retroactively and call into question past convictions where the prosecutor introduced at trial a confession that was not obtained in accordance with the Court's new ruling?

For more than two decades, the Court had decided this question on a case-by-case basis, balancing the purpose behind the new ruling against the potential costs of applying the rule retroactively.[11] Sometimes, as in *Miranda,* the Justices had given a new rule no retroactive effect—and had required that it be obeyed only in trials commencing after their decision. On other occasions, the Court had extended the benefit of a new rule to all defendants whose convictions were still subject to "direct review" (those whose appeals within the state system were not yet final). At yet other times, the Court also had allowed habeas petitioners

---

*In the 1987 case, *Batson* v. *Kentucky,* the Court had ruled that such race-based peremptories violated the Fourteenth Amendment's equal protection clause. Teague had raised his Sixth Amendment claim at least in part because his conviction had become final long before the Court handed down *Batson,* and he was probably ineligible to reap its benefits.

(whose direct appeals already were exhausted) to invoke new rules to challenge their convictions or sentences.

Justice Harlan and several scholars had criticized the inconsistency and unpredictability of this approach. McBride, however, had an additional complaint. The retroactive application of new criminal procedure decisions to cases on habeas review had been crucial to the abolitionist campaign against the death penalty. Time and again during the long process of death penalty appeals, defense lawyers had taken advantage of new Court rulings to raise new arguments (based on these rulings) challenging their clients' convictions and sentences. The result was a self-perpetuating cycle of delay as every defendant-friendly change in the criminal law became the basis of yet another federal habeas claim.

McBride wanted to use *Teague* to end all that. His proposal, put forward in a bench memo to O'Connor (and borrowed partly from Justice Harlan) was this: instead of deciding retroactivity on an ad hoc basis, set up a predictable formula. Whenever the Court established a "new" rule of criminal procedure, apply it retroactively to all defendants still on direct review; but, generally, do not apply the rule to defendants whose cases have moved into the habeas process.

If adopted, this scheme promised to cut down sharply federal habeas, especially death penalty appeals, and also would dramatically reduce the Court's unique role in the process of reviewing capital cases. Take Frank Teague, who was on first federal habeas. Under McBride's proposal, federal judges, including the Justices, would be required to decide the question of retroactivity *before* reaching the substance of a petitioner's claims. In other words, their first task would be not to look at the merits of Teague's discrimination claim but to determine whether, in making that claim, he was asking the Court to adopt a "new" rule. If the answer was yes—and McBride certainly thought Teague's Sixth Amendment argument was novel—then the Court would refuse even to consider his claim. The reason was this: even if the Court agreed theoretically with Teague that he'd been deprived of his Sixth Amendment right to an impartial jury, under McBride's scheme Teague would be ineligible to the benefit from the new ruling. And, according to McBride, since Teague couldn't benefit from the new rule, it would be wrong for the Supreme Court or any lower federal court to establish that rule in his case.

The practical effect of McBride's proposal would be to reduce drastically the kinds of arguments available to federal habeas petitioners. They would not be allowed to seek extensions of existing law, and they would lose the benefit of every favorable Court decision handed down after the end of their direct appeals through the state system. On the other side of the bench, federal judges, when considering habeas petitions, would be prohibited from adopting novel interpretations of federal law and from requiring states to bring their actions in line with evolving constitutional standards.

At the Supreme Court level, McBride's proposal would dramatically shrink the habeas docket or, as he bragged to his cabal cohort, "See: your IFP pile shrink in half . . . Hear: the libs scream bloody murder." McBride was setting up a whipsaw: if a habeas petitioner was seeking relief based on settled law (making him eligible for the Court's consideration), almost by definition his case did not raise the kind of novel and interesting issue that might cause the Justices to grant review. But if a petitioner raised a novel and interesting claim, he'd be "*Teagued*-out"— disqualified for seeking a new rule. For death row inmates, who were almost always seeking at least a modestly new wrinkle on established principles, this had the makings of a nightmare.

Justice O'Connor was certainly receptive to the basic idea behind McBride's approach. It tapped straight into the deep resentment of federal habeas that O'Connor had developed as a state court judge, when federal judges had the power to second-guess her work. Still, the Justice was leery of pushing such a dramatic legal change, including overturning long-settled precedent, in a case where the retroactivity issue had been neither briefed by the parties nor discussed in the lower court decisions.[12]

O'Connor's reluctance, though, did not dissuade McBride.* He quietly slipped his bench memo to a fellow cabalist in Rehnquist's Chambers, hoping that once the idea was planted, the Chief (an unrelenting opponent of federal habeas in the forty years since his clerkship with Justice Robert Jackson) would prove more daring than his own boss. Rehnquist did not disappoint. At conference he proposed deciding *Teague* according to McBride's retroactivity plan, and the other conservatives, including O'Connor, followed his lead. As a poetic touch, Rehnquist assigned the opinion to O'Connor, which meant that McBride had the

---

*When challenged about the propriety of using *Teague* to make a major change in the law on an issue neither briefed nor argued by the parties, McBride pointed out that the liberals of the Warren era had done the exact same thing in *Mapp* v. *Ohio*, the landmark case in which the Court, split 5–4, required states to exclude unconstitutionally obtained evidence from their criminal trials. On this point, *Teague* was another example of past liberal excesses coming home to roost.

pleasure of drafting the opinion that would enshrine his scheme into law.

As finally decided *Teague* was even more complicated than the preceding description would suggest. First, O'Connor's opinion included two exceptions to the general bar against applying new rules on federal habeas. These would become the source of continuing dispute, but so far they have proven to be of no practical import.[13]

Second, and more important, the Court in *Teague* did not provide a clear definition of what makes for a "new" rule. This definition was crucial. After all, the broader the definition of a "new" rule, the more federal judges would be disqualified from reviewing state court decisions. Suffice it to say, the Supreme Court adopted a very expansive definition of what rules are new. In a 1990 case, the Court (under Rehnquist's prodding) went so far as to suggest that a habeas petitioner is barred from challenging any state court decision having even a reasonable basis in existing precedent. In other words, a habeas petitioner is seeking a new rule not only when he seeks a truly novel interpretation of law, but even when his arguments are based on settled law—so long as the state court's rejection of those arguments was "reasonable."[14] In so doing, the Court has converted *Teague* from a significant case about the retroactive application of genuinely new law into a blockbuster potentially insulating from federal review every state court judgment presenting a minimally plausible view of current law.

The conservatives had good reasons for trying to reform a federal habeas process that had expanded exponentially since the Warren Court era and had become the pliable tool of death penalty abolitionists. Indeed, they could make a strong case for limiting petitioners to one "full and fair" crack at federal habeas, except in extraordinary circumstances (as, for example, the discovery of significant new evidence of actual innocence).

But one does not have to be a death penalty abolitionist or even a liberal to conclude that the Court's rulings in *McCleskey, Coleman, Teague,* and related cases were virtually indefensible. Rehnquist and the other Justices critical of federal habeas had no warrant to enact these reforms and change the terms of a statutory scheme that Congress, in the wake of the Powell report, had considered, reviewed, and seen fit to leave unchanged. Furthermore, the review process the Court jerry-rigged through *Teague, McCleskey, Coleman,* and other similar decisions was neither full nor fair. What the Court set up was a series of trapdoors where any procedural wrong step, no matter how trivial, resulted in a petitioner forfeiting his claims. Worse still, by telling states (in other rulings) that they need not provide petitioners with lawyers during this process, the Court encouraged, even guaranteed, a high percentage of missteps.* In so doing, the conservatives changed the habeas process from a broad opportunity for federal courts to remedy constitutional violations by state officials into an exitless maze shielding those officials from federal scrutiny even when they had clearly violated the Constitution.

The conservatives' habeas revolution, moreover, elevated an ideological passion for protecting state sovereignty over the plain realities of the judicial process. Underlying the Court's habeas innovations was the assumption that state judges were as well suited as federal judges to protect federal constitutional rights. Such faith in state court systems was simply blind. As practicing lawyers know, in aggregate, state court judges are just not as good as federal court judges. They tend to be less well educated and less distinguished in the profession. Many lack experience with or sophistication about federal constitutional law. State courts also lack the resources of federal courts, including top-flight law clerks and even, in some places, the rudiments of a federal law library.

But even assuming an equality of talent between state and federal judges, state judges remain intrinsically inferior for the purpose of deciding individual claims of constitutional right. The vast majority of state judges do not enjoy the life tenure that federal judges are guaranteed under the Constitution. And without life tenure state judges, however well intentioned, are hostages to passions of their communities.[15] Those passions run particularly hot in high profile criminal cases, especially the capital cases at which the Court's new states-friendly habeas regime was aimed. For state judges in many locales, issuing a pro-defendant ruling in a death penalty case, no matter how well justified, is tantamount to professional suicide. Even one or two "soft on crime" rulings can result in a

---

*The problem of petitioners forfeiting claims was especially severe in the South, where appointed trial counsel, even in capital cases, often bordered on incompetent and where little or no provision was made for the appointment of post-conviction legal assistance. Notably, the Powell report included strong incentives for states to provide lawyers from the very start of the habeas process. Yet the Court supplied the opposite incentive.

potentially career-ending and always costly recall campaign; any hope for promotion, by either appointment or election, vanishes instantly.*

The Constitution established an independent federal judiciary precisely to guard against such public pressures, and the value of that independence was evident from the record of federal habeas review in capital cases. Even after Presidents Reagan and Bush appointed hundreds of conservatives to the federal bench, federal habeas judges continued to find that state officials violated the Constitution in a stunning number of capital cases—roughly 50 percent, according to some studies.[16] (McCleskey is a case in point.) Even if, as a few academics charged, some federal reversals of state capital convictions and sentences were the result of liberal judges being overscrupulous, the numbers remained damning.[17]

In truth, over long practice federal habeas had served as an audit for how well state police, prosecutors, and judges were living up to constitutional requirements. In that sense the conservative habeas revolution resembled firing an accounting firm—in this case an accounting firm Congress had specifically authorized—for delivering bad news. This is, of course, a disastrous business practice. At a Court charged with upholding constitutional rights, it was even worse than forthright abdication. By eviscerating federal habeas and pretending to an equality between state and federal courts, the Justices legitimized for the public and every participant in the process a death penalty system that by any fair reckoning remained deeply flawed.[†]

At the Court itself the conservatives' habeas revolution provided a substantial buffer between the Justices and the everyday workings of the death penalty. As the nineties wore on, the terrible battles over emergency stays

---

*Of course, federal judges too are part of their communities and sometimes suffer intense repercussions for pro-defendant rulings. But on the local level, judicial recall campaigns, even for a single unpopular ruling, have become increasingly common. See, John Gibeaut, "Taking Aim," ABA Journal, November 1996, p. 50. Whatever pressure federal judges may have to endure, at least their jobs are not at risk.

†In 1996, Congress passed the Antiterrorism and Effective Death Penalty Act, codifying and even strengthening many of the habeas cutbacks adopted by the Rehnquist Court. The AEDPA, for example, limits second or successive habeas petitions (like McCleskey's) to claims involving either a new rule of law or new evidence that the petitioner is actually innocent of the crime for which he has been convicted and sentenced. While the AEDPA restrictions are open to substantive criticism—indeed, the American Bar Association has called for a temporary moratorium on executions until additional protections are added to the process—the new law has the undeniable virtue of being a creature of Congress, the appropriate institution for revising the habeas rules.

gradually abated. This was partly the result of Justices Brennan's and Marshall's retirement. But mainly it was due to *Teague, McCleskey,* and similar rulings which ensured that by the time almost every capital case filtered up to the Court, the defendant's claims were either *Teagued*-out or defaulted one way or another—and, thus, at least for the conservative majority, easily dismissed without ever looking at their merits.*

The conservative Justices, however, could not fully separate either the Supreme Court or the federal courts more generally from the bane of capital cases or from the cycle of illegitimate conduct into which these cases led both sides.[18] Like water pushing against a wall, abolitionist lawyers found the inevitable cracks in the system.

In April 1992, California prepared to break a long moratorium on capital punishment by executing Robert Alton Harris, who (together with his brother) had brutally murdered two teenage boys in 1978. In the intervening fourteen years, Harris had filed four unsuccessful federal habeas petitions, making any further habeas litigation almost certainly futile under the Court's recent *McCleskey* decision.[19] Abolitionists, however, devised a new strategy for trying to delay or avert Harris's execution—an event momentous both in its own right and for its implied threat to the hundreds of other residents of California's death row.

On April 17, four days before the scheduled execution, amid intense media coverage, the ACLU filed a class action lawsuit (covering all other members of California's death row, including Harris), claiming for the first time that California's method of execution, cyanide gas, caused an especially torturous death and was, therefore, unconstitutional under the Eighth Amendment. The ACLU's action was not a habeas petition. It was a claim under Section 1983, a statute regularly invoked to prevent state actions that will violate an individual's civil rights—in this case, the right not to be unconstitutionally executed. Naturally, among the relief sought by the ACLU was a temporary restraining order stopping California from moving forward with Harris's execution.

Under well-established law, granting a temporary restraining order is appropriate when a claim raises "serious questions" and "the balance of

---

*Ironically, in numerical terms, the habeas revolution, by streamlining the process, actually increased the flow of emergency stay applications that descended on the Court. These applications remained a terrible burden in the Chambers of the more liberal Justices—now including Stevens and Souter as well as the replacements for Justices White and Blackmun, Ruth Bader Ginsburg and Stephen Breyer. These four still scour each capital case for potentially certworthy issues, although in light of *Teague* and other developments, those cases are relatively rare.

hardships" tips in favor of the petitioner. The district judge assigned to the case, Marilyn Hall Patel, decided that the ACLU had met this test. In a recent opinion by Justice O'Connor, the Court had advised that judges should look to contemporary practice in the fifty states to determine whether a punishment qualified as unconstitutionally cruel and unusual. As Patel noted, only one active death penalty state still used lethal gas, and many states had recently abandoned that mode of execution. Considerable evidence, including recent reports of a lingering death in Arizona, suggested lethal gas to be an especially slow and painful method. Given the "hardship" of Harris's impending execution, on Saturday night, April 18, Patel granted the ACLU a ten-day delay to permit fuller consideration of its arguments.

California immediately asked the Ninth Circuit for a writ of mandate, a highly unusual special order overturning a district court ruling. The state's petition was referred to the same three-judge appellate panel (consisting of Judges Arthur Alarcon, Melvin Brunetti, and John Noonan) that had considered Harris's most recent federal habeas requests. This panel had split over his case before, and they split again now.* Over Judge Noonan's dissent, at 11:00 P.M. Sunday, Judges Alarcon and Brunetti granted the state's petition and dissolved Patel's stay. At the time of this order, the majority stated that it would describe the reasons for its decision in a soon-to-be-issued opinion. This elaboration emerged late Monday afternoon—only nine hours before Harris was scheduled to die.

The majority's reasons created great consternation within the circuit. Alarcon and Brunetti had reversed Patel, claiming that, under a case called *Younger* v. *Harris* (a different Harris), Patel did not have proper jurisdiction. According to the panel, *Younger* required that the ACLU present its claims to the state courts before proceeding in federal court. But to anyone familiar with *Younger*, this was patently wrong. As was well settled, the *Younger* doctrine instructed a federal court to abstain from action only when federal review might unduly interfere with a *pending* state court action (such as an ongoing criminal trial). *Younger* had nothing to do with the Harris situation, where there were no ongoing state proceedings. The panel majority had basically made up a doc-

---

*Although Alarcon, Brunetti, and Noonan were all conservative judges, Noonan, a devout Catholic, was deeply troubled by the death penalty.

trine to get the Harris execution—already delayed many years by what they considered specious arguments—back on track.

With the issuance of the panel opinion, chaos erupted on the twenty-eight-judge Ninth Circuit. The circuit's liberal judges, several of them among the nation's most liberal, were outraged that someone might be executed under a decision that was so clearly wrong as a matter of law. They began a series of frantic efforts, with the clock ticking down, to call for en banc review of the panel opinion. This process itself proved a disaster. The twenty-seven judges on the circuit, spread out over the entire western United States, could not even agree about what internal circuit rules governed the particular situation of reviewing a panel decision to grant a writ of mandate. As they lobbied, cajoled, and argued about what to do, the circuit's e-mail system broke down repeatedly, adding delay and confusion to the crisis. As midnight approached, two stays were issued, one by a group of ten judges, another by Judge Norris acting alone. Both were designed to preserve the status quo while the whole court came to some resolution.

Back in Washington the clerks on the death watch were replaying the old battle between those anxious to push for executions and those anxious to find reasons for a stay. Those eager to see Harris's sentence carried out had a strong upper hand. The conservative Justices were already predisposed to view stays issued within the Ninth Circuit as abolitionist guerrilla tactics. From their perspective, the liberal judges on the West Coast had a history of abolitionist maneuvering. Only a few months earlier, the conservatives had felt compelled to lecture one Ninth Circuit panel for stalling for more than two years in handing down a decision in a death case.[20] As far as the conservatives were concerned, the Harris stays showed that stalling had now escalated to pure obstructionism.

Over the dissents of Justices Blackmun and Stevens, at 3:00 A.M. the conservatives vacated both Ninth Circuit stays. In their view, the ACLU's suit, though styled as a Section 1983 action, was really a federal habeas in disguise, trying to sneak past *McCleskey*'s bar on successive habeas petitions. And, even if it was genuine, the suit challenging California's use of lethal gas was "an obvious attempt at manipulation. . . . [that] could have been brought a decade ago." As such, it was barred.

The majority made no mention of the Ninth Circuit's panel opinion misrelying on *Younger* or the ensuing en banc fight that had led to the stays it was dissolving. Nor did the conservatives deal with the inconvenient fact that under the Court's own Eighth Amendment doctrine (looking to contemporary practice), the ACLU had every reason, even perhaps a legal obligation, to delay for as long as possible filing a challenge to a mode of execution that more and more states were abandoning. For Rehnquist, who drafted the order, Harris was pulling another Rosenberg, and the Chief was determined, together with his allies, not to let him get away with it.

In California, state officials brought Harris to the apple green gas chamber and, at a few minutes before 4:00 A.M., strapped him into one of two chairs. Two minutes later, astonishingly, the phone rang. It was Judge Harry Pregerson of the Ninth Circuit, issuing yet another stay. Disregarding the Supreme Court's clear intent, he wanted to allow Harris a chance to present his current claim to the California state courts.

At the Supreme Court, where it was shortly after sunup, the clerks assigned to the Harris case were just heading home after a grueling and acrimonious all-nighter when runners from the clerk's office called them back to deal with Pregerson's stay. Justice O'Connor, the circuit justice, was not amused. "This is an outrage," she fumed upon arriving at her Chambers. "We'll just tell them no more stays." And she did. Again, over dissents from Justices Blackmun and Stevens, the conservatives dissolved Pregerson's stay and added, in an unprecedented assertion of power, "No further stays of Robert Alton Harris's execution shall be entered by the federal courts except upon the order of this Court."

Harris was pronounced dead at 6:21 A.M., West Coast time. The next day, in a move little noted, the original Ninth Circuit panel handling the case issued an order erasing from the books its trumped-up Monday afternoon opinion vacating Judge Patel's stay on *Younger* grounds. Continuing what already was the most acrimonious death penalty debate in years, Judge Noonan took to the op-ed pages of *The New York Times* to suggest that the Supreme Court's handling of the Harris case amounted to "treason" against the Constitution. On the other side, California Governor Pete Wilson denounced the Ninth Circuit's repeated stays as a "macabre legal circus."[21]

Actually, there was more than enough legitimate blame to go around. The seemingly devious manipulations of Alarcon and Brunetti were unjustifiable. And the actions of the conservative Justices pushed the outer limits of the law. The Court's first opinion never bothered to engage, much less refute, the ACLU's arguments. Its second represented a unique and perhaps insupportable claim to power. Neither was reasoned lawmaking. They were fits of pique.

But for all this, liberals—in particular liberal judges—must shoulder significant responsibility. In the death cases, illegitimacy had long ago begat illegitimacy, and *Harris* was but another offspring. Years of abolitionist or near-abolitionist maneuvering, led by Justices Brennan and Marshall but also widespread in the lower courts, had both created a conservative backlash and, crucially, robbed liberals of their credibility. The initial Ninth Circuit's stays in the Harris case were appropriate responses to the blatantly erroneous opinion of Alarcon and Brunetti. But there had been too many proverbial cries of wolf before, too many acts of abolitionist civil disobedience, such as Judge Pregerson's conscience-over-duty, last-gasp stay, the regrettable but fitting final act to the drama.[22]

A decade earlier, Norman Mailer had observed: "Capital Punishment is to the rest of all law as surrealism is to realism. It destroys the logic of the profession."[23] As *Harris* brought home once again, it also destroys the integrity of courts, and that tragedy continues to this day.*

The importance of the Court's habeas revolution was much deeper and broader than its obviously significant effect on the death penalty. From the dawn of the Warren era in 1953, habeas cases had served as a weathervane for the basic direction of the Court. *Teague*, *McCleskey*, and *Coleman* continued this function. Reflecting a powerful devotion to states' rights, they set the main course for the Rehnquist Court in recent

---

*Justice Blackmun became so discouraged and disheartened at the process that, as a swan song before retiring in 1994, he gave up on his agonizing case-by-case approach to capital punishment and announced his conversion to abolitionism. Although he still did not agree with Brennan and Marshall that the death penalty was inherently cruel and unusual, Blackmun had come to believe after twenty-four years' experience that, in practice, the system was incurably capricious and unfair, rife with inevitable "factual, legal, and moral error." Blackmun labored over his statement for months, waiting for the right case to issue his declaration that he would no longer "tinker with the machinery of death." Tellingly, he kept his plans secret from his colleagues. Here, as elsewhere, the idea of persuasion had long since disappeared and the liberals, wishing on the future, addressed themselves solely to the world beyond the Court. *Callins v. Collins*, 510 U.S. 1141 (1994).

Harris did not end the conflict between the liberal judges on the Ninth Circuit and the Court's conservatives. In the summer of 1997, the Ninth Circuit replayed its internal war over the death penalty in granting another highly publicized eleventh-hour stay to Thomas Thompson. Conservatives at the Court granted California's cert. petition in *Calderon v. Thompson* and are almost certain to reverse the Ninth Circuit before the end of the current term.

years. And that course heads in almost exactly the reverse direction from the one the Warren Court pursued in the 1960s.

In Warren's day, decisions expanding the availability of federal habeas had been part and parcel of the Court's Rights Revolution and its defining assault on race discrimination, especially in the South. Segregation in schools, restaurants, and every manner of public and private institution led the Court to expand the power of the federal government to override state laws and personal biases. Discrimination in the field of voting rights led to the adoption of the one-person/one-vote standard and to the outlawing of election practices that worked to the exclusion of blacks. Discrimination by police, prosecutors, and even state courts led to a nationalization of criminal procedure and a corresponding expansion of federal habeas.

Earlier, I described the animating force behind the Warren Court as the "spirit of Scottsboro," and the accomplishments of this era as the rediscovery, perhaps even the elevation, of the ideals that the victorious Union had enshrined in the Constitution during Reconstruction. Over time, that spirit gradually had expired, exhausted from the abuse of friends and foes alike as well as, importantly, from its own success in outlawing overt forms of discrimination.

With the rulings of the Rehnquist-led habeas revolution, a new spirit was emerging at the Court, the spirit of federalism—a less freighted term for states' rights. And just as the spirit of Scottsboro originally took hold at the Court mainly in cases involving the death penalty where the Justices expanded federal power and the scope of constitutional rights, so the spirit of federalism announced itself in a similar set of cases restricting federal power and the scope of those rights. As recent terms have shown, *Teague, McCleskey,* and *Coleman* were but signal bells for a new activist era.

The last several terms have been a roller-coaster ride of potentially landmark rulings—"epochal" in the words of Justice Souter—overturning precedent and major acts of federal legislation as the Court's new spirit has come of age. Naturally, the Court's emerging devotion to states' rights has had a profound effect in the area of race, where the Warren Court made its most crucial mark. The conservative majority, in several 5–4 decisions, has diluted the power of federal judges to continue enforcement of desegregation at public schools. By the same narrow margin, the conservatives have dismantled the "minority-majority" voting districts created in the South that brought the first black representatives to Congress since Reconstruction. The same five Justices, overruling Justice Brennan's last civil rights victory, have also cut back sharply on federal affirmative action programs, reiterating their view from *Richmond* v. *Croson* that race-conscious measures intended to help minorities are as suspect constitutionally as race-conscious measures intended to oppress them.[24]

Other pathbreaking, precedent-bending decisions have dramatically revised the balance of federal-state authority in favor of the states. Striking down federal efforts to combat guns near schools, the conservatives have—for the first time in fifty years—curtailed Congress' power under the Commerce Clause to interfere with local affairs. In so doing, they have cast doubt on the constitutional theory supporting the watershed civil rights laws of the 1960s. Similarly, in voiding part of the Brady handgun registration bill because it conscripts state law enforcement officers to carry out federal gun registration rules, the conservatives have put in jeopardy federal programs that rely on states for implementation.[25]

The parade of blockbusters continues. Last term the Justices struck down the Religious Freedom Restoration Act that Congress passed in 1993 to give greater legal protection to the practice of religion than the Court had found constitutionally required.[26] According to Justice Kennedy's majority opinion, Congress had exceeded its power under the Fourteenth Amendment to "enforce" against the states the Constitution's guarantee of religious freedom. By demanding that states specially justify laws affecting religious practice, the act was an unconstitutional "intrusion into the states' traditional prerogatives and general authority to regulate for the health and welfare of their citizens."*

Elsewhere, the conservatives limited Congress's power to penetrate the "sovereign immunity" of states and make them answerable in federal court. They also prevailed in two 5–4 decisions depriving federal courts of the power to hear cases where individual state and local officials were charged with violating federal law. Thus, Walter McMillian, who spent

---

*In passing the Religious Freedom Restoration Act, Congress attempted to overturn a 1990, Justice Scalia-authored, 5–4 ruling, *Employment Div.* v. *Smith*, which had substantially lessened constitutional protection for the free exercise of minority religious faiths. 494 U.S. 872 (1990). Ironically, Justice Souter, a critic of *Smith*, thought he had assembled a majority (including himself, O'Connor, Ginsburg, Breyer, and Thomas) to overrule *Smith*—before Congress stole his thunder. Whether Souter can reassemble such a coalition now that the Court has struck down RFRA is a question certain to arise in upcoming terms. And in any event, Souter's targeting of *Smith* will remain a sore spot for Scalia, who thinks the *stare decisis* touting Souter a hypocrite for seeking to jettison *Smith*.

six years falsely convicted on Alabama's death row because the Monroe county sheriff had concealed evidence of his innocence, was denied the right to sue that sheriff because, according to the majority, he was a state official immune from suit.[27]

These cases trace the fault line of the current Court. In virtually every one the Justices have split in the same configuration—Rehnquist, O'Connor, Scalia, Kennedy, and Thomas on one side, Stevens, Souter, Ginsburg, and Breyer on the other. Simply put, the Court today—in its continuing referendum on the merits of Warren's "Second Reconstruction"—is riven between those who see the federal government as the primary guarantor of constitutional rights and those who do not; between those Justices who still think that the federal government must intervene to achieve racial equality and those who do not; and between those for whom "states' rights" still carries the taint of its slaveholder legacy and those for whom it does not.

And, thus, while the Justices may have settled for the moment the great debate of the 1980s over abortion and the right to privacy, they carry on the Court's sharp and often nasty internal division in the two related areas that have haunted constitutional argument since the nation's founding: race and the relationship between the states and the federal government. In the mid-nineteenth century, the entire nation broke apart over these issues and fought a terrible war. This devastating schism is still with us and dominates the current Court.[28]

The More Things Change

Whenever I go back to the Court, I always feel part at home, part a stranger. Looking up at the Justices from the cushioned pews of the public section, eyeing their clerks off to one side, I can still recapture instantly the blinding intensity, exhilaration, anger, and nervous exhaustion I felt when this was my place, my battlefield. The flood of those emotions is always accompanied not only by a degree of nostalgia but also by some misgiving that no doubt formed the emotional seed for this book. Through years of research and reflection, I have tried to reach an understanding of the Court I experienced. In this book, I have tried to impart what I felt then, and later came to learn.

Visiting the Court in the mid-1990s, I saw a bench in some ways remarkably changed. The old liberal guard was gone. This Court had no Brennan aggressively championing a Constitution embodying his vision of liberal morality. It had no Marshall to serve as a standing reminder of the Jim Crow world that once was. And, most personal to me, the force of time has ushered Justice Blackmun into retirement and deprived the Court of its most compassionate voice.*

In 1993, on Byron White's retirement, President Clinton named to the Court Ruth Bader Ginsburg, a D.C. Circuit judge who had made her name as the nation's leading litigator for women's equality in the 1970s. In several important areas of law, this change has made little difference.

---

*These absences are evident in some major rulings, as in the physician-assisted suicide cases, where no Justice presented a strong affirmative case for why the Constitution protects a broad fundamental right to control the circumstances of one's death. That would never have been the case five years earlier. See *Vacco* v. *Quill;* 521 U.S. 993 (1999); *Washington* v. *Glucksberg,* 521 U.S. 702 (1997).

On the D.C. Circuit, the cautiously intelligent Ginsburg developed a record of solid conservatism on issues of criminal law. She also was a critic of bold liberal decisions, especially those (such as *Roe* v. *Wade*) based on substantive due process.* These views often allied Ginsburg with the Reagan/Bush wing of the circuit, including Scalia, her friend and fellow opera buff, when he served on that court. In three terms as a Justice, Ginsburg has held true to her past and, in so doing, has voted much as Justice White surely would have if he had not retired.†

At the same time, Ginsburg's sterling background in civil rights has been reflected in consistent support for gender equality (she wrote the opinion requiring the Virginia Military Institute to accept women),[1] the constitutionality of affirmative action, strong voting rights enforcement in the South, and federal power vis-à-vis the states. Generally, she may qualify as a judicial moderate. And, specifically, she is resistant to Brennanesque expansions of due process liberty. But on the litmus-test issues for this Court, she remains a firm partisan of the Warren Court innovations that laid the groundwork for her own career.

Stephen Breyer, the well-respected First Circuit judge and Harvard Law professor whom Clinton named to replace Justice Blackmun, has proven even more consistent in opposing the Court's states' rights ascendancy. Like Ginsburg, Breyer, too, has a strong tie to the Warren Court: he was a clerk to Justice Arthur Goldberg, Warren's stalwart ally in building his Second Reconstruction. Also, Breyer's long experience (in Washington and academia) dealing with federal bureaucracies seems to have left him with a cautious but basically liberal faith in the power of the national government to intervene beneficently in local affairs. In that vein, he has written several significant opinions defending federal power.[2]

What mark these new Justices may eventually leave on the Court is as yet uncertain. But for the moment, despite the changed faces, I see today's Court as distressingly familiar in crucial respects. It is still a Court of two camps divided intractably over the pressing issues of the day. And it is still a Court where the majority insists on making huge legal leaps on the slim authority of five votes triumphs over four.

---

*Though a public critic of *Roe*, Ginsburg has defended a woman's constitutional right to abortion on equality grounds.

†In this respect, Ginsburg had been portrayed accurately as a disciple of Harvard's "legal process" school of jurisprudence, once championed by Justice Felix Frankfurter, which counsels against bold and potentially divisive rulings by the Court.

By common account, the widening polarization over the issues of race and states' rights have shattered what hope emerged from *Casey* that the Court would find a meaningful center. Term by term, Justice Souter, the catalyst in *Casey*, has placed himself ever more firmly among the Court's liberals. As someone whose great-great-grandfather helped nominate Lincoln and whose ancestors worked the Underground Railroad, Souter has bred in his bones the brand of New England Republicanism that detested slavery, cherished the Union, died in Lincoln's war, and supported an aggressive federal Reconstruction of the South. This is not a Justice who could sign on to the conservatives' states' rights agenda. And his opinions—deeply appreciative of the effects of historical racism, increasingly skeptical of southern justice, and streaked with a Yankee libertarianism—put him ever more firmly at odds with the political party that named him.

Inside the Court, Kennedy and O'Connor have stopped thinking of Souter as "one of their own." Born in the West, their frontier Constitution does not bear the stamp of his Yankee history and the bloody war with the South. Theirs is a Constitution in which the states—the great "laboratories of democracy"—start afresh and where the chief threat to liberty comes not from local officials but from the behemoth of the federal government. Separated from Souter by this wide gorge of history and ideology, O'Connor and Kennedy have lost, seemingly irretrievably, the implicit trust that was so vital in forging their once-crucial and potentially Court-controlling coalition.

In the absence of such a center, at least a center with ballast, the Court remains, as it was in my day, a creature of Justices O'Connor and Kennedy, one or the other of whom holds sway in every major area of law. In case after case, these swing-vote Justices write separate concurrences, usually modulating the conservative insurgency, but always bending the Court and the law to their will. Occupying the pivot is often a deliberate strategy. Indeed, Kennedy has been known to brag about expressing views at conference designed to make him a necessary but distinctive fifth vote for a majority. O'Connor pursues the same policy more quietly. Both, in effect, hold constitutional interpretation hostage to their personal and often idiosyncratic views.*

---

*These views are not always conservative. Justice Kennedy wrote and Justice O'Connor joined one of the few liberal triumphs of the last few terms, the ruling striking down as a violation of the equal protection clause Colorado's voter initiative barring homosexuals from the benefits of local civil rights laws. See *Romer* v. *Evans*, 517 U.S. 620 (1996). They also joined a Ginsburg majority opinion requiring the admission of women at the Virginia Military Institute. These occasional

When the Court consistently decides the most important cases on its docket by a 5-4 division it is always unsettling, and doubly so when its rulings (as repeatedly with this Court) overturn or eviscerate settled precedents. How much worse when the monumental legal issues of the day are controlled not by five Justices, but rather by one. From lower court judges to prospective litigants to the lay public generally, we continue to be confused, uncertain, and dependent on the authority that now has fallen to O'Connor and Kennedy. That these two Justices should be in a position to wield such power, indeed that they undoubtedly feel compelled to do so by the persistent radicalism of their more "conservative" brethren, reveals the depth of the internal crisis that continues to plague a fractured Court.

Other destructive pathologies flourish as well. It is still a Court where Justices too often issue transparently inadequate or hypocritical opinions in highly significant, politically charged cases.[3] Stare decisis is passionately invoked in one case, blithely discarded in the next.[4] Avowed originalists conveniently forsake originalism; textualists forsake text.[5] And, throughout, ideologically driven clerks, especially in the swing-vote chambers, seek sometimes inappropriate influence over the law.[6]

There are hopeful signs. Although perhaps deficient in lawyers with real litigation experience, the current Court is, as a whole, remarkably intelligent by historical standards. Also, in some recent rulings—for example, the Court's unanimous denial of President Clinton's claim of immunity from the Paula Jones suit—the Justices have shown an ability, however rarely invoked, to set aside lurking partisanship and speak with a single institutional voice.

But the tests ahead are daunting. Outside the Court, especially in the vengeful post-Bork world of judicial confirmation, partisans on both sides wage a destructively misguided war against what they deride reflexively as judicial activism. For liberals, this judicial overstepping takes the form of every recent decision that has cut back or overturned a War-renesque ruling of the past. Meanwhile, conservatives cry foul at every decision in which a federal judge finds the police or prosecutors to have

----

apostasies arise from the same basic belief that leads O'Connor and Kennedy generally to oppose affirmative action: a belief that every person should be treated as an individual rather than as a member of a group. Such consistency nonetheless enrages Justice Scalia, who in one of his increasingly bitter dissents described such liberal decisions as "not the interpretation of a Constitution, but the creation of one." *United States v. Virginia*, 518 U.S. 515 (1996).

violated constitutional rights or those that impinge on favorite political causes such as school prayer.

Such convenient charges—which simply prove that activism is in the eye of the beholder—debase a crucial idea. Judicial "activism"—of the right or of the left—is no sin unto itself. Despite opportunistic complaints from liberals, precedent is no more sacrosanct now than when the Warren Court revised large swaths of constitutional law. *Stare decisis* mandates respect, not inviolability, for past decisions—which must stand the tests of reason and experience or ultimately fall. Nor is there anything intrinsically dismaying about judicial rulings that conservatives routinely decry. As part of the genius of our republican system, we have made it the business of the judiciary to enforce the Constitution against overzealous agents of state power or against invidious or overreaching expressions of the popular will. And conservatives do our liberties no favor by seeking to intimidate judges from performing that essential duty.

The sin is not judicial activism, which may be warranted and healthy, but judicial activism bereft of persuasion and its crucial ingredients: reason, consistency, and principle. It is this kind of activism that betrays the almost sacred trust we invest in our unelected, life-tenured judges and destroys our necessary faith that they pursue a method and ideal called law. It is this kind of activism that became endemic at the Court and has yet to abate.

Such corruption in the judicial process, as we have seen, invites reprisal upon reprisal. In an escalating spiral of illegitimacy, opposing Justices have lost faith in each other and then abandoned their own responsibilities. That loss of faith, that abandonment, is pure poison. From the inside, it undermines the Court's own justification for its existence. From the outside, it corrodes our belief in the Court's authority and puts at risk the liberties it was designed to protect.

For these ills there is no miracle cure. Our ideological divisions are certain to persist. And in confronting them, we cannot force the Justices to deliberate more conscientiously, or to bring greater candor and logic to their decisions, or to value more fully their obligations to the Court's institutional life.* The remedy, the power to restore the character of the

---

*This is not to deny the value of some reforms. Justice Scalia, for example, has advanced the excellent idea that the Justices refrain from joining a draft majority opinion until the main dissent in that case has circulated. Scalia's proposal, easily adopted, would have the salutary effect of promoting fuller consideration of opposing views.

Court and to repair its inner processes, lies only in the souls of the Justices themselves, both those who preside today and those who we—through our elected representatives—choose for the Court tomorrow.

Long ago, Nathaniel Hawthorne posed a question to which I return repeatedly when I ponder the Court's current ills. "Cannot you conceive," he asked, "that another man may wish well to the world and struggle for its good on some other plan than precisely that which you have laid down?" For too long, the Justices of our Supreme Court, liberal and conservative alike, have suffered from an arrogance of certainty. That arrogance is the purest and deadliest enemy of the self-restraint so vital to the wise and legitimate exercise of judicial power. Whatever other qualities we may seek in choosing heirs for the current Court—legal acumen, moral vision, scholarship, experience—the most important in my view will be open-mindedness and intellectual integrity. For without such strengths of character, the other qualities are for naught, and our belief in law and the possibility of justice will remain casualties in the cross fire of politics.

An Imperial Court
in a Troubled Democracy

Ten days before George W. Bush won the 2004 presidential election, word leaked out of a Washington hospital that Chief Justice Rehnquist had been diagnosed with thyroid cancer. Over the next few days, initial assurances from the Court press office that Rehnquist would return to work the following Monday gave way to increasingly grim assessments from cancer experts evaluating Rehnquist's course of treatment.

Although Rehnquist (as of this writing) has not submitted his resignation, he appears to be suffering from an aggressive cancer and is unlikely to resist retirement much longer, especially with the like-minded President Bush controlling his replacement. But even if Rehnquist perseveres for a few more years, his tenure is unlikely to see further innovations of great importance.

From 1986 when President Reagan elevated Rehnquist to Chief Justice, the Rehnquist era's steady shift to the right has always depended on the concurrence of O'Connor and Kennedy, the pivotal votes on a deeply but narrowly divided Court. While O'Connor and Kennedy lent the votes necessary to achieve the Rehnquist Court's rightward turn, they also set the boundaries for the Court's shift. Now, after seventeen years together on the bench, they have brought the Court to a political and jurisprudential equilibrium. Over time, O'Connor and Kennedy have managed to steer almost every aspect of constitutional law into their comfort zone—the place where their deeply ingrained but relatively moderate conservatism parts company with the more radical agenda of Rehnquist, Scalia, and Thomas. Simply put, the Rehnquist Court—the Court that O'Connor and Kennedy control—lacks an impetus (and the votes) for additional dramatic change.

Over the next few years, the political balance of the Court could change through additional retirement or unanticipated illness or death. If several more justices (say Stevens and O'Connor) left the Court and a Republican dominated Senate permits President Bush to replace both with hard-core conservatives, the Court could embark on a further journey to the right. It is easy to overstate the likelihood of mass departures, however. Although the current set of justices is aging, with the exception of Rehnquist, none is infirm, including Ginsburg, the most recent to suffer a cancer scare. Stevens (the oldest at eighty-four) appears as rigorous and acute as ever and, no doubt, recognizes the political implications of allowing Bush to appoint his successor. O'Connor, though more comfortable with Bush, has much to lose and little to gain by retiring. She remains the most powerful jurist in the world. With the Court reviewing only eighty cases or so a year, she does not have to work terribly hard. And as the Court's first woman, she is a heroine to a large national constituency. It is difficult to imagine why she would voluntarily cede such a magnificent position especially considering that she has watched Justices Stewart, Powell, Brennan, Marshall, Blackmun, and White rapidly deteriorate post-retirement. In sum, while dramatic short-term change in the Court's composition is certainly possible, it is not the foregone conclusion that many pundits and politicians suggest.

But whether or not a spate of retirements is forthcoming, the Court has reached an appropriate juncture for taking stock of the Rehnquist era—from its inception in 1986, through its single most significant decision (*Bush v. Gore*), to the Guantanamo cases, in which it has started to grapple with today's most pressing legal dilemma of how to meet the need for heightened national security in the age of terror while preserving our liberties at home.

In terms of bottom-line results, the Rehnquist revolution—the enterprise of erasing much of the Warren Court's legacy—has been a success, albeit a qualified one. Back in 1988, as Kennedy replaced Powell and the conservative juggernaut gained steam, a group of liberal clerks dashed off over dinner a potential target list for the Court's right wing. *Roe v. Wade* topped the list. Then came *Bakke v. Regents of the University of California*, which permitted affirmative action, followed by *Engle v. Vitale*, declaring public school prayer unconstitutional, and *Miranda v. Arizona*, with its famous warning to criminal suspects of their right to remain silent and to an attorney. Other goals were not so identified with a single case, but were clear nonetheless. The right wing of the legal world had never fully accepted the constitutional underpinnings for the modern administrative state or the broad expansion of federal power that accompanied the New Deal, the Great Society, and the civil rights revolution of the 1960s and '70s. Opponents of these developments had a variety of potential avenues for curbing the power of the federal government to regulate state officials and private industry—and we expected Rehnquist and his allies to explore them aggressively.

Since that time, the Rehnquist Court's conservatives have taken a run at all these targets, with remarkably consistent results. The Court's right wing recaptured a lot of territory seized by the liberals in an earlier day, but has not (yet) reached its ultimate goals. Every time the hardliners got close, either O'Connor or Kennedy (or sometimes both) balked, and the enterprise fell short.

Planned Parenthood v. *Casey* (1992) is an early but prime example. Although O'Connor and Kennedy previously had joined the Court's anti-*Roe* Justices in permitting greater state regulation of abortion, in *Casey* they (together with Souter) definitively refused to overturn *Roe* itself and, in what I dubbed the "fragile peace," tried to bring a measure of stability to the law of abortion. They succeeded. In the thirteen years since *Casey*, the Court has addressed abortion directly only once, in *Stenberg* v. *Carhart*, a 2000 decision in which the Court declared unconstitutional Nebraska's ban on so-called partial birth abortion, a rare late-pregnancy procedure.[1] With Justices O'Connor and Souter joining Stevens, Ginsburg, and Breyer, the Court applied *Casey*'s "undue burden" test and invalidated the Nebraska law because its criminal prohibition on the procedure failed to safeguard the health of the mother.

Notably, Justice Kennedy—the most reluctant participant in the *Casey* compromise—wrote an aggrieved dissent that made clear how much he felt betrayed by his *Casey* partners. For Kennedy, if states could not ban the late-pregnancy partial-birth method of abortion (as O'Connor and Souter now held), then *Casey*'s cutback on *Roe* was practically meaningless. Kennedy's regrets, however, have yet to translate into any new threat to *Roe*. Five years have passed since *Stenberg* with no change in abortion law and, the claims of politicians and activists notwithstanding, this Court is unlikely to achieve the right wing's ultimate objective—*Roe*'s overruling—any time soon, if ever.

A similar mixed result marks the Rehnquist Court's approach to affirmative action. Throughout the late 1980s and 1990s, O'Connor and Kennedy provided key votes for cutting back on race-conscious remedies in such cases as *Richmond* v. *Croson* and *Adarand Constructors* v. *Pena*. But while Rehnquist, Scalia, and Thomas long sought an outright ban on affirmative action, in the 2003 University of Michigan law school case (*Grutter* v. *Bollenger*), O'Connor and Kennedy rejected that position and, instead, endorsed Justice Powell's approach from *Bakke* affirming the value of affirmative action, so long as it was done modestly and carefully.[2]

The Court's *Miranda* decisions tell much the same tale. Through the '80s and '90s, the conservatives carved large loopholes in the rule prohibiting prosecutors from using evidence obtained through interrogations conducted in the absence of *Miranda* warnings. But thanks to O'Connor and Kennedy, in the 2001 case *Dickerson* v. *United States*, the Court explicitly reaffirmed *Miranda*, albeit in its diminished form.[3]

The list goes on. Consider the Court's decisions in the field of religion. The conservatives, including O'Connor and Kennedy, lowered considerably the metaphoric wall separating Church and State. Of greatest note, they abandoned the established line of cases prohibiting government from giving direct financial assistance to religious institutions or initiatives. Instead, the conservatives ruled that government, when administering broad funding programs, may include sectarian enterprises—thus giving legal support to school voucher programs that reach parochial schools as well as bolstering other faith-based initiatives the Bush Administration has pushed.[4]

But here, too, Kennedy and O'Connor, despite deep skepticism about the Warren Court's approach to religious issues, prevented really radical change. For example, both O'Connor and Kennedy rejected the idea that government not only *may* fund religious institutions as part of a general funding program but also that government *must* do so and on an equal basis with non-religious recipients.[5] Kennedy also cast the crucial vote and wrote the opinion in *Lee* v. *Weisman* (discussed earlier), preserving the Warren Court's ban on prayer in public school.

Even in the area of federalism, where the Rehnquist Court has dramatically remade the balance of power between the federal government and the states, O'Connor and Kennedy have stopped the revolution short of where the true believers would take it.

This field of law is complicated and unglamorous, but very important. Contrary to common belief, Congress cannot pass any law it wants. Rather, Congress can legislate only in furtherance of the legislative powers contained in the Constitution, which include, most significantly, the power to regulate interstate commerce and the power to enforce the equal protection, due process, and privileges and immunities clauses of the Fourteenth Amendment. Before the advent of a truly national economy, and while the country turned a blind eye to racial discrimination, these powers did not amount to much. But in the modern era, they provide the constitutional basis for Congressional regulation of food and drugs, worker safety, the environment, and most of the laws—from the Civil Rights Act and Voting Rights Act of the 1960s to the Americans with Disabilities Act of the 1990s—that define our modern commitment to civil rights.

The modern era's broader reading of federal power, moreover, inevitably comes at the expense of state power—as federal law imposes additional requirements on states and also intrudes on areas that states once exclusively regulated. This tug-of-war between state and national power first arose in the battle over slavery and the right of states to reject federal anti-slavery measures. The tension reemerged when the Supreme Court and Congress belatedly set about dismantling Jim Crow. Now, however, given the ubiquity of federal regulation, the potential implications go far beyond civil rights and extend to any area—from clean water to homeland security—where federal agencies exert substantial oversight and control.

What has the Rehnquist Court done about all this? A great deal. Using a variety of approaches, some of which are novel and others which reverse decades of precedent, it has struck down (almost always by 5–4 votes) parts of no fewer than ten federal statutes on federalism grounds.

The Court's federalism decisions fall into several overlapping categories. There are the decisions that, for the first time since the New Deal, find Congress to have overstepped its power to legislate pursuant to the interstate commerce clause—a clause that had been given a very elastic meaning in light of our increasingly nationalized economy.[6] Related to this category is another group of decisions holding that, when Congress exercises its commerce clause power, it cannot "commandeer" state officials to carry out federal law (as, for example, by requiring state officials to do background checks on gun buyers). Such commandeering, the conservatives ruled, violates the Tenth Amendment, which commands that "the powers not delegated to the United States . . . are reserved to the States respectively, or to the People." On these bases, the Court invalidated, for example, part of the Brady Bill regulating handguns and part of the Violence Against Women Act.[7]

In another line of decisions, the conservatives concluded that Congress has overstepped its authority to legislate under the Fourteenth Amendment, the post–Civil War Amendment that, generally speaking, makes the protections in the Bill of Rights applicable to the states. Basically, the justices ruled that Congress had to take a backseat to the Court in determining the scope of individual rights protected by the Fourteenth Amendment. Although the Constitution gives Congress the power to "enforce" the Fourteenth Amendment, according to the Court, Congress could only "enforce" rights as recognized by the Court—and could not expand the scope of constitutional rights independently. Thus, for example, the Court struck down the Religious Freedom Restoration Act because, in it, Congress sought to give individuals a broader First Amendment right to the "free exercise" of religion than the Court itself had recognized in its decisions.[8] Similarly, the conservatives voided parts of the American with Disabilities Act and the Age Discrimination in Employment Act because Congress had provided protection to the disabled and the elderly that was "disproportionate" to and "incongruent" with the level of constitutional protection that the Court afforded these groups.[9]

In related rulings, the Court also closely scrutinized a number of congressional enactments that stripped states of their sovereign immunity and, thus, subjected them to private lawsuits for violations of federal law. The first case in this line involved the Indian Gaming Regulatory Act, a 1988 law that directed states to engage in "good faith" negotiations with Indian tribes over gaming "compacts" to regulate casino-style gaming on reservations. Using its power under the commerce clause, Congress provided that tribes could sue states for not living up to this provision. The conservative justices, however, would not accept this. They ruled that Congress had absolutely no power under the commerce clause to abrogate state sovereign immunity and permit the tribes to sue.[10]

The conservatives did allow that Congress could abrogate sovereign immunity pursuant to its power to enforce the Fourteenth Amendment. But what the conservatives gave to Congress, they then partially took away. In the next set of cases, the conservatives made it much harder for Congress to use the Fourteenth Amendment to take away state immunity. And using this tougher standard, they declared unconstitutional the provisions allowing suits against states in the Age Discrimination in Employment Act, Title I of the American with Disabilities Act, and two laws dealing with patents and trademarks.[11]

More generally, the conservatives also broadened the circumstances where a state's sovereign immunity would come into play. The Eleventh Amendment (the only constitutional provision actually discussing suits against states) provides that the judicial power of federal courts will "not be construed to extend" to suits "prosecuted against one of the United States by Citizens of another State" or by a foreigner. Back in 1890, the Supreme Court had set aside the plain meaning of this text—which protected states from being hauled into hostile judicial venues by citizens of *other* jurisdictions—to protect states from suits by *their own* citizens.[12] The Rehnquist Court conservatives not only reaffirmed this much-criticized doctrine, they extended it to suits brought in state court (though the Eleventh Amendment was limited to federal court) and to actions before administrative agencies (which the Eleventh Amendment does not mention at all).[13] Although the conservatives conceded that their newly minted sovereign immunity doctrine lacked a foundation in the Constitution's text (or in much history), they ruled that the inherent "dignity" of states in the system of "dual sovereignty" implicit in the Constitution required the result. At bottom, this meant that, unless Congress invoked its Fourteenth Amendment power to wipe out state immunity (and the Court was making this increasingly difficult), individuals simply had no remedy if states (and their instrumentalities, like universities) violated their federal statutory rights.

These decisions mark a profound change in the structure of the union and the protections individuals enjoy against unlawful state action. Certainly, they have been viewed this way by the justices themselves, their clerks, and many academics. But it remains a stretch to say that the practical impact of these decisions on national governance has been momentous. True, the conservatives have tossed out sections of numerous statutes and the Religious Freedom Restoration Act (a law of more symbolic than substantive effect) entirely. They have also granted states a license to violate some federal laws. Still, the Court's conservatives have not yet seriously dented Congress's post–New Deal power to regulate a wide swath of American life. Nor have they overturned the core of any major civil rights or environmental legislation. Nor have they prohibited Congress from stripping states of immunity so long as Congress acts under the Fourteenth Amendment and creates a sufficient legislative record for why states need to be held accountable in the area in question.

Some predict that a more radical dismantling of the federal regulatory state is in the offing. But as with other radical potential departures, O'Connor and Kennedy hold the key—and O'Connor at least appears reluctant to take the federalism revolution much further. In the last two terms, she has sided with the liberals in two closely watched cases. With O'Connor's concurrence, the Court upheld the immunity stripping provisions in both the Family Medical Leave Act and Title II of the Americans with Disabilities Act.[14] Indeed, the states' rights movement generally seems to have hit a high-water mark, as O'Connor (and sometimes Kennedy) have also started to hold states to somewhat tighter account when it comes to habeas corpus review of death sentences, the area where (in cases like McCleskey and Coleman) the states' rights movement first gained traction.

The "O'Kennedy effect" on the Rehnquist Court's legacy, moreover, is more complicated than merely imposing a deep conservatism that lacks the more radical inclination of Rehnquist, Scalia, or Thomas. On rare but important occasions O'Connor and Kennedy have also joined with the Court's more liberal wing to expand individual rights. The signal example is Lawrence v. Texas, the 2003 decision that struck down the Texas law criminalizing homosexual but not heterosexual sodomy.[15] This landmark opinion overturned Bowers v. Hardwick and, in place of Bowers, held that the constitutional right to privacy includes the right to engage in private consensual acts of homosexual sex. Writing for the majority, Kennedy turned his back on thirty years of conservative efforts to limit the right to privacy and the doctrine of substantive due process that undergirds it. In seeking protection from Texas's bigoted law, Kennedy wrote sweepingly, Michael Lawrence was simply exercising the right of "persons in every generation to invoke [the Constitution's] principles in their own search for greater freedom." That was, as Scalia charged in a scathing dissent, as firm an embrace of a "living" and everevolving Constitution—the most hated of all legal concepts by rightwing theorists—as anything William Brennan had ever penned.

To merely describe the non-radical conservatism of the "O'Kennedy" Court, however, does not provide an underlying cause for the Court's actions. These do exist. The unifying theme is an unprecedented conception of judicial power that arises from O'Connor's and Kennedy's respective approaches to the law.

O'Connor's jurisprudence reflects almost perfectly the personal experience and political beliefs of the frontiersman's daughter who overcame longstanding prejudice against women professionals to become a successful attorney, local politician, state court judge and, finally, the first woman on the nation's highest court. A disciple of Arizona's then-preeminent politician Barry Goldwater, O'Connor is a small government, up by the bootstraps, country club tolerant, free-enterprise Republican (not a culture warrior and ideological theorist, like Scalia or Thomas)—and that is precisely how she votes at the Court.

Take O'Connor's position on abortion. She has never voiced a deep moral aversion to *Roe*, the sort of religiously based passion that animates Scalia and Thomas. Rather, O'Connor opposed *Roe*'s trimester framework, which struck her (reasonably enough) as legislating from the bench. She also thought *Roe* made all abortions, especially beyond the first trimester, too readily accessible. In the end, these flaws were not enough for O'Connor—the Court's self-conscious standard bearer for American women—to throw out *Roe* entirely. Instead, O'Connor rewrote abortion law to suit her own rather privileged perspective and created a legal regime that protects women who are in the world with which she is most familiar—while protecting others, such as those who cannot afford the procedure, not as well.

A similar story of fitting the law to personal preference could be told in many fields. O'Connor's states' rights anti-big government jurisprudence seems to spring straight from her experience as Arizona state legislator and judge. Her compromise views on affirmative action combine the skepticism of a frontier individualist uncomfortable with "group think" about racial issues with the recognition that comes with being a victim of discrimination herself. The same holds true for Church/State issues. O'Connor does not like hostility towards religion or longstanding religious traditions, but there's nothing evangelical about O'Connor—and her rewriting of First Amendment law follows her "gut" as to how much religion is too much religion. Reflecting this personalization of the law, O'Connor opinions are characteristically narrow, fact-driven affairs that employ "balancing tests" or other "I know it when I see it" standards for determining constitutional or other legal violations. Abortion regulations are okay unless they impose an "undue" burden; religious displays are okay unless they rise to the level of state "endorsement" of religion.[16]

Some have praised what they see as the judicial restraint in this "incremental" or "minimalist" approach.[17] But while O'Connor's self-referential caution may often minimize the scope of particular decisions, it maximizes O'Connor's power by making so many vital constitutional doctrines turn on her application of her own highly subjective tests. And O'Connor is not shy about wielding this power. On the couch in her office sits a pillow inscribed, "Maybe In Error, Never in Doubt." O'Connor is comfortable with her own judgments and with foisting those judg-ments on the country, even if that means overturning the acts of elected officials on what often amounts as a practical matter on this 5–4 Court to her say-so alone. Merely looking at the years 1995 to 2001 O'Connor voted fifty times to overturn state or federal laws, more than any other justice except Kennedy, who did so fifty-one times.[18]

Kennedy's penchant for overturning legislative judgments, however, arises from a different source than O'Connor's. Of all the justices, Kennedy holds the most romantic view of the Court's role in American life and of an individual justice's role on the Court. To Kennedy, the Court serves as a unique and irreplaceable moral beacon upholding the highest American traditions. And he often sees his role on the Court as either giving voice to American constitutional idealism or as protecting the Court's ability to serve as the ultimate arbiter of the law, even when doing so occasionally leads to results in individual cases that, on a per-sonal level, Kennedy regrets.

Kennedy has been mocked at the Court for a certain pomposity. When considering big cases, he has been known to pace back and forth across the interior flagstone courtyard outside his office, arms crossed, Rodin's *The Thinker* in motion, agonizing over yet another crisis of American constitutionalism and the heroic role he had been called upon to play. Such bouts of self-conscious reflection yield opinions filled with grandil-oquent statements that match Kennedy's expansive sense of mission. So it is that he began his defense of the decision to reaffirm *Roe* with the dec-laration that "liberty finds no refuge in a jurisprudence of doubt," and prefaced his most important federalism opinion by extolling the "genius" of the framers who "split the atom of sovereignty," or sought to protect the Court from the political fallout from its flag burning decision by pub-licly agonizing that "the hard fact is that sometimes we must make deci-sions we do not like." Kennedy is forever reaching for a phrase that will identify himself as defending an elevated vision of the law and of judging.

In political terms, this vision leads Kennedy sometimes right, other times left. The conflict between his personal abhorrence of abortion and his fear that overturning *Roe* would indelibly injure the Court brought him literally to tears—and also to the conclusion that he must serve the Court before his own morality. His almost mystical conception of liberty—what he described as "the right to define one's own concept of existence, of meaning, of the universe, and of the mystery of human life"—led him to extend constitutional protection to gay sex. And, by the same token, his conservative approach to federalism arises from a fealty to the superior wisdom of the founding generation and, at least as he perceives it, to the governmental architecture they designed. Thus, while O'Connor's jurisprudence is based on her own personal preferences, Kennedy's jurisprudence is based on his conception of the ideal judge, a black-robed knight-errant fighting for constitutional truth and beauty, however conservatively Kennedy often defines those terms.

By different roads O'Connor and Kennedy reach the same destination. Both are exceedingly comfortable exercising judicial power even if that means overturning the actions of the elected branches of government. This willingness to elevate judicial decision making above the judgments of elected legislatures or executive branch officials is the very definition of "judicial activism." And by this measure of activism, the Rehnquist Court, despite being "conservative" in ideological outlook, is also the most "activist" in Supreme Court history. Since 1994 alone, O'Connor and Kennedy's extreme self-confidence, coupled with the ideological commitments of other justices, has resulted in the Court striking down parts of more than thirty federal statutes and more than forty state statutes. This level of disdain for legislative enactments is unprecedented. (By comparison, between 1804 and 1856 the Court did not strike down a single federal law; and even the Warren Court, often criticized for its activism, did not strike down laws at this pace).

O'Connor and Kennedy, of course, cannot manage such extraordinary judicial intervention on their own. In the most contentious areas, they swing back and forth between the Court's competing ideological camps to create majorities in individual cases to invalidate legislative or executive actions. Sometimes that means joining Rehnquist, Thomas, and Scalia to nullify the kind of secularist, welfare state, government by regulation legislation that conservatives have been griping about for generations. Sometimes this means infuriating the Court's culture warriors Scalia and Thomas by joining the liberal bloc in repudiating attempts to legislate morality or religion. And sometimes the Court's usual voting blocs scramble themselves and (as in the fields of free speech and criminal sentencing) reorganize into doctrine-specific coalitions to strike down what they deem to be legislative overreaching. All told, however, the result has been an unmatched exercise of the power of judicial review.

The difference between the activism of this Court and the activism of other judicial eras is that, while historically the Court has gone through occasional periods when the justices have shown a willingness (even an eagerness) to second-guess the acts of state governments and state officials, the shifting coalitions on the Rehnquist Court has matched a skepticism about *state* action with an equal or even greater skepticism towards the other branches of the *federal* government. Indeed, the current Court's disrespect for Congress knows no parallel, even in the New Deal era when the Court's conservative wing (the Four Horsemen of the Apocalypse) tried to stop Congress' purportedly "socialist" attempts to revitalize the national economy.[19] No doubt Congress has earned some of this disrespect. Against the din of ever more partisan bickering, it serves up a welter of laws that seem more attuned to short-term political maneuvering than to coping with felt necessities of our time. With some frequency, moreover, Congress passes symbolic legislation of highly dubious constitutionality in the comfortable knowledge that the Court will likely correct its failed self-censorship.

But the Court's current penchant for judicial imperialism cannot simply be blamed on Congress or on the sometimes obstinate and arrogant bureaucracies that govern us. Two centuries ago, in *Marbury* v. *Madison*, the Court proclaimed that "It is emphatically the province and duty of the judicial department to say what the law is." At the time, and for a long time thereafter, this claim of judicial supremacy—the power to trump the judgments of other arms of government—had limits. In *Marbury*, the Court did strike down an Act of Congress (the Judiciary Act of 1789) as unconstitutional. The law in question, however, regulated the judiciary itself and the constitutional flaw that the Court identified was that it gave the Supreme Court broader jurisdiction than the Constitution allows. Strictly speaking, then, Chief Justice Marshall's opinion declared the Court to be the ultimate arbiter of the law only with regard to those laws governing the judiciary and not necessarily for all laws and all circumstances. But these limits, which long ago vanished from the popular imagination, no longer hold any sway at the Court. When it comes to the meaning of the Constitution, the justices view themselves not only as the final authority in the temporal sense of having the final say, but the only authority in an absolute sense. Without nuance or reticence or deference to the other national leaders or institutions, they act as though the Court's opinion is all that matters.

This concept of judicial supremacy helps explain a wide swath of Rehnquist era decisions. For example, it unites the Rehnquist Court's very worst decision, *Bush v. Gore*, with some of its very best, those involving the detainees held as "enemy combatants" in Guantanamo, Cuba. In all these cases, the ultimate touchstone was this Court's unwillingness to defer to Congress or the Executive on matters of unusual national import.

In *Bush v. Gore*,[20] the Bush campaign asked the justices to review a decision of the Florida Supreme Court ordering a statewide manual recount of "undervotes"—those ballots indicating that the voter may have intended to cast a vote for president but where the machine tabulation had registered no vote. The U.S. Supreme Court issued three rulings with respect to this challenge. First, on December 9, 2000, it stayed the Florida Supreme Court's order, thereby halting the recount that was underway. Second, on December 12, 2000, the Court ruled that the Florida Supreme Court's recount order violated the Constitution's equal protection clause because it did not specify uniform rules for what would be deemed a "legal vote" for president—that is, whether every Florida county had to count a "hanging chad" or a "dimpled chad" or some other indication of voter intent in a particular way. Third, the Court stopped the Florida election process instead of remanding the case to the Florida Supreme Court for it to cure the equal protection violation by establishing consistent vote-counting standards.

Leaving aside for the moment the merits of these rulings, the net result was to ensure that the U.S. Supreme Court—and the Court alone—would decide the 2000 presidential election. If the Court had never intervened or if it had returned the case to Florida to correct the perceived equal protection violation, the 2000 election would have been decided by a political process. Maybe the recount ultimately would have produced a clear winner (Hawaii's did in the 1960 presidential election when the recount shifted the state from Nixon's column into Kennedy's). Maybe the process would have produced competing Bush and Gore electoral slates from Florida. In that event, the dispute would have been decided in Congress, exactly as provided under the Constitution and the federal law enacted in 1887 after the disputed Hayes/Tilden presidential election. But this Court, or at least five members of it, did not want to risk having a decision of this magnitude made in the messy cauldron of politics. They stopped the recount once and for all, and called the election themselves.

In the Warren era, as the Court took on an expanding number of contentious national issues, it developed a "political question doctrine"—a doctrine of judicial humility recognizing that, even in a time of greater judicial intervention, that the resolution of some issues belongs wholly to the political process and the judiciary should play no role. On the current court, this doctrine has been replaced by the false rhetoric of humility. With a Caesar-like modesty, the conservative majority in *Bush* v. *Gore* claimed that, in deciding the case, they had been "forced to confront" an "unsought responsibility." But the Court could have declined the case (as most scholars prayed they would) or returned it to Florida (as almost all scholars thought they should).* Instead, by injecting themselves into the election and by then stopping the manual recount, the Court majority short-circuited the political process entirely and declared, in essence, that deciding the presidency was just too important to be trusted to the people's elected representatives or, indeed, by anyone (even by a one-vote margin) except themselves.

Bush v. *Gore* does not bear much resemblance to the Guantanamo cases in subject matter, scope, or effect, but the jurisprudential impulse driving the Court's decision is common to both. In the Guantanamo cases, the Bush Administration took the position that the Executive Branch may incarcerate anyone, even citizens, for an indefinite time, without meaningful judicial review (or in some circumstances no review at all) so long as the Executive, in its discretion, designates those persons "enemy combatants." This claim struck many observers as deeply troubling, even scary. The administration seem to be claiming the right to set up a modern-day Bastille where it could indefinitely warehouse foreign nationals without charge or access to lawyers or recourse to the protections of courts or international law, based on evidence and justifications known only to itself. And it seemed to be claiming an almost equal power over U.S. citizens, even ones apprehended on U.S. soil.

---

*Although styled as an unsigned *per curiam* opinion, the Court's *Bush* v. *Gore* majority was authored by Kennedy—and this makes the claim of "unsought responsibility" all the more insincere and ironic. Behind the scenes, Kennedy played an instigating role in getting the Court to grant review in the Florida election dispute—not just once, but twice—over the objection of the four more liberal justices. As often is forgotten, the Supreme Court first got involved in the election dispute after the Florida Supreme Court stopped Florida Secretary of State Katherine Harris from certifying Bush as the winner and extended the state law election certification deadline to permit the conclusion of certain ongoing recounts. When the Bush campaign sought review of this decision, Kennedy wrote the initial internal memo successfully advocating Court intervention over the bitter objection of the liberals. In the first go-round, the Court merely remanded to the Florida Supreme Court for clarification of the basis for its ruling. But this initial intervention laid the groundwork inside the Court for subsequent oversight and, at least in the view of Court liberals, to steering the election to Bush if that became necessary. To call such discretionary intervention "unsought" requires a high level of disingenuity.

Despite these misgivings, the administration's position enjoyed a modicum of support in some World War II era cases.[21] Furthermore, in this post–9/11 "age of terror," with some legal theorists calling for a "new paradigm" of executive power to combat the nation's elusive enemies, no one knew for sure whether courts would hold fast to old rules and old norms. The Judiciary has a history of deferring to the Executive when faced with claims of national security. The Japanese internment cases—where the Court accepted without challenge the military's claim that national security required the sequestration of West Coast Japanese Americans—are examples.[22]

Some commentators predicted that the Rehnquist Court would accept the position of this ideologically compatible administration. But those observers underestimated the pull of judicial supremacy on almost everything this Court does. By an 8–1 vote, the Justices rejected the administration's claim of unreviewable executive authority and affirmed the judiciary's jurisdiction to review the detentions of citizens imprisoned at Guantanamo; by a 6–3 vote, they also extended some judicial protection to non-citizen detainees.[23] In characteristic O'Connor fashion, the decisions did not sweep broadly. As a practical matter, they promised detainees a judicial forum and left for another day exactly what that forum had to look like and how rigorous a standard of judicial review need be applied. But on the big issue before the Court, the issue of Executive power in wartime, they held true to the lodestar of the Rehnquist era, which is that no act legislative or executive is beyond the reach of the judicial branch and, thus, of the Justices themselves.

To say, however, that the main hallmark of the Rehnquist Court is "judicial activism," even an unprecedented judicial activism—regardless of whether one embraces or fears that term—does not say much about the quality of the Court's judicial decision making. An activist Court can make equally good and bad decisions. To cite the most obvious illustrations, *Brown* v. *Board of Education* is surely activist and nearly universally accepted (even by self-described conservatives) as good. The Japanese internment decisions, by contrast, were profoundly restrained—and now are roundly condemned. Activism's virtue or vice can be measured only by considering the ends to which it is put and the means by which it is achieved. The proper test is one of justification. When the Court reverses course or overturns the judgment of the elected branches, the Justices have a duty to provide an especially compelling explanation for why their judgment must be substituted either for the judgment of their predecessors or for the judgment of officials who are actually answerable to the people whose government this is. Principled justifications for such actions do exist, right there in the Constitution, if fairly read and assessed in the light of history. But in their absence, judicial activism reduces quickly to the exercise of pure power and the line between what is law and what is politics—always fuzzy, never pure, and difficult to draw—vanishes altogether.

This is the standard against which the Rehnquist Court ultimately must be measured. And it is by this standard that the Rehnquist Court raises the profoundest concerns. *Bush* v. *Gore*, a case at once unique and troublingly characteristic, shows why. It is Rehnquist Era jurisprudence under a magnifying glass: outsized in its activism and outsized in its lack of justification, but no aberration at all.

As a matter of legal craft and logic, *Bush* v. *Gore* is stunningly weak.[24] At its core, the majority opinion nullifies the Florida Supreme Court's recount order on equal protection grounds because it allowed the statewide hand recount to proceed with different counties using modestly uneven standards for determining legal votes. Inside the Court, it appears that this equal protection theory had only a single genuine subscriber, Justice Kennedy, the author. Initially, Chief Justice Rehnquist had tried to get the conservative majority to coalesce around a completely different theory—that, by changing the counting rules midstream, the Florida Court had somehow violated Article II of the Constitution, which entrusts the making of election rules to state legislatures. Rehnquist had Scalia's and Thomas's votes and probably O'Connor's as well; but Kennedy would not sign on to Rehnquist's theory (which had plenty of its own problems). Kennedy's balking gave the conservatives the choice of splintering and having no majority opinion or accepting Kennedy's equal protection approach—and they chose the latter.

There was a reason none of the other justices, even those favoring Bush, wanted to decide the election based on a violation of the equal protection clause. The theory that the Constitution prohibited judicially supervised hand counting under somewhat different county-by-county standards simply could not be right. Indeed, the theory was so weak that Bush's lawyers consistently argued it like an embarrassing afterthought they felt compelled reluctantly to include.

Logic and history shows why. To begin with, the Court's ruling, if taken seriously, would mean that virtually every national election in U.S. history had, unbeknownst to us all, been conducted unconstitutionally. Different counties within states have always used somewhat different rules for counting votes (just as voting method and vote counting vary from state to state). In Florida during the 2000 election, different counties even used different ballots (including the infamous butterfly ballot, which generated thousands of mistaken Buchanan votes among Miami-Dade County Jews and without which Gore would have won without any recount). Different Florida counties also used different standards for counting absentee ballots. They even used different standards for determining which persons qualified as legal voters. Similar variations in vote counting techniques and voting standards existed all across the country and in every presidential election in the past. Yet no one had ever suggested that all these elections, present and past, violated the Constitution. To the contrary, election law had always allowed for variations of the type at issue in *Bush v. Gore*. And for that reason, the majority opinion could cite no case containing even remotely similar facts to support its analysis or result.*

In a perverse way, the majority opinion acknowledges that its equal protection holding would be unworkable as a general principle. It decrees that "[o]ur consideration is limited to the present circumstances." This extraordinary good-for-one-case-and-one-case-only pronouncement—which meant that the Court was deciding a presidential election in an opinion designed (in reverse of custom) to have no future consequence—stripped the decision of any pretense that it was based on principle as opposed to result.

These flaws, moreover, were compounded by the Court's decision to stop the vote count rather than let Florida's Supreme Court remedy the purported equal protection problem by creating a uniform vote-counting standard. In this regard, the majority opinion is just dishonest. It claims that the Court had no choice but to stop the recount because the Florida Supreme Court had decreed that, under state law, the vote-counting

---

*If anything, the Court's ruling disserved equal protection principles. The original and foremost purpose of the equal protection clause was to stop and to remedy centuries of racial subjugation of blacks. In Florida, black voters had suffered especially severe disenfranchisement in the original machine vote count because the voting machines in heavily minority (and, therefore, poor) districts tended to be more antiquated and inaccurate. The hand recount was designed in part to remedy this inequality—and, thus, the Court's equal protection ruling stopped a process that was increasing the equality of the very constituency that the equal protection clause was designed to help.

process had to be completed by December 12, the day of the Supreme Court's decision. Bad enough that the majority pretended that it had to honor the Florida Supreme Court's judgment in an opinion trashing the judgment of that court. Much more important, the Florida Supreme Court had never declared December 12 to be a firm deadline; state law did not decree it and neither did federal law. December 12 was only significant because, under federal law, if Florida resolved its internal election dispute by that date, its electoral slate would be immune from certain challenges in Congress. But nothing required resolution by December 12—and, case in point, Hawaii did not resolve its 1960 presidential election until December 28. In short, the Court called the election based on an invented deadline.*

This invention and the decision it supported tore the Court apart.[25] Although the ideological rancor at the Court had diminished somewhat as the more moderate Souter, Breyer, and Ginsburg supplanted Brennan, Marshall, and Blackmun, *Bush* v. *Gore* brought out all the old bitterness, despair, and distrust. The law clerks broke into warring factions, with the liberals and conservatives eating in separate rooms and exchanging epithet-laden charges of partisanship. Justice Souter, ashen-faced, brooded in his office about the damage being done to the Court. Trying to bridge the gap, he and Breyer flirted with Kennedy's equal protection argument provided the vote counting be allowed to continue. Breyer seemed to think that, if he went along, he could convince Kennedy not to stop the recount but instead to allow Florida to fix the problem. Kennedy, though, not only rebuffed Breyer, he used Breyer's willingness to entertain the equal protection argument as suggesting partial acquiescence in the majority opinion. Breyer's chambers stewed over this, but it was too late to do anything about it. As Breyer later rued, in his dealings with Kennedy, he had been "naïve" and was "taken to the cleaners."

In the lead dissent, Stevens concluded that, whoever the true winner of the 2000 election, the clear "loser" was "the nation's confidence in the

---

*Much attention has been given to the issue of whether Bush would have won the election anyway based on a completed recount (thus making the Court's decision, in some sense, academic). Although the answer cannot be known with certainty, it appears that Bush most likely would have won if only the "undervotes" were recounted, but that Gore most likely would have won if both undervotes and "overvotes" were recounted. (An overvote is a ballot rejected on the initial machine tabulation due to multiple indications of the voter's intent; some of these ballots, however, clearly indicated a single voter preference—as, for example, a ballot that had a punch out and a write-in for the same candidate—and, thus, some overvotes could have qualified as a legal votes). While hypothetical recounts shed important light on the 2000 election, such hindsight cannot provide additional justification for the Court's actions.

judge as an impartial guardian of the rule of law." From the liberal's perspective, the salt in the wound was not merely the legal deficiencies in the majority opinion, it was—as had been so often been true in less noted cases—the seeming hypocrisy of those who joined it. Here, the Court's five states' rights Justices, the Justices who had aggressively pushed deference to state court judges for as long as they had been on the bench, suddenly abandoned their usual principles and cooked up a facially implausible federal justification for overturning the Florida Supreme Court's interpretation of state election law without even giving that court a chance to redeem itself. And, more specifically, here were Rehnquist and O'Connor voting to overturn an election on dubious equal protection grounds even though, in 1983, they argued vehemently against applying federal equal protection principles to presidential elections because the conduct of elections was a matter of *state* law.[26] Such an election, they opined, could not violate the equal protection clause unless the state acted completely irrationally—and Florida, even with the acknowledged discrepancies, certainly was not doing that.

This intellectual flip-flopping is the most corrosive sin of all because it suggests that the justices involved are not acting in good faith but rather are simply invoking a convenient reason to reach a congenial result. Once the Court accepted review in *Bush v. Gore*, it was probably inevitable that the losers would impugn the motives of the prevailing side. But the majority's especially glaring intellectual about-face lent considerable credibility to charges that the conservatives were acting out of pure pro-Bush partisanship and, more parochially, trying to lock in their own legal legacies by ensuring the election of a conservative president.* These suspicions dated back (at a minimum) to December 9, 2000, when the Court, in a 5–4 opinion authored by Scalia, called a halt to the recount while the Court considered Bush's claims. Such stays are granted, as a legal matter, to avoid "irreparable harm." In the election case, Scalia identified that harm as the possibility (real at the time) that, if the recount was allowed to continue, Gore might overcome Bush's dwindling lead and, thereby, cast a pall over Bush's presidency if Bush ultimately prevailed. Never before had the Court deemed such a political harm (really a problem of public relations) to be irreparable legal

---

*The conservatives had their own mirror image gripe on the issue of hypocrisy. If the liberals could claim that the conservatives were flipping around on their usual federalism principles, by the same token, the liberals were suddenly discovering the value of judicial restraint and deference to state court judges, concepts they heretofore honored mainly in the breach.

harm. Worse, to liberals inside the Court and out, the stay signaled that the conservatives intended to wield their one-vote majority to elect Bush by whatever means necessary. As one clerk put it, Scalia "had made our case for us to the public about how crassly partisan the whole thing was."

There is a plausible and less cynical explanation for the conservatives' decision. Although few commentators defended the merits of the majority's analysis, a number explained and supported the decision on pragmatic grounds as necessary to avert what the most thoughtful, Judge Richard Posner, called "a potential political and constitutional crisis."[27] The Court was right to intervene and to stop the recount, these analysts explain, because (as the Justices surely understood) the alternative—letting the process play out in Florida—would have been protracted and potentially very ugly.

This pragmatic defense, however, at bottom a fear of too much politics, is almost as troubling as the problem it purports to solve. The pragmatist argument boils down to the idea that five unelected judges may avert a hypothetical crisis based on their ad hoc subjective assessment of the national psyche (vigorously disputed by the other four Justices) using as a fig leaf for this exercise in political judgment whatever constitutional justification best suits, even if not genuinely or convincingly applicable. To be sure, pragmatic and political considerations color many legal decisions. But if pragmatism, absent coherent legal theory, can justify *Bush* v. *Gore*, then the Justices really are our "Platonic guardians" saving democracy from itself. This is not the rule of law. It is the rule of power, however allegedly beneficial.

When *Bush* v. *Gore* was decided, many legal commentators, scholars, and citizens around the country reacted with shock and horror. Professor Akhil Amar, certainly one of the finest constitutional law scholars with a record of criticizing Warren and Rehnquist era decisions alike, wrote despairingly that the basic message he would now have to impart to his students was: "Put not your trust in judges."[28] Jeffrey Rosen, another thoughtful, middle-of-the-road analyst, headlined his commentary: "Disgrace: The Supreme Court Commits Suicide."[29] A basic premise behind both articles—and countless others like them—was that the Supreme Court had dangerously expended its reputational capital—the lifeblood of judicial authority—on a patently indefensible and political ruling. The dissenting Justices made exactly the same point. And many astute observers thought it might take a generation or more for the Court to recover from this self-inflicted wound.

Most of these critics recognized that many Rehnquist Court decisions were subject in varying degrees to the charges leveled at *Bush* v. *Gore*. They identified plenty of unconvincing opinions. They also understood the conservatives' intellectual inconsistency in the federalism cases, where Justices unalterably opposed to the finding of unenumerated individual rights in the Constitution (like the right to privacy in *Roe*), abandoned their textualism and originalism to find an unenumerated constitutional right to state sovereign immunity. But they were shocked nonetheless that the justices would expose these deeply problematic practices in a case where the whole world was watching. Surely, they thought, at some point people might start to question why we cede to the Court so much authority.

These assumptions, however, proved very wrong. Judicial supremacy, it would seem, has become bred into our very bones. In part, perhaps, this is because the Court rarely departs too far from prevailing public sentiment—or at least not for very long. Or perhaps this is because we are all cynics now and simply assume that the Court has always been and will always be more about politics than law.

As a matter of history, this quiet acceptance did not always prevail. From Andrew Jackson to Abraham Lincoln to Franklin Roosevelt, national leaders in the past have entered vigorous debates about the Constitution's meaning and the Court's hegemony over its interpretation. Not anymore. Even the Court's sharpest public critics do not meaningfully question the underlying scope of judicial power. Instead, they wait passively for justices to resign or die in the hope that new Justices will change the Court's direction more to their liking.[30]

Perhaps the modern Court's exceptional arrogation of power and its unprincipled use is not really cause for alarm. Perhaps our democratic traditions are so deeply entrenched that our constitutional system is, as one writer put it, a machine that runs by itself. Surely, our governmental institutions go through better and worse periods and, as Justice Blackmun was fond of saying, we may trust that "the pendulum swings and will swing again."

But we live in a strange and disquieting period. For the second time in our history, a president has been impeached and, like Andrew Johnson, acquitted.[31] In this matter, and in many others, not least the process for confirming federal judges, the divisions in Congress have grown only deeper and more angry as conscientious governance has yielded to blinding partisanship. A president has declared a new and amorphous type of war—a war on terror—and under that aegis claimed an unknown power to unilaterally prosecute the nation's enemies. After an especially divisive and emotional campaign season, we elected a president before the watchful eyes of thousands of lawyers—and escaped another judicially decided contest by the fortuity of about 50,000 votes in Ohio.

We observe these matters as political drama and ordinary (if vexing) dysfunction—but not crisis. Yet democracy is too rare in human history to be taken for granted. And thus, in reflecting on the modern Court, it is worth recalling that while, through ingenious design, the Court remains uniquely suited to protect our constitutional heritage against what Madison called the dangers of "temporary or partial considerations," it is not immune to hubris or irresponsibility of an especially anti-democratic kind. The Rehnquist Court has bequeathed us this problem. By the slimmest of margins and on the basis of opinions too often lacking in consistency and persuasiveness, the Justices control and rewrite the fundamental principles by which we govern ourselves. Changing this dynamic, a generation entrenched, is a momentous task not yet or, at best, barely begun—and it will not happen merely by the passing of the Rehnquist era. Although some of the Justices have engaged in a campaign of public fence-mending since *Bush* v. *Gore,* real and lasting change at the Court will depend on new Justices bringing a new integrity to the Court's decision making. Some might say—given the current poisonous dynamic for naming and confirming Justices—that finding appointees with the requisite character, temperament, and wisdom will require a political miracle. Maybe so. But it is a miracle upon which the Court's convalescence depends—and in this most legalistic of democracies, that is something very much worth wishing for.

NOTES

THE HIGHEST COURT IN THE LAND

1. Thucydides, *History of the Peloponnesian War*, 2.43.
2. See, e.g., E. J. Dionne, Jr., *Why Americans Hate Politics* (New York: Simon & Schuster, 1991); also Suzanne Garment, *Scandal: The Culture of Distrust in American Politics* (New York: Times, 1991); Jacob Weisberg, *In Defense of Government* (New York: Scribners, 1996).
3. Jack Rakove, *Original Meanings: Politics and Ideas in the Making of the Constitution* (New York: Knopf, 1996).
4. Anthony T. Kronman, *The Lost Lawyer: Failing Ideals of the Legal Profession* (Cambridge: Harvard Univ. Press, Belknap, 1993).
5. Between 1811 and 1823 the Court decided 457 cases, 437 of which were unanimous even though the Federalist Marshall presided over a Republican majority. See Gordon Wood, "The Father of the Court," *New Republic*, February 17, 1997 p. 38.
6. There are exceptions to this view of the Warren Court. Occasionally, the Justices did overreach, as in *Mapp v. Ohio*, 367 U.S. 643 (1961), in which a 5–4 majority for the first time required state courts to follow the "exclusionary rule" in dealing with unconstitutional police conduct. The parties in *Mapp* had not even raised the exclusionary rule in their appeal, and it had been neither briefed nor argued. Some other landmarks, such as *Miranda v. Arizona*, 384 U.S. 436 (1966), were decided by a single vote. But many of the Court's most controversial cases, such as those involving voting rights, school prayer, due process, and free speech, were decided by broad majorities. See generally, Ed Cray, *Chief Justice: A Biography of Earl Warren* (New York: Simon & Schuster, 1997).
7. Robert Bork, *Slouching Towards Gomorrah* (New York: HarperCollins, 1996), p. 117.

A CLERK'S EYE VIEW

1. Alex Kozinski, "Confessions of a Bad Apple," 100 *Yale Law J.* 1707, 1708 (1991).

2. Justice Brennan liked to refer to this as the Rule of Five. Generally speaking, for a Court opinion to have binding precedential effect, that is for it to become the definitive interpretation of a law or constitutional provision, it must reflect the views of at least five Justices. There are rare exceptions, such as when the Court is shorthanded or when the Court splits 4–1–4 and the views of the single Justice in the center are deemed to be controlling. See, e.g., *Regents of the University of California* v. *Bakke*, 438 U.S. 265 (1978) (opinion of Powell, J.). Notably, many journalists reporting on the Court neglect the Rule of Five and, thereby, dramatically misinform the public about the actual import of important Court decisions.

3. David M. O'Brien, *Storm Center: The Supreme Court in American Politics*, 3d ed. (New York: Norton, 1993), p. 319.

4. In a more recent development, Justice Ruth Bader Ginsburg has taken to using the literally self-effacing "pleased to join," a further deviation that some already have suggested reflects the Court's serious splintering on matters of actual substance.

5. Robert L. Stern, Eugene Gressman, and Stephen M. Shapiro, *Supreme Court Practice: For Practice in the Supreme Court of the United States*, 7th ed. (Washington, D.C.: Bureau of National Affairs, 1993).

6. Anthony Lewis, *Gideon's Trumpet* (New York: Random House, 1964).

7. This pooling system was originally proposed by Justice Lewis Powell.

8. In August 1991, Justices Blackmun and Kennedy both wrote memos expressing concern about the need for some checking function on the work of the cert. pool. Blackmun memorandum of August 6, 1991; Kennedy memorandum of August 1, 1997.

9. See, e.g., Bernard Schwartz, *Decision: How the Supreme Court Decides Cases* (New York: Oxford Univ. Press, 1996).

10. *Douglas* v. *Jeannette*, 319 U.S. 157, 182 (1943) (Jackson, J., concurring).

11. Preamble, U.S. Constitution.

12. 491 U.S. 397 (1989).

13. As part of the same suit, Judge Sand found Yonkers officials guilty of maintaining an unconstitutionally segregated public school system through the deliberate manipulation of attendance zone boundaries, school closings, and faculty assignments.

14. Paul D. Gewirtz, "Remedies and Resistance," 92 *Yale Law J.* 585 (1983).

15. The Court of Appeals did modify Judge Sand's order in one respect. It limited the fine against the city to an additional $1 million a day after day 15. 856 F. 2d 444 (2d Cir. 1988).

16. 358 U.S. 1 (1958).

17. 347 U.S. 483 (1954).

18. 493 U.S. 265 (1990).

THE GRAND CANYON

1. 492 U.S. 361 (1989).

2. *Booth*, 482 U.S. 476 (1987); *Gathers*, 492 U.S. 302 (1989). The Court took up the issue again in 1991, overturning both *Booth* and *Gathers*. See *Payne* v. *Tennessee*, 501 U.S. 808 (1991).

3. Tompkins's petition of certiorari contained a third claim, challenging the Texas death penalty statute on vagueness grounds, but this was dismissed by the Court before briefing.

4. 476 U.S. 79 (1986).
5. 447 U.S. 625 (1980).
6. 428 U.S. 153 (1976).
7. *Gardner* v. *Florida*, 430 U.S. 349, 357–58 (1977) (opinion of Justice Stevens for a plurality).
8. *Gregg*, 428 U.S. at 193.
9. In *Gregg*, the Court invalidated statutes that made the death penalty mandatory upon conviction for certain crimes in part because of a mirror-image concern. Jurors convinced of a defendant's guilt but reluctant to impose the death penalty would vote to acquit rather than trigger an automatic sentence of death.
10. See Karl Llewellyn, *The Common Law Tradition* (Boston: Little, Brown, 1960); Anthony T. Kronman, "Jurisprudential Responses to Legal Realism," 73 *Cornell Law Rev.* 335 (1988).
11. 100 U.S. 303 (1880).
12. *Norris* v. *Alabama*, 294 U.S. 587 (1935).
13. 380 U.S. 202 (1965).
14. For an excellent discussion of *Swain*, *Batson*, and the use of peremptory challenges, see Randall Kennedy, *Race, Crime, and the Law* (New York: Pantheon, 1997).
15. As the Court itself had emphasized in a 1984 case, *Spaziano* v. *Florida*, "The element [we] found essential to a fair trial in *Beck* was not simply a lesser included offense instruction in the abstract, but the enhanced rationality and reliability the instruction introduced into the jury's deliberations." 468 U.S. 447 (1984).
16. One of Marshall's former clerks, the Harvard Law School professor Randall Kennedy, recently singled out the Justice's opinions in this area as among his most influential and important. 114 U.S. CCCXVII.
17. Richard Kluger, *Simple Justice: The History of Brown v. Board of Education and Black America's Struggle for Equality* (New York: Vintage, 1977), p. 224.
18. 407 U.S. 493 (1972).
19. 491 U.S. 164 (1989).

THE SPIRIT OF SCOTTSBORO

1. James E. Goodman, *Stories of Scottsboro* (New York: Pantheon, 1994), p. 15.
2. *Ibid.*, p. 41 and n. 5.
3. Lawrence M. Friedman, *Crime and Punishment in America* (New York: Basic, 1993), p. 376.
4. More precisely, in March 1932, the Alabama Supreme Court upheld seven of the eight Scottsboro convictions, reversing the other on the ground that Eugene Williams may have been a juvenile improperly tried as an adult.
5. Alpheus T. Mason, *Harlan Fiske Stone: Pillar of the Law* (New York: Viking, 1956).
6. *Powell* v. *Alabama*, 287 U.S. 45 (1932).
7. *Norris* v. *Alabama*, 294 U.S. 587 (1935).
8. *Strauder* v. *West Virginia*, 100 U.S. 303 (1880).
9. *New York Times*, November 13, 1932.
10. The scholarship on the purpose behind the Civil War amendments is to say the least exhaustive. For a brief and persuasive treatment of the best reading of the Four-

teenth Amendment, see John Hart Ely, *Democracy and Distrust: A Theory of Judicial Review* (Cambridge: Harvard Univ. Press, 1980), pp. 11–41. See also Eric Foner, *Reconstruction: America's Unfinished Revolution, 1863–1877* (New York: Harper & Row, 1988).

11. *Palko* v. *Connecticut*, 302 U.S. 319 (1937).

12. *Gitlow* v. *New York*, 268 U.S. 652 (1925).

13. 367 U.S. 643 (1961).

14. 384 U.S. 436 (1966).

15. 391 U.S. 145 (1968).

16. 370 U.S. 660 (1962).

17. The depth of the Court's building concern about the racist conduct of southern law enforcement officials appears in many cases, though none more vividly than *Screws* v. *United States*, in which a white sheriff was accused of brutally beating a black prisoner. As Justice Douglas began his opinion, "This case involves a shocking and revolting episode in law enforcement." 325 U.S. at 92 (1945).

SAND IN THE MACHINE

1. *Louisiana ex. rel. Francis* v. *Resweber*, 329 U.S. 459 (1947).

2. E.g., *Fikes* v. *Alabama*, 352 U.S. 191 (1957) (establishing inadmissibility of involuntary confessions).

3. Goldberg's memorandum is reprinted in full in 27 *South Texas Law Rev.* 493 (1986).

4. 217 U.S. 349 (1910).

5. 356 U.S. 86 (1958).

6. Justice Brennan discusses this candidly in "Constitutional Adjudication and the Death Penalty: A View from the Court," 100 *Harvard Law Rev.* 313, 314 (1986).

7. *Trop* v. *Dulles*, 356 U.S. 86, 99 (1958) (Warren, C. J., plurality opinion).

8. *The Douglas Letters*, ed. Melvin Urofsky. (Bethesda, Md.: Adler & Adler, 1987).

9. Similarly, the Fifth Amendment dictates that "no person shall be held to answer for a capital, or otherwise infamous crime, unless on a presentment or indictment of a grand jury."

10. For a full account of the early stages of the LDF's battle against the death penalty, see Michael Meltsner, *Cruel and Unusual: The Supreme Court and Capital Punishment* (New York: Random House, 1973).

11. The most famous Amsterdam story runs as follows: Once while prosecuting a case before the D.C. Circuit Court of Appeals, Amsterdam responded to a question from the bench by citing from memory a case, complete with the volume number and page on which it could be found. The judge called for the book but could not find the cited case on the page Amsterdam had indicated. Upon being upbraided for his incorrect citation, Amsterdam immediately responded, "Your Honor, your volume must be misbound." It was.

12. *Congressional Globe*, 39th Cong., 1st sess., 2765 (1866).

13. In Florida, for example, of the six whites sentenced to death for rape since 1940, five received clemency or had their convictions reversed while only six of forty-eight blacks rapists escaped death row.

14. Meltsner, *Cruel and Unusual*, p. 71.

15. U.S. Congress, House Subcomm. No. 3 of the Committee on the Judiciary, 1972.

16. *Fay v. Noia,* 372 U.S. 391, 401–2 (1963).
17. U.S. Constitution, art. I, sec. 9.
18. *Fay v. Noia.*
19. *Martin v. Hunter's Lessee,* 14 U.S. (1 Wheat) 304, 349 (1816).
20. *Maxwell v. Bishop,* 257 F. Supp. 710 (1966).
21. Lee Epstein and Joseph Kobylka, *The Supreme Court and Legal Change: Abortion and the Death Penalty* (Chapel Hill: Univ. of North Carolina Press, 1992), p. 52.
22. For a critique of the LDF's death penalty campaign, see Eric L. Muller, "The Legal Defense Fund's Capital Punishment Campaign: The Distorting Influence of Death," 4 *Yale Law & Policy Rev.* 158 (1985).
23. Meltsner, *Cruel and Unusual,* p. 107.
24. 391 U.S. 510 (1968).
25. According to the polls cited in *Witherspoon,* as of 1966 42 percent of Americans favored capital punishment and 47 percent opposed it, with 11 percent undecided.
26. Meltsner, *Cruel and Unusual,* p. 114.
27. Epstein and Kobylka *Supreme Court and Legal Change,* p. 59.

THE STRIKE OF LIGHTNING

1. See William Brennan, "Constitutional Adjudication and the Death Penalty: A View from the Court," 100 *Harvard Law Rev.* 313, 317 (1986).
2. 402 U.S. 183 (1970). In conjunction with *McGautha,* the Court reviewed *Crampton v. Ohio,* but the two cases are customarily lumped together under the *McGautha* rubric, and I have done so here.
3. Learned Hand, *The Bill of Rights* (Cambridge: Harvard Univ. Press, 1958).
4. *McGautha,* 402 U.S. at 214.
5. Here I am following Brennan's own account. See "Constitutional Adjudication." It conflicts substantially with the account given in *The Brethren,* which has Marshall and Douglas but *not* Brennan unalterably opposed to capital punishment even before *McGautha.* Bob Woodward and Scott Armstrong, *The Brethren: Inside the Supreme Court* (New York: Simon & Schuster, 1979).
6. The other cases were *Jackson v. Georgia, Branch v. Texas,* and *Aikens v. California.* The Court later dismissed *Aikens* because the California Supreme Court struck down the state's death penalty statute while the case was still pending.
7. *Fay v. New York,* 332 U.S. 261, 282 (1947) (Jackson, J., concurring).
8. *Furman v. Georgia,* 408 U.S. 238 (1972).
9. Robert Weisberg, "Deregulating Death," *Supreme Court Rev.* 315 (1983).
10. Stewart's turmoil is recounted in Woodward and Armstrong, *The Brethren,* for which the Justice himself was a prominent source.
11. 408 U.S. at 411 (Blackmun, J., dissenting).
12. Lee Epstein and Joseph Kobylka, *The Supreme Court and Legal Change: Abortion and the Death Penalty* (Chapel Hill: Univ. of North Carolina Press, 1992), p. 80; Woodward and Armstrong, *Brethren,* p. 219.

BACKLASH

1.   See John C. Jeffries, *Justice Lewis F. Powell, Jr.: A Biography* (New York: Scribners, 1994), p. 422.
2.   *Roberts*, 428 U.S. at 335 (1976).
3.   *Gregg*, 428 U.S. at 183 (footnote omitted) (1976).
4.   *Woodson v. North Carolina*, 428 U.S. at 305 (1976).
5.   This, of course, had been precisely the view of Justice Harlan's majority opinion in *McGautha*.
6.   Jeffries, *Justice Powell*, p. 429.

THE DEATH WATCH

1.   Cesare Beccaria, *An Essay on Crimes and Punishments* (1764), trans. Henry Paolucci, 1963). Beccaria, a strong influence on early American criminal law reformers, was also the father of the modern penitentiary and the idea that imprisonment should be designed as much to reform as to punish.
2.   Immanuel Kant, *The Metaphysical Elements of Justice* (1797), trans. John Ladd (New York: MacMillan, 1985).
3.   Walter Berns, *For Capital Punishment: Crime and the Morality of the Death Penalty* (New York: Basic, 1979).
4.   See Clifford Sloan, "Death Row Clerk," *New Republic*, February 16, 1987, pp. 18–21.
5.   The Adams case subsequently became the subject of the documentary film *The Thin Blue Line*.
6.   To be more precise, Brandley was tried twice, the first proceeding having ended in a hung jury.
7.   More such stories continue to be revealed, including the recent case of Walter MacMillan, a black man who spent six years on Alabama's death row because the local sheriff concealed evidence of his innocence. For a compilation of cases in which probably innocent people were sentenced to death, see Michael Radelet, Hugo Adam Bedau, and Constance Putnam, *In Spite of Innocence: The Ordeal of 400 Americans Wrongly Convicted of Crimes Punishable by Death* (Boston: Northeastern Univ. Press, 1992).
8.   See Stephen B. Bright, "Counsel for the Poor: The Death Sentence Not for the Worst Crime but for the Worst Lawyer," 103 *Yale Law J.* 1835 (1994).
9.   Alexander M. Bickel, *The Least Dangerous Branch: The Supreme Court at the Bar of Politics* (New Haven: Yale University Press, 1986), p. 50.

THE LONE RANGER

1.   Regardless of Gilmore's wishes, three Justices (Brennan, White, and Marshall) insisted that Utah should not be allowed to carry out an execution until at least its own court system had determined that the state's death penalty statute was constitutional. Justice Blackmun thought the Court should give further consideration to the right of Gilmore's mother to prevent her son's death. The remaining bare majority, however, found Gilmore competent to waive his rights.

2. *Coker v. Georgia*, 433 U.S. 584 (1977).

3. *Edmund v. Florida*, 458 U.S. 782 (1982).

4. *Lockett v. Ohio*, 438 U.S. 586 (1978); *Eddings v. Oklahoma*, 455 U.S. 104 (1982).

5. *Godfrey v. Georgia*, 446 U.S. 420 (1980).

6. In another instance, the Court overturned restrictions on a defendant's access to the presentence offender evaluations that many states prepared for sentencing judges (thereby allowing defendants to challenge their accuracy). *Gardner v. Florida*, 430 U.S. 349 (1977).

7. *Godfrey v. Georgia*, 420.

8. See James S. Liebman, "More Than 'Slightly Retro': The Rehnquist Court's Rout of Habeas Corpus Jurisdiction in *Teague v. Lane*," 18 *N.Y.U. Rev. Law & Social Change* 537, 541, n. 15 (1990–91). See also *Murray v. Giarrantano*, 492 U.S. 1 (1989) (Stevens, J., dissenting).

9. As one pro–death penalty group asserted in an amicus brief, "The persistent, *ex cathedra* interference of an all-knowing, overarching Federal judiciary which constantly expands and tinkers with the procedural protections afforded to capital defendants interferes with the right of the States to protect their citizens." Brief for the Washington Legal Foundation in *Zant v. Stephens* at 31.

10. At trial, Spenkelink claimed that the victim had robbed him and forced him to commit homosexual acts and that the killing had occurred in self-defense during a struggle.

11. Ramsey Clark, "Spenkelink's Last Appeal," *Nation*, October 27, 1979, pp. 385–402.

12. Lower court judges enter stays under the authority of the All Writs Act, 28 *U.S. Code*, sec. 1651. As a general rule, the Court defers to lower court judgments about the propriety of granting a stay and will vacate only those stays that are "palpably erroneous." See *O'Brien v. Brown*, 409 U.S. 1 (1972).

13. *Wainwright v. Spenkelink*, 442 U.S. 901 (1979).

14. 451 U.S. 949, at 956–63 (Rehnquist, J., dissenting).

15. So much was the killing on Rehnquist's mind that he made specific reference to it in his *Balkom* dissent.

16. David G. Savage, *Turning Right: The Making of the Rehnquist Supreme Court* (New York: Wiley, 1992), p. 38.

17. Article 3, sec. 3, provides that "No Person shall be convicted of Treason unless on the Testimony of two Witnesses to the same overt Act, or on Confession in open Court."

18. For example, Saypol had held an inflammatory and widely reported news conference, undoubtedly heard by the unsequestered jury, describing the sworn statement of the prosecution witness Jed Perl, who would corroborate the most damaging testimony against the Rosenbergs. Yet Saypol never called the witness, who later recanted under oath.

19. Rehnquist to Jackson Memo, Papers of Justice Robert Jackson, Library of Congress.

20. Quoted in Frankfurter memo recounting the Rosenberg ordeal placed for the sake of posterity in Jackson's papers.

21. Joseph H. Sharlitt, *Fatal Error: The Miscarriage of Justice that Sealed the Rosenbergs' Fate* (New York: Scribners, 1985), p. 119 (relying on Frankfurter's papers).

22. Philip Elman, an oral history, interviewed by Norman Lilber, Columbia Univ., vol. 4, p. 227.

23.   Minton to Jackson, April 22, 1953, letter re. *Stein et al.* v. *New York*, Jackson Papers.

24.   Stuart Taylor, "Opposition to Rehnquist Nomination Hardens," *New York Times*, July 27, 1986, sec. 1, p. 18; Savage, *Turning Right*, p. 34.

25.   H. Jefferson Powell, "The Compleat Jeffersonian: Justice Rehnquist and Federalism," 91 *Yale Law J.* 1317 (1982). *Brown* v. *Allen*, 344 U.S. 443 (1953).

26.   See *Testa* v. *Katt*, 330 U.S. 386 (1947).

27.   Actually, Congress had shown concern about southern retribution against Union interests as early as 1833. In response to the so-called Nullification Crisis, Congress made federal habeas available to federal offices in state custody under certain circumstances.

28.   See Richard Kluger, *Simple Justice: The History of Brown v. Board of Education and Black America's Struggle for Equality* (New York: Vintage, 1977), pp. 113–14.

29.   261 U.S. 86 (1923).

30.   *United States* v. *Carolene Products, Co.*, 304 U.S. 144 n. 4 (1938).

31.   Humphrey's speech quoted in William Safire, *Lend Me Your Ears: Great Speeches in History* (New York: Norton, 1992), p. 800.

32.   "HABEAS CORPUS, revisited," p. 2, WHR to RHJ, Jackson Papers. Jackson echoed Rehnquist's view in the most famous section of his *Brown* v. *Allen* concurrence: "There is no doubt that if there were a super-Supreme Court, a substantial proportion of our reversals of state courts would also be reversed. We are not final because we are infallible, but we are infallible only because we are final." 440 U.S. 443, 540.

33.   321 U.S. 649 (1944).

34.   345 U.S. 461 (1953).

35.   Cert. memo for *Terry* v. *Adams*; Rehnquist memo to Jackson, "Re: Opinions of Black and FF in *Terry* v. *Adams*," Jackson Papers.

36.   "A Random Thought on the Segregation Cases," in Jackson Papers.

37.   Although district judges evaluating habeas petitions were entitled to respect relevant state court findings of fact in individual cases, they enjoyed significant discretion to conduct their own evidentiary hearings.

38.   Here Rehnquist was quoting from Justice Jackson's opinion in *Stein* v. *New York*, 346 U.S. 156, 197 (1953), another criminal case in which Rehnquist the clerk had staked out a strong states' rights position. See argument memo: "In Re *Stein, Cooper*, and *Wissner*," Jackson Papers.

STAY OF EXECUTION

1.   372 U.S. 391 (1963).

2.   Elena Kagan, "For Justice Marshall," 71 *Texas Law Rev.* 1125, 1127 (1993).

3.   See Burt Neuborne, "The Myth of Parity," 90 *Harvard Law Rev.* 1105 (1977).

4.   *Barefoot* v. *Estelle*, 463 U.S. 880, 915 (1983) (Marshall, J., dissenting).

5.   For a defense of this oft-criticized practice, see Jordan Steiker, "The Long Road Up from Barbarism: Thurgood Marshall and the Death Penalty," 71 *Texas Law Rev.* 1141 (1993).

6.   William J. Brennan, "The Constitution of the United States: Contemporary Ratification," 27 *South Texas Law Rev.* 433, 444 (1986).

7.   *Stone* v. *Powell*, 428 U.S. 465 (1976). As Powell saw it, the only justification for the wasteful and insulting redundancy of federal habeas was to serve as a double check

against convicting the innocent. Fourth Amendment claims, while alleging unconstitutional police conduct, never related to the reliability of a conviction. Inmates bringing such claims to a federal habeas court may have suffered error if the state courts misapplied search and seizure law, but that error would not have increased the possibility that an innocent person had been sent to jail.

8. *Wainwright* v. *Sykes*, 433 U.S. 72 (1977). Before *Sykes*, a defendant had to show only that he had not "deliberately bypassed" a constitutional objection at trial in order to raise it on federal habeas. *Fay* v. *Noia*, 372 U.S. 391 (1963).

9. Sandra Day O'Connor, "Trends in the Relationship Between the Federal and State Courts from the Perspective of a State Court Judge," 22 *William & Mary Law Rev.* 801 (1981).

10. *Engle* v. *Isaac*, 456 U.S. 107 (1982). See also *Rose* v. *Lundy*, 455 U.S. 509 (1982).

11. See Robert Weisberg, "Deregulating Death," *Supreme Court Rev.*, 305 (1983).

12. *Barefoot* v. *Estelle*, 800.

13. *Gray* v. *Lucas*, 463 U.S. 1237 (1983); *Autry* v. *Estelle*, 464 U.S. 1 (1983); *Sullivan* v. *Wainwright*, 464 U.S. 109 (1983).

14. Justice Blackmun dissented in *Autry*, the only one of the three cases still on first federal habeas.

15. 464 U.S. 377 (1984).

16. *Wainwright* v. *Adams*, 466 U.S. 964, 966 (1984). The second case was *Autry* v. *McKaskle*, 465 U.S. 1085 (1984).

17. See *Knighton* v. *Maggio*, 468 U.S. 1229 (1984); *Dobbert* v. *Wainwright*, 468 U.S. 1231 (1984).

18. This landmark case, 481 U.S. 279 (1987), is the subject of the next chapter.

19. 464 U.S. 1027 (1984).

20. 469 U.S. 1043 (1983).

21. David A. Kaplan, "The Court and the Switch," *New York Times*, December 6, 1984, p. A31.

22. 469 U.S. 1099 (1984).

23. Justice Brennan took note. At the next opportunity, he would file a grisly dissent arguing that electrocution, originally intended as a merciful way of killing, was itself a cruel and unusual punishment. See *Glass* v. *Louisiana*, 471 U.S. 1080 (1985).

24. John Jeffries, *Justice Lewis F. Powell, Jr.: A Biography* (New York: Scribners, 1994), pp. 538–39.

25. See Richard L. Revesz and Pamela S. Karlan, "Nonmajority Rules and the Supreme Court," 136 *Univ. of Pennsylvania Law Rev.*, 1067 (1988).

26. In *Ford* v. *Wainwright*, 477 U.S. 399 (1986), the Court would rule that executing an insane person would violate the Eighth Amendment.

27. 470 U.S. 68 (1985).

28. See Brennan, "Memorandum to the Conference: Stays of Execution in Capital Cases," September 19, 1985, Papers of William J. Brennan, Library of Congress.

29. 464 U.S. 1, 2 (1983).

30. The Darden letter was not completely without precedent. In *Barefoot* v. *Estelle*, the Justices had decided on their own to convert Barefoot's stay application into a cert. petition and then to grant it. Alpha Stephens had tried a similar maneuver just before his execution in 1984, but while four Justices voted to grant him a stay, only two, Brennan and Marshall, also favored a cert. grant.

31. See Harold H. Koh, "A Justice for Passion," 1990 *Annual Survey of American Law*, xxxi.

32. *Darden v. Wainwright,* 473 U.S. 927, 928–29 (1985) (Powell, J., concurring).

33. Letter of September 4, 1985, "85-5319 Darden v. Wainwright," Brennan Papers.

34. Brennan, "Stays of Execution."

35. David Lauter, "Recent Supreme Court Term Blackman's 'Most Difficult,'" *Washington Post,* July 26, 1986, p. A2.

36. See Robert A. Burt, "Disorder in the Court," 85 *Michigan Law Rev.* 1741 (1987).

A COP KILLER'S CASE

1. In addition to their race-based arguments, the abolitionists attempted to show that the new statutes were unconstitutionally arbitrary and irrational in that they produced numerous "disproportionate" death sentences—that is, sentences that appeared unjustified and excessive in comparison with the sentences handed down in many other factually similar cases. But this line of argument came to an abrupt dead end in 1983, when the Court rejected its underlying assumption that the Eighth Amendment, as interpreted in *Gregg* and elsewhere, required "comparative proportionality" among death sentences. See *Pulley v. Harris,* 465 U.S. 37 (1984).

2. What is called the Baldus study actually consisted of two separate analyses: a "Procedural Reform" study, which focused on defendants tried and sentenced for murder between March 1973 and July 1978; and a "Charging and Sentencing" study, which looked also at defendants who pleaded guilty to murder and manslaughter or were charged with manslaughter rather than murder between 1973 and 1980. See generally David Baldus, George Woodworth, and Charles A. Pulaski, Jr., *Equal Justice and the Death Penalty: A Legal and Empirical Analysis* (Boston: Northeastern Univ. Press, 1990).

3. Defendant-victim racial composition:
    1. Black defendant–white victim: 50 of 233 cases
    2. White defendant–white victim: 58 of 748 cases
    3. Black defendant–black victim: 18 of 1,443 cases
    4. White defendant–black victim: 2 of 60 cases

4. This particular model accounted for the thirty-nine nonracial variables believed to be most likely to play a role in Georgia's capital punishment scheme.

5. See memo from Eric S. Mulhaup to Sam Gross, October 14, 1982, found in LDF files on the McCleskey case. The race of the victim orientation of Baldus's numbers not only diminished the emotional impact of the study but also raised technical legal difficulties. Specifically, it was not obvious that a convicted murderer had the necessary standing to bring a lawsuit based on a legal injury (discrimination) that he himself had not suffered. Although several judges expressed concern about this issue, in the end it did not impede the LDF's claims.

6. Trial transcript, p. 214 (testimony of Cassie Barnwell).

7. My version of the Dixie Furniture robbery and the McCleskey investigation, trial, and posttrial legal proceedings is compiled from contemporary coverage in the *Atlanta Constitution,* official police reports, the relevant hearing and trial transcripts, and the files of the NAACP Legal Defense Fund, as well as interviews with McCleskey's appellate counsel, Jack Boger and Robert Stroup, the prosecuting attorney, Richard Parker, and Mary Beth Westmorland, who handled the McCleskey case in the state Attorney General's office.

8. State habeas hearing January 30, 1981, p. 58.
9. The trial judge had turned down Turner's request for funds to hire an investigator.
10. Turner admitted as much. State habeas hearing, p. 37.

EQUAL PROTECTION OF THE LAWS

1. Randall Kennedy, *Race, Crime, and the Law* (New York: Pantheon 1997), pp. 340–41.
2. *McCleskey v. Zant*, 580 F. Supp. 338 (ND Ga 1984).
3. 405 U.S. 150 (1971).
4. *McCleskey v. Kemp*, 753 F. 2d 877 (11th Cir. 1985) (en banc).
5. Ibid., 877, 891.
6. The LDF had presented this issue in *Witherspoon*, but the Court had reserved judgment on it. 391 U.S. at 517.
7. 476 U.S. 162 (1986).
8. Robert A. Burt, "Disorder in the Court," 85 *Michigan Law Rev.* 1741, 1788 (1987).
9. As the author of the Court's opinion in the second case for which *McCleskey* was held (*Rose v. Clark*), Powell had the responsibility to circulate a hold memo suggesting how to dispose of every petition being held pending the issuance of his opinion.
10. John C. Jeffries, *Justice Lewis F. Powell, Jr.: A Biography* (New York: Scribner's, 1994), p. 439.
11. *Brown v. Board of Education*, 349 U.S. 294, n. 11 (1954); Symposium, "The Court's Social Science and School Desegregation," 39 *Law & Contemporary Problems* (1975).
12. President Reagan expressed the conservative view in a campaign speech only weeks before the Court was scheduled to evaluate the Baldus study: "We don't need a bunch of sociology majors on the bench. What we need are strong judges." Mark Gitenstein, *Matters of Principle: An Insider's Account of America's Rejection of Robert Bork's Nomination to the Supreme Court* (New York: Simon & Schuster, 1992), p. 45.
13. See generally David Savage, *Turning Right: The Making of the Rehnquist Supreme Court* (New York: Wiley, 1993).
14. Ibid., p. 23.
15. Bernard Schwartz, *A History of the Supreme Court* (New York: Oxford Univ. Press, 1993), pp. 289–91.
16. See *Washington v. Davis*, 426 U.S. 229 (1976).
17. David C. Baldus, George Woodworth, and Charles A. Pulaski, Jr., "Reflections on the 'Inevitability' of Racial Discrimination in Capital Sentencing and the 'Impossibility' of Its Prevention, Detection, and Correction," 51 *Washington & Lee Law Rev.* 359 (1994).
18. See *Gregg*, 428 U.S. at 225 (White, J. concurring) (assuming the validity of the Georgia statute "[a]bsent facts to the contrary"); LDF brief at 25.
19. See *Bazemore v. Friday*, 478 U.S. 385 (1986).
20. *Batson v. Kentucky*, 476 U.S. 79 (1986).
21. 118 U.S. 356 (1886).
22. Jeffries, *Justice Powell*, p. 182.

23. See *Turner* v. *Murray*, 476 U.S. 28 (1986). Also, Randall Kennedy, "*McCleskey* v. *Kemp*: Race, Capital Punishment, and the Supreme Court," 101 *Harvard Law Rev.* 1388, 1418 (1988).

24. In later years, Powell recalled thinking that *Brown* was overdue in 1954, but his own sympathetic biographer describes this as "edit[ing] the past to bring it more nearly in line with his current values." Jeffries, *Justice Powell*, p. 298.

25. See generally *McCleskey* v. *Kemp*, 481 U.S. 282 (1987).

26. Here, as in many places in his draft, Powell closely followed the reasoning of the Eleventh Circuit.

27. Kennedy, "McCleskey and the Court," 1415.

28. *Enmund* v. *Florida*, 458 U.S. 782 (1982); *Cabana* v. *Bullock*, 474 U.S. 376 (1986).

29. 481 U.S. 137 (1987).

30. *Turning Right*, pp. 55–56.

31. *Furman*, 408 U.S. 238, 405 (1972) (Blackmun, J., dissenting).

32. See *Castaneda* v. *Partida*, 430 U.S. 482 (1977).

33. See Nina Totenberg, "A Tribute to Justice Harry H. Blackmun: 'The Kind Voice of Friends,'" 43 *American Univ. Law Rev.* 745, 747–48 (1994).

34. Sandra Day O'Connor, "Thurgood Marshall: The Influence of a Raconteur," 44 *Stanford Law Rev.* 1217, 1218 (1992). O'Connor does not say that Marshall told the story at the *McCleskey* conference, but she does describe the case under consideration as one "in which an African American defendant challenged his death sentence as racially biased." I assume that this case was *McCleskey*, the only such challenge on which the Court has heard argument.

35. See Carol S. Steiker and Jordan M. Steiker, "Sober Second Thoughts: Reflections on Two Decades of Constitutional Regulation of Capital Punishment," 109 *Harvard Law Rev.* 355 (1995).

36. 309 U.S. 227 (1940).

ROBERT BORK AND CIVIL WAR

1. This account of Powell's resignation owes much to the longer treatment in John C. Jeffries, *Justice Lewis F. Powell, Jr.: A Biography* (New York: Scribners, 1994), pp. 535–48.

2. See ibid., "Appendix," pp. 565–72.

3. See, e.g., *Thornburgh* v. *American College of Obstetricians and Gynecologists*, 476 U.S. 747 (1986); *Harris* v. *McRae*, 448 U.S. 297 (1980); *Bowers* v. *Hardwick*, 478 U.S. 186 (1986).

4. Compare *Wygant* v. *Jackson Board of Education*, 476 U.S. 267 (1986) with *United States* v. *Paradise*, 480 U.S. 149 (1987).

5. 482 U.S. 496 (1987).

6. Bork expressed his views in numerous articles and speeches and, most fully, in his book *The Tempting of America: The Political Seduction of the Law* (New York: Free Press, 1990).

7. Mark Gitenstein, *Matters of Principle: An Insider's Account of America's Rejection of Robert Bork's Nomination to the Supreme Court* (New York: Simon & Schuster, 1992), pp. 55–57.

8. Richard Lacayo, "The Battle Begins," *Time*, July 13, 1987, p. 10.

9. David M. O'Brien, *Storm Center: The Supreme Court in American Politics*, 3d ed. (New York: Norton, 1993), p. 107.

10. The most public airing of this heated debate appears in *Bartlett on behalf of Neuman* v. *Bowen*, 824 F. 2d 1240 (D.C. Cir. 1987).

11. *Dronenberg* v. *Zech*, 741 F. 2d 1388 (D.C. Cir. 1984).

12. *Bartlett*, 824 F. 2d at 1243.

13. For a complete discussion of the Solicitor General's Office and the liberal critique of the Reagan administration's subversion of its traditional role, see Lincoln Caplan, *The Tenth Justice: The Solicitor General and the Rule of Law* (New York: Knopf, 1987).

14. Charles Fried, *Order and Law* (New York: Simon & Schuster, 1991), p. 14.

15. *Bob Jones University* v. *United States*, 461 U.S. 574 (1983).

16. Caplan, *Tenth Justice*, p. 90 and generally chap. 7.

17. Ibid., p. 201.

18. Richard Lacayo, "Supreme or Not Supreme; That Is the Question, Says the Attorney General," *Time*, November 3, 1986, p. 46.

19. Meese somewhat overstated Lincoln's point. As evident from his first inaugural address, Lincoln carefully circumscribed his attack on the Court to include only an extraordinary case such as *Dred Scott*: "I do not forget the position assumed by some, that constitutional questions are to be decided by the Supreme Court; nor do I deny that such decisions must be binding in any case, upon the parties to a suit, as to the objects of that suit, while they are also entitled to very high respect and consideration in all parallel cases by all other departments of the Government. . . . [But] if the policy of the Government upon vital questions, affecting the whole people, is to be irrevocably fixed by decisions of the Supreme Court, the instant they are made, in ordinary litigation between parties in personal actions, the people will have ceased to be their own rulers, having to that extent practically resigned their government into the hands of that eminent tribunal." For the best treatment of Lincoln's thinking, see Robert A. Burt, *The Constitution in Conflict* (Cambridge: Harvard Univ. Press, Belknap, 1992).

20. See the Southern Congressional Manifesto of 1956.

21. This is by Bork's own account in his book *Slouching Towards Gomorrah* (New York: HarperCollins, 1996).

22. Ibid., p. 1.

23. See Alexander Bickel, "The Tolerance of Violence on the Campus," *New Republic*, June 13, 1970, p. 15, and "The Revolution of Unreason," *New Republic*, October 17, 1970, p. 18.

24. Robert H. Bork, "Neutral Principles and Some First Amendment Problems," 47 *Indiana Law J.* 1 (1971).

25. Mary Ann Glendon, *A Nation Under Lawyers: How the Crisis in the Legal Profession Is Transforming American Society* (New York: Farrar, Straus & Giroux, 1994), p. 216.

26. J. Mark Tushnet, "Critical Legal Studies: A Political History," 100 *Yale Law Rev.*, 1515, 1516 (1991).

27. See Glendon, *Nation Under Lawyers*; Eleanor Kerlow, *Poisoned Ivy: How Egos, Ideology, and Power Politics Almost Ruined Harvard Law School* (New York: St. Martin's Press, 1994).

28. Bork, *Tempting of America*, p. 264.

29. As Charles Fried put it, Bork "was responding above all to the dissolution of the idea of law." *Order and Law*, p. 61.

30. This point-counterpoint between the Warren Court's value-laden method of constitutional interpretation and Bork's originalism was not new to legal history. Such originalism has appeared periodically as a response to perceived judicial "activism" and dates from at least as early as President Thomas Jefferson's complaints about the Court under Chief Justice John Marshall. See Jeffrey Rosen, "Originalist Sin," *New Republic*, May 5, 1997 p. 26.

31. See, for example, Lino Graglia, "How the Constitution Disappeared," *Commentary*, February 1986, pp. 19–27.

32. Ethan Bronner, *Battle for Justice: How the Bork Nomination Shook America* (New York: Norton, 1989), p. 160.

33. Robert Bork, "Civil Rights—A Challenge," *New Republic*, August 31, 1963, p. 22.

34. As yet another example, Bork did not think the Constitution constrained the federal government from engaging in race discrimination as the Court had held in *Bolling v. Sharpe*, 347 U.S. 497 (1954).

35. Nomination of Robert H. Bork to Be Associate Justice of the Supreme Court of the United States: Hearings Before the Senate Comm. on the Judiciary, 100th Cong., 1st sess., 1004 (1987). See also Philip Bobbitt, *Constitutional Interpretation* (Cambridge: Blackwell, 1991), p. 106. William Coleman, a black Republican who had served as President Ford's secretary of transportation, opposed Bork for the same reason.

36. See, e.g., Edwin Meese, Address to the Federalist Society Lawyers Division, November 15, 1985.

37. William J. Brennan, "The Constitution of the United States: Contemporary Ratification," address delivered at Georgetown Univ., October 12, 1985.

38. John Paul Stevens, Address to the Federal Bar Association, October 23, 1985.

39. *United States* v. *Moreland*, 258 U.S. 433, 451 (1922). See also Richard A. Posner, *Overcoming Law* (Cambridge: Harvard Univ. Press, 1995), pp. 237–55. As Posner notes, Bork's argument that original intent jurisprudence is required because it is the interpretive method most compatible with democracy depends entirely on his unconvincing definition of democracy.

40. Fried, *Order and Law*, p. 62.

41. Jack Rakove, *Original Meanings: Politics and Ideas in the Making of the Constitution* (New York: Knopf, 1996), pp. 3–22.

42. See Jefferson Powell, "The Original Understanding of Original Intent," 98 *Harvard Law Rev.* 885 (1985).

43. Bork, *Tempting of America*, p. 76.

44. See Raoul Berger, *Government by Judiciary: The Transformation of the Fourteenth Amendment*, (Cambridge: Harvard Univ. Press, 1977), pp. 118–19. Also Ronald Dworkin, "The Bork Nomination," *New York Review of Books*, August 13, 1987, pp. 3–10. For an alternative perspective, see Michael McConnell, "Originalism and the Desegregation Opinions," 81 *Virginia Law Rev.* 947 (1995).

45. Bork, *Tempting of America*, p. 82.

46. For a more detailed version of this argument, see Dworkin, "Bork Nomination," pp. 3–10.

47. Posner, *Overcoming Law*, p. 251. In my view, Posner is too harsh. The search for what our Founding Fathers might have thought about modern legal conundrums has more than rhetorical value. Arguments from history are appeals to the closest thing we have to a set of shared political values and symbols. They provide us a useful constraint in this postmodernist world of anything goes interpretation and, in exploring the thinking of our Madisons and Hamiltons, they still yield a cache of distinctly American polit-

ical wisdom that remains stirringly, atypically profound. See Rakove, *Original Meanings*, pp. 366–68.

48. 381 U.S. 479 (1965).

49. Philip B. Kurland, *Politics, The Constitution and the Warren Court* (Chicago: Univ. of Chicago Press, 1970).

50. See Paul D. Gewirtz, "Remedies and Resistance," 92 *Yale Law J.* 585, 677 (1983).

51. Alexander M. Bickel, *The Morality of Consent* (New Haven: Yale Univ. Press, 1975), p. 123.

52. See Suzanne Garment, "The War Against Robert Bork," *Commentary*, January 1988, p. 17.

53. Caplan, *Tenth Justice*, p. xxi.

THE CABAL AGAINST THE LIBS

1. See, e.g., *Neuschafer v. Whitley*, 816 F. 2d 1390 (9th Cir. 1987).

2. *AFSCME v. State of Washington*, 770 F. 2d 1401 (9th Cir. 1985).

3. *Havens Realty Corp. v. Coleman*, 455 U.S. 363 (1982).

4. *TOPIC v. Circle Realty & Co.*, 532 F. 2d 1273 (9th Cir. 1976).

5. *United States v. Leon*, 468 U.S. 897 (1984).

6. David G. Savage, *Turning Right: The Making of the Rehnquist Supreme Court* (New York: Wiley, 1992), p. 177.

7. *Beller v. Middendorf*, 632 F. 2d 788 (9th Cir. 1980).

8. *Dronenberg v. Zech*, 741 F. 2d 1388 (D.C. Cir. 1984). In 1985, the Supreme Court agreed with Bork. See *Bowers v. Hardwick*, 478 U.S. 186 (1986).

9. Savage, *Turning Right*, p. 175.

10. Ibid., p. 177.

11. Mark Gitenstein, *Matters of Principle: An Insider's Account of America's Rejection of Robert Bork's Nomination to the Supreme Court* (New York: Simon & Schuster, 1992), pp. 317–18.

12. 392 U.S. 409 (1968).

13. 427 U.S. 160 (1976). Although Justices Powell and Stevens concurred in *Runyon*, both wrote separately to express their doubt that the Court had been correct in *Jones v. Alfred Mayer* to interpret the 1866 act as reaching private conduct. Nonetheless, they felt that, unless *Jones* was to be overruled, it required the conclusion that Section 1981 as well as Section 1982 did prohibit private discrimination.

14. See J. Mark Tushnet, "Patterson and the Politics of the Judicial Process," *Supreme Court Rev.* 43–60 (1988).

15. Stevens had expressed reservations in a concurrence to *Runyon*. Blackmun, an appellate judge, had written the Eighth Circuit opinion which the Supreme Court reversed in *Jones*, in which he had concluded that Section 1982 did not reach private conduct. Despite that initial view, he did join the Court's decision in *Runyon* respecting Section 1981.

16. 485 U.S. 617 (1987).

17. See *Gulfstream Aerospace Corp. v. Mayacamas Corp.*, 485 U.S. 271 (1988).

18. *Watson v. Butler*, 483 U.S. 1037 (1987).

19. William Rehnquist, "Who Writes Decisions of the Supreme Court," *U.S. News & World Report*, December 13, 1957, p. 74.

20. Alexander Bickel, "Supreme Court Law Clerks," *New York Times*, April 27, 1958, sec. 6, p. 16.

21. Code of Conduct for Law Clerks of the Supreme Court of the United States (effective March 3, 1989), p. 2.

22. For an academic discussion of cert. strategy, see H. W. Perry, *Deciding to Decide: Agenda Setting at the Supreme Court* (Cambridge: Harvard Univ. Press, 1991), pp. 198–215.

23. The opportunity for pursuing defensive denials from the liberal side was substantially limited by that fact that three of the liberal Justices—Brennan, Marshall, and Stevens—didn't participate in the cert. pool and made their own decisions about whether a particular case was certworthy.

24. William H. Rehnquist, *The Supreme Court: How It Was, How It Is* (New York: Morrow, 1987), p. 300. This description of the drafting process, however, is at odds with another of Rehnquist's observations: that the Justices' discussion at conference often produces only the vague contours of how a case should be decided and that the details usually must "come out in the writing."

25. See, e.g., Joseph Vining, "Justice Bureaucracy, and Legal Method," 80 *Michigan Law Rev.* 248–58 (1981); Anthony T. Kronman, *The Lost Lawyer: Failing Ideals of the Legal Profession* (Cambridge: Harvard Univ. Press, Belknap, 1993); Richard A. Posner, *The Federal Courts: Challenge and Reform* (Cambridge: Harvard Univ. Press, 1996).

26. See, e.g., *Arizona v. Fulminante*, 499 U.S. 279 (1991).

27. Kronman, *Lost Lawyer*, p. 347.

28. Ibid., p. 349.

29. 377 U.S. 583 (1964).

30. 376 U.S. 254 (1964).

31. *United States v. Nixon*, 418 U.S. 683 (1974).

32. Earl Warren, "Mr. Justice Brennan," 80 *Harvard Law Rev.* 1–2 (1966).

33. *Johnson v. Santa Clara Transportation Agency*, 480 U.S. 616 (1987).

34. 490 U.S. 228 (1989).

35. Terry Eastland, "While Justice Sleeps," *National Review*, April 21, 1989, p. 24.

36. *In re Amendment to Rule 39*, 500 U.S. 13 (1991).

37. For a detailed view of this period in the Court's history, see Alpheus T. Mason, *Harlan Fiske Stone: Pillar of the Law* (New York: Viking, 1956).

38. See *Lochner v. New York*, 198 U.S. 45 (1905) (Holmes, J., dissenting).

39. See, e.g., *Schechter Poultry Corp. v. United States*, 295 U.S. 495 (1935).

40. Arthur M. Schlesinger, *The Politics of Upheaval* (Boston: Houghton Mifflin, 1960), p. 463.

41. Ibid., p. 461.

42. Ibid., p. 455.

43. Ibid., pp. 483–88.

44. *West Coast Hotel v. Parrish*, 300 U.S. 379 (1937).

45. Schlesinger, *Politics of Upheaval*, pp. 471, 483.

46. Mason, *Harlan Fiske Stone*, p. 424.

47. See Rehnquist, *Supreme Court*, pp. 290–91.

48. David M. O'Brien, *Storm Center: The Supreme Court in American Politics*, 3d ed. (New York: Norton, 1993), p. 244.

THE TEST OF SINCERITY

1. See Herbert Weschler, "Toward Neutral Principles of Constitutional Law," 3 *Harvard Law Rev.* 1 (1959).

2. *Green* v. *County School Board*, 391 U.S. 430 (1968).

3. The busing issue shattered the Justices' previously unified front on issues of desegregation and ended in an unsatisfactory compromise: in pursuit of racial balance, judges could order the intrusive and race-conscious remedy of busing but not across district lines. This bus-the-cities-not-the-suburbs policy led in many metropolitan areas to a distressing "target" pattern of largely resegregated public schools with a nearly all-black bull's-eye in the inner-city center, surrounded by a white ring.

4. See John C. Jeffries, *Justice Lewis F. Powell, Jr.: A Biography* (New York: Scribners, 1994), pp. 282–331; also Tom Wicker, *Tragic Failure: Racial Integration in America* (New York: Morrow, 1996).

5. Speech at Howard University titled "To Fulfill These Rights," quoted in Andrew Kull, *The Color Blind Constitution* (Cambridge: Harvard Univ. Press, 1992), pp. 186–87.

6. See Charles Fried, *Order and Law* (New York: Simon & Schuster, 1991), p. 99.

7. Much the same holds true for affirmative action based on gender.

8. Stephen L. Carter, *Affirmative Action Baby* (New York: Basic, 1991); also Shelby Steele, *The Content of Their Character: A New Vision of Race in America* (New York: St. Martin's Press, 1990).

9. March on Washington, August 26, 1963.

10. See Paul D. Gewirtz, "Remedies and Resistance," 92 *Yale Law J.* 585 (1983).

11. See Kathleen Sullivan, "Sins of Discrimination: Last Term's Affirmative Action Cases," 100 *Harvard Law Rev.* 78 (1986).

12. 438 U.S. 265 (1978).

13. Notably, White had approved of the affirmative action quota at issue in *Bakke* but had shifted position subsequently.

14. Compare *Wygant* v. *Jackson Board of Education*, 476 U.S. 267 (1986) with *Paradise* v. *United States*, 480 U.S. 149 (1987).

15. In recent years, the Court has sometimes given real teeth to rational relations review and struck down legislation on that basis. See, e.g., *Zobel* v. *Williams*, 457 U.S. 55 (1982); *City of Cleburne* v. *Cleburne Living Center*, 473 U.S. 432 (1985); *Romer* v. *Evans*, 116 S. Ct. 1620 (1996). This more robust type of rational relations review is discussed in "Transitions."

16. Gerald Gunther, "In Search of an Evolving Doctrine on a Changing Court: A Model for a Newer Equal Protection," 86 *Harvard Law Rev.* 1 (1972).

17. *Korematsu* v. *United States*, 323 U.S. 214 (1944).

18. See *Craig* v. *Boren*, 429 U.S. 190, 211 (1976) (Stevens, J., concurring).

19. *Regents of the University of California* v. *Bakke*, 407 (separate opinion of Blackmun, J.).

20. For a complete discussion of the legislation and Supreme Court decision, see Drew Days, "Fullilove," 96 *Yale Law J.* 453 (1987).

21. 448 U.S. 448 (1980).

22. *City of Richmond* v. *J. A. Croson Co.*, 488 U.S. 469 (1989).

23. "The Congress shall have power to enforce this article by appropriate legislation."

24. *Bradley* v. *School Board of Richmond, Virginia*, 463 F. 2d 1058 (4th Cir. 1972).

25. *Richmond* v. *United States*, 422 U.S. 358 (1975).

26. Bradley v. *School Board Richmond*, 463 F.2d, at 1065.

27. Stephen Carter, "When Victims Happen to Be Black," 97 *Yale Law J.* 420, 433–34 (1988).

28. O'Connor was known to be especially proud of her opinions in *Michigan* v. *Long*, 463 U.S. 1032 (1983), and *Strickland* v. *Washington*, 466 U.S. 668 (1984). In *Michigan*, she carefully guarded state court judgments from federal judicial review; in *Strickland*, she sharply limited the ability of convicted state court defendants to challenge their convictions on the ground that they lacked adequate legal representation as required by the Sixth Amendment. For other important examples of O'Connor's states' rights views, see, e.g., *New York* v. *United States*, 505 U.S. 144 (1992); *FERC* v. *Mississippi*, 456 U.S. 742 (1982); *Garcia* v. *San Antonio Metropolitan Transit Authority*, 469 U.S. 528 (1985).

29. See *Associated General Contractors of California* v. *City and County of San Francisco*, 813 F. 2d 922 (9th Cir. 1987).

30. *Adarand Constructors, Inc.* v. *Pena*, 515 U.S. 200 (1995).

31. See Randall Kennedy, *Race, Crime, and the Law* (New York: Pantheon, 1997), p. 6.

32. Indeed, at the cert. stage, Solicitor General Charles Fried's office had urged the Court to review the *Croson* case instead of another set-aside case emanating from Dade County, Florida, because the facts surrounding the adoption of the Richmond plan presented the potential problems with affirmative action in a particularly stark way. Fried, *Order and Law*, p. 120.

33. John Hart Ely, *Democracy and Distrust: A Theory of Judicial Review* (Cambridge: Harvard Univ. Press, 1980).

34. 490 U.S. 642 (1989).

35. Specifically, the Court held that white firefighters in Birmingham, Alabama, could challenge an affirmative action plan that a federal court had approved eight years earlier to remedy the Birmingham fire department's long-standing policy of keeping blacks out of senior positions. 490 U.S. 755 (1989).

36. 491 U.S. 164 (1989).

37. As in other chapters, my reconstruction here of internal events at the Court is based in very large part on the Thurgood Marshall Papers and on extensive interviews with former clerks. My reconstruction of *Patterson*, however, also relies on James Simon's *The Center Holds: The Power Struggle Inside the Rehnquist Court* (New York: Simon & Schuster, 1995). Although I differ with Professor Simon over many issues of interpretation, his discussion is informed by access to private correspondence between Justice Brennan and Justice Kennedy not otherwise available. I have gratefully borrowed this material.

38. See Kenneth Karst, "Private Discrimination and Public Responsibility: *Patterson* in Context," *Supreme Court Rev.* 1, 22 (1989).

39. Report of C. Schurz, 39th Cong., 1st sess., S. Exec. Doc. 2, 20 (1866).

40. Other examples include Brennan's drafts in *Price Waterhouse* v. *Hopkins* and *Texas* v. *Johnson*, the so-called flag-burning case, where Brennan's sweeping language very nearly cost him Justice Kennedy's crucial fifth vote.

41. Kennedy also objected to the manner in which Brennan justified reaffirming *Runyon*. Although Brennan's draft was hardly strident on this point—relying on stare decisis rather than defending *Runyon* as correct originally—Kennedy quibbled with its suggestion that Congress had implicitly ratified *Runyon* in the intervening decade. This was, however, a secondary concern.

42. Actually, White's opinion was a partial concurrence and a partial dissent. He

agreed with Brennan's reaffirmance of *Runyon* and with another noncontroversial aspect of the case, involving Patterson's claim that she had been denied a promotion on account of race.

43. Although I refer to Kennedy's draft as a dissent, like Justice White's, it was also a partial concurrence.

44. Because Brennan would have ruled against Patterson on technical grounds, his subsequent discussion of Section 1981 would have been purely gratuitous or, in the language of the law, dicta. Such expressions of opinion not necessary to the resolution of the case at hand carry no weight as precedent. And although the line between dicta and holdings is often hard to discern, it would have been clear under these circumstances.

45. Linda Greenhouse, "Court Upholds Use of Rights Law but Limits How It Can Be Applied," *New York Times,* June 16, 1989, sec. 1, p. 1.

46. Simon, *Center Holds,* pp. 81–82.

47. Kennedy also targeted a fourth (less noteworthy) case, *Lorance* v. *AT&T Techs.,* 490 U.S. 900 (1989), which dealt with the time period for filing employment discrimination claims.

48. See Anthony T. Kronman, *The Lost Lawyer: Failing Ideals of the Legal Profession* (Cambridge: Harvard Univ. Press, Bellnap, 1993), pp. 342–43.

49. *Felix Frankfurter Reminisces,* ed. Phillips Harlan (New York: Reynal, 1960), pp. 344–46. For a contrary view, see Joseph Goldstein, *The Intelligible Constitution* (New York: Oxford Univ. Press, 1992).

50. See Sanford Levinson, "The Rhetoric of the Judicial Opinion," in *Law Stories: Narrative and Rhetoric in Law,* ed. Peter Brooks and Paul D. Gewirtz (New Haven: Yale Univ. Press, 1996).

51. Arthur M. Schlesinger, Jr., *The Disuniting of America: Reflections on a Multicultural Society* (New York: Norton, 1992).

THE RIGHT TO PRIVACY

1. Bernard Schwartz, *Decision: How the Supreme Court Decides Cases* (New York: Oxford Univ. Press, 1996), p. 23.

2. Charles Fried, *Order and Law,* (New York: Simon & Schuster, 1991), p. 88.

3. 462 U.S. 416 (1983).

4. By common account, Lee had guaranteed himself an abbreviated tenure as solicitor general when he overrode administration hard-liners. Lincoln Caplan, *The Tenth Justice: The Solicitor General and the Rule of Law* (New York: Knopf, 1987), pp. 105–7.

5. 476 U.S. 747 (1986).

6. David G. Savage, *Turning Right: The Making of the Renquist Supreme Court* (New York: Wiley, 1992), p. 227.

7. David J. Garrow, *Liberty and Sexuality: The Right to Privacy and the Making of Roe v. Wade* (New York: Macmillan, 1994), p. 673.

8. 367 U.S. 497 (1961).

9. Garrow, *Liberty and Sexuality,* p. 184.

10. Fried's memo quoted in Garrow, *Liberty and Sexuality,* p. 174.

11. *Pierce* v. *Society of Sisters,* 268 U.S. 510 (1925).

12. *Meyer* v. *Nebraska,* 262 U.S. 390 (1923).

13. The constitutional edict that government shall not deprive citizens of "life, liberty, or property, without due process of law" appears in both the Fifth and Fourteenth

Amendments—the former directed at the federal government, the latter directed at the states.

14. *Meyer v. Nebraska*, 262 U.S. at 399.

15. *West Coast Hotel Co. v. Parrish*, 300 U.S. 379 (1937).

16. *Palko v. Connecticut*, 302 U.S. 319 (1937).

17. *Adamson v. California*, 332 U.S. 46 (1947).

18. In reaching this conclusion, Black relied not only on the due process clause but on the entire text of the Fourteenth Amendment, which, significantly, also commanded that "no State shall make or enforce any law which shall abridge the privileges or immunities of citizens of the United States." See *Duncan v. Louisiana*, 391 U.S. 145 (1968). By its terms, this "privileges and immunities" clause would have been a better vessel for many of the rights the Court ultimately recognized to be protected by the due process clause, but in the Slaughterhouse cases of 1873 the Court rendered the privileges and immunities clause all but meaningless—and it remains so in all but the academic literature to this day.

19. Black's approach was not without its own difficulties, not least that a leading constitutional scholar of the time claimed that he had badly misconstrued the intentions of the Fourteenth Amendment's Framers. Charles Fairman, "Does the Fourteenth Amendment Incorporate the Bill of Rights? The Original Understanding," 2 *Stanford Law Rev.* 5 (1949).

20. The history of right to privacy from *Poe* to *Roe* is exhaustively canvassed in Garrow's *Liberty and Sexuality*. While I do not always subscribe to Garrow's point of view, I am indebted to his extraordinary research.

21. 381 U.S. 479 (1965).

22. Douglas, one of *Lochner's* fiercest critics, carefully avoided any explicit reliance on substantive due process, even to the point of inaccurately recharacterizing two child-rearing due process cases from the *Lochner* era, *Meyer* and *Pierce*, as First Amendment cases. He also tried to distinguish *Lochner* as a case involving economic rights, whereas the rights at issue in *Griswold* were personal. Most critics, however, find his fancy footwork unavailing and his opinion in *Griswold* to be an application of substantive due process in everything but name.

23. Byron White also penned a concurrence, adopting a significantly different methodology. Rather than entrench marital privacy as a specially protected fundamental right, White concluded simply that Connecticut's sweeping ban on contraceptives did not fit its espoused purpose of curtailing promiscuous or illicit sexual relationships and, therefore, could not stand under even the lowest level of judicial scrutiny.

24. "We do not sit as a superlegislature to determine the wisdom, need, and propriety of laws that touch economic problems, business affairs, or social conditions. This law, however, operates directly on an intimate relation of husband and wife and their physician's role in one aspect of that relation."

25. See generally, Bruce A. Ackerman, *We the People* (Cambridge: Harvard Univ. Press, Belknap, 1991).

THE PRICE OF GOOD INTENTIONS

1. See Lee Epstein and Joseph Kobylka, *The Supreme Court and Legal Change: Abortion and the Death Penalty* (Chapel Hill: Univ. of North Carolina Press, 1992), pp. 139–40.

2. David J. Garrow, *Liberty and Sexuality: The Right to Privacy and the Making of Roe v. Wade* (New York: Macmillan, 1994), p. 272.

3. Ibid., p. 277.

4. Ibid., p. 339. Additional support for a *Griswold*-based argument for abortion rights came from an essay written by retired Supreme Court Justice Tom Clark (who had stepped off the Court when President Johnson named his son, Ramsey, to be attorney general). Without endorsing the argument, Clark did suggest that "abortion falls within the sensitive area of privacy" that *Griswold* recognized.

5. *People* v. *Belous*, 458 p. 2d 194 (1969).

6. See, e.g., *United States* v. *Vuich*, 305 F. Supp. 1032 (1969) (vagueness); *McCann* v. *Babbitz*, 310 F. Supp. 293 (1970) (privacy); for a comprehensive summary of lower court abortion regulation, see Epstein and Kobylka, *Supreme Court and Legal Change*, pp. 164–66.

7. *Doe* v. *Bolton*, 319 F. Supp. 1048 (1970).

8. 305 F. Supp. 1032 (1969).

9. 402 U.S. 62 (1971).

10. The William O. Douglas, William J. Brennan, and Thurgood Marshall Papers all contain notes about the Justices' conferences concerning *Roe* and *Doe*. In addition, James Simon, author of *The Center Holds: The Power Struggle Inside the Rehnquist Court* (New York: Simon & Schuster, 1995), seems to have had access to Justice Blackmun's private notes. Reconstructions of the conferences appear in that book as well as Bob Woodward and Scott Armstrong's *The Brethren: Inside the Supreme Court* (New York: Simon & Schuster, 1979), and Garrow's *Liberty and Sexuality*. I have considered all these accounts—which differ somewhat in detail—and have chosen to rely on the original sources as well as Garrow and Simon.

11. Simon, *Center Holds*, p. 106.

12. Garrow, *Liberty and Sexuality*, p. 606.

13. John H. Ely, "The Wages of Crying Wolf: A Comment on *Roe* v. *Wade*," 82 *Yale Law J.* 920 (1973).

14. *New York Times*, Editorial, January 24, 1973, p. 40.

15. Phillip B. Heymann and Douglas E. Barzelay, "The Forest and the Trees: *Roe* v. *Wade* and Its Critics," 53 *Boston Univ. Law Rev.* 765 (1973).

16. See, e.g., Sylvia A. Law, "Rethinking Sex and the Constitution," 132 *Univ. of Pennsylvania Law Rev.* 955 (1984); Cass R. Sunstein, "Neutrality in Constitutional Law (with Special Reference to Pornography, Abortion, and Surrogacy)," 92 *Columbia Law Rev.* 1, 29–44 (1992).

17. Laurence H. Tribe, *American Constitutional Law*, 2d ed. (Mineola, N.Y.: Foundation Press, 1988), pp. 1349–50 and nn. 87–88; Andrew Koppelman, "Forced Labor: A Thirteenth Amendment Defense of Abortion," 84 *Northwestern Univ. Law Rev.* 480 (1990).

18. Richard A. Posner, *Overcoming Law* (Cambridge: Harvard Univ. Press, 1995), p. 180.

19. Robert Bork, *The Tempting of America, The Political Seduction of the Law* (New York: Free Press, 1990), p. 31.

20. It is true that the Connecticut statute at issue in *Griswold* also banned the manufacture of contraceptives—an activity that hardly involved the physical invasion of a home. The *Griswold* majority, however, did not focus on this aspect of the case.

21. See also *Skinner* v. *Oklahoma*, 316 U.S. 535 (1942), a case from the 1940s invalidating a law compelling sterilization of "habitual offenders" for crimes of "moral turpitude." Although the Court decided the case on equal protection grounds (because the law exempted white-collar crimes such as embezzlement), it referred to procreation as "one of the basic civil rights of man. . . . [a matter] fundamental to the very existence and survival of the race."

22. 405 U.S. 438 (1972) (emphasis added).

23. Garrow, *Liberty and Sexuality*, p. 542.

24. Ely, "Wages of Crying Wolf," p. 926.

25. See, e.g., Laurence H. Tribe, *Abortion: The Clash of Absolutes* (New York: Norton, 1990).

26. In my view, the best defense of *Roe* appears in Justice Stevens's concurring opinion in *Thornburgh* v. *American College of Obstetricians and Gynecologists*, 476 U.S. 747, 772 (1986).

27. John C. Jeffries, *Justice Lewis F. Powell, Jr.: A Biography* (New York: Scribners, 1994), p. 347.

28. *Olmstead* v. *United States*, 277 U.S. 438, 478 (1928).

29. Jeffries, *Justice Powell*, p. 350.

30. For a further discussion of this comparison, see Robert A. Burt, *The Constitution in Conflict* (Cambridge: Harvard Univ. Press, Belknap, 1992), pp. 344–52.

31. See, e.g., Law, "Rethinking Sex," 955; Cass R. Sunstein, "Neutrality in Constitutional Law (with Special Reference to Pornography, Abortion, and Surrogacy)," 92 *Columbia Law Rev.* 29 (1992). For a contrary view, see Posner, *Overcoming Law*, pp. 181–85.

32. Judith J. Thompson, "A Defense of Abortion," 1 *Philosophy & Public Affairs* 47 (1971).

33. See, e.g., James C. Mohr, *Abortion in America: The Origins and Evolution of National Policy, 1800–1900* (New York: Oxford Univ. Press, 1978).

34. Ruth C. Ginsburg, "Some Thoughts on Autonomy and Equality in Relation to *Roe* v. *Wade*, 63 *North Carolina Law Rev.* 371 (1985).

THE TRIUMPH OF POLITICS

1. Lee Epstein and Joseph Kobylka, *The Supreme Court and Legal Change: Abortion and the Death Penalty* (Chapel Hill: Univ. of North Carolina Press, 1992), pp. 269–73.

2. Ibid., p. 273.

3. A comprehensive history of the anti-abortion movement appears in Cynthia Gorney, *Articles of Faith: A Frontline History of the Abortion Wars* (New York: Simon & Schuster, 1998).

4. See, e.g., *Maher* v. *Roe*, 432 U.S. 464 (1977); *Harris* v. *McRae*, 448 U.S. 297 (1980). Brennan, Marshall, and Blackmun strongly dissented in all these cases. Stevens took a somewhat different view. He thought government could refuse to fund elective abortions but not therapeutic ones.

5. *Maher* v. *Roe*.

6. See, e.g., *Planned Parenthood of Central Missouri* v. *Danforth*, 428 U.S. 52 (1976); *Bellotti* v. *Baird*, 443 U.S. 622 (1979).

7. *Akron* v. *Akron Center for Reproductive Health, Inc.*, 462 U.S. 416, 420 and n. 1 (1983).

8. 439 U.S. 379 (1979).

9. Nina Totenberg, "Harry A. Blackmun: The Conscientious Conscience," 43 *American Univ. Law Rev.* 745, 749 (1994).

10. *Beal* v. *Doe*, 432 U.S. 438, 463 (1977) (Blackmun J., dissenting).

11. The final section of Blackmun's published opinion in *Thornburgh*, 476 U.S. 747, 771–72 (1986), contains an explicit reaffirmance of *Roe* and the citation to *Cooper* v. *Aaron*. The depth of his anger at persistent efforts to undermine *Roe* appears more clearly

in his comments at conference and in earlier drafts of this section, ultimately toned down at the suggestion of Justices Stevens and Powell. See Papers of Justice William J. Brennan, Library of Congress.

12.   *Thornburgh*, 476 U.S. at 772 (Stevens, J., concurring).

13.   Mark Gitenstein, *Matters of Principle: An Insider's Account of America's Rejection of Robert Bork's Nomination to the Supreme Court* (New York: Simon & Schuster, 1992), p. 318. When pressed about *Griswold* by Senator Biden, Kennedy responded, "If you were going to propose a statute or a hypothetical that infringed upon the core values of privacy that the Constitution protects, you would be hard put to find a stronger case than *Griswold*." David J. Garrow, *Liberty and Sexuality: The Right to Privacy and the Making of Roe v. Wade* (New York: Macmillan, 1994), p. 672.

14.   Ibid., p. 673.

15.   Howard Kohn, "The Lady and the Court," *Los Angeles Times Magazine*, April 18, 1993, p. 14.

16.   462 U.S. 416 (1983).

17.   In creating her new standard, O'Connor was also following the lead of Rex Lee, Reagan's solicitor general at the time, whose amicus brief also had focused on the "unduly burdensome" language of some past cases.

18.   491 U.S. 110 (1989).

19.   478 U.S. 186 (1986).

20.   John C. Jeffries, *Justice Lewis F. Powell, Jr.: A Biography* (New York: Scribners, 1994), p. 523.

21.   This is to say not that Justice Harlan would have agreed with *Roe* and disagreed with *Bowers* but only that his process for deciding these cases would have been very different from Scalia's. How Harlan would have voted in Roe is pure conjecture. It's worth noting, however, that in *Poe*, he specifically affirmed the right of government to proscribe homosexuality.

22.   Indeed, Scalia made this point specifically in another newly added footnote, which stated that an interest could not be deemed protected under due process when society had enacted laws *denying* that specific interest. This footnote was tailor-made for the right to abortion, an interest that many states had denied through their criminal laws.

23.   Jeffrey Rosen, "The Agonizer," *New Yorker*, November 11, 1996, p. 82.

24.   As Taney stated, "An act of Congress which deprives a citizen of the United States of his liberty or property [including slave property] merely because he came himself or brought his property into a particular territory of the United States, and who had committed no offense against the laws, could hardly be dignified with the name of due process of law."

25.   As a little payback to Blackmun, Rehnquist adorned his brief stare decisis discussion with a prominent citation to *Garcia* v. *San Antonio Metropolitan Transportation Authority*, 469 U.S. 528 (1985), in which Blackmun had overturned a major states' rights precedent (*National League of Cities* v. *Usery*, 426 U.S. 833 [1976]) that Rehnquist had written and to which he was especially devoted.

26.   Blackmun (who found Rehnquist's benign reading of the other statutory provisions implausible) would have struck down the Missouri law in its entirety, but he relegated his discussion of the preamble, the public facilities ban, and the encouraging and counseling provision to a single giant footnote.

27.   In the end, while Scalia commanded four votes for his plurality opinion in *Michael H.* (Justice Stevens concurred in the judgment for very different reasons), Scalia's due process footnote garnered only two votes, Rehnquist's and his own.

28.   David M. O'Brien, *Storm Center: The Supreme Court in American Politics*, 3d ed. (New York: Norton, 1993), p. 286.

29.   See *Teague* v. *Lane*, 489 U.S. 288 (1989).

30.   Don E. Fehrenbacher, *The Dred Scott Case: Its Significance in American Law and Politics* (New York: Oxford Univ. Press, 1978), p. 559.

TRANSITIONS

1.   Terry Eastland, "The Tempting of Justice Kennedy," *American Spectator*, February 1993.

2.   Richard Reuben, "Man in the Middle," *California Lawyer*, October 1992, p. 35.

3.   See Henry Monaghan, "Our Perfect Constitution," 56 *New York Univ. Law Rev.* 353 (1981).

4.   *Turnock* v. *Ragsdale*, 493 U.S. 987 (1989).

5.   See, e.g., *Turner* v. *Safley*, 482 U.S. 78 (1987); *Cleburne* v. *Cleburne Living Centers*, 473 U.S. 432 (1985).

6.   *Romer* v. *Evans*, 116 S. Ct. 1620 (1996).

7.   More specifically, Stevens was responding to O'Connor's concern for precedent. Previously, the Court had upheld a statute that required one-parent consent before a minor obtained an abortion because the law provided for judicial bypass. *Belloti* v. *Baird*, 443 U.S. 622 (1979). The question was whether this case required upholding Minnesota's system of two-parent notification with bypass. And Stevens argued no: an escape hatch (judicial bypass) from a reasonable general rule (one-parent notification) could save an otherwise unconstitutional statute. An escape hatch from an irrational general rule (two-parent notification) could not.

8.   A statistical study of this phenomenon is provided in Richard A. Posner, *The Federal Courts: Challenge and Reform* (Cambridge: Harvard Univ. Press, 1996), pp. 357–59. As Justice Jackson wrote in *Douglas* v. *Jeannette*, 319 U.S. 157, 182 (1943), "We must do our utmost to make clear and easily understandable the reasons for deciding these cases as we do. Forthright observance of rights presupposes their forthright definition."

9.   *Metro Broadcasting, Inc.* v. *FCC*, 497 U.S. 547 (1990).

10.   For the details of Souter's selection, see David G. Savage, *Turning Right: The Making of the Rehnquist Supreme Court* (New York: Wiley, 1992), pp. 349–58; David J. Garrow, "Justice Souter Emerges," *New York Times*, September 25, 1994, sec. 6, p. 36.

11.   Savage, *Turning Right*, p. 358.

12.   Garrow, "Justice Souter Emerges," p. 54.

13.   Ibid.

14.   Ibid.

15.   500 U.S. 173 (1991).

16.   *Harmelin* v. *Michigan*, 501 U.S. 957 (1991). Justice Scalia, writing also for Rehnquist, asserted (contrary to precedent) that the Constitution "contains no proportionality guarantee." Kennedy, joined by O'Connor and Souter, concurred separately. They thought the Constitution prohibited punishments "grossly disproportionate" to the crime yet concluded, in light of the nation's drug crisis, that Harmelin's sentence did not qualify.

17.   501 U.S. 808 (1991).

18.   791 S.W. 2d 10 (1990).

19.   490 U.S. 805 (1989).

20.   498 U.S. 1076 (1991).

21.   500 U.S. 110 (1991).

22.   This was how Marshall described his condition in his postannouncement news conference.

23.   There was at least one other obvious black Republican candidate to fill Marshall's seat: Amalya Kearse, a well-respected judge on the Second Circuit. Kearse, however, was a known moderate and she was never seriously considered.

24.   Savage, *Turning Right*, p. 429.

25.   The circumstances surrounding Thomas's nomination are covered exhaustively in Jane Mayer and Jill Abramson, *Strange Justice: The Selling of Clarence Thomas* (Boston: Houghton Mifflin, 1994).

26.   Ibid., p. 30.

27.   This phrase belongs to Garry Wills. See his "The Selling of Clarence Thomas," *New York Review of Books*, February 2, 1995, p. 36.

28.   Mayer and Abramson, *Strange Justice*, p. 219.

29.   See Stephen Carter, "The Candidate," *New Republic*, February 22, 1993, p. 29.

30.   John C. Danforth, *Resurrection: The Confirmation of Clarence Thomas* (New York: Viking, 1994); David Brock, *The Real Anita Hill: The Untold Story* (New York: Free Press, 1993).

31.   This conspiracy theory is dramatically presented in Brock, *Real Anita Hill*.

32.   The extremes of the Thomas defense are captured in Senator Danforth's penitent memoir, *Resurrection*.

33.   Higgenbotham has since resigned from the bench to become a professor at Harvard.

34.   Higgenbotham's letter, dated November 29, 1991, was published in the *University of Pennsylvania Law Review* and reprinted in *Race-ing Justice, Engendering Power: Essays on Anita Hill, Clarence Thomas, and the Construction of Social Reality*, ed. Toni Morrison (New York: Pantheon, 1992).

35.   This theme in Thomas's life is well explored in both Mayer and Abramson, *Strange Justice*, and Jeffrey Toobin, "The Burden of Clarence Thomas," *New Yorker*, September 27, 1993, p. 38.

36.   Ronald Dworkin, "Justice for Clarence Thomas," *New York Review of Books*, November 7, 1991, p. 41.

37.   Toobin, "Burden," p. 48.

38.   Jeffrey Rosen, "Confirmations," *New Republic*, December 19, 1994, p. 27.

A FRAGILE PEACE

1.   947 F. 2d 682 (3d Cir. 1991).

2.   The merits of the Third Circuit's decision to follow a prediction about what the Supreme Court would do in a future case as opposed to following still standing precedent received some scholarly attention. See, e.g., Evan H. Caminker, "Why Must Inferior Courts Obey Superior Court Precedents?" 46 *Stanford Law Rev.* 817 (1994).

3.   Although strongly opposed to abortion, Pennsylvania Governor Robert Casey did not want his state to pass an abortion law that directly flouted *Roe*, and his view prevailed in the legislative process.

4.   *Thornburgh v. American College of Obstetricians and Gynecologists*, 476 U.S. 747 (1986).

5.   A comprehensive account of how pro-choice advocates reacted to the Third Circuit's decision appears in Gorney, "End of the Line for *Roe* v. *Wade*," *Washington Post*

Magazine, February 23, 1992, p. 6. I have supplemented the information contained there with my own interviews of Kathryn Kolbert and other participants in *Casey*.

6.   David J. Garrow, "The Rehnquist Reins," *New York Times*, October 6, 1996, sec. 6, p. 64.

7.   Previous accounts of *Casey* have suggested that seven Justices (Rehnquist, White, O'Connor, Scalia, Kennedy, Souter, and Thomas) voted to uphold the entire Pennsylvania law. Of these, Rehnquist, White, Scalia, and Thomas allegedly wanted to overrule *Roe*, while the rest felt that the law could be upheld without overruling *Roe*. See David J. Garrow, "Justice Souter Emerges," *New York Times*, September 25, 1994, sec. 6, p. 36; Jeffrey Rosen, "The Agonizer," *New Yorker*, November 11, 1996, p. 82. Although the *Casey* Conference remains shrouded in some mystery, these previous reconstructions are inaccurate. Rehnquist did not push for overruling *Roe*, and O'Connor, Souter, and Kennedy were not of one mind to uphold the Pennsylvania law while leaving *Roe* intact.

8.   Garrow, "Souter Emerges," p. 38.

9.   *Mapp* v. *Ohio*, 367 U.S. 643, 677 (1961) (Harlan, J., dissenting).

10.   Howard Kohn, "The Lady and the Court," *Los Angeles Times Magazine*, April 18, 1993, p. 14.

11.   For example, Kennedy took particular pride in his opinions extending the Court's 1986 decision in *Batson* v. *Kentucky*, which barred prosecutors from using peremptory challenges to exclude jurors for race-based reasons. Pursuing his vision of judicial integrity, Kennedy played a leading role in expanding the ban on race-based peremptories from prosecutors to defense attorneys and from criminal cases to civil ones. His conservative clerks were so incensed at his votes in these cases that they declined to work on the opinions—which Scalia would deride in dissent as "enormously self-satisfying, [but] unmeasured and misdirected." See *Powers* v. *Ohio*, 499 U.S. 400 (1991); *Edmonson* v. *Leesville Concrete*, 500 U.S. 614 (1991). *Texas* v. *Johnson*, 491 U.S. 397 (1989). The best profile of Justice Kennedy is Rosen, "The Agonizer."

12.   *County of Allegheny* v. *ACLU*, 492 U.S. 573 (1989).

13.   These quotations are from the published joint opinion in *Casey*, 505 U.S. 833 (1992), and may differ, at least in minor ways, from the original draft.

14.   For example, Blackmun implausibly summarized the trio's undue burden standard subjecting to strict scrutiny "all no–*de minimis* abortion regulations." Were this accurate, the trio would have struck down the twenty-four-hour waiting period—which surely was not a *de minimis* restriction.

15.   Terry Carter, "Crossing the Rubicon," *California Lawyer*, October 1992, p. 39.

16.   *Congressional Quarterly*, June 27, 1992, p. 1883.

17.   On this point, the joint opinion damned itself with embarrassingly inadequate explanations, such as "In our considered judgment, an undue burden is an unconstitutional burden."

18.   In this respect, the joint opinion differed substantially from the three-Justice coalition in *Gregg* v. *Georgia*. While Stewart, Powell, and Stevens committed the Court to an ongoing policing of the death penalty process, the trio in *Casey* led the Court away from the issue of abortion. As discussed elsewhere, the centrist enterprise in *Gregg* has largely failed. Whether *Casey*'s solution to the dilemma of abortion will prove more enduring remains to be seen.

19.   *Vacco* v. *Quill*, 117 S. Ct. 2293 (1997); *Washington* v. *Glucksberg*, 117 S. Ct. 2258 (1997).

OLD BATTLES, NEW WOUNDS

1. 377 U.S. 201 (1964).

2. See *Sanders* v. *United States*, 373 U.S. 1 (1963).

3. *McCleskey* v. *Zant*, Brief for Respondent, p. 52.

4. *McCleskey* v. *Zant*, 890 F. 2d 342 (11th Cir. 1989).

5. Linda Greenhouse, "Judges Challenge Chief Justice's Role on Death Penalty," *New York Times*, October 6, 1989, at p. A1.

6. In other contexts, such as when trying to excuse a procedural default, a defendant could also show "cause" in two additional circumstances: (1) when his lawyer had been so inept as to violate the constitutional guarantee of effective assistance of counsel; and (2) when a defendant was raising a novel legal claim. These circumstances, however, were unavailable to a habeas petitioner such as McCleskey. Under *Teague* v. *Lane*, 489 U.S. 288 (1989), he could not raise a novel claim. And he could not claim unconstitutionally ineffective assistance of counsel because habeas petitioners did not have a constitutional right to a lawyer. *Pennsylvania* v. *Finley*, 481 U.S. 551 (1987).

7. *United States* v. *Frady*, 456 U.S. 152 (1982).

8. There was an added irony in applying the new standard to McCleskey. Under *Teague*, the conservatives had made it impossible for petitioners like him to benefit from new rules expanding the rights of criminal defendants. Yet in *McCleskey* they enthusiastically gave states the retroactive benefit of a new rule shrinking the rights of criminal defendants.

9. Bowers's threat was reported by a friendly columnist, Bill Shipp, in the *Marietta Daily Journal*, September 15, 1991, p. D1.

10. 501 U.S. 722 (1991).

11. See *Stovall* v. *Denno*, 388 U.S. 293 (1967).

12. The retroactive issue was raised in an amicus brief filed by the Criminal Justice Legal Foundation, a conservative advocacy group.

13. Under *Teague*, two kinds of new rules could be considered on habeas review: (1) rules that would categorically immunize certain behavior from punishment; and (2) rules that implicated fundamental fairness and were related to the defendant's guilt or innocence. Generally speaking the Court has defined both exceptions narrowly. See *Penry* v. *Lynaugh*, 492 U.S. 302 (1989); *Sawyer* v. *Smith*, 497 U.S. 227 (1990); *Saffle* v. *Parks*, 494 U.S. 484 (1990).

It is important to note that *Teague* itself was a plurality opinion, representing the views of four Justices with the separate concurrence of Justice White. Also *Teague* specifically did not address whether its new approach to retroactivity would apply to death cases. Several months later, in *Penry*, Justice White joined fully to make a majority for the *Teague* approach, and the Court applied its new retroactivity doctrine to capital cases. By the time *Teague* was handed down, however, the handwriting on these points was on the wall.

14. See *Butler* v. *McKellar*, 494 U.S. 407 (1990).

15. Stephen B. Bright, "Political Attacks on the Judiciary," 72 *New York Univ. Law Rev.* 308 (1997).

16. Stephen B. Bright, "Death by Lottery," 92 *West Virginia Law Rev.* 679 (1990).

17. Charles Fried, "Impudence," 1992 *Supreme Court Rev.* 155, 160.

18. In recent years, for example, the Court has wrestled with the problem of protecting against the execution of someone truly innocent of any crime. This possibility sufficiently haunted Justices O'Connor, Kennedy, and Souter that they kept open a nar-

row window of federal habeas review for this kind of claim. See *Herrera v. Collins*, 506 U.S. 390 (1993). Indeed, Justice Souter, after his first few terms, emerged as a fairly consistent defender of federal habeas, and his apostasy combined with O'Connor's occasionally heightened caution in capital cases to frustrate the efforts of Rehnquist, Scalia, and Thomas to do away entirely with independent federal review of state criminal trials. See *Wright v. West*, 505 U.S. 277 (1993).

19. One of Harris's habeas petitions had become the subject of a Supreme Court decision holding that states did not have to review each death sentence to determine if it was "proportional" to others in the state. *Pulley v. Harris*, 484 U.S. 37 (1984).

20. *In re Blodgett*, 502 U.S. 236 (1992).

21. John Noonan, "Should State Executions Run on Schedule?" *New York Times*, April 27, 1992, sec. A, p. 17. (Similar sentiments were expressed by Judge Stephen Reinhardt, the Ninth Circuit's most outspoken liberal.) *Los Angeles Times*, April 23, 1997, sec. A, p. 36.

22. For an excellent analysis of the Harris case from the conservative perspective, see Fried, "Impudence"; for a liberal counterpart, see Evan H. Caminker and Erwin Chemerinsky, "The Lawless Execution of Robert Alton Harris," 104 *Yale Law J.* 225 (1992). In my view, each side fails to appreciate the errors of the other. Liberals exonerate Judge Pregerson and ignore the degree to which conservatives see themselves as merely responding to the incessant irresponsibility of abolitionist judges. Conservatives do not acknowledge the near lawlessness of their response.

23. Norman Mailer, "Until Dead: Thoughts on Capital Punishment," *Parade*, February 6, 1981, p. 6.

24. On school desegregation, see, e.g., *Freeman v. Pitts*, 503 U.S. 467 (1992); *Missouri v. Jenkins*, 515 U.S. 70 (1995). On voting districts, see, e.g., *Shaw v. Reno*, 509 U.S. 630 (1993); *Miller v. Johnson*, 515 U.S. 900 (1995); *Bush v. Vera*, 517 U.S. 952 (1996); *Abrams v. Johnson*, 520 U.S. 74 (1997). On affirmative action, see *Adarand Contractors, Inc. v. Pena*, 515 U.S. 200 (1995) (overruling *FCC v. Metro Broadcasting, Inc.*).

25. On the issue of guns near schools, see *United States v. Lopez*, 514 U.S. 549 (1995). On the Brady Bill, see *Printz v. United States*, 521 U.S. 898 (1997).

26. *City of Boerne v. Flores*, 521 U.S. 507 (1997). It must be added that the Court did not divide along quite the same lines in this case as in the other federalism cases. This deviation, however, is readily explained by the fact that some Justices, Stevens and O'Connor particularly, viewed the case more in terms of religious freedom than in terms of federalism.

27. *Seminole Tribe of Florida v. Florida*, 517 U.S. 44 (1996). *McMillian v. Monroe County, Alabama*, 20 U.S. 781 (1997). See also *Idaho v. Coeur d'Alene Tribe of Indians*, 521 U.S. 261 (1997).

28. Some of the preceding material appeared in somewhat different form in E. Lazarus, "The Geography of Justice," *U.S. News & World Report*, July 7, 1997, p. 21.

THE MORE THINGS CHANGE

1. *United States v. Virginia*, 518 U.S. 515 (1996).

2. See, e.g., *United States v. Lopez*, 514 U.S. 549 (1995).

3. Leading candidates in the category of inadequate or hypocritical opinions would include the entire roster of the Court's vague, unconvincing, and self-contradictory opinions on voting rights and Chief Justice Rehnquist's cursory, ahistori-

cal, and atextual (yet precedent-reversing) opinion in *Seminole Tribe of Florida v. Florida,* 517 U.S. 44 (1996), strengthening the sovereign immunity of states under the Eleventh Amendment.

4.   An obvious example of inconsistent use of *stare* decisions emerges from a comparison of Justice O'Connor's opinion in *Planned Parenthood v. Casey,* 505 U.S. 833 (1992), with her opinion in *Adarand Contractors, Inc. v. Pena,* 515 U.S. 2001 (1995).

5.   That Justices Scalia and Thomas joined Chief Justice Rehnquist's avowedly nonoriginalist Eleventh Amendment opinion in *Seminole Tribe* is but one example of originalists abandoning originalism. Another is Scalia's own opinion striking down part of the Brady bill under a theory of "dual federalism" which nowhere appears in the Constitution and for which the originalist evidence is, by his own admission, weak. See *Printz v. United States,* 521 U.S. 898 (1997). Such hypocrisies have led Justice Souter to question Scalia's intellectual honesty and to act as a purposeful check on Scalia's historical analyses.

6.   In 1993, for example, conservative clerks from various chambers formed what they called the "Mastodon" group, another cabal-like effort to promote a hardline conservative agenda at the court.

AN IMPERIAL COURT IN A TROUBLED DEMOCRACY

1.   *Stenberg v. Carhart,* 530 U.S. 914 (2000).

2.   *Grutter v. Bollenger,* 539 U.S. 306 (2003).

3.   *Dickerson v. United States,* 530 U.S. 438 (2000). The *Dickerson* majority was actually written by Rehnquist, though his hand was almost certainly forced by O'Connor and Kennedy. Rehnquist had been a strong and persistent *Miranda* critic. But once it became apparent that O'Connor and Kennedy did not favor overruling *Miranda,* Rehnquist faced the very real possibility that, unless he joined the emerging majority, Stevens (as the senior justice on that side) would take the writing assignment and craft an opinion resoundingly reaffirming a decision Rehnquist opposed. Rather than let that happen, it appears that Rehnquist joined the *Dickerson* majority and took the writing assignment for himself so that the Court would ultimately issue only a very tepid pro-*Miranda* ruling.

4.   See, e.g., *Rosenberger v. University of Virginia,* 515 U.S. 819 (1995); *Agostini v. Felton,* 521 U.S. 203 (1997).

5.   *Locke v. Davey,* 540 U.S. 712 (2004).

6.   *United States v. Lopez,* 514 U.S. 549 (1995).

7.   *United States v. Morrison,* 529 U.S. 598 (2000); *Printz v. United States,* 521 U.S. 898 (1997).

8.   *City of Boerne v. Flores,* 521 U.S. 507 (1997).

9.   *University of Alabama v. Garrett,* 531 U.S. 356 (2001); *Kimel v. Florida Board of Regents,* 528 U.S. 62 (2000).

10.   *Seminole Tribe of Florida v. Florida,* 517 U.S. 44 (1996).

11.   *University of Alabama v. Garrett,* 531 U.S. 356 (2001); *Kimel v. Florida Board of Regents,* 528 U.S. 62 (2000); *College Savings Bank v. Florida Prepaid Postsecondary Educ. Exp. Bd.,* 527 U.S. 666 (1999).

12.   *Hans v. Louisiana,* 134 U.S. 1 (1890).

13.   *Alden v. Maine,* 527 U.S. 706 (1999); *Federal Maritime Commission v. South Carolina State Ports Authority,* 535 U.S. 743 (2002).

14.   *Nevada Department of Human Resources v. Hibbs*, 538 U.S. 721 (2003); *Tennessee v. Lane*, 541 U.S. 509 (2004).

15.   *Lawrence v. Texas*, 539 U.S. 558 (2003).

16.   For a similar view, see Jeffrey Rosen, "A Majority of One," *The New York Times*, June 3, sec 6, p. 32, col. 1.

17.   See, e.g., Cass R. Sunstein, *One Case at a Time: Judicial Minimalism on the Supreme Court* (Cambridge: Harvard University Press 1999).

18.   For the best study of Rehnquist era activism, see Thomas M. Keck, *The Most Activist Supreme Court in History: The Road to Modern Judicial Conservatism* (Chicago: The University of Chicago Press, 2004).

19.   The Court has also shown much greater disregard for administrative agencies whose actions used to receive far greater deference from the Court. See, e.g., *AT&T Corp. v. Iowa Utilities Bd.*, 525 U.S. 360 (1999).

20.   *Bush v. Gore*, 531 U.S. 98 (2000).

21.   See, e.g., *Ex Parte Quirin*, 317 U.S. 1 (1942) ; *Johnson v. Eisentrager*, 339 U.S. 763 (1950).

22.   *Hirabayashi v. United States*, 320 U.S. 81 (1943); *Korematsu v. United States*, 323 U.S. 214 (1994).

23.   *Hamdi v. Rumsfeld*, 124 S. Ct. 2633 (2004); *Rasul v. Bush*, 124 S. Ct. 2686 (2004).

24.   Naturally, *Bush* v. *Gore* has been the subject of nearly endless commentary and I do not profess that the points made here are particularly original. The best single volume is *Bush v. Gore: The Question of Legitimacy* (ed. Bruce Ackerman, New Haven: Yale University Press, 2002). I found especially interesting or persuasive the essays by Jed Rubenfeld, Robert Post, Steven Calabresi, Jeffrey Rosen, Charles Fried, and Jack Balkin.

25.   This account of what happened inside the Court owes its detail to the intrepid reporting of David Margolick, who managed to get several law clerks from that year to talk about the Court's internal deliberations. His work appeared in "The Path to Florida," *Vanity Fair*, October 2004, p. 310.

26.   See *Anderson v. Celebrezze*, 460 U.S. 780 (1983).

27.   Richard A. Posner, *Breaking the Deadlock: The 2000 Election, the Constitution, and the Courts* (Princeton, N.J.: Princeton University Press, 2001).

28.   Akhil Reed Amar, "Should We Trust Judges," *Los Angeles Times*, pg. M1, December 17, 2000.

29.   Jeffrey Rosen, "Disgrace: The Supreme Court Commits Suicide," *New Republic*, December 25, 2000.

30.   For an exceptionally thorough and insightful discussion of this point, see Larry D. Kramer, *The People Themselves: Popular Constitutionalism and Judicial Review* (New York: Oxford University Press, 2004).

31.   The Court itself opened the door to this constitutional confrontation between Congress and the president when, in *Clinton v. Jones*, 520 U.S. 681 (1997), it allowed Paula Jones to proceed with her civil suit against a sitting president, thereby setting the stage for Bill Clinton's fateful (and untruthful) deposition and all that followed. Had the Justices not naively dismissed the notion that "politically-motivated harassment and frivolous litigation" might undermine the president's ability to carry out his duties, the nation might have been spared this tawdry tangle of sex, lies, and Javert-like prosecution.

INDEX

abortion: ALI model law about, 344, 348,
349; and Bill of Rights, 356, 362;
Brown v. *Board of Education* as model
for fight about, 352, 376–77, 378; and
Bush administration, 373; call for reform of laws about, 343–46; and confirmation hearings, 247, 254, 372; and
conservative agenda, 372, 429, 485–86;
demonstrations about, 463, 465; and
divisiveness within Court, 13–14, 420,
480–81, 486; and fetus, 348, 357–59,
361–62, 365–68, 370–71, 377, 382–83,
391, 392–93, 395, 403–16, 466, 477,
484; and Fifth Amendment, 356; and
First Amendment, 356, 361, 402–3,
406, 407–8, 416, 442, 443; and Fourteenth Amendment, 246, 352, 356,
466; and Fourth Amendment, 356;
funding for, 330, 331, 375–76, 377,
380, 399, 402–3, 406, 407, 408, 413,
414, 416, 442–43; and *Griswold*, 345,
346, 347, 351, 356, 359, 363–64,
366–67, 369, 390, 395, 397; history of,
343–44, 356, 364; Hot Springs conference about, 345; and *Michael H.*,
384–85, 389, 390; and mother's health,
343, 344, 345, 348, 349, 353, 356, 357,
358, 377, 404, 477; NAACP as model
in fight about, 376–77; national ambivalence about, 346; and Ninth
Amendment, 350, 352–53, 356, 366;
and original intent, 360, 371; and
precedents/stare decisis, 344, 348, 352,
363, 366, 392, 393, 395, 398, 404, 441,
465, 468, 469, 472, 475–77, 478, 479,
480, 483–84; Rehnquist Court's undermining of, 7, 262; and rule of law, 381;
standard of review for, 351, 357, 358,
365, 370, 382–83, 392, 399, 404, 405,
409, 412, 432–33, 435–36, 459–81; and
Thirteenth Amendment, 361; and timing (trimester) system, 330, 350,
357–59, 365, 377, 382–83, 391,
392–93, 397, 399, 403–6, 407, 408,
409, 414, 415, 475, 477; vagueness of
laws about, 346, 353, 355. *See also specific person, opinion, or organization*
academia, 223, 284, 286, 307; affirmative
action in, 237, 265, 292; conservatives
in, 264–65; culture wars in, 235–36;
feminism in, 265; hiring and tenure
process in, 237; liberals in, 235–36
affirmative action: in academia, 237, 265,
292; amicus briefs about, 374;